The Gender, Culture, and Power Reader

Dorothy L. Hodgson
Rutgers University

New York   Oxford
OXFORD UNIVERSITY PRESS

Oxford University Press is a department of the University of Oxford.
It furthers the University's objective of excellence in research,
scholarship, and education by publishing worldwide.

Oxford   New York
Auckland   Cape Town   Dar es Salaam   Hong Kong   Karachi
Kuala Lumpur   Madrid   Melbourne   Mexico City   Nairobi
New Delhi   Shanghai   Taipei   Toronto

With offices in
Argentina   Austria   Brazil   Chile   Czech Republic   France   Greece
Guatemala   Hungary   Italy   Japan   Poland   Portugal   Singapore
South Korea   Switzerland   Thailand   Turkey   Ukraine   Vietnam

For titles covered by Section 112 of the US Higher Education
Opportunity Act, please visit www.oup.com/us/he for the
latest information about pricing and alternate formats.

Published by Oxford University Press
198 Madison Avenue, New York, New York 10016
http://www.oup.com

Oxford is a registered trademark of Oxford University Press

Library of Congress Cataloging-in-Publication Data
Hodgson, Dorothy Louise, author.
  The gender, culture, and power reader / Dorothy L. Hodgson.
    pages cm
  Includes bibliographical references.
   ISBN 978-0-19-020177-7 (pbk. : alk. paper) 1. Women--Cross-cultural
studies. 2. Sex role--Cross-cultural studies. 3. Women--Social conditions.
4. Power (Social sciences) I. Title.
  GN479.7.H64 2016
  305.4--dc23

                                                                  2015017548

Printing number: 9 8 7 6 5 4 3 2 1

Printed in the United States of America
on acid-free paper

For all of my students—past, present, and future—who have inspired, surprised, and taught me so much about the world of gender, culture, and power

Contents

Preface   xi
Acknowledgments   xiii
Key Terms   xv
About the Editor   xix

PART ONE   **KEY DEBATES, PAST AND PRESENT**   **1**

1. Challenging Universals   **5**

1.1   Is Female to Male as Nature Is to Culture? - Sherry B. Ortner   5

1.2   Female Forms of Power and the Myth of Male Dominance: A Model of Female/Male Interaction in Peasant Society - Susan Carol Rogers   17

1.3   Lifeboat Ethics: Mother Love and Child Death in Northeast Brazil - Nancy Scheper-Hughes   28

2. Power, Agency, and Structure   **36**

2.1   The Romance of Resistance: Tracing Transformations of Power Through Bedouin Women - Lila Abu-Lughod   36

2.2   Feminist Theory, Embodiment, and the Docile Agent: Some Reflections on the Egyptian Islamic Revival - Saba Mahmood   45

2.3   Transnational Surrogacy in India: Interrogating Power and Women's Agency - Daisy Deomampo   56

3. Gender, Sex, and Sexuality   **65**

3.1   The Gender of Brazilian Transgendered Prostitutes - Don Kulick   65

3.2 "Playing with Fire": The Gendered Construction
of Chicana/Mexicana Sexuality ~ Patricia Zavella   76

3.3 On the Edge of Respectability: Sexual Politics
in China's Tibet ~ Charlene E. Makley   86

4. Complicating Gender   **98**

4.1 "Like a Mother to Them": Stratified Reproduction
and West Indian Childcare Workers and
Employers in New York ~ Shellee Colen   98

4.2 Ethnically Correct Dolls: Toying with the
Race Industry ~ Elizabeth Chin   110

4.3 "Strong Women" and "Pretty Girls":
Self-Provisioning, Gender, and Class Identity
in Rural Galicia ~ Sharon R. Roseman   118

5. Politics of Representation   **128**

5.1 Under Western Eyes: Feminist Scholarship and
Colonial Discourses ~ Chandra Talpade Mohanty   128

5.2 A Homegirl Goes Home: Black Feminism
and the Lure of Native Anthropology
~ Cheryl R. Rodriguez   141

5.3 Do Muslim Women Really Need Saving?:
Anthropological Reflections on Cultural
Relativism and Its Others ~ Lila Abu-Lughod   150

PART TWO   **BECOMING/BEING GENDERED**   **157**

6. Growing Up Gendered   **160**

6.1 Growing Girls/Closing Circles: Limits
on the Spaces of Knowing in Rural Sudan
and U.S. Cities ~ Cindi Katz   160

6.2 "Do It for All Your Pubic Hairs!": Latino Boys,
Masculinity, and Puberty ~ Richard Mora   171

6.3 Trans Youth, Science, and Art: Creating (Trans)
Gendered Space ~ Alison Rooke   180

7. Language and Performance   **190**

7.1 Anger, Gender, Language Shift, and the Politics
of Revelation in a Papua New Guinean Village
~ Don Kulick   190

7.2 Performing Gender Identity: Young Men's Talk and the Construction of Heterosexual Masculinity ~ Deborah Cameron　201

7.3 Do Clothes Make the Woman?: Gender, Performance Theory, and Lesbian Eroticism ~ Kath Weston　212

8. Bodies/Embodiment　**223**

8.1 Weighty Subjects: The Biopolitics of the U.S. War on Fat ~ Susan Greenhalgh　223

8.2 Middle-Class Compassion and Man Boobs ~ Thaïs Machado-Borges　235

8.3 The Production of Possession: Spirits and the Multinational Corporation in Malaysia ~ Aihwa Ong　242

9. Mediated Lives　**253**

9.1 Warriors, Hunters, and Bruce Lee: Gendered Agency and the Transformation of Masculinity in Amazonia ~ Casey High　253

9.2 Women on the Market: Modernity, Marriage, and the Internet in Cameroon ~ Jennifer Johnson-Hanks　264

9.3 Negotiating Identities/Queering Desires: Coming Out Online and the Remediation of the Coming-Out Story ~ Mary L. Gray　272

PART THREE　GENDERED NEGOTIATIONS　**283**

10. Gender at Home　**285**

10.1 "Gone to Their Second Husbands": Marital Metaphors and Conjugal Contracts in The Gambia's Female Garden Sector ~ Richard A. Schroeder　285

10.2 Black Women Have Always Worked: Is There a Work–Family Conflict Among the Black Middle Class? ~ Riché J. Daniel Barnes　295

10.3 Scoring Men: Vasectomies, Gender Relations, and Male Sexuality in Oaxaca ~ Matthew C. Gutmann   304

11. Gender at Work   **313**

11.1 Designing Women: Corporate Discipline and Barbados's Off-Shore Pink-Collar Sector ~ Carla Freeman   313

11.2 Mothering, Work, and Gender in Urban Asante Ideology and Practice ~ Gracia Clark   322

11.3 Man Enough to Let My Wife Support Me: Gender and Unemployment Among Middle-Class U.S. Tech Workers ~ Carrie M. Lane   333

12. Gendered States   **342**

12.1 State Versus Islam: Malay Families, Women's Bodies, and the Body Politic in Malaysia ~ Aihwa Ong   342

12.2 Creating Citizens, Making Men: The Military and Masculinity in Bolivia ~ Lesley Gill   355

12.3 The Intimacy of State Power: Marriage, Liberation, and Socialist Subjects in Southeastern China ~ Sara L. Friedman   366

PART FOUR   **GENDER MATTERS**   **377**

13. Global Connections of Life, Labor, and Love   **379**

13.1 Filipina Migrants in Rural Japan and Their Professions of Love ~ Lieba Faier   379

13.2 "Now I Am a Man and a Woman!": Gendered Moves and Migrations in a Transnational Mexican Community ~ Deborah A. Boehm   390

13.3 Homeland Beauty: Transnational Longing and Hmong American Video ~ Louisa Schein   399

14. Structures of Violence   **410**

14.1 The Intimacies of Power: Rethinking Violence and Affinity in the Bolivian Andes ~ Krista Van Vleet   410

14.2 Reconstructing Masculinities: The Disarmament, Demobilization, and Reintegration of Former Combatants in Colombia ~ Kimberly Theidon   420

14.3 The Construction of Indigenous Suspects: Militarization and the Gendered and Ethnic Dynamics of Human Rights Abuses in Southern Mexico ~ Lynn Stephen   430

15. Politics of Human Rights and Humanitarian Interventions   **440**

15.1 Feminist Negotiations: Contesting Narratives of the Campaign Against Acid Violence in Bangladesh ~ Elora Halim Chowdhury   440

15.2 "These Are Not Our Priorities": Maasai Women, Human Rights, and the Problem of Culture ~ Dorothy L. Hodgson   449

15.3 International Human Rights, Gender-Based Violence, and Local Discourses of Abuse in Postconflict Liberia: A Problem of "Culture"? ~ Sharon Abramowitz and Mary H. Moran   460

Author Bios   471
Additional Resources for Teaching and Learning   475

Preface

My guiding vision for this reader is to introduce students to contemporary debates and perspectives in the study of gender, culture, and power through short, engaging, clearly written articles that demonstrate the power of rich ethnography to pose, elaborate, complicate, and challenge theoretical claims. Through the readings, they will explore different approaches to the study and conceptualization of gender, the value and limitations of gender as an analytic category, and the theoretical insights about gender produced by ethnographic research into the everyday lives, labors, loves, and livelihoods of people throughout the world. Why does gender "matter"? How are dominant ideas and practices of gender perceived, produced, experienced, and contested in different societies? How does ethnographic research provide access to these stories, perspectives, and experiences? Why is this important? What is the relationship between evidence and theory? All of these articles apply critical understandings of the cultural, social, political, and economic dimensions of gender as dynamic, relational, contingent, contested, and co-produced through and within other forms of social difference like "race," class, and sexuality.

The distinctive features of this reader include:

- Examples from the Global North and Global South to expose students to critical texts that resonate with their own experiences and to confront them with examples that challenge their normative worldviews
- Attention to key classical debates (such as nature/culture, domestic/public) as well as topics of contemporary relevance and interest (transgender, media representations, gender-based violence, human rights)
- Articles from scholars of diverse backgrounds, origins, and perspectives
- Exploration of the production and contestation of masculinities as well as femininities
- Short articles (around 5,000 words) that have been edited and abridged for clarity, accessibility, and coherence
- Brief section introductions and discussion questions for each article
- An appendix with additional teaching and learning resources

The book is designed to serve as the primary text for either a large lecture-style class (where the instructor can use the readings to explain and illustrate key theoretical concepts and debates) or smaller, discussion-style seminars (where the instructor can use questions, prompts, and short "mini-lectures" to help students understand, compare, and critically assess the texts in order to derive their own theoretical insights). As such, it is divided into 15 topics, each of which includes three different readings that illustrate key positions and diverse perspectives on the issue. These topics are themselves organized into four sections that gradually introduce students to fundamental debates and insights, and then complicate and apply those understandings so that students learn about both the centrality and the complexity of gender as both an analytic and a lived reality. By the conclusion of a course based on this reader, students will be able to:

- understand that "gender" is not a synonym for "women"
- demonstrate that ideas and practices of gender shape and are shaped by culture and power
- analyze gender in terms of other cross-cutting forms of social difference like class, generation, and "race"
- apply gender as a category of analysis to ethnographic material
- understand the value of ethnographic perspectives to the study and theorization of gender

The reader is appropriate for courses on gender in anthropology, geography, sociology, and other social sciences that rely, in part, on qualitative research, as well as classes in women's, gender, and sexuality studies that seek a comparative, global perspective.

Acknowledgments

Many people have contributed ideas, advice, and assistance to me as I developed and produced this reader. First and foremost, I am grateful to Sherith Pankratz, my wonderful editor at Oxford University Press, for inviting me (and then convincing me) to edit a reader. Her enthusiasm and encouragement have stimulated and guided me through the long process. I have also enjoyed working closely with her assistant, Meredith Keffer, as we navigated and negotiated the nitty-gritty of selections, permissions, and production.

I would also like to thank all of the authors who kindly provided me permission to include their pieces and worked with me to shorten them. Many of them are colleagues and friends who I have known for years. But the process of searching for fresh, accessible, smart pieces that would "teach well" led me to learn about and introduce myself to other scholars. Indeed, one of the many joys of producing this reader has been both to revisit "classic" works and to discover new material and people. I am grateful to the numerous members of the Association for Feminist Anthropology (AFA) listserv who responded to my appeal for suggestions with copies of their own work and ideas about others—I just regret that I had to make such hard decisions about what to include. Colleen Grimes, a fabulous former undergraduate student at Rutgers, also helped me early in the process to identify prospective selections and reformat some of the earlier works into debugged word documents.

The book has also benefitted from the helpful and generous feedback of numerous reviewers:

Mary M. Cameron, Florida Atlantic University
Jennifer Erickson, Ball State University
Vance Geiger, University of Central Florida
Theresa J. Gilbertson, University of South Florida Sarasota-Manatee
Nila G. Hofman, DePaul University
Anna Jaysane-Darr, Tufts University and Newbury College
Melinda Leach, University of North Dakota
Angela Montague, University of Oregon

Mary L. Russell, Pierce College Fort Steilacoom
Jose Leonardo Santos, Metropolitan State University
Patricia Taber, University of California, Santa Barbara

Additionally, students in my fall 2014 undergraduate "Anthropology of Gender" class read the draft essays and provided incisive comments and thoughtful questions. Perhaps most importantly, however, they shared my excitement in the structure and content of the reader.

Finally, I am grateful to my colleagues, students, friends, and family for their support. I have had the pleasure of teaching at Rutgers University for almost 20 years in the Department of Anthropology, which is now internationally recognized for its strengths in gender and feminist anthropology. Rutgers is also known for the excellence of its faculty in women's and gender studies more broadly, both in the Department of Women's and Gender Studies (with which I am affiliated) and in the many centers and institutes that are part of the Institute for Women's Leadership Consortium. My time at the Institute for Research on Women, first as a Faculty Fellow and later as the Director, taught me much about how to communicate and debate work on gender in an interdisciplinary, accessible, and engaged manner. But none of my intellectual pursuits would be possible without the nurturance of my family—especially my partner Rick and son Luke—and friends. Thanks, as always, for all that you do to sustain my mind, body, and spirit.

Key Terms

The following "working definitions" of key terms are provided to give you a basic understanding of important concepts. The meanings of some of these terms are the subject of intense debates between scholars (including some in this reader). The meanings of others have changed and will continue to change over time. But these brief definitions are at least a beginning . . .

Affine A relative by marriage (instead of birth)

Binary Characterized by two opposing parts, such as male/female, nature/culture

Biopolitical The application of political power to all aspects of peoples' lives

Bisexual A person who is attracted to both males and females (based on a *binary* understanding of gender and sexuality)

Bridewealth Gifts that are exchanged between the family of the groom and the family of the bride to legitimate a marriage

Butch A lesbian who intentionally displays a deeply masculine appearance or manner (often in contrast to *femme*, below)

Cisgender A person who conforms to dominant gender and sexual norms (sometimes referred to as "gender-straight")

Class A hierarchical grouping of people in a society usually based on differences of wealth, occupation, and status

Culture Learned patterns of thought and practices shared by a social group

Embodiment Expressing and experiencing something through one's body

Essentialism A belief that a certain set of attributes (like gender) is inherent, stable, and fixed, regardless of such differences as history and culture

Ethnocentrism The assumption that one's own worldview, ideas, and practices are superior to those of other people and societies in the world

Ethnography A research methodology in which scholars spend time learning about the world from the perspective of the people they are studying through conversations, interviews, participant-observation, and other primarily qualitative methods

Femininity/femininities Having qualities that are usually associated with the female gender in a society defined by a binary gender system; ways of expressing female gender attributes

Femme A lesbian who intentionally displays a deeply feminine appearance and manner (often in contrast to *butch*, above)

F2M/FtM An abbreviation for a female-to-male trans person

Gay A person who is sexually attracted to people of the "same" gender

Gender Identity A person's sense of their gender, which may differ from the gender they were assigned at birth or with which other people identify them

Gender Ideology A shared set of beliefs about appropriate gender practices, relations, dress, and so forth

Gender Nonconforming A person who does not conform to dominant gender systems, especially those based on binary concepts of male/female

Hermaphrodite A dated term for what people now prefer to call "intersexed" (see below)

Heteronormativity The assumption that heterosexual relations, or sexual relations between a man and a woman, are the "natural" and "normal" form of sexuality

Heterosexual Based on a binary view of gender as either male or female, describes a sexual preference for people of the "opposite" gender

Homosexual A sexual preference for people of the "same" gender

Ideology A shared set of beliefs

Intersectionality The belief that one form of social difference (like gender) cannot be understood or studied without attention to how it interacts with and is often differentiated by other forms of social difference (like class or race)

Intersexed A condition in which a person is born with ambiguous external genitalia, reproductive organs, or chromosome patterns that do not fit dominant biological categories of "male" or "female"

Lesbian A woman who is sexually attracted to other women

LGBTQ An acronym for "Lesbian Gay Bisexual Trans Queer," an umbrella term used to designate a group of people whose sexual or gender identities create a shared set of political and social concerns (sometimes additional letters are added such as "A" for "Ally" or "Asexual," "I" for "Intersex," or "Q" for "Questioning")

Masculinity/masculinities Having qualities that are usually associated with the male gender in a society defined by a binary gender system; ways of expressing male gender attributes

Matriarchy A society in which women dominate political, economic, and social life

Matrilineal A society in which descent and inheritance are traced through females

M2F/MtF An acronym for a male-to-female trans person

Nongovernmental Organizations (NGOs) A voluntary group of individuals or organizations that operate independently of governments to provide certain services or advocate for certain causes

Patriarchy A society in which men dominate political, economic, and social life

Patrilineal A society in which descent and inheritance are traced through males

Performativity The idea that people produce (and reproduce) certain identities (like gender) by selecting and repeating certain practices, appearances, postures, and other "signs" from a range of possibilities. In other words, the idea that an identity like gender is not something we *have* but something we *do*.

Polyandry Marriage between one woman and two or more men

Polygamy Marriage of one person to more than one partner at the same time

Polygyny Marriage between one man and two or more women

Queer A formerly negative term that some lesbians, gays, and trans people have reclaimed as an umbrella term to identify themselves. Includes people who identify as queer and those who feel like their desires, practices, and beliefs do not conform to dominant gender and sexual norms in their society.

Race A socially constructed category that is used to identify and distinguish groups of people because of presumed biological or physical traits such as skin color that they supposedly share

Reproductive Labor The physical, mental, and emotional work of bearing and caring for children, and creating and maintaining households

Sex A biological term designating a certain combination of genitalia, secondary sex characteristics (like breasts), and chromosomes

Sexuality The beliefs and practices associated with erotic desires, pleasures, and prohibitions

Sexual Orientation A person's sense of their own sexual identity and desires

Social Constructionism The belief that identities like gender, race, and class do not have an inherent, essential, static meaning or expression but are instead "constructed" through the ways that we are socialized and interact with one another in the world

Social Stratification A system in which society ranks certain people in hierarchical groups based on differences of wealth, power, status, and privilege

Stratified Reproduction How hierarchies of class, nationality, and gender shape the possibilities and constraints of work, mobility, and motherhood for different groups of women

Surrogate A woman who undergoes egg implants or artificial insemination in order to bear a baby for someone else

Trans An umbrella term that includes transgendered, transsexual, and transvestite and people who do not identify as either male or female or men or women

Travesti Transgendered Brazilian men who use silicone and hormones to change their bodies, but keep their male genitalia

About the Editor

DOROTHY L. HODGSON received her B.A. degree from the University of Virginia and her M.A. and Ph.D. degrees from the University of Michigan. She is Professor and Graduate Director in the Department of Anthropology at Rutgers University, where she has taught since 1995. She is the Vice-President of the African Studies Association and has previously served as Chair of the Department of Anthropology, Director of the Rutgers Institute for Research on Women, President of the Association for Feminist Anthropology, and on the Editorial Boards of *Signs*, *Women's Studies Quarterly*, and *Social Text*, among other journals. As a historical anthropologist, she has worked in Tanzania, East Africa, for almost thirty years on such topics as gender, ethnicity, cultural politics, colonialism, nationalism, modernity, the missionary encounter, transnational organizing, and the indigenous rights movement. She is the author of *Being Maasai, Becoming Indigenous: Postcolonial Politics in a Neoliberal World* (2011), *The Church of Women: Gendered Encounters Between Maasai and Missionaries* (2005), and *Once Intrepid Warriors: Gender, Ethnicity and the Cultural Politics of Maasai Development* (2001); and editor of *Gender and Culture at the Limit of Rights* (2011), *Gendered Modernities: Ethnographic Perspectives* (2001), and *Rethinking Pastoralism in Africa: Gender, Culture and the Myth of the Patriarchal Pastoralist* (2000); and co-editor of *"Wicked" Women and the Reconfiguration of Gender in Africa* (2001). She has also published many journal articles and book chapters. Her research and writing have been supported by awards from the John Simon Guggenheim Memorial Foundation, Rockefeller Foundation's Bellagio Center, National Endowment for the Humanities, Fulbright-Hays, American Council for Learned Societies, National Science Foundation, American Philosophical Society, Wenner-Gren Foundation, Social Science Research Council, and Center for Advanced Study in the Behavioral Sciences.

PART ONE

Key Debates, Past and Present

From the beginning, debates and studies of gender have engaged or produced ideas about culture and power, whether searching for explanations for the presumed "universal" oppression of women or relying on static, ahistorical, bounded ideas of "tradition" to argue for the terrible plight of "Third World women" as "victims" of their "culture." Many early studies relied on *essentialist* concepts of gender; that is, the idea that what it meant to be a "man" or a "woman" was always the same in different times and places because, in great part, of the presumed clear biological differences between men and women, whether of genitalia or chromosomes. Other scholars drew on comparative historical and ethnographic research to challenge these claims of essentialism, arguing instead that gender was *socially constructed*; that is, it was produced through the ideas, practices, and interactions of people. Even then, gender had to be understood in relation to other forms of social difference, like *race* and *class* through an *intersectional* analysis. Moreover, what about people and societies who embraced *gender ideologies* that were not predicated on the *binary* of male/female, or for whom gender was not related in any way to biological *sex*? And who should conduct this research? How did prior assumptions about gender, "race," and class shape the design, conduct, and conclusions of such research and writing?

The topics in this section will introduce you to some of these significant debates and developments in the study of gender in order to provide you with a shared theoretical vocabulary and common foundation.

1

1. *Challenging Universals:* The readings explore and question continuing efforts to propose all-encompassing explanations for the supposedly "universal" oppression of women by men, such as the symbolic equation of women with "nature" and men with "culture" and the confinement of women to "domestic" rather than "public" domains because of the demands of childbirth and childcare. In her classic article, "Is Female to Male as Nature Is to Culture?," Sherry B. Ortner searches for the underlying cultural logic that explains what she believes is the universal oppression of women throughout the world. Although Ortner argues that it is important to distinguish between "the universal fact" of women's "second-class status" in every society and "observable on-the-ground details" of women's activities, contributions, powers and so forth, the readings by Susan Carol Rogers and Nancy Scheper-Hughes challenge some of Ortner's assumptions and claims. Rogers draws on her fieldwork in rural France to examine forms of "informal" female power and compare their efficacy with forms of male authority and "formal" power. She compares the *ideologies* about gender and power with the realities of women's and men's everyday lives and interactions in the home, at work, and in politics. Scheper-Hughes confronts normative assumptions about the childcare choices and the inherent nurturing qualities of "mothers" through the wrenching stories of women in a Brazilian shantytown whose difficult economic and social circumstances force them to make hard decisions about the lives and deaths of their children.

2. *Power, Agency, and Structure:* These readings introduce and complicate key terms in the analysis of gender: power, agency, and structure. Gender differences, especially inequalities, are often the product of power relations between and among men and women. Moreover, gender dynamics reflect and produce broader structures of power such as colonialism, capitalism, racism, and religion. But people are not passive victims; they act on and within their worlds in compliance with or sometimes resistance to dominant sociocultural norms and expectations. Lila Abu-Lughod applies Michel Foucault's ideas about power and resistance to examine changing gendered dynamics among Bedouin women in Egypt as they experience the shift from kin-based power to the more elusive forms of power exerted by states and capitalism. Saba Mahmood challenges liberal ideas of agency as the expression of individual freedom through her study of a Muslim women's piety movement in Egypt in which women seek to demonstrate their faith through obedience, modesty, and veiling. Daisy Deomampo's study of Indian women who work as birth *surrogates* (or intermediaries) for parents in other countries provides yet another ethnographic example of how gendered agency is produced and constrained by such structures as class, education, and language.

3. *Gender, Sex, and Sexuality:* Different assumptions about and ideas of *sex* and *sexuality* are inevitably part of most analyses of gender. These readings help to clarify (and perhaps confound) the differences between each term, examine distinct and shifting articulations among them, and demonstrate that, like gender, dominant ideas of sex and sexuality are cultural and historical products. For example, in Brazil, according to Don Kulick, gender differences are not based on ideas about biological sex (males and females) but rather on differences of sexuality, or sexual practices: Brazilians distinguish between those who penetrate ("men") and those who are penetrated ("not-men"). Patricia Zavella uses the stories of two women to explore how Chicana/Mexicana sexuality is shaped by cultural discourses and relations of power. Charlene E. Makley examines how dramatic changes in the political economy of China have reshaped dominant ideas about appropriate gender, marriage, and sexual practices in Tibet.

4. *Complicating Gender:* Gender, of course, is only one of several forms of social difference. Scholars often use the term *intersectionality* to refer to approaches that examine the articulations and interactions of gender with other hierarchies such as class, "race," ethnicity, sexuality, and nationality. An intersectional analysis complicates our understanding of gender by revealing the distinctions among men and women and how gender shapes other forms of difference. Shellee Colen introduces the concept of *stratified reproduction* to explain how inequalities of race, class, nationality, and gender shape the possibilities and constraints of work, mobility, and motherhood for women in New York City and their West Indian childcare providers. The assumptions and experiences of racial, class, and gender inequalities are also central to Elizabeth Chin's study of the differences between the intentions of Mattel in producing racially diverse Barbie dolls and the realities of young, poor, black girls in Newhallville, Connecticut. Sharon R. Roseman examines expressions of gender and class differences in her article on "strong women" and "pretty girls" in rural Spain.

5. *Politics of Representation:* One way that power is expressed is through producing and reproducing images and representations of marginalized men and women that erase, silence, essentialize, or demean their agency, contributions, histories, contexts, meanings, and diversity. These readings explore the politics of representation: who has the power to represent others, how they do so, and what the consequences are for the lives of those who are represented. Chandra Talpade Mohanty examines how the stereotype of "Third World women" is produced in certain Western feminist writing. She analyzes both the limited explanatory potential and the damaging political effects of these problematic representations of "Third World women" as ignorant, tradition

bound, and victimized. Cheryl R. Rodriguez discusses the benefits and challenges of being a Black feminist anthropologist, as a "homegirl" and "native anthropologist" who conducts research on Black women's activism in Tampa, Florida. Lila Abu-Lughod probes the "political work" that representations of Muslim women as passive and oppressed have done to justify support for, among other things, American bombing and intervention in Afghanistan.

IS FEMALE TO MALE AS NATURE IS TO CULTURE?

DISCUSSION QUESTIONS

1. According to Ortner, why are women universally subordinated to men?
2. What kinds of evidence does she provide to support her arguments?
3. How do women's bodies and biological functions as mothers contribute to their subordination?

Much of the creativity of anthropology derives from the tension between two sets of demands: that we explain human universals, and that we explain cultural particulars. By this criterion, woman provides us with one of the more challenging problems to be dealt with. The secondary status of woman in society is one of the true universals, a pan-cultural fact. Yet within that universal fact, the specific cultural conceptions and symbolizations of woman are extraordinarily diverse and even mutually contradictory. Further, the actual treatment of women and their relative power and contribution vary enormously from culture to culture, and over different periods in the history of particular cultural traditions. Both of these points—the universal fact and the cultural variation constitute problems to be explained.

My interest in the problem is of course more than academic: I wish to see genuine change come about, the emergence of a social and cultural order in which as much of the range of human potential is open to women as is open to men. The universality of female subordination, the fact that it exists within every type of social and economic arrangement and in societies of every degree of complexity, indicates to me that we are up against something very profound, very stubborn, something we cannot rout out simply by rearranging a few tasks and roles in the social system, or even by reordering the whole economic structure. In this paper I try to expose the underlying logic of cultural thinking that assumes the inferiority of women; I try to show the highly persuasive nature of the logic, for if it were not so persuasive, people would not keep

An abridged version of Sherry B. Ortner, 1974. "Is female to male as nature is to culture?" pp. 68–87. Adapted from *Woman, Culture, and Society*. Edited by Michelle Zimbalist Rosaldo and Louise Lamphere. Copyright 1974 by the Board of Trustees of the Leland Stanford Jr. University. All rights reserved. Used with the permission of Stanford University Press, www.sup.org, and of the author. Ellipses are used to mark the deletion of large sections of text.

subscribing to it. But I also try to show the social and cultural sources of that logic, to indicate wherein lies the potential for change.

It is important to sort out the levels of the problem. The confusion can be staggering. For example, depending on which aspect of Chinese culture we look at, we might extrapolate any of several entirely different guesses concerning the status of women in China. In the ideology of Taoism, *yin*, the female principle, and *yang*, the male principle, are given equal weight; "the opposition, alternation, and interaction of these two forces give rise to all phenomena in the universe" (Siu, 1968: 2). Hence we might guess that maleness and femaleness are equally valued in the general ideology of Chinese culture. Looking at the social structure, however, we see the strongly emphasized patrilineal descent principle, the importance of sons, and the absolute authority of the father in the family. Thus we might conclude that China is the archetypal patriarchal society. Next, looking at the actual roles played, power and influence wielded, and material contributions made by women in Chinese society—all of which are, upon observation, quite substantial—we would have to say that women are allotted a great deal of (unspoken) status in the system. Or again, we might focus on the fact that a goddess, Kuan Yin, is the central (most worshiped, most depicted) deity in Chinese Buddhism, and we might be tempted to say, as many have tried to say about goddess-worshiping cultures in prehistoric and early historical societies, that China is actually a sort of matriarchy. In short, we must be absolutely clear about *what* we are trying to explain before explaining it.

We may differentiate three levels of the problem:

1. The universal fact of culturally attributed second-class status of woman in every society. Two questions are important here. First, what do we mean by this; what is our evidence that this is a universal fact? And second, how are we to explain this fact, once having established it?
2. Specific ideologies, symbolizations, and social-structural arrangements pertaining

to women that vary widely from culture to culture. The problem at this level is to account for any particular cultural complex in terms of factors specific to that group—the standard level of anthropological analysis.

3. Observable on-the-ground details of women's activities, contributions, powers, influence, etc., often at variance with cultural ideology (although always constrained within the assumption that women may never be officially preeminent in the total system). This is the level of direct observation, often adopted now by feminist-oriented anthropologists.

This paper is primarily concerned with the first of these levels, the problem of the universal devaluation of women. The analysis thus depends not upon specific cultural data but rather upon an analysis of "culture" taken generically as a special sort of process in the world. A discussion of the second level, the problem of cross-cultural variation in conceptions and relative valuations of women, will entail a great deal of cross-cultural research and must be postponed to another time. As for the third level, it will be obvious from my approach that I would consider it a misguided endeavor to focus only upon women's actual though culturally unrecognized and unvalued powers in any given society, without first understanding the overarching ideology and deeper assumptions of the culture that render such powers trivial.

THE UNIVERSALITY OF FEMALE SUBORDINATION

What do I mean when I say that everywhere, in every known culture, women are considered in some degree inferior to men? First of all, I must stress that I am talking about *cultural* evaluations; I am saying that each culture, in its own way and on its own terms, makes this evaluation. But what would constitute evidence that a particular culture considers women inferior?

Three types of data would suffice: (1) elements of cultural ideology and informants' statements that *explicitly* devalue women, according them, their roles, their tasks, their products, and their social milieux less prestige than are accorded men and the male correlates; (2) symbolic devices, such as the attribution of defilement, which may be interpreted as *implicitly* making a statement of inferior valuation; and (3) social-structural arrangements that exclude women from participation in or contact with some realm in which the highest powers of the society are felt to reside. These three types of data may all of course be interrelated in any particular system, though they need not necessarily be. Further, any one of them will usually be sufficient to make the point of female inferiority in a given culture.

Certainly, female exclusion from the most sacred rite or the highest political council is sufficient evidence. Certainly, explicit cultural ideology devaluing women (and their tasks, roles, products, etc.) is sufficient evidence. Symbolic indicators such as defilement are usually sufficient, although in a few cases in which, say, men and women are equally polluting to one another, a further indicator is required—and is, as far as my investigations have ascertained, always available.

On any or all of these counts, then, I would flatly assert that we find women subordinated to men in every known society. The search for a genuinely egalitarian, let alone matriarchal, culture has proved fruitless. An example from one society that has traditionally been on the credit side of this ledger will suffice. Among the matrilineal Crow, as Lowie (1956) points out, "Women . . . had highly honorific offices in the Sun Dance; they could become directors of the Tobacco Ceremony and played, if anything, a more conspicuous part in it than the men; they sometimes played the hostess in the Cooked Meat Festival; they were not debarred from sweating or doctoring or from seeking a vision" (p. 61). Nonetheless, "Women [during menstruation] formerly rode inferior horses and evidently this loomed as a source of contamination, for they were not allowed to approach either a wounded man or men starting on a war party. A taboo still lingers against their coming near sacred objects at these times" (p. 44). Further, just before enumerating women's rights of participation in the various rituals noted above, Lowie mentions one particular Sun Dance Doll bundle that was not supposed to be unwrapped by a woman (p. 60). Pursuing this trail we find: "According to all Lodge Grass informants and most others, the doll owned by Wrinkled-face took precedence not only of other dolls but of all other Crow medicines whatsoever. . . . This particular doll was not supposed to be handled by a woman" (p. 229).

In sum, the Crow are probably a fairly typical case. Yes, women have certain powers and rights, in this case some that place them in fairly high positions. Yet ultimately the line is drawn: menstruation is a threat to warfare, one of the most valued institutions of the tribe, one that is central to their self-definition; and the most sacred object of the tribe is taboo to the direct sight and touch of women.

Similar examples could be multiplied ad infinitum, but I think the onus is no longer upon us to demonstrate that female subordination is a cultural universal; it is up to those who would argue against the point to bring forth counterexamples. I shall take the universal secondary status of women as a given, and proceed from there.

NATURE AND CULTURE[1]

How are we to explain the universal devaluation of women? We could of course rest the case on biological determinism. There is something genetically inherent in the male of the species, so the biological determinists would argue, that makes them the naturally dominant sex; that "something" is lacking in females, and as a result women are not only naturally subordinate but in general quite satisfied with their position, since it affords them protection and the opportunity to maximize maternal pleasures, which to them are the most satisfying experiences of life. Without going into a detailed refutation of this position, I think it fair to say that it has failed to be established to the satisfaction of almost anyone in academic anthropology. This is to say, not that biological facts are irrelevant, or that men and women are not different, but that these facts and differences only take on significance of superior/inferior within the framework of culturally defined value systems.

If we are unwilling to rest the case on genetic determinism, it seems to me that we have only one way to proceed. We must attempt to interpret female subordination in light of other universals, factors built into the structure of the most generalized situation in which all human beings, in whatever culture, find themselves [. . .]

I translate the problem, in other words, into the following simple question. What could there be in the generalized structure and conditions of existence, common to every culture, that would lead every culture to place a lower value upon women? Specifically, my thesis is that woman is identified with—or, if you will, seems to be a symbol of—something that every culture devalues, something that every culture defines as being of a lower order of existence than itself. Now it seems that there is only one thing that would fit that description, and that is "nature" in the most generalized sense. Every culture, or, generically, "culture," is engaged in the process of generating and sustaining systems of meaningful forms (symbols, artifacts, etc.) by means of which humanity transcends the givens of natural existence, bends them to its purposes, controls them in its interest. We may thus broadly equate culture with the notion of human consciousness, or with the products of human consciousness (i.e., systems of thought and technology), by means of which humanity attempts to assert control over nature.

Now the categories of "nature" and "culture" are of course conceptual categories—one can find no boundary out in the actual world between the two states or realms of being. And there is no question that some cultures articulate a much stronger opposition between the two categories than others—it has even been argued that primitive peoples (some or all) do not see or intuit any distinction between the human cultural state and the state of nature at all [. . .]

[M]y point is simply that every culture implicitly recognizes and asserts a distinction between the operation of nature and the operation of culture (human consciousness and its products); and further, that the distinctiveness of culture rests precisely on the fact that it can under most circumstances transcend natural conditions and turn them to its purposes. Thus culture (i.e. every culture) at some level of awareness asserts itself to be not only distinct from but superior to nature, and that sense of distinctiveness and superiority rests precisely on the ability to transform—to "socialize" and "culturalize"—nature.

Returning now to the issue of women, their pan-cultural second-class status could be accounted for, quite simply, by postulating that women are being identified or symbolically associated with nature, as opposed to men, who are identified with culture. Since it is always culture's project to subsume and transcend nature, if women were considered part of nature, then culture would find it "natural" to subordinate, not to say oppress, them. Yet although this argument can be shown to have considerable force, it seems to oversimplify the case. The formulation I would like to defend and elaborate on in the following section, then, is that women are seen "merely" as being closer to nature than men. That is, culture (still equated relatively unambiguously with men) recognizes that women are active participants in its special processes, but at the same time sees them as being more rooted in, or having more direct affinity with, nature [. . .]

WHY IS WOMAN SEEN AS CLOSER TO NATURE?

It all begins of course with the body and the natural procreative functions specific to women alone. We can sort out for discussion three levels at which this absolute physiological fact has significance:

(1) woman's body and its functions, more involved more of the time with "species life," seem to place her closer to nature, in contrast to man's physiology, which frees him more completely to take up the projects of culture; (2) woman's body and its functions place her in social roles that in turn are considered to be at a lower order of the cultural process than man's; and (3) woman's traditional social roles, imposed because of her body and its functions, in turn give her a different *psychic structure,* which, like her physiological nature and her social roles, is seen as being closer to nature. [. . .]

1. *Woman's physiology seen as closer to nature.*
This part of my argument has been anticipated, with subtlety, cogency, and a great deal of hard data, by de Beauvoir (1953). De Beauvoir reviews the physiological structure, development, and functions of the human female and concludes that "the female, to a greater extent than the male, is the prey of the species" (p. 60). She points out that many major areas and processes of the woman's body serve no apparent function for the health and stability of the individual; on the contrary, as they perform their specific organic functions, they are often sources of discomfort, pain, and danger. The breasts are irrelevant to personal health; they may be excised at any time of a woman's life. "Many of the ovarian secretions function for the benefit of the egg, promoting its maturation and adapting the uterus to its requirements; in respect to the organism as a whole, they make for disequilibrium rather than for regulation—the woman is adapted to the needs of the egg rather than to her own requirements" (p. 24). Menstruation is often uncomfortable, sometimes painful; it frequently has negative emotional correlates and in any case involves bothersome tasks of cleansing and waste disposal; and—a point that de Beauvoir does not mention—in many cultures it interrupts a woman's routine, putting her in a stigmatized state involving various restrictions on her activities and social contacts. In pregnancy many of the woman's vitamin and mineral resources are channeled into nourishing the fetus, depleting her own strength and energies. And finally, childbirth itself is painful and dangerous (pp. 24–27 *passim*). In sum, de Beauvoir concludes that the female "is more enslaved to the species than the male, her animality is more manifest" (p. 239). [. . .]

In other words, woman's body seems to doom her to mere reproduction of life; the male, in contrast, lacking natural creative functions, must (or has the opportunity to) assert his creativity externally, "artificially," through the medium of technology and symbols. In so doing, he creates relatively lasting, eternal, transcendent objects, while the woman creates only perishables—human beings. [. . .]

At the same time, however, woman cannot be consigned fully to the category of nature, for it is perfectly obvious that she is a full-fledged human being endowed with human consciousness just as a man is; she is half of the human race, without whose cooperation the whole enterprise would collapse. She may seem more in the possession of nature than man, but having consciousness, she thinks and speaks; she generates, communicates, and manipulates symbols, categories, and values. She participates in human dialogues not only with other women but also with men.

[. . .] Indeed, the fact of woman's full human consciousness, her full involvement in and commitment to culture's project of transcendence over nature, may ironically explain another of the great puzzles of "the woman problem"—woman's nearly universal unquestioning acceptance of her own devaluation. For it would seem that, as a conscious human and member of culture, she has followed out the logic of culture's arguments and has reached culture's conclusions along with the men. [. . .] In other words, woman's consciousness—her membership, as it were, in culture—is evidenced in part by the very fact that she accepts her own devaluation and takes culture's point of view.

[. . .] Because of woman's greater bodily involvement with the natural functions surrounding reproduction, she is seen as more a part of nature than man is. Yet in part because of her consciousness and participation in human social dialogue, she is recognized as a participant in culture. Thus she appears as something intermediate between culture and nature, lower on the scale of transcendence than man.

2. *Woman's social role seen as closer to nature.*

[. . .] I now wish to show not only how woman's physiological functions have made her appear more involved in "species life," but have also tended universally to limit her social movement, and to confine her universally to certain social contexts which *in turn* are seen as closer to nature. That is, not only her bodily processes but the social situation in which her bodily processes locate her may carry this significance. And insofar as she is permanently associated (in the eyes of culture) with these social milieux, they add weight (perhaps the decisive part of the burden) to the view of woman as closer to nature. I refer here of course to woman's confinement to the domestic family context, a confinement motivated, no doubt, by her lactation processes.

Woman's body, like that of all female mammals, generates milk during and after pregnancy for the feeding of the newborn baby. The baby cannot survive without breast milk or some similar formula at this stage of life. Since the mother's body goes through its lactation processes in direct relation to a pregnancy with a particular child, the relationship of nursing between mother and child is seen as a natural bond, other feeding arrangements being seen in most cases as unnatural and makeshift. Mothers and their children, according to cultural reasoning, belong together. Further, children beyond infancy are not strong enough to engage in major work, yet are mobile and unruly and not capable of understanding various dangers; they thus require supervision and constant care. Mother is the obvious person for this task, as an extension of her natural nursing bond with the children, or because she has a new infant and is already involved with child-oriented activities. Her own activities are thus circumscribed by the limitations and low levels of her children's strengths and skills: she is confined to the domestic family group; "woman's place is in the home."

Woman's association with the domestic circle would contribute to the view of her as closer to nature in several ways. In the first place, the sheer fact of constant association with children plays a role in the issue; one can easily see how infants and children might themselves be considered part of nature. Infants are barely human and utterly unsocialized; like animals they are unable to walk upright, they excrete without control, they do not speak. Even slightly older children are clearly not yet fully under the sway of culture. They do not yet understand social duties, responsibilities, and morals; their vocabulary and their range of learned skills are small. One finds implicit recognition of an association between children and nature in many cultural practices. For example, most cultures have initiation rites for adolescents (primarily for boys; I shall return to this point below), the point of which is to move the child ritually from a less than fully human state into full participation in society and culture; many cultures do not hold funeral rites for children who die at early ages, explicitly because they are not yet fully social beings. Thus children are likely to be categorized with nature, and woman's close association with children may compound her potential for being seen as closer to nature herself. [. . .]

The second major problematic implication of women's close association with the domestic context derives from certain structural conflicts between the family and society at large in any social system. [. . .] The notion that the domestic unit—the biological family charged with reproducing and socializing new members of the society—is opposed to the public entity— the superimposed network of alliances and relationships that *is* the society—is also the basis of Lévi-Strauss's argument in the *Elementary Structures of Kinship* (1969a). [. . .] And although not every culture articulates a radical opposition between the domestic and the public as such, it is hardly contestable that the domestic is always subsumed by the public; domestic units are allied with one another through the enactment of rules that are logically at a higher level than the units themselves; this creates an emergent unit—society—that is logically at a higher level than the domestic units of which it is composed.

Now, since women are associated with, and indeed are more or less confined to, the domestic context, they are identified with this lower order of social/cultural organization. What are the implications of this for the way they are viewed? First, if the specifically biological (reproductive) function of the family is stressed, then the family (and hence woman) is identified with nature pure and simple, as opposed to culture. But this is obviously too simple; the point seems more adequately formulated as follows: the family (and hence woman) represents lower-level, socially fragmenting, particularistic sort of concerns, as opposed to interfamilial relations representing higher-level, integrative, universalistic sorts of concerns. Since men lack a "natural" basis (nursing, generalized to child care) for a familial orientation, their sphere of activity is defined at the level of interfamilial relations. And hence, so the cultural reasoning seems to go, men are the "natural" proprietors of religion, ritual, politics, and other realms of cultural thought and action in which universalistic statements of spiritual and social synthesis are made. Thus men are identified not only with culture, in the sense of all human creativity, as opposed to nature; they are identified in particular with culture in the old-fashioned sense of the finer and higher aspects of human thought—art, religion, law, etc.

Here again, the logic of cultural reasoning aligning woman with a lower order of culture than man is clear and, on the surface, quite compelling. At the same time, woman cannot be fully consigned to nature, for there are aspects of her situation, even within the domestic context, that undeniably demonstrate her participation in the cultural process. It goes without saying, of course, that except for nursing newborn infants (and artificial nursing devices can cut even this biological tie), there is no reason why it has to be mother—as opposed to father, or anyone else—who remains identified with child care. But even assuming that other practical and emotional reasons conspire to keep woman in this sphere, it is possible to show that her activities in the domestic context could as logically put her squarely in the category of culture.

In the first place, one must point out that woman not only feeds and cleans up after children in a simple caretaker operation; she in fact is the primary agent of their early socialization. It is she who transforms newborn infants from mere organisms into cultured humans, teaching them manners and the proper ways to behave in order to become full-fledged members of the culture. On the basis of her socializing functions alone, she could not be more a representative of culture. Yet in virtually every society there is a point at which the socialization of boys is transferred to the hands of men. The boys are considered, in one set of terms or another, not yet "really" socialized; their entree into the realm of fully human (social, cultural) status can be accomplished only by men. We still see this in our own schools, where there is a gradual inversion in the proportion of female to male teachers up through the grades: most kindergarten teachers are female; most university professors are male.

Or again, take cooking. In the overwhelming majority of societies cooking is the woman's work. No doubt this stems from practical considerations—since the woman has to stay home with the baby, it is convenient for her to perform the chores centered in the home. [. . .] Yet it is also interesting to note that when a culture (e.g. France or China) develops a tradition of *haute cuisine*—"real" cooking, as opposed to trivial ordinary domestic cooking—the high chefs are almost always men. Thus the pattern replicates that in the area of socialization—women perform lower-level conversions from nature to culture, but when the culture distinguishes a higher level of the same functions, the higher level is restricted to men.

In short, we see once again some sources of woman's appearing more intermediate than man with respect to the nature/culture dichotomy. Her "natural" association with the domestic context (motivated by her natural lactation functions) tends to compound her potential for being viewed as closer to nature, because of the animal-like nature of children, and because of the infrasocial connotation of the domestic group as against the rest of society. Yet at the same time her socializing and cooking functions within the domestic context show her to be a powerful agent of the cultural process, constantly transforming raw natural resources into cultural products. Belonging to culture, yet appearing to have stronger and more direct connections with nature, she is once again seen as situated between the two realms.

3. *Woman's psyche seen as closer to nature.*

The suggestion that woman has not only a different body and a different social locus from man but also a different psychic structure is most controversial. I will argue that she probably does have a different psychic structure, but I will draw heavily on Chodorow's paper (1974) to establish first that her psychic structure need not be assumed to be innate; it can be accounted for, as Chodorow convincingly shows, by the facts of the probably universal female socialization experience. Nonetheless, if we grant the empirical near universality of a "feminine psyche" with certain specific characteristics, these characteristics would add weight to the cultural view of woman as closer to nature.

It is important to specify what we see as the dominant and universal aspects of the feminine psyche. If we postulate emotionality or irrationality, we are confronted with those traditions in various parts of the world in which women functionally are, and are seen as, more practical, pragmatic, and this-worldly than men. One relevant dimension that does seem pan-culturally applicable is that of relative concreteness vs. relative abstractness: the feminine personality tends to be involved with concrete feelings, things, and people, rather than with abstract entities; it tends toward personalism and particularism. A second, closely related, dimension seems to be that of relative subjectivity vs. relative objectivity: [. . .] roughly, that men are more objective and inclined to relate in terms of relatively abstract categories, women more subjective and inclined to relate in terms of relatively concrete phenomena—as "general and nearly universal differences" (Chodorow 1974, p. 48).

But the thrust of Chodorow's elegantly argued paper is that these differences are not innate or genetically programmed; they arise from nearly universal features of family structure, namely that "women, universally, are largely responsible for early child care and for (at least) later female socialization" (p. 48) and that "the structural situation of child rearing, reinforced by female and male role training, produces these differences, which are replicated and reproduced in the sexual sociology of adult life" (p. 44). Chodorow argues that, because mother is the early socializer of both boys and girls, both develop "personal identification" with her, i.e. diffuse identification with her general personality, behavior traits, values, and attitudes (p. 51). A son, however, must ultimately shift to a masculine role identity, which involves building an identification with the father. Since father is almost always more remote than mother (he is rarely involved in child care, and perhaps works away from home much of the day), building an identification with father involves a "positional identification," i.e. identification with father's male role as a collection of abstract elements, rather than a personal identification with father as a real individual (p. 49). Further, as the boy enters the larger social world, he finds it in fact organized around more abstract and universalistic criteria; thus his earlier socialization prepares him for, and is reinforced by, the type of adult social experience he will have.

For a young girl, in contrast, the personal identification with mother, which was created in early infancy, can persist into the process of learning female role identity. Because mother is immediate and present when the daughter is learning role identity, learning to be a woman involves the continuity and development of a girl's relationship to her mother, and sustains the identification with her as an individual; it does not involve the learning of externally defined role characteristics (Chodorow 1974, p. 51). This pattern prepares the girl for, and is fully reinforced by, her social situation in later life; she will become involved in the world of women, which is characterized by few formal role differences (Rosaldo 1974, p. 29), and which involves again, in motherhood, "personal identification" with *her* children. And so the cycle begins anew.

Chodorow demonstrates to my satisfaction at least that the feminine personality, characterized by personalism and particularism, can be explained as having been generated by social-structural arrangements rather than by innate biological factors. [. . .] Woman's relationships tend to be, like nature, relatively unmediated, more direct, whereas man not only tends to relate in a more mediated way, but in fact ultimately often relates more consistently and strongly to the mediating categories and forms than to the persons or objects themselves.

It is thus not difficult to see how the feminine personality would lend weight to a view of women as being "closer to nature." Yet at the same time, the modes of relating characteristic of women undeniably play a powerful and important role in the cultural process. For just as relatively unmediated relating is in some sense at the lower end of the spectrum of human spiritual functions, embedded and particularizing rather than transcending and synthesizing, yet that mode of relating also stands at the upper end of that spectrum. Consider the mother–child relationship. Mothers tend to be committed to their children as individuals, regardless of sex, age, beauty, clan affiliation, or other categories in which the child might participate. Now any relationship with this quality—not just mother and child but any sort of highly personal, relatively unmediated commitment—may be seen as a challenge to culture and society "from below," insofar as it represents the fragmentary potential of individual loyalties vis-à-vis the solidarity of the group. But it may also be seen as embodying the synthesizing agent for culture and society "from above," in that it represents generalized human values above and beyond loyalties to particular social categories. Every society must have social categories that transcend personal loyalties, but every society must also generate a sense of ultimate moral unity for all its members above and beyond those social categories. Thus that psychic mode seemingly typical of women, which tends to disregard

categories and to seek "communion" (Chodorow, p. 55, following Bakan, 1966) directly and personally with others, although it may appear infra-cultural from one point of view, is at the same time associated with the highest levels of the cultural process.

THE IMPLICATIONS OF INTERMEDIACY

My primary purpose in this paper has been to attempt to explain the universal secondary status of women. Intellectually and personally, I felt strongly challenged by this problem; I felt compelled to deal with it before undertaking an analysis of woman's position in any particular society. Local variables of economy, ecology, history, political and social structure, values, and world view—these could explain variations within this universal, but they could not explain the universal itself. And if we were not to accept the ideology of biological determinism, then explanation, it seemed to me, could only proceed by reference to other universals of the human cultural situation. Thus the general outlines of the approach—although not of course the particular solution offered—were determined by the problem itself, and not by any predilection on my part for global abstract structural analysis.

I argued that the universal devaluation of women could be explained by postulating that women are seen as closer to nature than men, men being seen as more unequivocally occupying the high ground of culture. The culture/nature distinction is itself a product of culture, culture being minimally defined as the transcendence, by means of systems of thought and technology, of the natural givens of existence. This of course is an analytic definition, but I argued that at some level every culture incorporates this notion in one form or other, if only through the performance of ritual as an assertion of the human ability to manipulate those givens. In any case, the core of the paper was concerned with showing why women might tend to be assumed, over and over, in the most diverse sorts of world views and in cultures of every degree of complexity, to be closer to nature than men. Woman's physiology, more involved more of the time with "species life"; woman's association with the structurally subordinate domestic context, charged with the crucial function of transforming animal-like infants into cultured beings; "woman's psyche," appropriately molded to mothering functions by her own socialization and tending toward greater personalism and less mediated modes of relating—all these factors make woman appear to be rooted more directly and deeply in nature. At the same time, however, her "membership" and fully necessary participation in culture are recognized by culture and cannot be denied. Thus she is seen to occupy an intermediate position between culture and nature.

This intermediacy has several implications for analysis, depending upon how it is interpreted. First, of course, it answers my primary question of why woman is everywhere seen as lower than man, for even if she is not seen as nature pure and simple, she is still seen as achieving less transcendence of nature than man. Here intermediate simply means "middle status" on a hierarchy of being from culture to nature.

Second, intermediate may have the significance of "mediating," i.e. performing some sort of synthesizing or converting function between nature and culture, here seen (by culture) not as two ends of a continuum but as two radically different sorts of processes in the world. The domestic unit—and hence woman, who in virtually every case appears as its primary representative—is one of culture's crucial agencies for the conversion of nature into culture, especially with reference to the socialization of children. Any culture's continued viability depends upon properly socialized individuals who will see the world in that culture's terms and adhere more or less unquestioningly to its moral precepts. The functions of the domestic unit must be closely controlled in order to ensure this outcome; the stability of the domestic unit as an institution must be placed as far as possible beyond question. (We see some aspects of the protection of the integrity and stability of the domestic group in the powerful

taboos against incest, matricide, patricide, and fratricide.) Insofar as woman is universally the primary agent of early socialization and is seen as virtually the embodiment of the functions of the domestic group, she will tend to come under the heavier restrictions and circumscriptions surrounding that unit. Her (culturally defined) intermediate position between nature and culture, here having the significance of her *mediation* (i.e. performing conversion functions) between nature and culture, would thus account not only for her lower status but for the greater restrictions placed upon her activities. In virtually every culture her permissible sexual activities are more closely circumscribed than man's, she is offered a much smaller range of role choices, and she is afforded direct access to a far more limited range of its social institutions. Further, she is almost universally socialized to have a narrower and generally more conservative set of attitudes and views than man, and the limited social contexts of her adult life reinforce this situation. This socially engendered conservatism and traditionalism of woman's thinking is another— perhaps the worst, certainly the most insidious— mode of social restriction, and would clearly be related to her traditional function of producing well-socialized members of the group.

Finally, woman's intermediate position may have the implication of greater symbolic ambiguity. Shifting our image of the culture/nature relationship once again, we may envision culture in this case as a small clearing within the forest of the larger natural system. From this point of view, that which is intermediate between culture and nature is located on the continuous periphery of culture's clearing; and though it may thus appear to stand both above and/or below culture, it is simply outside and around it. We can begin to understand then how a single system of cultural thought can often assign to woman completely polarized and apparently contradictory meanings, since extremes, as we say, meet. That she often represents both life and death is only the simplest example one could mention.

For another perspective on the same point, it will be recalled that the psychic mode associated with women seems to stand at both the bottom and the top of the scale of human modes of relating. The tendency in that mode is to get involved more directly with people as individuals, and not as representatives of one social category or another; this mode can be seen as either "ignoring" (and thus subverting) or "transcending" (and thus achieving a higher synthesis of) those social categories, depending upon the cultural view for any given purpose. Thus we can account easily for both the subversive feminine symbols (witches, evil eye, menstrual pollution, castrating mothers) and the feminine symbols of transcendence (mother goddesses, merciful dispensers of salvation, female symbols of justice, and the strong presence of feminine symbolism in the realms of art, religion, ritual, and law). Feminine symbolism, far more often than masculine symbolism, manifests this propensity toward polarized ambiguity—sometimes utterly exalted, sometimes utterly debased, rarely within the normal range of human possibilities.

If woman's (culturally viewed) intermediacy between culture and nature has this implication of generalized ambiguity of meaning characteristic of marginal phenomena, then we are also in a better position to account for those cultural and historical "inversions" in which women are in some way or other symbolically aligned with culture and men with nature. A number of cases come to mind: the Siriono of Brazil, among whom, according to Ingham (1971: 1098), "nature, the raw, and maleness" are opposed to "culture, the cooked, and femaleness"; Nazi Germany, in which women were said to be the guardians of culture and morals; European courtly love, in which man considered himself the beast and woman the pristine exalted object—a pattern of thinking that persists, for example, among modern Spanish peasants (see Pitt-Rivers, 1961; Rosaldo, 1974). And there are no doubt other cases of this sort, including some aspects of our own culture's view of women. Each such instance of an alignment of women with culture rather than nature requires detailed analysis of specific historical and ethnographic data. But in indicating how nature in general, and the feminine

mode of interpersonal relations in particular, can appear from certain points of view to stand both under and over (but really simply outside of) the sphere of culture's hegemony, we have at least laid the groundwork for such analyses.

In short, the postulate that woman is viewed as closer to nature than man has several implications for further analysis, and can be interpreted in several different ways. If it is viewed simply as a *middle* position on a scale from culture down to nature, then it is still seen as lower than culture and thus accounts for the pan-cultural assumption that woman is lower than man in the order of things. If it is read as a *mediating* element in the culture-nature relationship, then it may account in part for the cultural tendency not merely to devalue woman but to circumscribe and restrict her functions, since culture must maintain control over its (pragmatic and symbolic) mechanisms for the conversion of nature into culture. And if it is read as an *ambiguous* status between culture and nature, it may help account for the fact that, in specific cultural ideologies and symbolizations, woman can occasionally be aligned with culture, and in any event is often assigned polarized and contradictory meanings within a single symbolic system. Middle status, mediating functions, ambiguous meaning—all are different readings, for different contextual purposes, of woman's being seen as intermediate between nature and culture.

CONCLUSIONS

Ultimately, it must be stressed again that the whole scheme is a construct of culture rather than a fact of nature. Woman is not "in reality" any closer to (or further from) nature than man—both have consciousness, both are mortal. But there are certainly reasons why she appears that way, which is what I have tried to show in this paper. The result is a (sadly) efficient feedback system: various aspects of woman's situation (physical, social, psychological) contribute to her being seen as closer to nature, while the view of her as closer to nature is in turn embodied in institutional forms that reproduce her situation. The implications for social change are similarly circular: a different cultural view can only grow out of a different social actuality; a different social actuality can only grow out of a different cultural view.

It is clear, then, that the situation must be attacked from both sides. Efforts directed solely at changing the social institutions—through setting quotas on hiring, for example, or through passing equal-pay-for-equal-work laws—cannot have far-reaching effects if cultural language and imagery continue to purvey a relatively devalued view of women. But at the same time efforts directed solely at changing cultural assumptions—through male and female consciousness-raising groups, for example, or through revision of educational materials and mass-media imagery—cannot be successful unless the institutional base of the society is changed to support and reinforce the changed cultural view. Ultimately, both men and women can and must be equally involved in projects of creativity and transcendence. Only then will women be seen as aligned with culture, in culture's ongoing dialectic with nature.

REFERENCES

Bakan, David. 1966. *The Duality of Human Existence.* Boston.

Chodorow, Nancy. 1974. "Family Structure and Feminine Personality." In *Woman, Culture and Society.* Michelle Rosaldo and Louise Lamphere, eds. Stanford.

De Beauvoir, Simone. 1953. *The Second Sex.* New York.

Ingham, John M. 1971. "Are the Sirionó Raw or Cooked?" *American Anthropologist* 73:1092–9.

Lévi-Strauss, Claude. 1969a. *The Elementary Structures of Kinship.* Trans. J.H. Bell and J.R. von Sturmer; ed. R. Needham. Boston.

———. 1969b. *The Raw and the Cooked.* Trans J. and D. Weightman. New York.

Lowie, Robert. 1956 [1935]. *The Crow Indians.* New York.

Pitt-Rivers, Julian. 1961. *People of the Sierra.* Chicago.

Rosaldo, Michelle. 1971. "Women, Culture and Society: A Theoretical Overview." In *Woman, Culture and Society.* Michelle Rosaldo and Louise Lamphere, eds. Stanford.

Siu, R. G. H. 1968. *The Man of Many Qualities.* Cambridge, Mass.

NOTE

1. With all due respect to Lévi-Strauss (1969a, b, and *passim*).

2 • *Susan Carol Rogers*

FEMALE FORMS OF POWER AND THE MYTH OF MALE DOMINANCE
A Model of Female/Male Interaction in Peasant Society

DISCUSSION QUESTIONS

1. What is the difference between "formal" and "informal" power?
2. What are the forms of informal power exerted by women in the village of G.F.?
3. Why does Rogers argue that male dominance is a "myth"?
4. Why do women support the myth rather than acknowledge the reality of their power?

INTRODUCTION

[In all societies] the men usually exercise control . . . the sheer physiological facts of existence make [the female] role secondary to that of the male in the decision-making processes at any level higher than the purely domestic . . . [In non-primitive societies] for a good part of her life a woman may be free to make some impact on the male world. It is curious therefore that this has not been felt more. Even with these increased opportunities, the woman's role is still secondary. (Fox 1969:31–32)

That women virtually everywhere play a subordinate role is a recurrent implicit or explicit assumption in anthropological literature. Whether this is due to the androcentrism of anthropologists or of human societies in general remains an open question. This paper challenges simple assumptions of

male dominance, asking what forms it takes in traditional societies, what is the actual position of women in such settings, and how these two are related.

In most societies, males evidently tend to monopolize positions of authority and are more involved with formal political institutions than women are. If anthropologists limit their interests to formal political processes, assuming these to be the most significant, men obviously appear to be dominant, and women to be relatively powerless. This dominance/subordination pattern gains further credence in the fact that in many societies, both men and women behave as if men were dominant and as if formal decision-making processes, controlled by men, were actually the most important. Anthropologists seem generally to have accepted this behavior at face value, and we are left

An abridged version of Susan Carol Rogers, 1975. "Female Forms of Power and the Myth of Male Dominance: a Model of Female/Male Interaction in Peasant Society." *American Ethnologist*, Volume 2, Issue 4, pages 727–756, November 1975. Reprinted with the kind permission of the author and of the publisher.

with an assumption of virtually universal male dominance and a preoccupation with formal forms of power.

The result is the formulation of power models which leave no room for informal power. Recently, scholars have turned more attention to women's roles, finding that women often wield significant amounts of power in the sense of having considerable involvement in important decision-making processes. But because women tend to wield power without directly participating in formal political institutions, their power does not fit into earlier models and so has not been explained in terms of larger societal-level processes. In an attempt to redress the imbalance in extant male-oriented data, students of female power have tended to dismiss outright, or to treat as a relatively uninteresting given, male forms of power and culturally elaborated ideologies of male dominance. Because of a lack of appropriate analytical tools or (until recently) relevant data, the relationship between female and male forms of power has not been explored.

The purpose of this paper is to explore the larger structural dimensions of women's power, using peasant society as an example. I will demonstrate that although peasant men monopolize positions of authority and are shown public deference by women, thus superficially appearing to be dominant, they wield relatively little real power. Theirs is a largely powerless authority, often accompanied by a felt sense of powerlessness in the face both of the world at large and of the peasant community itself. On the other hand, within the context of peasant society, women control a lion's share of important resources and decisions. So if we limit our investigation to the relative actual power of peasant men and women, eliminating for the moment those sources of power which are beyond the reach of either sex group, women appear to be generally more powerful. At the same time, the symbolic power of men should not be underestimated, nor can it be left unexplained.

I will argue that a non-hierarchical power relationship between the categories "male" and "female"

is maintained in peasant society by the acting-out of a myth of male dominance. I take myth to be the expression of an idea which may form a significant part of the belief system of its perpetuators, but which articulates a "truth which . . . does not relate to the ordinary matter-of-fact world of everyday things" (Leach 1969:107). Thus, one cannot understand the significance of a myth by interpreting it as a literally-believed idea which defines, in any very direct or complete way, ordinary behavior. In this case, it may be factually demonstrated that peasant society is not male dominated yet a myth of male dominance paradoxically serves to order social relationships in a non-hierarchical manner. Except for specific patterns of behavior directly linked with its expression, this myth does not directly determine ordinary behavior: males do not actually dominate, nor do either men or women literally believe them to be dominant.

The perpetuation of this myth is in the interests of both peasant women and men because it gives the latter the appearance of power and control over all sectors of village life, while at the same time giving to the former actual power over those sectors of life in the community which may be controlled by villagers. The two sex groups, in effect, operate within partially divergent systems of perceived advantages, values, and prestige, so that the members of each group see themselves as the winners with respect to the other. Neither men nor women believe that the myth is an accurate reflection of the actual situation. But each sex group believes (or appears to) that the opposite sex perceives the myth as reality, with the result that each is actively engaged in maintaining the illusion that males are, in fact, dominant.

I propose that the myth of male dominance will occur within societies having the characteristics listed below. These are associated with a wide variety of peasant societies but are undoubtedly also characteristic of other social contexts. These features include: (1) Women are primarily associated with the domestic. (2) The society is domestic-oriented: the domestic sphere is of central importance, at least socially, and has important implications for life beyond the domestic. (3) To the extent that formal positions and forms of power are not accessible to women, most ordinary and important interactions occur in the context of a face-to-face community, where informal relationships and forms of power are at least as significant a force in everyday life as formalized, authorized positions of power. (4) Men have greater access to jural and other formal rights. (5) They engage in activities which can be treated as important. (6) Men and women are approximately equally dependent on each other economically, socially, politically, or in other important ways. This last feature insures that both groups will play along and a relatively even balance of power will be maintained. It also renders inappropriate the analytical strategy of using autonomy as a measure of relative power: because the two sex groups are mutually interdependent, neither can be more autonomous than the other.

The extant literature on peasant societies offers ample evidence of the conditions sketched above: peasant male lack of real power; public behavior suggesting that peasant societies are male dominated; substantial power (generally informal or supernatural) wielded by peasant women, both in the household and the community; high degree of mutual interdependence between peasant men and women. These data suggest several contradictions which are resolved by a myth of male dominance, operating as I have suggested. More detailed ethnographic data from G.F., a French peasant village, further illustrates the themes in the literature through specific examples of the interplay of male and female power in a peasant community.

G.F.[1]

G.F., for centuries a peasant village, lies in the fertile rolling hills of the northeastern corner of France. Its population of 350, clustered in a nucleated settlement surrounded by outlying fields, has remained constant since the turn of the century. Village land once supported virtually all of its approximately eighty-five households, but since the

1950s, tiny family farms have become unviable. Increasing numbers of men have left farming for work in nearby steel mills; now only eleven households still farm (mixed grains and dairy). Farm households are the most admired within the village, and farmers monopolize local positions of prestige. Those who have left farming rent their land to kin or neighbors and retain close ties with their tenants, lending a hand during busy seasons. As far as possible, factory families have retained the behavior patterns and values of farm families. Farmers and factory workers alike feel alienated from, and hostile to, urban life. In spite of the daily commute to work in the city, factory workers do not identify with urban workers and do not participate in workers' organizations or activities. All households, farm and factory alike, raise their own garden vegetables, fruits and poultry.

The village may be conceptualized as three spheres, each affecting the size and shape of the others. The domestic sphere is solid and strong, the core of village life. The village sphere surrounds it and is more visible and more fragile. This complex, in turn, fits into the much larger sphere of the outside world. Women are in control of the domestic sphere and leave concerns and activities beyond that to the men. As directress of the household, a woman is responsible for growing, buying, and preparing food for her family, carrying out day-to-day duties of child-rearing, maintaining relationships with kin beyond the nuclear family, keeping household (and farm) records, and managing the family budget. Farm wives have as their major responsibility the feeding and care, including milking, of farm animals, which are housed in the barn adjoining the kitchen of each house. No married women are employed outside of the home.

Women form informal groups based on kin and neighborhood ties. These groups include several generations of individuals, belonging to both farm and factory households. The village is divided into about fifteen neighborhoods, invisible to an outsider, but clearly defined for villagers. Each morning, the baker's wife drives a van through the village, stopping in each neighborhood so that neighbor women come out together to buy their bread and chat. The baker's wife acts as a gossip broker, spreading news between neighborhoods. In the evening, those women who do not have their own cows gather in the barn of the nearest woman who does to buy the day's supply of milk. All village houses are built very close to the street and to each other, with the kitchen in the front. Women keep one eye on the window during much of the day, so that little happens in the neighborhood without their knowledge. Although women rarely visit each other's homes or leave their own neighborhoods, they keep in close contact with each other in the course of their daily work.

In contrast to the women, men spend most of their time away from home. Their work takes them to outlying fields or to factories outside of the village; otherwise, they gather in the cafe or the forge in the center of the village, choosing their closest associates from the village at large and forming informal groups of age mates of the same occupation. While women's conversations and interests are largely restricted to discussions of local activities and individuals, men's conversations often cover topics which extend beyond the village such as regional and national politics. These discussions almost invariably end with a shrug of the shoulders and "Well, that's life; what can you expect?" They are interested in the outside world, but regard it with marked resignation and fatalism.

There are several male voluntary associations in the village: hunting and fishing societies, a local chapter of the farmers' union (FNSEA) as well as the village governing body, the Municipal Council. But few local men belong to the hunting and fishing societies. All village farmers belong to the farmers' union, and, as a farmers' organization, it is quite prestigious. But its members say privately that the local chapter is powerless, dominated by national headquarters run by "capitalist farmers" who take little interest in the problems of peasant farmers. The Municipal Council is highly prestigious too and great excitement surrounds local elections, amounting to public judgment of the prestige of the candidates. Soon after elections, however, interest

dwindles. The café is regularly frequented only on Sunday afternoons when a group of old men come to play cards. Other men stop by occasionally during the week, but it is often deserted, and some men never go at all.

Men and women play complementary roles in G.F. The family is considered an inviolable unit: divorce is not tolerated, and unmarried individuals are rare and treated with ambivalence. Prestige accrues to families, not individuals. Especially in the farm families, but in factory families as well, men and women perform different but essential economic functions. The farms and commercial enterprises in the village are family enterprises, requiring the full-time commitment of both husband and wife. On the farms, there is some infraction of the sexual division of labor: men help their wives in the barns during slack seasons, and women help in the fields during the busy haying and harvest periods. Men dislike intensely working in the barns, considering it the most demeaning of the work they do. At the same time, women complain bitterly about working in the fields. A man in the barn is helping his wife and is under her orders, while a woman in the fields is helping her husband and is under his orders. No men help their wives with other domestic work or gardening, and women never help with ploughing or planting field crops. Factory wives have, at most, only a vague notion of the kind of work their husbands do.

Men and women inherit equally so husband and wife both bring property to the family. For this reason, intravillage marriages have been common and still comprise about a third of all village marriages. Land remains in the name of its heir, even after marriage. Because non-farmers prefer to rent land to close kin, a farmer may gain access to more land through his wife's, as well as his own, kin ties.

In their relationships with men, women seem to be subdued and respectful. If, by exceptional circumstances, a woman finds herself in the male domain—in the mayor's office on Election Day, for instance—she is visibly ill-at-ease, retiring, and ignored by the men. If a group of men are in her home, she silently serves them food or drinks and then retires to a corner to watch and listen. She is unlikely to leave the room, but she is equally unlikely to participate. Even when her own husband is the only man present, she is apt to be quiet. My conversations with women, even those who were very outspoken, usually ended when the husband came home. He was allowed to take over the conversation and always seemed to assume that I would be more interested in talking to him.[2] This outward deference does not, however, mean that women are necessarily subordinated. Male and female spheres are very clearly defined, and a member of one sex group simply does not belong in the domain of the other; the male sphere includes dealings with the outside world, including visiting outsiders.

One gets a very different impression of women when they are observed in a room of men, on one hand, and with a group of women, on the other. The woman in the corner is a sharp observer; what she sees is later reported to other women amidst clicking tongues, shaking heads, or gales of laughter. Women are not particularly awestruck by men, despite the impression they give when publicly in their presence. If a man happens on a group of women in the street or in a barn, they invariably disperse, fall silent, or change their conversation, losing their feminine ambiance. Thus, while women are non-participating observers of the male world, men have even less access to the female world. Women's behavior and men's tendency to take over in public prevent the latter from acquiring the same amounts of information as women can. Women do not seem to be overwhelmingly interested in male attention or concerns. In gatherings of the extended family or other mixed groups, the sexes segregate themselves, and there is little interchange between men and women. Each prefers, and feels more comfortable in, the company of his or her own sex group.

Specific examples of power processes illustrate the power wielded by G.F. women both in the household and in the community at large. For instance, women are responsible for managing the family budget, including the allocation of pocket money to their husbands. Mme. Gabin, a factory wife, does not give her husband any part of his paycheck, so he has to do odd jobs around the village to earn money for cigarettes and an occasional trip to the cafe. While most wives are more generous, they find nothing particularly remarkable about this behavior. Men grumble privately about their wives' refusal to give them more money, but are reluctant to complain too loudly, as that would imply that they were not fully in charge at home. "My wife," said one farmer, "is my minister of finance . . . I'm the one who gives out the money in my house, even though sometimes I need to ask for some of it back again." Ideally, major budget decisions are made mutually, with the husband as final authority. When there is a disagreement, however, it is the wife who usually wins, although the final decision is often attributed to the husband's change of heart. For instance, Mme. Francois wanted a motorbike for fetching the cows from pasture. She argued at length with her husband, who insisted that they could not afford one for at least a year. Two weeks later, she had a motorbike. When I asked her about it, she might have said, "I control the budget and I wanted it, so too bad for him, I went out and bought it." But rather, she winked and said simply, "Pierre changed his mind."

Women are also responsible for child rearing. Farm children of both sexes work with their mothers, until boys become their fathers' assistants at adolescence. Factory wives have less contact with their children, since little or no work is demanded of them at home. In both farm and factory households, children are considered important, but family life does not revolve around them, and mothers are not notably child-oriented. Nonetheless, it is mothers who help children with their schoolwork and are responsible for day-to-day discipline and guidance. Fathers act as disciplinarians and are quite distant from their children. Until recently, for instance, girl children addressed their fathers by the formal *vous*. A mother's control over her children is enhanced by an authoritarian father: The threat of appealing to the rather frightening figure of "papa" is generally enough to keep the children in line when her own efforts fail.

Major decisions about the children's future are made in a similar way to budget decisions. In marriage arrangements, the father ideally has the final word. A young man who wants to marry a girl must first gain permission to come see her at home (*entrer*). This is arranged through an intermediary, usually an individual related by marriage or blood to both the prospective bride and groom. Formal permission to come in is granted by the girl's father and is tantamount to permission to marry.

Claire Nicolas (22), a farmer's daughter, met a young man from outside the village whom she wanted to marry. Her father was unenthusiastic about the match, but her mother was adamantly opposed, saying that she still needed Claire's help at home. When Claire finally ran away to get married, her mother refused to go to the wedding or to let other family members go. Later, when Claire came home to visit, her mother threw her out of the house. According to village women, Claire's father would have accepted the marriage were it not for his wife's unreasonable (in their minds) opposition.

Christine Motelet (20), another farmer's daughter, had as a suitor a young farmer from a neighboring village. Her father was pleased with the match and promptly granted permission to come in. Christine, however, met a factory worker, Gilbert, whom she preferred. Her father was violently opposed to this match, but her mother was not. After five months, he granted Gilbert permission to come in. For her wedding, Christine and her mother wanted to hold two banquets but were not sure if Papa would consent. M. Motelet explained to me innumerable times that the old custom of holding two or three wedding banquets was very nice, but simply too expensive nowadays; Christine would only have one. Shortly before the wedding, he began explaining that, after all, "you don't marry off your daughter every day . . . we might as well do it right." Two banquets were held. No reference was made to the wishes of Christine or her mother in the course of any of my discussions of the subject with M. Motelet, and although they were usually present, they remained silent.

I do not know exactly what means are used to cajole, bully, or convince men to accept their wives' positions in these kinds of decision-making processes. Clearly, a wife is in control of her household; it is her sphere of activity and interest, and she is selective in the information she shares with her husband about it. His dependence on her to run the household, manage its finances and, in the case of farmers and shopkeepers, contribute to the family enterprise, gives her an important power base from which to operate.

Because activities in the village sphere are closely linked to the household unit, women's power extends beyond the domestic even though the village sphere falls in the male domain. For example, the Municipal Council is made up of nine village men, elected every six years. Immediately following elections, they choose a mayor from among themselves. Within the highly centralized French state, the decision-making powers of Municipal Councils—especially those in small villages—are very limited. A seat on the Council, however, is a mark of high status within the community. Two parties are always represented in the elections, but they reflect village factions and have no ties with national parties. Because prestige accrues to families rather than individuals, it is to a woman's advantage that her husband be elected to the Council. Because of its lack of actual important decision-making powers, it is not especially in her interest to be on the Council herself.

Within a priori limits as to who may be seriously considered for a seat (i.e., no factory workers or shopkeepers), women play a powerful role in influencing the composition of the Council. A farm wife may alternatively push her husband into the political arena, or, by demanding more help from him at home and refusing to help him in his work, prevent him from entering the race. Furthermore, because of the well-organized communications network among women, they are able to influence public opinion and so affect the outcome of the elections. The wife of a contender in the 1971 elections said: "Women fight with each other to get their husbands on the Municipal Council . . . there are aunts and cousins who don't even speak to each other because it's always between two groups, so they spread ugly rumors and all that to get people to vote for one or the other side." Even women whose husbands are not running actively participate in the "fight." Just before the 1971 elections, the wife of a factory worker spread a rumor that one of the contenders had molested her daughter. This man, a farmer, a member of an old village family, and part of the slate put up by the group who won most of the Council seats, was defeated.

Each party unofficially decides before the elections who its choice for mayor will be. The position of mayor carries the highest prestige, but its incumbent must spend a great deal of time attending to mayoral duties and there are few contenders for the job. Women undoubtedly have a great deal of influence here. Although most wives are eager for their husbands to get a seat on the Council, they are unwilling to make the sacrifices necessary for their husbands to spend so much time away from the family enterprise. The wife of one contender for a Council seat said that she threatened to divorce her husband if he put himself up for mayor. Later, she said that she had only been joking, but that "really, he's already hardly ever at home and if he were mayor, we wouldn't have any family life left. I couldn't stand that" (Karnoouh and Arlaud 1973).

In the early 1960s, six of the village farmers formed a machine cooperative (CUMA), as peasants have been urged by the national government to do since the late 1940s. They have been unusually successful in that they not only own many farm machines in common, but they also work together during the busy seasons, working each member's fields in turn. They complain constantly about the organization. "It's too democratic. We need a chief, but no one is willing to let anyone else be chief or to take the responsibility himself, so it takes forever to decide anything, or else we just don't decide." They give two compelling reasons for not abandoning the effort: the cost of farm machinery is prohibitive

for ordinary farmers, and they do not want their wives to have to work in the fields anymore. An individual farmer needs extra help during the busy seasons. The wives of non-CUMA farmers—and all farm wives in pre-CUMA days—are expected to provide it. But this has never, strictly speaking, been women's work. Women are outspoken in their dislike of it, considering it dirty, exhausting, and demeaning, although before CUMA, they had little choice. It might be more accurate, then, to phrase the second reason for CUMA's success as the wives' refusal to work in the fields anymore. In fact, CUMA wives speak very warmly of CUMA, never criticizing it. They undoubtedly encourage (at the least) their husbands to make it continue to work.

Another example of women's influence on the shape of the male village sphere is their part in the move from farm to factory. Because the success of a farm depends largely on the wife's willingness to make extensive work contributions as well as on her careful financial management, she must be fully committed to the farm or it will certainly fail. She thus has sufficient power to make her husband give up farming. In so doing, she assures her family of an income that is lower than that of farmers on average, but more dependable. Further, by pushing her husband to the factory, she relieves herself of a great deal of labor, especially the daily drudgery of animal care. On the other hand, leaving farming entails a considerable drop in her family's prestige in the community. This is a dilemma which each woman—and family—resolves for herself in her own circumstances. Virtually all of the young girls in the village say that they will absolutely refuse to marry a farmer. Few of the young men in the village are so disparaging of farming, but farmers' sons are ambivalent about their future occupations, usually citing the reputed difficulty of finding a girl willing to be a farmer's wife as their main reason for indecision. Thus women, within limits set by external economic conditions, have a great deal of influence on occupation patterns quite exterior to their domestic spheres.

FEMALE FORMS OF POWER AND THE MYTH OF MALE DOMINANCE

In G.F. as in many other peasant societies, sex roles are clearly defined and largely non-overlapping, with men and women performing very different but equally essential and mutually interdependent tasks. In general, peasant women center their activities in the domestic sphere, which is apt to include frequent interaction with relatively heterogeneous groups of female kin and/or neighbors. Men, on the other hand, tend to form groups which are more homogeneous and loosely knit, to do work which is located outside of the domestic sphere, and to participate more often in community- rather than domestic-based activities. The domestic unit, however, is central to peasant society as the major production, consumption, and social unit. The work men do outside of its physical bounds is their contribution to the family enterprise.

The work done by women in the domestic sphere is far more regulated and controllable than that done by men. It varies little from day to day, in contrast to work in the fields, with its seasonal variations and its vulnerability to such vagaries as the weather and plant disease. Even the factory work done by G.F. men is regulated by forces no more controllable by workers than is the weather controllable by farmers. This theme of impotence outside the domestic sphere and control within extends to the realm of political and social activities. Because of the peasant community's position in the larger society and internal attitudes, peasants have little control over extra-household political and economic decisions: they have practically no influence over government policy on farm prices, taxes, social security, and the like. From their positions in the household, women have significant input into the only aspect of village government over which villagers have any control: who will be elected to the Municipal Council. Because they remain in the domestic sphere, they have little impact on the actual decisions made by the Council, but these are, in effect, trivial.

Female solidarity in neighborhood and kin groups also provide women with relatively more emotional security than men have. As Blaxter (1971:122–123) points out, the women in these groups are not consistently charitable to each other. However, because each is securely in control of her own domestic sphere and not attempting to deal with what is beyond her reach in the world outside, her relationships with other women are likely to be less colored with the distrust, competition, and caution which characterize relationships between men. This may also be an important reason why "you don't find [peasant] women in this [beaten] condition, no matter how hard their lives have been" (Blythe 1969:105).

Given these observations, it seems that Fox's assumption—because women tend to be limited to domestic level decision-making, they universally play a secondary role (1969:31–32)—is a false one. Clearly, domestic decision-making is of primary importance in peasant societies, because there are few extra-domestic decisions of importance to community life which are within the power of peasants to make.

But the fact remains that high prestige does accrue to male activities, whatever their actual importance. No matter who ultimately makes household decisions, male peasants are usually considered to be the heads of households, to hold authority positions there, and overtly to make important decisions. In G.F., as undoubtedly elsewhere, women play an important part in shaping their husbands' positions in the community, but it is his position which determines family status. I do not believe, therefore, that the male impact can be so summarily dismissed.

I would argue that a kind of dialectic operates in peasant society, a delicately balanced opposition of several kinds of power and authority: overt and covert, formal and informal, direct and indirect. For this reason, the claim that one sex group is necessarily in a "primary" or dominant role and the other in a "secondary" one is a specious oversimplification.

But several crucial questions remain unanswered: why are peasant men so widely characterized by a felt lack of power, yet just as frequently shown to be deferred to, to monopolize positions of authority and prestige, and assumed to be dominant? If women actually do wield a significant amount of power, why do they behave as if men monopolize it? Why do women in G.F. insist that "Pierre changed his mind" when Pierre is only, as usual, doing what his wife told him to do? Why do both men and women in so many peasant societies publicly grant such high prestige to the relatively insignificant extra-household activities of men?

These apparent anomalies are resolved by the model positing that male dominance exists in peasant society as a "myth," acting to maintain a non-hierarchical power balance between men and women. Even though men are not literally dominant, both sex groups act publicly as if they were because each maintains its own power by doing so. The kinds of overt power and authority exercised by men obviously depend on the perpetuation of the myth. Women's power also stems from it in a variety of ways. Because extra-household activities are given highest prestige, it is to men's advantage to claim the village sphere as their own. It is to the peasant woman's advantage as well, because it leaves her in control of the domestic sphere, which is the only sphere over which villagers may have much control. Here we have a power/prestige balance between the two. It remains balanced as long as prestige is accorded to activities and actors in one, while actual power emanates from the other.

Within the domestic sphere, it is also to the woman's advantage that her husband be a figure of authority. This may enhance her control over children. Further, by acting as if her husband had the final word in those decisions requiring a joint agreement, she protects herself from mistakes or omissions: "We don't have such and such because my husband wouldn't buy it." More important, if he is allowed to be the overt decision maker, his status as "head of the family" is preserved, and with it, his—and his family's—image in the community. Here, the exchange is between power and image: "I'll give you credit for making the decisions here, if you'll make the ones I tell you to."

The model I have sketched can function only if no one explicitly admits that it is only a myth. Both men and women must publicly act as if men actually do the most important activities and are fully in charge. But in spite of their public deference toward men, women are clearly aware that men's political and social activities are relatively trivial and their economic activities no more important than those of women. They are also aware that they have significant power in shaping their husbands' activities and that it is most often themselves who make decisions in the home. In G.F. women seem to be cognizant of the situation: condescending winks and smiles passed when no men are looking, Mme. Rouyer's confidence: "Most of the wives here really control their husbands, even if it doesn't look like it." More oblique, "humorous" comments are sometimes made between women: "*Vous savez, les hommes, c'est une drole de race,*" "Men! They think they're being such a big help and all they do is make a mess . . . Oh, they're no good for anything!"

At the same time, men act publicly as if they believed the myth. They take seriously the village government and other village level activities, and interpret any public implication of their lack of control over their wives and families as a slur on their manliness. For instance, in G.F., the purchaser (a farmer from a neighboring village) at a land auction which village farmers tried unsuccessfully to prevent incurred a great deal of hostility and verbal abuse from villagers. One farmer later remarked with great disgust, "He probably bought that land because his wife told him not to come home without it, and he was more afraid of her than of us." On the other hand, their well-documented fatalism and felt lack of power, in G.F. their constant shoulder shrugging and "That's life, what can you expect?," their private belittling of village government or farmers' organizations and their resigned complaints of overbearing wives indicate that they believe no more than their wives do that men actually dominate much of anything.

It is significant that these remarks, indicating that neither men nor women believe males to be dominant, are expressed only privately, and well out of earshot of members of the opposite sex. It indicates that both sexes believe that it is important to act and speak publicly in mixed groups as if males were dominant, because they assume that the other group believes it to be true. By operating in this manner, they avoid any overt challenge to the whole system of rewards and perceived advantages. Even if men are not so sure how important male activities are, they continue to act as if they are the most important because women expect them to. If men are aware that women may have more effective power than they, it is acceptable to them as long as there is no public challenge, so they may continue to think that women do not realize it. If they are given credit for running things, that is good enough. Women, on the other hand, buy their power by granting men authority and respect, assuming that if they allow men to believe that male dominance actually exists, men will not notice that women actually wield considerable power. Male behavior would lead women to believe that they have succeeded in their ruse. From this point of view, too, the system would collapse if women were forced to recognize publicly that men were not actually being taken in either.

THE MYTH OF MALE DOMINANCE AND BEYOND

My analysis seriously undermines claims that women in "traditional" societies are necessarily the downtrodden, subordinated creatures they have been assumed to be. By the same token, it leaves in limbo another familiar claim: that women are necessarily emancipated in the process of modernization. Certainly, if male dominance is mythical in some societies, there are others (including our own), where it exists as a lived reality. How might we understand the difference between the two situations or processes of transition from one to the other? The set of conditions I have proposed as necessary for male dominance to be mythical provides a framework for thinking about the dynamics of change in gendered power relationships.

If the first three elements (those relating to female power) remain unchanged, while either of the second two (relating to male power) are negated, men will become relatively more dependent upon women, women's power will increase, and male dominance will no longer be expressed, even as a myth. On the other hand, the reverse may happen if the female forms of power described here are undermined, while males retain greater access to formal rights and participation in activities viewed as important. In that case, women may become more dependent on men and lose power such that male dominance becomes a reality. In these two cases, I have assumed that men and women remain interdependent. A third possibility may result from the negation of male/female interdependence. If women and men become largely autonomous categorically, power (or types of power) will not be distributed on the basis of gender. In this case, the concept of a power balance between the two sex groups becomes meaningless. These are but three of the possible transformations of the system, chosen as among the most probable.

CONCLUSION

In this paper, I have addressed the problem of power distribution between women and men in peasant societies. Beginning with the assumption that males are universally dominant, I showed that this generalization is based on definitions and models which deal with only a limited and male-oriented range of phenomena and is clearly contradicted by considerable empirical evidence of real power wielded by peasant women. But several anomalies remain: both men and women behave publicly as if males were dominant, while at the same time male peasants seem to be characterized by a felt lack of power. I have proposed a model to explain these apparent contradictions: male dominance operates as a myth that sustains a balance between the informal power of women and men's overt power. Both kinds of power depend on the persistence of the myth, which itself is maintained by a degree of ignorance—feigned or real—on the part of both groups as to how the system actually operates.

This analysis implies a new set of problems and a new way of viewing old ones, thus raising far more questions than it can answer. The most important point to be made is that it is only when we stop looking at male roles and forms of power as the norm and begin to look at female arrangements as equally valid and significant, though perhaps different in form, that we can see how male and female roles are intertwined and so begin to understand how human societies operate.

REFERENCES

Blaxter, Lorraine. 1971. Rendre Service and Jalousie. In Gifts and Poison. F. G. Bailey, Ed. New York: Schocken Books. pp. 119–138.

Blythe, Ronald. 1969. Akenfield: Portrait of an English Village. New York: Dell.

Fox, Robin. 1969. Kinship and Marriage. Baltimore: Penguin Books.

Karnoouh, Claude, and Jean Arlaud. 1973. Quiet Days in the Lorraine. 16 mm film produced by CNRS, Musée de I'Homme (Paris). US. distributor: Film Images, New York.

Leach, Edmund. 1969. Genesis as Myth and Other Essays. London: Jonathan Cape.

Michaelson, Evalyn, and Walter Goldschmidt. 1971. Female Roles and Male Dominance among Peasants. Southwestern Journal of Anthropology 27:330–352.

NOTES

1. All proper names used in this section are pseudonyms. The data on "G.F." were collected during my six-month field study in the village (March–September 1971), and supplemented by return trips in 1972 and 1973. I am grateful to Claude Karnoouh for initial introductions and many helpful discussions of village life. I also owe a debt to Henri Mendras, director of the Groupe de Recherches Sociologiques (Nanterre), for making available to me data collected earlier in G.F. by members of his research team.

2. This pattern largely accounts for the view we have been given by male anthropologists of the "androcentrism" of peasant societies (e.g., Michaelson and Goldschmidt 1971), which obscures or negates the female power reported by female anthropologists. A male anthropologist has no opportunity to see or talk to women except when they are in the presence of at least one man. He is thus continually used as part of the set for enacting the myth of male dominance and is given little reason to believe that it might be a myth. I was introduced to G.F. by a male anthropologist whose earlier work on informal political strategies in the village had led him to suspect that women might play a crucial role; he was interested in my project precisely because, as a man, he had been unable to obtain the data to confirm or elaborate this idea.

3 • *Nancy Scheper-Hughes*

LIFEBOAT ETHICS
Mother Love and Child Death in Northeast Brazil

DISCUSSION QUESTIONS

1. What does "lifeboat ethics" mean?
2. Why do mothers in El Alto decide to neglect certain infants and nurture others?
3. How does the indifference of institutions like the government and the church contribute to this situation?
4. How do these stories of maternal neglect challenge assumptions that mothers are universally nurturing and caring?

> I have seen death without weeping
>
> The destiny of the Northeast is death
>
> Cattle they kill
>
> To the people they do something worse
>
> —Anonymous Brazilian singer (1965)

"Why do the church bells ring so often?" I asked Nailza de Arruda soon after I moved into a corner of her tiny mud-walled hut near the top of the shantytown called the Alto do Cruzeiro (Crucifix Hill). I was then a Peace Corps volunteer and a community development/health worker. It was the dry and blazing hot summer of 1965, the months following the military coup in Brazil, and save for the rusty, clanging bells of N.S. das Dores Church, an eerie quiet had settled over the market town that I call Bom Jesus da Mata. Beneath the quiet, however, there was chaos and panic. "It's nothing," replied Nailza, "just another little angel gone to heaven."

Nailza had sent more than her share of little angels to heaven, and sometimes at night I could hear her engaged in a muffled but passionate discourse with one of them, two-year-old Joana. Joana's photograph, taken as she lay propped up in her tiny cardboard coffin, her eyes open, hung on a wall next to one of Nailza and Ze Antonio taken on the day they eloped.

Nailza could barely remember the other infants and babies who came and went in close succession. Most had died unnamed and were hastily baptized in their coffins. Few lived more than a month or two. Only Joana, properly baptized in a church at

From Nancy Scheper-Hughes, 1989. "Death without weeping: Has poverty ravaged mother love in the shantytowns of Brazil?" *Natural History* 98(10): 8–16. Reprinted with the kind permission of the author.

the close of her first year and placed under the protection of a powerful saint, Joan of Arc, had been expected to live. And Nailza had dangerously allowed herself to love the little girl.

In addressing the dead child, Nailza's voice would range from tearful imploring to angry recrimination: "Why did you leave me? Was your patron saint so greedy that she could not allow me one child on this earth?" Ze Antonio advised me to ignore Nailza's odd behavior, which he understood as a kind of madness that, like the birth and death of children, came and went. Indeed, the premature birth of a stillborn son some months later "cured" Nailza of her "inappropriate" grief, and the day came when she removed Joana's photo and carefully packed it away.

More than fifteen years elapsed before I returned to the Alto do Cruzeiro, and it was anthropology that provided the vehicle of my return. Since 1982 I have returned several times in order to pursue a problem that first attracted my attention in the 1960s. My involvement with the people of the Alto de Cruzeiro now spans a quarter of a century and three generations of parenting in a community where mothers and daughters are often simultaneously pregnant.

The Alto do Cruzeiro is one of three shantytowns surrounding the large market town of Bom Jesus in the sugar plantation zone of Pernambuco in Northeast Brazil, one of the many zones of neglect that have emerged in the shadow of the now tarnished economic miracle of Brazil. For the women and children of the Alto do Cruzeiro, the only miracle is that some of them have managed to stay alive at all.

The Northeast is a region of vast proportions (approximately twice the size of Texas) and of equally vast social and developmental problems. The nine states that make up the region are the poorest in the country and are representative of the Third World within a dynamic and rapidly industrializing nation. Despite waves of migrations from the interior to the teeming shantytown of coastal cities, the majority still live in rural areas on farms and ranches, sugar plantations, and mills.

Life expectancy in the Northeast is only forty years, largely because of the appallingly high rate of infant and child mortality. Approximately one million children in Brazil under the age of five die each year. The children of the Northeast, especially those born in shantytowns on the periphery of urban life, are at a very high risk of death. In these areas, children are born without the traditional protection of breast-feeding, subsistence gardens, stable marriages, and multiple adult caretakers that exists in the interior. In the hillside shantytowns that spring up around cities or, in this case, interior market towns, marriages are brittle, single parenting is the norm, and women are frequently forced into the shadow economy of domestic work in the homes of the rich or into unprotected and oftentimes "scab" wage labor on the surrounding sugar plantations, where they clear land for planting and weed for a pittance, sometimes less than a dollar a day. The women of the Alto may not bring their babies with them into the homes of the wealthy, where the often-sick infants are considered sources of contamination, and they cannot carry the little ones to the riverbanks where they wash clothes because the river is heavily infested with schistosomes and other deadly parasites. Nor can they carry their young children to the plantations, which are often several miles away. At wages of a dollar a day, the women of the Alto cannot hire baby sitters. Older children who are not in school will sometimes serve as somewhat indifferent caretakers. But any child not in school is also expected to find wage work. In most cases, babies are simply left at home alone, the door securely fastened. And so many also die alone and unattended.

Bom Jesus da Mata, centrally located in the plantation zone of Pernambuco, is within commuting distance of several sugar plantations and mills. Consequently, Bom Jesus has been a magnet for rural workers forced off their small subsistence plots by large landowners wanting to use every available piece of land for sugar cultivation. Initially, the rural migrants to Bom Jesus were squatters who were given tacit approval by the mayor to put up temporary straw huts on each of the three hills overlooking the town. The Alto do Cruzeiro is the oldest, the largest, and the poorest of the shantytowns. Over the past three decades many of the original migrants have become permanent residents, and the primitive and temporary straw huts have been replaced by small homes (usually of two rooms) made of wattle and daub, sometimes covered with plaster. The more affluent residents use bricks and tiles. In most Alto homes, dangerous kerosene lamps have been replaced by light bulbs. The once tattered rural garb, often fashioned from used sugar sacking, has likewise been replaced by store-bought clothes, often castoffs from a wealthy *patrão* (boss). The trappings are modern, but the hunger, sickness, and death that they conceal are traditional, deeply rooted in a history of feudalism, exploitation, and institutionalized dependency. My research agenda never wavered. The questions I addressed first crystallized during a veritable "die-off" of Alto babies during a severe drought in 1965. The food and water shortages and the political and economic chaos occasioned by the military coup were reflected in the handwritten entries of births and deaths in the dusty, yellowed pages of the ledger books kept at the public registry office in Born Jesus. More than 350 babies died in the Alto during 1965 alone—this from a shantytown population of little more than 5,000. But that wasn't what surprised me. There were reasons enough for the deaths in the miserable conditions of shantytown life. What puzzled me was the seeming indifference of Alto women to the deaths of their infants, and their willingness to attribute to their own tiny offspring an aversion to life that made their death seem wholly natural, indeed all but anticipated.

Although I found that it was possible, and hardly difficult, to rescue infants and toddlers from death by diarrhea and dehydration with a simple sugar, salt, and water solution (even bottled Coca-Cola worked fine), it was more difficult to enlist a mother herself in the rescue of a child she perceived as ill-fated for life or better off dead, or to convince her to take back into her threatened and besieged home a baby she had already come to think of as an angel rather than as a son or daughter.

I learned that the high expectancy of death, and the ability to face child death with stoicism and equanimity, produced patterns of nurturing that differentiated between those infants thought of as thrivers and survivors and those thought of as born already "wanting to die." The survivors were nurtured, while stigmatized, doomed infants were left to die, as mothers say, *a mingua*, "of neglect." Mothers stepped back and allowed nature to take its course. This pattern, which I call mortal selective neglect, is called passive infanticide by anthropologist Marvin Harris. The Alto situation, although culturally specific in the form that it takes, is not unique to Third World shantytown communities and may have its correlates in our own impoverished urban communities in some cases of "failure to thrive" infants.

I use as an example the story of Zezinho, the thirteen-month-old toddler of one of my neighbors, Lourdes. I became involved with Zezinho when I was called in to help Lourdes in the delivery of another child, this one a fair and robust little tyke with a lusty cry. I noted that while Lourdes showed great interest in the newborn, she totally ignored Zezinho who, wasted and severely malnourished, was curled up in a fetal position on a piece of urine- and feces-soaked cardboard placed under his mother's hammock. Eyes open and vacant, mouth slack, the little boy seemed doomed.

When I carried Zezinho up to the community day-care center at the top of the hill, the Alto women who took turns caring for one another's children (in order to free themselves for part-time work in the cane fields or washing clothes) laughed at my efforts to save Ze, agreeing with Lourdes that here was a baby without a ghost of a chance. Leave him alone, they cautioned. It makes no sense to fight with death. But I did do battle with Ze, and after several weeks of force-feeding (malnourished babies lose their interest in food), Ze began to succumb to my ministrations. He acquired some flesh across his taut chest bones, learned to sit up, and even tried to smile. When he seemed well enough, I returned him to Lourdes in her miserable scrap-material lean-to, but not without guilt about what I had done. I wondered whether returning Ze was at all fair to Lourdes and to his little brother. But I was busy and washed my hands of the matter. And Lourdes did seem more interested in Ze now that he was looking more human.

When I returned in 1982, there was Lourdes among the women who formed my sample of Alto mothers—still struggling to put together some semblance of life for a now-grown Ze and her five other surviving children. Much was made of my reunion with Ze in 1982, and everyone enjoyed retelling the story of Ze's rescue and of how his mother had given him up for dead. Ze would laugh the loudest when told how I had had to force-feed him like a fiesta turkey. There was no hint of guilt on the part of Lourdes and no resentment on the part of Ze. In fact, when questioned in private as to who was the best friend he ever had in life, Ze took a long drag on his cigarette and answered without a trace of irony, "Why my mother, of course." "But of course," I replied.

Part of learning how to mother in the Alto de Cruzeiro is learning when to let go of a child who shows that it "wants" to die or that it has no "knack" or no "taste" for life. Another part is learning when it is safe to let oneself love a child. Frequent child death remains a powerful shaper of maternal thinking and practice. In the absence of firm expectation that a child will survive, mother love as we conceptualize it (whether in popular terms or in the psychobiological notion of maternal bonding) is attenuated and delayed with consequences for infant survival. In an environment already precarious to young life, the emotional detachment of mothers toward some of their babies contributes even further to the spiral of high mortality—high fertility in a kind of macabre lock-step dance to death.

The average woman of the Alto experiences 9.5 pregnancies, 3.5 child deaths, and 1.5 still-births. Seventy percent of all child deaths in the Alto occur in the first six months of life, and 82 percent by the end of the first year. Of all deaths in the community each year, about 45 percent are of children under the age of five.

Women of the Alto distinguish between child deaths understood as natural (caused by diarrhea and communicable diseases) and those resulting from sorcery, the evil eye, or other magical or supernatural afflictions. They also recognize a large category of infant deaths seen as fated and inevitable. These hopeless cases are classified by mothers under the folk terminology "child sickness" or "child attack." Women say that there are at least fourteen different types of hopeless child sickness, but most can be subsumed under two categories—chronic and acute. The chronic cases refer to infants who are born small and wasted. They are deathly pale, mothers say, as well as weak and passive. They demonstrate no vital force, no liveliness. They do not suck vigorously; they hardly cry. Such babies can be this way at birth or they can be born sound but soon show no resistance, no "fight" against the common crises of infancy: diarrhea, respiratory infections, tropical fever.

The acute cases are those doomed infants who die suddenly and violently. They are taken by stealth overnight, often following convulsions that bring on head banging, shaking, grimacing, and shrieking. Women say it is horrible to look at such a baby. If the infant begins to foam at the mouth or gnash its teeth or go rigid with its eyes turned back inside its head, there is absolutely no hope. The infant is "put aside"—left alone—often on the floor in a back room, and allowed to die. These symptoms (which accompany high fevers, dehydration, third-stage malnutrition, and encephalitis) are equated by Alto women with madness, epilepsy, and worst of all, rabies, which is greatly feared and highly stigmatized.

Most of the infants presented to me as suffering from chronic child sickness were tiny, wasted famine victims, while those labeled as victims of acute child attack seemed to be infants suffering from the deliriums of high fever or the convulsions that can accompany electrolyte imbalance in dehydrated babies.

Local midwives and traditional healers, praying women, as they are called, advise Alto women on when to allow a baby to die. On midwife explained: "If I can see that a baby was born unfortuitously, I tell the mother that she need not wash the infant or give it a cleansing tea. I tell her just to dust the infant with baby powder and wait for it to die." Allowing nature to take its course is not seen as sinful by these often very devout Catholic women. Rather, it is understood as cooperating with God's plan.

Often I have been asked how consciously women of the Alto behave in this regard. I would have to say that consciousness is always shifting between allowed and disallowed levels of awareness. For example, I was awakened early one morning in 1987 by two neighborhood children who had been sent to fetch me to a hastily organized wake for a two-month-old infant whose mother I had unsuccessfully urged to breast-feed. The infant was being sustained on sugar water, which the mother referred to as *soro* (serum), using a medical term for the infant's starvation regime in light of his chronic diarrhea. I had cautioned the mother that an infant could not live on *soro* forever.

The two girls urged me to console the young mother by telling her that it was "too bad" that her infant was so weak that Jesus had to take him. They were coaching me in proper Alto etiquette. I agreed, of course, but asked, "And what do *you* think?" Xoxa, the eleven-year-old, looked down at her dusty flip-flops and blurted out, "Oh, Dona Nanci, that baby never got enough to eat, but you must never say that!" And so the death of hungry babies remains one of the best-kept secrets of life in Bom Jesus da Mata.

Most victims are waked quickly and with a minimum of ceremony. No tears are shed, and the neighborhood children form a tiny procession, carrying the baby to the town graveyard where it will join a multitude of others. Although a few fresh flowers may be scattered over the tiny grave, no stone or wooden cross will mark the place, and the same spot will be reused within a few months' time. The mother will never visit the grave, which soon becomes an anonymous one. What, then, can be said of these women? What emotions, what sentiments motivate them?

How are they able to do what, in fact, must be done? What does mother love mean in this inhospitable context? Are grief, mourning, and melancholia present, although deeply repressed? If so, where shall we look for them? And if not, how are we to understand the immoral visions and moral sensibilities that guide their actions?

I have been criticized more than once for presenting an unflattering portrait of poor Brazilian women, women who are, after all, themselves the victims of severe social and institutional neglect. I have described these women as allowing some of their children to die, as if this were an unnatural and inhuman act rather than, as I would assert, the way any one of us might act, reasonably and rationally, under similarly desperate conditions. Perhaps I have not emphasized enough the real pathogens in this environment of high risk: poverty, deprivation, sexism, chronic hunger, and economic exploitation. If mother love is, as many psychologists and some feminists believe, a seemingly natural and universal maternal script, what does it mean to women for whom scarcity, loss, sickness, and deprivation have made that love frantic and robbed them of their grief, seeming to turn their hearts to stone?

Throughout much of human history—as in a great deal of the impoverished Third World today—women have had to give birth and to nurture children under ecological conditions and social arrangements hostile to child survival, as well as to their own well-being. Under circumstances of high childhood mortality, patterns of selective neglect and passive infanticide may be seen as active survival strategies.

They also seem to be fairly common practices historically and across cultures. In societies characterized by high childhood mortality and by a correspondingly high (replacement) fertility, cultural practices of infant and childcare tend to be organized primarily around survival goals. But what this means is a pragmatic recognition that not all of one's children can be expected to live. The nervousness about child survival in areas of northeast Brazil, northern India, or Bangladesh, where a 30 percent or 40 percent mortality rate in the first years of life is common, can lead to forms of delayed attachment and a casual or benign neglect that serves to weed out the worst bets so as to enhance the life chances of healthier siblings, including those yet to be born. Practices similar to those that I am describing have been recorded for parts of Africa, India, and Central America.

Life in the Alto do Cruzeiro resembles nothing so much as a battlefield or an emergency room in an overcrowded inner-city public hospital. Consequently, morality is guided by a kind of "lifeboat ethics," the morality of triage. The seemingly studied indifference toward the suffering of some of their infants, conveyed in such sayings as "little critters have no feelings," is understandable in light of these women's obligation to carry on with their reproductive and nurturing lives.

In their slowness to anthropomorphize and personalize their infants, everything is mobilized so as to prevent maternal overattachment and, therefore, grief at death. The bereaved mother is told not to cry, that her tears will dampen the wings of her little angel so that she cannot fly up to her heavenly home. Grief at the death of an angel is not only inappropriate, it is also a symptom of madness and of a profound lack of faith.

Infant death becomes routine in an environment in which death is anticipated and bets are hedged. While the routinization of death in the context of shantytown life is not hard to understand, and quite possible to empathize with, its routinization in the formal institutions of public life in Bom Jesus is not as easy to accept uncritically. Here the social production of indifference takes on a different, even a malevolent cast.

In a society where triplicates of every form are required for the most banal events (registering a car, for example), the registration of infant and child death is informal, incomplete, and rapid. It requires no documentation, takes less than five minutes, and demands no witnesses other than office clerks. No questions are asked concerning the circumstances of the death, and the cause of death is left blank, unquestioned and unexamined. A neighbor, grandmother, older sibling, or common-law husband may register the death. Since most infants die at home, there is no question of a medical record.

From the registry office, the parent proceeds to the town hall, where the mayor will give him or her a voucher for a free baby coffin. The full-time municipal coffin maker cannot tell you exactly how many baby coffins are dispatched each week. It varies, he says, with the seasons. There are more needed during the drought months and during the big festivals of Carnaval and Christmas and São Joao's Day because people are too busy, he supposes, to take their babies to the clinic. Record keeping is sloppy.

Similarly, there is a failure on the part of city-employed doctors working at two free clinics to recognize the malnutrition of babies who are weighed, measured, and immunized without comment and as if they were not, in fact, anemic, stunted, fussy, and irritated starvation babies. At best, the mothers are told to pick up free vitamins or health "tonic" at the municipal chambers. At worst, clinic personnel will give tranquilizers and sleeping pills to quiet the hungry cries of "sick-to-death" Alto babies.

The church, too, contributes to the routinization of, and indifference toward, child death. Traditionally, the local Catholic church taught patience and resignation to domestic tragedies that were said to reveal the imponderable workings of God's will. If an infant died suddenly, it was because a particular saint had claimed the child. The infant would be an angel in the service of his or her heavenly patron. It would be wrong, a sign of a lack of faith, to weep for a child with such good fortune. The infant funeral was, in the past, an event celebrated with joy. Today, however, under the new regime of "liberation theology," the bells of N.S. das Dores parish church no longer peal for the death of Alto babies, and no priest accompanies the procession of angels to the cemetery where their bodies are disposed of casually and without ceremony. Children bury children in Bom Jesus da Mata. In this most Catholic of communities, the coffin is handed to the disabled and irritable municipal gravedigger, who often chides the children for one reason or another. It may be that the coffin is larger than expected and the gravedigger can find no appropriate space.

The children do not wait for the gravedigger to complete his task. No prayers are recited and no sign of the cross made as the tiny coffin goes into its shallow grave.

When I asked the local priest, Padre Marcos, about the lack of church ceremony surrounding infant and childhood death today in Bom Jesus, he replied: "In the old days, child death was richly celebrated. But those were the baroque customs of a conservative church that wallowed in death and misery. The new church is a church of hope and joy. We no longer celebrate the death of child angels. We try to tell mothers that Jesus doesn't want all the dead babies they send him." Similarly, the new church has changed its baptismal customs, now often refusing to baptize dying babies brought to the back door of a church or rectory. The mothers are scolded by the church attendants and told to go home and take care of their sick babies. Baptism, they are told, is for the living; it is not to be confused with the sacrament of extreme unction, which is the anointing of the dying. And so it appears to the women of the Alto that even the church has turned away from them, denying the traditional comfort of folk Catholicism.

The contemporary Catholic church is caught in the clutches of a double bind. The new theology of liberation imagines a kingdom of God on Earth based on justice and equality, a world without hunger, sickness, or childhood mortality. At the same time, the church has not changed its official position on sexuality and reproduction, including its sanctions against birth control, abortion, and sterilization. The padre of Bom Jesus da Mata recognizes this contradiction intuitively, although he shies away from discussions on the topic, saying he prefers to leave questions of family planning to the discretion and the "good consciences" of his impoverished parishioners. But this, of course, sidesteps the extent to which those good consciences have been shaped by traditional church teachings in Bom Jesus, especially by his recent predecessors. Hence, we can begin to see that the seeming indifference of Alto mothers toward the death of some of their infants is but a pale reflection of the official indifference of church and state to the plight of poor women and children.

Nonetheless, the women of Bom Jesus are survivors. One woman, Biu, told me her life history, returning again and again to the themes of child death, her first husband's suicide, abandonment by her father and later by her second husband, and all the other losses and disappointments she had suffered in her long forty-five years. She concluded with great force, reflecting on the days of Carnaval '88 that were fast approaching:

> No, Dona Nanci, I won't cry, and I won't waste my life thinking about it from morning to night. Can I argue with God for the state that I'm in? No! And so I'll dance and I'll jump and I'll play Carnaval! And yes, I'll laugh and people will wonder at a *pobre* like me who can have such a good time.

And no one did blame Biu for dancing in the streets during the four days at Carnaval—not even on Ash Wednesday, the day following Carnaval '88 when we all assembled hurriedly to assist in the burial of Mercea, Biu's beloved *casual*, her last-born daughter who had died at home of pneumonia during the festivities. The rest of the family barely had time to change out of their costumes. Severino, the child's uncle and godfather, sprinkled holy water over the little angel while he prayed: "Mercea, I don't know whether you were called, taken, or thrown out of this world. But look down at us from your heavenly home with tenderness, with pity, and with mercy." So be it.

AUTHOR'S UPDATE

Readers should consult my book, *Death Without Weeping: the Violence of Everyday Life in Brazil* (University of California 1993). Times and political and economic conditions have since changed radically in Brazil and on the Alto do Cruzeiro. Infant mortality is virtually eliminated and Brazilian women have a lower birth rate than American women. For a discussion of how this reproductive revolution came about, readers should consult my article, "No More Angel Babies on the Alto do Cruzeiro—A Dispatch from Brazil's Child Survival Revolution," published in *Natural History Magazine*, fall 2013. <http://www.naturalhistory mag.com/features/282558/no-more-angel-babies-on-the-alto-do cruzeiro>

1 · *Lila Abu-Lughod*

THE ROMANCE OF RESISTANCE
Tracing Transformations of Power Through Bedouin Women

DISCUSSION QUESTIONS

1. What types of resistance does Abu-Lughod document for Bedouin women?
2. What do these forms of resistance reveal about the forms of power that women confront in their daily lives?
3. How and why have the forms of resistance and forms of power changed over time?

INTRODUCTION

One of the central problematics in the human sciences in recent years has been the relationship of resistance to power. Unlike the grand studies of peasant insurgency and revolution of the 1960s and early 1970s, what one finds now is a concern with unlikely forms of resistance, subversions rather than large-scale collective insurrections, small or local resistances not tied to the overthrow of systems or even to ideologies of emancipation. Scholars seem to be trying to rescue for the record and to restore to our respect such previously devalued or neglected forms of resistance.

The popularity of resistance provokes a number of interesting questions. First, what is the relationship between scholarship or theorizing and the world-historical moment in which it takes place—why, at this particular time, are scholars from diverse disciplines and with extremely different approaches converging on the topic of resistance? Second, what is the ideological significance in academic discourse of projects that claim to bring to light the hitherto ignored or suppressed ways in

An abridged version of Lila Abu-Lughod, 1990. "The Romance of Resistance: Tracing
Transformations of Power through Bedouin Women." Reproduced by permission of the American
Anthropological Association and of the author from *American Ethnologist* Volume 17, Issue 1,
Pages 41–55, February 1990. Not for sale or further reproduction.

which subordinate groups actively respond to and resist their situations? In this article I want to consider a different question: what are the implications of studies of resistance for our theories of power?

For at the heart of this widespread concern with unconventional forms of noncollective, or at least nonorganized, resistance is, I would argue, a growing disaffection with previous ways we have understood power, and the most interesting thing to emerge from this work on resistance is a greater sense of the complexity of the nature and forms of domination. For example, work on resistance influenced by Bourdieu and Gramsci recognizes and theorizes the importance of ideological practice in power and resistance and works to undermine distinctions between symbolic and instrumental, behavioral and ideological, and cultural, social, and political processes.

Despite the considerable theoretical sophistication of many studies of resistance and their contribution to the widening of our definition of the political, it seems to me that because they are ultimately more concerned with finding resistors and explaining resistance than with examining power, they do not explore as fully as they might the implications of the forms of resistance they locate. There is perhaps a tendency to romanticize resistance, to read all forms of resistance as signs of the ineffectiveness of systems of power and of the resilience and creativity of the human spirit in its refusal to be dominated. By reading resistance in this way, we collapse distinctions between forms of resistance and foreclose certain questions about the workings of power.

I want to argue here for a small shift in perspective in the way we look at resistance—a small shift that will have serious analytical consequences. I want to suggest that we should use resistance as a *diagnostic* of power. In this I am taking a cue from Foucault, whose theories, or, as he prefers to put it, analytics of power and resistance, although complex and not always consistent, are at least worth exploring. One of his central propositions, advanced in his most explicit discussion of power, in the first volume of *The History of Sexuality,* is the controversial assertion that "where there is power, there is resistance" (1978:95–96). Whatever else this assertion

implies, certainly Foucault is using this hyperbole to force us to question our understanding of power as always and essentially repressive. As part of his project of deromanticizing the liberatory discourse of our 20th-century so-called sexual revolution, he is interested in showing how power is something that works not just negatively, by denying, restricting, prohibiting, or repressing, but also positively, by producing forms of pleasure, systems of knowledge, goods, and discourses.[1] He adds what some have viewed as a pessimistic point about resistance by completing the sentence just quoted as follows: "Where there is power, there is resistance, and yet, or rather consequently, this resistance is never in a position of exteriority in relation to power" (1978:95–96).

This latter insight about resistance is especially provocative, but to appreciate its significance one must invert the first part of the proposition. This gives us the intuitively sensible "where there is resistance, there is power," which is both less problematic and potentially more fruitful for ethnographic analysis because it enables us to move away from abstract theories of power toward methodological strategies for the study of power in particular situations. As Foucault (1982:209, 211) puts it when he himself advocates this inversion, we can then use resistance "as a chemical catalyst so as to bring to light power relations, locate their position, find out their points of application and the methods used." We could continue to look for and consider nontrivial all sorts of resistance, but instead of taking these as signs of human freedom we will use them strategically to tell us more about forms of power and how people are caught up in them.

In the ethnography of the Awlad 'Ali Bedouins that follows, I want to show how in the rich and sometimes contradictory details of resistance the complex workings of social power can be traced. I also want to show that these same contradictory details enable us to trace how power relations are historically transformed—especially with the introduction of forms and techniques of power characteristic of modem states and capitalist economies. Most important, studying the various forms of resistance will allow us to get at the ways in which intersecting and often conflicting structures of power work together these days in communities that are gradually becoming more tied to multiple and often nonlocal systems. These are central issues for theories of power which anthropologists are in a unique position to consider.

FORMS OF RESISTANCE/FORMS OF POWER

I will be taking as my case the changing situation of women in a Bedouin community in Egypt's Western Desert, not because I want to make an argument about women in particular, but because first, few studies of resistance have focused on women; second, gender power seems to be one of the more difficult forms of power to analyze; and third, the circumstances of doing field work in a sex-segregated society are such that I have more of the kind of rich and minute detail needed for this sort of analysis from women than I do from men. The group of Bedouins I will be discussing are known as Awlad 'Ali and are former sheepherders settled along the Egyptian coast from west of Alexandria to the Libyan border. Although sedentary, they describe themselves as Arabs and claim an affiliation with the Bedouin tribes of eastern Libya. They insistently distinguish themselves from the rural and urban Egyptians of the Nile Valley.

Although I did not begin with any sort of interest in Bedouin women's resistance, I discovered various forms. The first arena for resistance, one I have described elsewhere (Abu-Lughod 1985), is the sexually segregated women's world where women daily enact all sorts of minor defiances of the restrictions enforced by elder men in the community. Women use secrets and silences to their advantage. They often collude to hide knowledge from men; they cover for each other in minor matters, like secret trips to healers or visits to friends and relatives; they smoke in secret and quickly put out their cigarettes when children come running to warn them that men are approaching. These forms of resistance indicate that one way power is exercised in

relation to women is through a range of prohibitions and restrictions which they both embrace, in their support for the system of sexual segregation, and resist, as suggested by the fact that they fiercely protect the inviolability of their separate sphere, that sphere where the defiances take place.

A second and widespread form of resistance is Bedouin girls' and women's resistance to marriages. Indeed, one of the major powers families, and especially elder male relatives like fathers and paternal uncles, wield is control over the arrangement of marriages. Despite their apparent power, actual marriage arrangements are always complicated and involve many people, especially mothers and female relatives. Mothers sometimes successfully block marriages their daughters do not want, even though fathers or other male guardians are supposed to have control. When men are stubborn, however, or are so caught up in strategies and relations of obligation with other men that they will not or cannot reverse a decision, the women may not succeed. Yet even then, they do not necessarily remain silent. One woman whose daughter was forced to marry a cousin sang a song as the groom's relatives came to pick up her daughter for the wedding:

> You're not of the same stature as these your true
> match is the man with the golden insignia . . .
> *intī mā gadā hādhōl*
> *gadāk bū dabābīr yilihban . . .*

The song taunted them with the suggestion that her daughter was more worthy of an officer than of the poor man who was getting her.

Neither are unmarried girls always silent about their feelings about marriages. Girls sing songs as they get water from the wells and publicly at weddings, songs in which they object in particular to older men and their paternal cousins, two categories of men who tend to have binding ties on their fathers that would make their marriage requests hard to refuse.

The most interesting cases are those where women themselves actually resist marriages that have been arranged for them. Their retrospective narratives of resistance were among the most popular storytelling events I heard. The following one was told to me and a group of her daughters-in-law and grandchildren by the old matriarch of the community in which I lived. The events had occurred 60 years earlier.

> He was a first cousin, and I didn't want him. He was an old man and we were living near each other, eating out of one bowl [sharing meals or living in one household]. They came and slaughtered a sheep [to seal the engagement] and I started screaming, I started crying. And my father had bought a new gun, a cartridge gun. He said, "If you don't shut up I'll send you flying with this gun."
>
> Well, there was a ravine and I went over and sat there all day. I sat next to it, saying, "Possess me, spirits, possess me." I wanted the spirits to possess me; I wanted to go crazy. Half the night would pass and I'd be sitting there. I'd be sitting there, until Braika [a relative] came. And she'd cry with me and then drag me home by force and I'd go sleep in her tent. After 12 days, my cousin's female relatives were dyeing the black strip for the top of the tent. They were about to finish sewing the tent I'd live in. And they had brought my trousseau. I said, "I'll go get the dye for you." I went and found they had ground the black powder and it was soaking in the pot, the last of the dye, and I flipped it over—Pow!—on my face, on my hair, on my hands until I was completely black.
>
> My father came back and said, "What's happened here? What's the matter with this girl? Hey you, what's the matter?"
>
> The women explained. He went and got a pot of water and a piece of soap and said, "If you don't wash your hands and your face I'll . . ." So I wash my hands, but only the palms, and I wipe my face, but I only get a little off from here and there. And I'm crying the whole time. All I did was cry.
>
> Then they went and put some supper in front of me. He said, "Come here and eat dinner." I'd eat and my tears were salting each mouthful. I had spent 12 days, and nothing had entered my mouth.

This old woman's narrative, which had two more episodes of resisted marriages before she agreed to one, follows the pattern of many I heard—of women who had resisted the decisions of their fathers, uncles, or older brothers and eventually won.

A third form of Bedouin women's resistance is what could be called sexually irreverent discourse. What I am referring to are instances when women make fun of men and manhood, even though official ideology glorifies and women respect, veil for, and sometimes fear them. In this irreverence one can trace the ways the code of sexual morality and the ideology of sexual difference are forms of men's power. Women seem only too glad when men fail to live up to the ideals of autonomy and manhood, the ideals on which their alleged moral superiority and social precedence are based, especially if they fail as a result of sexual desire. Women joke about certain men behind their backs and they also make fun of men in general ways. For example, Bedouin men and women avow a preference for sons, saying people are happier at the birth of a boy. And yet in one discussion, when I asked what they did when a baby turned out to be a boy, one old woman said, "If it's a boy, they slaughter a sheep for him. The boy's name is exalted. He has a little pisser that dangles." And all the women present laughed.

In my book (Abu-Lughod 1986) I analyzed what I consider to be the most important of the subversive discourses in Bedouin society—a kind of oral lyric poetry. This is the fourth type of resistance. These poem/songs, known as *ghinnāwas* (little songs), are recited mostly by women and young men, usually in the midst of ordinary conversations between intimates. What is most striking about them is that people express through them sentiments that differ radically from those they express in their ordinary-language conversations, sentiments of vulnerability and love. Many of these songs concern relationships with members of the opposite sex toward whom they respond, outside of poetry, with anger or denial of concern. I argued that most people's ordinary public responses are framed in terms of the code of honor and modesty. Through these responses they live and show themselves to be living up to the moral code. Poetry carries the sentiments that violate this code, the vulnerability to others that is ordinarily a sign of dishonorable lack of autonomy and the romantic love that is considered immoral and immodest. Since the moral code is one of the most important means of perpetuating the unequal structures of power, then violations of the code must be understood as ways of resisting the system and challenging the authority of those who represent and benefit from it. When examined for what it can tell us about power, this subversive discourse of poetry suggests that social domination also works at the level of constructing, delimiting, and giving meaning to personal emotions.

The everyday forms of Bedouin women's resistance described above pose a number of analytic dilemmas. First, how might we develop theories that give these women credit for resisting in a variety of creative ways the power of those who control so much of their lives, without either misattributing to them forms of consciousness or politics that are not part of their experience—something like a feminist consciousness or feminist politics—or devaluing their practices as prepolitical, primitive, or even misguided? Second, how might we account for the fact that Bedouin women both resist and support the existing system of power (they support it through practices like veiling, for example), without resorting to analytical concepts like false consciousness, which dismisses their own understanding of their situation, or impression management, which makes of them cynical manipulators? Third, how might we acknowledge that their forms of resistance, such as folktales and poetry, may be culturally provided without immediately assuming that even though we cannot therefore call them cathartic personal expressions, they must somehow be safety valves? I struggled with some of these dilemmas in my earlier work and I find them in the work of others.

With the shift in perspective I am advocating, asking not about the status of resistance itself but about what the forms of resistance indicate about the forms of power that they are up against, we are

onto new ground. In addition to questions such as whether official ideology is really ever hegemonic or whether cultural or verbal resistance counts as much as other kinds, we can begin to ask what can be learned about power if we take for granted that resistances, of whatever form, signal sites of struggle. The forms I have described for Bedouin women suggest that some of the kinds of power relations in which they are caught up work through restrictions on movement and everyday activities, through elder kinsmen's control over marriage, through patrilateral parallel cousin marriage, through a moral system that defines superiority in terms of particular characteristics (like autonomy) that men are structurally more capable of achieving, through a set of practices that imply that maleness is sufficient justification for privilege, and through the linking of sets of sentiments to respectability and moral worth. These are not the only things at work—there are also such things as elder kinsmen's or husbands' control over productive resources, things which may or may not be resisted directly. But to discount the former as merely ideological is to fall into the familiar dichotomies that have kept people from looking at the most significant aspect of this situation: that power relations take many forms, have many aspects, and interweave. And by presupposing some sort of hierarchy of significant and insignificant forms of power, we may be blocking ourselves from exploring the ways in which these forms may actually be working simultaneously, in concert or at cross-purposes.

TRANSFORMATIONS OF POWER AND RESISTANCE

The other advantage of using resistance as a diagnostic of power is, as I argued at the outset, that it can help detect historical shifts in configurations or methods of power. In this final section, I want to turn to the ways in which Bedouin women are living a profound transformation of their social and economic lives. From a careful look at what may initially appear to be trivial matters, something important can be learned about the dynamics of power in situations where local communities are being incorporated into modern states and integrated into a wider economy.

I will make three observations about resistance. The first concerns the fate of traditional subversive forms. Some of these, such as folktales, seem to be dying out as Egyptian television and radio usurp young people's interest. Others, like the kind of poetry described above, are being incorporated into other projects and appropriated by different groups. I had thought, when I left Egypt in 1980, that this form of poetry was also disappearing. In recent years, however, the new popularity of semi-commercial, locally produced cassettes has given traditional Bedouin poetry new life. At the same time, though, its social uses are changing. These poem/songs, always before recited equally by women *and* young men, are becoming in their new form an almost exclusively male forum for resistance. Young men use it to protest or resist the growing power of older kinsmen. The Bedouins' involvement in the market economy has enhanced and rendered more inflexible the power of these older kinsmen in two ways: first, monetarization and the privatization of property, especially land, give patriarchs more absolute economic power; second, as hierarchy in general is becoming more fixed and wealth differences between families are growing more extreme, the tribal ideology of equality which limited the legitimacy of domination by elders is eroding. The shifting deployments of this poetic form of resistance are related to and reveal these complex changes.

The second observation about resistance is that new signs of women's resistance to restrictions on their freedom of movement are beginning to appear. On the one hand, I witnessed a number of arguments between older women and their younger nephews and sons about how harshly these young men were restricting the movements of their sisters and female cousins. Among themselves and in the presence of the young men, the older women expressed outrage and recalled the past, when they had freely gone off to gather wood

and draw water from wells, occasionally on the way exchanging songs and tokens of love with young men. Adolescent girls and young women began to complain that they felt imprisoned or that they were bored. This resistance to the restrictions on movement and the smears of reputation intended to enforce them do not index any new spirit or consciousness of the possibilities of freedom on the part of women. Rather, I would argue, they index women's sense of the new forms of the powers of restrictions which have come with sedentarization and the consequently more extreme division between men and women.

Third, a new and very serious form of resistance is developing in the women's world, one that—unlike the two just discussed, which widen the gap between women and men—pits young women against older women and indirectly against their fathers and uncles, while putting them in alliance with young men of their own generation. These generational conflicts involve a deceptively frivolous issue: lingerie. In the early 1980s, I witnessed the following incident. Two of the adolescent girls in our community had bought negligees from a peddler. (Most people sleep in their ordinary clothes.) The girls' grandmothers were furious, and they threatened to set the negligees on fire if the girls did not sell them back. When the grandmothers had some visitors, they demanded that one of the girls bring out her nightgown to show them. The women all touched it and pulled at it, and one old grandmother in the midst of hilarity put the sheer lime-green gown over her layers of clothing, danced around the room and made for the doorway, as if to go out and show the men. She was pulled back.

By 1987, it had become almost routine for brides to display nylon slips and negligees with their trousseaus. Most adolescent girls bought such items for their marriages, and their older female relatives would no longer try so hard to thwart them. Now the frontier has shifted to bras, cosmetics, and bobby pins. In the household in which I lived, for example, many of the tensions between one of the daughters and her mother were over the homemade bra the girl insisted on wearing. Her mother was scandalized by the way it drew attention to her chest, and she frequently criticized her. The daughter persisted, as Bedouin children nearly always do in the face of parental pressure, retaliating by criticizing her mother for having so many children and running such a chaotic household.

What the older women object to in the purchase of lingerie is not just the waste of precious money on useless items, but the immodesty of these emergent technologies of sexualized femininity to be deployed in the pleasing of husbands. Not that *they* had not worked to remain in their husbands' good graces; they had fulfilled their duties in maintaining their households and their moral reputations. But they had relied on their kinsmen for assurance of good treatment and redress of mistreatment by husbands. They had gained their right to support through their status as kinswomen or mothers and through the work they contributed to the extended household. Members of this older generation, at least as I saw them, were often dignified in comportment, but at the same time they were usually loud, sure of themselves, and hardly what we would consider feminine.

Young women, in resisting for themselves the older women's coarseness by buying moisturizing creams and frilly nylon negligees are, it could be argued, chafing against expectations that do not take account of the new set of socioeconomic circumstances into which they are moving. Some of the girls with whom I spoke still, like their grandmothers, want to resist marriages. They do not object to the fact that marriages are arranged for them, but they do resist particular matches, mostly those which do not promise to fulfill certain fantasies. What they say they want, and often sing about in short public wedding songs, are husbands who are rich (or at least wage-earning) and educated (or at least familiar with a more Egyptian way of life), husbands who will buy them the things they want—the dressing tables, the beds, the clothes, the shoes, the watches, the baby bottles, and even the washing machines that mean the end of back-breaking outdoor work. Sedentarized and more

secluded, these girls aspire to be housewives in a way their mothers never were. Their well-being and standard of living now depend enormously on the favor of husbands in a world where everything costs money, where there are many more things to buy with it, and where women have almost no independent access to it. Men's powers now importantly include the power to buy things and to punish and reward women through giving them.

As the veils they wear get sheerer and these young women become more involved in the kind of sexualized femininity associated with the world of consumerism, they are becoming increasingly enmeshed in new sets of power relations of which they are scarcely aware. These developments are tied to their new financial dependence on men but at the same time are directed pointedly at, and are a form of resistance to, their elders of both sexes. If resistance signals power, then this form of resistance may indicate the desperation with which their elders are trying to shore up the old forms of family-based authority which the moral code of sexual modesty and propriety supported.

Like the older forms of women's resistance described earlier, these young women's forms are also culturally given, not indigenously as before, but rather by emulation of and borrowing (not to mention buying) from Egyptian society. These resistances are again, therefore, neither outside of nor independent from the systems of power. Nevertheless, what is peculiar to these new forms of resistance is how they travel between two systems and what this can tell us about relations of power under such conditions. For instance, along with the lingerie and cosmetics goes a pleasure in listening to Egyptian rather than Bedouin songs and watching Egyptian television. Ironically, in taking up these Egyptian forms and deploying them against their elders, these young Bedouins are also beginning to get caught up in the new forms of subjection such discourses imply. These new forms are part of a world in which kinship ties are attenuated while companionate marriage, marital love based on choice, and romantic love are idealized, making central women's attractiveness and individuality as enhanced and perhaps necessarily marked by differences in adornment (hence the importance of cosmetics, lingerie, and differentiation in styles and fabrics of clothing).

In resisting the axes of kin and gender, the young women who want the lingerie, Egyptian songs, and fantasies of private romance their elders resist are perhaps unwittingly enmeshing themselves in an extraordinarily complex set of new power relations. These bind them irrevocably to the Egyptian economy, itself tied to the global economy, and to the Egyptian state, many of whose powers depend on separating kin groups and regulating individuals. For the Awlad 'Ali Bedouins the old forms of kin-based power, which the resistances described above have allowed us to see clearly, are becoming encompassed and crosscut by new forms, methods, and sources of subjection. These new forms do not necessarily displace the old. Sometimes, as in the case of the demands of sexual modesty and settling down, they run along the same tracks. Sometimes, as in the case of older men's greater control of resources and precedence in the political realm, they just catch up the old forms into larger, nonlocal networks of economic and institutional power, something which gives them a new kind of rigidity. Some, however, like the penetration of consumerism and the disciplines of schooling and other institutions of the state, with their attendant privatization of the individual and the family, are altogether new and just add to the complex ways that Bedouin women are involved in structures of domination.

Although their elders are suspicious of many of these new forms, the young women (and young men, I should add) do not seem to suspect the ways in which their forms of rebellion against their elders are backing them into wider and different sets of authority structures, or the ways in which their desires for commodities and for separation from kin and gender groups might be producing a kind of conformity to a different range of demands. This raises a final question: do certain modern techniques or forms of power work in such indirect ways, or seem to offer such positive attractions, that

people do not as readily resist them? There is some evidence for this, and it is a question worth exploring comparatively.[2] In the case of the Awlad 'Ali Bedouins, though, there seem to be new forms of resistance to just these kinds of processes. If that is so, then such resistances can be used as diagnostics as well.

One sign that these new forms of subjection *are* felt as such is that among those Awlad 'Ali who have become most involved with and have had most contact with secular Egyptian state institutions (especially schools) and cultural life (especially through television, radio, fashions and consumerism)—those Awlad 'Ali living in major towns and the city of Marsa Matruh, for example—there has been a growing interest in the Islamic movement. These Awlad 'Ali signal their participation in the movement by adopting Islamic dress, engaging in Koran study, and changing their behavior, especially toward members of the opposite sex. If within the Arab world generally the Islamic movement represents a resistance to Western influence, consumerism, and political and economic control by a Westernized elite, within the Awlad 'Ali community it serves as a perfect response to, symptom of, and therefore key to understanding the kinds of contradictory sets of power relations in which the Awlad 'Ali are currently caught. For young Bedouin women and men, it is a kind of double resistance to two conflicting sets of demands—the demands of their elders and the system of face to face kin-based authority they represent, on the one hand, and on the other the demands of the national westernized and capitalist state in which, because of their cultural differences, lack of education, and lack of ties to the elite, they participate only marginally. For young women, adopting modest Islamic dress has the added advantage of allowing them to distinguish themselves from their uneducated sisters and their elders while leaving them irreproachable in matters of morality.

This may seem like boxes within boxes within boxes. But that is the wrong image. A better one might be fields of overlapping and intersecting forms of subjection whose effects on particularly placed individuals at particular historical moments vary tremendously. As I have tried to show, tracing the many resistances of old and young Awlad 'Ali, men and women, and those from the desert and the town, gives us the means to begin disentangling these forms, helps us to grasp the fact that they interact and helps us to understand the ways in which they do. It also gives us the means to understand an important dynamic of resistance and power in nonsimple societies. If the systems of power are multiple, then resisting at one level may catch people up at other levels.

This is the kind of contribution careful analyses of resistance can make. My argument in this paper has been that we should learn to read in various local and everyday resistances the existence of a range of specific strategies and structures of power. Attention to the forms of resistance in particular societies can help us become critical of partial or reductionist theories of power. The problem has been that those of us who have sensed that there is something admirable about resistance have tended to look to it for hopeful confirmation of the failure—or partial failure—of systems of oppression. Yet it seems to me that we respect everyday resistance not just by arguing for the dignity or heroism of the resistors but by letting their practices teach us about the complex interworkings of historically changing structures of power.

REFERENCES

Abu-Lughod, Lila. 1985. A Community of Secrets. Signs: Journal of Women in Culture and Society 10:637–657.

———. 1986. Veiled Sentiments: Honor and Poetry in a Bedouin Society. Berkeley and Los Angeles: University of California Press.

Bourdieu, Pierre. 1977. Outline of a Theory of Practice. Cambridge: Cambridge University Press.

———. 1979. The Disenchantment of the World. *In* Algeria 1960. Pp. 1–94. Cambridge: Cambridge University Press and Maison des Sciences de l'Homme.

Foucault, Michel. 1977. Discipline and Punish. New York: Pantheon.

———. 1978. The History of Sexuality. Vol. 1: An Introduction. New York: Random House.

———. 1980. Power/Knowledge. Colin Gordon, ed. New York: Pantheon.

———. 1982. Afterword: The Subject and Power. *In* Beyond Structuralism and Hermeneutics. Hubert Dreyfus and Paul Rabinow. Pp. 208–226. Chicago: University of Chicago Press.

NOTES

1. A particularly clear statement of his view of power as productive is the following: "What makes power hold good, what makes it accepted, is simply the fact that it doesn't only weigh on us as a force that says no, but that it traverses and produces things, it induces pleasure, forms of knowledge, produces discourse. It needs to be considered as a productive network that runs through the whole social body, much more than as a negative instance whose function is repression" (Foucault 1980:119). His position on resistance is more ambiguous. Despite his insistence that resistance is always tied to power, he occasionally implies the persistence of some residual freedom (Foucault 1982:225).

2. Bourdieu (1977, 1979) and Foucault (especially 1977), among others of course, offer useful ways of thinking about the effects of new forms of power associated with modern states in a capitalist world because they attend to the microprocesses that affect individuals in seemingly trivial ways.

2 · *Saba Mahmood*

FEMINIST THEORY, EMBODIMENT, AND THE DOCILE AGENT
Some Reflections on the Egyptian Islamic Revival

DISCUSSION QUESTIONS

1. How does Mahmood define "agency"? How does this definition challenge liberal feminist ideas of agency and power?
2. Why do women in the piety movement veil?
3. How does veiling express their understanding of the relationship between bodies and norms, between "outward behavior" and "inward dispositions"?

Over the last fifty years, one of the key questions that has occupied many feminist theorists is how issues of historical and cultural specificity should inform both the analytics and politics of any feminist project. While this questioning has resulted in serious attempts at integrating issues of sexual, racial, class, and national difference within feminist theory, questions of religious difference have remained relatively unexplored. The vexed relationship between feminism and religious traditions is perhaps most manifest in discussions of Islam. This is partly because of the historically contentious relationship that Islamic societies have had with what has come to be called "the West," and partly because of the challenges contemporary Islamic movements pose to secular-liberal politics of which feminism has been an integral (if critical) part. The

suspicion with which many feminists tended to view Islamist movements only intensified in the aftermath of the September 11, 2001, attacks on the United States, especially the immense groundswell of anti-Islamic sentiment that has followed since. If supporters of the Islamist movement were disliked before for their social conservatism and their rejection of liberal values (key among them "women's freedom"), their association with terrorism—now almost taken for granted—has served to further reaffirm their status as agents of a dangerous irrationality.[1]

In this essay, I analyze the conceptual challenges that women's participation in the Islamist movement poses to feminist theorists and anthropologists of gender through an ethnographic account of an urban women's piety movement, organized

An abridged version of Saba Mahmood, 2001. "Feminist Theory, Embodiment, and the Docile Agent: Some Reflections on the Egyptian Islamic Revival." Reproduced by permission of the American Anthropological Association and of the author from *Cultural Anthropology*, Volume 16, Issue 2, Pages 202–236, May 2001. Not for sale or further reproduction. A later version appears in Saba Mahmood, *The Politics of Piety: The Islamic Revival and the Feminist Subject* (Princeton University Press, 2005).

through a loose network of mosques, which is part of the Islamic Revival in Cairo, Egypt.[2] "Islamic Revival" is a term that refers not only to the activities of state-oriented political groups but more broadly to a religious ethos or sensibility that has developed within Muslim societies more generally, particularly in Egypt, since the 1970s.[3] This essay is based on two years of fieldwork (1995–97) with a grassroots women's piety movement based in Cairene mosques. This movement is composed of women from a variety of socio-economic backgrounds who gather in mosques to teach each other about Islamic scriptures, social practices, and forms of bodily comportment considered germane to the cultivation of the ideal virtuous self.[4] Even though Egyptian Muslim women have always had some measure of informal training in Islam, the mosque movement represents an unprecedented engagement with scholarly materials and theological reasoning that had to date been the purview of learned men. Movements such as this, if they do not provoke a yawning boredom among secular intellectuals, certainly conjure up a whole host of uneasy associations such as fundamentalism, the subjugation of women, social conservatism, reactionary atavism, cultural backwardness, and the rest. My aim in this essay is not to analyze the reductionism of an enormously complex phenomenon that these associations entail; nor am I interested in recovering a redeemable element within the Islamist movement by recuperating its liberatory potentials. Instead, I want to focus quite squarely on the conceptions of self, moral agency, and embodiment that undergird the practices of this nonliberal movement so as to come to an understanding of the ethical projects that animate it.

I want to begin by exploring how a particular notion of human agency in feminist scholarship— one that seeks to locate the political and moral autonomy of the subject in the face of power—is brought to bear upon the study of women involved in patriarchal religious traditions such as Islam. I will argue that despite the important insights it has provided, this model of agency sharply limits our ability to understand and interrogate the lives of women whose sense of self, aspirations, and projects have been shaped by nonliberal traditions. In order to analyze the participation of women in religious movements such as the Egyptian piety movement I describe, I want to suggest we think of agency not as a synonym for resistance to relations of domination but as a capacity for action that historically specific relations of subordination enable and create. This relatively open-ended understanding of agency draws upon poststructuralist theory of subject formation but also departs from it, in that I explore those modalities of agency whose meaning and effect are not captured within the logic of subversion and resignification of hegemonic norms. As I will argue, it is only once the concept of agency is detached from the trope of resistance that a series of analytical questions open up that are crucial to understanding nonliberal projects, subjects, and desires whose logic exceeds the entelechy of liberatory politics. In conclusion I will discuss the political effects of such a modality of analysis.

TOPOGRAPHY OF THE MOSQUE MOVEMENT

The women's piety movement occupies a somewhat paradoxical place in relationship to feminist politics. It represents the first time in Egyptian history that such a large number of women have mobilized to hold lessons in Islamic doctrine in mosques, thereby altering the historically male-centered character of mosques as well as Islamic pedagogy.[5] This trend has, of course, been facilitated by the mobility and sense of entitlement engendered by women's greater access to education and employment outside of the home in post-colonial Egypt. In the last forty years women have entered new social domains and acquired new public roles from which they were previously excluded. A paradoxical effect of these developments is the proliferation of forms of piety that seem incongruous with the trajectory of the transformations that enabled them in the first place.[6] Notably, even though this movement has empowered women to enter the field of Islamic pedagogy in the institutional setting of mosques, their participation is critically structured by, and seeks to uphold, the limits of a discursive tradition that regards subordination to a transcendent will (and thus, in many instances, to male authority) as its coveted goal.

AGENCY, RESISTANCE, FREEDOM

The pious subjects of the women's mosque movement occupy an uncomfortable place in feminist scholarship: they pursue practices and ideals embedded within a tradition that has historically accorded women a subordinate status, and they seek to cultivate virtues that are associated with feminine passivity and submissiveness (e.g. shyness, modesty, perseverance, and humility—some of which I discuss below). In other words, the very idioms that women use to assert their presence in previously male-defined spheres are also those that secure their subordination. While it would not have been unusual in the 1960s to account for women's participation in such movements in terms of false consciousness, or the internalization of patriarchal norms through socialization, there has been an increasing discomfort with explanations of this kind. Drawing on work in the humanities and the social sciences since the 1970s that has focused on the operation of human agency within structures of subordination, feminists have sought to understand the ways women resist the dominant male order by subverting the hegemonic meanings of cultural practices and redeploying them for their own interests and agendas. A central question explored within this scholarship has been: how do women contribute to reproducing their own domination, and how do they resist or subvert it? Scholars working in this vein have thus tended to explore religious traditions in terms of the conceptual and practical resources they offer which women may usefully redirect and recode to secure their "own interests and agendas," a recoding that stands as the site of women's agency.

The focus on locating women's agency, when it first emerged, played a critical role in complicating and expanding debates about gender in non-Western societies beyond the simplistic registers of submission and patriarchy. In particular, the focus on women's agency provided a crucial corrective to scholarship on the Middle East that had portrayed Arab and Muslim women for decades as passive and submissive beings, shackled by structures of male authority. This scholarship performed the worthy task of restoring the absent voice of women to analyses of Middle Eastern societies, showing women as active agents who live an existence far more complex and richer than past narratives had suggested.

While such an approach has been enormously productive in complicating the oppressor/oppressed model of gender relations, I would submit such a framework remains not only encumbered by the binary terms of resistance and subordination, but is also insufficiently attentive to motivations, desires, and goals that are not necessarily captured by these terms. Notably, the female agent in this analysis seems to stand in for a sometimes repressed, sometimes active feminist consciousness, articulated against the hegemonic male cultural norms of Arab Muslim societies. Even in instances when an explicit *feminist* agency is difficult to locate, there is a tendency to look for expressions and moments of resistance that may suggest a challenge to male domination. When women's actions seem to reinscribe what appear to be "instruments of their own oppression," the social analyst can point to moments of disruption of, and articulation of points of opposition to, male authority that are either located in the interstices of a woman's consciousness (often read as a nascent feminist consciousness), or in the objective effects of the women's actions, however unintended they may be. Agency, in this form of analysis, is understood as the capacity to realize one's own interests against the weight of custom, tradition, transcendental will, or other obstacles (whether individual or collective). Thus the humanist desire for autonomy and expression of one's self-worth constitute the substrate, the slumbering ember that can spark to flame in the form of an act of resistance when conditions permit.

What is seldom problematized in such an analysis is the universality of the desire to be free from relations of subordination and, for women, from structures of male domination, a desire that is central for liberal and progressive thought, and presupposed by the concept of resistance it authorizes. This positing of women's agency as consubstantial with resistance to relations of domination, and its concomitant naturalization of freedom as a social ideal, I would argue is a product of feminism's dual character as both an *analytical* and a *politically prescriptive* project. Despite the many strands and differences within feminism, what accords this tradition an analytical and political coherence is the premise that where society is structured to serve male interests the result will be either a neglect, or a direct suppression of, women's concerns. Feminism, therefore, offers both a *diagnosis* of women's status across cultures as well as a *prescription* for changing the situation of women who are understood to be marginal/subordinate/oppressed.[7] Thus the articulation of conditions of relative freedom that enable women both to formulate and enact self-determined goals and interests remains the object of feminist politics and theorizing.

A number of feminist scholars over the years have offered trenchant critiques of the liberal notion of autonomy from a variety of perspectives. For example, while earlier critics drew attention to the masculinist assumptions underpinning the ideal of autonomy, later scholars faulted this ideal for its emphasis on the atomistic, individualized, and bounded characteristics of the self at the expense of its relational qualities formed through social interactions within forms of human community.[8] Consequently, there have been various attempts to redefine autonomy so as to capture the emotional, embodied, and socially embedded character of people, particularly of women.[9] A more radical strain of poststructuralist theory has situated its critique of autonomy within a larger challenge posed to the *illusory* character of the rationalist, self-authorizing, transcendental subject presupposed by Enlightenment thought in general,

and the liberal tradition in particular. Rational thought, these critics argue, secures its universal scope and authority by performing a necessary exclusion of all that is bodily, feminine, emotional, nonrational, and intersubjective.[10] This exclusion cannot be substantively or conceptually recuperated through recourse to an unproblematic feminine experience, body, or imaginary (*pace* Beauvoir and Irigaray), but must be thought through the very terms of the discourse of metaphysical transcendence that enacts these exclusions.

In what follows, I question the overwhelming tendency of poststructuralist feminist scholarship to conceptualize agency in terms of subversion or resignification of social norms, to locate agency within those operations that resist the dominating and subjectivating modes of power. In other words, the normative political subject of poststructuralist feminist theory often remains a liberatory one whose agency is conceptualized on the binary model of subordination and subversion. This scholarship thus elides dimensions of human action whose ethical and political status does not map onto the logic of repression and resistance. In order to grasp these modes of action that are indebted to other reasons and histories, I want to argue that it is crucial to detach the notion of agency from the goals of progressive politics.

Freedom and liberty as key political or personal ideals are relatively new in modern history. Many societies, including Western ones, have flourished with aspirations other than these. Nor, for that matter, does the narrative of individual and collective liberty exhaust the desires of people in liberal societies. If we recognize that the desire for freedom from, or subversion of, norms is not an innate desire that motivates all beings at all times, but is also profoundly mediated by cultural and historical conditions, then a question arises: How do we analyze operations of power that construct different kinds of bodies, knowledges, and subjectivities whose trajectories do not follow the entelechy of liberatory politics?

If the ability to effect change in the world and in oneself is historically and culturally specific (both in terms of what constitutes "change" and the means by which it is effected), then the meaning and sense of agency cannot be fixed in advance, but must emerge through an analysis of the particular concepts that enable specific modes of being, responsibility, and effectivity. Viewed in this way, what may appear to be a case of deplorable passivity and docility from a progressivist point of view, may actually be a form of agency—but one that can be understood only from within the discourses and structures of subordination that create the conditions of its enactment. In this sense, the capacity for agency is entailed not only in acts that resist norms but also in the multiple ways in which one inhabits norms.

It may be argued in response that this kind of challenge to the natural status accorded to the desire for freedom in analyses of gender runs the risk of Orientalizing Arab and Muslim women all over again—repeating the errors of pre-1970s Orientalist scholarship that defined Middle Eastern women as passive submissive Others, bereft of the enlightened consciousness of their "Western sisters," and hence doomed to lives of servile submission to men. I would contend, however, that to examine the discursive and practical conditions through which women come to cultivate various forms of desire and capacities of ethical action is a radically different project than an Orientalizing one that locates the desire for submission in an innate ahistorical cultural essence. Indeed, if we accept the notion that all forms of desire are discursively organized (as much of recent feminist scholarship has argued), then it is important to interrogate the practical and conceptual conditions under which different forms of desire emerge, including desire for submission to recognized authority. We cannot treat as natural and imitable only those desires that ensure the emergence of feminist politics.

Consider, for example, the women from the mosque movement that I worked with. The task of realizing piety placed these women in conflict with several structures of authority. Some of these structures were grounded in instituted standards of Islamic orthodoxy, others in norms of liberal discourse; some were grounded in the authority of parents and male kin, and others in state institutions. Yet the *rationale* behind these conflicts was not predicated upon, and therefore cannot be understood only by reference to, arguments for gender equality or resistance to male authority. Nor can these women's practices be read as a reinscription of traditional roles, since the women's mosque movement has significantly reconfigured the gendered practice of Islamic pedagogy and the social institution of mosques. One could, of course, argue in response that, the intent of these women notwithstanding, the actual effects of their practices may be analyzed in terms of their role in reinforcing or undermining structures of male domination. While conceding that such an analysis is feasible and has been useful at times, I would nevertheless argue that it remains encumbered by the binary terms of resistance and subordination, and ignores projects, discourses, and desires that are not captured by these terms, such as those expressed by the women I worked with.

My argument should be familiar to anthropologists who have long acknowledged that the terms people use to organize their lives are not simply a gloss for universally shared assumptions about the world and one's place in it, but are actually constitutive of different forms of personhood, knowledge, and experience. For this reason I have found it necessary, in what follows, to attend carefully to the specific logic of the discourse of piety: a logic that inheres not in the intentionality of the actors, but in the relationship articulated between words, concepts, and practices that constitute a particular discursive tradition.[11] I would insist that an appeal to understanding the coherence of a discursive tradition is neither to justify that tradition, nor to argue for some irreducible essentialism or cultural relativism. It is, instead, to take a necessary step toward explaining the force that a discourse commands.

DOCILITY AND AGENCY

In order to elaborate my theoretical approach, let me begin by examining the arguments of Judith

Butler, who remains, for many, the preeminent theorist of poststructuralist feminist thought, and whose arguments have been essential to my own work. Drawing on Foucault's insights, Butler asks a key question: "if power works not merely to dominate or oppress existing subjects, but also forms subjects, what is this formation?"[12] The issue for Butler is not how the social enacts the individual (as it was for generations of feminists), but what the discursive conditions are that sustain the entire metaphysical edifice of contemporary individuality. Butler departs from the notions of agency and resistance that I criticized earlier in that she questions an "emancipatory model of agency," one that presumes that all humans *qua* humans are "endowed with a will, a freedom, and an intentionality" whose workings are "thwarted by relations of power that are considered external to the subject".[13] In its place, Butler locates the possibility of agency within structures of power (rather than outside of it) and, more importantly, suggests that the reiterative structure of norms not only serves to *consolidate* a particular regime of discourse/power but also provides the means for its *destabilization*.[14] In other words, there is no possibility of "undoing" social norms that is independent of the "doing" of norms; agency resides, therefore, within this productive reiterability.

I find Butler's critique of humanist conceptions of agency and subject very compelling and, indeed, my arguments are manifestly informed by it. I have, however, found it productive to argue with certain tensions that characterize Butler's work, in particular her tendency to focus on those operations of power that resignify and subvert norms. In other words, the concept of agency in Butler's work is developed primarily in contexts where norms are thrown into question or are subject to resignification. An important consequence of this is that Butler's analysis of the power of norms remains grounded in an agonistic framework, one in which norms suppress and/or are subverted, are reiterated and/or resignified—so that one gets little sense of the work norms perform beyond this register of suppression and subversion within the constitution of the subject.

I would like to push the question of norms further in a direction that I think allows us to deepen the analysis of subject formation and also address the problem of reading agency primarily in terms of resistance to the regulating power of structures of normativity. In particular, I would like to expand Butler's insight that norms are not simply a social imposition on the subject but constitute the very substance of her intimate, valorized interiority. But in doing so, I want to move away from an agonistic and dualistic framework—one in which norms are conceptualized on the model of doing and undoing, consolidation and subversion—and instead to think about the variety of ways in which norms are lived and inhabited, aspired to, reached for, and consummated. As I will argue, this in turn requires that we explore the relationship between the immanent form a normative act takes, the model of subjectivity it presupposes (specific articulations of volition, emotion, reason, and bodily expression), and the kinds of authority upon which such an act relies. Let me elaborate by discussing the problems a dualistic conception of norms poses when analyzing the practices of the mosque movement.

Consider, for example, the Islamic virtue of female modesty (*al-haya*) that many Egyptian Muslims uphold and value. Despite a consensus about its importance, there is considerable debate about how this virtue should be lived, and particularly about whether its realization requires the donning of the veil. A majority of the participants in the mosque movement (and the larger piety movement of which the mosque movement is an integral part) argue that the veil is a necessary component of the virtue of modesty because the veil both expresses "true modesty" and is the means through which modesty is acquired.[15] They posit, therefore, an ineluctable relationship between the norm (modesty) and the bodily form it takes (the veil) such that the veiled body becomes the necessary means through which the virtue of modesty is both created *and* expressed. In contrast to this understanding, a position associated with prominent secularist writers argues that the virtue of modesty is no different than any other human attribute, such as moderation or humility: it is a facet of character but does not commit one to any particular expressive repertoire such as donning the veil.[16] Notably, these authors oppose the veil but not the virtue of modesty which they continue to regard as necessary to appropriate feminine conduct. The veil, in their view, has been invested with an importance that is unwarranted when it comes to judgments about female modesty.

The debate about the veil is only one part of a much larger discussion in Egyptian society wherein political differences between Islamists and secularists, and even among Islamists of various persuasions, are expressed through arguments about ritual performative behavior. The most interesting features of this debate lie not so much in whether the norm of modesty is subverted or enacted, but in the radically different ways in which the norm is supposed to be lived and inhabited. Notably, each view posits a very different conceptualization of the relationship between embodied behavior and the virtue or norm of modesty: for the pietists, bodily behavior is at the core of the proper realization of the norm, and for their opponents, it is a contingent and unnecessary element in modesty's enactment.

Let me elaborate upon these points by analyzing an ethnographic example drawn from my fieldwork. The ethnographic here stands less as a signature for the "real," and more as a substantiation of my earlier call to tend to the specific workings of disciplinary power that enable particular forms of investment and agency.

CULTIVATING SHYNESS

Through my field work, I came to know four lower-middle-class working women, in their mid to late thirties, who were well tutored and experienced in the art of Islamic piety. Indeed, one may call them virtuosos of piety. In addition to attending mosque lessons, they met as a group to read and discuss issues of Islamic doctrine and Quranic exegesis. Notably, none of these women came from a devout family, and in fact some of them had had to wage a struggle against their kin in order to become devout. They told me about their struggles, not only with their families, but also, and more importantly, with themselves in cultivating the desire for greater religious exactitude.

Not unlike other devout women I worked with from the mosques, these women also sought to excel in piety in their day to day lives—something they described as the condition of being close to God (variously rendered as *taqarrab allah* and/or *taqwa*). While piety was achievable through practices that were both devotional as well as worldly in character, it required more than the simple performance of acts: piety also entailed the inculcation of entire dispositions through a simultaneous training of the body, emotions, and reason until the religious virtues acquired the status of embodied habits.

Among the religious virtues that are considered to be important to acquire for pious Muslims in general, and women in particular, is modesty or shyness (*al-haya*) a common topic of discussion among the mosque participants. To practice al-haya means to be diffident, modest, and able to feel and enact shyness. While all of the Islamic virtues are gendered (insofar as their measure and standards vary when applied to men and women), this is particularly true of shyness and modesty. The struggle involved in cultivating this virtue was brought home to me when in the course of a discussion about the exegesis of a chapter in the Quran called "The Story," one of the women, Amal, drew our attention to verse twenty-five. This verse is about a woman walking shyly—with al-haya—toward Moses to ask him to approach her father for her hand in marriage. Unlike the other women in the group, Amal was particularly outspoken and confident, and would seldom hesitate to assert herself in social situations with men or women. Normally I would not have described her as shy, because I considered shyness to be contradictory to qualities of candidness and self-confidence in a person. Yet as I was to learn, Amal had learned to be outspoken in a way that was in keeping with Islamic standards of reserve, restraint and modesty required of pious Muslim women. Here is how the conversation proceeded:

> Contemplating the word *istihya'*, which is form ten of the substantive haya',[17] Amal said "I used to think that even though shyness (*al-haya*) was required of us by God, if I acted shyly it would be hypocritical because I didn't actually feel it inside of me. Then one day, in reading verse twenty-five (of "The Story") I realized that al-haya was among the good deeds and given my natural lack of shyness (*al-haya'*), I had to make or create it first. I realized that making (*sana'*) it in yourself is not hypocrisy, and that eventually your inside learns to have al-haya too." Here she looked at me and explained the meaning of the word *istihya'*: "It means making oneself shy, even if it means creating it." She continued with her point, "And finally I understood that once you do this, the sense of shyness (*al-haya*) eventually imprints itself on your inside." Another friend, Nama, a single woman in her early thirties, who had been sitting and listening, added: "It's just like the veil (*hijab*). In the beginning when you wear it, you're embarrassed, and don't want to wear it because people say that you look older and unattractive, that you won't get married, and will never find a husband. But you *must* wear the veil, first because it is God's command (*hukm allah*), and then, with time, your inside learns to feel shy without the veil, and if you were to take it off your entire being feels uncomfortable about it."

To many readers this conversation may exemplify an obsequious deference to social norms that both reflects and reproduces women's subordination. Indeed, Amal's struggle with herself to become shy may appear to be no more than an instance of the internalization of standards of effeminate behavior, one that contributes little to our understanding of agency. Yet if we think of "agency" not simply as a synonym for resistance to social norms but as a modality of action, then this conversation raises some interesting questions about the relationship established between the subject and the norm, between performative behavior and inward disposition.

To begin with, what is striking here is that instead of innate human desires eliciting outward forms of conduct, one's practices and actions determine one's desires and emotions. In other words, action does not issue forth from natural feelings but *creates* them. Furthermore, it is through repeated *bodily acts* that one trains one's memory, desire, and intellect to behave according to established standards of conduct. Notably, Amal *does not* regard simulating shyness in her initial self-cultivation to be hypocritical, as it would be in certain liberal conceptions of the self, according to which a dissonance between internal feelings and external expressions is a form of dishonesty or self-betrayal (as captured in the phrase: "How can I do something sincerely when my heart is not in it?"). Instead, taking the absence of shyness as a marker of an incomplete learning process, Amal further develops the quality of shyness by synchronizing her outward behavior with her inward motives until the discrepancy between the two dissolves. This is an example of a mutually constitutive relationship between body learning and body sense—as Nama says, your body literally comes to feel uncomfortable if you do *not* veil.

Second, what is also significant in this program of self-cultivation is that bodily acts—like wearing the veil or conducting oneself modestly in social interactions (especially with men)—do not serve as manipulable masks detachable from an essential interiorized self in a game of public presentation. Rather they are the *critical markers* of piety as well as the *ineluctable means* by which one trains oneself to be pious. While wearing the veil serves at first as a means to tutor oneself in the attribute of shyness, it is simultaneously integral to the practice of shyness: one cannot simply discard the veil once a modest deportment has been acquired, because the veil itself partly defines that deportment. This is a crucial aspect of the disciplinary program pursued by the participants of the mosque movement, the significance of which is elided when the veil is understood solely in terms of its symbolic value as a marker of women's subordination or Islamic identity.

The complicated relationship among learning, memory, experience, and the self undergirding the model of pedagogy followed by the mosque participants has at times been discussed by scholars through the Latin term *habitus*, meaning an acquired faculty in which the body, mind, and emotions are simultaneously trained to achieve competence at something (such as meditation, dancing, or playing a musical instrument). While the term *habitus* has become best known in the social sciences through the work of Pierre Bourdieu, my own work draws upon a longer and richer history of this term, one that addresses the centrality of gestural capacities in certain traditions of moral cultivation.[18] Aristotelian in origin and adopted by the three monotheistic traditions, this older meaning of *habitus* refers to a specific pedagogical process by which moral virtues are acquired through a coordination of outward behavior (e.g. bodily acts, social demeanor) with inward dispositions (e.g. emotional states, thoughts, intentions). Thus *habitus* in this usage refers to a conscious effort at reorienting desires, brought about by the concordance of inward motives, outward actions, inclinations, and emotional states through the repeated practice of virtuous deeds.

CONCLUSION

A significant body of literature in feminist theory argues that patriarchal ideologies—whether nationalist, religious, medical, or aesthetic in character—work by objectifying women's bodies and subjecting them to masculinist systems of representation, thereby negating and distorting women's own experience of their corporeality and subjectivity.[19] In this view, the virtue of al-haya can be understood as yet another example of the subjection of women's bodies to masculinist or patriarchal valuations, images, and representational logic. A feminist strategy aimed at unsettling such a circumscription would try to expose al-haya for its negative valuation of women, simultaneously bringing to the fore alternative representations and experiences of the feminine body that are denied, submerged, or repressed by its masculinist logic.

The analysis I have presented of the practice of al-haya (and the practice of veiling) departs from this perspective. It is important to note that even though the concept of al-haya embeds a masculinist understanding of gendered bodies, far more is at stake in the practice of al-haya than this framework allows, as is evident from the conversation between Amal and her friend Nama. Crucial to their understanding of al-haya as an embodied practice is an entire conceptualization of the role the body plays in the making of the self, one in which the outward behavior of the body constitutes both the potentiality and the means through which interiority is realized. A feminist strategy that seeks to unsettle such a conceptualization cannot simply intervene in the system of representation that devalues the feminine body, but must also engage the very armature of attachments between outward behavioral forms and the sedimented subjectivity that al-haya enacts. Representation is only one issue among many in the ethical relationship of the body to the self and others, and it does not by any means determine the form this relationship takes.

For a scholar of Islam this issue is particularly fraught because the veil, more than any other Islamic practice, has become the symbol and evidence of Islam's essential patriarchy and misogyny toward women. I have seldom presented my argument about the veil in an academic setting without facing a barrage of questions from people demanding to know why I have failed to condemn the patriarchal assumptions behind this practice and the suffering it engenders. I am often struck by my audience's lack of curiosity about what else the veil might perform in the world beyond its violation of women. These exhortations to condemnation are only one indication of how the veil and the commitments it embodies, have come to be understood through the prism of women's freedom and subjugation such that to ask a different set of questions about the practice is to lay oneself open to the charge of indifference to women's oppression. The force this coupling of the veil and women's freedom commands is equally manifest in those arguments that endorse or defend the veil on the grounds that it is a product of women's "free choice" and evidence of their "liberation" from the hegemony of Western cultural codes.

In summary, my argument simply is that in order for us to be able to judge, in a morally and politically informed way, even those practices we consider objectionable, it is important to take into consideration the desires, motivations, commitments, and aspirations of the people for whom these practices are important. Thus, in order to explore the kinds of injury specific to women located in particular historical and cultural situations, it is not enough simply to point, for example, that a tradition of female piety or modesty serves to give legitimacy to women's subordination. Rather it is only by exploring these traditions in relation to the practical engagements and forms of life in which they are embedded that we can come to understand the significance of that subordination to the women who embody it.

NOTES

1. This dilemma seems to be further compounded by the fact that women's participation in the Islamic movement in a number of countries (such as Iran, Egypt, Indonesia, and Malaysia) is not limited to the poor and middle classes (classes often considered to have a "natural affinity" for religion), but also from the upper and middle income strata.

2. There are three important strands that constitute the Islamic Revival: state-oriented political groups and parties, militant Islamists (whose presence has declined since the 1980s), and a network of socioreligious non-profit organizations that provide charitable services to the poor and perform the work of proselytization. The women's mosque movement is an important subset of this network of socioreligious organizations and draws upon the same discourse of piety (referred to as "da'wa").

3. This sensibility has a palpable public presence in Egypt, manifest in the vast proliferation of neighborhood mosques and other institutions of Islamic learning and social welfare, in a dramatic increase in attendance at mosques by both women and men, and in marked displays of religious sociability. Examples of the latter include the adoption of the veil

(*hijab*), a brisk consumption and production of religious media and literature, and a growing circle of intellectuals who write and comment upon contemporary affairs in the popular press from a self-described Islamic point of view. Neighborhood mosques have come to serve as the organizational center for many of these activities.

4. My research is based on two years of fieldwork (1995–1997) conducted in five different mosques from a range of socio-economic backgrounds in Cairo, Egypt. I also carried out participant observation among the leaders and members of the mosque movement in the context of their daily lives. This was supplemented with a year-long study with a sheikh from the Islamic University of al-Azhar on issues of Islamic jurisprudence and religious practice.

5. Mosques have played a critical role in the Islamic Revival in Egypt: since the 1970s there has been an unprecedented increase in the establishment of mosques by local neighborhoods and non-governmental organizations, many of which provide a range of social services to the Cairene, especially the poor, such as medical, welfare, and educational services. Given the program of economic liberalization that the Egyptian government has been pursuing since the 1970s and the concomitant decline in state provided social services, these mosques fill a critical lacuna for many Egyptians.

6. Currently there are hardly any neighborhoods in this city of eleven million inhabitants where women do not offer religious lessons to each other. The attendance at these gatherings varies between 10–500 women, depending on the popularity of the teacher. The movement continues to be informally organized by women, and has no organizational center that oversees its coordination.

7. Marilyn Strathern, *The Gender of the Gift: Problems with Women and Problems with Society in Melanesia* (Berkeley: University of California Press, 1988), pp. 26–28.

8. In the first group, see Nancy Chodorow, *The Reproduction of Mothering: Psychoanalysis and the Sociology of Gender* (Berkeley and Los Angeles: University of California Press: 1978) and Carol Gilligan, *In a Different Voice: Psychological Theory and Women's Development* (Cambridge, MA: Harvard University Press, 1982); in the second, see Seyla Benhabib, *Situating the Self: Gender, Community, and Postmodernism in Contemporary Ethics* (New York: Routledge, 1992) and Iris Young, *Justice and the Politics of Difference* (Princeton, NJ: Princeton University Press, 1990).

9. Suad Joseph, ed. *Intimate Selving in Arab Families: Gender, Self, and Identity* (Syracuse: Syracuse University Press, 1999); Marilyn Friedman "Autonomy and Social Relationships: Rethinking the Feminist Critique," in *Feminists Rethink the Self* ed. D.T. Meyers (Boulder, CO: Westview Press: 2003); Jennifer Nedelsky, "Reconceiving Autonomy: Sources, Thoughts and Possibilities," in *Yale Journal of Law and Feminism* 1 (1): 7–36 (1989).

10. Judith Butler, *Bodies that Matter: On the Discursive Limits of "Sex"* (New York: Routledge, 1993); Moira Gatens, *Imaginary Bodies: Ethics, Power, and Corporeality* (London: Routledge, 1996); Elizabeth Grosz, *Volatile Bodies: Toward a Corporeal Feminism* (Bloomington: Indiana University Press, 1994).

11. The concept "discursive tradition" is from Talal Asad, *The Idea of an Anthropology of Islam* (Washington D.C.: Center for Contemporary Arab Studies, Georgetown University, 1986), Occasional Paper Series.

12. Judith Butler, *The Psychic Life of Power: Theories in Subjection*s (Stanford, CA: Stanford University Press, 1977), p. 18.

13. Seyla Benhabib, Judith Butler, Drucilla Cornell, and Nancy Fraser. *Feminist Contentions: A Philosophical Exchange* (New York: Routledge, 1995), 136.

14. Judith Butler, *Bodies that Matter*, p. 15.

15. See Muhammed Sayyid Tantawi, "Bal al-hijab farida islamiyya" in *Ruz al-Yusuf*, June 27, 68, (1994).

16. Said Muhammed Ashmawi, "Fatwa al-hijab ghair shar'iyya" in *Ruz al-Yusuf*, August 8 and 28 (1994).

17. Most Arabic verbs are based on a tri-consonantal root from which ten verbal forms (and sometimes fifteen) are derived.

18. Pierre Bourdieu, *Outline of a Theory of Practice*, trans. R. Nice (Cambridge: Cambridge University Press, 1997).

19. Nilüfer Göle, *The forbidden modern: Civilization and veiling* (Ann Arbor University of Michigan Press, 1996), Lati Mani, *Contentious Traditions* (Berkeley: University of California Press, 1999); Emily Martin, *The woman in the body: A cultural analysis of reproduction* (Boston: Beacon Press, 1987).

3 • *Daisy Deomampo*

TRANSNATIONAL SURROGACY IN INDIA
Interrogating Power and Women's Agency

DISCUSSION QUESTIONS

1. Why do some women in India become surrogates, surrogate agents, or caretakers?
2. What are some of the "forms of agency" and "structures of power" experienced by these women?
3. How has the growth of the transnational surrogacy business in India reflected and reproduced inequalities of gender and class within India and between India and other countries?

On a sweltering summer day in 2010 I sat in a restaurant on the outskirts of Mumbai, India, with Nishi, a young woman preparing to become a surrogate mother for a foreign couple outside of India. Though not yet pregnant, Nishi was hoping to enter the world of transnational surrogacy, in which would-be parents from around the world travel to India to make babies through in vitro fertilization (IVF), egg donation, and gestational surrogacy. India made commercial surrogacy legal a decade ago in an effort to boost the medical tourism industry; since then hundreds of women like Nishi have found their way into this global market, transacting their bodies, body parts, and reproductive labor in exchange for the monetary payment they hope will ease their families' financial burdens.

Nishi told me of how she had separated from her husband four years earlier; separation and divorce remain unusual in India, particularly among working-class women like Nishi, but several women in my study had left their husbands, some of whom had been abusive. Indeed, as one fertility doctor I interviewed explained, "You'd be surprised at the number of separations and divorces that are happening [among lower-class women]. . . . After we started doing surrogacy in the past three years, we realized that about 30–40 percent of them are separated." This doctor asserted that most of these women walk out of their marriages because of abuse and alcoholism; Nishi's case proved typical.

Following her separation from her husband, Nishi struck up a friendship with Nikhil, a young man from south India who managed an electronics shop in Mumbai. As their friendship evolved into a romantic relationship, Nikhil supported Nishi and her two daughters in times of need. Nishi related that she felt she also should support Nikhil, whom she planned to eventually marry. When Nishi learned about surrogacy, she viewed it as a potential financial windfall for her and her family and began preparing for surrogacy without telling Nikhil. When she told Nikhil of her surrogacy plans, he disapproved: "He is not agreeing to it. He says don't do this; he thinks it is illegal. Yet I am trying to convince him somehow and I am trying. I also told him that everything has been done. I told him I have done the ET [embryo transfer] and I cannot go back now. So, he is sitting quietly now, not saying anything." In fact, at the time of our interview Nishi had not yet undergone embryo transfer. She was still in the preparatory phases: taking hormone injections and undergoing tests and procedures to determine her viability as a candidate for surrogacy. Why did Nishi deceive Nikhil?

What are the strategies that Indian women contemplating surrogacy employ to negotiate and respond to the structural and social constraints they face daily? How do women enact agency in their efforts to meet or secure their self-defined needs and desires? And what are the consequences of such acts of agency, particularly as they challenge cultural norms and expectations? This chapter addresses these questions by tracing the complexities of agency, constraint, and inequality in the lives of women who pursue surrogacy in India.

The views and experiences of women I spoke with resist reduction to simplistic stereotypes and binary oppositions between agent and victim, rich and poor, East and West; indeed, the more I learned about surrogacy in India throughout my fieldwork, the more inadequate these notions became. This chapter shows how women indeed find ways to resist dominant constructions of surrogates as powerless victims. I argue that in expressing forms of resistance and individual and collective agency, women find ways to challenge everyday gender norms and create new opportunities for themselves and their families, albeit within larger structures of power.

However, such expressions of agency also depend on the particular roles and relationships that women have within transnational structures of surrogacy. I contrast the experiences of women who work as surrogates with those who occupy intermediary positions—particularly surrogate agents and caretakers. Women who act as agents or caretakers often share the same socioeconomic background as surrogates and egg donors; indeed, such women are usually former surrogates or egg donors themselves. Yet they occupy distinct subject positions, especially with respect to power and agency. I contend that while women who act as intermediary agents have increased access to power and opportunities that allow them to boost their own social and financial status, their positions simultaneously reinforce the ever more refined hierarchies inherent in transnational surrogacy. By revealing the diversity of ways that women enact agency, however limited, through their experiences as surrogates or agent-caretakers, I highlight the subtleties of the intraclass social divisions that transnational surrogacy engenders and illustrate how women both exert power and are subject to it.

This chapter focuses on the experiences and aspirations of surrogates, highlighting the nuances of their everyday lives. In attending to these experiences of women involved in surrogacy, so, too, must scholars acknowledge their power and agency in the context of constrained opportunities. Building on Foucault's argument that power is everywhere, this work joins anthropological scholarship focused on revealing instances of agency and resistance among the relatively powerless. In contrast to popular media images of helpless women in need of assistance, my research shows the subtle and explicit ways in which women express resistance and agency within the context of structural factors that limit opportunities.

Transnational surrogacy in India, as elsewhere, reflects many of these concerns with power, inequality, and stratified reproduction, in which disparities in gender, race, class, and nation place some women's reproductive projects above others' (Colen 1995). Yet, in drawing attention to the uneven terrain beneath transnational surrogacy, I want to avoid and go beyond depictions of women who become surrogates as powerless victims in need of aid. As Chandra Mohanty (1988) has eloquently argued, viewing Third World women primarily as victims creates a pattern of domination—a form of discursive colonization—that measures progress against the yardstick of western women. In most popular media accounts of surrogacy in India expressions such as "womb for rent" merge seamlessly with images of the "poorest of the poor" who readily sign up to become surrogates. Yet such homogenous images of Third World women who are helpless, oppressed, and thus in need of rescue predefines women as victims and prematurely rules out any possibility of their being otherwise. Indian surrogates may be, or may become, victims in the unequal relationships formed between surrogate and doctor or intended parent. Nonetheless, I contend that reliance on the image of the oppressed surrogate neglects the local voices and perspectives long sought by ethnographers and feminists.

The research described in this chapter is part of a larger study on reproductive travel in India, where I conducted thirteen months of ethnographic fieldwork between 2008 and 2010. I draw on participant observation at varied sites throughout Mumbai, including infertility clinics, hospitals, intended parents' hotel or apartment accommodations, and surrogates' homes. I conducted in-depth interviews with thirty-five Indian surrogates and egg donors, including six agent-caretakers. In addition I conducted interviews with Indian doctors and intended parents from around the world. Relying on the ethnographic methods of anthropology, I also drew on feminist methodologies in order to, in the words of Faye Harrison (2007: 24), "underscore the value of women's voices, experiences, and agency and the sociocultural and political-economic contexts in which they are situated."

NISHI'S STORY: SURROGACY AND CONSTRAINED AGENCY

Nishi was twenty-seven years old when we met in Mumbai in April 2010. She had been married at nineteen in what she called, speaking to me in English, a "love-cum-arranged marriage"; as the story goes, Nishi's husband was "in love with her from afar," though Nishi did not reciprocate his feelings at first. His mother approached Nishi's family with a proposal for marriage, and while Nishi's mother believed that the family was an appropriate match at the time, Nishi says her mother has come to agree with her that he is "crazy" and has a drinking problem. Following marriage, Nishi quickly had her first child at twenty; she now has two school-age daughters born a year apart. Nishi and her husband are now separated, and she has filed a case for divorce. Since then she has endeavored to distance herself from her parents and their burdensome financial problems, while working to support herself and her two daughters independently.

Nishi was similar to many of the women I interviewed, with respect to class and social status, household income, and family histories of conflict and turmoil (in Nishi's case she struggled to provide for two daughters as a single mother separated from an alcoholic husband, while also shouldering the financial debts of her parents). However, unlike most of the women I interviewed, Nishi spoke English. She was confident, articulate, and inquisitive, and she made a strong first impression. Yet Nishi's education had been brief, and she attended a school in which Marathi was the primary language of instruction. In a conversation with her friend Antara, Nishi lamented the structural constraints that limited her educational aspirations:

NISHI: Actually I wanted to become a doctor but my father told me he couldn't afford it.

ANTARA: You can become one now.

NISHI: No, it is financially very difficult. I'll have to attend the classes, which is not possible for me. I can study hard but can't attend the classes. I studied very hard in the seventh standard and got first class but I had to give up school after that [due to financial constraints].

Nishi's seventh-grade education allowed her to secure a job at a large telecom company, where she earned a monthly salary of $200. Her English-language skills came from this job.

Nishi revealed a profound curiosity about the surrogacy process and the risks involved, both physical and legal, particularly in comparison with many women who felt unable to pose questions to their doctors about any aspects of the surrogacy process. Describing how she came to accept surrogacy, Nishi relates:

> My friend Shanti told me about the idea of ET [embryo transfer] and I was surprised. By that time I was aware about the test tube baby, but this was new for me. I thought about it for one month. Then I had a quarrel with my brother. . . . That was the decisive moment for me.

Nishi had been staying with her brother; she was hoping that surrogacy would offer the means to move out.

> I called Shanti and told her that I'm ready for the process. After visiting the hospital, I went to an Internet café and searched for information about surrogacy to prepare myself for the process. Most importantly, I'm earning a substantial amount for my kids. In India we rarely get the chance to earn this much at one go.

In contrast to many women Nishi took steps to educate herself about surrogacy. She was the only woman I interviewed who mentioned conducting Internet research in order to learn more about the risks involved in surrogacy.

Yet once Nishi began the surrogacy process, her relationship with Shanti soured. Shanti herself had wanted to become a surrogate; she had undergone embryo transfer three times, with no success. She decided to become an agent herself, and her discussions with Nishi were in her mind related to that. After accompanying Nishi to the doctor, where she underwent blood tests and ultrasound scans, Shanti demanded a commission—approximately $45, which would be deducted from Nishi's payment of $220 at the time of embryo transfer—for

introducing Nishi to her doctor. Nishi's first reaction, as she sat in the recovery room following her initial blood tests and scans, was, "Well, if she hadn't told me about this, then how would I have known? I would have had no idea about this." But she later balked at the idea of paying Shanti out of her own earnings. Nishi explained, "She is such a careless agent. I was dying here in the first two months [of pregnancy] with vomiting and she didn't come at all. That's not done."

Nishi's comments suggest the impact of agents' intermediary positions on surrogate experiences, as well as the subtle ways in which social relationships change in the context of surrogacy. As Shanti's focus moved toward becoming an agent, she alienated Nishi. As I will discuss further in the following section, the agent plays a large role in surrogate women's experiences, in ways that both enhance and constrain surrogate's opportunities. In Nishi's case, though she tried to learn about the practical details of surrogacy, she still found herself in a vulnerable position as a surrogate, as her agent demanded payment and neglected to care for her in the early months of her pregnancy.

Nearly all of the surrogates with whom I spoke reported a lack of transparency and power in negotiating contracts. This process illustrated the social and structural inequalities that both propel them into the surrogacy industry and circumscribe their experiences within it. For Nishi, like most surrogates, the experience of signing the contract was confusing and mysterious, and despite her assertive nature Nishi could not advocate on her own behalf:

DAISY: Can you tell me about the contract process?

NISHI: The contract was in two copies; one is original and other was Xerox.

DAISY: Did you ask for a copy for yourself?

NISHI: No, actually I wanted one copy for myself, but I didn't dare to ask for one. In fact I don't prefer to sign any contract without knowing it in detail but . . . one page was also blank which I signed and also the amount was not filled in. And most importantly she didn't give us a chance to read the agreement. She was turning the pages very fast. If she had let me read the document, I would have read it quickly because I can read English and I can read fast.

While Nishi reported these objections to me, she said she could not speak up in front of the doctor and lawyer who were present when she signed. Indeed, this came up again and again in interviews: surrogates would not confront doctors and lawyers on crucial issues related to their payment for fear of losing their contract. They said that doctors often hinted at an ample supply of women ready and willing to take their place as surrogates.

These obstacles notwithstanding, Nishi endeavored to express subtle and explicit forms of agency within these larger structures of power, by taking steps to read and conduct research and independently making her own decisions about surrogacy. Yet despite her own assertiveness and self-education Nishi's possibilities for agency remained constrained due to her position in relation to doctors, agents, and other actors involved in transnational surrogacy. In contrast the story of Antara, who had socioeconomic status similar to Nishi's but worked as an agent, reveals a distinct set of possibilities for agency and power.

ANTARA: INTERROGATING POWER IN AGENT-CARETAKER WORK

Antara and her husband, Rahul, had two children, a fifteen-year-old daughter and a thirteen-year-old son. Rahul, who had the equivalent of a seventh-grade education, worked for a private company laying roads; for this work he earned a monthly wage of $110, but since such seasonal work is irregular, the family often found themselves struggling to get by. Antara had been educated until the tenth grade, and when we first met, she was thirty-six years old and described herself as a "housewife". However, over the months I came to know her and

her family, I watched as Antara's work as an agent-caretaker grew into a job that took her all over the city, into women's homes, doctor's clinics, and hospitals.

Antara's introduction to the surrogacy industry took place several years prior to our first meeting in 2010. When her sister-in-law, Sumita, told her about surrogacy as an income opportunity, Antara initially thought, "What are you talking about? I thought it was probably wrong, but then I realized that I've had my two children. I'm donating something." Rahul, however, did not support the idea, and Antara called on her elder sister and sister-in-law to convince him. Confronted by these determined women of the family, saying, "Look at your living conditions; you need something better," Rahul eventually agreed. Indeed, many women told me similar stories of needing to persuade their husbands to allow them to become surrogates, contradicting some concerns that Indian women were being forced into surrogacy by their husbands against their will.

Antara became pregnant and gave birth to a boy via cesarean section. For this work she earned around $2,700, which, in Antara's words, "is not enough." Antara and Rahul put away some of the money for their daughter and used the rest to repair her family's home in the village. In Mumbai Antara's family continued to live in a rented home.

In 2009 she came to work as an agent-caretaker for Dr. Desai, who originally facilitated Antara's surrogacy. In her role as agent Antara would bring women interested in egg donation or surrogacy to Dr. Desai, for which she would receive a commission of $90 to $180. Antara's role as an agent, however, frequently overlapped with her work as a "caretaker"; charged with everything from accompanying surrogates to the hospital for medical procedures, to ensuring surrogates receive their medications, caretakers can receive between $450 and $900 for their work throughout the duration of a surrogate pregnancy. Initially, Antara would roam around her community and speak with women to see who might be interested in egg donation or surrogacy. Eventually, however, as her reputation as a caretaker spread, I observed a significant boost to Antara's work. By the end of my fieldwork all of Antara's "patients" would come to her through word of mouth, and most of the women she works with are distant relatives or neighbors in her community.

Throughout the months that I met with Antara, I observed how she came to identify more and more as "agent" rather than housewife, and I noted her strength and confidence in this role many times. She typically had between four and seven patients; at her busiest Antara could be responsible for up to nine or ten patients at varying stages of egg donation and surrogate pregnancy. Antara viewed her work as a full-time job and conscientiously fulfilled her duties; it was not uncommon for her to be out from early morning to late evening, and she meticulously took notes and kept track of all her patients' medications, payments, and doctor's visits. Responsible for dispensing medications and administering hormone injections, Antara claimed, "I'm also a doctor by practice; I don't have a degree so you can consider me 'half-doctor'!" In addition Antara grew close to her patients on a personal and social level, and on more than one occasion I witnessed Antara serve as a mediator and advisor for women and their families, offering advice on how to deal with an abusive husband or mediating between dueling sisters. As Nishi told me, "Antara goes all the way in helping patients with their problems. She has earned the right to ask for money as an agent."

During my fieldwork I noted how Antara's financial situation changed over the course of the year, due largely to her work as an agent. When we first met, she and her family were renting a small, cramped, one-room flat; several months later they moved to a more spacious, airy home. She was later able to purchase a refrigerator (with a lock to secure the medications she stored for surrogates and egg donors), as well as a steel cupboard, tangible markers of upwardly mobile class status. Antara and Rahul also saved enough money to send both of their children to college, so that they could receive the education that neither Antara nor Rahul could

achieve. These significant details reveal the impact of Antara's work as an agent; I observed few surrogates achieve similar goals in their postsurrogacy lives.

It was not uncommon for Antara to confront angry or abusive husbands, in ways not typically expected of Indian women. Following Antara's experience as a surrogate, her sister Asha, too, wanted an opportunity to become a surrogate and earn much-needed income for her family. While Asha's husband was fully informed about the surrogacy process and the procedures Asha would undergo in order to become pregnant, he nonetheless became angry, insecure, and jealous, harassing Antara and her family following a misunderstanding. Like other surrogates in the program Asha was admitted to the hospital for twelve days after the embryo transfer. Asha's husband visited her in the hospital, and Antara thought he had been made uncomfortable by the hospital's policy that he couldn't go into her room, for the privacy of others, but had to see his wife in a more public visiting room. He suspected he was actually being barred because Asha was committing adultery. Antara said:

> After that we had so much fighting in the house! . . . He said if something goes wrong I will throw both of you out of the house. He just wouldn't listen. He said, "My wife would not even go to the shop by herself and all of you took her so far away." I waited until morning when he sobered up. I said to him, "How did she get so far away? Didn't she ask you? And how dare you use such words about me?" I said if you say this ever again to her and if you so much as touch her to harm her, you watch it.

I asked, "You threatened him?" Antara replied:

> Yes, I told him not to be a bully. I'm good with those who are good to me but bad to those who are bad to me. This is not wrong. There is nothing wrong in this work. If there was, would I have helped my own sister to do it? Then he started apologizing. He said, "Forget it, I will never say anything about it again." Then he said, "Please don't tell her I spoke like that."

But I told her [Asha]. If he could speak to us like that, he would have said things to her too. So I told her this is the way your husband spoke to us. Then she must have confronted him. She is also a very strong woman. And now, he's quiet.

Antara navigated threats and assertions of power in her family. The sudden increase in Asha's earning potential as a surrogate prompted Asha's husband to react strongly to the subtle shift in the balance of power in their relationship. I encountered several women who negotiated tense relationships with husbands who were uncomfortable with the significant incomes their wives earned as surrogates. Yet, while Antara acknowledged the right of Asha's husband to have the final say in her embodied affairs, saying, "How did she get so far away? Didn't she ask you?" she simultaneously resisted her brother-in-law's threats and called on Asha, too, to confront her husband, signaling subtle and complex expressions of power and agency within the household. The conflict between Antara, Asha, and Asha's husband provides valuable insights into the impact of surrogacy within the households of surrogate women themselves, revealing the complexities and consequences of female agency as women collide with gendered cultural expectations of female submissiveness and dependency.

In another instance Antara explained to me how she banded with other agents to demand equal payments for their patients. As Antara described the monthly payment plan for Dr. Desai, one of the several doctors she worked with, she noted how surrogates were to receive approximately $65 for monthly expenditures, in addition to monthly payments of $110 to cover their rent and housing (these payments would be deducted from the total salary of $5500 that Antara's surrogates earn for their reproductive labor). Yet sometimes Dr. Desai would give $45 to some patients and $65 to others. When Antara and her fellow agents realized this, Antara explained, in an account that called to mind the efforts of labor organizers or activists, "All the agents came together and forced her to give equal payments to everybody. So now everyone is getting $65 as allowance for other expenses."

Yet Antara's role as patient advocate sometimes clashed with her entrepreneurial self, revealing the nuanced ways in which agents must negotiate the two positionalities. Antara's work as an agent was often tenuous and insecure, and she told me of how she coordinated with fellow agents to approach Dr. Desai when their own payments were decreasing:

ANTARA: Last month all us agents, around twenty-five, conducted a meeting with her and we confronted her about her decreased payments to us. . . . She is looking to reduce costs as much as she can, and she is deducting from the agent's accounts. Things like injections, traveling from home to the hospitals for different sonographies used to be paid; these are no longer paid nowadays. We demanded the expenses from her.

DAISY: Did she give you what you asked for, in the end?

ANTARA: No, she gave us her notebook to write down the demands. And there is the problem of patients becoming agents. If a patient is bringing someone else as a patient, she makes her an agent, resulting in a rising number of agents. It creates problems for us, and we can't pressure her for more money. We have asked her not to appoint new agents anymore.

While Antara and her fellow agents demanded higher pay and transparent pay scales, they also raised issue with the doctor's tendency to favor certain agents and patients over others. At the same time, however, their objections stemmed from the fact that patients who sought to become agents challenged their positionality in the hierarchy among doctors, agents, and patient. In seeking to preserve their own power and positionality, Antara and her fellow agents aimed to limit the power of their patients to become agents themselves. Ultimately, however, Dr. Desai did not address any of the agents' demands, and with limited opportunities to find alternate forms of income, Antara continues to work for her as an agent-caretaker.

I was surprised, however, when one day Antara presented me with several pages of computer printouts. With little knowledge of English, and having few opportunities to do research or access the Internet, Antara had approached a local vendor—the person who helped her secure identification cards for her patients—with a request to research payments for surrogates. When I asked why she had collected this information, Antara replied:

ANTARA: I wanted to know the actual payment to a surrogate from the client [intended parents]. If I know the actual payment, it will help me to make the process with patients more transparent, which eventually helps me to reach more women.

DAISY: What are you going to do with this information?

ANTARA: I'm not sure yet, but if we contact the clients directly, it will be more beneficial for everyone.

DAISY: Is this possible?

ANTARA: Why not? There are a lot of people who have asked me to approach the clients.

Displaying a canny sense of entrepreneurship, Antara imagined that she might eventually be able to reach clients directly, avoiding third parties such as Dr. Desai and increasing financial returns for herself and her patients.

Yet Antara also understood that particular social and structural factors circumscribed the range of possibilities available for women like her to negotiate their own livelihoods. When I asked her whether surrogates should be able to meet the future parents of the child they were carrying, Antara replied:

> It should be absolutely acceptable, but the main problem is being capable of having a dialogue with them. The language barrier hampers those who really want to communicate with their couple. Couples from abroad usually speak their own language, and it is difficult for many illiterate women to respond. These women are really uneducated. In my

sister's case the couple visited her so many times and really wanted to communicate with her, but she didn't utter a word. If a smart and educated surrogate had been there, she would have asked them about the details of the actual payment and other things. But here the patients are totally dependent on the doctor. So any added gifts or payment that might have been given by the client but did not reach its destination cannot be tracked.

As Antara's comments reveal, lack of education and lower social status in relation to the doctors and commissioning parents largely shape surrogates' experiences. Indeed, while Antara acknowledges the challenges language barriers between surrogates and intended parents pose, her comments illustrate that the factors that limit access to resources and motivate women to become surrogates (lack of education, low socioeconomic status) also restrict women's ability to confront intended parents and doctors and to ensure transparency in surrogate arrangements. Indeed, Antara was acutely aware of the inequalities at the heart of transnational surrogacy arrangements as she worked hard to use her own constrained agency to provide opportunities for herself and her family members.

CONCLUSION

Indian women involved in surrogacy take up a diverse set of roles and responsibilities, and in contrasting the relative positions of the surrogate and the agent/caretaker, I have shown how these intermediary roles have resulted in intraclass divisions that engender further stratification among women. In Antara's case her experience as a surrogate facilitated her ascension to her role as a sought-after surrogate agent, and this role afforded her power and agency, however constrained.

Both Nishi and Antara expressed forms of resistance to the larger structural forces that constrained their own opportunities as working-class Indian women. Yet their narratives reveal how their efforts at resistance actually recreated structural inequalities. Though Nishi sought to improve her own family's financial future through surrogacy and took proactive steps to educate and protect herself against the risks involved, she remained unable to negotiate key aspects of her surrogacy contract. Antara, too, worked to increase payments for her surrogates, yet her negotiations of power as an agent-caretaker did not represent interventions against structural processes. Rather, her actions intensified and recreated hierarchies among working-class women involved in surrogacy.

This chapter offered a critical examination of transnational surrogacy in order to reveal how women express agency in the context of structural constraints and social inequalities. The narratives of Antara and Nishi illustrate the unique contours of stratified reproduction in the context of transnational surrogacy, while simultaneously challenging popular portrayals of surrogates as powerless victims. While the system treats surrogates as though they are no more than wombs-for-rent, their voices and hopes reveal complex histories of women and families struggling to get into a global market on the best terms they can muster.

REFERENCES CITED

Colen, Shellee. 1995. ""Like a Mother to Them": Stratified Reproduction and West Indian Childcare Workers and Employers in New York." In *Conceiving the New World Order*, edited by Faye Ginsburg and Rayna Rapp, 78–102. Berkeley: University of California Press.

Harrison, Faye. 2007. "Feminist Methodology as a Tool for Ethnographic Inquiry on Globalization," in *The Gender of Globalization: Women Navigating Cultural and Economic Marginalities*, ed. Nandini Gunewardena and Ann Kingsolver. Santa Fe: School of Advanced Research Press.

Mohanty, Chandra T. 1988. "Under Western Eyes: Feminist Scholarship and Colonial Discourses." *Feminist Review* no. 30:61–88.

1 · *Don Kulick*

THE GENDER OF BRAZILIAN TRANSGENDERED PROSTITUTES

DISCUSSION QUESTIONS

1. What is the relationship among gender, sex, and sexuality in Brazil, according to Kulick?
2. How do the practices and desires of travestis reflect these gender ideologies?
3. How does the concept of gender promoted by Kulick challenge dominant "Western" ideas that gender differences are based on sexual/biological differences between men and women?

Males who enjoy being anally penetrated by other males are, in many places in the world, an object of special cultural elaboration. Anywhere they occur as a culturally recognized type, it is usually they who are classified and named, not the males who penetrate them (who are often simply called "men"). Furthermore, to the extent that male same-sex sexual relations are stigmatized, the object of social vituperation is, again, usually those males who allow themselves to be penetrated, not the males who penetrate them. Anywhere they constitute a salient cultural category, men who enjoy being penetrated are believed to think, talk, and act in particular, identifiable, and often cross-gendered

manners. What is more, a large number of such men do in fact behave in these culturally intelligible ways. So whether they are the *mahus*, *hijras*, *kathoeys*, *xaniths*, or *berdaches* of non-Western societies, or the mollies and fairies of our own history, links between habitual receptivity in anal sex and particular effeminate behavioral patterns structure the ways in which males who are regularly anally penetrated are perceived, and they structure the ways in which many of those males think about and live their lives.

One area of the world in which males who enjoy being anally penetrated receive a very high degree of cultural attention is Latin America. Any student

An abridged version of Don Kulick, 1997. "The Gender of Brazilian Transgendered Prostitutes." Reproduced by permission of the American Anthropological Association and of the author from *American Anthropologist*, Volume 99, Issue 3, Pages 574–585, September 1997. Not for sale or further reproduction.

of Latin America will be familiar with the effervescent figure of the effeminate male homosexual. Called *maricón*, *cochón*, *joto*, *marica*, *pajara*, *loca*, *frango*, *bicha*, or any number of other names depending on where one finds him, these males all appear to share certain behavioral characteristics and seem to be thought of in quite similar ways.

Throughout Latin America, sex between males does not necessarily result in both partners being perceived as homosexual. The crucial determinant of a homosexual classification is not so much the fact of sex as it is the role performed during the sexual act. A male who anally penetrates another male is generally not considered to be homosexual. He is considered, in all the various local idioms, to be a "man"; indeed, in some communities, penetrating another male and then bragging about it is one way in which men demonstrate their masculinity to others (Lancaster 1992:241; cf. Brandes 1981:234). Quite different associations attach themselves to a male who allows himself to be penetrated. That male has placed himself in what is understood to be an un-masculine, passive position. By doing so, he has forfeited manhood and becomes seen as something other than a man. This cultural classification as feminine is often reflected in the general comportment, speech practices, and dress patterns of such males, all of which tend to be recognizable to others as effeminate.

A conceptual system in which only males who are penetrated are homosexual is clearly different from the modern heterosexual–homosexual dichotomy currently in place in countries such as the United States, where popular understanding generally maintains that a male who has sex with another male is gay, no matter how carefully he may restrict his behavior to the role of penetrator.[1] But what does this kind of difference mean to how we can think about things like 'gender'? Might it be that the fundamental differences that exist between northern Euro-American and Latin American regimes of sexuality can also result in, or be reflective of, different regimes of gender?

In the literature on Latin America, this question has not been pursued, even in light of the obvious and important links between sexuality and gender that exist in a system where a simple act of penetration has the power to profoundly alter a male's cultural definition and social status. Instead of exploring what the differences in the construction of sexuality might mean for differences in the construction of gender, however, analysis in the literature on Latin American sexualities falls back on familiar concepts. So just as gender in northern Europe and North America consists of men and women, so does it consist of men and women in Latin America, we are told. The characteristics ascribed to and the behavior expected of those two different types of people are not exactly the same in these two different parts of the world, to be sure, but the basic gender categories are the same.

This article contests that view. I will argue that the *sexual division* that researchers have noted between those who penetrate and those who are penetrated extends far beyond sexual interactions between males to constitute the basis of the *gender division* in Latin America. Gender, in this particular elaboration, is grounded not so much in sex (like it is, for example, in modern northern European and North American cultures) as it is grounded in sexuality. This means that gender in Latin America should be seen not as consisting of men and women, but rather of men and not-men, the latter being a category into which both biological females and males who enjoy anal penetration are culturally situated. This specific situatedness provides individuals—not just men who enjoy anal penetration, but everyone—with a conceptual framework that they can draw on in order to understand and organize their own and others' desires, bodies, affective and physical relations, and social roles.

THE BODY IN QUESTION

I will make this argument by drawing on my fieldwork in the Brazilian city of Salvador, among a group of males who enjoy anal penetration. These males are effeminized prostitutes known throughout

Brazil as *travestis* (a word derived from *transvestir*, to cross-dress).[2] Travestis occupy a strikingly visible place in both Brazilian social space and in the Brazilian cultural imaginary. All Brazilian cities of any size contain travestis, and in the large cities of Rio de Janeiro and Sao Paulo, travestis number in the thousands. Travestis are most exuberantly visible during Brazil's famous annual Carnival, and any depiction or analysis of the festival will inevitably include at least a passing reference to them, because their gender inversions are often invoked as embodiments of the Carnival spirit. But even in more mundane contexts such as popular television shows, travestis figure prominently. And most telling of the special place reserved for travestis in the Brazilian popular imagination is the fact that the individual widely acclaimed to be most beautiful woman in Brazil in the mid-1980s was . . . a travesti. That travesti, Roberta Close, became a household name throughout the country. She regularly appeared on national television, starred in a play in Rio, posed nude (with demurely crossed legs) in *Playboy* magazine, was continually interviewed and portrayed in virtually every magazine in the country, and had at least three songs written about her by well-known composers. Although her popularity declined when, at the end of the 1980s, she left Brazil to have a sex-change operation and live in Europe, Roberta Close remains extremely well-known.

Regrettably, the fact that a handful of travestis manage to achieve wealth, admiration, and, in the case of Roberta Close, an almost iconic cultural status, says very little about the lives of the vast majority of travestis. Those travestis, the ones that most Brazilians only glimpse occasionally standing along highways or on dimly lit street corners at night or read about in the crime pages of their local newspapers, comprise one of the most marginalized, feared, and despised groups in Brazilian society. In most Brazilian cities, travestis are so discriminated against that many of them avoid venturing out onto the street during the day. They are regularly the victims of violent police brutality and murder. The vast majority of travestis come from very poor backgrounds and remain poor throughout their lives, living a hand-to-mouth existence and dying before the age of 50 from violence, drug abuse, health problems caused or exacerbated by the silicone they inject into their bodies, or, increasingly, AIDS.

The single most characteristic thing about travestis is their bodies. Unlike drag performers, travestis do not merely don female attributes temporarily. On the contrary, they incorporate them. Sometimes starting at ages as young as ten or twelve, boys who self-identify as travestis begin ingesting or injecting themselves with massive doses of female hormones in order to give their bodies rounded features, broad hips, prominent buttocks, and breasts. Boys discover hormones from a variety of sources. Most of my travesti friends told me that they learned about hormones by approaching adult travestis and asking them how they had achieved the bodies they had. Others were advised by admirers, boyfriends, or clients, who told them that they would look more attractive and make more money if they looked more like girls.

Hormones are valued by travestis because they are inexpensive, easy to obtain, and fast working. Most hormones produce visible results after only about two months of daily ingestion. But they can also result in chronic nausea, headaches, heart palpitations, burning sensations in the legs and chest, extreme weight gain, and allergic reactions. The doses of female hormones required to produce breasts and wide hips also make it difficult for travestis to achieve erections. This can be quite a serious problem, since, as we shall see, a great percentage of travestis' clients want to be penetrated by the travesti. What usually happens after several years of taking hormones is that most individuals stop, at least for a while, and begin injecting silicone into their bodies.

Just as hormones are procured by the individual travesti themselves, without any medical intervention or interference, so is silicone purchased from and administered by acquaintances or friends. The silicone available to the travestis in Salvador is industrial silicone, which is a kind of plastic normally used to manufacture automobile parts such as dashboards. Although it is widely thought to be illegal for industrial outlets to sell this silicone to private individuals, at least one or two travestis in any city containing a silicone manufacturing plant will be well connected enough to be able to buy it. Those travestis will resell it at a hefty profit to others.

Most travestis in Salvador over the age of seventeen have some silicone in their bodies, often between two and five liters (i.e. 0.5–1.3 US gallons). The majority have it in their buttocks, hips, knees, and inner thighs. This strategic placement of silicone is in direct deference to Brazilian aesthetic ideals that consider fleshy thighs, expansive hips, and a prominent, teardrop-shaped *bunda* (buttocks) to be the hallmark of feminine beauty. The majority of travestis do *not*, however, have silicone in their breasts because they believe that silicone in breasts (but not elsewhere in the body) causes cancer. In addition, large breasts are not an essential feature of an attractive woman in Brazil, and many travestis are satisfied with the size of the breasts they have achieved through hormone consumption.

THE BODY IN PROCESS

Why do they do it? One of the reasons habitually cited by travestis seems self-evident. Elizabeth, a 29-year-old travesti with 1½ liters of silicone in her hips and one water-glass of silicone in each breast, explained it to me this way: "To mold my body, you know, be more feminine, with the body of a woman." But why do travestis want the body of a woman? When I first began asking travestis that question, I expected them to tell me that they wanted the body of a woman because they felt themselves to be women. That was not the answer I received. No one ever offered the explanation that they might be women trapped in male bodies, even when I, exasperated, sometimes suggested it. In fact, there is a strong consensus among travestis in Salvador that any travesti who claims to be a woman is mentally disturbed. A travesti is not a

woman and can never be a woman, they tell one another, because God created them male. As individuals, they are free to embellish and augment what God has given them, but their sex cannot be changed. Any attempt to do so would be disastrous. Not only do sex-change operations not produce women (they produce, travestis say, only *bichas castradas*, "castrated homosexuals"), they also inevitably result in madness. I was told on numerous occasions that, without a penis, semen cannot leave the body. When trapped, it travels to the brain, where it collects and forms a "stone" that will continue to increase in size until it eventually causes insanity.

So Roberta Close notwithstanding, travestis modify their bodies not because they feel themselves to be women but because they feel themselves to be "feminine" (*feminino*) or "like a woman" (*se sentir mulher*), qualities most often talked about not in terms of inherent predispositions or essences but rather in terms of behaviors, appearances, and relationships to men.[3] When I asked Elizabeth what it meant when she told me she felt feminine, for example, she answered, "I like to dress like a woman. I like when someone—when men—admire me, you know? . . . I like to be admired, when I go with a man who, like, says: 'Sheez, you're really pretty, you're really feminine.' That . . . makes me want to be more feminine and more beautiful every day, you see?" Similar themes emerged when travestis talked about when they first began to understand that they were travestis. A common response I received from many different people when I asked that question was that they made this discovery in connection with attraction and sexuality. Eighteen-year-old Cintia told me that she understood she was a travesti from the age of seven:

> I already liked girls' things, I played with dolls, played with . . . girls' things; I only played with girls. I didn't play with boys. I just played with these two boys; during the afternoon I always played with them . . . well, you know, rubbing penises together, rubbing them, kissing on the mouth.
>
> *{Laughs.}*

Forty-one-year-old Gabriela says that she knew that she was a travesti early on largely because "since childhood I always liked men, hairy legs, things like that, you know?" Banana, a 34-year-old travesti, told me "the [understanding that I was a] travesti came after, you know, I, um, eight, nine years, ten years old, I felt attracted, really attracted to men." The attraction that these individuals felt for males is thus perceived by them to be a major motivating force behind their self-production as travestis, both privately and professionally. Travestis are quick to point out that, in addition to making them feel more feminine, female forms also help them earn more money as prostitutes. At night when they work on the street, those travestis who have acquired pronounced feminine features use them to attract the attention of passing motorists, and they dress (or rather, undress) to display those features prominently.

But if the goal of a travesti's bodily modifications is to feel feminine and be attractive to men, what does she think about her male genitals?

The most important point to be clear about is that virtually every travesti values her penis: "There's not a better thing in the whole world," 19-year-old Adriana once told me with a big smile. Any thought of having it amputated repels them. *"Deus é mais"* (God forbid), many travestis interject whenever talk of sex-change operations arises. "What, and never cum (i.e., ejaculate, *gozar*) again?!" they gasp, horrified.

Despite the positive feelings that they express about their genitals, however, a travesti keeps her penis, for the most part, hidden, "imprisoned" (*presa*) between her legs. That is, travestis habitually pull their penises down between their legs and press them against their perineums with their underpanties. This is known as "making a cunt" (*fazer uma buceta*). This cunt is an important bodily practice in a travesti's day-to-day public appearance. It is also crucial in another extremely important context of a travesti's life, namely in her relationship to her *marido* (live-in boyfriend). The *maridos* of travestis are typically attractive, muscular, tattooed young men with little or no education and no jobs.

Although they are not pimps (travestis move them into their rooms because they are impassioned [*apaixionada*] with them, and they eject them when the passion wears thin), *maridos* are supported economically by their travesti girlfriends. All these boyfriends regard themselves, and are regarded by their travesti girlfriends, as *homens* (men) and, therefore, as non-homosexual.

One of the defining attributes of being a *homem* (man) in the gender system that the travestis draw on and invoke is that a man will not be interested in another male's penis. A man, in this interpretative framework, will happily penetrate another male's anus. But he will not touch or express any desire for another male's penis. For him to do so would be tantamount to relinquishing his status as a man. He would stop being a man and be reclassified as a *viado* (homosexual, faggot), which is how the travestis are classified by others and how they see themselves.

Travestis want their boyfriends to be men, not *viados*. They require, in other words, their boyfriends to be symbolically and socially different from, not similar to, themselves. Therefore, a travesti does not want her boyfriend to notice, comment on, or in any way concern himself with her penis, even during sex. Sex with a boyfriend, consists, for the most part, of the travesti sucking the boyfriend's penis and of her boyfriend penetrating her, most often from behind, with the travesti on all fours or lying on her stomach on the bed. If the boyfriend touches the travesti at all, he will caress her breasts and perhaps kiss her. But no contact with the travesti's penis will occur, which means, according to most travestis I have spoken to, that travestis do not usually have orgasms during sex with their boyfriends.

What surprised me most about this arrangement was that the ones who are the most adamant that it be maintained are the travestis themselves. They respect their boyfriends and maintain relationships with them only as long as the boyfriends remain "men." If a boyfriend expresses interest in a travesti's penis, becomes concerned that the travesti ejaculate during sex, or worst of all, if the boyfriend expresses a desire to be anally penetrated by the travesti, the relationship, all travestis told me firmly, would be over. They would comply with the boyfriend's request, they all told me, "because if someone offers me their ass, you think I'm not gonna take it?" Afterward, however, they were agreed, they would lose respect for the boyfriend. "You'll feel disgust (*nojo*) toward him," one travesti put it pithily. The boyfriend would no longer be a man in their eyes. He would, instead, be reduced to . . . a *viado*. And as such, he could no longer be a boyfriend. Travestis unfailingly terminate relationships with any boyfriend who deviates from what they consider to be proper manly sexuality.

This absolute unwillingness to engage their own penises in sexual activity with their boyfriends stands in stark contrast to what travestis do with their penises when they are with their clients. On the street, travestis know they are valued for their possession of a penis. Clients will often request to see or feel a travesti's penis before agreeing to pay for sex with her, and travestis are agreed that those travestis who have large penises are more sought after than those with small ones. Similarly, several travestis told me that one of the reasons they stopped taking hormones was because they were losing clients. They realized that clients had begun avoiding them because they knew that the travesti could not achieve an erection. Travestis maintain that one of the most common sexual services they are paid to perform is to anally penetrate their clients.

Most travestis enjoy this. In fact, one of the more surprising findings of my study is that travestis, in significant and highly marked contrast to what is generally reported for other prostitutes, enjoy sex with clients. That is not to say they enjoy sex every time or with every client. But whenever they talk about thrilling, fulfilling, or incredibly fun sex, their partner is always either a client or what they call a *vício*, a word that literally means "vice" or "addiction" and that refers to a male, often encountered on the street while they are working, with whom they have sex for free. Sometimes, if the *vício* is especially attractive, is known to have an

especially large penis, or is known to be especially versatile in bed, the travesti will even pay *him*.

THE BODY IN CONTEXT

At this point, having illustrated the way in which the body of a travesti is constructed, thought about, and used in a variety of contexts, I am ready to address the question of cultural intelligibility and personal desirability. Why do travestis want the kind of body they create for themselves? What is it about Brazilian culture that incites and sustains desire for a male body made feminine through hormones and silicone?

By phrasing that question primarily in terms of culture, I do not mean to deny that there are also social and economic considerations behind the production of travesti bodies and subjectivities. As I noted above, a body full of silicone translates into cash in the Brazilian sexual marketplace. It is important to understand, however—particularly because popular and academic discourses about prostitution tend to frame it so narrowly in terms of victimization, poverty, and exploitation—that males do not become travestis because they were sexually abused as children or just for economic gain. Only one of the approximately forty travestis in my close circle of acquaintances was clearly the victim of childhood sexual abuse. And while the vast majority of travestis (like, one must realize, the vast majority of people in Brazil) come from working-class or poor backgrounds, it is far from impossible for poor, openly effeminate homosexual males to find employment, especially in the professions of hairdressers, cooks, and housecleaners, where they are quite heavily represented.

Another factor that makes it problematic to view travestis primarily in social or economic terms is the fact that the sexual marketplace does not require males who prostitute themselves to be travestis. Male prostitution (where the prostitutes, who are called *michês*, look and act like men) is widespread in Brazil. Also, even transgendered prostitution does not require the radical body modifications that travestis undertake. Before hormones and silicone became widely available (in the mid-1970s and mid-1980s, respectively) males dressed up as females, using wigs and foam-rubber padding (*pirelli*), and worked successfully as prostitutes. Some males still do this today.

Finally, it should be appreciated that travestis do not need to actually have sex with their clients to earn money as prostitutes. A large percentage of a travesti's income from clients is derived from robbing them. In order to rob a client, all that is required is that a travesti come into close physical proximity with him. Once a travesti is in a client's car or once she has begun caressing a passerby's penis, asking him seductively if he *"quer gozar"* (wants to cum), the rest, for most travestis, is easy. Either by pickpocketing the client, assaulting him, or if she does have sex with him, by threatening afterward to create a public scandal, the travesti will often walk away with all the client's money (Kulick 1996a). Thus it is entirely possible to derive a respectable income from prostitution and still not consume hormones and inject silicone into one's body.

In addition to all those considerations, I also phrase the question of travestis in terms of culture because, even if it were possible to claim that males who become travestis do so because of poverty, early sexual exploitation, or some enigmatic inner psychic orientation, the mystery of travestis as a sociocultural phenomenon would remain unsolved. What is it about the understandings, representations, and definitions of sexuality, gender, and sex in Brazilian society that makes travesti subjectivity imaginable and intelligible?

Let me begin answering that question by noting an aspect of travesti language that initially puzzled me. In their talk to one another, travestis frequently refer to biological males by using feminine pronouns and feminine adjectival endings. Thus the common utterance *"ela ficou doida"* (she was furious) can refer to a travesti, a woman, a gay male, or a heterosexual male who has allowed himself to be penetrated by another male. All of these different people are classified by travestis in the same manner. This classificatory system is quite subtle,

complex, and context sensitive: travestis narrating their life stories, for example, frequently use masculine pronouns and adjectival endings when talking about themselves as children but switch to feminine forms when discussing their present-day lives. In a similar way, clients are often referred to as "she" because they want to be penetrated. But when a travesti recounts that she struggled with a client over money or when she describes the client as handing over money to pay for the travesti's services, his gender will often change from feminine to masculine.

The important point here is that the gender of males is subject to fluctuation and change in travesti talk. Males are sometimes referred to as "she" and sometimes as "he." Males, in other words, can shift gender depending on the context and the actions they perform. The same is not true for females. Females, even the several brawny and conspicuously unfeminine lesbians who associate with the travestis I know, are never referred to as "he" (Kulick 1996b). So whereas the gender of females remains fixed, the gender of males fluctuates and shifts continually.

Why can males be either male or female, but females can only be female? The answer, I believe, lies in the way that the gender system that the travestis draw on is constituted. Debates about transgendered individuals such as 18th-century mollies, Byzantine eunuchs, Indian hijras, Native American berdaches, U.S. transsexuals, and others often suggest that those individuals constitute a third, or intermediate, gender, one that is neither male or female or one that combines both male and female. Journalists and social commentators in Brazil sometimes take a similar line when they write about travestis, arguing that travestis transcend maleness and femaleness and constitute a kind of postmodern androgyny.

My contention is the opposite. Despite outward physical appearances and despite local claims to the contrary, there is no third or intermediate sex here. Travestis only arise and are only culturally intelligible within a gender system based on a strict dichotomy. That gender system, however, is structured according to a dichotomy different from the one with which many of us are familiar, anchored in and arising from principles different from those that structure and give meaning to gender in northern Europe and North America.

The fundamental difference is that, whereas the northern Euro-American gender system is based on sex, the gender system that structures travestis' perceptions and actions is based on sexuality. The dominant idea in northern Euro-American societies is that one is a man or a woman because of the genitals one possesses. That biological difference is understood to accrete differences in behavior, language, sexuality, perception, emotion, and so on. As others have pointed out, it is within such a cultural system that a *transsexual* body can arise, because here biological males, for example, who do not feel or behave as men should, can make sense of that difference by reference to their genitals. They are not men; therefore they must be women, and to be a woman means to have the genitals of a female.

While the biological differences between men and women are certainly not ignored in Brazil, the possession of genitals is fundamentally conflated with what they can be used for, and in the particular configuration of sexuality, gender, and sex that has developed there, the determinative criterion in the identification of males and females is not so much the genitals as it is the role those genitals perform in sexual encounters. Here the locus of gender difference is the act of penetration. If one *only* penetrates, one is a man, but if one gets penetrated, one is not a man, which, in this case, means that one is either a *viado* (a faggot) or a *mulher* (a woman).

Anal penetration figures prominently as an engendering device in another important dimension of travestis' lives, namely, their self-discovery as travestis. When I asked travestis to tell me when they first began to understand that they were travestis, the most common response, as I noted earlier, was that they discovered this in connection with attraction to males. Sooner or later, this attraction always led to sexuality, which in practice means that the young proto-travesti began allowing himself to be penetrated anally. This act is always cited

by travestis as crucial in their self-understanding as travestis.

A final example of the role that anal penetration plays as a determining factor in gender assignment is the particular way in which travestis talk about gay men. Travestis frequently dismiss and disparage gay men for "pretending to be men" (*andar / passar como se fosse homem*), a phrase that initially confounded me, especially when it was used by travestis in reference to me. One Sunday afternoon, for example, I was standing with two travesti friends eating candy in one of Salvador's main plazas. As two policemen walked by, one travesti began to giggle. "They see you standing here with us," she said to me, "and they probably think you're a man." Both travestis then collapsed in laughter at the sheer outrageousness of such a profound misunderstanding. It took me a long time to figure out what was so funny.

I am a gay man, and I finally came to realize that as a *viado*, I am assumed by travestis to *dar* (be penetrated by men). I am, therefore, the same as them. But I and all other gay men who do not dress as women and modify our bodies to be more feminine disguise this sameness. We hide, we deceive, we pretend to be men, when we really are not men at all. It is in this sense that travestis can perceive themselves to be more honest, and much more radical, than "butch" (*machuda*) homosexuals like myself. It is also in this sense that travestis simply do not understand the discrimination that they face throughout Brazil at the hands of gay men, many of whom feel that travestis compromise the public image of homosexuals and give gay men a bad name.

What all these examples point to is that for travestis, as reflected in their actions and in all their talk about themselves, clients, boyfriends, *vícios*, gay men, women, and sexuality, there are two genders; there is a binary system of opposites very firmly in place and in operation. But the salient difference in this system is not between men and women. It is, instead, between those who penetrate (*comer*, literally "to eat" in Brazilian Portuguese) and those who get penetrated (*dar*, literally "to give"), *in a system where the act of being penetrated has transformative force.* Thus those who *only* "eat" (and *never* "give") in this system are culturally designated as "men". Those who give (even if they *also* eat) are classified as being something else, a something that one might call "not men."

What this particular binary implies is that females and males who enjoy being penetrated belong to the same classificatory category, they are on the same side of the gendered binary. They share, in other words, a gender.

This sharing is the reason why the overwhelming majority of travestis do not self-identify as women and have no desire to have an operation to become a woman even though they spend their lives dramatically modifying their bodies to make them look more feminine. Culturally speaking, travestis, because they enjoy being penetrated, are structurally equivalent to, even if they are not biologically identical to, women. Because they already share a gender with women, a sex-change operation would (again, culturally speaking) give a travesti nothing that she does not already have. All a sex-change operation would do is rob her of a significant source of pleasure and income.

It is important to stress that the claim I am making here is that travestis share a gender with women, not that they *are* women (or that women are travestis). Individual travestis will not always or necessarily share individual women's roles, goals, or social status. Just as the worldviews, self-images, social statuses, and possibilities of, say, a poor black mother, a single mulatto prostitute, and a rich white businesswoman in Brazil (to draw on stereotypes that have great salience in the country) differ dramatically, even though all those individuals share a gender, so will the goals, perspectives, and possibilities of individual travestis differ from those of individual women, even though all those individuals share a gender. But inasmuch as travestis share the same gender as women, they are understood to share (and feel themselves to share) a whole spectrum of tastes, perceptions, behaviors, styles, feelings, and desires. And one of the most important of those desires is understood and felt to

be the desire to attract and be attractive for persons of the opposite gender. The desire to be attractive for persons of the opposite gender puts pressure on individuals to attempt to approximate cultural ideals of beauty, thereby drawing them into patriarchal and heterosexual imperatives that guide aesthetic values and that frame the direction and the content of the erotic gaze.[4] And although attractive male bodies get quite a lot of attention and exposure in Brazil, the pressure to conform to cultural ideals of beauty, in Brazil as in northern Euro-American societies, is much stronger on females than on males. In all these societies, the ones who are culturally incited to look (with all the subtexts of power and control that that action can imply) are males, and the ones who are exhorted to desire to be looked *at* are females.

In Brazil, the paragon of beauty, the body that is held forth, disseminated, and extolled as desirable in the media, on television, in popular music, during Carnival, and in the day-to-day public practices of both individual men and women is a feminine body with smallish breasts, ample buttocks, and high, wide hips. Anyone wishing to be considered desirable to a man should do what she can to approximate that ideal. And this, of course, is precisely what travestis do. They appropriate and incorporate the ideals of beauty that their culture offers them in order to be attractive to men: both real men (i.e., boyfriends, some clients, and *vícios*), and males who publicly "pretend to be men" (clients and *vícios* who enjoy being penetrated).

CONCLUSION: PENETRATING GENDER

What exactly is gender and what is the relationship between sex and gender? Despite several decades of research, discussion, and intense debate, there is still no agreed-upon, widely accepted answer to those basic questions. Researchers who discuss gender tend to either not define it or, if they do define it, do so by placing it in a seemingly necessary relationship to sex. It is only when one realizes that sex stands in no particularly privileged, or even necessary, relation to gender that one can begin to understand the various ways in which social groups can organize gender in different ways.

My work among travestis has led me to define gender, more or less following Eve Sedgwick (1990:27–28), as a social and symbolic arena of ongoing contestation over specific identities, behaviors, rights, obligations, and sexualities. These identities and so forth are bound up with and productive of male and female persons, in a hierarchically ordered cultural system in which the male/female dichotomy functions as a primary and perhaps a model binarism for a wide range of values, processes, relationships, and behaviors. Gender, in this rendering, does not have to be about "men" and "women." It can just as probably be about "men" and "not-men," a slight but extremely significant difference in social classification that opens up different social configurations and facilitates the production of different identities, understandings, relationships, and imaginings.

My main point is that for the travestis with whom I work in Salvador, gender is thought to be determined by one's sexual behavior. Travestis have distilled and clarified a relationship between sexuality and gender that seems to be widespread throughout Latin America. Past research on homosexual roles in Latin America has conflated sex and gender. Researchers have assumed that gender is a cultural reading of biological males and females and that there are, therefore, two genders: man and woman. Effeminate male homosexuals do not fit into this particular binary; they are clearly not women, but culturally speaking they are not men either. So what are they? Calling them "not quite men, not quite women," as Roger Lancaster (1992:274) does in his analysis of Nicaraguan cochones, is hedging. It is also not hearing what cochones, travestis, and other effeminate Latin American homosexuals are saying. When travestis, maricas, or cochones call each other "she" or when they call men who have been anally penetrated "she," they are not just being campy and subcultural; I suggest that they

are incisively reading off and enunciating core messages generated by their cultures' arrangements of sexuality, gender, and sex.

I realize that this interpretation of travestis and other effeminate male homosexuals as belonging to the same gender as women will seem counterintuitive for many Latin Americans and students of Latin America. Certainly in Brazil, people generally do not refer to travestis as "she," and many people, travestis will be the first to tell you, appear to enjoy going out of their way to offend travestis by addressing them loudly and mockingly as "o senhor" (Sir or Mister). The very word travesti is grammatically masculine in Brazilian Portuguese (o travesti), which makes it not only easy but logical to address the word's referent using masculine forms. There are certainly many reasons why Brazilians generally contest and mock individual travestis' claims to femininity, not least among them being travestis' strong associations with homosexuality, prostitution, and AIDS—all highly stigmatized issues that tend to elicit harsh condemnation and censure from many people.

Refusal to acknowledge travestis' gender is one readily available way of refusing to acknowledge travestis' right to exist at all. It is a way of putting travestis back in their (decently gendered) place, a way of denying and defending against the possibilities that exist within the gender system itself for males to shift from one category to the other.

REFERENCES CITED

Brandes, Stanley. 1981. Like Wounded Stags: Male Sexual Ideology in an Andalusian Town. *In Sexual Meanings: The Cultural Construction of Gender and Sexuality.* S. B. Ortner and H. Whitehead, eds. Pp. 216–239. Cambridge: Cambridge University Press.

Kulick, Don. 1996a. Causing a Commotion: Public Scandals as Resistance among Brazilian Transgendered Prostitutes. *Anthropology Today* 12(6):3–7.

———. 1996b. Fe/male Trouble: The Unsettling Place of Lesbians in the Self-images of Male Transgendered Prostitutes in Salvador, Brazil. Paper presented at 95th annual meeting of the American Anthropological

Association, San Francisco; later published in 1998 in *Sexualities* 1(3): 299–312.

Lancaster, Roger N. 1992. *Life Is Hard: Machismo, Danger, and the Intimacy of Power in Nicaragua.* Berkeley: University of California Press.

Sedgwick, Eve Kosofsky. 1990. *Epistemology of the Closet.* Berkeley: University of California Press.

Wooden, Wayne S., and Jay Parker. 1982. *Men behind Bars: Sexual Exploitation in Prison.* New York: Da Capo Press.

NOTES

1. One of the few contexts in which ideas similar to Latin American ones are preserved in North American and northern European understandings of male sexuality is prisons. See, for example, Wooden and Parker 1982.

2. This article is based on 11 months of anthropological fieldwork and archival research and more than 50 hours of recorded speech and interviews with travestis between the ages of 11 and 60 in Salvador, Brazil's third-largest city, with a population of over 2 million people. The material sketched here is presented and analyzed in detail in the book *Travesti: Sex, Gender and Culture among Brazilian Transgendered Prostitutes.* Chicago: University of Chicago Press, 1998.

3. The literal translation of *se sentir mulher* is "to feel woman," and taken out of context, it could be read as meaning that travestis feel themselves to be women. In all instances in which it is used by travestis, however, the phrase means "to feel like a woman," "to feel as if one were a woman (even though one is not)." Its contrastive opposite is *ser mulher* (to be woman).

4. I use the word *heterosexuality* purposely because travesti–boyfriend relationships are generally considered, by travestis and their boyfriends, to be *heterosexual.* I once asked Edison, a 35-year-old *marido* who has had two long-term relationships in his life, both of them with travestis, whether he considered himself to be heterosexual, bisexual, or homosexual. "I'm heterosexual; I'm a man," was his immediate reply. "I won't feel love for another heterosexual," he continued, significantly, demonstrating how very lightly the northern Euro-American classificatory system has been grafted onto more meaningful Brazilian ways of organizing erotic relationships: "[For two males to be able to feel love], one of the two has to be gay."

2 • *Patricia Zavella*

"PLAYING WITH FIRE"
The Gendered Construction of Chicana/Mexicana Sexuality

DISCUSSION QUESTIONS

1. What are some of the cultural, social, political, and economic influences that shaped Mirella's and Maria's changing sexual identities and desires?
2. How was power coded into their sexual practices and relationships?
3. What do we learn about Mexican ideas of gender and sexuality from these narratives?

Mexican sexual/gender discourse expresses a particular version of the Catholic "honor-shame" configuration (Pitt-Rivers 1968). Rooted in the history of Spanish conquest, colonization and repression of indigenous peoples, the Mexican "national allegory" began with betrayal by Malinche, Cortés' translator and concubine, instituting notions that sexual intercourse (*chingar*) is linked to conquest, violation, and devaluation of women where men avenge their honor through sexual conquest. The Virgin of Guadalupe's appearance after the conquest symbolizes proper servility and modesty for Mexican women, as well as the subversive spiritual power of indigenous peoples who accepted Spanish Catholicism yet incorporated their own beliefs. Male dominance and the double standard are integral in the cultural polemics of *macho/chingón* and virgin/whore.

The research on Chicana/Mexicano sexuality in contemporary times confirms the continuing importance of Catholic repression and the double standard (Alonso and Koreck 1989, Ascencio 2010, Zavella and Castañeda 2005). Further, U.S. Mexicans—like others—do not always follow church doctrines when it comes to decisions about contraception or abortion (NLIRH, 2011). Beyond the Church, cultural constructions in Mexico and the United States are influenced by other forces—popular culture, state policies, or increased incidents of sexually transmitted diseases. Feminists, gay men, and lesbians contest this interpretive framework and transgress these gendered scripts, struggling to dismantle Mexican heterosexism and homophobia by creating discourse and social spaces for acknowledging homoerotic sexuality. Lesbian theorists also claim La Virgen de Guadalupe as their icon, reconfiguring her as symbol of indigenous liberation and women's empowerment.

How do individuals construct their sense of sexual pleasure or subjectivity in relation to cultural discourse? How is power coded into sexual behavior and relationships? This piece explores

An abridged version of Patricia Zavella, 1997. "Playing with Fire": The Gendered Construction of Chicana/Mexicana Sexuality. In R. N. Lancaster and Micaela di Leonardo (eds), *The Gender/Sexuality Reader: Culture, History, Political Economy*. New York: Routledge, pp. 392–408. Adapted by the author with permission of John Wiley and Sons.

these questions in relation to Chicana/Mexicana sexuality through ethnographic interviews.[1]

Interviews are challenging for understanding sexuality because knowledge is often "nondiscursive," assumed rather than explicit. The people I interviewed struggled to convey their ambivalent feelings or describe experiences previously repressed. I heard a common refrain: "We just *knew*. There were certain things you did not talk about, and sex was one of them." The interviews, then, were transgressions of the silencing expected of women. Further, interviewees may suffer memory lapses. Women I interviewed often had difficulty recalling what they were taught and by whom, which was telling. In these instances I culled from their recollections of childhood experiences and admonitions to understand their enculturation regarding gender and sexuality. For others, memories were "brilliant frozen moments" (Lively 1994, vii) because of their significance; yet they were "distorted by the wisdom of maturity" and the social context of the interview setting. These narratives are thus representations and should be read critically.

My purpose is to explicate the political economy of gender and sexuality among low income Chicanas and Mexicanas and illustrate how social meaning is culturally constructed. This analysis begins with two women's narratives that took place in an arena of plural and often conflicting social narratives about sexual practices and meanings by a heterosexual Chicana, Mirella Hernández (a pseudonym), and a *lesbiana Mexicana*—María Pérez.[2]

To understand the meaning of sexuality, I will examine women's "cultural poetics" where the metaphors "playing" and "fire" recurred about desire among Chicana and Mexicana interviewees.[3] Heterosexuals and lesbians indicated that in seeking sexual desire they were "playing"—flirting, teasing, or testing potential lovers. Fire contained dual meanings, signifying both the repressive forces of culturally sanctioned silence regarding Eros in Mexican society; and simultaneously, in seeking the "powers of desire" (Snitow et al. 1983) women imagined sexual pleasure as fire—"hot," "passionate," "boiling," "explosive"—and difficult

to stop. They envisioned seeking out potential sexual partners as a "game" played within the limits imposed by church doctrines, family practices, and the sanctions of conventional society. While women did not always "win" the game, and indeed sometimes "got burned," playing was pleasurable, often because the game was taboo. Seeking a partner, then, often pushed societal parameters and made these women feel powerful in their ability to pursue desire. During interviews, women recalled even failed loves occasionally with tears of pain, but more often with smiles and joy.

In presenting these narratives, I do not impose binary oppositions—cultural vs. essential self, heterosexual and homosexual, feelings and logic. Rather, I illustrate women's agency in contesting traditional expectations. I argue that these women's cultural poetics of sexuality entailed struggling with the contradictions of repressive discourses and social practices that were often violent toward women and their desires. I chose these women because their narratives represent "incandescent moments when different configurations of gender and knowledge are illuminated" (Franco 1989, xxiii).

MIRELLA HERNÁNDEZ

Her mother immigrated from a rural Mexican village with limited education; her father was from New Mexico with high school education. Born in California and 21 years old, Mirella identified herself ethnically as Mexican.

Mirella had vivid memories of experiences related to sexuality: "I've always been curious about sex." She told me about an incident that occurred when she was eight. She and a neighbor boy were in a swimming pool and they began exposing their bodies. When her brother tattled to her mother, Mirella had to apologize to the boy's parents. She recalled: "That was the worst." Mirella was taught that sex was not to be discussed openly:

I remember this really clearly. This lady came over when my mom was pregnant, and she told me "when your Mom buys the baby." I thought, "you're so stupid, I know where they come from." My Mom gave me the eye like "don't you dare say a word." Later I asked her, "why can't I say anything?" And she told me, "out of respect."

Clearly, respect—for herself or for elders—meant that openness about sex should be avoided.

Mirella's mother was a battered woman whose alcoholic spouse would rape her, sometimes in front of the children, which was traumatic for Mirella: "When I was old enough Mom told me about it and sometimes I saw. I felt really sick. I remember thinking how dirty a person could feel. I hated my father when that happened. I didn't want him to touch me. And even my Mom, I wouldn't let my Mom touch me." Mirella's mother would occasionally call the police to stop the battering, but would not press charges. Mirella kept silent about the violence at home: "I kept it a secret from everybody so they would think that my family was just fine."

As Mirella became an adolescent, adults gave her mixed messages about her body. When she began menstruating, her mother and aunts offered congratulations for her new status as a woman, which she found to be embarrassing but pleasing. Mirella also experienced a new reticence towards men:

> I knew that I could have kids now, which was really scary yet also exciting. Then after that I hated men. I didn't want them to get too close to me, for about six months. I don't know if it was because of my Dad, or it was just me; it was a weird feeling I got. My Mom would always say, "all men are alike, they're bastards." So I thought maybe they really are.

Mirella was also encouraged more to be "ladylike," foregoing her usual attire of pants for dresses, curly hair, and makeup. Her father warned her about impregnation in clinical terms: "My Dad told me you have to be in love and usually when you marry. And 'intercourse' was the word; it wasn't sex. He explained that certain times of the month you could get pregnant, or you couldn't, which was

confusing for me." Her mother was more direct: "She told me not to throw myself at boys: 'Have respect,' and 'I was never with anybody until I got married.' I always told myself, because of my mother's values, that I would not have sex until I was married." The strategy of saving her virginity for marriage would provide her with the expectation of economic stability where a man would support her in exchange for her unsullied reputation.

Mirella never received any sense that a homosexual relationship was a possibility: "I heard the word 'fag,' but I didn't know what it meant. I just laughed along with everybody else." Thus she was encouraged to be feminine and celebrate her apparent fecundity, but only to a limited degree. Becoming a woman meant the possible threat of pregnancy, distasteful intimacy with men, the importance of self-respect, and the prospect of economic support.

At age fifteen, Mirella's family celebrated her *quinceañera*, a religious ritual when young woman become adults: "At first I didn't want one because I didn't know what it meant. When I started going to catechism, I learned the meaning of a *quinceañera* and why my Mom wanted me to have one. It represents purity, your virginity, which was neat. But I thought I was one of the only virgins at 15. I had so much fun!" Over three hundred people attended, including relatives from far away. She and family members worked to save enough to cover the costs. Mirella's parents had separated just prior to the *quinceañera*. "It was a real turning point for us, as a family, to be able to do this on our own." This celebration of virginity and family, then, was meaningful at several levels.

Mirella then had permission to date but her mother applied different standards of behavior to her and her brother. Mirella had to report where she was going, with whom, obey a strict curfew, and report if she changed her plans. Perhaps because she was parenting by herself, Mirella's mother seemed particularly vigilant: "My Mom would tell me to have fun, but '*cuídate*,' be careful. I know what that means now."

Mirella's mother informed her she would be able to tell if a woman has lost her virginity:

> My Mom says she can tell 'cause you get bags under your eyes. And she can tell when someone's pregnant, even if they're not showing, by their face, if they look drained. Our neighbor came over once and Mom asked her. And she'd be, "no, I'm not planning on having any kids," and she turned out pregnant. I think that my Mom was trying to scare me to think, if I have sex, she is going to know.[4]

Her mother advised Mirella to date a lot of different men so she would not end up "tied down" as she had been: "She loves the guys that I've gone out with, but she never wanted me to have a serious relationship with anybody. She was open to birth control and I can talk to her about sex if I wanted to." Again, the message was mixed, with the openness about discussing sex with her mother tempered by the caution: "She said, 'don't have sex until you get married, then you don't have to worry about birth control.'"

Clearly Mirella was expected to remain a virgin until marriage. She was trained to repress her own sexual desires. She came of age in northern California during the late 1980s, however, a time when Madonna was the popular cultural icon and the seductive Kenny G. was her favorite musician. Mirella received different messages from the dominant culture and her friends than she received at home and at church.

Mirella started dating her first boyfriend at 16, after years of flirting and "playing hard to get." Michael was four years older, white, and from a wealthy family. Mirella found him attractive because, "I think it was his body and his eyes talked. They were sending out these messages, like he always got what he wanted. And I wasn't the girl who gave what you wanted, which was a big challenge for him and it was a challenge for me." With her long, black hair and "olive" skin, Mirella's beauty was classically Mexican. Michael's mother did not approve of the relationship, was

blatantly rude, and Mirella's brother did not approve either:

> He told me Michael was bad news, 'cause he did drugs in high school and he was a rebel. He said. "this guy just wants one thing, to get you in the sack." I knew if I went out with him I couldn't talk to my brother about it. At first it was hush-hush; only Mom knew. When I finally told him, he said "well you gotta do what you have to do," and "Be careful." But that's not what I saw, because it took a long time for me to even sleep with this guy. Michael was very respectful. He was my first real love, even though then I really didn't know what love was.

Mirella, then, was playing with fire, drawn to this dangerous man but wanting to preserve her reputation as a "good girl." His membership in the local powerful white community added to the sense of taboo and enhanced the challenge. Proving her brother wrong was an added enticement. Mirella was asserting her own independence within the confines of her family's control. That she was in love with the man provided a rationale in which a young woman was considered respectable despite the loss of her virginity.[5]

The relationship with Michael lasted nine months before Mirella discovered he had dated another woman.

> When I found out he had cheated on me, it broke my heart. And I didn't give him any chances either. It was over. I said to myself, "Why am I so stupid? I should have listened to my Mom; I shouldn't have had sex until I get married." I was so afraid that if anyone found out, they're going to think I'm a tramp. Especially if my Mom found out, she would kill me. I was the worst person.

Since neither her mother nor brother found out she had lost her virginity, her reputation remained unscathed.

It was another year and a half before Mirella could trust a man enough to go out with him. During this period she reflected upon how she would conduct herself in relationships, and made a profound change in her thinking: "I thought maybe I shouldn't fall in love. It's okay just to date someone and sleep with them." Mirella was beginning to reconfigure her own sense of pleasure within the confines of her life.

Her next relationship was with another white boy, Jim, of working class background. Even though he was very handsome, and had an "even better body" than Michael, Mirella said: "I wasn't looking for a boyfriend. But he was really sweet and fun. I thought 'okay, not all guys are the same.'" Still, Mirella would not have sex with Jim for quite some time. Then an opportunity for privacy presented itself:

> My grandmother went away and I was taking care of her house. My grandma's fairly religious and everywhere there's a crucifix or saints. I remember being in her room and there's this cross looking at me, and I thought "oh my God, how evil I am." But then things happened, and I could care less about what was on the walls.

Their relationship lasted three years and the couple discussed marriage. Jim had drinking problems, however, and Mirella asserted her independence from him: "I'm not going to put up with that, not after what my mom went through. Despite "still being in love with him," Mirella ended the relationship. She enrolled in a nursing program and worked part-time, moving toward economic self-sufficiency.

Mirella began dating another man, a university student and friend of her brother's. This was the first "Hispanic" she had ever dated, and she found that their same ethnic background "really makes a difference" and was a powerful attraction:

> Now that I've dated Ray, I realize that I don't have to teach him anything, and he knows what I'm saying when I talk to my mom in Spanish. And he's got this little saying, he calls me "*mija*" (my little daughter) which I think is the cutest thing. It gives me the neatest feeling. And I could see my mom's face light up the first time they met. Ray can dance and everything. I'm happy when I go out with him.

Mirella was attracted to Ray because of his good looks, but this time she appreciated something more: "He's so smart, and that's a turn on for me. He's going to school and he's got goals and he's going for it. And that's what I'm doing too. I can talk to him about school and he understands."

The couple delayed initiating sex. Mirella was taking the pill to regulate her menstrual cycle and made it clear that nevertheless she was not "easy": "I explained it wasn't because I was sleeping around or anything." An educated man himself, Ray was not judgmental about Mirella's sexual past. The couple was making plans to solidify their relationship:

> We were talking the other night. I haven't told Ray "I love you" straight out and he hasn't told me either. But I think I'm getting there. He asked me "are you falling in love?" And I told him how I felt about him and he told me. He says that he can see himself marrying me.

Mirella's ideal relationship would "work 50-50," where each was committed to the relationship, and they spent as much time on their relationship as on their careers.

When I asked her "what would you desire in a sexual relationship," Mirella got flustered and then responded: "I don't think I'm turned on by just the thought of having sex. I do have to care for the person. I don't think if I wanted it, I just could have it because that hasn't happened. If something could work out between us." Later she clarified, "I think it's a turn on to think that Ray's got so much going for him. He can make a life out of what he's doing, and I know I can too." Anticipating meeting Ray's family and developing their relationship, Mirella admitted, "I'm excited. I'm really excited."

A maturing young woman, Mirella Hernández now realizes that sexual relationships are not inherently dangerous and that all men are not stupid, abusive, or mistrustful. She incorporated some of her mother's advice and Catholicism as guides for her behavior so that she would not be considered "easy." But she also resisted her family's preoccupation with virginity and her mother's model of a traditional role within marriage. Now closer to economic stability herself, Mirella prefers a relationship with a man working toward a career and she claims the right to sexual pleasure outside of marriage.

MARÍA PÉREZ

Reared in a small town in Mexico, María Pérez was 35 year old. She attended all-girls schools in Mexico on scholarships and completed a master's degree. While she was raised Catholic, she no longer attends church. Like Mirella, María received traditional gender socialization as a child:

> I was taught that you should marry and the husband will take care of you. You need to learn how to cook, sew, clean up the house, and make good food for your husband. You've got to have children because that's your role in life, as a woman, and sacrifice for your family.

Her family assumed that heterosexuality would be the norm.

María received clear messages that sex was sinful and sexual pleasure was to be avoided. She recalled that as a five-year-old, she and a male cousin of the same age exposed their bodies. María's mother became angry and slapped María, saying "I don't want you doing this." María recalled, "One time my mother found me exploring myself and she was pretty pissed off. She slapped me and said, 'those things you don't do.' Later I learned about masturbation, the concept, but it was like, 'that's a sin, and God will punish you.' The Ten Commandants were mandatory." When María became older, "I learned that you should be a virgin when you get married, and then you should be sexually available for your husband." Other than warning her to preserve her virginity, however, María's kin offered no information about sexual relationships.

At twelve, María realized that females could have intimate relationships through the discovery

of two girls at school: "Everyone said 'dykes' with horrible contempt, and I was scared." María fell in love for the first time herself with a young woman. But she was afraid of her desires: "I passed through a denial stage, 'how can I be in love with a girl?' Later, at secondary school I would see popular guys surrounded by girls, and I would say 'I wish I could *be* that boy.'" María began a period where she perceived herself as "the most popular boy," when she had "a heap of admiring girls." She began a process of sexual exploration and play, only with women and usually with more than one. In a classic Mexican sense, María was solidifying her sense of herself as male and predator.

She met a younger woman and the relationship became serious: "She was so young, and beautiful." They were open with each other about the sexual nature of their relationship, which was cast in a heterosexist mold where María played the male and her lover the female when they made a commitment. María would tell her lover "you cannot go out with other boys," and her lover responded,

> "You can't go out with other girls." And I would say, "well, I didn't seek them out." I was copying the male patriarchs because I didn't have anyone else to copy. It was not easy for a girl to play the role of a boy. The role of a woman is defined. But I was a girl who desired to be a boy, and with no one to learn from. Also there was much about boys that I did not like. I didn't know much in this interior struggle. Anyway, at that time I was very male, very butch.

Talking about her behavior over two decades later, María was embarrassed about her past mimicry of what to her were the negative male qualities of jealousy, infidelity and possessiveness towards her girlfriend. She said, "I was a *macho* Mexican *cabrón*." María's experience parallels that of Cherríe Moraga (1983, 125), who noted: "In the effort to avoid embodying *la chingada*, I became the *chingón*. In the effort not to feel fucked, I became the fucker, even with women."

At fifteen, María became involved with "the love of my life," Josefina, who "had the most beautiful eyes and hair. She was all woman, the self-denying mother, the suffering woman. It was very appropriate for me to get in that relationship because I was the macho prototype in the tradition of values." As the prototypical female, Josefina was protective and nurtured María:

> She believes that no one would love me like her. She's right. She was a mother, nurturing me. I became a baby sometimes in her arms. Sometimes when she embraced me, she made me feel like I had regained something that I missed when I was a child. I became mature with her. And I taught her how to be independent and fight for good grades.

María's vision of gender roles for women, then, was "defined" and restricting, complementing those for men which were assertive and strong.

The lovers suffered through an initial period of denial, then admitted their feelings for one another. "It was really a Romeo and Juliet thing; it was very passionate and intense. I had my first real sexual relationship with her. She taught me how to kiss, the giving part and the exchanging part of the kiss where you lose yourself in the pleasure." The lovers would be together for nine years and experienced the full panoply of feelings:

> We did it all. We had passion, we had confrontations, we had growing, we had turbulence, we had the caring. It was a struggle against everything. We were claiming our right to be in love. We couldn't avoid touching each other in front of everybody. It was like water boiling over. It was not possible for us to deny we loved each other. We would hold hands and walk in front of everybody, we said, "we don't care; our love is meant to be and we are gonna defend it."

The school officials sent the girls to a psychologist who was sympathetic: "She knew what was happening and wanted us to not sleep together. But that was our sanctuary, even though it was in the middle of a large building." The other girls began protecting them with an unwritten code of honor in which no one would "break the ice" and tell the authorities. María and Josefina knew they were in love, but did not understand exactly what was happening to them. María investigated through books and found a term for her desires—lesbianism.

During this period María and Josefina dated boys, "to play the role that I had a boyfriend. But the boyfriends were only a mask to cover up that there was more between Josefina and I. It was just because I was general secretary so I needed to do that. I had to be normal." The boyfriends did not interest María—"not even a kiss. They asked me why, and I said 'no, I take care of my honor.' And they believed in that and I manipulated that." María used the subterfuge of virgin honor to mask her blossoming homosexuality.

The lovers' relationship was made public inadvertently when María's mother opened a letter from Josefina, which caused a scandal. The discovery pushed the lovers together: "We would say, 'if the world doesn't want us we will leave this world.' We would commit suicide if necessary." The breach with her mother has never fully healed. Josefina's parents were more accepting and María became like an adopted daughter yet they were not open about their relationship:

> It was a big unspoken secret. That is a concept in the family in Mexico, whenever some sin is going on, we have a social psychology protecting the victim and victimizer. And it has come here [to the U.S.]. They say, "don't say anything about your aunt, poor thing, she has a big problem." And now I'm guilty too. You break the guilty feeling in pieces and distribute it among the whole family over a long period of time. Whenever someone gets pissed, they say "enough, I'm going to tell the secret!"

María and Josefina's relationship was an unspoken secret: "Everyone pretended that we were great friends."

María and Josefina's relationship was premised on three vows they made to one another: During sex they would not engage in vaginal penetration, so they would preserve their virginity: María explained the significance of giving up one's virginity:

"The social oppression to marry as a virgin was so strong that it was a sacrifice to lose one's virginity." The second was: "If we wanted to give our virginity to anyone, it would be among ourselves first." Like Mirella, María was told that one could tell if a woman lost her virginity—the backs of her knees would change. They waited two years before agreeing to vaginal penetration. The third agreement was: "If we found a man who became the love of our life, we would end our relationship." In some ways this was a quixotic promise, for as María noted, "that was very far from happening after nine years."

During this time María had several sexual relations with other women, describing herself as "promiscuous," but clarified, "I'm not the type of person to make out on the first date. I needed something more from the person." In one of these relationships, her lover pressured her for sex with penetration. María asked the lover to wait: "I told her, 'I'm not ready.' I directed the thing with Josefina emotionally so that we complied with my promise to have that experience with her. It was a good experience, very satisfying." María was successful with other women because of the clarity of the boundaries she established with them: "I couldn't promise those women the heavens and the stars. I would say, 'I have this relationship with another woman but I can play with you sexually.'" She took pleasure in her identification with the sexual prowess of men:

I was very fortunate because I received the gift of a woman's virginity from many women. A true man would envy me enormously and ask, "how did you do that? You had all these virgins and didn't have to marry any of them?" And I did not have to violate them either. I guess I was charming.

María viewed herself as male—in control, guiding the relationship with Josefina, having multiple lovers, and gaining the ultimate male conquest, a woman's virginity. María sought the entitlements of Mexican masculinity even as she constructed a lesbian identity that was in opposition to patriarchal authority.

After nine years, the relationship between the women soured because Josefina wanted children. María's voice broke as she explained the crisis:

We would make love at night and fight during the day. It was painful to make love because we knew that we couldn't have children. But we wanted a consummation of our relationship. When we made love, she usually ended up crying. And I felt so impotent, without reason. I was not at fault for that.

Josefina then had her own affair with a man, fell in love, and became pregnant. She got an abortion and created an irreparable rift in their relationship.

The abortion is what hurt me, more than her being in love with somebody else. I didn't understand, why did she do that? She said, "I knew that you were jealous, and feeling sad." I said, "Let's have it, it will be our child. It's good that you are pregnant. Yes, I am jealous but when you have the child, those jealousies will be gone. Let me process this." No. That was a very strong breach.

Unable to control Josefina on something so important, María resumed her macha ways: "I started being unfaithful again, with two more women at the same time. I started being promiscuous."

In 1978, María moved to Mexico City where she became involved in a network of other lesbianas. But without public safe spaces such as the lesbian bars and a nascent gay and lesbian rights movement centered in Guadalajara, she remained closeted: "We didn't say 'we're lesbianas,' but we would just be together. Whenever people would say something about it, we would look at them like, 'you better shut up.'" Looking for adventure and still grieving the loss of her relationship with Josefina, María moved to the United States in 1986.

Here María experienced a new awareness of racism and more openness regarding sexuality. Economically her life took a tailspin; despite her credentials, she worked as a farmworker before becoming a bilingual staffperson in a social service agency. Her social life was a different story: She met a number of women who were out of the closet and a national magazine dubbed Santa Cruz a "lesbian utopia." In this context, María began dating women, and with their encouragement she underwent a profound transformation. María came out of the closet and began accepting herself as female: "One lover was very beautiful and made me realize if women were with me, it wasn't because I was pretending to be a man. It was because I was a *woman*. So I confronted that. Now I say, 'yeah I'm a woman and I love women.'" This reconciliation with herself even had a dramatic effect on her body. "Before, I didn't have large breasts. I looked like a boy." She gained weight and became more curvaceous: "Because of the comfort of being accepted, I have learned to cope. And my body changed after I accepted that I was a woman. I think it was psychosomatic."

María was living with her lover in an open lesbian relationship, proud of their fidelity and honesty. The couple experienced economic difficulties, as the defunding of social services in California often meant that one or both of them was unemployed. Their financial difficulties led to flexible gender roles: "In the beginning I was the provider and then I became the housewife. And I'm the mom sometimes, because she's younger than me, and I'm the teacher most of the time. She's a very good student." María described their love: "I'm very lucky to be with Frida. When I am in love with a woman, I'm very passionate. I'm a Scorpio so it's extreme: It's like a big explosion—boom."

María's coming out story, however, is not a simple process of self-actualization. Frida occasionally bullies María by throwing furniture or hitting walls during arguments, although Frida did not hit María. The couple sought help at an agency that provides lesbian-sensitive services for battered women so María sees herself as a survivor. She laments those services are not offered in Spanish, the language of their intimacy. María hopes to start an organization of *lesbianas Mexicanas* that could provide culturally sensitive, bilingual services for lesbians experiencing domestic violence. She seeks a new kind of power—collective mutual aid with women.

CONCLUSION

Despite differences of generation, nationality, and sexual identity, these women articulated similar cultural poetics regarding gender and sexuality. They expected to conform to traditional Catholic expectations that women forego sexual exploration or pleasure, guard their virginity and reputations for marriage and children, and denigrate homosexuality. Both were told their bodies would reveal their deviation from "purity" and a loss of status, confirming other research about the importance of virginity for Mexican women. When these women did "give up" their virginity, their lovers playfully called them little daughters. Both heard echoes of honor and respect for their conformity to these ideals of proper womanhood, or experienced shame, anguish, and scandal for the transgressions. This cultural message promised economic support by a man in exchange for playing the part. These women learned few culturally sanctioned messages that confirmed their yearning and faced contending ideas about sexuality in the United States.

These women, however, are not the subjugated, essentialized woman in the Mexican allegory of virgin/whore. As historical actors, they both regarded Catholic ideology as a template to be contested. Their own volition and support of others shaped how they came to know their bodies, whom they found attractive, and the pleasure they found in sexual relationships. Each struggled to create a discourse about the power of love in this culturally mediated world of male dominance.

Mirella's "plot" involved desiring an economically mobile man despite the emotional scarring of male violence and Catholic-inspired control over her body, and having been "singed" through her social transgressions with white men. Despite the cadences of "valley girl" speech with inferences of nonchalance, her dreams carry serious economic consequences. The potential stable life together with Ray, with their combined income as a professional couple, would provide prospects of economic and social mobility much beyond what she could provide for herself. Mirella links the vision of a companionate ideal family—one sanctioned by institutionalized heterosexuality—with sexual pleasure.

María also recoiled from the crucible of patriarchy and Catholicism even as she was drawn to the entitlements of masculinity. She, too, was "scorched" for her desire for women and for flaunting the conventions of virginity and femininity. As a lesbian, she would not have the economic support afforded to women who marry well.[6] María's and Frida's work in marginally funded social services that made economically stability challenging.

These women's narratives illustrate Mexican notions of gender, sexuality and racialized bodies in American society that profoundly affect individual decisions. While the boundaries proscribed for women are rigid and limiting, these women created space for themselves. In following her desires, each woman subverted male dominance and reconstructed power, claiming an autonomous life and subjectivity. Each maneuvered through the fires of control to embrace the body enflamed.

BIBLIOGRAPHY

Alonso, Ana María and María Teresa Koreck. 1989. "Silences: 'Hispanics,' AIDS, and Sexual Practices." *Differences: A Journal of Feminist Cultural Studies* 1:101–124.

Asencio, Marysol. 2010. *Latina/o Sexualities: Probing Powers, Passions, Practices, and Policies*. New Brunswick: Rutgers University Press.

Franco, Jean. 1989. *Plotting Women: Gender and Representation in Mexico*. New York: Columbia University Press.

Lively, Penelope. 1994. *Oleander, Jacaranda: A Childhood Perceived*. New York: Harper Collins.

Moraga, Cherrie. 1983. *Loving in the War Years: lo que nunca pasó por sus labios*. Boston: South End Press.

National Latina Institute for Reproductive Health. 2011. "Poll: Latino Voters Hold Compassionate Views on Abortion." National Latina Institute for Reproductive Health and Lake Research Partners, New York.

Olaiz, Francisca Angulo. 1995. "Struggling to Have a Say: How Latino Adolescents Construct Themselves as Sexual Adults and What this Means for HIV Prevention Programs." Anthropology Department, University of California, Los Angeles.

Pitt-Rivers, Julian. 1968. "Honor." *International Encyclopedia of the Social Sciences*: 131–51.

Snitow, Ann, Christine Stansell, and Sharon Thompson. 1983. *Powers of Desire: The Politics of Sexuality*. New York: Monthly Review Press.

Zavella, Patricia. 2003. "Talkin' Sex: Chicanas and Mexicanas Theorize about Silences and Sexual Pleasures." Pp. 228–253 in *Chicana Feminisms: A Critical Reader*, edited by G. Arredondo, A. Hurtado, N. Klahn, O. Nájera Ramírez, and P. Zavella. Durham: Duke University Press.

———. 2011. *I'm Neither Here nor There: Mexicans' Quotidian Struggles with Migration and Poverty*. Durham: Duke University Press.

Zavella, Patricia and Castañeda Xóchitl. 2005. "Sexuality and Risks: Young Mexican Women Negotiate Gendered Discourse about Virginity and Disease." *Latino Studies* 3:226–245.

NOTES

1. I did historical and ethnographic research on the construction of family and sexuality among the poor in Santa Cruz County, California, interviewing mainly women—Mexicanas, Chicanas and whites, heterosexual and queer (Zavella, 2011). I queried how people were socialized regarding sex, family and marriage, inquiring about early experiences with sexual experimentation, messages they received about their bodies, experiences regarding starting to menstruate (for women), sexual histories, notions of sexual pleasure, and experiences and values regarding family and sex.

2. María preferred that I use her real name and viewed this disclosure as part of her process of coming out as a lesbian: "I know it's a tremendous risk but this is reality, this is not fiction. They cannot deny me."

3. Although this trope emerged with white women as well, that analysis is beyond the scope of this paper.

4. Other Chicanas and Mexicanas reported changes that occur in women's bodies after losing their virginity, including that women's hips get wider, that they walk differently, or that their faces become more "knowing." See Zavella (2003).

5. Olaiz (1995) finds that young women do not denigrate a woman who lost her virginity if she was in love with the man and expected permanence in the relationship.

6. This research was conducted prior to marriage equality legislation in California.

3 • *Charlene E. Makley*

ON THE EDGE OF RESPECTABILITY
Sexual Politics In China's Tibet

DISCUSSION QUESTIONS

1. What were the dominant ideas and practices of gender and sexuality in Labrang, especially about marriage, before incorporation into China?
2. How and why did the meanings of some of these practices change under Chinese rule?
3. Why do concepts of "respect" and "respectability" become central sites of contestation in asserting and challenging certain gender ideologies?

A PICNIC

On a rainy July day during the community festival season in 1995, my husband and I joined a Tibetan village family we knew in the famous Buddhist monastery town of Labrang (now southwest Gansu province, China) for a picnic in their tent pitched high on a peak above the Sang (Ch. Daxia) river valley. During that long, damp day of our visit, I was reminded of the ways in which the performance of such a communal Tibetan unity critically relied on the maintenance of hierarchical differences in gendered sexuality, differences which, in the contemporary context, could produce seemingly absurd contradictions (to an outsider) as well as greatly unequal moral and physical burdens for men and women.

Drolma, the daughter-in-law of the family in her late twenties, had married in from a neighboring region.[1] She bustled about helping her mother-in-law cook and serve refreshments. Meanwhile, her father-in-law, her husband and her husband's closest male friend affectionately lounged against each other on the cushions, keeping each other warm under wool blankets, and intermittently napping, telling jokes and playing cards. My husband and I, as guests, perched on the cushions opposite the men. But as the day wore on, we became increasingly uncomfortable, not because of any major change in the situation, but because we could not get warm! To rely, as did the men, on each other's body heat to do so would have been extremely inappropriate because in the Labrang region, any public behavior suggestive of desirous heterosexual contact was considered improper—especially in the presence of parents.[2]

When, in desperation, my husband tried to put a blanket across the two of us, we immediately

An abridged version of Charlene E. Makley, 2002. "On the Edge of Respectability: Sexual Politics in China's Tibet," in *positions*, Volume 10, no. 3, pp. 575–630. Copyright, 2002, Duke University Press. All rights reserved. Republished by permission of the copyright holder, Duke University Press, and of the author. www.dukeupress.edu

encountered the standard reprimand—Drolma's urgent glance in the direction of her sleeping father-in-law and the quick, discreet brush of her index finger across her cheek. That gesture is the one widely used among Tibetans to remind one of the shameful or "face-warming" (Tib. *ngo tsha*) nature of certain behavior. We got the point and quickly, miserably, removed the blanket. In my cold discomfort I bitterly noted the irony that, while such seemingly innocent behavior (to us) was deemed so dangerously sexual, the cards with which the men casually played were adorned with photos of Chinese women in tiny string bikinis, posed to display as much as possible of the material assets offered by modernity—ample breasts, curvaceous buttocks, glittering televisions and motorcycles. In the context of 1990s Labrang, where even the sex workers would not publicly bare their ankles, such images of nearly-naked female bodies seemed to me strikingly obscene, yet they circulated among the men with little notice from anyone in the tent that day.

THE EROTICS OF THE EXOTIC

Sex sells. So goes the oft-repeated maxim that conveys the inevitability of both biological imperatives and capitalist profit motives. But as many social theorists have recently argued, recourse to this seemingly explanatory phrase elides the historicity of the relationship between sexuality and consumption, as well as the particularity of its local operations. To stop there would be to foreclose an exploration of such questions as, why and what does it sell? How? And with what consequences? Foucault's groundbreaking work provided the seminal insight that the power of the erotic to attract (and repel) lies not in universally experienced biological drives, but in the uniquely compelling ways it links bodily processes with the social within a specific cultural politics.[3] This then is the starting-point for my analysis of the shifting cultural politics of sexuality, or beliefs and practices

associated with erotic desire, pleasure and prohibition, and their differential impacts on Tibetan men and women situated on the Sino-Tibetan cultural frontier in China's marginalized western regions.

In this article, I focus on sexuality as a way to reveal the dynamic articulations between local and translocal socioeconomic processes as Tibetans in Labrang coped with the intensifying encroachments of capitalist market forces after post-Mao reforms (1980s on). Such a perspective can reveal particularly dynamic relationships among sex, gender, ethnic or national identity and power because the (dangerous) capacity of sexuality to titillate or even to liberate is premised upon the simultaneous construction and transgression of foundational social and biological differences.

In this predominately rural region, the peculiar status of Labrang past and present makes it an ideal place to examine the role of sexuality in the construction of key boundaries. That is, as an erstwhile monastic polity and Buddhist pilgrimage center, the political and economic power of Labrang's Tibetan elite was premised on the huge monastic fraternity's claim to lifelong celibacy. Yet the market town that grew up alongside the monastery has all along been a site of urban, transgressive liminality and relatively promiscuous sexual relations. The situation at Labrang actually epitomized a cultural politics of the body that runs throughout Tibetan regions: the (often hidden) symbiotic relationship between practices of asceticism and sexuality.[4] And what kept that relationship safely neutral and socially vital in the past was local adherence to certain gendered proscriptions on public, bodily performance. However, in recent years in Labrang and elsewhere, the ambiguous nature of traditional Tibetan authorities under Chinese rule and the demands of competing visions of modernity have opened possibilities for new types of participation in work and leisure, reconfiguring gendered spaces and thus rendering newly problematic the traditionally close relationship between ritually powerful asceticism and sexuality.

The context of post-Mao China, ushered in with Deng Xiaoping's sweeping economic reforms in the early eighties, provided a fascinating test case of post-socialist transition and the introduction of global capitalist forces. Theorists focused on the restructuring of the economy, the rise of mass media production and the seeming rush to consumerism among the Chinese populace, all processes which eluded the Communist Party (CCP)'s pretensions to regulate them. As many have pointed out, the status of the nation-state, which during the Maoist years (1949–1976) was constructed as a totalizing force, was increasingly in question. In this context, the state was deeply implicated in recruiting its multiethnic citizens into the shared dream of a new, modern "socialist" nation built on capitalist foundations.[5] In line with trends noted by observers in other urban centers in the PRC by the mid-nineties, including in Lhasa, I found in Labrang that a new form of commodified sexuality worked to sell not only bodies and products, but also visions of capitalism and modernity—promises of sparkling futures and (ironically) the immediate lure of opportunities to participate in a new form of private agency, the ability to experience personal power through consumption.

This new "erotics of the exotic" on the Sino-Tibetan frontier drew Tibetans in through the fantasy appeal of the spectacular sexuality of foreigners and Chinese urbanites, even as those very processes objectified Tibetan men and women as sexualized objects for the consumption of foreign and Chinese tourists. Yet in urbanizing locales like Labrang, the resulting contestations over crucial cultural boundaries were occurring along gendered lines, as the valorization of personal agency associated locally with maleness and masculinity (including Buddhist monkhood) increasingly polarized ideas of sexed bodies and gendered spaces. The unfortunate consequence for Tibetan women was that state and local interests converged on containing, regulating and objectifying female sexuality above all.

SPATIALIZED GENDER POLARITIES: ENCLOSING FEMALE SEXUALITY

Labrang is located in a narrow farming valley at the very edge of the grassland steppes and just beyond what was the western extent of Chinese settlement and control. Since the founding of the famous Geluk sect monastery of Labrang Tashi Khyil in 1709, the place developed into both a frontier trading town and a powerful regional center controlled by celibate monastic hierarchs. During its heyday in the 19th and early 20th centuries, Labrang monastery housed up to 4,000 monks, some 68 resident incarnate lamas, and administered thousands of lay households in the region. In the market town that grew up alongside it, called Tawa (Tib. *mtha' ba*, The Edge), all manner of Tibetans and ethnic others met and mingled, including pilgrims, state officials, foreign travelers, and a sizable population of Muslim Chinese merchants. Such a space of close juxtapositions under Tibetan rule was fertile ground for representations on the part of Chinese and foreign visitors of Tibetans' exotic or chaotic sexual promiscuity.[6]

However, Tibetans in the Labrang region did have cultural practices for the relative enclosure and control of female corporality and sexuality, practices which have taken on heightened rhetorical value in recent years. This most generally played out in the widespread insistence on a particular spatialized gender polarity: associating women with the mundane life of the body inside the household domain (Tib. *nang*), and men with prestigious affairs of the mind outside of it (Tib. *phyi*). Tibetan sexual discretion focused on maintaining the ongoing *appearance* of this distinction at junctures that were particularly salient for locals, thereby protecting the grounds of male ritual and social authority. Negotiations and judgments of behavior occurred with reference to prescriptions for ideally gendered bodily performance so that public judgment of illicit or lewd behavior (Tib. *'dod log* or *log g'yem*) could be avoided or duly brought to bear. In that context, the most important grounds for sexual discretion were the everyday bodily disciplines of monasticism and marriage under public scrutiny and gossip in the narrow valley, not frequent punishment or complete confinement.

Women whose public comportment was deemed too independently desirous or instrumental risked being associated with negative agencies by the community—bad mothers, unclean housekeepers, witches, gossips and whores, that is, those women who came to embody the draining effects of female desire out of control, and thereby gave vent to the impure and socially destructive agencies of demons.[7] In the Labrang region, the most important practices for enclosing female agency were the coming-of-age and marriage rites aimed at publicly appropriating a woman's sexuality to benefit the (ideally) male-headed household. Despite the diversity that scandalized outside observers, Tibetan androcentrism meant that the ideal forms of inheritance and marriage were not that far from local Chinese practices.[8] Tibetans widely preferred sons and arranged, patrilocal, monogamous marriages that kept the household patrimony intact and established beneficial alliances by bringing in a daughter-in-law.[9] The common practice in the valley of "Taming the Hair" (Tib. *skra phab*), in which girls between 16–17 years old donned the bejeweled headdress and ornaments of adult laywomen, publicly asserted a daughter's sexual maturity and her status as a good prospect for a patrilocal marriage.

A marriage was paradigmatically accomplished through the rites of negotiation and feasting that brought the bride into the purview of her new husband's home, and legitimized their sexual relations and subsequent children as belonging to that household. In contemporary Labrang, the phrases "*gnas la 'gro*" (lit. "to go home") and "*ston mo byed*" (lit. "to throw a feast party") were widely used to refer to marriage in general, yet they specifically connoted this type of union. In practice, a wide range of relationships could be legitimized under that rubric, distinguishing the relative purity and

virtue of female sexual behavior that brought offspring and income to the household from that of "prostitutes" (Tib. *smad 'tshong ma*),[10] that is, "unmarried," unattached women who "sold" sexual intercourse for personal gain and lust.

As numerous oral histories and travel accounts I collected attest, Labrang was renowned among male travelers throughout Tibetan regions for the beautiful, sexually available women of Tawa town (Tib. *mtha' ba mdza' ma, bla brang mtha' mo*). But such women did not necessarily think of themselves as "prostitutes." Instead, in many cases they competed for lovers and called their unions "temporary marriages," living all the while in their natal households and contributing the monetary or in-kind "gifts" of their lovers to the household's income. Thus such women could be locally powerful and proud—they were real locals after all, surrounded by friends and relatives in their villages versus the daughters-in-law (Tib. *mna' ma*) who had more ideally married in. Having undergone the "Taming the Hair" rite, their bodies were adorned as adult laywomen, and thus displayed their association with a household. They went about usual daily activities of married women, tending the household's fields and livestock, worshipping appropriately at and supporting the monastery. In this way, they were not dangerously different from daughters-in-law because they were still "discreet" by Tibetan standards, that is, they did not performatively disrupt key gendered boundaries by making inappropriate heterosexuality socially visible.

CONTEMPORARY CONTESTS: A SEXUAL MISRECOGNITION

Drolma, my friend from the picnic, was not an ideal *nama*, or daughter-in-law. In fact, she had eloped with her husband, the eldest son of a prominent Labrang village family. The two had met in college in the provincial capital and Drolma often nostalgically told me how she had been swayed by his romantic persistence in courting her. At the time, she was convinced of the "modern" virtue of choosing her own mate based on mutual "love" or "feelings" (Tib. *brtse dung*). Drolma persevered against her own prominent family's pressure to marry a local man and stay in her home region, foregoing a proper wedding feast and moving to Labrang to live with her new husband.

A story Drolma once recounted further illustrated the continued salience of traditional Tibetan boundaries on female sexuality. In the course of lamenting the increasingly immoral sexuality she saw among young people in the valley, Drolma told me of the time she had been walking down the main street one afternoon in Labrang. A young Tibetan man she didn't recognize approached her, grabbed her arm and entreated her to stop, telling her, "Girl, I'll pay whatever you ask!" Significantly, her first move was to insist, to the man in the story and to me as listener, on the man's misrecognition of her as a "prostitute" (a group of women in town she had just labeled using the Chinese word: *jinu*). And despite her ambiguous status as a daughter who had defied the obligations of arranged, patrilocal marriage, Drolma did this by repeatedly telling him, "I am a daughter-in-law!" (Tib. *nga mna' ma zig yin*). This, she explained, was her way of telling him that she had married out (Tib. *gnas song sdod gi*), and thus that she was not the kind of person who did that. According to her, on that and another occasion in which she ran into him outside a pool hall, he ignored her and continued to pull her arm and ask her price. She said only when she recognized him as the married son of a local family and scolded him for running around on his poor wife did his face warm up with embarrassment, and he tried to appease her by saying, "no harm done! That's just how young guys are nowadays!"

CONVERGING GAZES AND DISPROPORTIONATE BURDENS

As this interaction and Drolma's framing of it indicate, the transformed social context under Chinese rule had greatly altered the grounds for the performance of sexual discretion in Labrang. Thus the meanings attached to sexed bodies and gendered spaces had dangerously shifted, thereby threatening the enclosure of female sexuality that underwrote Tibetan culture and power in the region. 1990s commentary in international news media and pro-Tibet activist writings tended to depict these developments throughout Tibetan regions as the direct result of Chinese colonization efforts, the intentional "sexual degradation" of the people in order to demoralize and thus better control them.

As I found in my fieldwork, such portrayals could resonate strongly with local Tibetans' views about the spatial and temporal structure of change. In Labrang, the rapid and ultimately violent way the Chinese Communists finally overthrew monastic authorities in 1958 seemed for Tibetans to have abruptly sealed an idealized Tibetan society in the past (Tib. *'jig rten rnying pa*), rendering them hapless victims of outside forces. But after the death of Mao Zedong and the advent of Deng Xiaoping's "Reform and Opening up" era, Tibetans' defensive conservatism could not mitigate the transformed parameters for sexual discretion. Most importantly, the erosion of the ritual infrastructure of the monastery and state limits on monk admissions to assemblies drastically reduced the power of the Tibetan leadership to regulate monastic and lay bodies. Hundreds of young robed men thus lived outside of monastic structures individually seeking teachings, contacts or modern forms of masculine leisure. And the imposition of state-arbitrated spaces and times had desacralized much of the space within monastic grounds, bringing in laypeople and non-Tibetans, including women, as state officials, tourists and vendors at all times of the ritual year.

As I found during my fieldwork, local Tibetans' efforts to control sexuality in this transformed context and thus re-establish powerful Tibetan difference ironically brought them onto shared ground with the Chinese state and popular media. This is so because the weight of public scrutiny and negative social consequences came down not on trangressing males (robed or not) but on publicly visible female bodies as markers of inappropriate and disruptive sexual agency. Thus, as young Tibetan men sought ways to stave off the emasculating effects of their cooptation by the state and reclaim their traditional mobility—out of households and across public spaces, young women found their movements curtailed, by increasing demands that they simultaneously shore up the household economy and exhibit a Tibetan feminine respectability and bodily purity that would maintain the sacred inviolability of male celibacy. Aspiring women like Drolma were thus pulled between such local demands, their own newly possible aspirations for social mobility and independent sexual agency, and the profound sexism of the market and the state which into the nineties increasingly collaborated to commodify women as sexual objects to be consumed.

By the early nineties, Labrang, with its unique opportunities for secular and monastic education, and for contacts with cosmopolitan others, had become a gathering place for unmarried, ambitious Tibetan women and men from rural regions. In the midst of this onslaught, local Tibetans across the community often characterized the change to the town as the extraordinarily promiscuous intermingling of males and females in public spaces. And I found that they tended to express their anger and disgust in the terms set down in state discourses. Echoing state anxiety about the "spiritual pollution" let into China with the "opening up" process, locals, especially the older generations, were appalled and perplexed by the moral ambiguity and social "chaos" (often expressed using the Chinese loanword "*luan*") they felt came in from the outside.

In this light, local Tibetan and state gazes converged on female bodies as the simultaneous objects of lust and social controls. Chinese discourses about "scientific" sexuality had for decades focused on "naturally" compulsive male sex drives and the need to control "deviant" females pursuing sexual encounters—for the good of society and for the girl herself. As Harriet Evans argues, in CCP

rhetoric the female "third party" (Ch. *di sanzhe*) was "constructed as the single most important—and dangerous—threat to marital and familial stability".[11] Thus since the 1980s, "cautionary tales" widely circulated in newspapers, youth magazines and local rumors and aimed at curbing extramarital sexuality had different messages for men and women. For men, they emphasized the great danger of being duped and drained (of vital physical energy and money) by wily oversexed women. For women, they emphasized their vulnerability to being exploited by men and discarded, their reputations ruined forever. I found that this gendered construction of sexuality resonated strongly with Tibetans in Labrang, who lamented what they saw as young men's precarious hold on vows of marriage or celibacy. The ironic consequence of this was a confluence of conscious and unconscious responses that together worked to narrow the traditional parameters of sexual discretion for Tibetan women in town.

By the early 1990s, Tibetans in Labrang widely accepted the state's discourse on prostitution as a social evil and a crime that gave inappropriate sexual license to unattached women. Thus, indignant men and women in our conversations tended to blame the increasing divorce rate and flagging Buddhist monastic discipline on unmarried women in town they now labeled "prostitutes". Drolma, switching to Chinese to make the point, even explicitly called them "third parties," the ones responsible for breaking up families.

In effect, the presence in Labrang of foreign and urban Han women tourists, as well as of rural Tibetan women, exhibited an unprecedented translocal mobility of female bodies. And this had dangerously sexualized and desacralized public spaces in and outside of the monastery. It thus had become paramount for local women to distinguish themselves from the unrestrained sexuality associated with tourist women and prostitutes—even though for many young laywomen in town their own aspirations for independent social mobility and their desire to postpone the disproportionate burdens of marriage were precisely the motivations that were increasingly leading young women of every stripe to accept money for sex, not only in Labrang, but across the country.

In the Labrang Tibetan community, this process took the form of an intensifying insistence on the correctness of an ideally Tibetan feminine respectability, and the progressive devaluation of forms of marriage other than ideally negotiated patrilocal unions. In 1995, upstanding village families had revived the "Taming the Hair" coming-of-age rite for teen-age daughters, who now donned the traditional headdress for only a few days before returning to work or school. In this way, daughters whose activities had expanded outside the household could be publicly recognized as earmarked for a future patrilocal marriage. Further, as one old laywoman complained to me, it had become much harder for a household without sons to find a man willing to marry in and become a son-in-law (Tib. *mag pa*). And I couldn't count the number of people who expressed embarrassment at the term "temporary wives," equated it with "prostitution" and disgustedly echoed the sentiment that in Labrang, kids didn't know their fathers, only their mothers.

The performative burden of bodily shame and ritual-social purity thus disproportionately fell on young women. Respectably feminine women were expected to demonstrate their distance from inappropriate heterosexuality in their discreet speech, dress and physical distance from laymen and monastic bodies and spaces. And Tibetan language stories, comic routines and drama extolled the virtues of a Tibetan wife who kept an industrious, clean household and properly propitiated household deities.

In everyday conversation, the phrase most widely used to characterize the behavior of brazenly public women was the Tibetan idiom "*nyag gi nyog gi*", which locals often interchanged with the Chinese idiom "*qi da ba da*". Both carry connotations of extraordinary disorder, but the Tibetan adds the sense of corporeal filth—due to indiscriminate and polluting intermingling. Drolma often used the Tibetan phrase to describe "prostitutes"

in town, and in our talk, she sought my acknowledgment of her difference from them: "we two are correct, aren't we? We found husbands and got married!"

THE AESTHETICS OF DECONTEXTUALIZATION: COMMODIFYING FEMALE CORPORALITY

Yet, as many of my women friends in Labrang discovered, their efforts to keep their sexuality appropriately invisible in this way could not prevent the increasing visibility adhering to all young female bodies concomitant with their commodification in the globalizing media. As with elsewhere in China, one of the most compelling attractions of a cosmopolitan modernity for young Tibetans was the vision of open, erotic heterosexuality premised on the heightened pleasures of a hyper-empowered man possessing a hyper-sexualized woman. Since the 1980s, in China the promise of such pleasure had been coded on the nude or semi-nude bodies of western, and increasingly, Chinese or other Asian women models, who were then posed and framed to sell everything from playing cards to state-sponsored scholarly journals. Images of ideal sexualized others thus offered Tibetan consumers the pleasures and power of a new form of decontextualized looking, a kind of voyeurism based on a refigured aesthetics of gendered bodies as objects to be desired and envied.

This "culture industry" as it played out in Labrang both participated in and intensified the on-going re-configuration of gendered spaces accompanying the urbanizing town's integration into capitalist markets (e.g., the town's development as a tourist site and the rise of private enterprises as the backbone of its economy). In such a locale, the realm of the private became increasingly elaborated and valorized, associated with secret aspirations for both resistance to Chinese state hegemony and for transcending the limitations of the state and the now feminized local/domestic order. In this context, consumption and voyeurism emerged as the most accessible expressions of masculine translocal agency. And that newly valorized masculine agency in turn produced a bifurcated feminine other that marked the refigured boundary between public/translocal and private/local: the female sexual commodity outside and the respectable feminine (ethnic) reproducer inside.

In contrast to Chinese urban centers, in Labrang the public exposure of young women's bodies was still strikingly other, signaling to many locals I spoke with an almost completely unfettered sexuality. Tibetan women never appeared in public or in images with their bodies bared. In fact, I never saw a Tibetan woman there wearing a western-style dress. Instead, the most fashionable of young women in town preferred to feminize pants and long sleeve shirts—wearing high heels, large earrings and baseball caps. By contrast, western and Chinese women tourists who walked through town in shorts and sandals sent ripples through Tibetan onlookers, and one traumatized Chinese woman in a halter top was chased down the main street by a group of Tibetan boys.

But Tibetan women themselves could not escape the ordering power of the new consumerist voyeurism. By the early 1990s in Labrang, female bodies in public drew looks—whether it was to scrutinize them for their opposition to the undressed commodity, or to judge them in terms of the new corporeal eroticism. As many observers have noted, since the 1980s the state and Tibetans themselves had collaborated to commodify Tibetan women as icons of exotic, ethnic Tibetanness. And tourism literature about Labrang (produced both locally and elsewhere) featured young Tibetan women in tight-fitting "traditional" dress, as dancers and hotel hostesses. In these ways, the pressures of a repressive state and a sexist market drew Tibetans themselves into capitalizing on longstanding fantasies among Chinese and westerners about the exotic sexuality of Tibetan women. As Gail Hershatter reported, in the 1990s wealthy Chinese businessmen in the coastal regions were willing to pay as much as five times more for sex with an exotic "minority" woman than with an urban Chinese woman.[12]

In places like Labrang, this new kind of eroticized looking was so powerfully insidious because it was so eminently gender-appropriate, and therefore unmarked or invisible. As elsewhere, Tibetan women were drawn in as they identified with the power and pleasure of attracting looks and thus exercising public sexuality. One of the things that most angered Labrang locals was the apparently unabashed pride of a group of young women who took money for sex in town. These were local village women who identified with the traditional reputation of beautiful Labrang women and as before lived at home while competing for clients among Tibetan male pilgrims and traders.

For their part, the women considered themselves to be at the pinnacle of a hierarchy of women selling sex in town. And they considered their high earnings and ability to purchase consumer goods direct evidence of their superior beauty. As one young woman, who had moved to Labrang from a neighboring nomad region to earn money this way, proudly told me, her gold tooth glinting jauntily, the most successful women could bring in thousands of yuan a month, especially during festival seasons. This was several times the average salary of a government cadre in town, and it provided them with a large disposal income to buy the accouterments of modern femininity—makeup, jewelry and leather jackets. In recent years, the intensification of their corporeal competition was indexed by the nicknames they acquired in town which ranked them according to their physical beauty: "number one body," "number two body," "number three body."

Despite the increasing outrage of some local Tibetans, these women were elite in some ways, proudly reprising forms of female sexual agency that had been tolerated in pre-Communist Labrang. Further, many continued to contribute income to their natal households, and, it was rumored, some families even collaborated with daughters to host their "temporary husbands" for a fee. Several I knew were very pious supporters of the monastery, worshipping often and donating labor to its reconstruction or to cook and clean for monks. Meanwhile, the lower end of the sex work hierarchy were the poor and sometimes desperate rural Tibetan women who came to Labrang as pilgrims or wage workers and sold sex for a couple yuan a night. Locals still tended to associate the most polluting promiscuity with them.

However, the expansion of Tibetan men's gender-appropriate agency into activities and sexual pursuits associated with prestigious "modernity" meant that *all* Tibetan women had to work harder—in household labor and in protecting their bodies and reputations. Contrary to state feminist rhetoric, in the Labrang region there were still very few opportunities for women's education or participation in market enterprises. Rural families preferred to keep daughters and daughters-in-law at home, where their work was supposed to demonstrate their virtuous devotion to the household. And the moral flux of the sexist marketplace had diminished the public spaces and times through which young women could pass with their sexuality unmarked, thus remaining safe from assumptions of easy availability. Even the most elite of the sex workers had to work hard to keep men's advances in forms and in times and spaces they agreed to—as I witnessed myself, they were often subject to the drunken violence of young men.

Drolma ruefully explained that it was essential for a respectable young woman to keep her sexuality discreet and not to be seen with "prostitutes," or else her "reputation" (Ch. *mingsheng*) would be lost for good, humiliating her husband and family and exposing herself to the advances of strange men. Yet as several of my young unmarried women friends told me, knowledge of sex and use of contraceptives (something widely assumed to be women's exclusive responsibility) was associated with sex workers. Thus unmarried women who indulged in sex with boyfriends (and there were many!) risked humiliating pregnancies or subjected themselves to multiple abortions in order to protect their reputations.[13]

As Drolma's narrative about her daytime encounter with the young Tibetan man in the street illustrates, the great difficulty for young Tibetan women was that even the diligent performance of devotion to an ideal household was not enough to stave off the insidious reach of the commodifying gaze. After all, the ultimate message of Deng Xiaoping's economic reforms was that anything—or any female body—could be possessed with money. Hers was only one of the many stories I was told by Labrang Tibetan women ranging in age from teens to their mid-fifties of being accosted on the street and offered money for sex by men young and old. The most dangerous spaces and times, the ones in which women risked men's physical violence, were those most closely associated with the performance of men's modern sexual agency—nighttimes and the bars and dance halls (several of them Tibetan-owned) where Tibetan men and women performed traditional courtship songs and dances to hook up for the night. Young Tibetan women on the street at night were fair game—subject to harassment and physical advances. I was told of several such incidents by young women who had attempted to go out at night on errands.

The intensifying cultural politics of gender and sexuality in this still-subordinate Tibetan frontier region under Chinese rule meant that young Tibetan men and women were faced with the painful dilemma of increasing state and local demands for the display of idealized Tibetan masculinities and femininities even as they encountered a diminished capacity or willingness to perform them. As I found during my fieldwork, this process could place aspiring men and women at tragic odds with each other—while young men sought to shore up masculinities and transcend the local by feminizing it, young women in unprecedented numbers sought to participate in modernity by expanding their horizons.

Thus the most public form of legitimized male violence against wives or girlfriends was when a woman asserted herself and participated in the "modern" fun of going to a dance hall in the evening with friends. Stories abounded of great public dramas in which husbands and boyfriends in a jealous rage burst in on office parties at restaurants or bars, making a show of roughing their women up, and dragging them off home. Drolma's life perhaps epitomized the potentially tragic consequences of such a gendered process. Over time, she could do little to keep her husband, an underpaid, low-level cadre, from spiraling down into depression and indolence. She gave up hopes for the romantic, modern union she had left home for, and instead found herself more and more limited by his jealous anger. As his drinking binges and excursions with male friends increased, so too did his reprimands of her for being out too long, for singing love songs during a party, for being at work. No matter how much Drolma fought back—physically, during his increasingly vicious beatings, and socially, by striving to be an ever more pious wife and daughter-in-law, she could never convince him of her wholehearted commitment to him and his household.

CONCLUSION: CONSUMPTION FOR POWER?

I have shown that Labrang on the eve of the Communist victory was not the debauched and chaotic community of Chinese and foreigners' colonial fantasies. Instead, by looking at sexuality as the ways in which people negotiated embodied moral ideals through the gendered performance of sexual discretion, we could appreciate the complex sociohistorical conditions in which a particularly Tibetan hierarchy of sexed bodies and purified agencies could keep the crucial relationship between celibate asceticism and sexuality in Labrang mutually beneficial and thus ritually powerful. The bodily disciplines of monasticism and marriage marked inappropriate heterosexuality, not homosexuality, as the most dangerous of transgressions to Tibetans. And ritualized constraints on polluting female sexuality maintained the possibility for transcendent male subjectivity. But Tibetans' forced assimilation to a new socialist moral order, and the sudden social flux of the capitalist reform years had profoundly altered the performative grounds for sexual discretion

in town—resulting in the unprecedented intermingling of male and female bodies and ethnic others in and around monastic spaces.

I have tried to demonstrate in this article the difficult and differential consequences for men and women of a new eroticism of the frontier—in which state and local gazes converged on Tibetan women's bodies as commodified objects of both sexual desire and efforts to contain it. In effect, as Tibetan men's sexual agency expanded in unmarked ways to meet modernity, Tibetan women's sexuality was increasingly marked and curtailed in order to maintain the integrity of Tibetan households and sacred places.

This perspective then sheds light on the significance of a story circulating in Labrang in 1995 and 1996. I heard several versions of this narrative from men and women and it was repeated to me as the oath-swearing truth, always in the context of conversations about chaotic sexuality in town: a Tibetan village woman accepted several hundred yuan to have sex with a western man. But her client's huge penis, typical of western men, punctured her, nearly killing her and scarring her for life. She was forced to go to the state-run hospital, where the doctors refused treatment until she admitted what she had done, and then they required her to pay an exorbitant fee—much more, emphasized the tellers, than she had earned in her sexual transaction. She was informed (too late!) by the doctors that it is impossible for Tibetan women to have intercourse with western men because such men are too big.

We can see this narrative as a local Tibetan version of a "cautionary tale" for Tibetan women: it singles out Tibetan women as the problematic agents in the perilous local encounter with the global. And it emphasizes their inherent, inescapably physical handicap and vulnerability in the face of the overpowering sexuality of the West. Drawing on the authority of "scientific sexuality," the narrative punishes the female protagonist for her greedy, independent, and public intercourse with modernity by condemning her to permanent damage to her body and reputation.

To recall the picnic scene with which I began this discussion, Drolma's quick and silent insistence on reminding my husband and I of a Tibetan sense of face-warming shame in that situation illustrates, like the narrative above, how women in Labrang carried the burden of keeping inappropriate heterosexuality invisible. Meanwhile, Tibetan men's expanding participation in the commodification of women as sex objects could be as unmarked and casual as exchanging girlie cards in a game among male friends. However, the danger for all Tibetans, men and women, was that the erotic appeal of a Chinese-mediated modernity substituted consumption for local autonomy and power, and diverted attention from the ways in which the state appropriated Tibetan androcentrism to its purposes, thereby facilitating the on-going assimilation of the frontier into the Chinese nation-state.

NOTES

1. All personal names of contemporary people in this paper are pseudonyms.
2. This was something I heard expressed in many different contexts as my contrasting assumptions about the parameters of (hetero)sexual discretion encountered those of my Tibetan interlocutors. For example, in a conversation with a widowed woman in her thirties who lived in town and made her living as a local petty trader, she was embarrassed by a picture I showed her of my husband and I holding hands. She said that here, we cannot touch each other like that in front of our parents or we would be very embarrassed (Tib. *ngo res tsha gi*).
3. Foucault, Michel. *The History of Sexuality, Vol. 1, An Introduction.* (New York: Random House, 1978).
4. Tibetan Buddhism, in its emphasis on tantric forms of yogic practice which rely on sexual metaphors for liberation that are based on a refigured, although not entirely inversed, notion of male-female sex-gender polarity, perhaps epitomizes this more than other Buddhist cultures.
5. The state regulates ethnicity in 56 officially recognized "*minzu*" groups, of which the Han *minzu* are the vast majority at around 92%. Tibetans, labeled

"*Zangzu*", number only about 6 million, distributed throughout the 5 provinces of the Tibetan Autonomous Region, Yunnan, Sichuan, Gansu and Qinghai.
6. Chinese writers for centuries have depicted the frontiers of empires as spaces outside the civil propriety of a Chinese cultural order emanating from imperial courts. Frontiers in those texts appear as peripheries populated by carnal, barbarian others and the criminal dregs of Chinese populations. In Labrang, both Chinese and foreign visitors tended to depict Tibetan sexuality and religious practices as either "absolutely free" (Ch. *wanquan ziyou*) or grossly debauched and chaotic (Ch. *hunluan*).
7. Wives were widely considered to be responsible for the propitiation of household deities or "stove gods" (Tib. *thab lha*). Any behavior not in line with ritual-social propriety was potentially "unclean" (Tib. *mi gtsang ma*) and offensive to the stove gods, thus capable of bringing harm to the whole household.
8. My monk friend Konchog explicitly made this analogy in our conversation and he cited as emphasis the Chinese saying which plays on the different gender connotations of the Chinese homophones *jia* 1 and *jia* 4, "*nande dang jia, nude gei jia*" (lit. Men bear up the household while women are married into them).
9. In a wedding song reprinted in a 1981 Qinghai Tibetan language magazine, the male singer representing the groom's family locates the divine/historical precedent for this type of marriage in that of the great 7th century king and founder of the Tibetan Yarlung dynasty Song tsan gampo and the Chinese princess who traveled to Tibet to be his bride. Note the association of such patrilocal marriage with the proud strength of a unified Tibetan state.
10. This term, still in use today to gloss the Chinese "*jinu*", literally means "woman who sells the lower (body parts)". Note that in Tibetan regions to sell the body in this way is exclusively associated with women. There is no equivalent word for men.
11. Evans, Harriet. 1997. *Women and Sexuality in China: Dominant Discourses of Female Sexuality and Gender Since 1949* (Cambridge: Polity Press), p. 200.
12. Hershatter, Gail. 1997. *Dangerous Pleasures: Prostitution and Modernity in 20th Century Shanghai* (Berkeley: University of California Press), p. 348. During the four year period I visited Labrang and

other Tibetan regions, I heard many stories of western men seeking sexual encounters with Tibetan women. I even got to read the dismissive "love letter" sent by an Australian man in response to the pleas of his erstwhile Tibetan woman lover in Labrang for him to return. He told her that what they had had was "special" but right now he was taking a "well-deserved rest" on a beach. The flipside of this eroticization of Tibetans by outsiders is the recent fascination among Chinese men and women with Tibetan masculinity, which they imagine to epitomize virile, brutish sexuality, or in the case of some women writers, virile, yet tender sexuality in contradistinction to uncaring Han men.

13. As I mentioned above, the state was implicated in this as well, in that state family planning policies widely assumed that women alone were responsible for contraception and they focused on making contraception proper and available to married women, not to young women before marriage.

1 • *Shellee Colen*

"LIKE A MOTHER TO THEM"
Stratified Reproduction and West Indian Childcare Workers and Employers in New York

DISCUSSION QUESTIONS

1. How and why do ideas about the responsibilities of "mothers" and the value and behavior of children differ between female employers in New York City and their West Indian childcare workers?
2. What is the concept of "stratified reproduction," according to Colen? Do you think it helps to understand and analyze her evidence?

> You have these kids sometimes from . . . seven in the morning to seven at night. Twelve hours of a day. You feed them. You clothe them. You take them out. You play with them. You're like a mother to them.
>
> —A Guyanese Mother of Four,
> Speaking of her Childcare work in New York City

The experiences of West Indian childcare workers in New York and their white U.S.-born employers reveal the operation of a transnational, highly stratified system of reproduction.[1] By *stratified reproduction* I mean that physical and social reproductive tasks are accomplished differentially according to inequalities that are based on hierarchies of class, race, ethnicity, gender, place in a global economy, and migration status and that are structured by social, economic, and political forces. The reproductive labor—physical, mental, and emotional—of bearing, raising, and socializing children and of creating and maintaining households and people (from infancy to old age) is differentially

An abridged version of Shellee Colen, 1995. "'Like a Mother to Them': Stratified Reproduction and West Indian Childcare Workers and Employers in New York." In F. D. Ginsburg and Rayna Rapp (eds), *Conceiving the New World Order, The Global Politics of Reproduction*. Berkeley: University of California Press, pp. 78-102. Reprinted with permission from the author.

experienced, valued, and rewarded according to inequalities of access to material and social resources in particular historical and cultural contexts. Stratified reproduction, particularly with the increasing commodification of reproductive labor, itself reproduces stratification by reflecting, reinforcing, and intensifying the inequalities on which it is based (Rollins 1985, 1990; Colen and Sanjek 1990). The hiring of West Indian childcare labor in the United States, which linked New York City and the English-speaking Caribbean in the 1970s and 1980s, opened a window on a transnational system of stratified reproduction in which global processes are evident in local, intimate, daily events, and in which stratification itself is reproduced, as childcare occurs across class lines, kin lines, and oceans.

In this chapter, I outline some of the economic, social, and legal factors shaping West Indian women's migration to New York and their work as household childcare givers for white U.S.-born employers. Discussion of West Indian experiences and meanings of motherhood and fostering localizes the transnational experience of stratified reproduction. Employers' ideas about motherhood and childcare are contextualized in changing socioeconomic realities and ideologies about reproductive labor and by media representations of motherhood. I draw on the daily, lived experiences of stratified reproduction and the reproduction of stratification, highlighting and contrasting workers' and employers' perspectives on childcare.[2]

MOTHERS, MIGRATION, AND REPRODUCTIVE LABOR: TRANSNATIONAL CONTEXTS

The differential experiences of reproduction, particularly of parenting and childcare, for West Indian workers and New York employers are framed by a transnational stratified system. In this system, West Indian women confront the legacies of slavery, colonialism, underdevelopment, and Caribbean articulation into a world capitalist system and the constraints these place on fulfilling their gender-defined obligations. They face, on the one hand, un- and underemployment, rising costs of living, and limited educational and occupational opportunities, and, on the other, gender expectations that they bear, raise, and carry the bulk of the financial responsibility for children and for other kin. The West Indian women in my study viewed migration to New York as a means of constituting their families. Often leaving middle-class jobs at home, they migrated to support themselves, their families, and others in the short run and to secure better opportunities (through obtaining legal residence in the United States) for themselves and their kin in the long run.

U.S. immigration policies mediated migration in two crucial ways (Colen 1990). First, if West Indian women were without permanent resident status they had to migrate alone, leaving children behind. Some of those few who migrated with legal status were prevented by immigration policy from bringing their children (and a few chose to spare their children some of the trauma of migration until they themselves were settled into jobs and homes). Second, women seeking legal status were directed by immigration policies to private household work as a way to gain employer sponsorship for legal permanent-resident status (the green card).

Even migrants with green cards confronting this system of a racially stratified division of labor had difficulty translating their skills and job histories from home into comparable employment in New York yet found household childcare work with relative ease. This system of reproduction assigns paid reproductive labor to working-class women, often of color, and the system itself reproduces such stratification. For undocumented, live-in workers, especially those seeking legal status, this often meant exploitative, indenture-like conditions. For those with green cards working full-time, increased autonomy was accompanied by low wages without medical, retirement, or other benefits, which exacerbated their own household difficulties. While some women left household work after obtaining legal status through employer sponsorship, stratification created labor-market conditions often unfavorable to finding the kinds of higher paying non-household jobs with benefits and better conditions that they sought. Some found childcare preferable to the alternatives, at least temporarily.

Workers perceived a hierarchy of household reproductive labor in which live-in jobs with responsibility for all of a household's maintenance and childcare occupy the bottom, especially for undocumented workers needing sponsorship. On the next rungs, daywork housecleaning is followed by full-time, live-out household maintenance and childcare jobs. Childcare jobs with minimal or no housework are at the top. Most workers interviewed had worked at each level at some point. With green cards, workers enjoyed the relative power to set the parameters of private household work that their undocumented sisters lacked in their indenture-like positions, which they often compared to slavery. Whereas undocumented workers often had to "do everything" in the household to get their green cards and reunite with their children, those with legal status had more power to define their job responsibilities, to limit or eliminate housecleaning, and to devote themselves to childcare.

Social and economic shifts in the United States in the 1970s and 1980s created an acute need for childcare across classes. Such factors as the baby boomers' own baby boom coupled with the rising labor-force participation of mothers and continued expectations of female responsibility for reproductive labor left more families confronting inadequate options for childcare. The ideology of privatized childcare, the virtual absence of state- or employer sponsored childcare, and severely limited day-care options all served to increase the stratification of childcare solutions. In New York, as upper-middle- and upper-class women found higher-end positions, more women, especially women of color, including new immigrants, found positions on lower rungs. Limited options and the valuing of private, in-home childcare created a demand for reproductive laborers in upper-middle- and upper-class households at the same time as the pool of native-born workers willing to work in private households shrank and as a large pool of West Indian and other immigrant

workers sought employment. Many New York parents with the means hired West Indian (and other immigrant) childcare workers on a full-time or live-in basis (Colen 1990).[3] In contrast, most middle- and working-class parents used family day care, day-care centers, care by relatives in New York, or, for migrants, care by fosterers in home countries.

Within employing households, workers interacted primarily with female employers who managed the tasks they did not themselves perform and who calculated childcare expenses in relation to their individual not their household incomes. Although several female employers stated that their husbands shared or "helped" with household or childcare work, workers in homes rarely reported male employers' doing so. Employing households seeking parenting help rarely challenged gender divisions of labor. Instead they crossed class, race, and national lines and hired West Indian caregivers whose own tenuous, often transnational, household reproduction was accomplished on low wages, in part with help from kin and family daycare arrangements.

"THESE ARE MY RICHES": WEST INDIAN MOTHERHOOD AND FOSTERING

Motherhood is a major organizing principle of West Indian women's identities and the marker of adult status in West Indian communities. Children provide access to material and social resources from the father, kin, and community. "Baby fathers" and their kin are expected to provide some material support for the child. However, nonelite West Indian men's limited access to resources often means that nonelite women (with less access) bear most of the responsibility for children (Bolles 1986; D'Amico-Samuels 1986, 1993). Children link their mothers to the broader community, creating networks of economic, social, and emotional support that expand over time. As they reach adulthood, children (especially daughters) are expected to provide and care for their parents.

For women regardless of class, childbearing and child rearing are major sources of respect—a crucial component of West Indian social relations. Stigma is attached to childlessness (Durant-Gonzalez 1982). Raising more than one generation of children increases the respect earned. Entry into the "big-woman" role is signaled by becoming a grandmother and having adult children who provide goods and services. Both the grandmother role and fostering prolong mothering over a woman's life (Durant-Gonzalez 1982, Smith 1956). This role is marked linguistically as grandmothers are often called "mommy" by the grandchildren they raise.

Childcare tasks may be shared by a community of West Indian women rather than left to the mother or specified caregiver in both the West Indies and New York, as the common practice of fostering makes clear. Older children and adults look out for children in homes and public or semi-public spaces (the street, shared yards), and caregivers in New York watch and caution other women's charges as well as their own.

Children are considered women's wealth in West Indian cultures. A woman in New York spoke of her mother in rural St. Vincent who had nine children, forty grandchildren, and twelve great-grandchildren and who cared for many of the "grands" and "great-grands." Her mother said of the children, "These are my riches." Children resemble a kind of social capital that yields benefits both immediately and over time.

In New York the valuing of motherhood is expressed in many forms. Not only are baby showers important West Indian women's gatherings, but christenings are often marked by an elaborateness of preparation and presentation (in dress, food) that parallels that of weddings in dominant North American culture. Several women reported that the three days they attend church (whether or not they go at other times) are Christmas, their wedding day, and Mothers' Day.

Fostering is an extension of the activities, relationships, and values associated with motherhood in West Indian culture. It carries rich meanings and creates webs of interdependent ties in which social and economic resources are shared across time and space through the temporary transferal of parental rights in children. Fostering is central to the experience of migration and reproduction for the West Indian mothers working in New York homes. Many of the women had themselves been fostered while their mothers migrated for work. Children are also fostered when parents cannot afford to raise them. Generally female maternal kin such as grandmothers or aunts or, less often, paternal kin, fathers, or close friends foster children. Through fostering, childless women have the opportunity to parent and to gain emotional satisfaction as well as ties to growing children and increased status and respect. Fostering may also provide households with additional child helpers. For those with few or grown children, it extends the benefits of parenting. It intensifies emotional and economic ties between fosterers and fostered, as well as between fosterers and migrants, and it generally provides fosterers with access to material goods from migrant parents and from adults whom they have fostered.

West Indian women migrate to New York to provide for their families as a normative aspect of motherhood. Immigration restrictions force them to leave children behind in foster care, which is considered temporary until mothers can legally and financially sponsor children to join them. West Indian mothers in New York support their children, the fosterers, and other kin with remittances of as much as one-half of their income. Remittances take the form of shipped barrels filled with soap, oil, rice, flour, sugar, toothpaste, clothing, and other items unavailable or unaffordable at home. Money is also remitted for school fees and uniforms, medical care, home improvements, and other expenses.

Fostering can create complicated relationships over the life cycle. It is not without emotional costs to parents, children, fosterers, and other family members. Parents and children may endure a variety of negative affects because of their separations. Children may feel like second-class citizens in fostering households, while fosterers complain of insufficient remittances from parents abroad. While close attachments to fostering adults may develop, children may feel confusion, loss, or resentment due to their mothers' absence. These feelings complicate children's altogether difficult adjustment to life in New York when they eventually join their mothers.

The costs of the social reproduction of West Indian children are borne in the West Indies. The prolonged, legally dictated sponsorship process ensures that the responsibility for socialization and education of children remains with the home community after the mother migrates since many children remain there through most of primary school. While the majority of mothers sent for their children as soon as legally possible, a few made painful but strategic choices to keep their children at home a bit longer. The long hours workers devoted to childcare jobs and commuting left little time for their own children who might be isolated in hazardous New York neighborhoods without kin and community attending to them. The alien values, physical danger, and poor scholarship that characterize their local New York public schools shocked some mothers into keeping their children at home, where primary education takes place in a safe environment steeped in West Indian values. Mothers tended to send for children by adolescence to ensure that they earned a high school diploma in the United States and which might ease their way into employment and further education. In these and other ways, West Indian mothers strategized for their children in their struggle in a stratified transnational system of reproduction.

IDEOLOGICAL AND SOCIOECONOMIC CONTEXTS OF REPRODUCTIVE LABOR

Childcare workers' and employers' differential experiences of stratified reproduction are contextualized, in part, in the complex shifting, and conflicting ideologies and behaviors surrounding reproductive labor in dominant North American culture since the 1950s. A central strand of 1950s gender ideology, which masked women's wage work, continued to be influential in the 1970s and 1980s. It assigned reproductive labor to women, held motherhood and waged work in opposition, and prescribed that mothers "stay home" to raise their children. Reproductive labor was devalued and trivialized as unskilled, unwaged women's work in homes (even though many working-class women, especially of color, performed it in other women's homes for minimal wages).

However, economic realities, social behaviors, and changing beliefs and expectations increasingly contradicted this ideology. Motivated by economic necessity, by the pursuit of financial security and personal fulfillment, and, eventually, by feminism, mothers of young children increasingly joined the labor force (Hartmann 1987, Ryan 1983). Household survival or the maintenance of living standards or both were key economic factors in women's entrance into the labor market. Women's labor-force participation itself and contemporary feminist ideas changed attitudes about working mothers. Mothers increasingly needed and felt entitled to work outside the home more or less continuously.

Yet little corresponding reconceptualization of responsibility for reproductive labor occurred; it was still women's "nonwork" (Kessler-Harris and Sacks 1987: 76) with little or no state, corporate, or community support for childcare, poor parental leave policies, inflexible job schedules and minimal cross-gender sharing of reproductive tasks. Instead, a racially/ethnically stratified commodification of child care and other reproductive labor with low-waged women workers, often immigrant and of color, grew.

Under these rapidly shifting conditions, the views of female employers with whom I spoke often seemed contradictory and tension-filled. Before the birth of their first child, many believed they would immediately return to work and felt superior to stay-at-home mothers. But the realities of new-borns sent many I interviewed to negotiate part-time or less demanding working conditions, often unsuccessfully. One employing mother of two indicated that she had not intended to work until her children started school (replicating the conditions of her own upbringing), but financial necessity drove her back to teaching nursing: "I never imagined that I would be working—want to be working, need to be working—when I had little kids. And in fact I do want to work because I do feel like there's just so much your brain can take of sitting on the floor and playing, making farmyard noises. Although it's great, but to do it all day, every day, it's too much. There are some women that do it and probably do it well. But I think it's important also to know what you can manage, and I know I need to do something else—and not like go out for lunch with my friends either—the thing that's going to make the brain cells fire up occasionally." Like others she experienced this ambivalence in daily ways: "Even when I'm thinking 'I can't wait to get rid of these kids, they're driving me crazy,' when I actually turn around and walk out of the door, I always feel ambivalent."

Unlike the West Indian women, who were extremely articulate about children being women's wealth, the employers I interviewed had a hard time articulating what having children meant to them. Shifting media images of motherhood and children in New York in the 1980s provide a backdrop for employers' conceptions of having children. In the early 1980s, mothering and reproductive labor were devalued, while overflowing datebooks and "dressing for success" were in vogue and careers were valorized. By the mid-1980s babies surfaced in television, movies, and advertisements as commodities that people collected. As the *New York Times* headline declared, "In TV and Films as in Life, Babies are in Fashion Again" (Hirsh 1987). The message was that children were a valuable commodity and could fill a void that work and other activities could not.

WEST INDIAN CAREGIVERS' PERSPECTIVES ON THEIR WORK

For West Indian women, paid childcare work entailed complex and contradictory experiences. They generally valued childcare activity, were proud of their knowledge and skills, and were comfortable caring for children. However, inadequate pay, the lack of health, pension, and other benefits, and the lack of respect from employers offended them. Workers expected respect from parents who entrusted them with children. Yet every worker (including those with the "best" employers) related incidents in which they experienced profoundly disrespectful attitudes or behavior. Doing childcare for money in New York was different from doing it in the kin network at home for love.

Workers had difficulty reconciling employers' dependence on them or care of their children with behavior that they felt denied them status as adult human beings with thoughts, feelings, and families of their own. This contradiction was especially powerful for undocumented workers who were "living in" and dependent on employers for sponsorship because of the complex interdependence and structural aspects of live-in work such as isolation, the intimacies of sharing household space, twenty-four-hour on-call status, and relationships that are at once waged, hierarchical, and personal. Workers endured exploitation and indignities only to obtain green cards and to allow their children to join them. Ms. T. expressed the sentiments of many when she responded to her employers' humiliating behavior this way: "I want to be treated as a full adult. . . . Once I had a husband and kids and had the same responsibility as you all . . . but now I am in this situation."

Despite the crucial contributions caregivers made to employing households, they frequently felt invisible (as female, working-class reproductive workers of color often are made to feel), particularly when employers regularly failed to inquire about them or their families or to note work that they had accomplished. As one worker put it, they expect you to "give extra to these children" and yet they "treat you as if you were part of the furniture." With more autonomy, full-time live-out workers still contended with long, often erratic hours, low wages, a lack of benefits, the asymmetrical relations of waged work in homes, and employers' lack of consideration for workers' family lives and responsibilities. While many workers regularly worked about 11–12 hours a day, several worked more hours and a few worked less. In fact, workers questioned why some employers had had children when they were too busy to care for them, "even morning and night." Nearly two-hour commutes each way to and from work were not unusual, so it is no surprise that workers strongly resented employers' tendency to stay out late without warning or to call in just as they were preparing to leave and ask them to stay later than the usual or agreed time. Workers wondered whether employers saw that they too had lives and families: "It's O.K. for them to ask me to stay extra time because they have their family together, but what about me? . . . They don't think that I have my family waiting for me."

Differential notions of appropriate behavior for and discipline of children disturbed many West Indian workers whose expectations that children act "respectfully" toward adults were often unmet, particularly when they started a job with older (post-toddler) children who treated them "rudely." Many workers criticized employers' lax discipline and attempted to teach children "manners." One worker voiced her frustration at trying to teach a seven-year-old boy not to drink from a juice pitcher at the refrigerator when he repeatedly retorted, "Why not? My father does." Workers were given the responsibility for socializing children often without being accorded the authority to discipline them.

Countless other contradictions arose out of the emotional fallout from caring for children as waged work. The daily work of childcare itself—the caring, the socializing, the investment of physical and emotional labor—promoted ties between workers and children. Twelve- or twenty four-hour childcare responsibility forged bonds between workers and children, especially when workers had raised their charges since infancy. The emotional devastation of separation from their own children often intensified bonds. As one worker told her employer, "I really love my job and I really love [the employer's son]. . . . I never raised my own kids, and I'm raising him." However, emotional involvement with children can make workers vulnerable. Although Ms. H. resented her employer's behavior, she stayed on because she loved the child. Her tolerance eventually ran out, and she left saying, "It's still just a job." The crucial aspect of workers' relations with children is controlled by employers: they have the power to hire, fire, and change the conditions of employment. Even after employment ended, many workers maintained informal contact with their charges, and some attended graduations and other events years later.

Workers reported that children often called them "mommy." One worker said her employers told their daughter that she was "lucky to have two mommies who love her," and another worker received Mothers' Day presents from employers in the name of the infant for whom she cared. Nevertheless, many workers were aware that employers harbored jealousy toward them. A Barbadian woman told of the jealousy she sensed in her employer, whose little boy "cried 'mommy' behind" her every night when she left work: "Every evening he'd cry, 'I need mommy.' He did it many times. But that particular evening . . . I was going home, and he cried to get in the elevator with me. And she would say, 'That's not your mommy! I'm your mommy!' And she said [with forced calm] . . . 'But I don't mind you calling her mommy because she's nice to you.' . . . Probably when I went home, she said, 'That's not your mommy. That's not your mommy. Don't call her mommy!'"

EMPLOYERS' PERSPECTIVES ON CAREGIVERS

Employers depended on caregivers to take responsibility for children for eight to twenty-four hours a day and to stabilize and make possible their busy lives. They acknowledged that "your life depends on your childcare person." One mother who employed a valued caregiver since her son's birth said, "I want her to stay at least until [my son] goes to college." I concentrate here on employers' conceptualizations of childcare, the qualities sought from workers, notions of appropriate age-specific care, and cultural discord between employers and caregivers in these arenas.

Even when most of the child's waking hours were spent in the worker's care, most employing mothers felt that they were still the primary caretakers. Employers wanted substitute caregivers who would provide daily care, nurturance, and socialization. As one employer said when questioned about whether she had considered a live-in situation, "I don't need somebody to take over taking care of my children. I need somebody to help me take care of my children. And that's an important distinction to me . . . . I'm the person who does primary childcare here. And our sitter is the person who fills in for us. Even though she's here eight hours a day, I'm the one."

The majority of employers in my sample hired caregivers on a full-time basis. In most of these cases, childcare and associated tasks such as doing children's laundry, tidying their rooms, and preparing their meals were considered the workers' primary responsibility. Workers often performed more general housekeeping tasks as well, which a few employers expected to be done during naptime so as not to distract workers from children's needs. In addition, workers took children to parks, play dates, and programs. Most employers also indicated that workers did household errands at the post office, dry cleaners, and grocery store. A few employers in my sample hired childcare workers on a live-in basis with responsibility for all housekeeping and childcare. A couple of employers shared their childcare workers' services with another household, either with joint care of children or with the caregiver splitting her workweek between two households.

Employers' profound dependence on caregivers determined the qualities they most valued in them: trustworthiness and reliability. Employers wanted workers they could count on to handle any eventuality responsibly. As one mother of two noted, "You're relinquishing control of your children." They sought workers who would arrive punctually every day—"never sick and never late"—and

provide their households with the security of steady, stable childcare. One employer said that in the interest of reliability she would not hire a worker whose life appeared to be "chaotic." Behind this word lurked a set of assumptions about the complicated family lives of immigrant workers as well as a need to deny workers' lives and family responsibilities outside of the job. This denial allowed employers to focus only on their own dependence on workers' labor and not on the interdependence of worker and employer for both their households. In fact, employers generally remained ignorant of their workers' family situations, a strategy that may have enabled them to make demands such as working extra hours.

Many employers felt strongly that they wanted to know what their children did every day in order to feel part of the milestones of child development. As one employer phrased it, when parents aren't there, they want to know "all the idiot details" of their children's activities. Yet a line of inquiry directed toward that end might have insulted a worker by making her feel she was not trusted.

Most employers cited "warmth" and "love for children" as crucial qualities they found in West Indian caregivers. They favored workers who "connected" with children during initial interviews. One employer spoke of what she called West Indian caregivers' "naturalness and warmth" with children and of her preference for hiring them because they "do not see it as inherently degrading work." Although her use of the term *naturalness* is problematic for its overtones of racial/ethnic and gender stereotyping, her perception of West Indian women's feelings about childcare was valid for most of the workers in my sample.

While discipline was often a sore spot for workers, employers tended to be pleased with West Indian women's care in this arena (as long as they perceived no verbal, emotional, or physical abuse). One employer liked that her sitter was "loving and firm." Another appreciated the worker's setting limits. A third was pleased when the child's grandmother approved of the child's new habit of wiping her mouth after eating or drinking, a behavior taught by her sitter. Few were aware of the potential negative effects that their own more relaxed standards of discipline and acceptable children's behavior might have on workers.

Beyond basic characteristics—all employers sought competent, trustworthy, patient, intelligent workers to provide physical and affective care—what employers sought in caregivers was age-specific. For infants and toddlers they especially desired physical warmth and affection and expressed gratitude that West Indian workers seemed to "love" babies, held them, and gave them what one called "warm, laid-back nurturing." However, in discussions of what constituted appropriate childcare for older, preschool children, employers focused on particular kinds of child-rearing practices and enculturation. Many echoed the mother who said, "What you want for infancy tends to be different from what you want later, as opposed to a play partner or something like that." As children grew, many wanted workers to read to and provide other intellectual stimulation for children; take them to parks, playgrounds, and play dates where they could socialize with other children; engage in interactive play; and enculturate them in particular ways. Although employers appreciated when workers read to children and provided sociability, often through sitters' networks, several thought West Indian sitters might not engage "enough" in interactive play or "get down on the floor and play with" children at home or at playgrounds. As one teacher noted, "I didn't see a lot of caretakers getting their butts in the sand. I didn't see a lot of women up on the slide." One academic employer reacted negatively to the difference in cultural styles she saw: "Watching the style of the West Indian babysitters in one corner sitting, and by my, I'll admit, my white middle-class standards . . . doing nothing. Or not intervening enough in the play. . . . The white middle-class mothers are just running in and intervening and settling disputes, or helping with disputes is how we see it, and there will be a tendency for the West Indian babysitters to let go. . . . It's just a very different head set. And even though I understand that intellectually, emotionally I find

that I disapprove often of the things I see in the playground." Employers who remarked on this sought to hire workers who were more interactive with children. This couple had hired a young West Indian woman whom they described as "unusual." "She was always with the children in the sandbox and stuff like that."

Differential notions of appropriate childcare practices resulted in a clash of cultural styles between West Indian workers and their employers. Employers' expectations that sitters hold babies fit with the workers' cultural codes. But workers were likely to sit on the floor entertaining three-year-olds less than employers desired because of norms of behavior for grown women and their own beliefs about raising children. West Indian women, who do not play on the floor (especially as they age), believe that children should learn independence through play as well as in other ways. Thus, the play dates or park gatherings of sitters and children share elements with West Indian patterns of child-caring. When children play in these situations, West Indian sitters look out for the well-being of all the children in the group but may not continuously intervene in their activity. As in West Indian settings, children play together under adults' protective gaze with infrequent adult involvement; when intervention occurs, it might be by any of the adults present, not only the specified caregiver.

One employer couple appreciated their Barbadian worker's affectionate caring, "great" skill with babies, fierce protectiveness, and teaching of manners, but voiced uncertainty about her capacity to provide other appropriate enculturation for their daughter. Like several parents, they expressed concern that their sitter did not speak "standard English" with the children. One said, "My reservations about [my sitter] increase as [my daughter—then three] gets older. . . . It would certainly be nice to have a nice well-educated nanny at this point, and we don't. But . . . school hopefully makes up for that." Like other parents with similar concerns, they enrolled their daughter in a part-time preschool program. They were delighted when they thought a female college student who sat for them at night might work days. They assumed the college student would pick the child up from school and take her to museums and so on, which their West Indian sitter did not do.

While more employers resembled that couple, the veterinarian mother of two children (aged three years and eight months) was an unusual exception. She expressed complete confidence in the competent child rearing of her Jamaican worker and was pleased when the children stayed over with the worker's family in Brooklyn from time to time. While she valued the reading and other learning activities her worker did regularly with the children, she quite clearly stated that nurturance was the key element she sought from caregivers: "I like the Caribbean women who take care of children. There's love there and there's care for the kids. I think children should have a childhood. I don't need to do flash cards with them."

Many employers chose to enroll children in preschool programs (at eighteen to thirty-six months old), supplementing the care of West Indian workers with additional stimulation, educational activity, and interaction with other children and adults. With these expanded services parents could shepherd children from the "nurturance" of West Indian caregivers to preschool programs geared toward Ivy League futures.

Employers' discourse about age-specific childcare expectations reflected a separation between a domain of love and nurturance and one of achievement and "obtaining culture," and stereotyped West Indian caregivers as warm, loving nurturers with questionable educational abilities. In fact, West Indian workers share with their employers a highly developed achievement orientation that motivated their difficult transnational move to New York and their struggles to support, educate, and empower their own kin. Both workers and employers sought to provide their children with what they considered "the best." But employers could afford to buy a range of reproductive services beyond the reach of workers. Such differences and similarities in values were open to substantial cultural misunderstanding.

COMMUNICATION IN EMPLOYER/WORKER RELATIONS

Communication, crucial in private childcare, was one of the most significant problems for West Indian childcare workers and their employers. Simultaneously hierarchical and personal relationships in isolated private households, a lack of formal contracts and grievance procedures and the interdependence of worker and employer intensify the importance of communication. Communication was stressful for both worker and employer. Each operated from different sets of assumptions about appropriate behavior, communication, and conflict resolution, yet each often entered into relations thinking that the other shared basic attitudes and behaviors.

Fear and tension constrained some employers' relationships with childcare providers. Several pointed to the same fear: the potential negative consequences of indicating anger toward or criticizing a worker. One expressed her reluctance to criticize her sitter out of fear that the sitter would "take it out on the children." She didn't think that would ever happen, "but there's always that fear." As she put it, "[These are] employer–employee relationship[s] except these are dealing with something very precious to you—as opposed to just your job." A related concern is what one employer called the "Jamaican babysitter syndrome"—an offended worker walks out the door on Friday and does not return on Monday—which few had experienced but of which many had heard. Dependence on caregivers underlies most employers' fears.

Employers tended toward models of conflict resolution in which people express their grievances verbally and work them through to resolution by talking. Although some were fearful of expressing themselves, some, when they sensed worker dissatisfaction, attempted to probe and coax workers into conversations to identify and talk out problems. However, this model of conflict resolution was not part of the cultural repertoire of most of the West Indian women. While some expressed grievances verbally, most did not expect talking to resolve problems but feared it might lead to potentially explosive conflicts, jeopardizing relationships with employers, job security, and more. Avoidance of conflict was especially crucial to childcare workers who depended on employer sponsorship for legal residence, as their jobs were the means to reunite their families. Without green cards, West Indian workers felt silenced by their powerlessness, subordinate roles, and dependence. And all workers felt that engaging in angry discussion also could erode West Indian women's respectability.

West Indian women also brought assumptions about appropriate attitudes and behavior to interactions with employers. First, they assumed that employers shared a model of reciprocal respect; if one gives respect, one gets it back. Second, they assumed that employers shared their basic conceptions of appropriate behavior. They were taken aback when employers exhibited what they perceived as disrespectful behavior, which they felt was knowingly offensive. This perceived breach in employer conduct made the kind of communication that some employers sought all the more unlikely. Why engage in risky verbal conflict with people who had already offended and insulted them? Many remained silent. Employers found the silence troubling and perhaps threatening.

For employers' models of conflict resolution to be effective, participants must share values and relevant interpersonal skills. However, initiating this kind of conversation, with its veneer of equality and friendliness, masks the power relations of employer and employee. Such conversations are especially problematic when the workplace is the employer's home and workers are isolated from one another. But silence and other nonverbal communication can result in greater miscommunication and dissatisfaction on both sides.

CONCLUSION

Examining the cultural construction of parenting and childcare for West Indian workers and their U.S.-born employers illustrates some of the many ways in which reproduction is stratified. Although parenthood and reproductive labor are central in the lives of both West Indian childcare workers and their employers, they are valued and experienced differently. Both groups are caught in the squeeze of reproduction—both try "to do the best for" their children, sharing similar aspirations for them, while maintaining different notions about children and appropriate childcare. However, in a transnational system in which households have vastly disparate access to resources (according to class, race/ethnicity, gender, and place in a global economy), inequalities (themselves historically structured by social, economic, and political forces) shape and stratify experiences of reproduction for workers and employers. Moreover, this very stratification tends to reproduce itself by reinforcing the inequalities on which it is based.

REFERENCES

Bolles, A. Lynn. 1986. Economic Crisis and Female-Headed Households in Urban Jamaica. In *Women and Change in Latin America,* edited by June Nash and Helen Safa. South Hadley, Mass.: Bergin and Garvey.

Colen, Shellee. 1990. "Housekeeping" for the Green Card: West Indian Household Workers, the State, and Stratified Reproduction in New York. In *At Work in Homes: Household Workers in World Perspective,* edited by Roger Sanjek and Shellee Colen. American Ethnological Society Monograph 3. Washington, D.C.: American Anthropological Association.

Colen, Shellee, and Roger Sanjek. 1990. At Work in Homes I: Orientations. In *At Work in Homes: Household Workers in World Perspective,* edited by Roger Sanjek and Shellee Colen. American Ethnological Society Monograph 3. Washington, D.C.: American Anthropological Association.

D'Amico-Samuels, Deborah. 1986. "You Can't Get Me Out of the Race": Women and Economic Development in Negril, Jamaica, West Indies. Ph.D. diss., Graduate Center of the City University of New York.

———. 1993. A Way Out of No Way: Female Headed Households in Jamaica Reconsidered. In *Where Did All the Men Go? Female Headed/Female Supported Households: Cross-Cultural Comparisons,* edited by Joan

Mencher and Anne Okongwu. Boulder, Colo.: Westview Press.

Durant-Gonzalez, Victoria. 1982. The Realm of Female Familial Responsibility. In *Women and the Family,* edited by Joycelin Massiah. Women in the Caribbean Project, vol. 2. Cave Hill, Barbados: Institute for Social and Economic Research, University of the West Indies.

Ginsburg, Faye D., and Rayna Rapp. 1991. The Politics of Reproduction. *Annual Review of Anthropology* 20: 311–43.

Glenn, Evelyn Nakano. 1992. From Servitude to Service Work: Historical Continuities in the Racial Division of Paid Reproductive Work. *Signs: Journal of Women in Culture and Society* 18(1): 1–43.

Hartmann, Heidi I. 1987. Changes in Women's Economic and Family Role in Post–World War II United States. In *Women, Households, and the Economy,* edited by Lourdes Beneria and Catherine R. Stimpson. New Brunswick, N.J.: Rutgers University Press.

Hirsch, James. 1987. In TV and Films, as in Life, Babies Are in Fashion Again. *New York Times,* 12 October, B5.

Kessler-Harris, Alice, and Karen Brodkin Sacks. 1987. The Demise of Domesticity in America. In *Women, Households, and the Economy,* edited by Lourdes Beneria and Catherine R. Stimpson. New Brunswick, N.J.: Rutgers University Press.

Rollins, Judith. 1990. Ideology and Servitude. In *At Work in Homes: Household Workers in World Perspective,* edited by Roger Sanjek and Shellee Colen. American Ethnological Society Monograph 3. Washington, D.C.: American Anthropological Association.

Ryan, Mary P. 1983. *Womanhood in America: From Colonial Times to the Present.* New York: Watts.

Sanjek, Roger, and Shellee Colen, eds. 1990. *At Work in Homes: Household Workers in World Perspective.* American Ethnological Society Monograph 3. Washington, D.C.: American Anthropological Association.

Smith, Raymond T. 1956. *The Negro Family in British Guiana.* London: Routledge & Kegan Paul.

NOTES

1. By reproduction I refer to the recent conception of social reproduction as "the creation and recreation of people as cultural and social, as well as physical human beings" (Glenn 1992:4) and as "the array of activities and relationships involved in maintaining people both on a daily basis and intergenerationally" (Glenn 1992:1). See also Ginsburg and Rapp (1991) and Colen and Sanjek (1990).

2. From 1984 to 1986 I conducted research in New York through participant observation, extended interviews, and gathering life histories from twenty-five English-speaking Afro-Caribbean women who had performed household and childcare work at some point since migrating to New York City after 1965. Brief fieldwork in St. Vincent and Barbados, West Indies, in 1986 centered on migrants' return visits, childcare and fostering, and migration processes. In 1988–89, I conducted twenty interviews with white U.S.-born employers of West Indian childcare workers in the New York area. They were not employers of the workers interviewed. Seventeen interviews were with mothers only and three included fathers. All of the employers in this urban and suburban sample had attended college and had annual household incomes ranging from $40,000 to over $200,000, with most falling between $50,000 and $120,000. All female employers were married to or living with men except for one single, lesbian mother.

3. Employers' advertisements in newspapers like the *New York Times* and the *Irish Echo* drew an overwhelmingly West Indian response, although other ethnic groups did respond. Employers generally preferred English-speaking West Indian women to non-English speakers or to other African-diaspora women (who had previously dominated private household work in New York). Many employers perceived West Indians as better educated, more achievement-oriented, and less threatening than working-class African American women.

2 • *Elizabeth Chin*

ETHNICALLY CORRECT DOLLS
Toying with the Race Industry

DISCUSSION QUESTIONS

1. Why did Mattel start producing racially diverse Barbie dolls? According to Chin, what was the problem with their approach?
2. How do "race," class, and gender shape the daily lives of girls and boys in Newhallville? Give examples.
3. How do Asia, Natalia, and other girls interviewed by Chin challenge (or "queer") these racial and class boundaries by playing with their Barbies?

On a July afternoon in 1992, I sat talking with ten-year-old Natalia and her cousin Asia on Natalia's front stoop. We were in Newhallville, a working-class and poor African American neighborhood in New Haven, Connecticut. Spying a frazzle-haired white Barbie doll beneath Natalia's seat, and holding my tape recorder, I asked the girls to tell me about the doll. Without missing a beat, Natalia and Asia commandeered the machine and began to speak:

ASIA: You never see a fat Barbie. You never see a pregnant Barbie. What about those things? They should make a Barbie that can have a baby.

NATALIA: Yeah . . . and make a fat Barbie. So when we play Barbie . . . you could be a fat Barbie.

ASIA: OK. What I was saying is that Barbie . . . how can I say this? They make her like a stereotype. Barbie is a stereotype. When you think of Barbie you don't think of fat Barbie . . . you don't think of

pregnant Barbie. You never, ever . . . think of an abused Barbie.

Speaking into the tape recorder, Natalia announced: "I would like to say that Barbie is *dope*. But y'all probably don't know what that means, so I will say that Barbie is *nice*!" The tape recorder was the girls' conduit to an imaginary audience, one located outside their own neighborhood, and one that is not black. In substituting the bland word "nice" for the tastiness of "dope," Natalia demonstrated a devastating sensitivity to the gap between her own world and the one where the "y'all" whom she addressed live. In wondering why there wasn't a Barbie that is "fat," "pregnant," or "abused," Natalia and Asia also wondered why these dolls represent social and cultural worlds so foreign to them.

In 1991, a year before these girls spoke their minds, the makers of Barbie had introduced their first ethnically correct fashion dolls to the market.

Abridged version of Elizabeth Chin, 1999. Ethnically Correct Dolls: Toying with the Race Industry. Reproduced by permission of the American Anthropological Association and of the author from *American Anthropologist*, Volume 101, Issue 2, Pages 305-321, June 1999. Not for sale or further reproduction.

Shani and her friends Asha and Nichelle were unlike other black dolls Mattel had produced: they came in light, medium, and dark skin tones; they had newly sculpted facial features; and there were reports that their bodies had been changed to accurately represent African American figures. These toys were designed and marketed specifically to reshape a territory dominated by an assumption of whiteness, but paradoxically, they have integrated the toy world while at the same time fixing racial boundaries more firmly.

In Newhallville, however, girls tended to have white dolls that they worked to bring into their own worlds, often through styling their hair. These interactions highlight children's understandings that racialized commodities like Shani can only incompletely embody the experiences of kids who are not simply racial beings, but also poor, working class, young, ghettoized, and gendered. Embodied in these children's activities is a profound recognition that race is not only socially constructed but has potential to be imaginatively reconstructed. Girls in Newhallville worked on their dolls materially and symbolically, blurring racial absolutes by putting their hair into distinctively African American styles using beads, braids, and foil. The question of race and dolls suggests ways in which feminist notions of multiple subjectivity and queer theory ideas about the flexibility of designations such as "straight" or "gay," "girl" and "boy" are relevant to the study of race and racism. In looking at the interactions of Newhallville girls and their white dolls, ways of thinking between and outside of bounded racial categories emerge. However, the radical potential of these girls' playful efforts is just that: potential, since Asia and Natalia—like other kids in their neighborhood—live lives constrained by the contingencies of social inequality.

After my field work was over, I saw that multiple photographs I had taken showed black girls with white dolls whose hair had been elaborately braided, twisted, or styled in ways racially marked as black. Understanding these hair stylings meant looking in several territories. White dolls with black hairdos required looking into the ethnically correct toy industry, since these toys have been manufactured for children like Natalia and Asia. But few Newhallville children had such dolls; for the most part, their significance in these kids' lives was specifically in their absence. The social, economic, historical, and political factors that have engineered the absence of ethnically correct toys from Newhallville children's rooms are the same forces that have helped to form poor, racially segregated, and embattled communities in urban areas across the nation. It is precisely in the context of multiple social inequalities that ethnically correct toys like Shani and Newhallville's racially transformed white dolls need to be understood. This context breeds silence, and kids like those I knew in Newhallville rarely speak or are heard beyond their sequestered sphere. However, when they are heard, their experiences, observations, and talk form a foundation for understanding how white dolls with braids have a profound and radical meaning that confounds the commercial rhetoric of ethnically correct toys like the Shani doll.

QUEERING RACE

Queer, feminist, and cultural studies analyses have already yielded incisive critiques of Barbie and her ilk, ethnically correct and otherwise. These analyses have moved well beyond the familiar observation that Barbie, with her sadistically pointed breasts, waspy waist, and permanently high-heel prepared feet, does not look much like any real woman who has not had extensive plastic surgery.

In the Barbie realm, the work of Erica Rand is an important model for how to think critically about toys, children, and culture—even though she excludes children from the scope of her inquiry. In *Barbie's Queer Accessories* (1995) Rand has collected women's recollections of Barbie in their lives. Central to Rand's analysis is the way she conceptualizes the notion of queer. In *Barbie's Queer Accessories,* making Barbie queer is not necessarily about sex or sexuality. Rand's notion of queering highlights the bending, twisting, or flipping of apparently real or natural or accepted social states, and she explores a variety of ways in which Barbie gets queered: consumer activists switch the voice boxes of talking G.I. Joe with talking Barbie, adult women remember cross-dressing Barbie or making her fuck Midge, 'zines generate faux ads for such items as AIDS Barbie. The fundamental tension is between a commodity with a packaged identity and the consumers who put her to work in their own lives; the deliciousness of the images is their transgression of Mattel's carefully managed Barbie profile.

As radical as these queerings may be in a given cultural space and social moment, they also make use of and take place within powerful ideological discourses: transgression does not make up its own rules, or exist in a world apart from hegemonic influences, and the power of resistance should not be overstated (Sholle 1990). As Abu-Lughod has argued, when we look at resistance and the sites where it emerges, we stand to learn more about structures of power than arenas of freedom (1990). Rand's description of one of her own Barbie queerings illustrates the ways in which the layered and multiple meanings of race, sexual identity, and gender can reflect back upon each other, creating a hall-of-mirrors effect in which the subversion suddenly is itself subverted. In positioning two dolls in a staged "top/bottom dyke sex scene" between her White Barbie and "Chicana" Barbie (which, according to the package, was an American Indian Barbie) she writes:

> I struggled with how to assign roles to my two Barbies. Putting Chicana Barbie on top reinforces racial stereotypes of the dark brute overpowering the less animalistic white girl; the hair contrast alone places my Dream Loft firmly within the hetero-generated tradition of lesbian representation, which often features an aggressive, dark-haired vixen seducing a blond innocent. Putting blond Barbie on top would have subverted these stereotypes but performed white supremacy. In terms of race, there was no way out of dominant discourse. (1995:172–173)

Despite a growing literature examining hybridity or mixed-race ethnicity and identity, in the U.S., discussions and analyses of race tend to make use of a polarized black/white framework. Ethnically correct toys, too, draw upon these notions of difference and phenotype, paradoxically making use of oppressive distinctions to try to create progressive change. The braided heads of white dolls in Newhallville at least make a dent in the concreteness of race boundaries. Neither hybrid nor multicultural, they are instead queer. Seeing these dolls as racially queered is appropriate not only because naturalized categories of race are being bent, but also because it is a notion which, unlike hybridity, is fundamentally playful. These children have made a play on whiteness. Race that has been queered in this way challenges "pure" forms by disconnecting racial markers from particular bodies, much in the way that queer and gender studies have recognized that gender and sexuality are not inherently, predictably, or inevitably rooted in physical "male" or "female" individuals. These playfully imagined, resistant realities are not separable, however, from the context of discrimination, segregation, and oppression in which they have been generated, to which they ultimately refer, and with which they remain enmeshed.

NEGOTIATING NEWHALLVILLE, THE MALL, AND SHANI'S WORLD

Harsh economic contrasts and racial tensions characterize New Haven today. Located in the wealthiest of the fifty states in terms of per capita income, this city of 130,000 was in 1980 the seventh-poorest of its size in the nation (U.S. Bureau of the Census 1980). Newhallville is almost completely segregated and has a 91.7% minority population, but it borders the richest (and whitest) neighborhood in town.

Newhallville kids' sense of danger and possibility changed depending on the location. Downtown, the atmosphere was charged with racial tensions, but girls' romantic fantasies took wing. The downtown mall was an especially racially charged space where they felt embattled and unwelcome (Chin 1996, 1998): bus stops used to be on the same block as the mall, but were moved several blocks away. Frank Sinatra dominates the sound system. These strategies specifically target poor and minority shoppers.

In contrast, their neighborhood was a racially safe but sexually dangerous place, where teenage boys and older men were seen as threats but increasingly interesting. Not trusting in my ability to negotiate the neighborhood, the girls would escort me, guiding me past stores, streets, and people. One summer afternoon when Natalia decided I had let an impromptu conversation with a man last too long, she deftly cut the interaction short. "He's probably a drug dealer," Natalia said with assurance as we walked away. "He probably rapes little girls." For Newhallville girls, the concerns about rape and pregnancy begin early. But actively negotiating these issues at the age of ten is less the impact of gender, perhaps, than it is of class, race, social, and economic issues.

In contrast to the streets, girls' homes typically were places of safety where they could still be like little kids. Doll play, as Natalia's cousin Asia pointed out, was a sign of being a little kid. "We might play with Barbies like this," she said, miming the way kids bounce a doll along a tabletop to make it walk, "but we don't let anybody see us." At ten years old, the girls could allow themselves to be vulnerable only inside their houses, whose windows were shrouded by shades and curtains. Boys their age still gathered together outside on stoops to play with their action figures and vehicles.

In general, getting to stores was difficult and expensive. For example, the nearest Toys 'R' Us was all but inaccessible by public transport and could only be reached by taking a highway to the next town. Nearly half of Newhallville households did not have a car; friends and relatives could provide rides, but often charged for "gas money." Most kids I knew in Newhallville visited Toys 'R' Us at most only once or twice a year. Some had never been there.

Newhallville kids learned early and well that they were expensive to house and feed, and that whatever they got usually meant that someone else had to do without. Tionna, like many of her peers, had nearly fully incorporated the lesson that she should harbor few expectations and make few demands. On Christmas morning, in 1992, Tionna got up early and ran to look under the tree. She didn't see any gifts. Thinking that there just weren't any gifts that year, she went back to bed. There were presents, she just hadn't seen them. But despite her fierce (if temporary) disappointment, Tionna accepted the possibility that there were no presents at all because the possibility was real.

The primary appeal toy makers offer with their ethnically correct playthings is the idea that such toys can help minority kids to feel more at home in the world through allowing them to play with dolls that look like them. In a community where kids can accept the idea that Santa just didn't come this year, and where even getting to a toy store is a major undertaking, having ethnically correct toys on the shelves of Toys 'R' Us seems unlikely to have much impact. By framing the representation problem as one solely of race, makers of ethnically correct toys miss issues that for Newhallville children were often more immediately pressing. Despite the overt physical changes that Mattel made when they produced Shani, she still inhabits a fantasy world remarkably similar to Barbie's, the world where the word "dope" must be replaced with "nice," as the product packaging suggests:

> Shani, Asha, and Nichelle invite you into their glamorous world to share the fun and excitement of being a top model. Imagine appearing on magazine covers, starring in fashion shows, and going to Hollywood parties as you, Shani, Asha, and Nichelle live your dreams of beauty and success, loving every marvelous minute!

THE UNBEARABLE WHITENESS OF BARBIE

Psychologists Kenneth and Mamie Phipps Clark in the late 1930s and early 1940s conducted their groundbreaking "doll studies." These studies used black and white dolls as a way to unearth black children's views about race, asking them to point out, for example, which doll "looks nice." In a series of publications, the Clark studies revealed that black children often thought the white doll "looks nice," while the black doll "looks bad" (Clark and Clark 1939, 1947). The Clarks argued that these choices resulted from "self-rejection" or "self-hatred." However, the impetus for these feelings was not internally generated. Rather, the Clarks said, kids understood all too well that the larger society disrespected and devalued blacks. As a result, children's feelings about themselves were contaminated by this knowledge. The doll studies gained additional clout when they became associated with the landmark civil rights case *Brown v. the Board of Education of Topeka, Kansas*, in which the Supreme Court ruled segregated schooling to be unconstitutional.

Mattel recruited the psychologist Darlene Powell-Hopson as a consultant in designing the Shani dolls. Powell-Hopson, who had replicated the Clark studies in the early 1980s, found that children's perceptions of race had hardly improved since the 1930s (Powell-Hopson 1985).

Powell-Hopson's involvement in developing Shani dolls provided a direct line of descent from the Clarks' work. But Mattel added a commercial twist: the message became that children who play with dolls that look like them will not suffer from self-hatred. With ethnically correct toys, the Clark studies' logic is reversed: it is the *toys* that determine children's perceptions, not the society that produces the toys.

With the introduction of Shani and her friends, the makers of Barbie herself have recognized the unbearable whiteness of Barbie in minority children's experience. But the type of diversity that has developed in the toy industry's products is problematic; while mounting a challenge to whiteness as a norm, the diversity under manufacture in the form of "ethnically correct" playthings does not significantly transform the understanding of race, or even racism. Rather, ethnically correct dolls simply refashion racist discourses and market them to minority buyers.

SHANI AND THE MARKETING OF BLACKNESS

The signature aspects of ethnically correct dolls are resculpted faces, skin tones, hair types, and ethnic fashions. While these toys do enshrine difference in a way that preceding black dolls and toys do not, the emphasis on race as a collection of visible markers masks the complexity of race both as a social construct and as a social experience.

Moreover, the Shani dolls, with their light, medium, and dark skin tones, were designed to signify different kinds of blackness. But the progressive notion that black does not look just one way is not as progressive as it might appear. When one looks closely at the Shani dolls, their facial features seem to get more stereotypically "black" the darker the doll's skin color: Asha, the light-skinned doll, has the smallest nose and thinnest lips; meanwhile Nichelle, the darkest doll, has lips that are much wider than the outlines of her stamped-on pink lipstick, and her nose is the largest and widest of the Shani dolls. Light as Asha is, she is not so light that there is any danger that she might be able to "pass" as white.

In the mind of at least one Newhallville child, the meaning of the various skin colors was not kinds of blackness, but rather kinds of racial mixing. When Carlos and I were in Toys 'R' Us, I pointed out to him that the dolls came in three skin tones. As I held one of each color in my hand, Carlos spontaneously began to describe them. "She's African American," he said, about Nichelle, the darkest-skinned doll. "She must be part Indian," he said, referring to Shani. "This one is like Puerto Rican or a light-colored black person," he finished, as he examined Asha. When Carlos describes Asha as being "Puerto Rican or a light-colored black person" he captures the difficulty in being able to know race simply by looking.

Carlos has also pinpointed that in depicting kinds of blackness, Mattel has inadvertently roused the specter of miscegenation. There is (of course) no Interracial Barbie, no Mulatto or Quadroon Barbie, no Eurasian Barbie, nor a Barbie that like golf champion Tiger Woods might be described as "Cablinasian"—Caucasian, black, Indian and Asian—a mixture not of two races, but of several. Tiger Woods' insistence on creating a name for what he is, like Carlos' description of the racial backgrounds of Shani, Asha, and Nichelle, speaks to the inability of our racial categories to capture the finely tuned perceptions of kids (or adults), who may not understand how to put the "one drop rule" to work in their everyday lives, especially when they may be the offspring of parents who are themselves of two or more different races. Racial identity, in other words, is complex and multifaceted experientially, socially, and historically. In the made-up world of Mattel, and much American public discourse, however, the current option is to check the boxes that apply: "White, Black (not of Hispanic origin), Hispanic, Asian, Native Hawaiian or Pacific Islander, American Indian or Alaska Native, or Other."

Shani, like white Barbie, is deeply in need of the kind of racial queering that has been going on for years in relation to Barbie's gender. Even Erica Rand (1995), with her keen critical eye, couldn't see a way to queer the racial boundaries of her "Chicana" and "White" Barbies. Why didn't it occur to her to switch the dolls' heads? That would say a lot about minds and bodies, about perception and experience. In another form, this is precisely what the girls I knew in Newhallville were doing with their own dolls.

BRAIDS AND THE BLONDE DOLL

I have a photograph of Clarice sitting on the front steps of her porch, next to her younger brother Joey. Clarice has a doll snuggled on her lap. Against the dark color of Clarice's T-shirt, the doll's light skin and blond hair are blazingly white. The front section of the doll's long, silky hair is done up in braids, each held at the end with a small plastic barrette, just like Clarice's.

When the long blond hair of white dolls is heavy with beads and foil, or tucked up into a braid-upon-braid 'do, what has happened to the boundary between white and black? Power relationships and conceptual boundaries between white and black are destabilized as Newhallville girls braid their dolls' hair. This destabilization is delicate, fleeting even, and is likely to have little social impact beyond the realm of these children's own personal spheres, because it is undertaken in the context of far-reaching and multiple oppressions. Such destabilization is not likely to have any real or lasting impact on these kids' living relationships with either white people or the idea of whiteness: the elements of play and control present in doll hairstyling are markedly missing in kids' interactions with their white teachers, shopkeepers, police. But although fleeting and precarious, what these girls are doing subtly works away at the constricted and constricting notions of race that continue to dominate current discourse. It is a form of racial integration that has been largely unimagined by adult activists, scholars, politicians, or toy manufacturers.

The question of hair in African American culture is a particularly contentious one, especially for girls and women. Hair emerges as an almost living character in scores of novels, memoirs, magazine articles, and scholarly works by or about African American women. As a primary racial marker, hair has become increasingly politicized as a medium through which racial identity potentially may be embraced or erased (Mercer 1990). Debates over whether black women and girls should do things to their hair that make it approximate the straight, silky, flowing hair associated with whiteness have been especially heated. At an extreme, curly, nappy hair has been judged "bad" hair, while flowing, silky hair is "good" hair.

Given this situation, it is no wonder that Darlene Powell-Hopson encouraged Mattel to produce dolls that had a variety of hair textures. However, because hair play has become an increasingly central element of toy marketing to girls, Mattel did not comply. Each of the Shani dolls has what kids in Newhallville called "Barbie Doll Hair," styled in ways similar to those typical of white Barbie dolls: curls for Nichelle and Asha and a crimped style similar to that found on "Totally Hair Barbie" for Shani. In a half-hearted stab at African-Americanizing this hair, my "Beach Dazzle" Shani dolls come not with the brush that my white Barbie has, but with wide-toothed implements that the company describes as "hair picks," even though Shani's and Barbie's hair is essentially the same.

Accepting stereotypical notions about black hair makes light of the fact that the "good" and "bad" hair debate would not be possible if black kids had hair that only comes in tight, nappy curls. It also comes in straight or curly versions as silky, and even as blond as Veronica Lake's famous eye-obscuring cascade. There are some indications that the absolute line between what constitutes "black" or "white" hair was originally enforced by whites who claimed long silky hair as a marker of their racial identity: there are accounts of slave-owning women, who, when faced with female slaves who had long, silky hair, would remove the offending tresses from the slave's head to enforce their blackness (White and White 1995).

If one accepts that racial divisions are absolute and unbridgeable, what these girls are doing with their dolls makes little sense. Why put a black hairstyle on a white doll? And yet, if these dolls belong to these black girls, and live in the worlds they inhabit, how white are they? Remember Asia and Natalia's ruminations on Barbie, which urgently pointed out that the main difference between them and the doll could be summarized with a nod to race, but really rested in their life situations. The girls seem to recognize the socially constructed nature of race, the ambiguity of a racialized existence, and the flexibility of racialized expression: it is not always or only the color of their dolls that makes them hard to relate to or identify with. Moreover, what these girls are doing emphasizes that they do not need to buy racial difference, or even to buy dolls that look like them; they can create dolls that look like them in fundamental ways through their own imaginative and material work.

The girls' refusal to accept racial boundaries as absolute and unbridgeable spilled over into my relationships with them, since from the very beginning they were fascinated with my own waist-length "Barbie Doll Hair." As I grew to know the girls better, they began to get their hands in my hair, styling it in ways that made me look better to them, while also demonstrating their nearness to me both physically and emotionally. They'd yank and gel and twist my practical ponytail into a sleek topknot with long, twirling curls just in front of each ear, or part my hair into five or six sections and braid each one. These girls were changing my head around on days like this, and when they'd finished their creations and sent me into the bathroom to look at their work, it seemed that it wasn't quite me in the mirror. Their work of transformation was not to rearrange my race or racial identity in some biological sense; nevertheless, they were working to make me more like them just as they did with their dolls. Their joy in being able to re-create me was tangible, and during the week that my braids stayed in kids greeted me with surprised glee: "Ooooh, Miss Chin, you got your hair braided! You look so nice!"

CONCLUSION

Kenneth Clark himself wrote that "Our society can mobilize itself to wage a dramatic and successful war against racial prejudice and its effects upon human beings. In doing so it will eliminate the situation where the prejudiced individuals are the ones who have higher status, and where they compel others to conform to their prejudices" (Clark [1955] 1963:139). While making reference to the pioneering work of the Clarks' "doll studies," ethnically correct dolls embody a fundamentally different social project than the one Kenneth Clark envisioned. The effort to manufacture racial diversity in the form of ethnically correct dolls is not in the end an effort to transform the assumptions and beliefs that dominate racial discourse. Consider, for example, this comment by Yvonne Rubie, president of the International Black Toy Association: "If children grow up with things that are like themselves, they will tend to like themselves or at least identify themselves with that positive image" (Ebony 1993:66). Ms. Rubie's assertion that it is children's relationships with *things* rather than people that is most critically important for their sense of self is utterly startling, and yet utterly in line with a consumerist ethic. This perspective fits in well with the emergence of an industry ready to supply the things kids need in order to have a "positive self-image" while sidestepping the question of fundamental social, political, and historical issues that impinge on children's experiences and hence their perceptions of themselves as people in the world.

It is perhaps because kids like those in Newhallville do not have a ready ability to buy the commodities being marketed to them that they are able to bend racial boundaries as readily as they do. From Cabbage Patch Kids with hair heavy with beads and foil to long-haired blond dolls sporting elaborately braided 'dos, white dolls in Newhallville were, over and over again, not quite recognized as such. The dolls' whiteness did not stop girls from integrating them into their worlds. And yet, I have already noted that these transformations are probably fleeting, at best, even in the consciousness of the children who create them. This is what Fiske (1993) calls "weak power," a concept that recognizes the transformative potential of processes like those being undertaken by these Newhallville children, but that also places that potential within the oppressive structure of the larger society.

Toy makers' rigid understanding of race is based on notions of the fixity of genetics. They attempt to turn racism on its head but not to reimagine race itself, ultimately perpetuating a vision of race that anthropologists, at least, have been endeavoring to dismantle for well over a century. But in having their white dolls live in black worlds, Newhallville girls reconfigure the boundaries of race. In so doing, these girls challenge the social construction not only of their own blackness, but of race itself.

REFERENCES CITED

Abu-Lughod, Lila. 1990. "The Romance of Resistance: Tracing Transformations of Power Through Bedouin Women." *American Ethnologist* 17 (1): 41–55.

Chin, Elizabeth. 1996. "Fettered Desire: Consumption and Social Experience among Minority Children in New Haven, Connecticut,". Graduate School of the City University of New York, Anthropology.

———. 1998. "Social Inequality and Servicescape: Local Groceries and Downtown Stores in New Haven, Connecticut." In *Servicescapes: The Concept of Place in Contemporary Markets*, edited by Jr. John F. Sherry, 591–617. Chicago: NTC Group.

Clark, Kenneth B. [1955] 1963. *Prejudice and Your Child*. Boston: Beacon Press.

Clark, Kenneth B., and Mamie K. Clark. 1939. "The Development of Consciousness of Self and the Emergence of Racial Identification in Negro Preschool Children." *The Journal of Social Psychology, SPSSI Bulletin* 10: 591–99.

Clark, Kenneth B., and Mamie Phipps Clark. 1947. "Racial Identification and Preference in Negro Children." In *Readings in Social Psychology*, edited by T.M. Newcomb and E.L. Hartley, 169–78. New York: Henry Holt.

Ebony. 1993. "New Boom in Ethnic Toys: Experts Say the Trend Is More than Skin Deep." *Ebony*.

Fiske, John. 1993. *Power Plays, Power Works*. London and New York: Verso.

Mercer, Kobena. 1990. "Black Hair/Style Politics." In *Out There: Marginalization in Contemporary Cultures,* ed. Russell Ferguson, Martha Gever, Trinh T. Minh-Ha and Cornel West, 247–64. New York and Cambridge, MA: The New Museum of Contemporary Art and MIT Press.

Powell-Hopson, Darlene. 1985. "The Effects of Modeling, Reinforcement, and Color Meaning Word Associations on Doll Color Preferences of Black Preschool Children and White Preschool Children." Hofstra University, Psychology.

Rand, Erica. 1995. *Barbie's Queer Accessories*. Durham: Duke University Press.

Sholle, David. 1990. "Resistance: Pinning Down a Wandering Concept in Cultural Studies Discourse." *Journal of Urban and Cultural Studies* 1 (1): 87–105.

U.S. Bureau of the Census. 1980. *Census of Population and Housing*. Washington, D.C.: Government Printing Office.

White, Shane, and Graham White. 1995. "Slave Hair and African American Culture in the Eighteenth and Nineteenth Centuries." *Journal of Southern History* 61 (1): 45–76.

3 • *Sharon R. Roseman*

"STRONG WOMEN" AND "PRETTY GIRLS"

Self-Provisioning, Gender, and Class Identity in Rural Galicia

DISCUSSION QUESTIONS

1. How and why do women in rural Spain position themselves as "strong women" or "pretty girls" through their work, appearance, and practices?
2. Why do men and women value working their own land over wage work, or even no productive work at all?
3. What is "code switching," according to Roseman? Do you think this is a useful concept for understanding how people alternate between different expressions of gender and class identity?

I opened the sturdy wooden door swiftly, shaking the raindrops from my hair, and called out: "*E . . . is anyone here?*" Concepción's muffled reply, "*Estamos aquí dentro*" [We're in here] could be heard from behind the door to the *salón* or small living room that Concepción and her family rarely use. I was surprised at the sight: Concepción and her 21-year-old granddaughter María were standing in the midst of several large reed baskets, two plastic buckets, and a roughly hewn wooden bench—all covered with the parts of a freshly butchered pig. Concepción was wielding a small ax, and María was holding a basket lined with fresh bay leaves upon which more pork would be placed.

I had only been in their living room once before. It was my impression that it was mainly used to entertain *festa* guests twice a year. Our conversations had normally taken place in the kitchen, the cowshed, the yard, or the family's fields. Similar to other living rooms in the Galician village of Santiago de Carreira,[1] Concepción's was furnished with a sofa, two easy chairs, a low coffee table, a varnished dining room table, and an open-shelved sideboard where ornaments were displayed. María had ushered me there one previous time for a brief tour of some of the family's most prized possessions. On another occasion, Concepción had showed me their new bathroom on the second floor of the house.[2] At that time, in 1990, the family had had an indoor bathroom for only three years.

The *salón* space, the objects exhibited there, and the bathroom and its porcelain accouterments were some of the symbols of prosperity that served to differentiate households in the village of

Abridged version of Sharon R. Roseman, 2002. "Strong Women" and "Pretty Girls": Self-Provisioning, Gender, and Class Identity in Rural Galicia. Reproduced by permission of the American Anthropological Association and of the author from *American Anthropologist,* Volume 104, Issue 1, Pages 22-37, March 2002. Not for sale or further reproduction.

Carreira during the 1990s. Many families lacked the new furniture and ornaments. For almost two decades, Concepción's only son Alberto worked on heavy construction jobs in Switzerland and Galicia whenever he could secure contracts. For a few years during the 1980s, his wife Susana joined him in Switzerland, where she cleaned private homes. It was through a combination of these types of wage jobs performed mainly by Alberto in migrant destinations and the women's work raising cattle and crops at home that the family was able to survive as well as make improvements to the house.

On the rainy day in late November 1990 when I encountered Concepción and María butchering their pig, the *salón* was cold and dark. The two women had placed layers of sheets and blankets over the already thick curtains and blinds that covered the room's windows. Concepción explained that the *salón* was the best place in the house for butchering because it was clear of other activities and they could ensure that little or no moonlight would enter it overnight. In rural Galicia, *luceiro* or moonlight is believed by many to cause raw, unprocessed meat to spoil. Over the next several days and weeks, Concepción and María would salt some of the meat and prepare the sausages and lard. The men who earlier in the day had cut the pig's throat, bled its body, cleaned and burnt its hide, and quartered it were no longer anywhere in sight. As I looked more closely into the gloom, I noticed that the cherished furniture was covered with sheets to protect it from being stained. The long dark skirt and gray, striped apron that Concepción almost always wore were splattered with blood. As we talked, she wiped her hair away from her face where it had escaped the homemade, black kerchief and pushed up the sleeves of the black sweater she wore under her apron. Like many of the other middle-aged and older women in the village, Concepción protected her feet from the chilly, wet Galician weather with a pair of thick black stockings and handmade wooden-soled boots with black, leather uppers. Her granddaughter María, home from university for the weekend, was also dressed for work, albeit in navy blue rubber-soled canvas shoes, a baggy pair of dark-colored sweatpants, and a full-body apron. Uncharacteristically, she also wore on this day a kerchief over her hair.

RURAL LIVELIHOOD PRACTICES AND CLASS IDENTITY IN LATE-20TH-CENTURY GALICIA

At first, it appeared incongruous to me that Concepción would choose to complete what has come to be regarded in Galicia as a stereotypic "peasant" task in the most "bourgeois" and least functional room in the house. That evening I wrote in my field notes that the apparent juxtaposition Concepción had achieved in her choice of a room in which to butcher eloquently represents the mixed livelihood practices of many rural people in this part of northwestern Spain. With further analytical hindsight, however, Concepción's decision to use the *salón* as a butchery seemed more significant than it having simply been a practical accommodation to a multi-occupational livelihood or the unconscious construction of a collage representing that livelihood.

The imagery of the blood-splattered sheets overlaying the pristine, polished furniture has remained vivid. I would argue that Concepción's behavior in this instance emerged out of her participation in the active cultural remaking of gender and class identities in a rural smallholders' settlement in late-20th-century Europe. Concepción and María were, after all, splattering blood on precious commodities in the process of completing a key provisioning task for their family. For months, Concepción had provided the young pig with the table scraps and additional nourishment that it needed in order to grow into an animal that could fulfill the family's annual requirements for pork products. She had also watched over it assiduously to make sure that it did not fall ill and talked to it affectionately as it grew to be healthy and strong. When the fall chill came into the air and it looked to be the right size, Concepción's male relatives set about slaughtering the pig, and she and María used the skills women learn in villages such as

Carreira to properly butcher and preserve the dead animal.[3]

I adopt the concept of a worker peasantry to analyze how these rural inhabitants of southern Europe have maintained mixed livelihood practices that include provisioning activities performed on land that families rented or owned, the sale of agricultural and craft commodities, a variety of wage labor opportunities both locally and in migrant destinations, and a partial or periodic reliance on remittances from state programs including the old-age pension scheme and unemployment insurance. People in Carreira say that they have to "go out" (that is, leave the household or village) to earn *o xornal* (an old Galician term that refers literally to "day wages" earned performing either agricultural or non-agricultural work). They also say that they must continue to raise and process their own foodstuffs, for one must "work to eat" (*traballar pra comer*).

In her study of Puerto Rican shantytowns, Safa writes that "viewing class consciousness from a feminist perspective permits one to question whether the narrow focus on [paid] work roles is even appropriate. As the marginal labor force grows larger it also becomes harder for men to find stable employment or to identify with their [paid] work role" (1980:71). Her conclusions fit the case of some areas in rural Galicia. I focus on the social process of defining an alternative class positionality in Carreira by examining both women's ability to "code switch," and men's acknowledgment of women's unpaid labor as central to family and community survival. I am extending the concept of "code switching" to the broad array of cultural expressions of class identity from its original use in sociolinguistic analysis to describe individuals switching between different languages or between language varieties such as standard and vernacular dialects of the same language. (e.g., Coupland 1980; Roseman 1995, 1997; Scotton 1979). Unlike urban-based men who may not emphasize the economic significance of their female relatives' unpaid labor expended in activities such as shopping, meal preparation, and cleaning, men from Carreira highlight their families' partial reliance

on the unpaid provisioning labor of women who work the land and prepare food from their own kitchen gardens, animal pens, and fields. Women, in turn, somewhat ambivalently acclaim both their maintenance of a "peasant" work regime and their ability to consume the clothing, household décor, and other products that characterize a dominant late-20th-century Spanish public female identity defined by a notion of womanhood that is not preoccupied with daily, hard manual labor.

My data draw attention to the importance of considering the differences in labor activity, consciousness, and identity between women and men and the way in which different labor relationships can be gendered not only as part of the hegemony of the dominant classes but also as components of critiques generated by subaltern people. My discussion of women's complex class and gender identities responds to Henrietta Moore's (1994:85) call for us to pay increasing attention not just to the social construction of gender but also to the gendering of individuals' identities through their bodies. Much research has been done on women's bodies under the headings of sexuality and reproduction. One of my aims is to suggest that we should also focus on how laboring bodies become gendered. Women in Carreira self-consciously "code switch" between "peasant" and "non-peasant" demeanors as part of their negotiation of where they fit into a broader economic and social system. Their ability to transform themselves from "strong women" into "pretty girls" and back again is tied to a layered appropriation of different images of femininity and the variable consumption of commoditized and non-commoditized products. A full study of class and gender should entail a consideration of ideas and behaviors associated with both labor and consumption.

These Galicians' cultural understanding of global capitalism and their place within it can be compared with cases reported by ethnographers working in different contexts. Women and men reassert the priority of unwaged provisioning work on a continual basis through its daily visible performance in outside spaces such as people's yards and fields, and through detailed discussions (Butler

1989). In addition to their recognition of women's contributions to household income through unwaged *traballo* (a Galician word that can be translated as either "labor" or "work"), men also actively participate in subsistence activities when they return to the village. The contrast that they draw between the conditions of waged and unwaged labor appears to enable men in Carreira to negotiate their own vulnerable situations as workers: for the most part, they are not members of the securely employed working class but, rather, constitute a reserve army of "flexible," contract laborers for employers in Spain as well as in other European countries.

Some younger and middle-aged women from Carreira have also formed part of the army of migrant laborers. Most, however, have spent the majority of their working lives in the village performing a range of activities that have always included substantial amounts of unwaged subsistence, domestic, and caregiving work; they are also the individuals who are mainly engaged in unwaged labor exchange relationships with other households. Women, more than men, signify clearly that they are not members of the urban-based Spanish working and middle classes through their bodies. They also symbolize this situation by dressing like the "peasants" they consider themselves (in part) to be. Men, in contrast, when helping with farmwork wear the blue *monos* or coveralls that they also wear when working as paid laborers on construction projects or in other blue-collar jobs in Spain and abroad.

"WE WORK TO EAT": THE COUNTRYSIDE VERSUS THE CITY

A common theme of conversation in Carreira is the superiority of the rural mixed economy to the way of life of city dwellers who rely solely on cash wages. In contrast, some rural Galicians such as those living in Carreira continue to supply many of their daily subsistence needs by growing staple crops such as potatoes, kale, and cabbage as well as raising livestock including fowl, pigs, and cattle. Although many of the men (and some of the women) have lived in Spanish and

foreign cities for years and even decades as migrant laborers, they consider themselves to be "peasants" (*labradores/as, labregos/as,* or *campesiños/as*) as well as laborers who earn wages (*o xornal*). Many rural Galicians construct a peasant identity around the activities of "working the land" and eating food from the land—homegrown and homemade food (*comida caseira*). They do not trust fully either the wage market or the welfare state and do not rule out the possibility of being forced in the future to return to a less commoditized lifestyle. "You can't eat money" is a comment that I heard frequently.

Unlike wage earners in other contexts, men define their class positions as incompletely proletarianized workers partly through the unpaid subsistence work done by their female relatives. In one household, Pedro, a 63-year-old widowed grandfather, praised his daughter-in-law Teresa's work numerous times, sometimes within her hearing: "If she didn't do all this work, taking care of the crops and the chickens, cooking, cleaning, and caring for the children, we would have to pay someone to do it." The emphasis placed on continuing some degree of the subsistence provisioning done mainly by women reveals that neither women nor men pretend that the men have ever earned a "family wage" or are the sole "breadwinners."

The contention that life is "better" in the countryside also involves a discourse on productive autonomy. Men with extensive migrant labor, as well as more local, wage-earning experience, emphasize that the ability to organize production on one's own land for one's own benefit is something that fully proletarianized urban dwellers have lost. "I'll decide whether to plant my potatoes in the garden today. I'm not working 'under' anyone like I did in Switzerland," 72-year-old Pepe explained. His neighbor Esteban compared the mainly unskilled wage work that men perform in migrant destinations with the army service that most have also fulfilled—both experiences involve hierarchical, disciplinary arrangements and the frequent requirement that men at the bottom remain "silent."

Galicians and other migrant workers from the poorest regions of southern and eastern Europe have good cause to draw a sharp contrast between experiences of wage work and working on their own land, for they have often performed the most menial labor in countries such as Switzerland and Germany. Like other worker-peasants, they have tended to "accept wages and working conditions that others, that is, urban laborers, are loath to accept" (Holmes and Quataert 1986:194). This case confirms the argument that peasant production, housework, the "informal" economy, and other forms of unwaged or unregulated labor have been and continue to be structural, rather than conjunctural, features of capitalism. It should not be surprising to discover, therefore, that individuals who experience the economy as mixed (Fernandez 1986:119) develop a class consciousness based on contrasts between the different relationships they have to the means and distribution of production as well as to different modes of consumption—both commoditized and non-commoditized.

THE PEASANT WOMAN

Teresa was born in a rural parish, but raised in a city orphanage after losing both her parents. Although she had maintained ties with her godfather's home in the countryside, she did not feel comfortable performing many rural household chores when she came to Carreira as a young bride. She had to ask a male neighbor known for his slaughtering skills the best way to kill, clean, and butcher chickens and rabbits shortly after her marriage. By the time I met Teresa, she was accepted as a fully integrated member of the village who was knowledgeable about many aspects of subsistence agriculture and animal husbandry.

It would have been very difficult for Teresa to have resisted the social pressures to participate in the activities that dominate the village subsistence economy and culturally define sociality in Carreira. The same is true of returned female migrants. Women who are not seen working outside (in the fields and gardens) are either suspected of being lazy or open to suspicions of witchcraft or adultery. Like other women in the community, Teresa won acceptance through her dedication to "peasant" work, for being a "strong woman" (*muller forte*), and for the caring labor she performs for her children, her husband, her husband's father, and other relatives. She joined her neighbors in making sarcastic comments about the "fine" ladies of the city and nearby towns who are said to spend their days dusting and attending meetings of the local housewives' association.

One of the rhetorical strategies that people use to highlight the positive value of the subsistence production that "peasant" women in the village undertake is to contrast this work with indoor housework. Women who do not have much land in production, livestock, young children, or wage work are defined as not having anything to do. The category of "housewives" (*amas de casa*) is used for the wives (or daughters) of men with substantial incomes and they are said to appear to "have cash" all the time (*ten cartos*) rather than the financial worries and necessity to be frugal that characterize the lives of most people in Carreira. One of the key ways that such "fine ladies" spend money is in purchasing services and commodities that symbolize their families' class position and their own role. Houses are kept clean and are decorated with new furniture and other items. Women who live in rural communities but do not cultivate their fields or care for animals can wear daily the short skirts, high heels, makeup, and gold jewelry that, since the late 1970s, have signaled respectable femininity throughout Spain and other areas in southern Europe (Collier 1986). This layer of clothing and accessories is only the outer layer of other bodily differences between agriculturalist and non-agriculturalist women. The latter are described by women in Carreira as having smooth, white skin on their hands, faces, and necks; unbroken, painted fingernails; precisely cut, curled, and colored hair; shaved legs and underarms; and thin, nonmuscular arms, legs, and hips that are a result of little exercise and careful dieting. The majority of women in

Carreira, in contrast, have the hands and musculature of individuals who perform manual work; sunburned faces, necks, and forearms during the summer months; and other physical features that mark them as being women who labor outside in all kinds of weather, work in the earth, and take care of livestock.

In addition, most Carreira women over 45 years of age dress as "strong" peasant women, wearing the dark stockings, kerchiefs, long skirts and aprons, and wooden-soled shoes that Concepción is described as having had on in my opening vignette. Her granddaughter María, I have noted, was dressed in more up-to-date clothes; and it seems to me that her generation of women will be the ones to partially transform the image of "peasant woman" that is perpetuated not simply by women such as Concepción but also on postcards and other public images of Galicia sold as commodities in the cities (Roseman and Fife 1995). However, María's outfit—particularly her stained baggy sweatpants, old-fashioned body apron, and head kerchief—was not that different from Concepción's in the sense that it marked her as a manual worker rather than an urbanized housewife. It is a matter of pride to Concepción, Teresa, and other women in Carreira to do several hours of "outside" work prior to undertaking tasks such as making beds, airing bedrooms, and washing breakfast dishes.

Encarnación—the wife of one of the most successful small businessmen in surrounding villages—dressed in a manner similar to María whenever she appeared in public view in the village lanes. She continued to produce some garden and fodder crops; she also maintained a flock of hens, chickens, and other fowl. Encarnación regularly stopped in the center of the village on her way to and from her fields with a wheelbarrow piled high with produce that she had harvested. She was always "dressed for work" and engaged her financially less well-off neighbors in discussions about the weather, the state of her crops and fowl, and other topics related to subsistence production. However, despite the significance of public certifications of such provisioning work, women from Carreira frequently and adeptly "code switch" between being sturdy "peasant producers" and well-dressed "modern consumers."

"PRETTY GIRLS"

Married women like Teresa and Encarnación would dress carefully in polished shoes, knee-length dresses, and cardigans or suits when they visited cities or attended weddings. The young, unmarried women in María's generation went out to *discotecas* in nearby towns where most rural young people meet their future spouses. The hour before neighbors would convene to organize carpools to drive to these towns, they would bathe, fix their hair and makeup, and dress up in the short skirts or tight pants, high-heeled shoes, costume jewelry, and other consumer items that defined feminine beauty in Galicia in the 1990s and early 21st century. As in other countries, this ideal is promoted persuasively in magazine advertisements and articles, in television advertising and programming, and by the example of women in the hegemonic classes. As in past historical periods, even though women dress for *traballo* (work) most of the time, they are equally interested in dressing appropriately for *festas* (celebrations).

Another context in which villagers' self-possessed adoption of clothing and bodily styles considered to be *de moda* (of the latest style) becomes evident is the evening dances held in villages during patron saint and other *festas*. The live bands that play at these dances play a mix of musical styles, including the requisite *muiñeiras* (a Galician folkdance), classical waltzes, and the most recent dance music played in the discotheques. These bands include groups of up to six male musicians and singers, and young and attractive female dancers and singers in revealing outfits who dance in a sexually explicit manner and are a key part of a band's overall spectacle. Band members explicitly encourage those young people attending the dance to imitate the movements and gestures of the female dancers. There is a convergence in clothing and dance styles between the scenes at "modern" discotheques and those played out during these outdoor parish *festa* dances. Young women such as María might dance in a practiced way through the night at either of these venues dressed in short skirts and high heels but may, in an equally practiced way, head out the next day in rubber boots and aprons to hoe their elder relatives' potato fields.

Carreira provides an example of a rural locale in which women from both the older and the younger generational age cohorts are involved in the social production of emerging class identities that are openly resistive to the path toward the full commoditization of family livelihood and flexible enough to allow for both effective stylistic code switching and some degree of ambivalence on the part of participants. Young village women have mixed feelings about whether they wish to continue to live in Carreira and labor as subsistence producers. At times, María told me that she did not want to live the life of "servitude" of her grandmother and mother and that she preferred indoor housework to work in the fields. Moreover, she had attended university in pursuit of gaining entrance to a teaching position. However, María always stopped short in her criticisms of subsistence work, linking the "servitude" mainly to keeping cows rather than to growing crops. She was reluctant to criticize fully the lives of her parents and grandmother. Like others from villages, during her university years María returned to Carreira almost every weekend, socialized more with young people from her home area than with unknown cohorts from her university classes, made a point of downplaying her status as a student when at home, and subsisted in the apartment she shared in the city largely on the food products her grandmother and mother gave her. She told me that she could not bear to eat the poor-quality potatoes and meat available in the grocery stores. She continued to be firmly linked to the village as a result of her material and emotional attachment to non-commoditized provisioning practices and social ties,

expressed through her practices of linguistic and identity code switching.

Young women, like their older relatives, distinguished between activities that require steady, physical labor and the festive, leisure occasions when it is appropriate—especially for young, unmarried people—to dress up. Being able to purchase appropriate "pretty," "feminine" clothing depends on frugal spending patterns and subsistence production; participation in the consumption of femininity does not necessarily negate a continuing adherence to a "peasant" work role and self-provisioning activities.

CONSPICUOUS PRODUCTION: RESISTING FULLY COMMODITIZED CONSUMPTION

The blood-splattered sheets in Concepción's *salón* reminded me of Aihwa Ong's (1987, 1990) account of possession trances among alienated young Malaysian women working in multinational factories. *Bombohs* or religious specialists called in to ritually cleanse the factories use the blood of slaughtered chickens, producing images of chaos that contrast sharply with the normally "gleaming, sanitized world of multinational firms" (1990: 419). While these experiences of spirit possession cause the tools of capitalist production to be splattered with the blood of chickens, Concepción and María splattered capitalist commodities like factory-produced furniture with the blood of pigs that they raised. I had become used to seeing Galician rural women working with dead animals in their yards, sheds, and kitchens. However, I had rarely seen any productive activities taking place in the shrine-like *salóns* owned by only some families and used only for festive occasions and for the display of consumer items purchased with limited disposable income. Concepción and María were employing the "strong women" code in one of the few household spaces that is used normally to display "pretty girl" identities, their behavior serving to de-emphasize their status within a particular class segment by literally asserting the preeminence of subsistence production over conspicuous consumption.

Concepción was very proud of her ability to have a well-decorated *salón* and a granddaughter attending university, achievements that distinguished her from less well-off neighbors; at the same time, she and her daughter-in-law Susana insisted that, rather than always studying, María help with housework and subsistence production while she was home. As I describe above, María went to university because she aspired to supersede what she sometimes phrased as her mother and grandmother's "slavery" to the livestock and the land, but at the same time she remained emotionally and financially tied to her natal household and continued to assist her female elders with self-provisioning work whenever she was home.

This case demonstrates the importance of looking at the social relations of wage employment as well as provisioning strategies broadly when analyzing the bases for individuals' class consciousness and their daily expressions of gender and class identity. In Carreira, women resist full proletarianization partly by pursuing the provisioning activities that suit a mixed livelihood and partly by taking full ideological advantage of the status that they gain as contributors to the family's subsistence production and other nonwage labor requirements.

Women from Carreira who self-consciously "code switch" between "peasant" and "non-peasant" demeanors, or from *mulleres fortes* (strong women) into *chicas guapas* (pretty girls), do so through a variable consumption of commoditized and noncommoditized products. Their partial resistance to the superfluous consumption of "modern" food, household products, and clothing seems more radical than their notions of labor. However, in the end both consist of a necessary accommodation to global capitalism's "need" for "flexible" labor.

CONCLUSION

I have argued that members of a population of semi-proletarianized migrant laborers with a permanent tie to a village in northwestern Spain have collectively crafted a regularly enacted gender and class identity that is, in part, based on a public recognition of the value of women's unpaid provisioning labor. The "revelatory incident" (after Fernandez 1986:xi) with which I begin the article also points to these villagers' expressions of resistance to widespread commodity fetishism.[4]

Most worker-peasants from Carreira have never had job security or worked in one place long enough to affiliate strongly with labor unions or other forms of organization (Safa 1980). These men and women do, however, have firm ideas about their labor: what it is worth, when it is alienated from them, and when they can control it. And their class identity intersects with notions of a gendered self as it emerges out of the context of a multiple livelihood strategy that involves the pursuit of wage labor locally and in migrant destinations as well as the practice of subsistence production. There is a link between these rural Europeans' continuing commitment to subsistence production and their experiences of mainly insecure and fluctuating wage employment.

I have used the example of Carreira to talk about the importance of analyses of cultural expressions of class and gender identity that take into account the social relations of provisioning strategies. This article demonstrates that, because subsistence production is the crux of the alternative positioning of these Galician worker-peasants and is largely performed by women, it has resulted in men defining their own class identities at least partly through women's unpaid labor. This situation is the opposite of the more common case in which heterosexual married women's unwaged "domestic" labor is ideologically characterized by both men and women as "natural" and their class position is presumed to be tied directly to the occupations of their husbands, even if they also earn some cash wages.

Women living in Carreira designate their subsistence production as contributing more to households than the housework performed by other women who do not own agricultural land or have paid employment, just as men compare the different types of work they perform (both waged and unwaged) and often contrast themselves with other wage workers who have no access to land. Rather than having developed a gender consciousness whereby, as Safa puts it, "women recognize that they [as a group of laborers] are exploited and oppressed" (1980:71), women in Carreira who assert the value of the work they do in producing food may also denigrate the "clean" work of urban housewives and other women. Nor do they fully question why they, rather than men, are the ones who often sacrifice wage employment opportunities to maintain subsistence production. Furthermore, both women and men ultimately reinforce their designation within global capitalism as "flexible" laborers. Although they criticize the conditions of wage labor they experience abroad, by maintaining subsistence production, families allow themselves to continue to accept inadequate and insecure wage contracts.

The alternative class and gender identities expressed by women and men in Carreira and similar communities are, however, fragile. If more young women either leave Carreira permanently or cease to be engaged in unpaid subsistence production, the capacity for sustaining a mixed economy will be weakened. Under such circumstances, men's class identity of being semi-proletarianized producers and consumers might collapse as quickly as their valorization of women's non-wage provisioning labor would.

REFERENCES CITED

Butler, Judith. 1989. Gender Trouble: Feminism and the Subversion of Identity. New York: Routledge.

Collier, Jane. 1986. From Mary to Modern Woman. American Ethnologist 13(1):100–107.

Coupland, Nikolas. 1980. Style-Shifting in a Cardiff Work-Setting. Language in Society 9(1): 1–12.

Fernandez, James W. 1986. Persuasions and Performances: The Play of Tropes in Culture. Bloomington: Indiana University Press.

Holmes, Douglas R., and Jean Quataert. 1986. An Approach to Modern Labor: Worker Peasantries in Historic Saxony and the Friuli Region over Three Centuries. Comparative Studies in Society and History 28:191–216.

Moore, Henrietta. 1994. A Passion for Difference: Essays in Anthropology and Gender. Bloomington: Indiana University Press.

Ong, Aihwa. 1987. Spirits of Resistance and Capitalist Discipline: Factory Women in Malaysia. New York: State University of New York Press.

———. 1990. Japanese Factories, Malay Workers: Class and Sexual Metaphors in West Malaysia. In Power and Difference: Gender in Island Southeast Asia. Jane Manning Atkinson and Shelly Errington, eds. Pp. 385–422. Stanford: Stanford University Press.

Roseman, Sharon R. 1995. Falamos como Falamos: Linguistic Revitalization and the Maintenance of Local Vernaculars in Rural Galicia. Journal of Linguistic Anthropology 5(1):3–32.

———. 1997. "Lenguas de solidaridad" en el medio rural: El mantenimiento del gallego vernáculo. In As linguas e as identidades: Ensaios de etnografía e de interpretación antropolóxica. Xaquín Rodríguez Campos, ed. Pp. 105–122. Santiago de Compostela, Spain: Universidade de Santiago de Compostela.

Roseman, Sharon R., and Wayne Fife. 1995. Images of Peasants in Galician Public Culture. Paper presented at the Annual Meeting of the Northeastern Anthropological Association, Lake Placid, NY, April 2–5.

Safa, Helen Icken. 1980. Class Consciousness among Working-Class Women in Latin America: Puerto Rico. In Sex and Class in Latin America: Women's Perspectives on Politics, Economics, and the Family in the Third World. June Nash and Helen Icken Safa, eds. Pp. 69–85. New York: J. F. Bergin Publishers.

Scotton, Carol Myers. 1979. Codeswitching as a "Safe Choice" in Choosing a Lingua Franca. In Language and Society: Anthropological Issues. William C. McCormack and Stephen A. Wurm, eds. Pp. 71–87. The Hague: Mouton.

Taussig, Michael. 1980. The Devil and Commodity Fetishism. Chapel Hill: University of North Carolina Press.

NOTES

1. Fieldwork for this article was conducted during eight field trips between 1989 and 2000. Inhabitants of Carreira speak both Galician and Castilian (Spanish) (Roseman 1997).

2. Because the second floor of Galician rural houses is a private space, visiting takes place mainly on the bottom floor; acquaintances and even close friends are rarely invited upstairs.

3. Unlike the case of other families in Spain and other parts of Western Europe, their task of providing pork for the winter months did not involve the knowledge, currency, time, and transportation required to purchase meat in a grocery store or butcher's shop. However, I do not mean to imply that Concepción, María, and other women from Carreira did not have to employ these types of resources in other instances. Indeed, the ability to "shop well"—whether that be in the regional rural fairs, in the shops in nearby towns, or in the large shopping centers and grocery stores that had at the time of fieldwork been built recently in Galician cities—is a long-standing and highly valued capacity among rural Galicians. Furthermore, it is women who are said to be more frugal than men, and being frugal is regarded to be an important contribution to a household's economic survival.

4. See Taussig 1980.

1 • *Chandra Talpade Mohanty*

UNDER WESTERN EYES
Feminist Scholarship and Colonial Discourses

DISCUSSION QUESTIONS

1. What are the five ways that "Third World Women" as a category of analysis are used in Western feminist discourse?
2. What are the problems with these Western feminist representations of "Third World Women" in terms of both their "explanatory potential" and their "political effects"?
3. How and why is the production and circulation of such representations a form of power?

It ought to be of some political significance at least that the term "colonization" has come to denote a variety of phenomena in recent feminist and left writings in general. From its analytic value as a category of exploitative economic exchange in both traditional and contemporary Marxisms, to its use by feminist women of color in the U.S. to describe the appropriation of their experiences and struggles by hegemonic white women's movements, colonization has been used to characterize everything from the most evident economic and political hierarchies to the production of a particular cultural discourse about what is called the "Third World."[1] However sophisticated or problematical its use as an explanatory construct, colonization almost invariably implies a relation of structural domination, and a suppression—often violent—of the heterogeneity of the subject(s) in question. What I wish to analyze is specifically the production of the "Third World Woman" as a singular monolithic subject in some recent (Western) feminist texts. The definition of colonization I wish to invoke here is a predominantly *discursive* one, focusing on a certain mode of appropriation and codification of "scholarship" and "knowledge" about women in the third world by particular analytic categories employed in specific writings on the subject which take as their referent feminist interests as they have been articulated in the U.S. and Western Europe.

My concern about such writings derives from my own implication and investment in contemporary debates in feminist theory, and the urgent political necessity (especially in the age of Reagan) of forming strategic coalitions across class, race, and national boundaries. Clearly Western feminist discourse and political practice is neither singular nor homogeneous in its goals, interests or analyses. However, it is possible to trace a coherence of *effects* resulting from the implicit assumption of "the West" (in all its complexities and contradictions) as the primary referent in theory and praxis. My reference to "Western feminism" is by no means intended to imply that it is a monolith. Rather, I am attempting to draw attention to the similar effects of various textual strategies used by particular writers that codify Others as non-Western and hence themselves as (implicitly) Western. It is in this sense that I use the term "Western feminist." The analytic principles discussed below serve to distort Western feminist political practices, and limit the possibility of coalitions among (usually White) Western feminists and working class and feminists of color around the world. These limitations are evident in the construction of the (implicitly consensual) priority of issues around which apparently *all* women are expected to organize. Feminist scholarly practices (whether reading, writing, critical or textual) are inscribed in relations of power—relations which they counter, resist, or even perhaps implicitly support. There can, of course, be no apolitical scholarship.

The relationship between "Woman"—a cultural and ideological composite Other constructed through diverse representational discourses (scientific, literary, juridical, linguistic, cinematic, etc.)—and "women"—real, material subjects of their collective histories—is one of the central questions the practice of feminist scholarship seeks to address. I would like to suggest that the feminist writings I analyze here discursively colonize the material and historical heterogeneities of the lives of women in the third world, thereby producing/re-presenting a composite, singular "Third World Woman"—an image which appears arbitrarily constructed, but nevertheless carries with it the authorizing signature of Western humanist discourse. I argue that assumptions of privilege and ethnocentric universality on the one hand, and inadequate self-consciousness about the effect of Western scholarship on the "third world" in the context of a world system dominated by the West on the other, characterize a sizable extent of Western feminist work on women in the third world. An analysis of "sexual difference" in the form of a cross-culturally singular, monolithic notion of patriarchy or male dominance leads to the construction of a similarly reductive and homogeneous notion of what I call the "Third World Difference"—that stable, ahistorical something that apparently oppresses most if not all the women in these countries. And it is in the production of this "Third World Difference" that Western feminisms appropriate and "colonize" the fundamental complexities and conflicts which characterize the lives of women of different classes, religions, cultures, races and castes in these countries. It is in this process of homogenization and systematization of the oppression of women in the third world that power is exercised in much of recent Western feminist discourse, and this power needs to be defined and named.

It is both to the *explanatory potential* of particular analytic strategies employed by such writing, and to their *political effect* in the context of the hegemony of Western scholarship, that I want to draw attention here. While feminist writing in the U.S. is still marginalized (except from the point of view of women of color addressing privileged White women), Western feminist writing on women in the third world must be considered in the context of the global hegemony of Western scholarship—i.e., the production, publication, distribution and consumption of information and ideas. Marginal or not, this writing has political effects and implications beyond the immediate feminist or disciplinary audience. One such significant effect of the dominant "representations" of Western feminism is its conflation with imperialism in the eyes of particular third world women.[2] Hence the urgent need to examine the *political* implications of *analytic* strategies and principles.

My critique is directed at three basic analytic principles which are present in (Western) feminist discourse on women in the third world. Since I focus primarily on the Zed Press "Women in the Third World" series, my comments on Western feminist discourse are circumscribed by my analysis of the texts in this series.[3] This is a way of limiting and focusing my critique. However, even though I am dealing with feminists who identify themselves as culturally or geographically from the "West," what I say about these analytic strategies or implicit principles holds for anyone who uses these methods, whether third world women in the West, or third world women in the third world writing on these issues and publishing in the West. As a matter of fact, my argument holds for any discourse that sets up its own authorial subjects as the implicit referent, i.e., the yardstick by which to encode and represent cultural Others. It is in this move that power is exercised in discourse.

The first principle I focus on concerns the strategic location or situation of the category "women" vis-à-vis the context of analysis. The assumption of women as an already constituted, coherent group with identical interests and desires, regardless of class, ethnic or racial location or contradictions, implies a notion of gender or sexual difference or even patriarchy (as male dominance—men as a correspondingly coherent group) which can be applied universally and cross-culturally. The second principle consists in the uncritical use of particular methodologies in providing "proof" of universality and cross-cultural validity. The third is a more specifically political principle underlying the methodologies and the analytic strategies, i.e., the model of power and struggle they imply and suggest. I argue that as a result of the two modes—or, rather, frames—of analysis described above, a homogeneous notion of the oppression of women as a group is assumed, which, in turn, produces the image of an "average third world woman." This average third world woman leads an essentially truncated life based on her feminine gender (read: sexually constrained) and being "third world" (read: ignorant, poor, uneducated, tradition-bound, domestic,

family-oriented, victimized, etc.). This, I suggest, is in contrast to the (implicit) self-representation of Western women as educated, modern, as having control over their own bodies and sexualities, and the freedom to make their own decisions.

"WOMEN" AS CATEGORY OF ANALYSIS, OR: WE ARE ALL SISTERS IN STRUGGLE

By women as a category of analysis, I am referring to the critical assumption that all of us of the same gender, across classes and cultures, are somehow socially constituted as a homogeneous group identified prior to the process of analysis. What binds women together is a sociological notion of the "sameness" of their oppression. It is at this point that an elision takes place between "women" as a discursively constructed group and "women" as material subjects of their own history. Thus, the discursively consensual homogeneity of "women" as a group is mistaken for the historically specific material reality of groups of women. This results in an assumption of women as an always-already constituted group, one which has been labelled "powerless," "exploited," "sexually harassed," etc., by feminist scientific, economic, legal and sociological discourses. (Notice that this is quite similar to sexist discourse labeling women weak, emotional, having math anxiety, etc.) The focus is not on uncovering the material and ideological specificities that constitute a particular group of women as "powerless" in a particular context. It is rather on finding a variety of cases of "powerless" groups of women to prove the general point that women as a group are powerless.

In this section I focus on five specific ways in which "women" as a category of analysis is used in Western feminist discourse on women in the third world.[4] Each of these examples illustrates the construction of "Third World Women" as a homogeneous "powerless" group often located as implicit *victims* of particular socio-economic systems. The authors I deal with write with varying degrees of care and complexity. However, the *effect* of the representation of third world women in these texts is coherent and systematic, due to the use of "women" as a homogeneous category of analysis, and it is this effect I focus on. In these texts women are defined as victims of male violence (Fran Hosken); victims of the colonial process (M. Cutrufelli); victims of the Arab familial system (Juliette Minces); victims of the economic development process (B. Lindsay and the [liberal] WID School); and finally, victims of *the* Islamic code (P. Jeffery). This mode of defining women primarily in terms of their *object status* (the way in which they are affected or not affected by certain institutions and systems) is what characterizes this particular form of the use of "women" as a category of analysis. In the context of Western women writing/studying women in the third world, such objectification (however benevolently motivated) needs to be both named and challenged. As Valerie Amos and Pratibha Parmar argue quite eloquently in a recent essay, "Feminist theories which examine our cultural practices as 'feudal residues' or label us 'traditional,' also portray us as politically immature women who need to be versed and schooled in the ethos of Western Feminism. They need to be continually challenged."[5]

Women as Victims of Male Violence

Fran Hosken,[6] in writing about the relationship between human rights and female genital mutilation in Africa and the Middle East, bases her discussion/condemnation of genital mutilation on one privileged premise: the goal of genital mutilation is "to mutilate the sexual pleasure and satisfaction of woman" ("FGM," p. 11). This, in turn, leads her to claim that women's sexuality is controlled, as is their reproductive potential. According to Hosken, "male sexual politics" in Africa and around the world "share the same political goal: to assure female dependence and subservience by any and all means" ("FGM," p. 14). Physical violence against women (rape, sexual assault, excision, infibulation, etc.) is thus carried out "with an astonishing consensus among men in the world" ("FGM," p. 14). Here, women are defined consistently as the *victims* of male control—the "sexually oppressed." Although it is true that the potential of male violence against women circumscribes and elucidates their social position to a certain extent, defining women as archetypal victims freezes them into "objects-who-defend themselves," men into "subjects-who-perpetrate-violence," and (every) society into powerless (read: women) and powerful (read: men) groups of people. Male violence must be theorized and interpreted *within* specific societies, both in order to understand it better, as well as in order to effectively organize to change it. Sisterhood cannot be assumed on the basis of gender; it must be forged in concrete, historical and political practice and analysis.

Women as Universal Dependents

Beverly Lindsay's conclusion to the book *Comparative Perspectives of Third World Women: The Impact of Race, Sex and Class* states: ". . . dependency relationships, based upon race, sex and class, are being perpetrated through social, educational, and economic institutions. These are the linkages among Third World Women."[7] Here, as in other places, Lindsay implies that third world women constitute an identifiable group purely on the basis of shared dependencies. If shared dependencies were all that was needed to bind us together as a group, third world women would always be seen as an apolitical group with no subject status! Instead, if anything, it is the common context of political struggle against class, race, gender and imperialist hierarchies that may constitute third world women as a strategic group at this historical juncture. Similarly, examine statements like: "My analysis will start by stating that all African women are politically and economically dependent."[8] Or: "Nevertheless, either overtly or covertly, prostitution is still the main if not the only source of work for African women."[9] *All* African women are dependent. Prostitution is the only work option for African women as a *group.* Both statements are illustrative of generalizations sprinkled liberally through a recent Zed

Press publication, *Women of Africa: Roots of Oppression*, by Maria Rosa Cutrufelli. What is it about cultural Others that make it so easy to analytically formulate them into homogeneous groupings with little regard for historical specificities? Again, I am not objecting to the use of universal groupings for descriptive purposes. Women from the continent of Africa *can* be descriptively characterized as "Women of Africa." It is when "women of Africa" becomes a homogeneous sociological grouping characterized by common dependencies or powerlessness (or even strengths) that problems arise.

Descriptive gender differences are transformed into the division between men and women. Women are constituted as a group via dependency relationships vis-a-vis men, who are implicitly held responsible for these relationships. When "women of Africa" as a group (versus "men of Africa" as a group?) are seen as a group precisely because they are generally dependent and oppressed, the analysis of specific historical differences becomes impossible, because reality is always apparently structured by divisions—two mutually exclusive and jointly exhaustive groups, the victims and the oppressors. Here the sociological is substituted for the biological in order, however, to create the same—a unity of women. Thus, it is not the descriptive potential of gender difference, but the privileged positioning and explanatory potential of gender difference as the *origin* of oppression that I question. The problem with this analytic strategy is that it assumes men and women are already constituted as sexual-political subjects *prior* to their entry into the arena of social relations. Only if we subscribe to this assumption is it possible to undertake analysis which looks at the "effects" of kinship structures, colonialism, organization of labor, etc., on women, who are already defined as a group apparently because of shared dependencies, but ultimately because of their gender. But women are *produced through these very relations* as well as being implicated in forming these relations. For example, that women mother in a variety of societies is not as significant as the *value* attached to mothering in these societies. The distinction between the act of mothering and the status attached to it is a very important one—one that needs to be made and analyzed contextually.

Married Women as Victims of the Colonial Process

Another troubling example occurs when in discussing the marriage ritual of the Bemba, a Zambian matrilocal, matrilineal people, Cutrufelli in *Women of Africa* focuses on the *fact* of the marital exchange of women before and after Western colonization, rather than the *value* attached to the exchange in this particular context. This leads to her definition of Bemba women as a coherent group affected in a particular way by colonization. Cutrufelli asserts that *the effect of European colonization has changed this whole marriage system*. However, it is not possible to talk about Bemba women as a homogeneous group within the traditional marriage structure. Bemba women *before* the initiation are constituted within a different set of social relations compared to Bemba women *after* the initiation. To treat them as a unified group characterized by the fact of their "exchange" between male kin, is to deny the sociohistorical and cultural specificities of their existence, and the differential *value* attached to their exchange before and after their initiation.

Women and Familial Systems

It is *in* the family, as an effect of kinship structures, that women as women are constructed, defined within and by the group. Thus, for instance, when Juliette Minces (Zed Press, 1980)[10] cites *the* patriarchal family as the basis for "an almost identical vision of women" that *Arab* and *Muslim* societies have, she falls into this very trap. Not only is it problematical to speak of a vision of women shared by Arab and Muslim societies without addressing the particular historical, material and ideological power structures that construct such images, but to speak of *the* patriarchal family or *the* tribal kinship structure as the *origin* of the socio-economic status of women is to again assume that women are sexual-political subjects prior to their entry into the family. So while on the one hand women attain value or status *within* the family, the assumption of a singular patriarchal kinship system (common to all Arab and Muslim societies) is what apparently structures women as an oppressed group in these societies! This singular, coherent kinship system presumably influences another separate and given entity, "women." Thus, all women, regardless of class and cultural differences, are affected by this system. Not only are *all* Arab and Muslim women seen to constitute a homogeneous oppressed group, but there is no discussion of the specific practices within the family which constitute women as mothers, wives, sisters, etc. Arabs and Muslims it appears, don't change at all. Their patriarchal family is carried over from the times of the prophet Mohammed. They exist, as it were, "outside history."

Women and Religious Ideologies

A further example of the use of "women" as a category of analysis is found in cross-cultural analyses which subscribe to a certain economic reductionism in describing the relationship between the economy and factors such as politics and ideology. Here, in reducing the level of comparison to the economic relations between "developed and developing" countries, any specificity to the question of women is denied. Mina Moderes, in a careful analysis of women and Shi'ism in Iran, focuses on this very problem when she criticizes feminist writings which treat Islam as an ideology separate from and outside social relations and practices, rather than a discourse which *includes* rules for economic, social and power relations within society.[11] Patricia Jeffery's otherwise excellent work on Pirzada women in purdah (Zed Press, 1979)[12] considers Islamic ideology as a partial explanation for the status of women in that it provides a justification for the purdah. Here, Islamic ideology is reduced to a set of ideas whose internalization by Pirzada women contributes to the stability of the system. However, the primary explanation for purdah is located in the control that Pirzada men have over economic

resources, and the personal security purdah gives to Pirzada women. By taking a specific version of Islam as *the* Islam, Jeffrey attributes a singularity and coherence to it.

Women and the Development Process

The best examples of universalization on the basis of economic reductionism can be found in the liberal "Women in Development" literature. Proponents of this school seek to examine the effect of development on third world women, sometimes from feminist perspectives. At the very least, there is an evident interest in and commitment to improving the lives of women in "developing" countries. Cross-cultural comparison between women in different "developing" countries is made both possible and unproblematical by this assumption of women as a group affected (or not affected) by economic policies. For instance, Perdita Huston states that the purpose of her study is to describe the effect of the development process on the "family unit and its individual members" in Egypt, Kenya, Sudan, Tunisia, Sri Lanka and Mexico. She states that the "problems" and "needs" expressed by rural and urban women in these countries all center around education and training, work and wages, access to health and other services, political participation and legal rights. Huston relates all these "needs" to the lack of sensitive development policies which exclude women as a group or category. For her, the solution is simple: improved development policies which emphasize training for *women* field workers, use *women* trainees, *women* rural development officers, encourage *women's* cooperatives, etc. Here, again, women are assumed to be a coherent group or category prior to their entry into "the development process." Huston assumes that all third world women have similar problems and needs. Thus, they must have similar interests and goals. However, the interests of urban, middle-class, educated Egyptian housewives, to take only one instance, could surely not be seen as being the same as those of their uneducated, poor maids. Development policies do not affect both groups of women in the same way. Practices which characterize women's status and roles vary according to class. Women are constituted as women through the complex interaction between class, culture, religion and other ideological institutions and frameworks. They are not "women"—a coherent group—solely on the basis of a particular economic system or policy. Such reductive cross-cultural comparisons result in the colonization of the conflicts and contradictions which characterize women of different social classes and cultures.

What is problematical, then, about this kind of use of "women" as a group, as a stable category of analysis, is that it assumes an ahistorical, universal unity between women based on a generalized notion of their subordination. Instead of analytically demonstrating the production of women as socio-economic political groups *within* particular local contexts, this move limits the definition of the female subject to gender identity, completely bypassing social class and ethnic identities. What characterizes women as a group is their gender (sociologically not necessarily biologically defined) over and above everything else, indicating a monolithic notion of sexual difference. Because women are thus constituted as a coherent group, sexual difference becomes coterminous with female subordination, and power is automatically defined in binary terms: people who have it (read: men), and people who do not (read: women). Men exploit, women are exploited. As suggested above, such simplistic formulations are both reductive and ineffectual in designing strategies to combat oppressions. All they do is reinforce binary divisions between men and women.

What would an analysis which did not do this look like? Maria Mies's work is one such example which illustrates the strength of Western feminist work on women in the third world and which does not fall into the traps discussed above. Maria Mies's study of the lace-makers of Narsapur, India (Zed Press, 1982),[13] attempts to carefully analyze a substantial household industry in which "housewives" produce lace doylies for consumption in the world market. Through a detailed analysis of the structure of the lace industry, production and reproduction relations, the sexual division of labor, profits and exploitation, and the overall consequences of defining women as "non-working housewives" and their work as "leisure-time activity," Mies demonstrates the levels of exploitation in this industry and the impact of this production system on the work and living conditions of the women involved in it. In addition, she is able to analyze the "ideology of the housewife," the notion of a woman sitting in the house, as providing the necessary subjective and socio-cultural element for the creation and maintenance of a production system that contributes to the increasing pauperization of women, and keeps them totally atomized and disorganized as workers. This is a good example of what careful, politically focused, local analyses can accomplish. It illustrates how the category of women is constructed in a variety of political contexts that often exists simultaneously and overlaid on the top of one another. There is no easy generalization in the direction of "women" in India, or "women in the third world"; nor is there a reduction of the political construction of the exploitation of the lacemakers to cultural explanations about the passivity or obedience that might characterize these women and their situation. Finally, this mode of local, political analysis which generates theoretical categories from *within* the situation and context being analyzed, also suggests corresponding effective strategies for organizing against the exploitations faced by the lace makers. These Narsapur women are not mere victims of the production process, because they resist, challenge and subvert the process at various junctures. Here is one instance of how Mies delineates the connections between the housewife ideology, the self-consciousness of the lace makers and their inter-relationships as contributing to the latent resistances she perceives among the women:

> The persistence of the housewife ideology, the self-perception of the lace makers as petty commodity producers rather than as workers, is not only upheld by the structure of the industry as such but also by the deliberate propagation and reinforcement of

reactionary patriarchal norms and institutions. Thus, most of the lace makers voiced the same opinion about the rules of *purdah* and seclusion in their communities which were also propagated by the lace exporters. In particular, the *Kapu* women said that they had never gone out of their houses, that women of their community could not do any other work than housework and lace work etc. But in spite of the fact that most of them still subscribed fully to the patriarchal norms of the *gosha* women, there were also contradictory elements in their consciousness. Thus, although they looked down with contempt upon women who were able to work outside the house— like the untouchable *Mala* and *Madiga* women or women of other lower castes, they could not ignore the fact that these women were earning more money precisely because they were *not* respectable housewives but workers. At one discussion, they even admitted that it would be better if they could also go out and do coolie work. And when they were asked whether they would be ready to come out of their houses and work in one place in some sort of a factory, they said they would do that. This shows that the *purdah* and housewife ideology, although still full internalized, already had some cracks, because it has been confronted with several contradictory realities.[14]

It is only by understanding the *contradictions* inherent in women's location within various structures that effective political action and challenges can be devised.

METHODOLOGICAL UNIVERSALISMS, OR: WOMEN'S OPPRESSION IS A GLOBAL PHENOMENON

Western feminist writings on women in the third world subscribe to a variety of methodologies to demonstrate the universal cross-cultural operation of male dominance and female exploitation. I summarize and critique three such methods below, moving from the most simple to the most complex methodologies.

First, proof of universalism is provided through the use of an arithmetic method. The argument goes like this: the more the number of women who wear the veil, the more universal is the sexual segregation and control of women.[15] Similarly, a large number of different, fragmented examples from a variety of countries also apparently add up to a universal fact. For instance, Muslim women in Saudi Arabia, Iran, Pakistan, India and Egypt all wear some sort of a veil. Hence, this indicates that the sexual control of women is a universal fact in those countries in which the women are veiled.[16] However, it is the analytic leap from the practice of veiling to an assertion of its general significance in controlling women that must be questioned. While there may be a physical similarity in the veils worn by women in Saudi Arabia and Iran, the specific meaning attached to this practice varies according to the cultural and ideological context. For example, as is well known, Iranian middle class women veiled themselves during the 1979 revolution to indicate solidarity with their veiled working class sisters, while in contemporary Iran, mandatory Islamic laws dictate that all Iranian women wear veils. While in both these instances, similar reasons might be offered for the veil (opposition to the Shah and Western cultural colonization in the first case, and the true Islamicization of Iran in the second), the concrete *meanings* attached to Iranian women wearing the veil are clearly different in both historical contexts. In the first case, wearing the veil is both an oppositional and revolutionary gesture on the part of Iranian middle class women; in the second case it is a coercive, institutional mandate.[17] Only through such context-specific differentiated analysis does feminist theorizing and practice acquire significance. It is on the basis *of* such analyses that effective political strategies can be generated. To assume that the mere practice of veiling women in a number of Muslim countries indicates the universal oppression of women through sexual segregation would not only be analytically and theoretically reductive, but also prove quite useless when it comes to political strategizing.

Second, concepts like reproduction, the sexual division of labor, the family, marriage, household, patriarchy, etc., are often used without their specification in local cultural and historical contexts. These concepts are used by feminists in providing explanations for women's subordination, apparently assuming their universal applicability. For instance, how is it possible to refer to "the" sexual division of labor when the *content* of this division changes radically from one environment to the next, and from one historical juncture to another? At its most abstract level, it is the fact of the differential assignation of tasks according to sex that is significant; however, this is quite different from the *meaning* or *value* that the content of this sexual division of labor assumes in different contexts. In most cases the assigning of tasks on the basis of sex has an ideological origin. Superficially similar situations may have radically different, historically specific explanations, and cannot be treated as identical. For instance, the rise of female-headed households in middle class America might be construed as greater independence and feminist progress, whereby women are considered to have *chosen* to be single parents (there are increasing numbers of lesbian mothers, etc.). However, the recent increase in female-headed households in Latin America where women might be seen to have more decision-making power, is concentrated among the poorest strata, where life choices are the most constrained economically.[18] Thus, while it is possible to state that there is a rise in female-headed households in the U.S. and in Latin America, this rise cannot be discussed as a universal indicator of women's independence, nor can it be discussed as a universal indicator of women's impoverishment. The *meaning* and *explanation* for the rise obviously varies according to the socio-historical context. Similarly, the existence of a sexual division of labor in most contexts cannot be sufficient explanation for the university subjugation of women in the work force. That the sexual division of labor does indicate a devaluation of women's work must be shown through analysis of particular local contexts. In addition, devaluation of *women* must also be shown through careful analysis. Concepts like the sexual division of labor can be useful only if they are generated through local, contextual analyses.[19] If such concepts are assumed to be universally applicable, the resultant homogenization of class, race, religious, cultural and historical specificities of the lives of women in the third world can create a false sense of the commonality of oppressions, interests and struggles between and amongst women globally. Beyond sisterhood there is still racism, colonialism and imperialism!

Finally, some writers confuse the use of gender as a superordinate category of organizing analysis with the universalistic proof and instantiation of this category. In other words, empirical studies of gender differences are confused with the analytical organization of cross-cultural work. Beverly Brown's review of the book *Nature, Culture and Gender*[20] best illustrates this point. Brown suggests that nature:culture::female:male are superordinate categories which organize and locate lesser categories (like wild/domestic and biology/technology) within their logic. These categories are universal in the sense that they organize the universe of a system of representations. This relation is totally independent of the universal substantiation of any particular category. Her critique hinges on the fact that rather than clarify the generalizability of nature:culture::female:male as superordinate organizational categories, *Nature, Culture and Gender,* the book, construes the universality of this equation to lie at the level of empirical truth, which can be investigated through field work. Thus, the usefulness of the nature:culture::female:male formulation as a universal mode of the organization of representation within any particular socio-historical system is lost. Here, methodological universalism is assumed on the basis of the reduction of the nature:culture::female:male analytic categories to a demand for empirical proof of its existence in different cultures. Discourses of representation are confused with material realities, and the distinction made earlier between "Woman" and "women" is lost.

THE SUBJECT(S) OF POWER

This last section returns to an earlier point about the inherently political nature of feminist scholarship, and attempts to clarify my point about the possibility of detecting a colonialist move in the case of a hegemonic first-third world connection in scholarship. Each text assumes "women" have a coherent group identity within the different cultures discussed, prior to their entry into social relations. Thus, Omvedt can talk about "Indian Women" while referring to a particular group of women in the State of Maharashtra, Cutrufelli about "Women of Africa" and Minces about "Arab women" as if these groups of women have some sort of obvious cultural coherence, distinct from men in these societies. The "status" or "position" of women is assumed to be self-evident, because women as an already constituted group are *placed* within religious, economic, familial and legal structures. However, this focus on the position of women whereby women are seen as a coherent group in *all* contexts, regardless of class or ethnicity, structures the world in ultimately binary, dichotomous terms, where women are always seen in opposition to men, patriarchy is always necessarily male dominance, and the religious, legal, economic and familial systems are implicitly assumed to be constructed by men. Thus, both men and women are always apparently constituted whole populations, and relations of dominance and exploitation are also posited in terms of whole peoples-wholes coming into exploitative relations. It is only when men and women are seen as different categories or groups possessing different *already constituted* categories of experience, cognition and interests as *groups*, that such a dichotomy is possible.

What does this imply about the structure and functioning of power relations? The setting up of the commonality of third world women's struggles across classes and cultures against a general notion of oppression (primarily the group in power—i.e., men) necessitates the assumption of what Michel Foucault calls the "juridico-discursive" model of power, the principle features of which are:

"a negative relation" (limit and lack); an "insistence on the rule" (which forms a binary system); a "cycle of prohibition"; the "logic of censorship"; and a "uniformity" of the apparatus functioning at different levels. Feminist discourse on the third world which assumes a homogeneous category—or group—called women necessarily operates through the setting up of originary power divisions. Power relations are structured in terms of a source of power and a cumulative reaction to power. Opposition is a generalized phenomenon created as a response to power—which, in turn, is possessed by certain groups of people. The major problem with such a definition of power is that it locks all revolutionary struggles into binary structures—possessing power versus being powerless. Women are powerless, unified groups. If the struggle for a just society is seen in terms of the move from powerless to powerful for women as a *group,* and this is the implication in feminist discourse which structures sexual difference in terms of the division between the sexes, then the new society would be structurally identical to the existing organization of power relations, constituting itself as a simple *inversion* of what exists. If relations of domination and exploitation are defined in terms of binary divisions—groups which dominate and groups which are dominated—surely the implication is that the accession to power of women as a group is sufficient to dismantle the existing organization of relations? But women as a group are *not* in some sense essentially superior or infallible.

What happens when this assumption of "women as an oppressed group" is situated in the context of Western feminist writing about third world women? It is here that I locate the colonialist move. By focusing on the representation of women in the third world, and what I referred to earlier as Western feminisms' self-presentation in the same context, it seems evident that Western feminists alone become the true "subjects" of this counter-history. Third world women, on the other hand, never rise above their generality and their "object" status. In other words, Western feminist discourse, by assuming women as a coherent, already constituted group which is placed in kinship, legal and other structures, defines third world women as subjects *outside* of social relations, instead of looking at the way women are constituted as women *through* these very structures. Legal, economic, religious, and familial structures are treated as phenomena to be judged by Western standards. It is here that ethnocentric universality comes into play. When these structures are defined as "underdeveloped" or "developing" and women are placed within these structures, an implicit image of the "average third world woman" is produced. This is the transformation of the (implicitly Western) "oppressed woman" into the "oppressed third world woman." While the category of "oppressed woman" is generated through an exclusive focus on gender difference, "the oppressed third world woman" category has an additional attribute—the "third world difference!" The "third world difference" includes a paternalistic attitude towards women in the third world. Since discussions of the various themes I identified earlier are conducted in the context of the relative "underdevelopment" of the third world, third world women as a group or category are automatically and necessarily defined as: religious (read "not progressive"), family-oriented (read "traditional"), legal minors (read "they-are-still-not-conscious-of-their-rights"), illiterate (read "ignorant"), domestic (read "backward") and sometimes revolutionary (read "their-country-is-in-a-state-of-war-they-must-fight!"). This is how the "third world difference" is produced. When the category of "sexually oppressed women" is located within particular systems in the third world which are defined on a scale which is normed through Eurocentric assumptions, not only are third world women defined in a particular way prior to their entry into social relations, but since no connections are made between first and third world power shifts, it reinforces the assumption that people in the third world just have not evolved to the extent that the West has. This mode of feminist analysis, by homogenizing and systematizing the experiences of different groups of women in these countries, erases all marginal and resistant modes of experiences. It limits theoretical analysis as well as reinforcing Western cultural imperialism. For in the context of a first/third world balance of power, feminist analyses which perpetrate and sustain the hegemony of the idea of the superiority of the West produce a corresponding set of universal images of the "third world woman," images like *the veiled woman, the powerful mother, the chaste virgin, the obedient wife,* etc. These images exist in universal, ahistorical splendor, setting in motion a colonialist discourse which exercises a very specific power in defining, coding and maintaining existing first/third world connections.

To conclude, then, let me suggest some disconcerting similarities between the typically authorizing signature of such Western feminist writings on women in the third world, and the authorizing signature of the project of humanism in general—humanism as a Western ideological and political project which involves the necessary recuperation of the "East" and "Woman" as Others. The focus of this work can be stated simply as an uncovering of the political *interests* that underlie the binary logic of humanistic discourse and ideology whereby, as a valuable recent essay puts it, "the first (majority) term (Identity, Universality, Culture, Disinterestedness, Truth, Sanity, Justice, etc.), which is, in fact, secondary and derivative (a construction), is privileged over and colonizes the second (minority) term (difference, temporality, anarchy, error, interestedness, insanity, deviance, etc.), which is in fact, primary and originative.[21] In other words, only in so far as "Woman/Women" and "the East" are defined as *Others,* or as *peripheral,* that (Western) Man/Humanism can represent him/itself as the center. It is not the center that determines the periphery, but the periphery that, in its boundedness, determines the center.

As discussed earlier, a comparison between Western feminist self-presentation and Western feminist re-presentation of women in the third world yields significant results. Universal images of "the third world woman" (the veiled woman, chaste virgin, etc.), images constructed from adding the "third world difference" to "sexual difference" are predicated upon (and hence obviously bring into sharper focus) assumptions about Western women as secular, liberated, and having control over their own lives. This is not to suggest that Western women *are* secular, liberated and have control over their own lives. I am referring to a *discursive* self-presentation, not necessarily to material reality. If this were a material reality there would be no need for political movements in the West—a ridiculous contention in these days of the imperialist adventures of Jerry Falwell and Indiana Jones! Similarly, only from the vantage point of the West is it possible to define the "third world" as underdeveloped and economically dependent. Without the overdetermined discourse that creates the *third* world, there would be no (singular and privileged) first world. Without the "third world woman," the particular self-presentation of Western women mentioned above would be problematical. I am suggesting then that the one enables and sustains the other. However, in the context of the hegemony of the Western scholarly establishment in the production and dissemination of texts, and in the context of the legitimating imperative of humanistic and scientific discourse, the definition of "the third world woman" as a monolith might well tie into the larger economic and ideological praxis of "disinterested" scientific inquiry and pluralism which are the surface manifestations of a latent economic and cultural colonization of the "non-Western" world. It is time to move beyond the Marx who found it possible to say: They cannot represent themselves; they must be represented.

NOTES

1. Terms like "third" and "first" world are very problematical both in suggesting over-simplified similarities between and amongst countries labelled "third" or "first" world, as well as implicitly reinforcing existing economic, cultural and ideological hierarchies which are conjured up in using such terminology. I use the term "third world" with full awareness of its problems, only because this is the terminology available to us at the moment. The use of quotation marks is meant to suggest a continuous questioning of the designation "third world." Even when I *do* not *use* quotation marks, I mean to *use* the term critically.

2. A number of documents and reports on the U.N. International Conferences on Women, Mexico City, 1975, and Copenhagen, 1980, as well as the 1976 Wellesley Conference on Women and Development attest to this.

3. The Zed Press "Women in the Third World" series is unique in its conception. I choose to focus on this series because it is the only contemporary series I have found which assumes that "women in the Third World" is a legitimate and separate subject of study and research. A number of the texts in this series are excellent, especially those texts which deal directly with women's resistance struggles. However, a number of the texts written by feminist sociologists, anthropologists, and journalists are symptomatic of the kind of Western feminist work on women in the Third World that concerns me. Thus, an analysis of a few of these particular texts in this series can serve as a representative point of entry into the discourse I am attempting to locate and define.

4. My analysis in this section of the paper has been influenced by Felicity Eldhom, Olivia Harris and Kate Young's excellent discussions in "Conceptualising Women," *Critique of Anthropology,* "Women's Issue," 3 (1977), 101-103. Eldhom, Harris and Young examine the use of the concepts of "reproduction" and the "sexual division of labor" in anthropological work on women, suggesting the inevitable pull towards universals inherent in the use of these categories to determine "women's position."

5. Amos and Parmar, "Challenging Imperial Feminism," *Feminist Review,* 17 (Autumn 1984) p. 7.

6. Fran Hosken, "Female Genital Mutilation and Human Rights," *Feminist Issues,* 1 (Summer 1981), 3–24 (hereafter cited in the text as "FGM").

7. Beverly Lindsay, ed., *Comparative Perspectives of Third World Women: The Impact of Race, Sex and Class* (New York: Praeger Publishers, 1983), esp. pp. 298, 306.

8. Maria Rosa Cutrufelli, *Women on Africa: Roots of Oppression* (London: Zed Press, 1983), esp. p. 13.

9. Cutrufelli, *Women of Africa,* p. 33.

10. Juliette Minces, *The House of Obedience: Women in Arab Society* (London: Zed Press, 1980), esp. p. 23.

11. Mina Modares, "Women and Shi'ism in Iran," *m/f,* 5 & 6 (1981), 61–82.

12. Patricia Jeffery, *Frogs in a Well: Indian Women in Purdah* (London: Zed Press, 1979).

13. Maria Mies, *The Lace Makers of Narsapur: Indian Housewives Produce for the World Market* (London: Zed Press, 1982).

14. Mies, *The Lace Makers*, esp. p. 157

15. Ann Dearden, eds., *Arab Women* (London: Minority Rights Group Report No. 27, 1975), esp. pp. 4–5.

16. Dearden, *Arab Women*, pp. 7, 10.

17. See Azar Tabari, "The Enigma of the Veiled Iranian Women," *Feminist Review*, 5 (1980), 19–32, for a detailed discussion of these instances.

18. Olivia Harris, "Latin American Women—An Overview," in Harris, ed., *Latin American Women* (London: Minority Rights Group Report, No. 57, 1983), pp. 4–7.

19. See Eldhom, Harris and Young, "Conceptualising Women," for an excellent discussion of this.

20. Beverly Brown, "Displacing the Difference—Review, *Nature, Culture and Gender*," *m/f*, 8 (1983), 79–90; Marilyn Strathern and Carol McCormack, eds., *Nature, Culture and Gender* (Cambridge: Cambridge Univ. Press, 1980).

21. "William V. Spanos, "*boundary 2* and the Polity of Interest: Humanism, the 'Center Elsewhere,' and Power." *boundary 2* 12(3)/13(1) (1984), 173-214.

2 • *Cheryl R. Rodriguez*

A HOMEGIRL GOES HOME
Black Feminism and the Lure of Native Anthropology

DISCUSSION QUESTIONS

1. What challenges has Rodriguez encountered as a Black feminist anthropologist in terms of her life and research?
2. How have her life experiences as a Black feminist influenced her choice of research projects?
3. Given the politics of representation, do you think it is politically better or methodologically easier to be a "native anthropologist" or "homegirl" doing anthropology of one's home?

How do the experiences of homegirl and Black feminist intellectual merge with the identity of native anthropologist? How do these identities influence the researcher's areas of interest, her methodologies, and her ethnographic representations? How does a Black feminist anthropologist define and negotiate the politics of home in her research endeavors? These are questions I answer by considering my own evolving relationship to feminism. In particular I examine the intersection of three important elements of native Black feminist anthropology: the historical and contemporary struggles of the Black feminist intellectual, the significance of naming for Black feminists, and the politics of home. It is my position that an awareness of these underlying elements contributes to a richer field experience for the native ethnographer as she attempts to capture and define Black feminist anthropology. Drawing upon my own oral narrative research project about Black women's activism in Tampa, Florida, I demonstrate how a native Black feminist project is consciously constructed and designed, and I analyze the implications this approach has for teaching, community activism, and further research into local Black women's lives.

In her discussion of the boundaries and possibilities for women within patriarchal societies, feminist poet Adrienne Rich argues, "The most notable fact that culture imprints on women is the sense of our limits" (Rich 1976, 246). As Black feminist anthropologists, we represent resistance to the limitations of culture (including the culture of a colonized anthropology) that historically have been imposed on people of the Black community in general and Black women in particular. In our efforts to decolonize anthropology, we paint pictures of empowerment and strength where others have left bleak images of savagery and inferiority. Yet,

An abridged version of Cheryl Rodriguez, 2001. "A Home Girl Goes Home: Black Feminism and the Lure of Native Anthropology." In Irma McClaurin, ed. *Black Feminist Anthropology: Theory, Politics, Praxis and Poetics.* New Brunswick: Rutgers University Press, pps. 233-257. Reprinted with the kind permission of the author and of the publisher.

before we can laud the value of our work in identifying, resisting, and dismantling the limitations of culture, we must acknowledge that there are still critical questions to ponder. For example, what is a native Black feminist project? How do formal education, intellectualism, and feminism affect our interactions in the field with other women of the Black community? As researchers, how can we learn from and appreciate Black women's ways of knowing without assuming intellectual authority over their stories and without appearing to appropriate their cultural treasures for our own advancement? These are critical questions for the Black feminist anthropologist who is concerned not only about the integrity and truthfulness of her work but also about the impact of her feminist perspective on people of the Black community. Although a number of scholars have explored the dimensions of native anthropology for the Black anthropologist, few have pondered the specific issues of the self-identified feminist who turns her gaze on her home community. I argue that it is critical for Black feminist anthropologists to examine those issues we take with us to the field that are specifically related to personal history, self-identity, and our own perspectives about the purposes of modern anthropology.

In my research among Black women activists in Tampa, Florida, "the field" is my hometown as well as an ethnographic setting. Having been socialized in the ways of the Black community as well as those of the larger society, I enter and negotiate the field with multiple cultural perspectives. As a "home-girl," I have been socialized into the historic realities, cultural values, and linguistic norms of Black southern life. Thus, when conducting anthropological research among Black women, I perceive myself to be someone who has an intimate understanding of some of the most defining aspects of their lives. However, my education, my role as an anthropologist, and my own feminist activism have socialized me to "rename, recategorize, reclassify, and reconceptualize" many cultural phenomena associated with home (Vaster 1996, 216).

My own evolving relationship to feminism derives from some of the mysterious and personal contents of my own cultural knapsack. While I remain an unequivocal Black feminist, I am also aware of the problems and conflicts this identity can raise even as I attempt to engage in liberatory and empowering research. Although scholars and activists credit the second wave of the women's movement with the astounding changes in women's social, economic, and political lives, feminism—as the ideological foundation of these changes—remains woefully misunderstood. Theoretically, politically and socially, feminism continues to face numerous challenges. For example, Black feminism—as both political stance and lived experience—continues to be misrepresented, distorted, or dismissed as though being both Black and feminist are two mutually exclusive and/or conflicting experiences.

Because of the misconceptions and confusion surrounding Black women's varying relationships to feminism, it is important for me to identify the sources of my own feminist consciousness. This dictates a discussion of the intersection of three important elements of native Black feminist anthropology mentioned previously: the historical and contemporary struggles of the Black feminist intellectual, the significance of naming for the Black feminist, and the politics of home. I argue that an awareness of these underlying themes contributes to a richer field experience for the native ethnographer as she attempts to capture and define Black feminist anthropology.

Just as the definition of Black feminism continues to be elusive, so the definition of Black feminist anthropology will also remain nebulous if we fail to understand the critical components that form the core of our endogenous (or native) research. Toward this end, I wish to describe an oral narrative research project involving Black women's activism in Tampa. This study, which was consciously constructed and designed as a native Black feminist project, has implications for teaching, community activism, and further research on local Black women's lives. For me, the lure of anthropology at home springs from a very fundamental sense of respect and concern for my community. As I explain, my early observations and experiences with resistance and change in the Jim Crow South not only influenced my belief in the power of activism; these experiences also shaped my feminist sensibilities as well as my interest in contributing to an anthropology of truth and liberation.

BLACK FEMINISM: PERSONAL AND POLITICAL TRANSFORMATIONS

Black women's intellectual and political struggles with the racism and classism of Euro-American feminism have occurred simultaneously with our struggles to address sexism, colorism, and homophobia within the Black community. As Stanlie James argues, our feminism is rooted and nourished in Black communities even as we challenge those same communities to address issues of internal oppression (James 1993, 2). In retrospect, I realize that while growing up, I witnessed Black women enduring many forms of oppression within the Black community. Sexist beliefs and practices were as common as rain and often appeared to be the natural order of life. Yet those of us who were born in the 1950s grew up at the doorstep of a new era. Despite our subordinated positions as girls, as well as our seeming acceptance of social expectations of feminine clothing and behavior, many of us who came of age during the 1950s and 1960s were aware of sexual oppression before we could actually name it. That is, we had a sense of gender consciousness that came from the stories and admonishments of grandmothers and mothers who knew about the dual dangers and vulnerabilities of being both Black and female.

I gained my gender consciousness from my grandmother, who understood quite clearly how Black women were sexualized by men—through harassment and physical violation—in both public and private spheres. Working all her life as a domestic, my grandmother also taught me about the dignity and courage of Black women as they resisted—in very subtle ways—the dehumanizing treatment of their employers. I learned that Black women walked bravely through symbolic, ideological, and physical minefields that were as long and wide as life itself. Black grandmothers and mothers had the awesome task of teaching their daughters how to negotiate minefields daily. However, to grow up amid blatant racism and sexism is also to grow up in a culture of contradiction. Lessons on dignity, courage, and self-reliance were often taught within the context of achieving ladyhood. Yet ladyhood was only bestowed upon those girls who were compliant, obedient, and most of all, silent.

Reflecting on the ways that my relationship to sexism evolved, I contend that my own Black feminist consciousness derives from some very complex, multidimensional, and contradictory experiences with oppression. My feminist consciousness also derives from living with the wrenching realities of racism. I was a part of the generation of southern Black children whose nascent awareness of second-class citizenship matured even as we turned the stained and torn pages of our battered, secondhand textbooks in our segregated classrooms. Our separation from white children taught us that not only were white people the Other but that they were a superior and dangerous Other. At the same time, I learned that an enduring part of our lives as Black people was to confront the restrictions imposed by the dangerous Other.

I developed a sense of racial pride by observing, reading about, and absorbing the tumultuous changes occurring during the Civil Rights movement, and I became aware that people from all walks of life were resisting racism. Although it was the formally educated men whose leadership we all sought, I eventually learned that the work of intellectuals was intricately interwoven with that of grassroots activists.

My formal introduction to Black feminist ideas came through the literature that I discovered in the waning years of the Civil Rights movement. Black feminist writers asserted themselves and became visible in liberatory spaces that previously had been occupied and defined by Black men or white women. As Nancie Caraway argues, Black feminism "deconstructed the images, identities, presumptions, and methodology of hegemonic theory—not only androcentric world views but those of white feminism as well" (Caraway 1991, 5). Yet even more courageously, Black feminist writers challenged the blatant sexism of the Black community, including that of Black male revolutionaries. These writings would become the single most important influence in my life as an intellectual, a community member, a social scientist, a teacher, and as a Black woman in a racialized, sexualized, and certainly class-driven America.

In the 1980s I transformed my intellectual and theoretical relationship with feminism into a relationship that was defined by public activism. I became involved in a chapter of the National Organization for Women (NOW) in Chicago, Illinois. On the national, state, and local levels, NOW was predominantly white, more mainstream than radical, and painfully racist. However, in the absence of any other activist organization in suburban Chicago, NOW became the vehicle that ushered me into feminist and community politics. Through NOW I became involved in organizing reproductive rights marches, editing the chapter newsletter, building coalitions with other women's organizations, and bringing feminist education to local public schools. My leadership responsibilities increased, and eventually I became the chapter president. All of this was done while simultaneously challenging the local NOW membership to come to terms with their own individual and collective racism.

As I shifted my interests and gradually transitioned into the academic world, this multiple consciousness would serve me well, particularly in the execution and analysis of projects that focused on Black women's lives. As Harrison contends, "anthropologists with multiple consciousness and vision have a strategic role to play in the struggle for a decolonized science of humankind. Anthropologists with dual or multiple vision may be uniquely able to convert their 'extra eyes' into useful research tools and effective political weapons" (1991, 90). The ethnographer who is also a Black woman and a feminist thinker brings not only a multiple vision but a distinct consciousness to native anthropology. This consciousness is influenced by our own lived experiences with struggles against race, gender, and class oppression. It is also influenced by our knowledge of the historic struggles of our Black feminist foremothers. Accompanying this distinctive consciousness, I contend, should be an awareness of the themes and elements that form the core of native Black feminist anthropology.

NATIVE ANTHROPOLOGY: CORE ELEMENTS OF OUR WORK

Although some may question the efficacy, the objectivity, and even the methodological rigor of anthropology conducted in one's own society, the notion of anthropology at home is supported by a diverse and innovative body of research. As Donald Messerschmidt contends, "More than ever before we are staying home, where we study communal living, neighboring and cooperation, health and healing, old age and alienation" (1981, 4). Although it may not be considered an exotic or adventurous anthropology in the traditional sense, research conducted in our own environs challenges us to deconstruct notions of familiarity in that we are required to gaze deeper into the strangeness of the everyday realities we take for granted. We become students of our own communities and develop a more refined sense of who we are in relationship to the community. At the same time, anthropology at home can awaken us to the creativity, resiliency, and diversity of our communities. Just as we prepare and reinvent ourselves for living and working abroad, we must also change ourselves in some very distinctive ways so that we can work in our own culture. In some cases we must recapture some aspects of our former selves to reconnect with our home communities. For example, Linda Nelson describes her initial feelings of alienation upon returning to Brooklyn, the community of her youth, to conduct a study of cultural themes in Black women's narratives: "I was annoyed by my anxiety since these were the very streets I had traveled alone, regularly, day and night, with little more preparation than a reminder to myself to 'just be cool'. In short, I had lost much of my street savvy" (Nelson 1996, 195). As Nelson's revelation implies, fieldwork at home removes the façade we can comfortably assume when we are naïve strangers.

Anthropology at home has been called an anthropology of issues in that it implies an attempt to link the theory–practice dichotomy. As Messerschmidt (1981) argues, it is anthropology of action and planning. In addition, I believe it is an anthropology that explores the interconnectedness between history, social change, and the future. Anthropology at home does not relegate the ethnographer to a minor role in the discipline, nor does it diminish the meaning of the anthropological experience. "In turning homeward, we are abandoning neither our methodological heritage nor our holistic perspective. Rather, we are building on them with confidence and innovation" (Messerschmidt 1981, 4–5).

Anthropology *at* home becomes the anthropology *of* home for the native anthropologist. When we claim insider status with our informants on the basis of factors such as ethnicity, kinship, social class, or gender, one assumption is that accessibility and rapport are minor issues. As Nelson muses, "On first consideration, anthropological research among one's own people promises much of the certainty and ease of a tender voyage home" (Nelson 1996, 183). She goes on to explain the unwitting cultural blunders we commit and the varying degrees of acceptance from community informants that make this statement more idealistic than true. However, in general, native anthropology for the Black anthropologist promises a level of cooperation and a richness of spirit that is embedded in Black community traditions of racial uplift. Zora Neale Hurston alluded to this support when she wrote: "I hurried back to Eatonville because I knew that the town was full of material and that I could get it without hurt, harm or danger" (Hurston 1990, 2). Similarly, John Gwaltney discussed the fact that Black informants' cooperation with the native anthropologist is often seen as "an act of racial solidarity and civic responsibility" Gwaltney 1976, 236).

Assumptions of cooperation, racial solidarity, and even shared identity all relate to the anthropologist's general knowledge of the folks who compose her community of informants. Yet for us as Black feminists, what are some of the core elements that influence our approach to native anthropology? What do these core elements of native Black feminist anthropology tell us about ourselves as we engage in transforming the discipline and its relationship to the Black community? One of the first issues we must understand is the historic and contemporary struggles of Black women intellectuals. This issue is a core element in our work as native anthropologists.

When we engage in native anthropology, we often think of the corrective impact our research will have on the discipline. After all, we attempt to give voice to silence and to represent our communities in ways that are empowering. Moreover, in some respects, Black feminist anthropological analysis should be a vehicle for shedding new light on ongoing problems. Yet we must remember that our work as native anthropologists is intellectual work. In fact, I see native Black feminist anthropology as intellectual activism. We can examine the writings by and about our Black feminist foremothers in anthropology as well as the work of other Black women to find a very substantive tradition of intellectual activism.

Contemporarily, the ongoing struggles of the Black feminist intellectual occur in several dimensions and locations of our professional lives. We struggle with the irony of composing careers within a discipline whose origins are grounded in racist ideology and whose discourse has influenced the development of a highly racialized society. Adrienne Andrews speaks to this particular dilemma as she attempts to understand her own conflicted relationship with anthropology: "I am the other. As a member of a group whose members are often perceived of as others (African Americans) I have been plagued with feelings of ambivalence surrounding my membership in the group of others known as anthropologists" (Andrews 1993, 179).

Another core element of native Black feminist anthropology is the significance of naming. Bettina Aptheker contends, "Naming is a central motif in feminist thought. . . . Consider the connections between naming and identity, between naming and language, between naming and silence" (Aptheker 1989, 20). Gloria Hull and Barbara Smith, in a discussion of the critical need to study Black women's lives, argue, "Like any politically disenfranchised group, Black women could not exist consciously until we began to name ourselves" (Hull and Smith 1982, xvii). Naming is a political strategy; it is a foundation, a force that connects divergent and contradictory experiences. Naming ourselves as feminists always situates us at a very critical ideological and political juncture, from which we resist demands (from others) to rank the oppressive forces that subjugate Black women. Despite Pearl Cleage's definition of feminism as "the belief that women are full human beings capable of participation and leadership in the full range of human activities" (Cleage 1993, 28), Black women's identification as feminists is often interpreted as a sign of our disconnection to Black communities. Black feminist intellectuals engage in some deeply emotional struggles with this perception.

Despite a deep, reflexive sense of duty to ourselves and our people, we Black feminists navigate treacherous waters when we turn our gazes on the social conventions of our home communities. Collins raises two issues about Black feminism that have implications for our work as native anthropologists. First, she argues that Black feminism disrupts the historical and typically unquestioned code of Black racial solidarity (Collins 1996, 13). Thus, the implication is that our presence in Black communities might be less controversial (or threatening) if our questions were about race rather than the intersection of race and gender. How much overt and institutionalized resistance do native Black feminist researchers encounter when their inquiry involves topics such as domestic violence, rape, absentee fathers, or child support issues in Black communities? This would be an interesting question to explore among Black feminist anthropologists.

Second, Collins makes the point that Black feminism conflicts with certain elements of Black religious traditions. Thus, if our ethnographic interests led us to explore women's invisibility in leadership positions in the Black church, or if we wanted to examine the Black church's silence on issues such

as AIDS or sexual harassment, or if we wanted to conduct interviews with Black lesbians, would we risk a form of alienation from our communities that could permeate our research? How can we speak about these issues in professional settings if people in Black communities view our work as disrespectful or misguided? As difficult as these questions may be, they are basic challenges that the native Black feminist anthropologist must consider before making the journey home. While we struggle with the complexities of expressing ourselves as intellectuals and naming ourselves as feminists, we must remain aware that our engagement in these particular struggles signifies a certain privileged status. Our realities as feminist scholars and researchers are distinctly different from the realities of large numbers of Black women who remain illiterate, undereducated, or perpetually disempowered by poverty.[1] As Black feminists, we should be about the business of developing ethnographic projects that interweave our realities and struggles against patriarchy with those of all Black women. This includes giving voice to strengths and weakness, pain and troubles, the issues that affect Black women as women, and the issues that define Black women's relationships to Black men.[2] How we bridge the gap between the realities of the anthropologist and those of the informant is a critical aspect of the politics of home. I argue that the journey home for the Black feminist anthropologist should speak to intellectualism that embraces a range of experiences and worldviews, not simply those of the researcher.

Bridging the gap between ourselves and our informants does not mean that we attempt to use our research to change all of the social conventions of the Black community that we deem oppressive to Black women. For me, bridging the gap means theorizing about issues of identity, self-definition, power, difference, and privilege in Black women's lives. Bridging the gap means employing what Moraga and Anzaldua call "theory in the flesh" (1981, 23). That is, theory in which all of our divergent realities—those shaped by color, class, sexuality, and varying levels of privilege—all merge in the creation of a "politic born out of necessity" (1981, 23). In my work among local Black women, theory in the flesh makes Black women's history, beliefs, and agency a catalyst for understanding myself as well as the women who share their stories. In addition to an emphasis on activism, identity, resistance, and home, my native research projects focus on memory and connections.

Native Black feminist anthropology involves negotiating the challenges of our lives as Black women who are also feminists and researchers. It involves reinventing ourselves not only as anthropologists but also as those who are capable of building bridges across contradictory realities. This is something that is rarely done.

LOCAL KNOWLEDGE AND HOME TRUTHS: EXPLORING BLACK WOMEN'S ACTIVISM[3]

In 1994 I began a study of local Black women's grassroots activism. I consciously constructed this research as a native Black feminist ethnographic project, that is, a project that would explore the "multilayered texture of Black women's lives" (Combahee River Collective 1983, 276) from the perspective of a Black feminist researcher. The most immediate goal of this project was to document Black women's contributions to social change in Tampa. The larger and far-reaching goal of this ongoing project is to determine how Black women can gain more political visibility and electoral power in Tampa. Through recorded personal interviews, I sought to compare the stories, strategies, and insights of women who were activists during the years of Tampa's Civil Rights movement with the activist experiences of contemporary Black women. I also sought to explore the ways in which local Black women expressed their experiences with multiple forms of oppression. Further, I wanted to document the issues or situations that stimulated Black women's community activism during and after the civil rights years.

Local knowledge about Black women's historical and contemporary grassroots leadership in Tampa remains obscure, scattered, and sometimes difficult to uncover. There are several reasons for this. First, there is limited knowledge of African American community history in Tampa. Although African Americans established stable and enduring communities and traditions in Tampa, it has only been within the last ten to fifteen years that the systematic study of historic institutions, organizations, ceremonies, and practices has developed. There is also limited historical documentation of race relations in Tampa. In fact, few local citizens are aware of the activism that occurred in Tampa during the Civil Rights movement. Once again, scholarly efforts to document struggles against Jim Crow and other racist policies and practices are recent and few. Finally, the ethnohistorical literature on African American activism in Tampa focuses primarily on the work of educated African American men, particularly ministers, attorneys, and businessmen who were leaders of local, state, and national civil rights initiatives. Clearly, this history is of the highest import, yet the exclusion of African American women makes this history an incomplete one. Another reason for the invisibility of Black women's activism in Tampa's community history is that with few exceptions, scholars have not interviewed local Black women about the roles they have played in social change. All of these factors contribute to a gaping chasm in local knowledge about Black women's visions and voices in this southern community. Through a number of research projects (as well as through teaching and community activism), I hope to fill this void.

For this project, I conducted interviews with six women who have lived most of their adult lives in Tampa and who were involved in public forms of activism. Three of the women developed their activist consciousness during the civil rights era; however, only one informant from this group actually worked for a civil rights organization. The other two women were involved in community organizing, voter registration, and electoral politics. A second small group of women interviewed for this study consisted of three women who were (and continue to be) involved full time in grassroots activism in their respective communities.

One of the women heads a task force on gay and lesbian rights issues; the other two are involved in community organizing and public housing issues. I interviewed the activists in their homes or offices, most of which were located in historically Black neighborhoods. Prior to these meetings, I had not had extensive discussion with any of my informants; I knew of their activism through newspaper articles and, in some cases, mutual acquaintances. For one interview session, I sat on the porch of a rickety old house in Seminole Heights. Formerly an all-white neighborhood (and consequently not a community that I would have visited as a child), Seminole Heights is now a racially and economically integrated neighborhood. The young woman who agreed to the interview felt it would be better if we sat outside and watched my car while we talked. A few days before our interview, her own car had been vandalized right in her front yard. As we sat and talked on the porch, teenage boys cruised by blasting rap music from their car stereos. My informant was initially uncomfortable with the interview process, but after we shared our mutual concerns and confusion about the problems of today's youth, she became more receptive to my presence. We spent an afternoon sitting on her porch swing, sharing our thoughts and learning from each other, the way that Black women have done for centuries.

To learn about the life and work of two other activists, I made several visits to the rental office of the Central Park Village public housing complex to interview a mother and daughter who have been living and working in public housing all of their lives. The office is a gathering place for the women's children, grandchildren, friends, and neighbors. As I made myself comfortable listening to stories, laughing, and joking with the women and their children, I thought about my childhood experiences at my grandmother's apartment in the "projects" across town. On another day, I drove to West Tampa to visit a woman who lived in a splendid old house that had intrigued me as a child. In fact, my friends and I would pass this house every day on our way to George Washington Carver Elementary School. On the day of the interview, I entered her house in awe, never having dreamed that I would one day be invited to see its grandeur.

On another occasion, one rainy Halloween evening, I found myself at a mall that had been long abandoned by the local middle-class citizenry. The mall's clientele were mostly low-income people of color. Perhaps this was why it was an appropriate place for the office of the Tampa NAACP. Amid the squeals of delighted trick-or-treaters, I interviewed a longtime activist who had taken charge of the embattled local chapter. My desire to learn about these women's lives required me to leave the familiarity of the predominantly white, suburban world that I have inhabited since early adulthood.

In establishing a relationship with the field and in revisiting old memories and images, I am doing what Toni Morrison refers to as memory returning to the "archaeological site" (1987, 103). My memories help me to remain aware of my current roles as both an intellectual and a feminist. These memories also established a very effective connection between my informants and myself.

Like many Black women activists, most of the women I interviewed spoke more about the barriers erected by racism than those created by sexism. Nevertheless, their powerful and truthful narratives reveal an understanding of Black women's roles in institutional change. As I have argued previously, "narratives of African American women activists represent the complex knowledge and strategies that compose a Black women's activist tradition" (Rodriguez 1998, 108-109). Exploring and analyzing that tradition through this project is a very basic example of native Black feminist anthropology.

CONCLUSION

Determined to transform the anthropological canon so that Black women's stories will be told truthfully, I initiated a study involving interviews with women in my hometown. As I share these women's stories locally, my hope is that this research will raise awareness of the need for coalition building among Black women who work on diverse issues in Tampa. Without this kind of ethnographic work, the community has no systematic, written record of Black women's participation in social change and consequently gives the perception that we have no role models. Without the knowledge of these activist role models, young Black women may not feel empowered to become involved in local leadership.

A belief in the inherent value of Black women's lives—a guiding principle in Black feminist thought—is the essence of my anthropological endeavors. This, I strongly feel, is the nature of the home truths I have learned and the theory in flesh I seek to create. It is what draws me to work in my community, and it is the inspiration for my ever-evolving roles as both researcher and homegirl.

BIBLIOGRAPHY

Andrews, Adrienne. 1993. "Balancing the Personal and Professional." In *Spirit, Space, and Survival: African American Women in (White) Academe*, edited by Joy James and Ruth Farmer, 179. New York: Routledge.

Aptheker, Bettina. 1989. *Tapestries of Life: Women's Work, Women's Consciousness, and the Meaning of Daily Experience.* Amherst: University of Massachusetts Press.

Caraway, Nancie. 1991. *Segregated Sisterhood.* Knoxville: University of Tennessee Press.

Cleage, Pearl. 1993. *Deals with the Devil: And Other Reasons to Riot.* New York: Ballantine Books.

Collins, Patricia Hill. 1996. "What's in a Name? Womanism, Black Feminism and Beyond." *Black Scholar 26,* 1.

Combahee River Collective. 1983. "The Combahee River Collective Statement." In *Home Girls: A Black Feminist Anthology,* edited by Barbara Smith, 272–282. New York: Kitchen Table Women of Color Press.

Gwaltney, John L. 1976. "On Going Home Again—Some Reflections of a Native Anthropologist." *Phylon 30,* 236.

Harrison, Faye Venetia. 1997. "Ethnography as Politics." In *Decolonizing Anthropology: Moving Further Toward an Anthropology of Liberation,* edited by Faye V. Harrison, 88–110. Arlington, Va.: American Anthropological Association.

Hull, Gloria T. and Barbara Smith. 1982. "The Politics of Black Women's Studies." In *All the Women Are White, All the Blacks Are Men, but Some of Us Are Brave: Black Women's Studies,* edited by Gloria T. Hull, Patricia Bell Scott and Barbara Smith, xvii–xxxii. Old Westbury, N.Y.: Feminist Press.

Hurston, Zora Neale. 1990. *Mules and Men.* New York: Harper.

James, Stanlie. 1993. "Introduction." In *Theorizing Black Feminisms: The Visionary Pragmatism of Black Women,* edited by Stanlie James and Abena Busia, 1–12. New York: Routledge.

Messerschmidt, Donald A., editor. 1981. *Anthropologists at Home in North America: Methods and Issues in the Study of One's Own Society.* New York: Cambridge University Press.

Moraga, Cherrie and Gloria Anzaldua, editors. 1981. *This Bridge Called My Back: Writings by Radical Women of Color.* Watertown, Massachusetts: Kitchen Table Women of Color Press.

Morrison, Toni. 1987. "The Site of Memory." In *Inventing Truth: The Art and Craft of Memoir,* edited by William Zinsser, 103–124. Boston: Houghton Mifflin.

Nelson, Linda. 1996. "Hands in the Chit'lins: Notes on Narrative Anthropological Research among African American Women." In *Unrelated Kin: Race and Gender in Women's Personal Narratives,* edited by Gwendolyn Etter-Lewis and Michele Foster. New York: Routledge.

Rich, Adrienne. 1976. *Of Woman Born: Motherhood As Experience and Institution.* New York: Norton.

Rodriguez, Cheryl. 1998. "Activist Stories: Culture and Continuity in Black Women's Narratives of Grassroots Community Work." *Frontiers: Journal of Women's Studies* 19, 2: 94–112.

Vaster, Michele. 1996. "Like Us but Not One of Us: Reflection on a Life History Study of African American Teachers." In *Unrelated Kin: Race and Gender in Women 5 Personal Narratives,* edited by Gwendolyn Etter-Lewis and Michele Foster, 216. New York: Routledge.

NOTES

1. Collins challenges us to think about this issue: "One might ask how closely the thematic content of newly emerging black women's voices in the academy speak for and speak to the masses of African American women still denied literacy" (1996, 15).

2. I believe that Black feminist anthropology should address issues of masculinity as well as issues that are relevant to the political, social, and economic survival of Black men. In this essay, however, I am concerned with the origins of a Black feminist consciousness and the ways in which this consciousness becomes a part of our anthropological methodologies.

3. The fieldwork described in this chapter was supported by a grant from the Division of Sponsored Research at the University of South Florida. I express my appreciation to the Black women activists of my local community, who continue to inspire and guide my native Black feminist projects.

3 • *Lila Abu-Lughod*

DO MUSLIM WOMEN REALLY NEED SAVING?

Anthropological Reflections on Cultural Relativism and Its Others

DISCUSSION QUESTIONS

1. What are some of the dominant representations of Muslim women in the United States?
2. What is the "political work" that such representations have been used to accomplish?
3. What alternative kinds of representations and explanations does Abu-Lughod propose, and why?

What are the ethics of the current "War on Terrorism," a war that justifies itself by purporting to liberate, or save, Afghan women? Does anthropology have anything to offer in our search for a viable position to take regarding this rationale for war?

I was led to pose the question of my title in part because of the way I personally experienced the response to the U.S. war in Afghanistan. Like many colleagues whose work has focused on women and gender in the Middle East, I was deluged with invitations to speak. Why did this not please me, a scholar who has devoted more than 20 years of her life to this subject and who has some complicated personal connection to this identity? Here was an opportunity to spread the word, disseminate my knowledge, and correct misunderstandings.

My discomfort led me to reflect on why, as feminists in or from the West, or simply as people who have concerns about women's lives, we need to be wary of this response to the events and aftermath of September 11, 2001. I want to point out the minefields of this obsession with the plight of Muslim women. I hope to show some way through them using insights from anthropology, the discipline whose charge has been to understand and manage cultural difference. At the same time, I want to remain critical of anthropology's complicity in the reification of cultural difference.

CULTURAL EXPLANATIONS AND THE MOBILIZATION OF WOMEN

It is easier to see why one should be skeptical about the focus on the "Muslim woman" if one begins with the U.S. public response. I will analyze two

An abridged version of Lila Abu-Lughod, 2002. "Do Muslim Women Really Need Saving?" Reproduced by permission of the American Anthropological Association and of the author from *American Anthropologist*, Volume 104, Issue 3, Pages 783–790, September 2002. Not for sale or further reproduction.

manifestations of this response: some conversations I had with a reporter from the PBS *NewsHour with Jim Lehrer* and First Lady Laura Bush's radio address to the nation on November 17, 2001. The presenter from the *NewsHour* show first contacted me in October to see if I was willing to give some background for a segment on Women and Islam. I agreed to look at the questions she was going to pose to panelists. The questions were hopelessly general. Do Muslim women believe "x"? Are Muslim women "y"? Does Islam allow "z" for women? I asked her: If you were to substitute Christian or Jewish wherever you have Muslim, would these questions make sense? There was a consistent resort to the cultural, as if knowing something about women and Islam or the meaning of a religious ritual would help one understand the tragic attack on New York's World Trade Center and the U.S. Pentagon, or how Afghanistan had come to be ruled by the Taliban.

The question is why knowing about the "culture" of the region, and particularly its religious beliefs and treatment of women, was more urgent than exploring the history of the development of repressive regimes in the region and the U.S. role in this history. Such cultural framing, it seemed to me, prevented the serious exploration of the roots and nature of human suffering in this part of the world. Instead of political and historical explanations, experts were being asked to give religio-cultural ones. Instead of questions that might lead to the exploration of global interconnections, we were offered ones that worked to artificially divide the world into separate spheres—recreating an imaginative geography of West versus East, us versus Muslims, cultures in which First Ladies give speeches versus others where women shuffle around silently in burqas.

Most pressing for me was why Muslim women in general, and Afghan women in particular, were so crucial to this cultural mode of explanation, which ignored the complex entanglements in which we are all implicated, in sometimes surprising alignments. Why were these female symbols being mobilized in this "War against Terrorism" in a way they were not in other conflicts? Laura Bush's

radio address on November 17 reveals the political work such mobilization accomplishes. On the one hand, her address collapsed important distinctions that should have been maintained. There was a constant slippage between the Taliban and the terrorists, so that they became almost one word—a kind of hyphenated monster identity: the Taliban-and-the-terrorists. Then there was the blurring of the very separate causes in Afghanistan of women's continuing malnutrition, poverty, and ill health, and their more recent exclusion under the Taliban from employment, schooling, and the joys of wearing nail polish. On the other hand, her speech reinforced chasmic divides between the "civilized people throughout the world" whose hearts break for the women and children of Afghanistan and the Taliban-and-the-terrorists, who want to "impose their world on the rest of us." The speech enlisted women to justify American bombing and intervention in Afghanistan. As Laura Bush said, "Because of our recent military gains in much of Afghanistan, women are no longer imprisoned in their homes. They can listen to music and teach their daughters without fear of punishment. The fight against terrorism is also a fight for the rights and dignity of women" (U.S. Government 2002).

These words have haunting resonances for anyone who has studied colonial history. Many who have worked on British colonialism in South Asia have noted the use of the woman question in colonial policies where intervention into sati (the practice of widows immolating themselves on their husbands' funeral pyres), child marriage, and other practices was used to justify rule. As Gayatri Chakravorty Spivak (1988) has cynically put it: white men saving brown women from brown men. The historical record is full of similar cases, including in the Middle East. In Turn of the Century Egypt, what Leila Ahmed (1992) has called "colonial feminism" was hard at work. This was a selective concern about the plight of Egyptian women that focused on the veil as a sign of oppression but gave no support to women's education and was professed loudly by the same Englishman, Lord Cromer, who opposed women's suffrage back home. Sociologist Marnia Lazreg (1994) has (also) offered some vivid examples of how French colonialism enlisted women to its cause in Algeria.

Just as I argued above that we need to be suspicious when neat cultural icons are plastered over messier historical and political narratives, so we need to be wary when Lord Cromer in British-ruled Egypt, French ladies in Algeria, and Laura Bush, all with military troops behind them, claim to be saving or liberating Muslim women.

POLITICS OF THE VEIL

I want now to look more closely at those Afghan women Laura Bush claimed were "rejoicing" at their liberation by the Americans. This necessitates a discussion of the veil, or the burqa, because it is so central to contemporary concerns about Muslim women.

It is common popular knowledge that the ultimate sign of the oppression of Afghan women under the Taliban-and-the-terrorists is that they were forced to wear the burqa. Liberals sometimes confess their surprise that even though Afghanistan has been liberated from the Taliban, women do not seem to be throwing off their burqas. Someone who has worked in Muslim regions must ask why this is so surprising. Did we expect that once "free" from the Taliban they would go "back" to belly shirts and blue jeans, or dust off their Chanel suits?

First, it should be recalled that the Taliban did not invent the burqa. The burqa, like some other forms of "cover," has, in many settings, marked the symbolic separation of men's and women's spheres, as part of the general association of women with family and home, not with public space where strangers mingled. Twenty years ago the anthropologist Hanna Papanek (1982), who worked in Pakistan, described the burqa as "portable seclusion." She noted that many saw it as a liberating invention because it enabled women to move out of segregated living spaces while still observing the basic moral requirements of separating and protecting women from unrelated men. Such veiling

signifies belonging to a particular community and participating in a moral way of life in which families are paramount in the organization of communities and the home is associated with the sanctity of women. What had happened in Afghanistan under the Taliban is that one regional style of covering or veiling, associated with a certain respectable but not elite class, was imposed on everyone as "religiously" appropriate, even though previously there had been many different styles, popular or traditional with different groups and classes.

To draw some analogies, none of them perfect, why are we surprised that Afghan women do not throw off their burqas when we know perfectly well that it would not be appropriate to wear shorts to the opera? At the time these discussions of Afghan women's burqas were raging, a friend of mine was chided by her husband for suggesting she wanted to wear a pantsuit to a fancy wedding: "You know you don't wear pants to a WASP wedding," he reminded her. New Yorkers know that the beautifully coiffed Hasidic women, who look so fashionable next to their dour husbands in black coats and hats, are wearing wigs. This is because religious belief and community standards of propriety require the covering of the hair. They also alter boutique fashions to include high necks and long sleeves. As anthropologists know perfectly well, people wear the appropriate form of dress for their social communities and are guided by socially shared standards, religious beliefs, and moral ideals, unless they deliberately transgress to make a point or are unable to afford proper cover. If we think that U.S. women live in a world of choice regarding clothing, all we need to do is remind ourselves of the expression "the tyranny of fashion."

Second, not only are there many forms of covering, which themselves have different meanings in the communities in which they are used, but also veiling itself must not be confused with, or made to stand for, lack of agency (Mahmood 2001). As I have argued in my ethnography of a Bedouin community in Egypt in the late 1970s and 1980s (1986), pulling the black head cloth over the face in front of older respected men is considered a voluntary act by women who are deeply committed to being moral and have a sense of honor tied to family. One of the ways they show their standing is by covering their faces in certain contexts. They decide for whom they feel it is appropriate to veil.

Two points emerge from this fairly basic discussion of the meanings of veiling in the contemporary Muslim world. First, we need to work against the reductive interpretation of veiling as the quintessential sign of women's unfreedom, even if we object to state imposition of this form, as in Iran or with the Taliban. What does freedom mean if we accept the fundamental premise that humans are social beings, always raised in certain social and historical contexts and belonging to particular communities that shape their desires and understandings of the world? Is it not a gross violation of women's own understandings of what they are doing to simply denounce the burqa as a medieval imposition? Second, we must take care not to reduce the diverse situations and attitudes of millions of Muslim women to a single item of clothing. Perhaps it is time to give up the Western obsession with the veil and focus on some serious issues with which feminists and others should indeed be concerned.

Ultimately, the significant political-ethical problem the burqa raises is how to deal with cultural "others." How are we to deal with difference without the cultural relativism for which anthropologists are justly famous—a relativism that says it's their culture and it's not my business to judge or interfere, only to try to understand. Cultural relativism is certainly an improvement on ethnocentrism and the racism, cultural imperialism, and imperiousness that underlie it; the problem is that it is too late not to interfere. The forms of lives we find around the world are already products of long histories of interactions.

I want to explore the issues of women, cultural relativism, and the problems of "difference" from three angles. First, I want to consider what feminist anthropologists are to do with strange political bedfellows. I used to feel torn when I received the e-mail petitions circulating for the last few years

in defense of Afghan women under the Taliban. I was not sympathetic to the dogmatism of the Taliban; I do not support the oppression of women. But the provenance of the campaign worried me. I had never received a petition from such women defending the right of Palestinian women to safety from Israeli bombing or daily harassment at checkpoints, asking the United States to reconsider its support for a government that had dispossessed them, closed them out from work and citizenship rights, refused them the most basic freedoms. I do not think that it would be as easy to mobilize so many of these American and European women if it were not a case of Muslim men oppressing Muslim women—women of cover for whom they can feel sorry and in relation to whom they can feel smugly superior.

To be critical of this celebration of women's rights in Afghanistan is not to pass judgment on any local women's organizations, such as RAWA, the Revolutionary Association of Women of Afghanistan, whose members have courageously worked since 1977 for a democratic secular Afghanistan in which women's human rights are respected, against Soviet-backed regimes or U.S.-, Saudi-, and Pakistani-supported conservatives. Their documentation of abuse and their work through clinics and schools have been enormously important. It is also not to fault the campaigns that exposed the dreadful conditions under which the Taliban placed women. It is, however, to suggest that we need to look closely at what we are supporting (and what we are not) and to think carefully about why.

How should we manage the complicated politics and ethics of finding ourselves in agreement with those with whom we normally disagree? I do not know how many feminists who felt good about saving Afghan women from the Taliban are also asking for a global redistribution of wealth or contemplating sacrificing their own consumption radically so that African or Afghan women could have some chance of having what I do believe should be a universal human right—the right to freedom from the structural violence of global inequality and from the ravages of war, the everyday rights of having enough to eat, having homes for their families in which to live and thrive, having ways to make decent livings so their children can grow, and having the strength and security to work out, within their communities and with whatever alliances they want, how to live a good life, which might very well include changing the ways those communities are organized.

Suspicion about bedfellows is only a first step; we need to confront two more big issues. First is the acceptance of the possibility of difference. Can we only free Afghan women to be like us or might we have to recognize that even after "liberation" from the Taliban, they might want different things than we would want for them? What do we do about that? Second, we need to be vigilant about the rhetoric of saving people because of what it implies about our attitudes.

Again, when I talk about accepting difference, I am not implying that we should resign ourselves to being cultural relativists who respect whatever goes on elsewhere as "just their culture." I have already discussed the dangers of "cultural" explanations; "their" cultures are just as much part of history and an interconnected world as ours are. What I am advocating is the hard work involved in recognizing and respecting differences—precisely as products of different histories, as expressions of different circumstances, and as manifestations of differently structured desires. We may want justice for women, but can we accept that there might be different ideas about justice and that different women might want, or choose, different futures from what we envision as best (see Ong 1988)?

Although we must be careful not to fall into polarizations that place feminism on the side of the West because many people within Muslim countries who are trying to find alternatives to present injustices, who do not accept that being feminist means being Western, will be under pressure to choose (Are you with us or against us?), we must remain aware of differences, respectful of other paths toward social change that might give women better lives. Can there be a liberation that is Islamic? And, beyond this, is liberation even a goal

for which all women or people strive? Are emancipation, equality, and rights part of a universal language we must use? In other words, might other desires be more meaningful for different groups of people? Living in close families? Living in a godly way? Living without war? I have done fieldwork in Egypt over more than 20 years and I cannot think of a single woman I know, from the poorest rural to the most educated cosmopolitan, who has ever expressed envy of U.S. women, women they tend to perceive as bereft of community, vulnerable to sexual violence and social anomie, driven by individual success rather than morality, or strangely disrespectful of God.

Saba Mahmood (2001) has pointed out a disturbing thing that happens when one argues for a respect for other traditions. She notes that there seems to be a difference in the political demands made on those who work on or are trying to understand Muslims and Islamists and those who work on secular-humanist projects. She, who studies the piety movements in Egypt, is consistently pressed to denounce all the harm done by Islamic movements around the world—otherwise she is accused of being an apologist. But there never seems to be a parallel demand for those who study secular humanism and its projects, despite the terrible violences that have been associated with it over the last couple of centuries, from world wars to colonialism, from genocides to slavery. We need to have as little dogmatic faith in secular humanism as in Islamism, and as open a mind to the complex possibilities of human projects undertaken in one tradition as the other.

BEYOND THE RHETORIC OF SALVATION

Let us return, finally, to my title, "Do Muslim Women Need Saving?" The discussion of culture, veiling, and how one can navigate the shoals of cultural difference should put Laura Bush's self-congratulation about the rejoicing of Afghan women liberated by American troops in a different light. It is deeply problematic to construct the Afghan woman as someone in need of saving. When you save someone, you imply that you are saving her from something. You are also saving her *to* something. What violences are entailed in this transformation, and what presumptions are being made about the superiority of that to which you are saving her? Projects of saving other women depend on and reinforce a sense of superiority by Westerners, a form of arrogance that deserves to be challenged. All one needs to do to appreciate the patronizing quality of the rhetoric of saving women is to imagine using it today in the United States about disadvantaged groups such as African American women or working-class women. We now understand them as suffering from structural violence. We have become politicized about race and class, but not culture.

As anthropologists, feminists, or concerned citizens, we should be wary of taking on the mantles of those 19th-century Christian missionary women who devoted their lives to saving their Muslim sisters. One of my favorite documents from that period is a collection called *Our Moslem Sisters*, the proceedings of a conference of women missionaries held in Cairo in 1906 (Van Sommer and Zwemer 1907). The subtitle of the book is *A Cry of Need from the Lands of Darkness Interpreted by Those Who Heard It*. Speaking of the ignorance, seclusion, polygamy, and veiling that blighted women's lives across the Muslim world, the missionary women spoke of their responsibility to make these women's voices heard. As the introduction states, "They will never cry for themselves, for they are down under the yoke of centuries of oppression" (Van Sommer and Zwemer 1907:15). "This book," it begins, "with its sad, reiterated story of wrong and oppression is an indictment and an appeal. It is an appeal to Christian womanhood to right these wrongs and enlighten this darkness by sacrifice and service" (Van Sommer and Zwemer 1907:5). One can hear uncanny echoes of their virtuous goals today, even though the language is secular, the appeals not to Jesus but to human rights or the liberal West. The continuing currency of such imagery and

sentiments can be seen in their deployment for perfectly good humanitarian causes.

Could we not leave veils and vocations of saving others behind and instead train our sights on ways to make the world a more just place? The reason respect for difference should not be confused with cultural relativism is that it does not preclude asking how we, living in this privileged and powerful part of the world, might examine our own responsibilities for the situations in which others in distant places have found themselves. We do not stand outside the world, living under the shadow— or veil—of oppressive cultures; we are part of that world. Islamic movements themselves have arisen in a world shaped by the intense engagements of Western powers in Middle Eastern lives.

A more productive approach, it seems to me, is to ask how we might contribute to making the world a more just place. A world not organized around strategic military and economic demands; a place where certain kinds of forces and values that we may still consider important could have an appeal and where there is the peace necessary for discussions, debates, and transformations to occur within communities. We need to ask ourselves what kinds of world conditions we could contribute to making such that popular desires will not be overdetermined by an overwhelming sense of helplessness in the face of forms of global injustice. Where we can seek to be active in the affairs of distant places, can we do so in the spirit of support for those within those communities who goals are to make women's (and men's) lives better? Can we use a more egalitarian language of alliances, coalitions, and solidarity, instead of salvation?

Even RAWA, which was so instrumental in bringing to U.S. women's attention the excesses of the Taliban, has opposed the U.S. bombing from the beginning. They do not see in it Afghan women's salvation but increased hardship and loss. They have long called for disarmament and for peace-keeping forces. Spokespersons point out the dangers of confusing governments with people, the Taliban with innocent Afghans who will be harmed. They consistently remind audiences to take a close look at the ways policies are being organized around oil interests, the arms industry, and the international drug trade. They are not obsessed with the veil, even though they are the most radical feminists working for a secular democratic Afghanistan. Unfortunately, only their messages about the excesses of the Taliban have been heard, even though their criticisms of those in power in Afghanistan include previous regimes. A first step in hearing their wider message is to break with the language of alien cultures, whether to understand or eliminate them. Missionary work and colonial feminism belong in the past. Our task is to critically explore what we might do to help create a world in which those poor Afghan women, for whom "the hearts of those in the civilized world break," can have safety and decent lives.

REFERENCES

Abu-Lughod, Lila. 1986. Veiled Sentiments: Honor and Poetry in a Bedouin Society. Berkeley: University of California Press.

———. 2013. Do Muslim Women Need Saving? Cambridge: Harvard University Press.

Ahmed, Leila. 1992. Women and Gender in Islam. New Haven, CT: Yale University Press.

Lazreg, Marnia. 1994. The Eloquence of Silence: Algerian Women in Question. New York: Routledge.

Mahmood, Saba. 2001. Feminist Theory, Embodiment and the Docile Agent: Some Reflections on the Egyptian Islamic Revival. Cultural Anthropology 16(2):202–235.

Ong, Aihwa. 1988. Colonialism and Modernity: Feminist Re-Presentations of Women in Non-Western Societies. Inscriptions 3–4:79–93.

Papanek, Hanna. 1982. Purdah in Pakistan: Seclusion and Modern Occupations for Women. *In* Separate Worlds. Hanna Papanek and Gail Minault, eds. Pp. 190–216. Columbus, MO: South Asia Books.

Spivak, Gayatri Chakravorty. 1988. Can the Subaltern Speak? *In* Marxism and the Interpretation of Culture. Cary Nelson and Lawrence Grossberg, eds. Pp. 271–313. Urbana: University of Illinois Press.

U.S. Government. 2002. Electronic document, http://www.whitehouse.gov/news/releases/2001/11/20011117, Accessed January 10,

Van Sommer, Annie and Samuel Zwemer. 1907. Our Moslem Sisters: A Cry of Need from Lands of Darkness Interpreted by Those Who Heard It. New York: F. H. Revell.

PART TWO

Becoming/Being Gendered

If gender is *socially constructed*, then what are the various ways that humans become gendered? The topics in this section explore some key domains in which gender is learned and expressed, from the explicit and tacit messages that we are taught as children and youth, to our language, appearance, bodies, and the media.

6. *Growing up Gendered:* These readings examine and compare how children and adolescents learn (and sometimes challenge) dominant gender norms from their parents and peers, from their work and play, and from other sources. Cindi Katz compares differences and changes in the "home range" (distance that children can travel away from home without adult supervision) of boys and girls in rural Sudan and urban New York City, with some surprising conclusions. Richard Mora examines how Dominican and Puerto Rican boys use their bodies to create and change their masculine identities during puberty in relation to one another, to girls, and to other available models of masculinity. Alison Rooke analyzes the limits of gendered spaces that are premised on binaries of male/female, especially for trans youth, and explores one effort by trans youth in the United Kingdom to create transgendered spaces.

7. *Language and Performance:* One important way in which dominant gender codes are produced, reproduced, and sometimes transgressed is

through language and, more broadly, performance. Sometimes our words are also actions (such as the phrase "I promise"), which linguists call *performativity*, whereby speech is a form of social action. Judith Butler, among others, has applied and expanded this concept to theorize gender. She argues that gender is produced (and sometimes challenged and changed) through the repeated actions and expressions of language, appearance, behavior, and so forth. Thus, she argues, gender is a performative process, a set of continuous acts of "doing" gender rather than a static state of "being" gendered. These readings explore how we become, experience, and express gender through language and performance. Don Kulick compares dominant female and male language forms in a Papua New Guinean village, examining how these forms are understood as gendered and, in turn, reproduce gendered stereotypes about angry, "traditional" women and calm, "modern" men. Deborah Cameron complicates easy alignments of gender and language by demonstrating how our prior assumptions about gender differences can in fact shape our seemingly "objective" analysis of linguistic material through a reanalysis of a set of recorded conversations among five white, 21-year-old American college students. Kath Weston explores how lesbians in California produce and experience gendered differences (like *butch/femme*) in different historical moments, situations, meanings, and ways.

8. *Bodies/Embodiment:* These readings explore how, like language, our bodies can serve as sites for experiencing and expressing gender. Susan Greenhalgh examines how the medicalization of the "war on fat" in the United States has produced "fat-subjects" and "fat-talk" that, by making moral judgments about people who are only slightly heavier than "normal" weight, can often have deeply unhealthy, gendered effects. Thaïs Machado-Borges explores the gender and class dynamics of the Brazilian obsession with using plastic surgery to correct the "problem" of "man boobs" in adolescent boys. Aihwa Ong looks at women's bodies as sites of control where gender politics, health, educational practices, and, most recently, capitalist labor demands intersect in Malaysia. But these same bodies are also the vehicle for experiencing and expressing distress over these gendered practices, in this case through outbreaks of spirit possession among female factory workers.

9. *Mediated Lives:* Another key source for the production, expression, and contestation of dominant and alternative gendered ideas and practices is the media. New communication technologies like social media, the Internet, and films have enabled people across the world to imagine new possibilities of being and to establish virtual connections that transcend their physical locations. But these new media sources and resources do not appear on a blank landscape; they are understood,

absorbed, and reworked through the prism of prior and ongoing gendered, social, political, and economic dynamics. Casey High examines how young Waorani men in Amazonian Ecuador express specific generational forms of masculinity in reference to past violence, urban intercultural relations, and global film images like Bruce Lee and Rambo. Jennifer Johnson-Hanks explores how the Internet has transformed the marriage prospects of young women in Cameroon, who can now seek European husbands to fulfill their local conceptions of "proper" marriage and ideal husbands. Mary L. Gray analyzes how rural LGBTQ, queer, and questioning young people in the United States have drawn on media-generated source materials to create and rework their identities, depending on their material conditions, cultural context, and history.

1 · *Cindi Katz*

GROWING GIRLS/CLOSING CIRCLES
Limits on the Spaces of Knowing in Rural Sudan and U.S. Cities

DISCUSSION QUESTIONS

1. Why do boys and girls in rural Sudan and New York City have different "home ranges"? How and why have these changed over time?
2. What are the effects of the differences in access to and control over outdoor environments between boys and girls for their cognitive development?
3. How is gender learned, expressed and produced through such differences in spatial control and mobility?

Social power is reflected in and exercised through the production and control of space. These socio-spatial relations are gendered and vary across the life course, riddled by differences associated with class, ethnicity, race, and nationality. From "dad's chair" to occupied national territories, the spatial forms of control are charged with and interpenetrated by political-economic power, cultural meaning, and personal significance. These conjunctures are neither stable over time nor distributed evenly across space. This chapter explores their gendered form and significance in the shifts from childhood to youth and adulthood in two divergent settings—rural Sudan and urban United States.

The notions that access to and control of space are greater for males than females and increase with age, at least until middle adulthood, are so commonplace that they remain largely unexamined. Their significance in everyday life has been under-thematized and thus little explored in social science research. While Western social scientists have been vocal about restrictions on women's mobility in Islamic cultures—explicating and condemning *purdah* as a monolithic restraint on women—the constraints on women's access to space in the West have been less well recognized. But in many ways these are as formidable and as systemic as those associated with Islam. The spatial forms in which

An abridged version of Cindi Katz, 2001. "Growing Girls/Closing Circles: Limits on the Spaces of Knowing in Rural Sudan and United States Cities." In D. Hodgson (ed.), *Gendered Modernities: Ethnographic Perspectives.* New York: Palgrave, pp. 173-202. Reprinted with the kind permission of the author and of the publisher.

social control is manifested are emblematic of the contradictory intersections between public and private spheres in everyday life. This chapter addresses some of these issues cross-culturally to make more vivid the forms, variations, meanings and interpretations of different conjunctures of space and power over the life course of women.

Evidence from my research among children in rural Sudan contradicts the propositions that boys exercise greater control over space than girls; and that access to space expands with age. First, the home range (distance children travel away from home unaccompanied by adults) of boys did not appear to be greater than that of girls during early and middle childhood. Second, while boys' range continued to increase as they come of age, girls' access to space became constricted at puberty, and the spaces they controlled were close to home, at least until they passed their prime child-bearing years. While in the United States spatial range tends to increase with age for boys and girls alike, the reasons undergirding it and its differential consequences for men and women bear greater scrutiny. It remains that females' spaces are generally more circumscribed at all ages. Fear of personal injury or violation may be the *purdah* of the industrialized West, effectively curtailing girls' and women's access to public space. Yet Western scholars still often train their focus on *purdah* and its restrictive implications for women's lived experience, ignoring how girls and women in the industrialized West are similarly constrained in their access to and control of space.

In examining these relationships, both within each setting and between them, this piece explores the diversity of spatial experience and addresses some of the enduring consequences of women's restricted access to and control of the environment. The chapter contributes to breaking down stereotypical notions of *purdah* by demonstrating some of its asymmetries and examining the similarities between it and other strategies by which women's movements are restricted. In drawing these comparisons my intent is to deepen our understanding of how gendered and hierarchized power relations are manifested in the spatial forms and practices of girls' and women's everyday lives, and to reflect on their significance both in women's experience and for the social formations within which they live their lives.

CHILDREN'S SPATIAL RANGE IN RURAL SUDAN

In Howa, a rural Sudanese village of about 335 households where I conducted research intermittently between 1980 and 1995, spending a year there in 1980–81, girls and boys roamed widely and freely in the village, and the fields, pastures and wooded areas at its outskirts five kilometers away. The twinned plagues of supervision and lack of autonomy that have become the lot of children in United States cities and suburbs were not theirs. Not only did these children play independently around the village beginning in early childhood, but by nine or ten years of age they had responsibility for tasks that routinely led them out of the confines of the settlement. With this responsibility came a fair degree of autonomy in their control of time and space. Girls, for instance, collected fuelwood and gathered food and other resources from wooded areas up to an hour's walk away. Boys also left the village to collect fuelwood and other resources as well as to shepherd, which was the responsibility of about a third of all boys in Howa at some time during their late childhood or adolescence. In these tasks the children participated in making decisions concerning the terrain they worked, often choosing it themselves; were responsible for selecting their routes; and independently determined when to return to the village each day. Boys and girls also left the settlement to assist their elders in the farm tenancies bordering the village one to five kilometers away. In agriculture children's autonomy was more curtailed. Time and space were controlled by the elders, who set the pace, scheduling and daily limits for each task, which took place in clearly demarcated farm tenancies.

My research indicated that boys and girls alike shared a rich geographic knowledge that included an understanding of local spatial relationships and an extensive knowledge of the local environment and its resources (cf., Katz 1989, 1991, 2004). In large measure these were gained in the course of their work and play in and around the village. While the content of the girls' and boys' activities differed and was reflected in their knowledge, the arenas in which these activities took place did not. Unlike their U.S. counterparts, these children were at liberty to explore their "neighborhood," and its surrounds without undue surveillance. Their geographic knowledge was but one reflection of this freedom, which children in the industrialized West increasingly lack in their overscheduled and supervised daily lives.

From the age of three or four children in Howa delivered messages or carried food and other small items from one house to another within the house-yard of their extended family. When just slightly older, they began to run errands around the village—picking up something at the store, fetching small containers of water from the well, or conveying messages to neighbors. The age at which these activities commenced depended in part on the children's birth-order position. First born children tended to assume responsibilities at an earlier age than those with older siblings to do the work. Moreover, while certain chores were passed down, there was a tendency for older children to continue with many of them, sparing their younger brothers and sisters for other activities, like playing or going to school. By seven or eight years of age, all children in Howa did these tasks at least occasionally, and also began to work outside the confines of the settlement, accompanying their elders to assist in the fields or going with other children to collect wood and other plant resources. By nine or ten, boys started to herd their families' flocks. Through adolescence, boys continued to work at these and other activities, gradually assuming greater responsibility. But girls' access to the environment outside of the houseyard and especially outside of the village narrowed considerably as they reached puberty and married. While pubescent girls, particularly those without siblings available to take

on their work, continued to fetch water and wood, their movements around the village began to be restricted—they no longer played in the streets and rarely ran errands, for example. At this time girls began to wear flimsy shawls over their heads whenever they left their families' houseyards. As with adults, covering themselves, even tokenistically, was a sign of modesty that facilitated the girls' movements through public spaces. In the 1980s girls in Howa began to marry and bear children by their early teens, during which time their withdrawal from public space was intensified. Women were secluded to different extents depending upon their class position, life course stage and household circumstances. In places like Howa where women rarely participate in tasks that take them outside of their family compounds, the importance of children's work is magnified. In many ways children enabled the practice of *purdah* in Howa because they procured the means of existence and accomplished many of the tasks associated with household reproduction.

CHILDREN'S GEOGRAPHIES IN AN ALTERED SOCIAL SPACE

These spatialized relationships were undergoing a profound alteration in 1981 as a result of the changes brought about by inclusion in the large-scale Suki Agricultural Development Project ten years earlier. Given how tightly the patterns of each gender, age and occupational group were articulated with one another, any alterations within the constellation had individual and collective reverberations with serious implications for present and future. Of particular significance here because of their gender implications are: (1) that women were working in their households' agricultural tenancies and as piece workers during the three-month harvest period given the labor demands of picking cotton and the intensifying local need for cash; (2) that children's labor time and space were expanding due to the extension of the cash economy, the degradation of the local environment, and their mothers' changing work patterns; and (3) that male outmigration was beginning because of limitations on access to land and other productive resources resulting from the fixed number of farm tenancies allocated to the village at the start of the Project. Each of these spatio-temporal shifts raises issues in which production, reproduction and knowledge intersect with consequences for the contemporary work landscape, repercussions for intergenerational relationships, and resonance for rescripting modernity.

As the capitalist relations of production associated with the agricultural development project came to predominate in Howa, a growing need for cash led increasing numbers of women to pick cotton and harvest groundnuts both in their families' tenancies and as piece workers. Who engaged in these practices varied. Women from relatively well-off families worked neither in their households' fields nor those of others, and women in the younger childbearing years almost never worked the fields no matter how dire their household circumstances. However, just ten years after the Project was established, more than 42 per cent of the village households had earnings below subsistence level, and with growing impoverishment the strictures of *purdah* began to break down. About a third of the women in Howa reported working for cash during the harvest, and of these, virtually all who were from tenant households picked cotton in their own tenancies as well. To accommodate this new socioeconomic situation spatiotemporally, many families in Howa set up "camps" and moved their entire household to the fields during the harvest, bringing the tasks of production and reproduction together in a different setting, and enabling the maximum labor input from all family members including women with young children.

Children's work also expanded and intensified as a result of the twin processes of environmental degradation and commodification associated with Howa's inclusion in the agricultural project. In brief, to establish the Suki Project approximately 2,500 acres were cleared for farm tenancies in the immediate vicinity of the village, encompassing most of the grazing and wooded areas near the village. The transition put immense pressure on the remaining wood and grasslands, which were severely degraded within the first two decades of the Project's establishment. This destruction of the local environment required children and others to go further afield and to spend more time to procure adequate household fuel supplies and graze animals. As local resources were commodified and households' needs for cash grew, children's work increased. They earned cash for their households selling water, wood and food, for example, and working as paid field hands. They also played a key role in the seasonally intensive work of cotton picking.

In many households—particularly the poorer ones—these changes interfered with school enrollment and attendance. My research suggested that it was the poorest and richest households that appeared to require the most work of their children. In the impoverished households, male and female children's labor was necessary to maintain basic household subsistence and provide cash on occasion. In the wealthiest households the differentiation of household production activities required increased labor of children as well. In these households there was a process of specialization which affected boys in particular—certain sons worked the fields, others were sent to school, others learned about raising livestock, and still others learned about trading. As they worked these boys were groomed for their future roles in their extended families' economies. I did not discern any systematic variation in girls' roles, even in wealthier households, and the extremely low level of female school enrollment in Howa at the time precludes systematic analysis of whose daughters went to school.

In addition, by 1981 young men were beginning to leave Howa for nearby towns in search of work. Part of this shift was demographic. Only 250 tenancies were allocated to Howa when the Project was established in 1971, which fell short of the number of households in the village. Moreover, as new households were formed and tenants remained active, the chance to acquire a farm tenancy grew progressively slimmer for each prospective tenant. Prior to the Suki Project, when subsistence dryland cultivation was practiced in Howa, young men coming of age would have been given a small plot from their families' holdings, including fallow lands, or cleared new land at the margins of the village's cultivated area. As household needs grew young farmers would extend the area of cultivation into new areas or the fallowed land of their extended family, none of which were more than an hour's walk from the village. With the Suki Project all bets were off. Given (1) the fixed number of tenancies allocated to the village, (2) the fact that the average family in Howa included five children, and (3) the early age of marriage and childbearing (which meant, for example, that many twenty-year-old men had parents in their thirties and thus still economically active), few young men had access to land as they began to form their own households.

In the face of these conditions, lured by the "better" life they witnessed or heard about in the towns, young men in Howa began to seek employment in the nearby Project headquarters and market towns in the region. Male outmigration often leads to the increased participation of women and children in agricultural production. As this occurred in Howa, the practice of *purdah* was likely to be further eroded. But with more general rural depopulation and the creation of more urbanized households, male outmigration tended to reinforce *purdah* because female seclusion is more easily facilitated by town life where it is customary for male household members to do all marketing, and where, particularly among the middle class, there was heightened social pressure to conform with its strictures. If young couples move to towns without their extended families, as was happening in Howa, it may well come to mean greater seclusion for women than they experienced in in the village where the houseyard provided a setting that was anything but secluded.

These shifts in the activities of women, children, and men led not only to new sociospatial patterns over their life courses, but for the village and region as a whole. For example, as women began to work away from the household for certain tasks, the construction of *purdah* was altered to support the expansion of women's spatial domains. To the extent that women took on tasks previously performed by children—for example, fuelwood collection when the available sources become too distant—children's time was released and a growing number might then attend school. Such increases and decreases in children's labor are part of a matrix of sociospatial work relations, and were taking place in a political-economic field in which it was becoming increasingly clear to many parents that the new regime of accumulation in Sudan required a new kind of preparation of their children. As they witnessed the quest for work by the first generation to come of age after the establishment of the Project, their best hopes were that government schools would prepare their children for the changing circumstances they were facing.

The population was not passive in the face of external change. Within fifteen years of the Project's founding, the Village Council of Howa sponsored the construction of a girls' school using self-help funds generated through the village sugar cooperative. Cognizant of the complex space-time considerations of household work, however, the Council first sponsored the construction of standpipes throughout the village with the option for individual clans to bring piped water into their compounds. This local initiative, supported by the state, reduced children's and particularly girls' labor time substantially. In many cases it made the difference between attending school or not. In later years, hand pumps were installed around the village by a European NGO, further reducing the labor time involved in fetching water, and in tandem with this development the Village Council oversaw the construction of a secondary school in Howa.

It is not trite to note that school attendance was likely to expand the horizons of girls in Howa. As more of them went on to high school they might begin careers as teachers, health practitioners, midwives, and social workers. At the same time the increasing rate of male outmigration would also affect female horizons, resulting in less metaphoric expansions. In the face of a rising male exodus from the village, agricultural production was likely to be taken over by women in Howa. Under these conditions, the childhood work and learning experiences of girls in the fields, forests and open lands around the village, would prove useful to them in their adulthoods, and their social activity space upon reaching puberty might not be as constricted.

SPACE AND LEARNING

Children's knowledge in Howa was acquired in a "community of practice," rooted and developed in their extensive environmental experiences amongst elders and peers (Lave and Wenger 1991). Developmental psychologists working cross-culturally have demonstrated a positive relationship between "self-managed sequences" of work and play and the development of analytic ability (cf. Nerlove *et al.* 1974). Going out alone in the community is an important arena of self-managed behavior for children. Earlier research by Nerlove and her colleagues revealed direct links between children's autonomous environmental experience and the development of analytic ability, including the acquisition of large "cognitive maps" and the spatial ability that goes along with their construction and negotiation (Nerlove *et al.* 1971). In Howa children's spatial autonomy along with their work and play activities in a variety of shared settings lent themselves to and called for the development of a range of cognitive abilities through middle childhood when the options for girls began to narrow and when those (boys) who continued their formal education had to leave the village altogether.

Children in urban areas of many industrialized Western countries have far fewer opportunities for such "grounded" learning and free exploration. Their access to the outdoor environment is limited largely by parental concerns for their safety—physical and psychosocial. These concerns have arisen in large measure due to the deterioration of the urban environment brought about by capital disinvestment coupled with a steady and often shrill

public rhetoric concerning children's safety and the seeming omnipresence of threats to their well-being (e.g., Katz 2001b, 2006, 2012). At the same time as these threats are posed, there have been dramatic shifts in household composition over the last few decades in the U.S. and fewer women or other family members are available to care for children when they are not in school or other programs. The number of single-parent families has grown steadily and women increasingly have left home-based care-giving roles for the paid labor force out of economic necessity and/or in response to changing socioeconomic relations of production and reproduction. Under these circumstances safe access to the outdoor environment in the U.S. is becoming a class privilege available to children whose parents can afford child care, safer living environments and/or special programs. Even then, these options rarely allow the kind of unencumbered and autonomous access that children in Sudan had to the outdoor environment. The erosion of children's autonomy and outdoor experience in industrialized Western cities marks not only a deterioration in the quality of children's lives, but an arena of deskilling with long-term implications both for the children and for the society as a whole.

While it is easy for Western eyes to see the limits to mobility imposed by *purdah,* or the foreclosing of some of life's choices without a formal education, closer scrutiny of the lives of children in our industrialized cities reveals deep impoverishment of experience and a staggering disregard for its consequences except insofar as they impinge on middle-class concerns. The comparison of girls' and boys' lives in these diverse settings is intended to point to the need for change in both.

CHILDHOOD CITY

Children are curious about the life of their communities. They are intrigued by the activities of their elders and throughout childhood experiment with fitting themselves into the social fabric around them. In places like Howa children have easy access to much of this life. Their lives and those of their elders take place in sociophysical settings that are largely overlapping. Children not only witness but participate in much of the work undertaken by members of their households. The sociophysical domains of children and adults are more discrete in industrialized nations, particularly in urban areas where children's opportunities to observe the range of work and other activities of their elders are severely restricted. In these areas children learn a great deal about the comings and goings of their community by playing in the streets and other public spaces that give them visual access to its everyday life, even as these sites place their activities under the gaze of others.

For a variety of reasons many parents in U.S. cities are loath to allow their children to play outdoors without adult supervision, but are not around to provide it or pay others to do so. Many of these children are home alone after school. Unable to play with friends or explore outdoor environments on their own, these children lose important opportunities for social, physical and cognitive development. These problems are not evenly distributed. Girls are particularly restricted in this regard. Studies of children's outdoor play in industrialized settings have consistently found significant differences between girls' and boys' autonomy, the extent of their free range area, and the ways in which they use space. Hart (1979), for example, found not only that girls' home range was smaller than that of boys among all socioeconomic groups in a small town in Vermont, but that girls were not encouraged to explore and manipulate their environment to the same extent as the boys in their community. In Stockholm, Bjorklid (1985) found that boys were given more territorial freedom at an earlier age than girls. Noting that most of the outdoor spaces provided in urban areas, particularly those abutting high-rise housing, are flat open spaces preferred and dominated by boys, she found that girls' range was even more constrained in areas of high-rise buildings. Bjorklid argues that girls in the city lost out in three ways; there were few outdoor places for the quieter play activities that they preferred, such as dramatic play,

sitting games and socializing; these activities were difficult to undertake outdoors in the cold winter months; and the skills developed in the course of team sports—which predominated in the open spaces of the neighborhood—were more highly valued by the larger adult society than those developed in the course of the girls' outdoor activities. Our findings in a study of New York City schoolyards echoed Bjorklid's. When asked where girls played given that boys' sporting activities frequently consumed all available space, one boy blithely told us, "They play on the empty spots!"

LOST SPACES OF KNOWING

People often make a distinction between "dangerous" and "unsafe" environments, the former implying social hazards, and the latter physical. This distinction points to some common bonds in the experiences of girls and boys in Sudan and the urban United States, where many of the restrictions on children's movements were concerned primarily with access to girls' bodies. These patterns reflect the codes of control that define female experience in most of the world. While *purdah* is recognized as an explicit means to effect this control, equally powerful codes—implicit and explicit—limit female access to and control over space in the heart of the advanced capitalist industrialized world as well.

All studies of children's outdoor experience in Western industrialized settings—rural, suburban and urban—reveal that boys are allowed greater spatial freedom and range from an earlier age than girls. Yet boys are injured with greater frequency than girls from all manner of "unsafe" elements in the environment—traffic, falls, poor play equipment and the like, as well as from accidents incurred in the "normal" course of play. However concerned parents are about physical injury, it does not appear to motivate significant restrictions on their children's movements, especially for boys.

Fears concerning the social dangers to which children are exposed, however, seem to impel parents to limit children's, and particularly girls', autonomy outdoors. The data suggest that, at least in the U.S., boys are the more common victims of social dangers as well. Even as boys suffer more frequent sexual and physical abuse than girls or comprise the majority of adolescent prostitutes, parents continue to act as if their sons were immune to these social dangers (Smith 1991). Without minimizing the real and present dangers to which children outdoors alone in the U.S. are exposed, it appears, at least in part, that parents are responding more to the horrifying and headline-grabbing nature of social crimes against children than the actual incidence of them (most of which happen at home in any case). These perceptions lead parents to exercise greater precaution—especially concerning their daughters' movements—than these events might warrant. But that is the nature of risk perception, and parents make choices and rules for their children within a risk calculus that is as much a function of fear as fact, of statistical reality (whatever that is) as social custom, of emotion as economics. The result is that girls in urban industrialized areas are restricted from exploring and manipulating the outdoor environment perhaps even more so than girls in ostensibly more restrictive societies such as Islamic Sudan. I am, of course, mindful of the counter-argument that it is because parents keep their children indoors or under adult supervision that social crimes against them are not more prevalent. To a certain extent this is surely true. My argument here is that: (1) parents do not restrict their children's access to the outdoors to protect them from "unsafe" environments as much as from "dangerous" ones; (2) childhood injuries from "unsafe" environments exceed those from "dangerous" ones in number and in frequency; and (3) girls are perceived to be at disproportionate risk from the latter while boys are apparently at disproportionate risk from both. The net result is that boys have greater access to and control over the outdoor environment than girls despite the risks it poses to them; while perceptions of the less common but more violating threats to girls limit their control over space even in their own communities.

The loss of environmental experience has serious ramifications for all children. The life course implications of girls' restricted worlds are especially severe. I referred above to the demonstrated links between autonomous and self-directed sequences of behavior and the development of analytic ability; and suggested that autonomous exploration and manipulation of the outdoor environment were an important arena wherein children "self-direct" the sequencing of their behavior. Developmental, environmental and cognitive psychologists, as well as anthropologists and geographers, have found that boys tend to exceed girls in spatial and mathematical ability, that their cognitive maps and mapping skills are more elaborated, and that they are more skilled at related analytic operations (e.g., Nerlove *et al.* 1971; Saegert and Hart 1978; Harris 1981; Liben 1981). These differences are in part the result of children's uneven access to the public environment. My concern is not only that gendered differences in children's spatial experiences favor greater development of particular skills and abilities among boys than girls, but that, because of unequal social and economic relations, certain girls may be deprived of the chance to develop these skills at all, diminishing their life chances but also affecting overall socioeconomic productivity.

CONCLUSION

This chapter has attempted to demonstrate the nature of restrictions on female mobility in two distinct settings—rural Sudan and urban United States—and explored some of the life course implications of these spatial patterns. In comparing these two cases, what was striking for me was that despite obvious (potentially blinding) surface differences, there was so much in common in female experience and its meaning for the control over and production of space. Important commonalities were (1) how the particular configuration of the household affects children's spatial experience and how shifts in this configuration can have dramatic impacts upon children's access to the environment; (2) how restrictions upon girls' mobility were rooted in social codes that control access to the female body; and (3) how girls' relative lack of experience with the environment compared with boys' was a form of deskilling with enduring implications for them and the society as a whole.

Part of my intent in exploring these two cases was to "de-essentialize" *purdah* as a social practice by showing not only that it was deployed unevenly in Islamic areas, but that female mobility was restricted in the urban U.S. as well, perhaps more perniciously because it is masked by an ideology of equality. My work suggests that children in rural Sudan had a more extensive immediate world than their counterparts in many urban areas of the United States, and that, unlike the U.S., access to and control over space was not sharply divided by class or gender. Without romanticizing the experiences of children in rural Sudan, it appears that the variation and range in what they were able to encounter in their everyday lives enabled them not only to acquire an extensive knowledge of the surrounding environment but their freedom to explore and manipulate this environment endowed them with learning skills.

While in Sudan the sociospatial patterns of most females' adulthoods did not allow the full development of much of this knowledge, it is possible that their autonomous learning skills will empower them in the face of changed circumstances and novel possibilities. In the case of the United States it is hard to be optimistic. My work and that of others suggests that childhood experience is being eroded in a way that actively deskills children, and particularly girls, reducing their life chances in adulthood. This is aggravated by the structural shrinkage of life chances due to the crises of capitalism that affect the work landscapes of so many children coming of age at the dawn of the twenty-first century.

POSTSCRIPT

I returned to Howa in 1995 to follow up on what had happened to the village and the "children,"

now grown. I interviewed all but one of the surviving sixteen children with whom I had worked earlier. Much of what I anticipated might happen to Howa over the years did, but not quite in the ways I had anticipated. While these changes are discussed at length elsewhere (e.g., Katz 2000; 2001a; 2004), a number of them have resonance in light of the concerns outlined in this piece. By 1995, the continued deteriorations in the local landscape coupled with the exclusion of most newly formed households from the agricultural project had provoked something I call "time-space expansion." Through this surprising configuration, people were able to still carry out the old pattern of livelihood practices encompassing agriculture, animal husbandry and forestry but only in a much expanded field. Wood was cut and charcoal produced in areas 200 kilometers away, animals were grazed in pastures more than 100 kilometers from Howa, and seasonal agricultural work was taken in similarly far-flung places. This pattern—which often included a seasonal stint of work in regional or more distant towns—was a form of resilience that forestalled more permanent migration to urban areas at the levels I had anticipated, and enabled the endurance of some semblance of rural life in Howa.

The pattern was, of course, gendered. Virtually all of this work was undertaken by men, and the mobility it entailed increased the circumference of their everyday lives. While this sociospatial pattern—which straddled various arenas of work—did not leave women in the village in charge of agricultural production anywhere near the extent that I had imagined, it did alter substantially the patterns of their everyday lives as well. If men's spatial range expanded in the face of the political ecological deteriorations and political economic difficulties they faced in Howa, it was women's time that became more protracted.

As the first generations to come of age after the agricultural project were displaced from the easy assumption of tenancies and all that went with it, two concurrent and intertwined shifts occurred. Young men in growing numbers began to migrate away from the village in search of work, and local views concerning formal education changed markedly. This change was first demonstrated in the construction and staffing of a girls' school in Howa following the village-wide provision of standpipes in 1984 noted above. The results were startling. In 1981 only 4.2% of the girls 7–12 years old attended school (and very few of them got past second grade), but not fifteen years later more than 43% of the school-aged girls in Howa attended, with many of them not only graduating but going on to secondary school. Further, by the middle of the 1990s as the deskilling of their children became obvious to adults in Howa, there was another village-wide mobilization on behalf of schooling which resulted in the construction of a secondary school in the village, completed in 1995. This palpable transformation in local views on formal education was spurred, among other things, by the further-flung travels of young men and others from Howa as much as from the increased role of formal education itself. But the turn to formal schooling was also in response to the visceral experiences of displacement provoked by the agricultural project and all its broader entailments. Despite the substance and significance of this response, the deepening political-economic crises of Sudan rendered local attempts to rework the circumstances of young people largely moot. Even the most educated young men struggled to find work that compensated adequately, and many of them ended up participating in the mobile work patterns associated with "time-space expansion." And this, in part, was where the protraction of women's time came in.

Young women in Howa—those who had attended school and those who had not—were well prepared to continue the work of reproduction, but because young men—again, those that had attended school and those that had not—had a harder time raising a bride price than in previous times, the age of marriage was increasing. Not only was the bride price inflating rapidly by the 1990s, but it was outstripping wage rates significantly. The circumstances of Sudan's economy made it extraordinarily difficult for men in Howa to patch together the necessary goods and wealth to marry—the rise in education there and the creative strategies associated

with time-space expansion notwithstanding. These circumstances left women (and men) in a protracted adolescence, much like young people in the U.S. who cannot find steady work after completing their education. But while men at least had the freedom to travel for work, the women continued to live and work in their parents' households doing things post-pubertal girls rarely had done before, including gathering wood, fetching water and working in the fields during the harvest. *Purdah*'s mutability was clear in these altered practices.

These patterns suggest the spatio-temporal contours of a peculiarly, if not perversely, gendered modernity. With time-space expansion and growing awareness in Howa of social practices urban areas near and far—both of which suggest extraordinary resilience and agile patterns of reworking the conditions associated with increasingly difficult political economic and political ecological circumstances—young people's horizons were expanding as the possibilities of their reaching them seemed to recede. In the expanded field produced at the intersection of the material social practices of what I am calling time-space expansion and the structural processes akin to what Michel-Rolph Trouillot (1996) calls "fragmented globality," the young people with whom I worked in New York as much as in Howa have come of age with a growing sense of being marooned in the ferment of all that is possible. A sadder commentary on the promises of "development" is hard to imagine.

REFERENCES

Bjorklid, Pia. 1985. "Children's Outdoor Environment from the Perspectives of Environmental and Developmental Psychology." In Tommy Garling and Jaan Valsiner, eds., *Children within Environments: Toward a Psychology of Accident Prevention*. New York: Plenum.

Harris, L.J. 1981. "Sex-Related Variations in Spatial Skill." In Lynn S. Liben, Arthur H. Patterson and Nora Newcombe, eds., *Spatial Representation and Behavior across the Life Span*. New York: Academic Press.

Hart, Roger. 1979. *Children's Experience of Place*. New York: Irvington.

Katz, Cindi. 1989. "Herders, Gatherers and Foragers: The Emerging Botanies of Children in Rural Sudan." *Children's Environments Quarterly* 6(1): 46–53.

———. 1991. "Sow What You Know: The Struggle for Social Reproduction in Rural Sudan." *Annals of the Association of American Geographers* 81(3): 488–514.

———. 2000. "Fueling War: A Political-Ecology of Poverty and Deforestation in Sudan." In Vigdis Broch-Due and Richard Schroeder, eds., *Producing Nature and Poverty in Africa*. Uppsala: Nordic Africa Institute and Transaction Press.

———. 2001a. "On the Grounds of Globalization: Towards a Topography of Feminist Political Engagement." *Signs* 26(4).

———. 2001b. "The State Goes Home: Local Hypervigilance and the Global Retreat from Social Reproduction." *Social Justice* 28(3): 47–56.

———. 2004. *Growing Up Global: Economic Restructuring and Children's Everyday Lives*. Minneapolis: University of Minnesota Press.

———. 2006. "Power, Space and Terror: Social Reproduction and the Public Environment." In Setha M. Low and Neil Smith, eds., *The Politics of Public Space*. New York: Routledge, pp. 105–21.

———. 2012. "Just Managing: American Middle-Class Parenthood in Insecure Times." In Rachel Heiman, Carla Freeman, and Mark Liechty, eds., *The Global Middle Classes: Theorizing Through Ethnography*, Santa Fe: SAR Press, pp. 169–88.

Lave, Jean and Wenger, Etienne. 1991. *Situated Learning: Legitimate Peripheral Participation*. Cambridge and New York: Cambridge University Press.

Liben, Lynn S. 1981. "Spatial Representation and Behavior: Multiple Perspectives." In Lynn S. Liben, Arthur H. Patterson, and Nora Newcombe, eds., *Spatial Representation and Behavior across the Life Span*. New York: Academic Press.

Nerlove, Sara B., Munroe, Ruth H., and Munroe, Robert L. 1971. "Effect of Environmental Experience on Spatial Ability: A Replication." *Journal of Social Psychology* 84: 3–10.

Nerlove, S.B., Roberts, J.M., Klein, R.E., Yarbrough, C., and Habicht, J-P. 1974. "Natural Indicators of Cognitive Development: An Observational Study of Rural Guatemalan Children." *Ethos* 2(3): 265–295.

Saegert, Susan and Hart, Roger. 1978. "The Development of Environmental Competence in Girls and Boys." In M. Salter, ed., *Play: Anthropological Perspectives*. Cornwall, NY: Leisure Press.

Smith, P. 1991. Children's Defense Fund (personal communication).

Trouillot, Michel-Rolph. 1996. "Theorizing a Global Perspective: A Conversation with Michel-Rolph Trouillot." *Crosscurrents in Culture, Power and History: A Newsletter of the Institute for Global Studies in Culture, Power and History, Johns Hopkins University* 4(1): 1–4.

"DO IT FOR ALL YOUR PUBIC HAIRS!"

Latino Boys, Masculinity, and Puberty

DISCUSSION QUESTIONS

1. How do the boys studied by Mora use their bodies to express and enact certain masculine identities during puberty?
2. What are the main sources through which they learn about, absorb, and privilege these masculinities?
3. How does Mora apply ideas about power and intersectionality to analyze his ethnographic evidence?

Pubescence brings about the most noticeable changes to the male body, second only to neonatal development (Martin 1996). The social meanings ascribed to these physical changes, and puberty itself, are locally situated (Janssen 2006). Hence, understanding how boys make sense of puberty and how they interpret and socially construct their bodies during pubescence may illuminate how boys' bodies figure into their gender identities, given that gender involves bodies and that masculinity is a life-long project involving the changing physical body. Yet we lack thorough and sustained *in situ* examinations of how diverse boys employ their bodies to construct masculine identities during pubescence across a range of sociocultural contexts.

The present chapter contributes to our understanding of masculinity by examining how sixth-grade, second-generation, immigrant Dominican and Puerto Rican boys, who publicly acknowledge that they are experiencing puberty, both construct their masculine identities and employ their bodies while at school. The relationship between the boys' gender construction and physiological development emerged early on in a two-and-a-half year ethnographic study that followed a group of sixth graders at Romero Elementary and Middle School, a bilingual school in the greater metropolitan area of a Northeastern city. (All names, including that of the school, have been changed.) At the time of the study, Romero had a total student enrollment of approximately 380, of which approximately 85% were Latina/o. The middle school had approximately 90 students, of which more than 95% were Latina/o. More than 75% of all students received free lunches. Youth gangs in the area marked

An abridged version of Richard Mora, 2012. "Do it for all your pubic hairs!": Latino Boys, Masculinity, and Puberty," *Gender and Society* 26(3): 433-460. Adapted by the author with Permission of SAGE Publications.

their presence with graffiti near Romero, and some Latino and Black youth sported baseball caps associated with their respective gangs. At the end of the school day, it was common for local male youths to congregate near the campus to flirt with middle school girls and meet up with friends and girlfriends. The focus of this chapter is primarily on 10 of the boys—seven second-generation Dominicans and three second-generation Puerto Rican boys who acknowledged, enacted, and maintained their heritages, as described below. Throughout the school day, I observed the boys and their peers in and out the classroom.

At Romero, students of Latin American heritage referred to whites as Americanos (Americans) and regularly identified themselves and each other by their nations of origin. Students whose parents were born in the Dominican Republic, for example, referred to themselves as "Dominicans," and less often as "Latino," "Hispanic," or "Spanish." Many of the students publicly demonstrated their national pride by writing "DR#1" (i.e., Dominican Republic is no. 1) or "PR#1" (i.e., Puerto Rico is no. 1) on desks and in textbooks, and by wearing accessories with their home country's national flag. These students had such strong attachment to their Caribbean countries of origin because they visited regularly and participated in transnationalism, sustaining "multi-stranded social relations that link[ed] their societies of origin and settlement" (Basch, Glick-Schiller, and Blanc 1994, 8). During their visits, the boys were exposed to gender norms that gave primacy to dominant, heteronormative masculinity; gender norms that they brought with them to school.

BOYS' CHANGING BODIES AND MASCULINITY

In the following sections, representative data illustrate how Latino boys at Romero performed masculinity within their peer group during pubescence. The first section documents how the boys referenced their bodies and puberty during playful interactions. The second section considers the boys' longing for muscular male physiques like those in their multiple social worlds. The third section examines how the boys displayed physical strength and punished their bodies to prove their manliness. The last and final section briefly discusses how the boys enacted masculinity after the sixth grade. The data suggest that among the boys, puberty was a social accomplishment connected to masculine enactments informed by: the dominant gendered expectations of peers at school and in their neighborhoods; the hegemonic masculine practices espoused by commercial hip hop rappers; and the dominant gender orders in the United States and both Dominican and Puerto Rican societies.

"Puberty Is Now"

While in the sixth grade, the boys were experiencing sexual maturation—a fact they declared publicly. During a science class discussion on physical development, for example, one boy loudly interjected, "Puberty is now." In addition, the boys' exchanges regularly included references to puberty and the accompanying biological changes. When a boy appeared exceedingly "wild" (i.e., hyperactive), the other boys attributed it to hormonal changes brought on by puberty and, using language introduced by one of them, jokingly rebuked him with statements such as, "Control your hormones!" and "Let your hormones relax, c'mon. Your hormones are gonna get tired." Contrary to retrospective accounts of high school students (Martin 1996), the boys at Romero experienced puberty within their homosocial group, rather than alone.

The boys also referenced puberty in ways that defined the construction of and boundaries surrounding masculine status within their peer group. An exchange about male genitalia, for example, led Brandon to ask Steven whether he had experienced his first menstruation:

[In class] Michael makes fun of Steven by referencing an episode of *South Park* in which a boy has a penis and scrotum growing on his chin. Michael says: "Steven got a little dicky and scrotum on his chin. And it is growing every day."

Brandon joins in: "Steven, did you get your period yet?"

Brandon's depiction of Steven as a pre-menstrual girl called both Steven's gender and pubescent development into question. Here menarche, as a signifier of femininity, is used to interactionally undermine Steven's masculinity. Participating in banter and verbal one-upmanship was a cultural, gendered expectation the boys willingly met. Like other working-class Dominican (De Moya 2004) and Puerto Rican (Ramírez 1999) youth, the boys constructed gender identities and relations of power within their verbal exchanges.

Like other boys, the boys at Romero viewed penises as appendages distinguishing boys from girls and as associated with males' manhood and dominance. They frequently brought up male genitalia to playfully disparage one another's masculine identities, highlighting the interplay between the body and the construction of gendered identities. One afternoon, banter about a banana resulted in the charge that Rudy, the shortest boy, had an undersized penis:

During lunchtime, Michael holds out a peeled banana, wiggles it, and says, "Look, it's crooked." A two-inch long piece of banana breaks off and lands on the table. Michael says, "Look, Steven—he lost his manhood. It fell off."

Steven smiles and says, "That's Rudy's." Cesar chimes in, "Yeah, it's like this"—Cesar holds out his pinkie finger and smiles.

Steven and Cesar used Rudy to demarcate the low masculine status attributed to smaller male bodies. As the only boy referred to as "shrimp," "small fry," or "enano" ["midget"], Rudy was not perceived as physically dominant, which led to the accusation that he

had a small penis. In all, I documented 43 references to secondary sex characteristics during the sixth grade, of which nearly two dozen were public acts of verbal one-upmanship.

The boys mentioned penises much more during the sixth grade than during any other period thereafter, and stopped publicly referencing puberty after the sixth grade. This stark difference in the boys' interactions reveals just how significant the initial phases of their physical development were to them.

Bodies in Transition

The boys compared the size of their flexed biceps and the firmness of their abdomens on almost a daily basis. With comments like, "I'm stronger," they frequently vied to carry boxes and crates for teachers. Through these verbal interactions, the boys enacted a social hierarchy based on the gender status attributed to muscular development, which was proof of a boy's physical transition beyond boyhood and of his willingness to control and transform his physique. The boys openly shared their desire to possess the "sociocultural ideal male physique"—strong, lean, muscular, and fit (McCabe and Ricciardelli 2004). A telling example of how much they yearned for muscular bodies worthy of admiration is a portrait one of them drew of himself and his four closest classmates. The drawing, which according to the illustrator depicted his friends and him "in five or six years," was of five stoic young men, each wearing a tank top and baggy pants, with extremely muscular arms and chests, relatively small waists, and a weapon—either a knife, gun, or crowbar—in his hand. The figures represented the physiological aesthetic the boys were interested in replicating—namely, that of the muscular rappers they favored and of young men in their social worlds who valued strong, dominant bodies.

Both broad and localized cultural expectations associated with masculinity and male bodies informed the boys' imaginings of their future bodies and selves. Consider Michael's reference to gladiators in a fantasy replete with his desire for a tough, sculpted body:

> As students worked independently on an assignment on ancient Rome, Michael says to me, "Richard, I'm going to build a time machine and go back [to ancient Rome]. I'm going to work out so when I go I'm strong. I'm going to get a scar." He moves a finger along his right cheek. "I'm going to fight like the gladiators."

For both cultural and practical reasons, Michael and the rest of the boys valued tough, strong bodies skilled at fighting. Their cultural expectation was that men defend themselves. Practically, Michael and the boys were cognizant that in their neighborhoods strong male bodies became dangerous weapons during physical fights, and because of their association with the capacity to inflict harm, were also highly valued outside of fights.

Since the boys prized muscular definition, they were preoccupied with the amount of fat (or "flubber") on their bodies. Like other boys (James 2000), they held fatness in low regard, equating it with a lack of bodily control and strength. A telling incident transpired after the nurse summoned the entire class for an annual health examination. Pedro and Rodrigo came into the room smiling and in a celebratory tone simultaneously yelled, "I don't have no flubber!" Aware that others scrutinized their bodies, many of the boys "with flubber" masked their concerns with self-deprecating humor. Michael, who wanted to be a gladiator, occasionally lifted his shirt, exposing his stomach, and asked peers, "Do you think I'm fat?" The handful of boys who had flubber also sought to communicate that they were physically strong. For example, while discussing his physical appearance with a thinner, taller female classmate, a boy stated, "I don't care if I don't have a six-pack. I got muscles. That's why you couldn't take the ball away from me [during the basketball game]." Similarly, consider what James said to Michael during a tense dispute:

> Michael says James is fatter than he is. James frowns and says, "I work out with my [adult] brother. I bet

you don't even work out. I am better than you in every sport, except baseball. I don't play baseball."

By highlighting his superior athleticism, James dismissed Michael's comment and communicated that though fatter, his was the more "successful body" (Drummond 2003). As the data show, the boys ascribed masculine status to musculature, which they considered proof of a boy's physical transition beyond boyhood and of his willingness to transform his physique.

Physical Strength, Toughness, and Masculine Status

At Romero, there were no school-sanctioned sports teams. Thus, the boys at Romero lacked the opportunity to gain masculine status on the field or court. This may partially explain why boys opted to bring their masculinity "into action" through a wide array of other physical activities—arm wrestling matches, bloody knuckles, and slap hands—all of which the school banned to curtail confrontations. With these physical enactments, the boys sought to initiate themselves into manhood, while exploring, defining, and patrolling the boundaries of their collective masculine practices. They did this mostly in the lunch area, where it was easier to evade teachers' surveillance.

The boys regularly tried to convince each other to engage in public physical challenges. For example, one afternoon, Raul held out his right clenched fist and invited another boy to play "bloody knuckles" with him: "C'mon, punch my knuckles. It's like a massage. It doesn't hurt me. It's like a massage. C'mon, give me a massage." When rebuffed, boys usually tried to goad prospective competitors with statements such as "Don't be a sissy" and "Don't be a girl." More often than not, boys who declined a challenge were met with ridicule. All this peer pressure and gender policing rarely failed.

Perhaps because they craved external validation, the boys were quick to praise one another for exhibiting grit during physical activities. Such public praise was sometimes a form of gender policing that reinforced the notion that manhood required the withstanding of pain in "sporting situations" (Vaccaro 2011, 71). Here is a representative instance:

> Ignacio asks me to hold out my right hand. I do. He slaps my hand hard three times with his right hand. I pull my hand away. Ignacio smiles, looks over at James and says, "C'mon, James, *you're* a man." James holds out his right hand, and Ignacio slaps it hard twice. They smile. Then, Ignacio asks Jesse to hold his hand out. Jesse does so. Ignacio slaps Jesse's hand twice and announces, "Jesse, *you're* a man." Jesse and Ignacio smile again.

Note how Ignacio declared that James and Jesse were men because, unlike me, an adult male, they displayed toughness. With his declaration, Ignacio also acknowledged his own masculinity as he too withstood pain after delivering each slap. Like boys competing in sporting events, the boys at Romero valued physical toughness and sought out opportunities to demonstrate it.

Most notably, the boys publicly asserted masculine identities during arm wrestling matches, the outcomes of which the boys used to rank themselves. Each match was an opportunity for boys to display physical strength and acquire "physical capital" within their social world regardless of their physical size (Swain 2000, 2003). Note the following lunchtime arm wrestling session:

> Pedro, Ignacio, Bernardo, Adam, and Jason take turns arm wrestling one another.
>
> Jason beats Ignacio, looks over at me, and says nonchalantly, "Kids."
>
> Pedro points at Armando and says, "He's number one in arm wrestling."
>
> Jason nods and says, "Yeah, I don't know how he does it. I'm, like, number three." Pedro then says, "I'm, like, number four."

With his comment, Jason playfully associated his physically weaker peers with boyhood and, by contrast, himself with adolescence and manliness. Moreover, Armando, who despite being among the smallest boys in the group was the best arm wrestler, was praised for his feat. I observed roughly a dozen arm wrestling matches during each visit.

The boys arm wrestled older boys with bigger, more developed physiques. Most of the seventh- and eighth-grade boys accepted challenges only after the younger boys playfully took on tough personas and accused them of being "scared." The older boys won these matches decisively. However, interactions with older, male schoolmates were chances for the boys to test their physical strength and try on the stoic demeanor embodied by rappers and many of the youth in their social worlds.

Like many young men in their neighborhoods, the boys defined themselves as urban, working-class males with ties to their respective countries of origin. In line with the local "code of the street," the boys adopted tough personas and expressed a willingness to fight. They did so in part because in their neighborhoods fights among youths were regular occurrences, and those who did not defend themselves or seek retribution were ridiculed and called "pussies," "bitches," and/or "fags." What is more, they identified with Latino and Black rappers who view the streets as "the school of hard knocks." The boys especially liked rappers who embodied a tough, heterosexual masculinity and displayed dominance, physical strength, and a willingness to use violence. Conversely, the boys rejected wholesome-seeming singers, like the white Justin Timberlake, whose masculine embodiment did not reflect the urban, ethnoracial masculinities they imagined themselves achieving someday.

Over the course of the semester, the girls in the boys' class peer group and those in the other sixth-grade class challenged the boys to arm wrestle approximately two dozen times. The boys rebuffed these challenges because many of their female peers were physically stronger, a fact the boys acknowledged only among themselves. For the boys, to arm wrestle girls *and lose* would have been humiliating since they publicly claimed that males are physically stronger than females.

The banter punctuating arm wrestling matches reified their notions of masculine dominance and heteronormativity. The boys belittled any boy that did not adequately display physical strength or other perceived masculine traits by calling him "a girl" or "a woman"—a finding echoed in previous research (e.g., Thorne 1993; Fine 1987). They levied such accusations over 50 times. Consider the following exchange, for example:

> Santiago and James arm wrestle. James loses. Santiago screams to James, "You're a woman!" Santiago and James laugh. Brandon says to James, "Until you don't [sic] beat him you're a woman."

Both Santiago and Brandon insinuated that James had to display the physical might of a man during arm wrestling matches, rather than the presumed physical weakness of a woman. The boys reduced gender to a male–female binary and considered masculinity the opposite of femininity, much like the many neighborhood youths who also espoused male dominance and the patriarchal tenets of Dominican and Puerto Rican hegemonic masculinities.

Moreover, the boys' homosocial peer group also offered them "a performative space where heterosexuality and masculinity can be fused and displayed" (Kehily 2001, 179). Consistent with Pascoe's (2007) research, the boys also regularly lobbed joking accusations of homosexuality and unmanliness at one another. Here is a case in point:

> Ignacio asks Albert, "You're the son of a fag?"
>   Albert smiles and screams, "Do it [arm wrestle] for all your pubic hairs!"

Using a homophobic slur that was common within the boys' peer group (see Mora 2013), Ignacio implied that Albert's poor performance was evidence of his father's homosexuality. Like his peers, Ignacio coupled heterosexual masculinity and physical strength—a perspective in line with the hegemonic masculinities in the boys' neighborhoods, in their respective countries of origin, and in the United States.

Albert, for his part, then associated boys' corporeal might with pubic hairs, a key signifier of puberty.

Whenever they used their bodies to best male peers, the boys made public declarations of manliness. On average, there were six brash comments, like "I'm a man" or "I'm the man," per day of observation. These loud proclamations drew the attention of teachers, one of whom assured me the boys "don't think of themselves as boys; they think of themselves as men." However, in time, I learned that when they referred to themselves as "men," the boys were simply voicing masculine aspirations. In one another's presence, the boys readily admitted being—as they put it—"pre-teenagers." Thus, with their declarations, the boys attempted to both make sense of their ongoing and impending physical development and shored up what they imagined to be their future masculine identities.

No Longer Little Boys

The boys were viewed as children by both their female classmates and their teachers. Similar to girls in previous research (Dixon 1997), the sixth-grade girls at Romero, who were generally taller and appeared older than their actual age, viewed their bodies as being closer to adulthood and maturity than the boys' bodies and, thus, associated the boys with childhood. Throughout my observations, there were 26 instances in which girls publicly referred to the boys as "little boys" because of what they deemed their "childish" behavior, such as punching lockers, arm wrestling, and play fighting. Similarly, eighth-grade girls regularly called some of the boys "cute" and ruffled their hair, which the boys found condescending. In doing so, the girls at Romero voiced physical expectations for adolescent manliness and influenced the boys' construction of masculine identities.

Teachers also influenced the boys' perceptions of their own physical development. The boys' teachers also infantilized the boys with frequent, public chastisements for acting "like babies" when they "whined" about one another's behavior. Less often, teachers pointed out how particular boys were physically "changing." The boys readily engaged in such assessments:

A female teacher supervising the lunch area walks over to Pedro and Ruben, points to Ruben's face, and says, "You're starting to look sharp. Like a man." Ruben replies, "I *am* a man." The teacher smiles and says, "No, you're not. *He's* [points to me] a man. Do you have 36 teeth [i.e., wisdom teeth]?"

Pedro interjects, "I do." He opens his mouth and counts his teeth with his right index finger: "Owan . . . tuoo . . . threa . . ." The teacher looks at Pedro and says, "No, you don't."

The boys wanted recognition for their physical development, and did not want to hear how much they physically resembled younger boys. Consequently, partly to avoid derision, the boys maintained their homosocial peer group during the sixth grade, but their female peers and teachers nonetheless influenced their masculine identities.

After the summer between the sixth and seventh grade, the boys returned to school physically transformed. All of them were taller, most of them taller than their female classmates, and most of them had shed much of the "flubber" that had occupied their minds months earlier. At the beginning of the seventh grade, their teachers and female peers complimented them on their physiological development, which may explain why many walked with swagger and confidence. Furthermore, from the seventh grade on, the boys rarely engaged in the physical games and challenges of "little boys." That is, they hardly made a public show of their physical strength or their ability to endure physical pain.

Instead, they ventured beyond their homosocial peer group and turned much of their attention to public displays of heteronormative masculinity. More to the point, they flirted with and tried to woo teenage girls, much like peers in the Dominican Republic, who, by the age of 12 or 13, were expected to "show a vivid and visible erotic interest in all females that come close" (De Moya 2004, 74). The most common form of flirting involved *piropos*, or "'amorous compliments,' often undesired by the

females at whom they are directed" (Bailey 2000, 562). Among the 51 documented *piropos*, were phrases used in Spanish songs and by older peers and relatives in their neighborhoods and countries of origin. For example, some of the boys regularly said something like, *"¡Oh, mami! Tu sí 'tas buena* (Oh, baby! You *are* fine)." The boys delivered most of their *piropos* in the presence of male peers, who acknowledged particularly clever compliments and who were likely the *actual* audience for the boys' *piropos*.

Into the flirtatious exchanges, the boys and girls often incorporated sexual innuendos that called attention to their own developed bodies and to those of the individuals they desired. These sorts of interactions allowed the boys and girls to express their physical attraction to one another and to explore the personal and physical boundaries of potential boyfriends and girlfriends. Here is a representative observation that captures the playful manner in which the boys and girls held conversations with sexual undertones:

In class, Samuel is wearing his sweats well below his crotch. Valerie, who is near him, says to Samuel, "Pull 'em up." Samuel replies, "Why don't *you* pull 'em up?" Samuel smiles, and Valerie grins. Later, Samuel says to Valerie, "When my hair grows long you can braid it. And, the hair down here too." Samuel smiles, looking down at his crotch. Valerie smiles and says, "I'll pull it."

During these suggestive exchanges, boys displayed their compliance with compulsory heterosexuality and augmented their masculine status amongst male and female peers.

PUBERTY AND SOCIAL IDENTITIES

By showing how Dominican and Puerto Rican boys collectively construct masculinity during pubescence, this chapter provides important insights into how diverse boys viewed their bodies and how multiple cultures inform the intersection of masculinity, ethnicity and gender. The boys wanted height and physical musculature so that others, particularly their female peers and teachers, would no longer read them as "little boys." They yearned for muscular bodies that approximated the "sociocultural ideal male physique" highly valued by many males, including the young Dominican and Puerto Rican men in their urban neighborhoods, and their favorite rappers and wrestlers (McCabe and Ricciardelli 2004). Thus, with their declarations, banter and physical activities, each of the boys sought to communicate that he was way beyond childhood and was preparing his body for a social world wherein physical confrontations between males was commonplace. Ironically, female classmates, many of whom were taller and physically stronger, associated the boys' enactment of masculinity not with manliness but rather with childishness. Still, the boys enacted gender hierarchies based on, and espoused the male dominance of, their models of masculinity—rappers and older boys at Romero, and in their neighborhoods. They professed that male bodies were naturally strong and considered their female classmates' greater physical strength and height a temporary fact. Together, the cultural influences to which the boys were exposed reiterated the appropriateness of hegemonic masculinities and of those masculine practices that provided status and some level of protection in their social worlds.

Contrary to retrospective research on high school students (Martin 1996), the boys at Romero did not experience puberty on their own but rather within their homosocial group. Overall, the findings highlight pubescence as a *social* process as much as a biological transformation—a social process that is interactional, collective, embodied, and situated in classed, gendered, and ethnoracialized contexts. The data inform research examining masculinity and the body, heteronormativity at schools, and the intersection of racial identity and masculinity. This research also points to areas of further study. At present, the few studies on boys and puberty offer limited insight into how boys perceive and utilize their changing bodies, or the dialectic between *localized* masculine enactments and more macro-cultural interpretations of changing male bodies. The data presented herein, however, suggest the need for longitudinal ethnographic studies examining how boys from various social backgrounds experience the ongoing gendered process of "becoming" during their pubescent development. Lastly, scholarship on boys and masculinity would benefit from additional research on the intersection of masculine, ethnoracial, class, and sexual identities.

BIBLIOGRAPHY

Bailey, Benjamin. 2000. Language and negotiation of ethnic/racial identity among Dominican Americans. *Language in Society*, 29: 555–582.

Basch, Linda, Nina Glick Schiller, and Christina Szanton Blanc. 1994. *Nations unbound: Transnational projects, postcolonial predicaments, and deterritorialized nation-states*. Amsterdam: Gordon and Breach.

De Moya, E. Antonio. 2004. Power games and totalitarian masculinity in the Dominican Republic. In *Interrogating Caribbean masculinities: Theoretical and empirical analyses*, edited by R. E. Reddock. Kingston: University of West Indies Press.

Dixon, Carolyn. 1997. Pete's tool: Identity and sex-play in the design and technology classroom. *Gender and Education 9*: 89–104.

Drummond, Murray J.N. 2003. The meaning of boys' bodies in physical education. *Journal of Men's Studies 11*: 131–43.

Fine, Gary Alan. 1987. *With the boys: Little League baseball and preadolescent culture*. Chicago: University of Chicago Press.

James, Allison. 2000. Embodied being(s): Understanding the self and the body in childhood. In *The body, childhood, and society*, edited by A. Prout. Houndmills: Macmillan.

Janssen, Diederik F. 2006. "Become big, and I'll give you something to eat": Thoughts and notes on boyhood sexual health. *International Journal of Men's Health 5*: 19–35.

Kehily, Mary. 2001. Bodies in school: Young men, embodiment, and heterosexual masculinities. *Men and Masculinities 4*: 173–85.

Martin, Karin A. 1996. *Puberty, sexuality, and the self: Boys and girls at adolescence.* New York: Routledge.

McCabe, Marita P. and Lina A. Ricciardelli. 2004. A longitudinal study of pubertal timing and extreme body change behaviors among adolescent boys and girls. *Adolescence 39*: 145–66.

Mora, Richard. 2013. "Dicks are for chicks": Latino boys, homosexuality, and the abjection of homosexuality. *Gender and Education 25*(3): 340–56.

Pascoe, C.J. 2007. *Dude, you're a fag: Masculinity and sexuality in high school.* Berkeley: University of California Press.

Ramírez, Rafael L. 1999. *What it means to be a man: Reflections on Puerto Rican masculinity*, translated by Rosa E. Casper. New Brunswick, NJ: Rutgers University Press.

Swain, Jon. 2003. How young schoolboys become somebody: The role of the body in the construction of masculinity. *British Journal of Sociology of Education 24*: 299–314.

———. 2000. "The money's good, the fame's good, the girls are good": The role of playground football in the construction of young boys' masculinity in a junior school. *British Journal of Sociology of Education 21*: 95–109.

Thorne, Barrie. 1993. *Gender play: Girls and boys in school.* New Brunswick: Rutgers University Press.

Vaccaro, Christian Alexander. 2011. Male bodies in manhood acts: The role of body-talk and embodied practice in signifying culturally dominant notions of manhood. *Sociology Compass 5*: 65–76.

3 • *Alison Rooke*

TRANS YOUTH, SCIENCE, AND ART
Creating (Trans) Gendered Space

DISCUSSION QUESTIONS

1. How do dominant gender norms, especially the presumption that gender identity is binary (male/female), affect the lives, emotions, and experiences of trans youth?
2. How did the Sci:identity project work with trans youth to create a transgendered space? What were the effects of this "space of recognition" for trans youth?
3. What is the difference, according to Rooke, of studying trans lives rather than theorizing about trans subjects?

INTRODUCTION

This paper is concerned with the direct and subtle ways that space is gendered, and the ways transgendered space can be produced.[1] Here "transgendered space" refers to a space of comfort where transgendered subjectivities can be expressed, recognised and formed. It takes as its example a UK participatory arts and research project "Sci:dentity",[2] which took place over a year in London. An interrogation of the space Sci:dentity created is instructive in understanding ways in which social and cultural space is gendered and the consequences of that gendering for those of us who do not fit neatly within available predetermined gender categories. The paper also offers an example of the possibilities of grounding queer theory, which so often takes the trans subject as its object of inquiry, in the everyday lived experience of trans lives.

CREATING TRANSGENDER SPACE

In the UK transgender people have been actively creating trans and queer spaces organised around support, activism and the arts, producing spaces of grassroots mutual support, activism, self-expression, representation, and celebration. Some of these support spaces are aimed exclusively at trans people, others bring together trans, queer and non-queer people, providing spaces that aim to be inclusive on the basis of mutual respect of difference rather than investment in identity. Sci:dentity was distinct from these spaces in that it was an educational participative arts project specifically aimed at young people (who are often unable to participate in events in licensed venues). Sci:dentity had three main phases: first, a period of development and recruitment[3] and second a creative engagement phase, in which a series

An abridged version of Alison Rooke, 2010. "Trans Youth, Science and Art: Creating (trans) gendered Space." *Gender, Place and Culture* 19(5): 655-672. Adapted by the author with permission from Taylor and Francis.

of arts workshops and "science lessons" took place. The third phase of the project consisted of outreach workshops delivered to a variety of audiences including school and college students and teachers, young people including LGBT youth, youth workers, arts practitioners, educationalists, activists and those working in the area of equalities and diversity policy and its delivery. In the spirit of participation some of the participants went on to co-facilitate the outreach workshops. A documentary film of the process was shown in outreach workshops. This paper focuses on the creative engagement phase of the project.

A PARTICIPATORY PEDAGOGY

I learnt a lot about the lack of scientific/medical understanding about sex, or rather that understanding became less of a concept and more of a reality. It has driven me to learn more about sex and intersex. I think it has made me feel less like the female assignment and characteristics I have *make* me female. I think once you shed the ideal images of what a man and woman should be away it's easier to accept your own body, when you realize there is no clear line. It's like ok, I'm a short, unusual guy, and there's lots of them about and not all of them are even trans! The challenge becomes less of an internal battle (mind vs. matter), more of a process of getting the recognition of who you are! (Paul, FtM, aged 20)[4]

The creative engagement phase of Sci:dentity combined a pedagogical exploration of science with an encouragement to respond to the certainties of science with art (see Rooke 2010 for a discussion of the projects relational aesthetics). In "science lessons" participants listened to presentations on the science of sex, and interviewed medical experts in the field of sex reassignment. Participants explored scientific explanations of sex and gender: such as differences in the brain, hormones and their effect on behaviour, chromosomes and their function, hormonal and surgical sex reassignment, and associated moral and ethical issues. The "science lessons" did not simply educate young people about the science of

sex and gender; rather these encounters were a way of unpicking the variety of sciences which come together in the idea of sex. Paul's reflection on the project speaks of how learning about the science of sex and gender impacted upon his sense of himself as a transgendered young man. Learning about degrees of intersexuality, which are erased in the reiterative gendering declaration that "it's a boy" or "it's a girl', prompted Paul to rethink his relationship with gender. Participants became aware of the wide variation that exists beyond the apparent chromosomal simplicity of the XX and XY binary, and the extent to which physical appearances are dependant on a combination of growth and sex hormones.

A central pedagogical aim of the project was to encourage a critical exploration of scientific knowledge and the ways it is instrumentalised by medical practitioners such as endocrinologists, psychiatrists and surgeons in trans peoples' lives as they navigate the process of being diagnosed and treated. The work of these practitioners regulates the possibilities of embodied self-realisation in the production of coherent transsexual subjects. This occurs in the discursive production of what Butler (2001) describes as intelligible genders. i.e. those genders which maintain coherence and continuity within the cultural matrix of sex, gender, sexual practice and desire.

In this pedagogical space, participants had an opportunity to ask "experts" questions outside of a diagnostic encounter, by interviewing an endocrinologist and a consultant from a private gender clinic.[5] Rather than recreating a patient/doctor diagnostic dyad, in which the medical expert asks questions of the patient, the interrogative role here was reversed. These encounters revealed the considerable time already invested by participants researching and contemplating the medical aspects of sex and transsexuality. This included frameworks for diagnosis and hormone regimes which may be offered in the process of transition. For example, one group formulated the following questions, for a gender specialist regarding the ethics of "gender dysphoric" diagnostics:

What is the relationship between theories of hormones and theories of brain sex? Does endocrinology endorse "brain sex" theories? How do you feel about the rightness and wrongness of a person's transition? How do you feel about having the responsibility of making decisions about a person's transition process?

This opportunity to investigate the science of sex outside of the disciplinary site of the clinic was also valuable to one of the facilitators who is a transman:

> I benefited from the scientific investigations as much as the young participants. It empowered me to speak to these experts as an equal and not as a patient, which is what I have been. It was great to engage with how science gets produced—through evidence gathering and experiments in the lab—and to critique the authoritative voice in which it operates. (Sci:dentity Facilitator)

Significantly, this participative pedagogical space allowed the participants, some of whom were already being treated through National Health Service (NHS) Gender Identity Clinics, to express their reservations and concerns about the effects of a medical transition through hormones and surgery. This experience stands in contrast to a diagnostic situation which invites the speaking trans subject into being through adherence to a set of scripts that both social actors are arguably familiar with.

CREATIVE SPACE: RE-NARRATING GENDER

Sci:dentity opened up a creative space where young people could explore their self-understandings of their sexed and gendered selves and interrogate some of the cultural incitement to gender intelligibility that they were encountering in their daily lives. As well as offering a space to critique the discourse of sex as being a matter of certainty verified by scientific evidence, Sci:dentity offered arts practice as an expressive opportunity to communicate the humanity of trans lives, with dignity and pathos. The creative practice employed, such as drawing, cartoons, painting, song writing, performance and

filmmaking, gave the young people an opportunity to narrate their self-understanding—and crucially, their sense of their own gender—in creative ways which combined both community narratives of trans selfhood such as female-to-male (FtM) male-to-female (MtF) and genderqueer, with medical discourses of transsexuality to narrate a coherent trans-self (Rooke and McNamara, 2008).

The artwork created was shared with an audience of 150 people on the final weekend of the workshops. This included performances, screenings of short films, photography, a zine, sculpture and puppetry. The length of this article does not permit a detailed description or discussion of all the artwork produced in the project. However, I do want to focus on one piece of artwork and discuss its significance for the themes of this paper: a short film produced by Liam, an FtM young man aged twenty-two. Liam's film exemplifies how the learning and creativity at the heart of the project offered a space to respond to medical discourses about the science of sex and to articulate his self-understanding. This, in turn, offers insights into the space created by the project. After the first weekend of the creative workshops, Liam expressed some ambivalence about the "science lessons" presented that weekend when he wrote the following in the evaluation blog, "[T]he most challenging aspect of the weekend for me was the science talk and the thoughts and feelings it always evokes in me when biology is mentioned." However, by the end of the creative workshops he had used these feelings to critique the authority of science, by making a short film based on a first-hand encounter with medical discourses of sex and gender. This occurred when, several weeks into the project, he approached his General Practitioner (GP) to request referral to a gender identity clinic. The encounter was less than satisfactory, revealing his GP's lack of awareness of trans identities and NHS procedures. He describes his experience of the appointment in an interview:

> So I talked to him about things and he immediately turned away from me and listened to me, but

pretended to fiddle about on his computer and stuff, and then eventually he wrote this: "This twenty two year old asked me to refer her as she has not been feeling fully female, has felt more male gender in her physical and mental activities. Her menarche started late fourteen and her sexual organs showed reasonable development. She denies any hirsutism would you kindly see her for further investigations."

Discussing this encounter Liam stated in an interview, "My doctor called it the gender determination department. When I said to him, no, it's the gender identity clinic, and he didn't know any of the doctors names, so later on I wrote 'To Dr (X)[6]' on it." Clearly Liam had a negative and frustrating experience with this initial approach to his GP. From the content of the letter, it seems that the GP had little knowledge of transsexualism and may have referred for investigations into whether he was intersex (reflected in his notes about evidence of normal biological development). Liam took this medical text and proceeded to repurpose it with the intention of re-narrating the encounter until it reflected his sense of his gender.

The video intelligently explored the notion of transition. It begins with Liam clean-shaven, and as it plays backwards, we see Liam seemingly shaving on shaving foam, then with a beard prior to the shave, and finally putting a beard on (with the use of glue and hair clippings). The visual dimensions of the video achieve a transition from male to female (or at least imbue in the viewer some uncertainty). Simultaneously the voice-over which accompanies these visuals begins with Liam's (pre-transition) female-sounding voice reading out the doctor's letter referring to "her," "she" and female biology (such as a lack of hirsutism and menarche). As the film progresses the voice-over becomes deeper and the words of the letter change, until at the end, a deep male-sounding voice states:

This twenty two year old asked me to refer him as he has not been feeling fully male, has felt more male gender in his physical and mental activities. His menarche started late fourteen, and his sexual organs

showed unreasonable development. He denies any hirsutism, would you kindly see him for further investigations\\

This final statement is an account of transsexuality narrated from the perspective of the trans person. His body has not developed appropriately, and the absence of the external evidence of his male embodiment is hindering him in feeling fully male. When discussing this video later in an interview Liam stated, "There will be a progression; 'cause that's what a transition is; from what's not acceptable/not real to a better place." Liam's film is an example of how the creative space of the workshops enabled him to respond creatively to the provocations of the "science lessons" and his frustrating entry into spaces where medical discourses are at work. By using creative technologies, Liam was able to narrate his gendered self-hood in the very terms which had been used to dismiss it.

In curating the final show and exhibition, the participants came up with the idea of a "grey room" that explored the space between binary genders: a transgendered space. Rather than thinking about transgendered space through the identity politics of location, position and territoriality found in space such as clubs and bars, the artwork here foregrounded movement through time and space, and the everydayness of trans people's lives. This in turn reveals the inextricable matrix of gender normativity that they continually negotiate. The exhibition's grey room contained a series of sculptures and projections, which explored the ways that gender is "done" in the social world and attempted to undo gender. Installations included a collage titled "Buying into Gender" showing gendered consumer goods such as children's toys and clothes, typically coded in pink and blue colours. A video installation showed a participant playing with clothes and gender stereotypes in a shop changing-room, while a sculpture featured gender stereotypical clothes which had been ripped and burnt. Another installation in the grey room consisted of a large toilet with walls that on three sides were covered with the young people's writing. This writing spoke of their experience of the binary gendered space of the public toilet and how navigating these spaces was particularly treacherous.

TRANSGENDER RECOGNITION: FROM VIRTUAL TO "REAL" LIFE

I consider myself a newly "discovered" transboy as I only came out in February of this year. I am pretty new to everything, all the new terms and information makes my head hurt. Most of my research has been through various TG[7] sites on the Internet. Different websites say different things, but nothing beats meeting a transperson in person and talking to them. I got to do that this weekend and I am very happy I met the guys here, as it helps me divert text and websites into real-life experience. (Steven, FtM 19 years old)

The Sci:dentity project provided a space of recognition which points towards the limits of online interaction and the significance of offline embodied encounters. Transgender identities are often formed in physical isolation from other trans people through virtual encounters in cyberspace (Whittle, 2006). Transgender community knowledge is acquired, incorporated and managed between the boundaries of the virtual and the "non-virtual". This was evident in the participant's stories of the ways they came to identify as trans. Sixteen of the eighteen participants had never met another trans person in "real life" before coming along to the workshops. Most participants had developed their self-understanding as trans in on-line spaces where they could receive and pass on (trans)gendered cultural knowledge and form collective identities. The Internet offers alternative transgender identity narratives to those perpetuated by psychiatry (gender dysphoria) and broadcast media (the spectacular "freak show" material of talk show and makeover television). While it is doubtful that these spaces are free of bullying or harassment, they do offer a space of support which stands in contrast to the

difficulties of navigating the offline social world. Existing research shows that in "non-virtual" space transgendered people continue to face high levels of victimisation (Doan, 2006; Namaste, 2000; Hill and Willoughby, 2005; Lombardi et al, 2002). The cultural knowledge gained in virtual space, such as how to navigate gender-segregated spaces such as toilets and changing rooms is valuable once incorporated, embodied and improvised upon in the navigation of trans people's "off-line" lives. It also offers a valuable alternative to the routine dismissals of the participant's self-understandings encountered on an everyday basis.

In the Sci:dentity workshops a space of recognition was established in the first session by working as a group, establishing ground rules, and discussing with the participants the name and pronoun they preferred to be addressed by (he, she, either, neither). While this may be considered a fairly straightforward exercise its performative potential in offering its affirmation and recognition is significant. To ask someone which name and pronoun they would like to be addressed opens up a space of recognition and the possibility of "linguistic agency". As Butler observes:

[T]o be addressed is not merely to be recognized for what one already is, but to have the very term conferred by which the recognition of existence becomes possible. One comes to "exist" by virtue of this fundamental dependence on the address of the Other. One "exists" not only by virtue of being recognized, but, in a prior sense by being recognizable. (Butler 1996: 5)

It also enabled the speech act of stating their name in their felt gender, and allows others to hail them forth in their felt gender from there on, in the workshops. This exercise was repeated at the start of each week, giving the participants an opportunity to reiterate their gender and, at the same time, recreating the linguistic conditions of recognition. Some of the participants were clear at the outset that this was a space where they wanted to be recognised as being a gender which they were generally not routinely, officially or legally recognised by in their everyday lives. Some participants changed their name and choice of pronoun over the course of the workshop series as they experimented with the ways their gender could be expressed and received. This may reflect an increase in confidence and a sense of being in a safe trans space, or alternatively one could read this as an example of the ways in which the very incitement to be intelligible *as* trans amongst ones peers did its own performative work amongst the participants. Indeed I do not want to suggest that the project was a site that sat outside of identitarian or medical science discourses of the meaning of being trans.

This space of recognition provided by the workshops pointed implicitly toward the consequences of one's gendered agency *not* being recognised. At the end of each weekend the participants returned to families and their everyday lives of schools, colleges and work, where they were interpellated in ways that routinely foreclosed the very possibility of recognition that the project created. The boundary between the "here" of the project workshops and the "there" of the everyday was crossed when two social workers from the social service care team dropped off and collected one of the participants who identified as male-to-female. In spite of the project team clearly referring to this participant as "her" and "she" and using her chosen name (a female version of her male name), the social workers insisted on referring to "him," "he" and a male name. Their gendered speech was perhaps routinised rather than malicious, but it emphasised the space of recognition the project had created and its fragility. In a discussion of hate speech, Butler (1996) considers the disorientation of injurious speech and how, in suffering injurious speech, one can experience a loss of context. This is precisely the work that the social workers' speech act brought about. It was a temporary disruption to the context the project created. Most of the participants returned to worlds where their gendered agency would be contested repeatedly in these ways for some time. As one participant stated in an interview,

> David said to me at the end of the project, "I am going home now and I am not going to get called 'he' for months and months". Obviously someone can call you he on the Internet but it is not the same as that real experience that you are wanting to have. (John FtM, twenty-two years old)

The experience of "real-ness" that this participant refers to is the experience of one's embodied gendered presence being hailed forth and recognised. Similarly, in another interview, a participant discusses the embodied and intersubjective dimension of the project and the ways in which it provided a space where gendered expressions could be worked on:

> Yes, it gives you validation, when you meet other people in your situation, because not only can you have the words, but get tips on haircuts, binding and where to buy shirts and stuff. You can't get that on the Internet, like someone saying "that doesn't suit you. You need to buy different jeans". (Shannon, genderqueer, nineteen years old)

These participants' experiences speak to the relationship between on-line interactive trans culture and the visual culture of the heterosexual matrix in the "real" (i.e. off-line) world and the ways that transgender embodied cultural capitals and resources are acquired through off-line affective interactions. The workshop offered a space where gendered expressions and trans identities could be reflected upon, worked on and re-worked. As Browne (2006) argues, in a discussion of masculine-appearing women who are mistaken for men, it is not the case that the sexed body is an essential element of the individual. It is more the case that the sexed body is produced performatively in relation to others. As Browne argues, "[Thus] the creation of the sexed body is not a sole individual endeavour, rather it is produced through a nexus of interrelations" (Browne, 2006: 137). Crucially, it is through encounters with others that sexed bodies are constituted. The Sci:dentity project is an example of one nodal point in this nexus of interrelation and encounter.

BECOMING COMFORTABLE

A significant body of work concerned with sexual geographies has paid attention the relationship between the formation of lesbian, gay, bisexual and queer spaces and queer subjectivities. These sexual spaces are formed within the overall cultural logic of heterosexuality (even in its refusal) and crucially within the gendered binaries on which it rests and the ubiquitous performative work they do. In interrogating the gendered logic of heterosexuality, we must consider the ontological space it produces. In a consideration of the relationship between emotions, bodies and space, Ahmed (2004) describes the ways in which heterosexuality provides a space of comfort for those who can inhabit it with ease. This comfort is found in the fit between the body and the spaces surrounding it:

> To be comfortable is to be so at ease with one's environment that it is hard to distinguish where ones body ends and the world begins. One fits, and by fitting, the surfaces of bodies disappear from view. The disappearance of the surface is instructive: in feelings of comfort, bodies extend into spaces, and spaces extend into bodies. (Ahmed 2004: 147)

Ahmed argues that comfort is characterised by a kind of ontological osmosis between the unambiguously gendered heterosexual body and space it occupies; discomfort on the other hand is characterised by a feeling of disorientation, whereby one's body feels "out of place, awkward or unsettled" (ibid). A comfortable body relaxes—indeed, it is in moments of discomfort that we feel our bodies and their lack of fit in space more insistently. In the space of the Sci:dentity workshops the pressing, quotidian logic of gender normativity could be temporarily cast off and transgendered and transsexual embodiment could be expressed with comfort, as seemingly straightforward boundaries between male and female could be explored and blurred and crossed. At the end of the first weekend of creative workshops, the facilitators and I were left with a mental image which summed up some of the value of the project and the significance of the space it created for the young people taking part. On the first day many of the participants entered the workshops, uncertain, quiet, shy, speaking softly into their chests. They seemed to be holding their bodies in a way that took up as little space as possible. By the end of the weekend the same young people were laughing, playing physically and expressing themselves with boldness and confidence. This was, without doubt, due to the elation of being with other trans youth for the first time, but it was also due to the project teams' thoughtful work in conceptualising, creating and maintaining a space where young people could feel safe to explore and express their self-understandings of their own sex and gender without the ridicule, refusal or demands to account for themselves that they encountered on a regular basis in their everyday lives. When asked "What are the most important things you have got out of this project?" this participant stated:

> The chance to be entirely yourself for the duration of the weekends, to not have to hide anything or be worried about being misunderstood. That for me has been the most important thing I think and has contributed to a massive surge in confidence, in being myself and being out [. . .] Actually the most important thing I've got is friends. (Eddie, FtM, twenty years old)

Many of the participants spoke about how their participation in the project had impacted on their self-understandings and ability to articulate these in the social world. Here Aiden discusses the ways the project offered the possibility of "being who you are", in contrast to being "who you want to be":

> [W]hen you're allowed to express yourself more and more as who you are, it becomes more apparent who you're not and who you weren't when you were trying to act a different way. So having this full weekend where you can just without question be yourself and be who you are was a first for me. Like

I've gone to bars where for the night I can be who I wanna be—I've got friends who know me as who I am, but they still don't know the gender thing yet, don't know the sex thing yet, they just know who I am. The pronoun stuff . . . grating. But being here, for like a solid two days and being completely in this space is like one of the first times for the longest period of time that I've been able to do that, and feel better and better about it, and it being more comfortable with me. (Aiden, genderqueer, twenty two years old)

However, the comfort that the project opened up simultaneously highlighted the ways in which the navigation of a binary gendered social world—which routinely foreclosed any confirmation of the participants felt gender[8]—had emotional consequences:

It's a nasty shock leaving that safe environment and going in to a challenging one again that looks at you and sees something else. It was severely unpleasant going home sometimes. And I know, speaking to [name] she said, "I want to stay in there because that's the life that I want and life can't be like that". It was deeply disturbing for me as well. I remember going home the first time and thinking, "I am glad there are three more weekends of that 'cos that was fantastic. I will really miss it." (Shannon, genderqueer, nineteen years old)

Shannon speaks both of the possibilities that the workshop allowed and the ways in which these are foreclosed in the binary gendered everyday, a world which does not routinely afford cultural space for those who are transgendered. The "nasty shock" that this participant refers to can be understood in reference to the ways that sex and gender act as a set of discourses and a visual regime which limit our ways of seeing, in which you are looked at and not seen as you feel yourself to be. This is the visual matrix of cultural intelligibility that is central to the workings of both heterosexuality *and* homonormativity (Duggan, 2002; Halberstam, 2005; Rooke 2007).

CONCLUSION: THEORISING GENDERED SPACE

What counts as a coherent gender? What qualifies as a citizen? Whose world is legitimated as real? Who can I become in such a world where the limits and the meanings of the subject are set out in advance for me? By what norms am I constrained as I begin to ask what I may become? And what happens when I become that for which there is no place within the given regime of truth? (Butler 2004; 58)

Sci:dentity speaks more generally to the questions raised by Butler above. The project attempted to open up a transgender space, albeit small and temporary, within the "regimes of truth" regarding sex and gender. Sci:dentity's participative ethos speaks more broadly to the difference that engaged empirical research can make. If, as Whittle argues, trans theory is a project which aims to enable the coherent voices of trans people to be heard throughout the academy (Whittle, 2006; xv), we might ask, which voices are allowed to be heard and are considered coherent within emerging theory?

The trans subject has proven useful to think with within the disciplines of sociology and cultural theory. Indeed, we might argue that the trans subject is something of a fetish for the deconstructive project of queer theory. The "transgender phenomenon" (Ekins and King 2006) has been employed productively within queer theory to examine the way in which it epitomises the deconstruction of the categories male and female and the mechanisms of heterosexuality. It also speaks to concepts central to queer theory such as performance, performativity, visibility, recognition as well as to Deleuzian notions of becoming (Deleuze and Gautarri, 1972). However, within this body of theory there has been a neglect of the socially located, embodied materiality of transgender lives. Geographers of sexualities have focused on the significance of place and location, and the spatial dimensions of homophobia, heteronormativity and heterosexism.[9] Each of these bodies of theory have neglected the significance of the specificity of transgender and transsexual lives for theorising the interconnectedness of gender, sex, and sexuality, spatiality, the cultural and political consequences of gendered (mis)recognition *and* their potential for imagining what a less gender-normative world might look like. An emerging body of trans theory is shifting the intellectual focus from a queer and postmodern project, which employs the trans *subject* 'to think with', to one of thinking about trans *lives* in an engaged, interdisciplinary way. This shift enables us to focus on the relationship between materiality and representational practices, social and political recognition, the specificity of trans experience and its connection to other sites where social justice is fought for. Contemporary trans theory offers a welcome interrogation of the significance of trans lives to such theorisations of social and cultural spaces. It locates the critique of gender norms *within* the complexity of the lives of those who are living the consequences of not fitting neatly, within a social world which is organised primarily around a gendered and sexual normativity. Central to trans theory is a project of "enabling coherent trans voices to be heard throughout the academy" (Whittle, 2006:xv), bringing to fruition an intellectual and activist project whereby theorisation may make a difference to the lives of trans people, especially the more vulnerable trans people such as the young, the isolated, those with physical or mental health problems. This paper is a contribution to these debates by grounding such theorising in the materiality of the everyday and the routine negotiation and regulation of gender norms that it brings into force and asking important questions regarding the extent to which the theories we produce can work to shape trans lives and their liveability.

BIBLIOGRAPHY

Ahmed, S. 2004. *The Cultural Politics of Emotion.* Edinburgh: Edinburgh University Press.

Bell, D., and Valentine, G. 1995. *Mapping Desire, Geographies of Sexualities.* London: Routledge.

Browne, K. 2006. A Right Geezer Bird (man-woman): the sites and sights of "female" embodiment. *Acme,* Special Edition: Gender and Sex, 5, no. 2: 121–143.

Browne, K., Brown, G., and Lim, J. 2007. *Geographies of Sexualities. Theory, Practice and Politics.* Ashgate: Hampshire.

Butler, J. 1996. *Excitable Speech: A Politics of the Performative.* New York: Routledge.

———. 2001. Doing justice to someone. Sex reassignment and allegories of transsexuality. *GLQ, A Journal of Lesbian and Gay Studies* 7, no. 4: 621–636.

———. 2004 *Undoing Gender.* London, Routledge.

Deleuze, G., and Guatarri, F. 1972. *Anti-Oedipus: Capitalism and Schizophrenia* (translated from the French by Robert Hurley, Mark Seem, and Helen R. Lane); preface by Michel Foucault. Minneapolis, MN: University of Minnesota Press.

Doan, P. 2006. Violence and transgendered people. *Progressive Planning: Special Issue on Gender and Violence.* Planners Network. http://www.plannersnetwork.org/publications/mag 2006 2 spring.html

Duggan, L. 2002. The new homonormativity: The sexual politics of neoliberalism. In *Materializing Democracy: Toward a Revitalized Cultural Politics,* ed. Russ Castronovo and Dana D. Nelson, 175–194. Durham, NC: Duke University Press.

Ekins, R., and King, D. 2006. *The Transgender Phenomenon.* London, Thousand Oaks, New Delhi: Sage Publications.

Halberstam, J. 2005. *In A Queer Place and Time: Transgendered Bodies Subcultural Lives.* London: NYU Press.

Hill, D., and Willoughby, B. 2005. The development and validation of the genderism and transphobia scale. *Sex Roles* 53: 531–544.

Ingram, B.I., Bouthillette, A.M., et al. 1997. *Queers in Space: Communities, Public Places, Sites of Resistance.* Seattle, Washington: Bay Press.

Lim, J., and Browne, K. 2009. Senses of gender. *Sociological Research Online* 14,1.

Lombardi, E.L., Wilchins, R.A., Preising, D., and Malouf, D. 2002. Gender violence: transgender experiences with violence and discrimination. *Journal of Homosexuality* 42, no. 1: 89–101.

Namaste, K. 2000. *Invisible Lives: The Erasure of Transsexual and Transgendered People.* Chicago: University of Chicago Press.

Rooke, A. 2007. Navigating embodied lesbian cultural space: towards a lesbian habitus. *Space and Culture* 10: 231–252.

———. 2010. Telling trans stories: (un)doing the science of sex. In *Transgender Identities: Towards a Social Analysis of Gender Diversity*, ed. S. Hines and T. Sanger. London: Routledge.

Rooke, A., and McNamara C. 2008. Scientific autobiography. In *Creative Encounters,* 46–65. London: Wellcome Trust Publications.

Whittle, S. 2006 Foreword. In *The Transgender Studies Reade,* ed. Susan Stryker and Stephen Whittle. London: Routledge.

NOTES

1. Throughout this article certain terms are used that need explanation for the sake of clarity. *Trans* is used in this report to include transsexual and transgender. *Transsexual* is a medical term used to refer to a person who identifies as a gender which is different from that which they were assigned at birth. Transsexuals usually undergo a medical process of sex reassignment through the use of surgery and the administration of hormones. *Transgender* is a more colloquial term used to describe a person who feels that the gender assigned to them at birth is not a correct or complete description of what they feel. Transgender can be used to describe a wide range of gender expressions, which are a variation from the norms of society (for example including masculine or "butch" women, feminine men, cross-dressers). *Genderqueer* is also a colloquial or community term that describes someone who identifies as a gender other than "man" or "woman," or someone who identifies as neither, both, or some combination thereof. In relation to the male/female genderqueer people generally identify as more "both/and" or "neither/nor," rather than "either/or." Some genderqueer people may identify as a third gender in addition to the traditional two. The commonality is that all genderqueer people are ambivalent about the notion that there are only two genders in the world.

2. The Wellcome Trust is an independent biomedical research charity. Sci:dentity was funded as part of the Wellcome Trust's Pulse programme, which supports arts projects which work to engage young people with biomedical science and encourage them to tackle complex, emotive issues.

3. Eighteen young people, aged between fourteen and twenty-two, from across Britain and Northern Ireland, took part. Sci:dentity was formulated by three academics whose background was in queer theory, visual arts, participatory research and performance. The participants were recruited through LGBT youth groups, groups aimed at specifically at supporting trans youth and Social Services departments.

4. Participants' names have been changed to protect their anonymity.

5. The experts who kindly agreed to participate in the project were Prof. Andrew Levy and Dr. Richard Curtis.

6. Referring to a NHS gender specialist.

7. TG is shorthand for transgender.

8. See Lim and Browne (2009) for a discussion of the idea of gender as "felt" and sensed as a way of doing justice to research respondents' complex testimonies regarding their gender.

9. See collections by Browne, Brown and Lim, 2007; Bell and Valentine, 1995; Ingram et al. 1997 for an overview of this work.

1 · *Don Kulick*

ANGER, GENDER, LANGUAGE SHIFT, AND THE POLITICS OF REVELATION IN A PAPUA NEW GUINEAN VILLAGE

DISCUSSION QUESTIONS

1. Describe the language ideology in Gapun in terms of ideas about the relationship among language, transparency of meaning, knowledge, and danger.
2. What are the differences between female and male forms of language in Gapun? How are they shaped by the overall language ideology?
3. How do these differences both reflect and reproduce stereotypes about men and women, especially in relation to Christianity and "modernity"?

INTRODUCTION

Catherine Lutz's work (1986, 1990) has explored the network of associations in Western culture that link women with emotion, which in most cases is overtly devalued. A contrasting situation is described by Bambi Schieffelin (1990), E. L. Schieffelin (1976, 1985) and Steven Feld (1990), who all argue that among the Kaluli people of Papua New Guinea,

it is males who are "stereotypically culturally constructed as the emotional gender" (Feld 1990: 262). Those studies, as well as many others by anthropologists (e.g. Lutz & Abu-Lughod 1990; Bloch & Parry 1982; Watson-Gegeo & White 1990; White & Kirkpatrick 1985), have shown that in probably all communities throughout the world, the expression of affect is engendered, and that, therefore, "any discourse on emotion is also, at least implicitly, a

Abridged version of Don Kulick, 1992. Anger, Gender, Language Shift and the Politics of Revelation in a Papua New Guinean Village. *Pragmatics* 2 (3): 281–296. Reprinted with the kind permission of the author.

discourse on gender" (Lutz 1990: 69, see also Ochs 1988: 177-83, 215-16).

Because both emotion and gender are indexed and expressed in large measure through language, one might augment Lutz' generalization with the observation that discourses on emotion and gender will also be bound up with discourses, or ideologies, of language (Ochs 1992: 341). We can, furthermore, expect that at certain periods in the history of a language, the links that exist between discourses on affect, gender and language may come to salience and work to compel speakers to engage in linguistic practices that may result in changes in the language itself.

This paper focuses on a far-reaching process of ideological and linguistic change that is underway in a small village (population ca. 110) in Papua New Guinea called Gapun.[1] Gapun is located about ten kilometers inland from the northern coast of Papua New Guinea, roughly midway between the lower Sepik and Ramu rivers. It is a relatively isolated village, and the villagers are self-supporting through a combination of swidden agriculture, hunting with spears, and sago processing. Despite their isolation and their consequently low level of participation in cash cropping or other money generating projects, the villagers of Gapun are very keen to "develop" (*kamap*), and thinking about how this might happen occupies a great deal of their time. The villagers have been nominally Roman Catholic since the 1950s, and their hopes for development are pinned in elaborate ways on Christianity and on the immanent second coming of Christ.

In Gapun, a language shift is currently underway from the village vernacular—a Papuan language called Taiap—to Tok Pisin, the creole language that has become Papua New Guinea's most widely spoken national language. Children are no longer learning the vernacular, and no one under fourteen years of age actively commands it. The reasons for this language shift are complex and many-stranded, but here I will focus on one of the most central reasons behind the shift, namely links that exist in village discourses between gender, the expression of anger, and particular ideologies that link language to sociality and knowledge.

Two specific speech genres evoke these links very clearly for the villagers. The first is a kind of dramatic public display of anger that occurs virtually daily in the village. The word by which the villagers most commonly call this genre is a Tok Pisin word, *kros*, which literally means "anger" (in the village vernacular, the name is *pwapəŋar nam*[2], which literally means "angry talk"). *Kros*-es are considered by Gapuners—both men and women—to be stereotypically feminine expressive modes.

The second engendered speech genre is called "men's house talk" (*ambagaiŋa nam*). This talk is oratories, by men, that occur inside or in the immediate vicinity of the men's houses in the village. Men's houses (*haus boi* / *ambagai*) are large, open-air houses in which men sit and socialize. Women and girls over the age of about 8 are not allowed into them. Unlike *kros*-es, which foreground and proclaim anger, "men's house talk" is not explicitly and always concerned with anger as such. However, a central organizing characteristic of men's oratories is concern to downplay conflict and reframe disputes so that everyone appears to be content and harmonious. And on certain occasions, for example during meetings called to help heal a sick person, anger is made an explicit topic of discussion, and men are urged to "expose" their anger and "reveal" their complaints.

In both *kros*-es and oratories, discourses of gender, affect and language reinforce one another, and are sustained through specific linguistic practices. Villagers invoke those linguistic practices to justify their belief that women and men have different and opposing relationships to institutions and values that everyone agrees are important: namely, Christianity, modernity and civilization. This differential positioning of women and men in relation to Christianity, modernity and civilization is one of the main reasons why Taiap is dying.

LANGUAGE IDEOLOGY AND KNOWLEDGE

A basic tenet of village language ideology is that speakers do not normally say what they mean.

Unlike much Western philosophical tradition and contemporary middle-class values, which see language as a "transparent window to truths both formulable and communicable in it" (Silverstein 1985: 248), villagers in Gapun do not interpret a person's words as a reflection of their inner state or as an accurate representation of their opinions on a matter. Quite the opposite: the general assumption in Gapun is that language "hides" (*haitim / ambu-*) meanings that the speaker either cannot or will not state openly. Consequently, interpretation in the village is geared towards getting "inside" or "underneath" the words actually used in speech.

Language ideology in Gapun is also related to particular ideas about the nature and consequences of knowledge. In the village, knowledge is associated with danger. Many forms of knowledge that were traditionally valued, such as knowledge of healing chants, of certain myths, of the men's *tambaran* cult and of special skills such as yam planting or wood-carving—all these forms of knowledge are bound up with hazard. Knowledge about any facet of the *tambaran* cult, for example, is believed to have the power to cause the deaths of women who might somehow acquire such knowledge. Even men must carefully guard what they know about the cult secrets, because to reveal them to women or children could cause the cult deities to kill the speaker (as well as the addressee). Magic chants, even benevolent ones, link their knower to ancestral spirits or men's cult deities who may act entirely on their own to bring harm to anyone who displeases the knower, even if the knower does not wish this. Overhearing certain myths may cause sickness, and uttering secret names may cause environmental disturbances or death to large numbers of people.

Even private knowledge is fraught with danger. On one occasion, for example, a senior man explained to me that after repeated attempts, he had finally managed to recreate, on a fan he was weaving, a mythologically important pattern that he recalled seeing as a boy. "Nobody taught me to weave the design," he said, "I exposed (*kamapim*) it in my thoughts." This exposure, however, apparently angered the ancestral spirit-owners of the design, who

retaliated, he told me, by inflicting him with a serious illness.

This kind of understanding of knowledge makes possessing it and imparting it a risky business. Knowledge is valuable, but it is also—and this, of course, is part of what constitutes its value—potentially lethal. It must be handled, passed on and made public in very delicate ways.

Gapuners' language ideology privileges ambiguity, hidden meanings, and meanings construed by listeners rather than those conveyed by speakers. The way villagers think about and use language provides them with the means to traffic in knowledge without putting themselves or their interlocutors in too much danger. In their talk with one another, villagers oscillate between what they call "inside" talk and "outside" talk (i.e. hints and insinuations vs. speaking clearly). They make deliberately ambiguous, self-contradictory statements, and they deploy discursive features such as repetition and dissociation to reveal, discuss and circulate knowledge even as they conceal it (Kulick 1992, Stroud 1992). By using talk in particular ways, villagers gingerly sidestep many of the potentially fatal consequences that stark, unmitigated knowledge is known to have.

ANGER

Anger enters this discussion as a singularly inflamed object of knowledge. In village discourses on emotion and knowledge, anger in adults is always linked to danger. If anger is not voiced or acted upon, villagers say that it will remain in the stomach (the seat of emotions) and "rot" (*sting / pisimb-*). The putrefaction of anger may mobilize the ancestral spirits associated with the aggrieved person, and these may cause harm to whomever provoked anger in that person. Alternatively, rotting anger may "give bad thoughts" to the aggrieved, driving them to seek out the services of a sorcerer, who will be paid to murder the object of the anger.

If anger is voiced or acted upon, then there is a risk that its expression will provoke the wrath of the ancestral spirits associated with the person who is abused or attacked. Abusing or attacking another person may also drive *that person* to a sorcerer. So no matter how it is ultimately dealt with, anger is dangerous. People in Gapun die of anger. Village deaths (all of which are held to be caused by sorcery) are inevitably accounted for at least in part by recalling past arguments or fights that the deceased or his/her close family members or matrilineal relatives had with other people.

Anger (*kros* / *pwap-*) is one of the relatively few affects that villagers regularly speak about and attribute to themselves and others—the others being shame (*sem* / *maikar-*), concern and sadness (*wari* / *punat-*), dissatisfaction (*les* / *mnda-*) and fear (*pret* / *rεw-*). Of these emotions, anger and dissatisfaction are seen as the earliest and most basic. They are tied to a dimension of personhood that the villagers call *hed* in Tok Pisin, and *kɔkir* in their vernacular. Both these words mean "head". Each individual, the villagers maintain, has *hed*. Each individual, in other words, has a basic and volatile sense of personal will and autonomy. The concept of *hed* in Gapun signifies egoism, selfishness and maverick individualism. It denotes emotional bristliness and defiant anti-social behavior, and it is roundly condemned in village rhetoric.

For the villagers, one of the avatars of this flammable dimension of personhood is small children. Babies and toddlers in Gapun are routinely said to be, and treated as if they are, continually dissatisfied and angry. A child cooing softly on its mother's lap will suddenly be shaken lightly and asked, "Ai! What are you mad about? Ah?!" (*Ai! Yu belhat long wanem samting? Ah?!*). Likewise, a mother seeing her eight-month-old daughter reaching out towards a dog lying beside her will comment "Look, she's mad (*kros*) now, she wants to hit the dog," and she will raise the baby's hand onto the dog's fur telling the child, "That's it, hit it! Hit it!" One of the clearest indications of how villagers view the affective state of children is in the first words they attribute to them. In the village, a child's first word is said to be *ɔki*, which is a Taiap word that means "I'm getting out of here." Attributed to infants as

young as two months old, this word encapsulates the adult belief that babies "do what they want" (*bihainim laik bilong ol yet*) and go where they want to go regardless of the wishes of others.

The two words that villagers consider rapidly follow *ɔki* also underscore the notion of a baby as a gruff, independent individualist with a "strong" *hed*. These are the Taiap words *mnda* ("I'm sick of this") and *aiata* ("Stop it!").

In the villagers' view of what it means to grow up, children should come to understand that *hed* and the display of anger and dissatisfaction that typifies it must be suppressed (*daunim*). As they mature, children are expected to curtail their expressions of anger and to begin to accommodate others. They should share things with others and conduct themselves "quietly" (*isi* / *tɔwεrki*). So anger, in this cultural understanding, is not only fraught with danger, it is also seen as childish and immature. Although it is explicitly recognized to be a central component of all people, it is one that grown-ups should do their best to suppress and conceal.

Unfortunately, however, people do become angry at the actions of other people: other people who steal one's betelnut, who neglect to collect firewood for the evening meal, who forget to return a borrowed item, who engage in extramarital affairs, who spread rumors about one, and so on. Villagers have developed a number of ways of dealing with the anger that they see as being provoked in them, including destroying their own possessions and outright fighting. The single most common way in which anger is conveyed, however, is through the village speech genre known as a *kros*.

PROCLAIMING ANGER IN A *KROS*

The best way to give an impression of the general tenor of *kros*-es in Gapun is to present a brief extract from one that was recorded and transcribed in June 1991. This is a *kros* between two sisters living next door to one another. It arose because for several weeks the younger sister, a woman in her thirties named Sake, had been complaining loudly about the fact that children who played in the area near her house littered the ground with coffee beans, which they blew through bamboo pipes at each other and at the domesticated pigs that snuffle around through the village. One afternoon, Sake caught her sister's ten-year-old son red-handed as he stood shooting coffee beans at pigs underneath her house (Gapun is in a swamp, and houses are built on poles about six feet off the ground). Sake chased the boy and shouted at him. At one point she asked him in a loud voice: "Does your mother come and clean up around here?!" (the answer, Sake knew, was no).

Hearing this rhetorical question from inside her house, the boy's mother, a woman in her forties named Erapo, began yelling at Sake. Sake strode up into her own house and responded in full force. This segment occurs about five minutes into the shouting match:

SAKE: <u>No good rotten big black hole!</u>

ERAPO: Smelly cunt bloody bastard!

SAKE: <u>I was talking to Erapo</u> [sarcastic]. I was talking good about the rubbish [i.e. the coffee beans], Erapo gets up and swears at me. Fucking cunthole bastard you!

ERAPO: This hole of yours [(unintelligible)

SAKE: [Rotten! Your dirty cunt is <u>a big black hole</u>. Bastard. <u>Black guts! What is she, what is Erapo talking to me about, kros-ing me about, swearing at me for?! Ah?! Erapo [you have] a rotten black hole! Catfish cunt! Erapo has a black cunthole! A black cunthole Erapo! Erapo has a huge black cunthole! Erapo has an enormous black cunthole! Satan fucks you all the time, Satan is fucking you Erapo! Erapo! Satan is fucking you really good! Your cunt is sagging like loose mud on a riverbank. Catfish cunt!</u>

This is a typical Gapun *kros*. It exhibits many of the conventions which characterize the speech genre, such as vituperative insults and gross vulgarity, loud voices shouted out over the village, the spatial placement of the speakers inside their respective houses, and harsh, explicitly confrontational accusations of wrongdoing. As the *kros* continues, the insults that the women exchange become interwoven with direct threats, and Sake, especially, repeatedly challenges Erapo to come down from her house so that Sake can "beat her till she shits."

Kros-es in Gapun are gendered speech genres that are associated with and almost inevitably enunciated by women. Whenever Sake or some other woman has a loud *kros*, those village men not directly involved in some way make clucking sounds, shake their heads disparagingly and mutter knowingly that "this kind of rubbish talk is the habit of women, it's their way" (*desela kain rabis toke m we bilong ol meri, pasin bilong ol*). Women are collectively held by village men to be more *bikhed* (willful, big-headed) than men. They are associated with individualism, atomicity and anti-social behavior.

Until the late 1950s, men all slept in the communal men's house, apart from their wives and children. And through their roles as the organizers of funerary feasts, initiation rites and war raids, men embodied cooperation and social cohesion. The collective actions of men were considered the "bones" (*bun / <u>ning</u>*) of society. The actions of women, even though they, too, could be collective (women had their own initiation rites, and during funerary feasts many of them cooked collectively to feed the *tambaran* deities in the men's house), were not accorded the same type of cultural significance as those of men, and women were and continue to be represented as divisive troublemakers whose selfish actions constantly threaten the solid, manly group. Echoing a statement heard all over Papua New Guinea, Gapun men sometimes remind one another that "we fight over women"; that is, we would not fight if there were no women. Women, with their anger, their *kros*-es and their unwillingness to "suppress" their *hed*-s are the root of all conflicts.

Individual women in Gapun do not share this view of themselves as destructive troublemakers. Women who have *kros*-es do not interpret their own behavior in reference to the stereotype. When Sake, for example, has a *kros*, she does not consider that she is being divisive; she will tell you that she is legitimately defending herself from some violation or infringement. When *another* woman has a *kros*, however, then Sake will often be quick to sniff that the *kros* speaker is "a woman who always gets angry for no reason" (*meri bilong kros nating nating*).

The existence of a culturally elaborated stereotype of women as quarrelsome means that such a role is available for any woman to act out. And as a stereotypically female role, it is unattractive for men. Men in the village like to pretend that they have no conflicts with others, and they dismiss *kros*-es as *samting bilong ol meri / naŋrɔma ɔrak* (what women do). The village stereotype of what represents ideal male behavior puts pressure on the men to be more sociable, generous, dignified and temperate than their wives, who are expected to fly off the handle and have a *kros* at the slightest excuse. In most cases, a married man is able to uphold this stereotype and simultaneously announce infringements by simply informing his wife about some slight or infraction that he has been subjected to (such as somebody not returning a borrowed axe or shovel). The wife can usually be counted on to take it from there, and in doing so she reinforces the stereotype of quarrelsome, loud-mouthed women. Even on those occasions when men publicly *belhat* (get angry, shout), this anger is usually directed at that man's wife or his close female relatives. So public arguments almost inevitably involve women at some level. Both men and women blame (other) women for making trouble, for not being able to contain their anger and for "showing *hed*."

CONCEALING ANGER IN THE MEN'S HOUSE

In marked contrast to women's *kros*-es, oratories in the men's house are occasions on which men in Gapun engage in speeches that downplay tension, smooth over disagreement and stress consensus in the village. Oratories occur whenever meetings are called in the men's house to announce the need for labor to clear overgrown paths or repair rotten footbridges, to work out the arrangements that have to be made for funerary feasts, to discern the meaning of messages and news items which villagers bring back with them from their travels to other villages, to arrange to help a village man and his wife in some task which requires a number of laborers, such as carrying house posts, roofing a house, or clearing the forest to plant a garden, or to discuss any number of other public issues.

Because they are so strongly associated with the men's house, oratories, by definition, are male. Only men in Gapun are considered to orate. There is no rule or explicit consensus in the village that women cannot orate, and there are a few strong-willed women in Gapun, like Sake, who do occasionally speak in public gatherings that concern both men and women. Women's speeches contain many of the same rhetorical features, such as repetition, which are predominant in oratories, but they differ importantly in that they are much briefer than most men's speeches (which usually last about 10–15 minutes, but which can go on for as long as 45 minutes), and they never contain any of the particular formulaic tags that the men use to mark their speech as oratorical. Furthermore, women, who are not allowed inside the men's house, obviously cannot speak from there, and so their contributions to a discussion have a peripheral character that is underscored by their spatial placement. Because of factors like these, women who make short speeches at public gatherings are not considered to be orating; they are, rather, "complaining" (*komplain*).

Usually, anger is not an explicit topic of discussion in contexts dominated by oratorical speech-making. Quite the opposite. Skillful orators draw on a wide variety of paralinguistic cues (e.g. speakers are called and assembled under the same roof), metalinguistic cues (e.g. speakers address their talk directly to a general public, use politeness markers to assume and relinquish the floor), and linguistic cues (e.g. there is a marked preference for speakers to use diminutives to diminish their own status, and oratories are characterized by supportive repetition from listeners), to meaningfully ignore and downplay the tensions that infect daily life in the village and to promote an illusion that everyone is in agreement and that there really is no anger and consequently no conflicts at all. In creating this illusion and bringing the villagers together in this way, orators demonstrate their own social awareness and skills, even as they work to structure a context in which others can demonstrate their sociability by listening and contributing to the buildup of the consensus by repeating and agreeing.

Sometimes, however, village men focus explicitly on anger, and there are contexts in which they spend much time and talk urging one another to "expose" (*autim* / *arɔni ŋgur-*) their anger, to "break it open" (*brukim* / *kra-*), to "reveal" (*kamapim* / *mamanj-*) it. This kind of speechmaking occurs whenever somebody in the village is struck down by a serious illness that people conclude is being caused by ancestral spirits. When this happens, men gather together in a men's house and talk about conflicts. When everybody who wants to talk has had a turn, senior men invoke the village ancestors and call upon them to stop causing the sickness. Everyone present in the men's house then dips his finger in a glass of water, which is subsequently used to wash the sick person. The idea behind this procedure is that the men act as a channel for ancestral spirits, and by first "revealing" their anger, then dipping their finger in the water, they "cool" (*kolim* / *pɔkɛmb-*) the anger that is causing sickness in the afflicted person.

The following text is extracted from a meeting in the men's house, attended by all village men, called to effect a cure for me, the author of this paper. In June 1991, I became afflicted with disabling pains that the villagers, upon hearing the symptoms, immediately identified as "a sickness of the ground" (i.e. a sickness caused by village ancestral spirits). Note how anger is talked about here.

MONE: Whoever feels that something isn't right, alright expose it. It's like we're breaking open the talk now. It isn't good if this [anger] remains in our stomachs, because he [i.e. Don] will suffer. We have to expose all the little talk.

KAWRI: <u>Yeah.</u>

MONE: Like yesterday too I talked about doing work for him [Mone means that yesterday he exhorted the villagers to get to work building a house for me. Work on this house had been progressing extremely slowly, because even though the villagers had volunteered to build it, they were unwilling to work together because of various village conflicts]. We were all lazy [and therefore did no work]. Or maybe we have some worries, or maybe we're tired of doing work, or maybe we're just tired for no reason, or like that.

KRUNI: That's it.

MONE: Alright we're gonna reveal all these little worries: "This man said something to me and so I'm unwilling to work," this kind of thing. Alright, when we've finished talking we'll/or we'll talk about the spirits of the village, of the men's house, OK, and we'll put our fingers in the water alright Don will/we'll hold Don's pain, wash it in the water of our talk. Like just try it. It's not this [i.e. a sickness caused by a village spirit], it's a [white man's] sickness he's got, he'll go to the hospital.

KRUNI: At the hospital it'll finish. We'll try it our way [first].

MONE: <u>There's no talk</u> [i.e. no dissention]. Like we can/maybe we don't have any talk, or maybe we can talk about the spirits of the village, we don't think that something is as it should be/we can talk about work or about something that is amongst us giving illness to him, alright we'll talk straight about that. Talk straight and put fingers in the water.

Later, towards the end of this session, after several men had "revealed" "little" irritations or conflicts that they were involved in or had heard about, the talk is summarized like this:

KEM: We're gonna hold the water and rub his pain. <u>These things,</u> there's not plenty of complaints.

SAIR: <u>No.</u>

ANDON: <u>There's no</u> complaints.

KEM: Our [little talk, that's it.

KAWI: [little crumbs of talk.

KEM: We're making it.

The aspect of this talk to which I want to draw attention is the way in which anger, even though it is explicitly spoken about here, is consistently embedded in speech characterized by hedges ("maybe we don't have any talk"), the presentation of alternative positions ("or maybe we're just tired for no reason", "it's a [white man's] sickness he's got"), and specific denials that the anger the men are supposed to be exposing is in fact anger at all. Choruses like the one here, in which several men hasten to agree with one another that there are no complaints, occur throughout meetings like this, and they become particularly insistent whenever somebody actually does "expose" a happening or occurrence that caused them to feel angry. At one point during this meeting, for example, a senior man "revealed" that the men present were reluctant to work on my house because they were angry at Allan, my adoptive village "father". The anger, it was pointed out, stemmed from the fact that Allan and his wife, the indomitable Sake, had moved into my previous, communally built, house when I completed my original fieldwork and left the village in 1987. The couple made this move in defiance of received village opinion, and the other villagers now accused Allan and Sake of "ruining" (*bagarapim*) the house. Every person present at this meeting was acutely aware of the truth of this senior man's "revelation", because in private villagers routinely expressed bitter resentment towards Allan and Sake for having moved into the house. In the men's house, though, the revelation was handled in the following way:

KEM: Alright, you all gave up on poor Allan, he's by himself [i.e. working on building my new house by himself]. You all have this thought, I know, you can't cover it up it, we're showing Christian belief here. It's not anger (*kros*), it's like you're talking straight. OK, and you hold the water now and the spirit will go inside it. It's like that.

ANDON: Is it anger? [rhetorical question]

KRUNI: It isn't anger.

MARAME: There's no anger, it's talk.

MONE: Yes.

One of the most significant ways in which men's public talk about anger differs from women's is in this kind of cooperative re-contextualizing work, where speakers weave together their words to re-frame anger as not-anger, and where they sometimes even go so far as to congratulate themselves on talking about anger as a way of "showing Christian belief" (*autim bilip*). I interpret this kind of supportive discursive interaction between men as a linguistic manifestation of the village orientation to knowledge as something which in many cases is safely revealed only if it is somehow subsequently re-concealed.

That is the point. One of the most significant differences between women's *kros*-es and men's oratories—and the difference that seems to evoke the greatest degree of discomfort in villagers—is not so much that female speakers publicize anger: in many ways this is in fact commendable, since villagers agree that it is much better to express anger than to let it remain unexposed and rotting in one's stomach. What is unacceptable and dangerous about *kros*-es is that women only complete half the discursive equation. Women reveal anger without subsequently re-concealing it. They expose anger and leave it uncovered, where it is thought to act like a throbbing hot lightning rod of unleashed dissention, pulling sorcery, sickness and death into the village.

Women's linguistic practices for dealing with anger are in almost every way inversions of men's practices. In addition to exposing anger without hiding it again, women's *kros*-es emanate from inside or nearby private dwelling houses. Men's oratories, on the other hand, occur in or near the communal men's house. *Kros*-es are organized as competing monologues; in oratories, the people being orated at are free to contribute sympathetic interjections throughout the speech and follow the orator by producing a speech or a summation in which they "give support" to the orator. *Kros*-es are dramatic declarations of self-display in which speakers assert themselves and their personal autonomy by broadcasting throughout the village that these have been violated. Oratories are characterized by self-effacement, speakers repeatedly remind their listeners in polite muted tones that they only have "little crumbs of talk" or "a little worry" to draw to everyone's attention. *Kros*-es are meant to shame a specific, named person or a specific unknown, unnamed culprit; oratories are intended to generalize and address people as members of a group—even in those cases where the topic of an oratory is some sort of transgression committed by somebody, blame is inevitably diffused and generalized, and everyone is reminded that others in the village (though not necessarily they themselves) are just as lazy or uncooperative or big-headed as the (always unnamed) people who committed the transgression. For both men and women, *kros*-es are associated with (other) women and divisiveness; oratories, on the other hand, are seen as concrete evidence that men in Gapun really are more placid, consensus oriented, sociable and reasonable than their tempestuous, forever bickering wives.

LANGUAGE SHIFT

We can consider anger as a kind of locus where ideologies of language, gender and affect all converge, creating a discursive space in which gender stereotypes are both imagined and acted out. In large measure because of their linguistic practices for publicly dealing with anger, men in Gapun are credited by everybody with greater knowledge about how to handle knowledge, as it were. By exposing anger even as they deny it and conceal it, men present themselves as providing and embodying a protective buffer against the ravages that naked anger is known to be able to summon forth. Women, in contrast, brazenly expose anger and subsequently do nothing to mitigate the negative

consequences that may be generated by this exposure. This particular linguistic practice of handling anger has become representative of "what women do," and it permits the maintenance of a negative stereotype that demeans women as childish, destructive and irresponsible.

How is this convergence of anger, gender and the politics of revelation working to produce a tension in Gapun such that the linguistic situation of the village is moving towards new configurations?

The answer to that question lies in the ideology and practice associated with the two languages that villagers use in their day-to-day talk. Basically, the situation is one in which the vernacular language, Taiap, is nowadays associated with tradition, the land, the local concept of *hed,* and women. Tok Pisin, on the other hand, has come to be bound up with modernity and change. Tok Pisin is tied to Christianity, white people, money, schooling, and, significantly, it is also tied to men and those affective stances that are seen to typify men.

These associative networks are frequently made explicit in men's house talk. At some point during each meeting in the men's house, no matter what the original reason for the meeting happened to be, somebody will inevitably make a speech *in Tok Pisin* extolling Christian ideals, reaffirming the value of education, devaluing the ways of the ancestors and urging the villagers—specifically the village women—to suppress their anger and stop their fighting so everybody can "come up" (*kamap*— i.e. change, develop). The men's house has thus become an important arena in which individual men can publicly assert their familiarity with the modern world by reminding others that the Catholic Church, school, "Papua New Guinea" and *bisnis* (cash-generating enterprises) have altered the nature of village relationships and must be accorded a central role in village life. In making these assertions, Gapun men are able to substantiate their claims to knowledge about the modern world by choosing to orate primarily in the language through which that world is understood to be constituted, i.e. Tok Pisin. Angry women employ what amounts to a

Table 1. Summary of contrastive features of *kros*-es and oratories

KROS-ES	ORATORIES
• enunciated by women	• enunciated by men
• emanate from individual houses	• emanate from communal men's house
• vulgarity	• politeness
• self-display	• self-effacement
• competing overlapping monologues	• supportive serial monologues
• reveal anger	• reveal anger and re-conceal it again
• are about intra-village matters	• link village matters to outside world
	• Tok Pisin predominates

similar discursive strategy in their public speeches. They substantiate their dissatisfaction and foreground their claims to having been violated and impinged upon by choosing to announce those claims primarily in the language though which affective discourse is constituted, i.e. Taiap.

These practices and the ideas that inform them are moving the village vernacular towards extinction. Powered by its links with women and the stereotypes associated with them, it seems likely that the Taiap language itself will increasingly come to be tied to negatively valued aspects of life, such as affective access, discursive irresponsibility and dangerous knowledge. This process is already well underway, and is evidenced by situations such as when villagers sometimes pointedly refuse to speak their vernacular among themselves in order to prove that they are not "hiding" talk (this happens, for example, during periods of millenarian activity or during sensitive meetings with people from other village), or when village children understand purposeful parental switches from Tok Pisin into the vernacular as conveying anger and the threat of punishment (Kulick 1992: 217).

For reasons like these, it seems probable that the Taiap language will be abandoned. The Gapun case illustrates the way in which particular linguistic practices reinforce and are reinforced by particular ideas that exist in a community about language, affect and gender, and the relationship between those phenomena. By speaking in particular ways, women and men in Gapun activate complex webs of associations

that link a wide array of discourses. Women are not only spitting curses and men are not only making dispassionate, measured speeches that smooth over conflicts in the village: by using language in the specific ways they do, speakers are embodying and recreating salient stereotypes about what women and men are, they are engendering affect and they are positioning themselves socially in relation to Christianity, civilization and the modern world.

One of the contributions this example from Gapun can make to discussions about language ideology is the reminder that language ideologies seem never to be solely about language—they are always about entangled clusters of phenomena, and they encompass and comment on aspects of culture like gender and expression and being civilized. Furthermore, this inherently snarled and delicately-layered nature of language ideology provides a point of entry for colonial discourses of Christianity and modernity to penetrate and, as has happened in Gapun, to enmesh themselves with linguistic practice, and with local ideas about things like gender, affect and language.

REFERENCES

Bloch, M. & J. Parry (eds.) (1982) *Death and the regeneration of life*. Cambridge: Cambridge University Press.

Feld, S. (1990) *Sound and sentiment: birds, weeping, poetics and song in Kaluli expression*. 2nd ed. Philadelphia: University of Pennsylvania Press.

Kulick, D. (1992) *Language shift and cultural reproduction: socialization, self and syncretism in a Papua New Guinean village.* New York: Cambridge University Press.

Lutz, C. (1986) "Emotion, thought and estrangement: emotion as a cultural category." *Cultural Anthropology* 1: 405–36.

Lutz, C. (1990) "Engendered emotion: gender, power, and the rhetoric of emotional control in American discourse."In C. Lutz & L. Abu-Lughod (eds.). *Language and the politics of emotion.* Cambridge: Cambridge University Press.

Lutz, C. & L. Abu-Lughod (eds.) (1990) *Language and the politics of emotion.* Cambridge: Cambridge University Press.

Ochs, E. (1992) "Indexing gender." In A. Duranti & C. Goodwin (eds.), *Rethinking context: language as an interactive phenomenon.* New York: Cambridge University Press.

Ochs, E. (1988) *Culture and language development: language acquisition and language socialization in a Samoan village.* New York: Cambridge University Press.

Schieffelin, B. (1990) *The give and take of everyday life: language socialization of Kaluli children.* New York: Cambridge University Press.

Schieffelin, E. L. (1985) "The cultural analysis of depressive affect: an example from New Guinea." In A. Kleinman & B. Good (eds.), *Culture and depression: studies in the anthropology and cross-cultural psychiatry of affect and disorder.* Berkeley: University of California Press.

Schieffelin, E. L. (1976) *The sorrow of the lonely and the burning of the dancers.* New York: St. Martin's Press.

Silverstein, M. (1985) "Language and the culture of gender: at the intersection of structure, usage,and ideology." In E. Mertz & R. J. Parmentier (eds.), *Semiotic meditation: sociocultural and psychological perspectives.* New York: Academic Press.

Stroud, C. (1992) "The problem of intention and meaning in code-switching." *Text* 12(1): 127–55.

Watson-Gegeo, K. & G. White (eds.) (1990) *Disentangling: conflict discourse in Pacific societies.* Stanford: Stanford University Press.

White, G. & J. Kirkpatrick (eds.) (1985) *Person, self, and experience: exploring Pacific ethnopsychologies.* Berkeley: University of California Press.

NOTES

1. Fieldwork in Gapun was carried out during 15 months in 1986–87 and for 7 weeks in 1991.

2. Throughout this text, words that are underlined *and* italicised are vernacular language words. Words that are only italicised are Tok Pisin words. In the translations of village speech, which are not italicised, talk that occurred in Taiap is underlined; Tok Pisin speech is not. In the transcripts, a / indicates a false start, and [indicates overlapping talk.

2 • *Deborah Cameron*

PERFORMING GENDER IDENTITY
Young Men's Talk and the Construction of Heterosexual Masculinity

DISCUSSION QUESTIONS

1. What are the dominant assumptions about the differences between male and female conversational styles in the United States?
2. How did Danny's analysis of the conversation support such generalizations?
3. How and why does Cameron challenge his analysis?
4. How do the five men in the conversation use language to assert their heterosexual masculinity?

INTRODUCTION

In 1990, a 21-year-old student in a language and gender class I was teaching at a college in the southern USA tape-recorded a sequence of casual conversation among five men; himself and four friends. This young man, whom I will call "Danny",[1] had decided to investigate whether the informal talk of male friends would bear out generalizations about "men's talk" that are often encountered in discussions of gender differences in conversational style—for example that it is competitive, hierarchically organized, centres on "impersonal" topics and the exchange of information, and foregrounds speech genres such as joking, trading insults and sports statistics.

Danny reported that the stereotype of all-male interaction was borne out by the data he recorded. He gave his paper the title "Wine, women, and sports". Yet although I could agree that the data did contain the stereotypical features he reported, the more I looked at it, the more I saw other things in it too. Danny's analysis was not inaccurate, his conclusions were not unwarranted, but his description of the data was (in both senses) *partial*: it was shaped by expectations that caused some things to leap out of the record as "significant", while other things went unremarked.

I am interested in the possibility that Danny's selective reading of his data was not just the understandable error of an inexperienced analyst. Analysis is never done without preconceptions, we can never be absolutely non-selective in our observations, and where the object of observation and analysis has to do with gender it is extraordinarily difficult to subdue certain expectations.

One might speculate, for example, on why the vignettes of "typical" masculine and feminine behaviour presented in popular books like Deborah Tannen's *You Just Don't Understand* (1990) are so often apprehended as immediately *recognizable*.[2] Is it because we have actually witnessed these

Originally published as Deborah Cameron, 1998. "Performing Gender Identity: Young Men's Talk and the Construction of Heterosexual Masculinity." In Jennifer Coates, ed. *Language and Gender*. Malden, MA: Blackwell, pps. 270–284. Adapted with permission of John Wiley and Sons and of the author.

scenarios occurring in real life, or is it because we can so readily supply the cultural script that makes them meaningful and "typical"? One argument for the latter possibility is that if you *reverse* the genders in Tannen's anecdotes, it is still possible to supply a script which makes sense of the alleged gender difference. For example, Tannen remarks on men's reluctance to ask for directions while driving, and attributes it to men's greater concern for status (asking for help suggests helplessness). But if, as an experiment, you tell people it is women rather than men who are more reluctant to ask for directions, they will have no difficulty coming up with a different and equally plausible explanation—for instance that the reluctance reflects a typically feminine desire to avoid imposing on others, or perhaps a well-founded fear of stopping to talk to strangers.[3]

What this suggests is that the behaviour of men and women, whatever its substance may happen to be in any specific instance, is invariably read through a more general discourse on gender difference itself. That discourse is subsequently invoked to *explain* the pattern of gender differentiation in people's behaviour; whereas it might be more enlightening to say the discourse *constructs* the differentiation, makes it visible *as* differentiation.[4]

I want to that propose the conversationalists themselves often do the same thing I have just suggested analysts do. Analysts construct stories about other people's behaviour, with a view to making it exemplify certain patterns of gender difference; conversationalists construct stories about themselves and others, with a view to performing certain kinds of gender identity.

IDENTITY AND PERFORMATIVITY

In 1990, the philosopher Judith Butler published an influential book called *Gender Trouble: Feminism and the Subversion of Identity*. Butler's essay is a postmodernist reconceptualization of gender,

and it makes use of a concept familiar to linguists and discourse analysts from speech-act theory: *performativity*. For Butler, gender is *performative*—in her suggestive phrase, "constituting the identity it is purported to be". Just as J.L. Austin (1961) maintained that illocutions like "I promise" do not describe a pre-existing state of affairs but actually bring one into being, so Butler claims that "feminine" and "masculine" are not what we are, nor traits we *have*, but effects we produce by way of particular things we *do*: "Gender is the repeated stylization of the body, a set of repeated acts within a rigid regulatory frame which congeal over time to produce the appearance of substance, of a 'natural' kind of being" (p. 33).

This extends the traditional feminist account whereby gender is socially constructed rather than "natural", famously expressed in Simone de Beauvoir's dictum that "one is not born, but rather becomes a woman". Butler is saying that "becoming a woman" (or a man) is not something you accomplish once and for all at an early stage of life. Gender has constantly to be reaffirmed and publicly displayed by repeatedly performing particular acts in accordance with the cultural norms (themselves historically and socially constructed, and consequently variable) which define "masculinity" and "femininity".

This "performative" model sheds an interesting light on the phenomenon of gendered *speech*. Speech too is a "repeated stylization of the body"; the "masculine" and "feminine" styles of talking identified by researchers might be thought of as the "congealed" result of repeated acts by social actors who are striving to constitute themselves as "proper" men and women. Whereas sociolinguistics traditionally assumes that people talk the way they do because of who they (already) are, the postmodernist approach suggests that people are who they are because of (among other things) the way they talk. This shifts the focus away from a simply cataloguing of differences between men and women to a subtler and more complex inquiry into how people use linguistic resources to produce gender differentiation. It also obliges us to attend to the "rigid regulatory frame" within which people must make their choices—the norms that define what kinds of language are possible, intelligible and appropriate resources for performing masculinity or femininity.

A further advantage of this approach is that it acknowledges the instability and variability of gender identities, and therefore of the behaviour in which those identities are performed. While Judith Butler rightly insists that gender is regulated and policed by rather rigid social norms, she does not reduce men and women to automata, programmed by their early socialization to repeat forever the appropriate gendered behaviour, but treats them as conscious agents who may—albeit often at some social cost—engage in acts of transgression, subversion and resistance. As active producers rather than passive reproducers of gendered behaviour, men and women may use their awareness of the gendered meanings that attach to particular ways of speaking and acting to produce a variety of effects. This is important, because few, if any, analysts of data on men's and women's speech would maintain that the differences are as clear-cut and invariant as one might gather from such oft-cited dichotomies as "competitive/cooperative" and "report talk/rapport talk". People *do* perform gender differently in different contexts, and do sometimes behave in ways we would normally associate with the "other" gender. The conversation to which we now turn is a notable case in point.

THE CONVERSATION: WINE, WOMEN, SPORTS . . . AND OTHER MEN

The five men who took part in the conversation, and to whom I will give the pseudonyms Al, Bryan, Carl, Danny and Ed, were demographically a homogeneous group: white, middle-class American suburbanites aged 21, who attended the same university and belonged to the same social network on campus. This particular conversation occurred in the context of one of their commonest shared leisure activities: watching sports at home on television.[5]

Throughout the period covered by the tape-recording there is a basketball game on screen, and participants regularly make reference to what is going on in the game. Sometimes these references are just brief interpolated comments, which do not disrupt the flow of ongoing talk on some other topic; sometimes they lead to extended discussion. At all times, however, it is a legitimate conversational move to comment on the basketball game. The student who collected that data drew attention to the status of sport as a resource for talk available to North American men of all classes and racial/ethnic groups, to strangers as well as friends, suggesting that "sports talk" is a typically "masculine" conversational genre in the US, something all culturally competent males know how to do.

But "sports talk" is by no means the only kind of talk being done. The men also recount the events of their day—what classes they had and how these went; they discuss mundane details of their domestic arrangements, such as who is going to pick up groceries; there is a debate about the merits of a certain kind of wine; there are a couple of longer narratives, notably one about an incident when two men sharing a room each invited a girlfriend back without their roommate's knowledge—and discovered this at the most embarrassing moment possible. Danny's title "Wine, women, and sports" is accurate insofar as all these subjects are discussed at some length.

When one examines the data, however, it becomes clear there is one very significant omission in Danny's title. Apart from basketball, the single most prominent theme in the recorded conversation, as measured by the amount of time devoted to it, is "gossip": discussion of several persons not present but known to the participants, with a strong focus on critically examining these individuals' appearance, dress, social behaviour and sexual mores. Like the conversationalists themselves, the individuals under discussion are all men. Unlike the conversationalists, however, the individuals under discussion are identified as "gay".

The topic of "gays" is raised by Ed, only a few seconds into the tape-recorded conversation (6):[6]

ED: Mugsy Bogues (.) my name is Lloyd Gompers I am a homosexual (.) you know what the (.) I saw the new Remnant I should have grabbed you know the title? Like the head thing?

"Mugsy Bogues" (the name of a basketball player) is an acknowledgement of the previous turn, which concerned the on-screen game. Ed's next comment appears off-topic, but he immediately supplies a rationale for it, explaining that he "saw the new Remnant"—*The Remnant* being a deliberately provocative right-wing campus newspaper whose main story that week had been an attack on the "Gay Ball", a dance sponsored by the college's Gay Society.

The next few turns are devoted to establishing a shared view of the Gay Ball and of homosexuality generally. Three of the men, Al, Bryan and Ed, are actively involved in this exchange. A typical sequence is the following (14–16):

AL: gays=

ED: =gays w[hy? that's what it should read [gays why?

RYAN: [gays]   [I know]

What is being established as "shared" here is a view of gays as alien (that is, the group defines itself as heterosexual and puzzled by homosexuality: "gays, why?"), and also to some extent comical. Danny comments at one points, "it's hilarious", and Ed caps the sequence discussing the Gay Ball (23–5) with this witticism:

ED: the question is who wears the boutonniere and who wears the corsage, flip for it? Or do they both just wear flowers coz they're fruits

It is at this point that Danny introduces the theme that will dominate the conversation for some time: gossip about individual men who are said to be gay. Referring to the only other man in his language and gender class, Danny begins (27):

DANNY: My boy Ronnie was uh speaking up on the male perspective today (.) way too much

The section following this contribution is structured around a series of references to other "gay" individuals known to the participants as classmates. Bryan mentions "the most effeminate guy I've ever met" (29) and "that really gay guy in our Age of Revolution class" (34). Ed remarks that "you have never seen more homos than we have in our class. Homos, dykes, homos, dykes, everybody is a homo or a dyke" (64). He then focuses on a "fat, queer, goofy guy . . . [who's] as gay as night" [sic] (78–80), and on a "blond hair, snide little queer weird shit" (98), who is further described as a "butt pirate." Some of these references, but not all, initiate an extended discussion of the individual concerned. The contest of these discussions will bear closer examination.

"The Antithesis of Man"

One of the things I initially found most puzzling about the whole "gays" sequence was that the group's criteria for categorizing people as gay appeared to have little to do with those people's known or suspected sexual preferences or practices. The terms "butt pirate" and "butt cutter" were used, but surprisingly seldom; it was unclear to me that the individuals referred to really were homosexual, and in the one case where I actually knew the subject of discussion, I seriously doubted it.

Most puzzling is an exchange between Bryan and Ed about the class where "everybody is a homo or a dyke", in which they complain that "four homos" are continually "hitting on" (making sexual overtures to) one of the women, described as "the ugliest-ass bitch in the history of the world" (82–9). One might have thought that a defining feature of a "homo" would be his lack of interest in "hitting on" women. Yet not one seems aware of any problem or contradiction in this exchange.

I think this is because the deviance indicated for this group by the term "gay" is not so much *sexual* deviance as *gender* deviance. Being "gay" means failing to measure up to the group's standards of masculinity or femininity. This is why it makes sense to call someone "really gay": unlike same-versus other-sex preference, conformity to gender norms can be a matter of degree. It is also why hitting on an "ugly-ass bitch" can be classed as "homosexual" behaviour—proper masculinity requires that the object of public sexual interest be not just female, but minimally attractive.

Applied by the group to men, "gay" refers in particular to insufficiently masculine appearance, clothing and speech, To illustrate this I will reproduce a longer sequence of conversation about the "really gay guy in our Age of Revolution class", which ends with Ed declaring: "he's the antithesis of man".

BRYAN: uh you know that really gay guy in our Age of Revolution class who sits in front of us? he wore shorts again, by the way, it's like 42 degrees out he wore shorts again [laughter] [Ed: That guy] it's like a speedo, he wears a speedo to class (.) he's got incredibly skinny legs [Ed: it's worse] you know=

ED: =you know like those shorts women volleyball players wear? It's like those (.) it's l[ike

BRYAN: [you know what's even more ridicu[lous? when

ED: [French cut spandex]

BRYAN: you wear those shorts and like a parka on . . .

(5 lines omitted)

BRYAN: he's either got some condition that he's got to like have his legs exposed at all times or else he's got really good legs=

ED: =he's probably he'[s like

CARL: [he really likes

BRYAN: =he

ED: =he's like at home combing his leg hairs

CARL: his legs=

BRYAN: he doesn't have any leg hair though= [*yes* and oh

ED: =he *real* [*ly* likes

ED: his legs=

AL: =very long very white and very skinny

BRYAN: those ridiculous Reeboks that are always (indeciph) and goofy white socks always striped=   [tube socks

ED: =that's [right

ED: he's the antithesis of man

In order to demonstrate that certain individuals are "the antithesis of man", the group engages in a kind of conversation that might well strike us as the antithesis of "men's talk". It is unlike the "wine, women, and sports" stereotype of men's talk—indeed, rather closer to the stereotype of "women's talk"—in various ways, some obvious, and some less so.

The obvious ways in which this sequence resembles conventional notions of "women's talk" concern its purpose and subject-matter. This is talk about people, not things, and "rapport talk" rather than "report talk"—the main point is clearly not to exchange information. It is "gossip", and serves one of the most common purposes of gossip, namely affirming the solidarity of an in-group by constructing absent others as an out-group, whose behaviour is minutely examined and found wanting.

The specific subjects on which the talk dwells are conventionally "feminine" ones: clothing and bodily appearance. The men are caught up in a contradiction: their criticism of the "gays" centers on their unmanly interest in displaying their bodies, and the inappropriate garments they choose for this purpose (bathing costumes worn to class, shorts worn in cold weather with parkas which render the effect ludicrous, clothing which resembles the outfits of "women volleyball players"). The implication is that real men just pull on their jeans and leave it at that. But in order to pursue this line of criticism, the conversationalists themselves must show an acute awareness of such "unmanly" concerns as styles and materials ("French cut spandex", "tube socks"), what kind of clothes go together, and which men have "good legs". They are impelled, paradoxically, to talk about men's bodies as a way of demonstrating their own total lack of sexual interest in those bodies.

The less obvious ways in which this conversation departs from stereotypical notions of "men's talk" concern its *formal* features. Analyses of men's and women's speech style are commonly organized around a series of global oppositions, e.g. men's talk is "competitive", whereas women's is "cooperative"; men talk to gain "status", whereas women talk to forge "intimacy" and "connection"; men do "report talk" and women "rapport talk". Analysts working with these oppositions typically identify certain formal or organizational features of talk as markers of "competition" and "cooperation" etc. The analyst then examines which kinds of features predominate in a set of conversational data, and how they are being used.

In the following discussion, I too will make use of the conventional oppositions as tools for describing data, but I will be trying to build up an argument that their use is problematic. The problem is not merely that the men in my data fail to fit their gender stereotype perfectly. More importantly, I think it is often the stereotype itself that underpins analytic judgements that a certain form is cooperative rather than competitive, or that people are seeking status rather than connection in their talk. As I observed about Deborah Tannen's vignettes, many instances of behaviour will support either interpretation, or both; we use the speaker's gender, and our beliefs about what sort of behaviour makes sense for members of that gender, to rule some interpretations in and others out.

Cooperation

Various scholars, notably Jennifer Coates (1989), have remarked on the "cooperative" nature of informal talk among female friends, drawing attention to a number of linguistic features which are prominent in data on all-female groups. Some of these, like hedging and the use of epistemic modals, are signs of attention to others' face, aimed at minimizing conflict and securing agreement. Others, such as latching of turns, simultaneous speech where this is not interpreted by participants as a violation of turn-taking rights (cf. Edelsky, 1981), and the repetition or recycling of lexical items and phrases across turns, are signals that a conversation is a "joint production": that participants are building on one another's contributions so that ideas are felt to be group property rather than the property of a single speaker.

On these criteria, the conversation here must be judged as highly cooperative. For example, in the extract reproduced above, a strikingly large number of turns (around half) begin with "you know" and/ or contain the marker "like" ("you know like those shorts women volleyball players wear?"). The functions of these items (especially "like") in younger Americans' English arc complex and multiple,[7] and may include the cooperative, mitigating/face-protecting functions that Coates and Janet Holmes (1984) associate with hedging. Even where they are not clearly hedges, however, in this interaction they function in ways that relate to the building of group involvement and consensus. They often seem to mark information as "given" within the group's discourse (that is, "you know", "like", "X" presupposes that the addressee is indeed familiar with X); "you know" has the kind of hearer-oriented affective function (taking others into account or inviting their agreement) which Holmes attributes to certain tag-questions; while "like" in addition seems to function for these speakers as a marker of high involvement. It appears most frequently at moments when the interactants are, by other criteria such as intonation, pitch, loudness, speech rate, incidence of simultaneous speech, and of "strong" or taboo language, noticeably excited, such as the following (82–9):

ED: he's I mean he's like a real artsy fartsy fag he's like (indeciph) he's so gay he's got this like really high voice and wire rim glasses and he sits next to the ugliest-ass bitch in the history of the world

ED: [and

BRYAN: [and they're all hitting on her too, like
four

ED: [I know it's like four homos hitting
on her

BRYAN: guys[hitting on her

It is also noticeable throughout the long extract reproduced earlier how much latching and simultaneous speech there is, as compared to other forms of turn transition involving either short or long pauses and gaps, or interruptions which silence the interruptee. Latching—turn transition without pause or overlap—is often taken as a mark of cooperation because in order to latch a turn so precisely onto the preceding turn, the speaker has to attend closely to others' contributions.

The last part of the reproduced extract, discussing the "really gay" guy's legs, is an excellent example of jointly produced discourse, as the speakers cooperate to build a detailed picture of the legs and what is worn on them, a picture which overall could not be attributed to any single speaker. This sequence contains many instances of latching, repetition of one speaker's words by another speaker (Ed recycles Carl's whole turn, "he really likes his legs", with added emphasis), and it also contains something that is relatively rare in the conversation as a whole, repeated tokens of hearer support like "yes" and "that's right".[8]

There are, then, points of resemblance worth remarking on between these men's talk and similar talk among women as reported by previous studies. The question does arise, however, whether this male conversation has the other important hallmark of women's gossip, namely an egalitarian or non-hierarchical organization of the floor.

Competition

In purely quantitative terms, this conversation cannot be said to be egalitarian. The extracts reproduced so far are representative of the whole

insofar as they show Ed and Bryan as the dominant speakers, while Al and Carl contribute fewer and shorter turns (Danny is variable; there are sequences where he contributes very little, but when he talks he often contributes turns as long as Ed's and Bryan's, and he also initiates topics). Evidence thus exists to support an argument that there is a hierarchy in this conversation, and there is competition, particularly between the two dominant speakers, Bryan and Ed (and to a lesser extent Ed and Danny). Let us pursue this by looking more closely at Ed's behaviour.

Ed introduces the topic of homosexuality, and initially attempts to keep "ownership" of it. He cuts off Danny's first remark on the subject with a reference to *The Remnant*: "what was the article? cause you know they bashed them they were like". At this point Danny interrupts: it is clearly an interruption because in this context the preferred interpretation of "like" is quotative (see note 7)—Ed is about to repeat what the gay-bashing article in *The Remnant* said. In addition to interrupting so that Ed falls silent, Danny contradicts Ed, saying "they didn't actually (.) cut into them big". A little later on during the discussion of the Gay Ball, Ed makes use of a common competitive strategy, the joke or witty remark which "caps" other contributions (the "flowers and fruits" joke at 23–5, quoted above). This, however, elicits no laughter, no matching jokes and indeed no take-up of any kind. It is followed by a pause and a change of direction if not of subject, as Danny begins the gossip that will dominate talk for several minutes.

This immediately elicits a matching contribution from Bryan. As he and Danny talk, Ed makes two unsuccessful attempts to regain the floor. One, where he utters prefatory remark "I'm gonna be very honest" (20), is simply ignored. His second strategy is to ask (about the person Bryan and Danny are discussing) "what's this guy's last name?" (30). Firstly Bryan asks him to repeat the question, then Danny replies "I don't know what the hell it is" (32).

A similar pattern is seen in the long extract reproduced above, where Ed makes two attempts to interrupt Bryan's first turn ("That guy" and "it's worse"), neither of which succeeds. He gets the floor eventually by using the "you know, like" strategy. And from that point, Ed does orient more to the norms of joint and production; he overlaps others to produce simultaneous speech but does not interrupt; he produces more latched turns, recycling and support tokens.

So far I have been arguing that even if the speakers, or some of them, compete, they are basically engaged in a collaborative and solidary enterprise (reinforcing the bonds within the group by denigrating people outside it), an activity in which all speakers participate, even if some are more active than others. Therefore I have drawn attention to the presence of "cooperative" features, and have argued that more extreme forms of hierarchical and competitive behaviour are not rewarded by the group. I could, indeed, have argued that by the end, Ed and Bryan are not so much "competing"—after all, their contributions are not antagonistic to one another but tend to reinforce one another—as engaging in a version of the "joint production of discourse".

Yet the data might also support a different analysis in which Ed and Bryan are simply *using* the collaborative enterprise of putting down gay men as an occasion to engage in verbal duelling where points are scored—against fellow group members rather than against the absent gay men—by dominating the floor and coming up with more and more extravagant put-downs. In this alternative analysis, Ed does not so much modify his behaviour as "lose" his duel with Bryan. "Joint production" or "verbal dueling"—how do we decide?

Deconstructing Oppositions

One response to the problem of competing interpretations raised above might be that the opposition I have been working with—"competitive" versus "cooperative" behaviour—is inherently problematic, particularly if one is taken to exclude the other. Conversation can and usually does contain both cooperative and competitive elements: one could argue (along with Grice, 1975) that talk must by definition involve a certain minimum of cooperation, and also that there will usually be some degree of competition among speakers, if not for the floor itself then for the attention or the approval of others (see also Hewitt, 1997).

The global competitive/cooperative opposition also encourages the lumping together under one heading or the other of things that could in principle be distinguished. "Cooperation" might refer to agreement on the aims of talk, respect for other speakers' rights or support for their contributions; but there is not always perfect co-occurrence among these aspects, and the presence of any one of them need not rule out a "competitive" element. Participants in a conversation or other speech event may compete with each other and at the same time be pursuing a shared project or common agenda (as in ritual insult sessions); they may be in severe disagreement but punctiliously observant of one another's speaking rights (as if a formal debate, say); they may be overtly supportive, and at the same time covertly hoping to score points for their supportiveness.

This last point is strangely overlooked in some discussions of women's talk. Women who pay solicitous attention to one another's face are often said to be seeking connection or good social relations *rather than* status; yet one could surely argue that attending to others' face and attending to one's own are not mutually exclusive here. The "egalitarian" norms of female friendship groups are, like all norms, to some degree coercive: the rewards and punishments precisely concern one's status within the group (among women, however, this status is called "popularity" rather than "dominance"). A woman may gain status by displaying the correct degree of concern for others, and lose status by displaying too little concern for others and too much for herself. Arguable, it is gender-stereotyping that causes us to miss or minimize the status-seeking element in women friends' talk, and the connection-making dimension of men's.

HOW TO DO GENDER WITH LANGUAGE

I hope it will be clear by now that my intention in analysing male gossip is not to suggest that the young men involved have adopted a "feminine" conversational style. On the contrary, the main theoretical point I want to make concerns the folly of making any such claim. To characterize the conversation I have been considering as "feminine" on the basis that it bears a significant resemblance to conversations among women friends would be to miss the most important point about it, that it is not only *about* masculinity, it is a sustained performance *of* masculinity. What is important in gendering talk is the "performative gender work" the talk is doing; its role in constituting people as gendered subjects.

To put matters in these terms is not to deny that there may be an empirically observable association between a certain genre or style of speech and speakers of a particular gender. In practice this is undeniable. But we do need to ask: in virtue of what does the association hold? Can we give an account that will not be vitiated by cases where it does *not* hold? For it seems to me that conversations like the one I have analysed leave, say, Deborah Tannen's contention that men do not do "women's talk", because they simply *do not know how,* looking lame and unconvincing. If men rarely engage in a certain kind of talk, an explanation is called for; but if they do engage in it even very occasionally, an explanation in terms of pure ignorance will not do.

I suggest the following explanation. Men and women do not live on different planets, but are members of cultures in which a large amount of discourse about gender is constantly circulating. They do not only learn, and then mechanically reproduce, ways of speaking "appropriate" to their own sex; they learn a much broader set of gendered meanings that attach in rather complex ways to different ways of speaking, and they produce their own behaviour in the light of those meanings.

This behaviour will vary. Even the individual who is most unambiguously committed to traditional notions of gender has a range of possible gender identities to draw on. Performing masculinity or femininity "appropriately" cannot mean giving exactly the same performance regardless of the circumstances. It may involve different strategies in mixed and single-sex company, in private and in public settings, in the various social positions (parent, lover, professional, friend) that someone might regularly occupy in the course of everyday life.

Since gender is a relational term, and the minimal requirement for "being a man" is "not being a woman", we may find that in many circumstances, men are under pressure to constitute themselves as masculine linguistically by avoiding forms of talk whose primary association is with women/femininity. But this is not invariant, which begs the question: under what circumstances does the contrast with women lose its salience as a constraint on men's behaviour? When can men do so-called "feminine" talk without threatening their constitution as men? Are there cases when it might actually be to their advantage to do this?

WHEN AND WHY DO MEN GOSSIP?

Many researchers have reported that both sexes engage in gossip, since its social functions (like affirming group solidarity and serving as an unofficial conduit for information) are of universal relevance, but its cultural meaning (for us) is undeniably "feminine". Therefore we might expect to find most men avoiding it, or disguising it as something else, especially in mixed settings where they are concerned to mark their difference from women (see Johnson and Finlay, 1997). In the conversation discussed above, however, there are no women for the men to differentiate themselves from; whereas *there is* the perceived danger that so often accompanies Western male homosociality: homosexuality. Under these circumstances perhaps it becomes acceptable to transgress one gender norm ("men don't gossip, gossip is for girls") in order to affirm what in this context is a more important norm ("men in all-male groups must unambiguously display their heterosexual orientation").

In these speakers' understanding of gender, gay men, like women, provide a contrast group against whom masculinity can be defined. This principle of contrast seems to set limits on the permissibility of gossip for these young men. Although they discuss other men besides the "gays"—professional basketball players—they could not be said to gossip about them. They talk about the players' skills and their records, not their appearance, personal lives or sexual activities. Since the men admire the basketball players, identifying *with* them rather than *against* them, such talk would border dangerously on what for them is obviously taboo: desire for other men.

Ironically, it seems likely that the despised gay men are the *only* men about whom these male friends can legitimately talk among themselves in such intimate terms without compromising the heterosexual masculinity they are so anxious to display—though in a different context, say with their girlfriends, they might be able to discuss the basketball players differently. The presence of a woman, especially a heterosexual partner, displaces the dread spectre of homosexuality, and makes other kinds of talk possible; though by the same token her presence might make certain kinds of talk that take place among men *im*possible. What counts as acceptable talk for men is a complex matter in which all kinds of contextual variables play a part.

In this context—a private conversation among male friends—it could be argued that to gossip, either about your sexual exploits with women or about the repulsiveness of gay men (these speakers do both), is not just one way, but the most appropriate way to display heterosexual masculinity. In another context (in public, or with a larger and less close-knit group of men), the same objective might well be pursued through explicitly agonistic strategies, such as yelling abuse at women or gays in the street, or exchanging sexist and homophobic jokes. *Both* strategies could be said to do performative gender work: in terms of what they do for the speakers involved, one is not more "masculine" than the other, they simply belong to different settings in which heterosexual masculinity may (or must) be put on display.

CONCLUSION

I hope that my discussion of the conversation I have analysed makes the point that it is unhelpful for linguists to continue to use models of gendered speech which imply that masculinity and femininity are monolithic constructs, automatically giving rise to predictable (and utterly different) patterns of verbal interaction. As the same time, I hope it might make us think twice about the sort of analysis that implicitly seeks the meaning (and sometimes the *value*) of an interaction among men or women primarily in the style, rather than the substance, of what is said. For although, as I noted earlier in relation to Judith Butler's work, it is possible for men and women to performatively subvert or resist the prevailing codes of gender, there can surely be no convincing argument that this is what Danny and his friends are doing. Their conversation is animated by entirely traditional anxieties about being seen at all times as red-blooded heterosexual males: not women and not queers. Their skill as performers does not alter the fact that what they perform is the same old gendered script.

REFERENCES

Austin, J L. (1961) How to Do Things with Words. Oxford: Clarendon Press.

Butler, Judith (1990) Gender Trouble: Feminism and the Subversion of Identity. New York: Routledge.

Cameron, Deborah (1995) Verbal Hygiene. London: Routledge.

Coates, Jennifer (1989) "Gossip revisited", pp. 94–121 in J. Coates and D. Cameron (eds) Women in Their Speech Communities. London: Longman.

Edelsky, Carole (1981) "Who's got the floor?" Language in Society, 10, 3, 383–422.

Frank, Karsta (1992) Sprachgewalt. Tubingen: Max Niemeyer Verlag.

Grice, H. P. (1975) "Logic and conversation", pp. 41–58 in P. Cole and J. Morgan (eds) Syntax and Semantics, vol. 3: Speech Acts. New York: Academic Press.

Hewitt, Roger (1997) "'Box-out' and 'taxing'", pp. 27–46 in Sally Johnson and Ulrike Hanna Meinhof (eds) Language and Masculinity. Oxford: Blackwell.

Holmes, Janet (1984) "Hedging your bets and sitting on the fence: some evidence for hedges as support structures". Te Reo, 27, 47–62.

Johnson, Sally and Finlay, Frank (1997) "Do men gossip? An analysis of football talk on television", pp. 130–43 in Sally Johnson and Ulrike Hanna Meinhof (eds) Language and Masculinity. Oxford: Blackwell.

Lichterman, Paul (1992) "Self-help reading as a thin culture". Media, Culture and Society, 14, 421–47.

Simonds, Wendy (1992) Women and Self-Help Culture: Reading between the Lines. New Brunswick, NJ: Rutgers University Press.

Tannen, Deborah (1990) You Just Don't Understand: Women and Men in Conversation. New York: Ballantine Books.

NOTES

1. Because the student concerned is one of the speakers in the conversation I analyse, and the nature of the conversation makes it desirable to conceal participants' identities (indeed, this was one of the conditions on which the data were collected and subsequently passed on to me), I will not give his real name here, but I want to acknowledge his generosity in making his recording and transcript available to me, and to thank him for a number of insights I gained by discussing the data with him as well as by reading his paper. I am also grateful to the other young men who participated. All their names, and the names of other people they mention, have been changed, and all pseudonyms used are (I hope) entirely fictitious.

2. I base this assessment of reader response on my own research with readers of Tannen's book (see Cameron, 1995, ch. 5), on non-scholarly reviews of the book, and on reader studies of popular self-help generally (e.g. Lichterman, 1992; Simonds, 1992).

3. I am indebted to Penelope Eckert for describing this "thought experiment", which she has used in her own teaching (though the specific details of the example are not an exact rendition of Eckert's observations).

4. The German linguist Karsta Frank (1992) has provocatively argued that so-called gender differences in speech-style arise *exclusively* in reception: women and men are heard differently, as opposed to speaking differently. I do not entirely accept Frank's very strong position on this point but I do think she has drawn attention to a phenomenon of some importance.

5. I mention that this was "at home" because in the United States it is also common for men, individually or in groups, to watch televised sports in public places such as bars and even laundromats; but this particular conversation would probably not have happened in a public setting with others present. It appears to be a recurrent feature of male friends' talk that the men are engaged in some other activity as well as talking. The Swedish researcher Kerstin Nordenstam, who has an impressive corpus comprising data from twelve different single-sex friendship groups, has found that the men are far less likely than the women to treat conversation as the exclusive or primary purpose of a social gathering. Many of the women's groups recorded for Nordenstam were "sewing circles"—a traditional kind of informal social organization for women in Sweden—but they frequently did not sew, and defined their aim simply as "having fun"; whereas the men's groups might meet under no particular rubric, but they still tended to organize their talk around an activity such as playing cards or games. (Thanks to Kerstin Nordenstam for this information.)

6. Numbers in parenthesis refer to the lines in the original transcript. (Added by editor: Two of the main transcription conventions used in this article are: = Equal signs indicate "latching," that is, two utterances that follow one another without any perceptible pause. [A square bracket between turns indicates the point at which overlap by another speaker starts.)

7. For example, *like* has a "quotative" function among younger US speakers, as in "and she's like [= she said], stop bugging me, and I'm like, what do you mean stop bugging you?". This and other uses of the item have become popularly stereotyped as markers of membership in the so-called "slacker" generation.

8. It is a rather consistent research finding that men use such minimal responses significantly less often than women, and in this respect the present data conform to expectations—there are very few minimal responses of any kind. I would argue, however, that active listenership, involvement and support are not *absent* in the talk of this group; they are marked by other means such as high levels of latching/simultaneous speech, lexical recycling and the use of *like*.

3 • *Kath Weston*

DO CLOTHES MAKE THE WOMAN?
Gender, Performance Theory, and Lesbian Eroticism

DISCUSSION QUESTIONS

1. How do gay women themselves understand and interpret gender in their relationships?
2. What are the differences between how lesbians practiced and understood the gender categories of "butch" and "femme" in the past and in the present?
3. According to Weston, how does her ethnography of lesbian women challenge the idea that gender is a performative process?

Isn't it curious that from the time the women's movement first began to carve out a place for itself within the academy, "gender relations" has served primarily as a code word for male–female relations? After all, social constructionists have long argued that gender is the product of culture: certain societies may symbolically incorporate genitalia and other elements of anatomy into gender constructs, but those constructs are in no way determined by bodies or biology. Ethnographic research lent validity to this claim by demonstrating the sheer variability, from one society to another, of phenomena that "Western" observers studied under the rubrics of gender and sexuality. But what about the gendering of same-sex relations? What happens when an analysis pushes social constructionism to its limits by factoring anatomy—"sex differences"—out of the equation to see how gendered differences and continuities become incorporated into relations among women (or men)?

Historically the sites where gender intersects with sexual identities have produced and disseminated a wealth of cultural categories that combine gendered meanings with nuances of age, race, and class. Femme and butch, androgynous and ki-ki, swish and queen, lipstick lesbians, kids, and bulldaggers are all classifications that emerged from a century of queer community-building in North America.[1] When I began my study of the gendering of relationships among lesbians in the Bay Area, I intentionally focused on "femme" and "butch" as categories that cut across debates on gender identity.[2] I wanted to know how these terms figured in the lives of lesbians who condemned them or used them only in jest as well as those who called themselves butch or femme. I also assumed the possibility that such categories represent a creative transformation, rather than a straightforward reproduction, of the old opposition between male and female. In the rush to "prove" first that lesbians

A revised and abridged version of Kath Weston, 2002. "Do Clothes Make the Woman: Performing In and Out of Industrial Time," from *Gender in Real Time: Power and Transience in a Visual Age* (Routledge). Reprinted with the kind permission of the author.

really want to be men, then that lesbians are just as feminine as heterosexual women, and more recently that the practice of butch/femme offers a revolutionary subject position capable of subverting oppressive gender relations, scholars have paid little attention to how gay women themselves have interpreted gender in their relationships. How do successive attempts to re-theorize gender in literary studies, theater/film criticism, and philosophy stack up against an ethnographic analysis that examines what lesbians of different backgrounds and political persuasions have been doing and saying while scholars debate gender's fate?

DANCE AND STANCE

The 1985 Prom Nite dance at the Women's Building of the Bay Area was one of several events I attended in the course of my research that highlighted the possibility—perhaps the inevitability—of gendering same-sex relationships. While Rachel Becker was getting ready to go to the dance, styling and restyling her collar-length hair in the mirror, another woman in our group came into the bathroom to offer her opinion on the overall effect.[3] "It looks good," she said, "only you've got it parted on the girls' side." "Is there anything that gender doesn't permeate in this society?" I wondered, still grappling with its complexities after a year of the close attention to detail and compulsive note-taking that characterize anthropological fieldwork.

On several previous occasions Rachel had insisted that she seldom thought of herself in terms of what she called "roles." When other lesbians categorized her, she believed they tended to see her as femme; that had certainly been the case with her last girlfriend. Like many lesbians who claimed that the categories butch and femme had little to do with their self-perception, however, Rachel was prepared to accept the classification others attributed to her, "if I have to choose." For the dance she had decided to add her new leather vest to a tailored shirt, dress pants, and a pair of shoes that everyone agreed sent out "mixed messages." On

our way over to San Francisco's Mission District, she tried to enlist the group's support for her (re) gendering project, saying with a laugh, "You guys remind me to act butch, okay?"

The auditorium, one of the few rooms in the Women's Building large enough to hold a gathering of hundreds, bore a marked resemblance to a high school gym. Volunteers from the local clean-and-sober organization sponsoring the dance had spent hours decorating the space to invoke lesbian identity and carry through the prom night motif. On one wall a slide show created a montage of images of women from different cultures. Here and there posters proclaimed "Sappho Lives" or "Dyke of Earl" in a graffiti scrawl.

When our group had originally walked in the door, the first people we encountered were a woman in a black sheath dress escorted by another in a white pleated shirt and bow tie. Behind me someone exclaimed with delight, "Oh, good, I'm glad people dressed!" It took us several minutes to work our way into the auditorium, where pink, yellow, and black helium-filled balloons drifted slowly across the ceiling, trailing ribbons that threaded their way through a room packed with dancers. On one side of the floor a woman in a pin-striped shirt and red tie leaned against the stage, hair slicked back, with just a few strands falling—carelessly? artfully?—over her forehead. In her arms was a woman in a sleeveless gold top that glittered under the lights, her outfit accented with lipstick, fishnets, and costume jewelry. Someone had on a full set of leathers; another wore handcuffs hooked through a belt loop. More than a few were clad in the natural fibers usually attributed to the lesbians known as "East Bay dykes" or "crunchy granola types" (depending on one's perspective).

On some women earrings dangling neatly, symmetrically, while women without jewelry turned their heads to reveal a row of earrings arrayed on one side. There were those who had created their own version of "gender fuck" drag by juxtaposing symbols of femme and butch: earrings with a flashy tie or nylons with combat boots. As women in jeans and button-down shirts kissed one another in the hallways, women in short skirts paired off for a song or two. Lesbians in ball gowns, all tulle and satin, joined partners in tuxes with red cummerbunds or suspenders and bow ties. Some of the women could have danced their way unobtrusively through any school prom in the state—unobtrusively, that is, unless they had walked in together, hand in hand.

An hour or so later, Rachel found me in the crowd and confided, "It's amazing what dressing butch will do for you. I already asked three women to dance! And I'm saying the most incredible things." What sort of things? "Well you know . . . flirting. And here I was worried I'd be a wallflower!" "Wallflower—now there's a term I haven't heard since junior high," I thought to myself. If I remembered correctly, it was a term reserved for the girls, not the boys. Objects of pity or desire, the girls who sat out the dances came under the boys' scrutiny at the very moment they seemed most marginalized.

After a few dances, I wasn't the only one eyeing the carrot cake that stood, still uncut, amidst the remnants of someone's birthday potluck. By 10:30 the place was jammed and sweat began to mingle with the scents of perfume. More and more people were eager to move their bodies to the beat, with less and less room left to work out that energy on the dance floor. Following through on the prom night theme, the DJ began to mix in hits from the 1950s and early 1960s. Little Richard screamed "Lucille" until Ritchie Valens cut in with "La Bamba." During the slow dances, the floor hardly cleared. Cornrows and perms rested on shoulders beneath flattops and dreds, wedges and buzz cuts. When "I Love How You Love Me" came over the speakers, I shouted, "It's the Paris Sisters!" to a new acquaintance sitting across the table. "The who?" she yelled back. Judging from appearances, half the women in the room (including myself) had not yet entered elementary school when that single was released in 1961. Given the noise that both enveloped and elevated the crowd, appearances were about all anyone had to go on.

GENDER IS AS GENDER DOES?

In the search for a theoretical framework that could illuminate what had transpired at the dance, I turned to theories that analyze gender as a matter of performance or performativity. Performance theories of gender, which weave together strands of postmodernist, speech act, and feminist theory, responded to a stalemate in the debate between social constructivist and essentialist accounts of gender, which explained gender differentiation as an outgrowth of culture or biology, respectively. Because determinisms of either sort attempt to isolate a foundation for a fixed identity that is subsequently expressed, they afford little insight into the *production* of gendered subjectivity, much less its anomalies and contradictions. According to Judith Butler, gender is not a core identity or essence that precedes expression but rather a social product created through the *practice* of relating to other people. As people perform gender, they orchestrate the play of gendered symbols upon and through the body's surface to create an illusion of a fixed interior reality.

One way to characterize Prom Nite would be as an event that takes the volume and "pumps it up," an image that condenses several aspects of postmodernist accounts of gender. In the first sense of "volume," the music, dance, and encompassing sound of urban nightlife establish a social arena for the lesbians in attendance to create gendered presentations through movement, dress, and interaction. The "loudness" of their displays drew attention to this process of cultural construction through parody, humor, and an overall accentuation of gendered signification. As the volume of performances picked up, the possibilities multiplied for gendering relations in ways that some would argue offer an alternative to the restrictions of a two-gender system.

At an event such as Prom Nite, performance theory would say that people play with—as they play on—cultural representations of gender by the juxtaposition of certain styles of clothing, hair, makeup, stance, and even the long-term reconfiguration of musculature through bodybuilding or sport. Rachel Becker's sense that the gendering of her body was largely a matter of presentation, for instance, allowed her to believe in the possibility of moving between femme and butch personae.

Performance theory grants no ontological status to the psychic space that many people in the United States image as the locus of a "true" or core self. The spectacle created by the constant play of gendered signification across the body's surface implies an inner substance, but the fixed gender of that "real me" simply does not exist. The hands in the pockets and the bouffant hairdo point to the possession of a substantive identity as surely as they mask its absence. For performance theorists, it's all in the act—not the essence. According to Butler, practices such as butch/femme are radicalizing precisely because they expose and break apart the fiction of a neat, natural correspondence among anatomy, gender identity, and desire.

Lesbians have every reason to be critical of the putative correspondence of gender to genitalia and eroticism. In Euro-American societies where gender inversion theories of homosexuality prevail, heterosexuals often confuse homosexuality with transgender identification. Popular stereotypes continue to associate lesbianism with masculinity and male homosexuality with effeminacy. On occasion after occasion, lesbians and gay men are subjected to searches for the gendered signs inscribed in bodies (the low-pitched voice, the limp wrist) that people in the United States use to infer gay identity. Because passing for straight requires the careful management of symbols that are more specifically linked to gender than to sexuality per se, coming out to oneself as a gay person generally entails coming *into* a heightened consciousness of gender.

Many accounts of gender as performance rely heavily upon an analogy between butch/femme and gay male drag or more precisely, on an analysis that interprets butch/femme as an instance of drag or camp style. While I was in the Bay Area, someone had written in large letters on a wall where Castro Street turns into Divisadero: "There are no women—there are only drag queens." If a feminist version of performance theory were to add anything to the writing on the wall, it would be that there are also no men—only stone butches and diesel dykes. By this logic no performer exists, no fixed subject, no authentic femininity or masculinity waiting to be learned or recovered. Each performance refers to other performances, rather than to some originating standard of femaleness and maleness. It is in this sense that Butler calls gender a "citational practice." The performance offers but an "imitation" of an "imitation," like a remake of a movie that never had its first release.

As an exposé of the gendering of social relations, performance theories of gender can be very seductive. Most of their tenets initially seemed applicable to the way I saw lesbians gendering their relationships. Prom Nite, for instance, combined many elements customarily mentioned in attempts to distinguish the postmodern era from its modernist predecessor: nostalgia; a fragmentation that isolates artifacts (earrings, boots, hair) and presses them into the service of parody or pastiche; an overriding emphasis on fashion and style; and the distanced approach to gender epitomized by Rachel's sense of playing a part. Like performance theorists, ethnographers have recognized the image of an atomized inner self as the product of a peculiarly "Western" way of ordering experience. Performance theory's focus on the social significance of bodily movement and adornment is quite compatible with anthropological studies of how people use ritual, work style, and dance to produce culturally specific notions of gender and selfhood.

More troubling is the question of whether butch/femme and drag work to denaturalize and subvert because they help viewers "see through" identity, or whether their political merits are supposed to reside in an altered consciousness that people acquire through "doing" gender. As Butler herself notes, drag's ambivalent implication in power relations, its willingness to borrow literally and figuratively from the trappings that cloak inequalities of all sorts, means that drag can just as easily shore up gendered hegemonies as make a case for sedition. In everyday life butch/femme may sometimes be associated with a playful, irreverent, anti-essentialist approach to gender, but this association has been confined to a limited number of "players" in relatively specialized historical circumstances.

BEHIND THE SCENES WITH PERFORMANCE THEORY

Prom Nite cannot legitimately be isolated and reduced to a setting for a string of gendered performances; it must also be understood as an activity that took shape in a distinctive context. Organizers staged the dance as a one-time celebration that invoked a theme which invited satire and costume. Clearly no one interpreted the advance advertisements as invitations to an actual school prom. As a result, many women attended who probably would not have systematically integrated the sorts of gendered representations they made visible at the dance into other arenas of their lives. The gendering of clothing was much more marked at Prom Nite than at most other gatherings of lesbians I attended in the Bay Area. Several of the people I encountered that night mentioned that having people dress up made the experience fun, outrageous, "a kick": precisely the sorts of words gay men might use when they're camping it up. None of the women I knew who went to the dance considered herself "seriously into" butch/femme.

This broader context for the representations of femme and butch observed at Prom Nite hints at significant changes that separate the butch/femme of the 1980s–1990s from that of the 1920s–1950s. For some lesbians, "eighties butch-femme—if it accurately can be termed as such—is a self-conscious aesthetic that plays with style and power, rather than an embrace of one's 'true' nature against the constraints of straight society."[4] Many felt free to style themselves femme or butch, perhaps for an evening, perhaps for the duration, without necessarily following through in bed, without claiming femme or butch as identities, and without adhering to any particular logic for dividing up the chores. Herein lies the novelty, relative to past decades.

To the extent that theories of gender performativity ignore these historical shifts, they cannot differentiate phenomena specific to the butch/femme of the 1980s–1990s from the gendered practices of earlier periods. Insightful though they are, applications of the concept of performativity to the gendering of lesbian relationships can be considered period pieces in the sense that they could only have been written in the wake of butch/femme's second wave. By the late twentieth century it had become possible for at least some lesbians to pursue butch/femme as a fashion statement without the expectation that other aspects of daily life would be gendered accordingly. Roberta Osabe, for instance, left a lover because the woman had an "old-fashioned" idea of how femmes were supposed to conduct themselves. As Roberta explained, "I only wanted to do it, really, through looks, and certain small little behavior things. . . . I didn't want to do all the dishes!" This focus on style and presentation, as well as a certain resistance to using gender as a scaffolding for inequality, allows the "second wave" of butch/femme to lend itself easily to an analysis of gender as performance. Yet that same focus is rooted in *historical* developments that have sundered any presumed congruence between the gendered ways that a woman identifies herself (butch, femme, what have you) and gendered domains of dress, behavior, or sex.

The marginalization of femme- and butch-*identified* lesbians in the late twentieth century also contrasted sharply with pre-feminist working-class lesbian communities in which members generally adopted one or the other of these categories as a persona, if not always an identity. By the 1980s, the crucial question had become not "Which are you?" but "Are you into it?" To characterize butch/femme as a paradigm for resistance to essentialist models of gender collapses a multitude of meanings, contexts, uses, and practices into a timeless "butch/femme couple." The Femme and The Butch cannot stand for the entire range of lesbians who have employed these categories any more than Woman can adequately represent the concrete women who people the planet.

Even today, it is dangerous to mistake a small, though eye-catching, segment of lesbian nightlife for the totality of the gendering of lesbian relations. Although bodies may be culturally malleable, it is important to remember that not all people experience them as such. A study of gay women conducted as early as the mid-1970s found that while some approached butch/femme with playfulness or irony, others considered femme and butch unalterable personal attributes.[5] In the Bay Area during the 1980s, notions of a coherently gendered self were alive and well. Complaints about façades and calls to "drop the act" are usually voiced because a person expects that something will be there to enjoy once the mask has been ripped away. For both the women who embraced butch or femme as identities and the ones who flirted with these categories in a more limited way, essentialism could exist in conjunction with the very practice that performance theory expected to undermine it.

While Sarah Voss believed that she could, to a degree, control others' perceptions of her gender and sexual identity, she could not conceive how a new suit of clothes or a shortened stride could ever touch her sense of herself as a butch. One day Sarah decided to trade clothes with a friend she placed "on the femme side of the scale":

> We were having one of these arguments about, "Well, if you walked a mile in my shoes." And here they are! Right, let's do it! Her immediate hit on my clothes is that they were uncomfortable, and mine was that hers were vulnerable. They made me sexually vulnerable in ways I didn't like, like these loose, flowing pants that could fall off at any time, and this loose, flowing blouse. . . . Clothing, especially on a motorcycle, has got to be armor in some sense. You know, skin is expensive. Also, it didn't work, but it may not have worked because all the people we hung out with all day were people who already knew us in our roles. So, of course, their immediate take on seeing us wearing each other's clothes was to lie

down on the floor and throw up laughing so hard. I still don't think we could have passed, though. You can say it's body language; you could say it's attitude.

Compare Vicki Turner's comments on her former roommate, a self-described butch: "She's worn skirts and things like that. But I couldn't see her in these [gestures at her Spandex pants] and carrying it off to be really this ultra-Jessica Rabbit kind of thing. Sorry, girlfriend! It's like me being the daddy butch. They'd look at me and go, 'Sorry, hon. You just don't have it.'" Drawing on notions of fit and coherence, some women claimed that any outfit can feel like putting on drag if it is not "right for you." Like many of the lesbians I interviewed, Vicki used autobiographical anecdotes to establish the "naturalness" or "rightness" of gendered traits that she attributed to herself. "I was bred to primp," she explained, so identifying as a femme offered "an easier way to live."

For Vicki, style was the *least* important part of being a femme, although she enjoyed getting ready to go out in dresses and pumps: "I'm not one of those halfway middlers, that 'go in between' kind of thing. I really am feminine in poofy stuff. And I can dress up to the epitome of feminine. I mean, I can go *all* the way. Which some women can't, because they can't carry it off." Many butch- and femme-identified women described clothes and presentation becoming less important to them as they grew older and came to feel "secure" in their identities. While these self-portraits were not incompatible with performance theory's emphasis on aesthetics, since gestures that appealed to the eye sometimes preceded the consolidation of identity, their accounts demonstrated how essentialist interpretations of identity can reassert themselves even for those whose practice fractures any "natural" correspondence between gender and action or desire.

Vicki, who worked as a stripper, drew upon her experience of playing a part on a literal stage to make a distinction between acting and "real life." Significantly, she considered her femme identity and her partnership with a butch-identified woman to be part of that reality, rather than just another act. By rejecting the language of "roles" as inadequate to describe the complexity of their everyday lives, other femme- and butch-identified women also distinguished between act and essence. "Roles" in this formulation came to represent something false and prepackaged; something readily adopted and just as easily cast off. Both these concepts were at odds with their conceptualization of butch and femme as authentic extensions of a core self.

Another way women reinstated the notion of a gendered identity waiting to be expressed was through imagery of the butch who "goes overboard" and the "ultra-femme." "When you've got a scale, you always have the people who are over here off the scale . . . like overly femme and kind of false, and the same for butch," explained Marilyn Daniels, who described herself as "a 2½" on a scale from 1 to 10, where 1 was femme and 10 was butch. According to Jeanne Riley, who disliked the whole notion of butch/femme, "I know [lesbians] who actually have long red fingernails and mince around in skirts and do all those right things. And I can sort of see it as a drag queen, effectively. For me to do that, that's what I would have to be." Interestingly, Jeanne's account was not very different from how Vicki said she felt after she had spent an hour "grooming" for a night out: "flamboyant, like more of a drag queen." Although Jeanne condemned the practice and Vicki reveled in it, both used the "ultra" category to distinguish between gendering as artifice and gendering as an extension of self. Not all femmes "foreground cultural femininity" in such a way as to expose its social construction, and of those who do, not all do so consistently.[6]

Of course, not everyone who participates in butch/femme finds herself invested in creating coherence. Like Rachel Becker, Louise Romero (who told me, "They all call me femme, so I go as femme") accepted the attribution contextually but did not construct "femme" as a personal identity. Other women seemed quite comfortable with incongruities, relocating themselves up and down a butch/femme scale as they moved from one relationship or one cultural domain to another. Teresa

Ramirez associated butch/femme with style and superficiality—"it's more on the surface, more of a front"—but that did not prevent her from drawing a second-order contrast between butch/femme and what she called her "feminine and masculine sides."

> You change depending on your mood, on the situation. I don't know if you feel this way, but with certain people I feel very vulnerable, and the vulnerability brings out my feminine qualities and I want to be very giving and I want to take care of the person and I want to kiss them, I want to hug them, I want to feed them, I want to do all this stuff, right? And with . . . certain other people, I feel very in control. Like, hey, I'm cool, I got it, and I'm gonna take care of this person: sort of like this other attitude. I think it's partly chemistry that you have with people, that certain people bring out something, a part of your life that is beyond words. . . . So with certain people I'm much more feminine than with other people.

The variety in these women's conceptions of how their relationships were gendered should not come as a great surprise to anyone familiar with the many paths that lead to the adoption of an identity such as lesbian or gay. Although coming out does facilitate—perhaps even demand—a reflective stance toward gender (as theorists of performativity contend), it can also incorporate an essentialist model of self-discovery in which an individual arrives at the final "truth" of her or his sexual identity. That person may or may not incorporate such a model into a politics of resistance.

Performance theory elaborates an extended theatrical metaphor that works very well to illuminate the mechanics and demystify the organics of gender's production. Yet metaphor cannot carry the weight of all that theory leaves unexamined. Despite an overt commitment to respecting differences of race, class, history, and culture, performance theory's restricted focus on process leaves little room for the complexities and contradictions that appear as soon as an event like Prom Nite is located in sociohistorical context. As a result, theories of gender performativity rest their political aspirations on a foundation as ethereal as the groundwork believed to prop up gender identity.

A DIFFERENT KIND OF CLOSET

It is one thing to understand the limitations of performance theory; it is another to comprehend its appeal. Accounts of performativity tend to cast femmes and butches as "spin doctors" of gender, actors whose performances may be limited by contingency, but who nevertheless enjoy great interpretive leeway to manipulate their audiences. Who wouldn't be attracted to the competence implicit in this image of the "new lesbian," whose savvy approach to gender allows her to orchestrate self-presentation so as to create others' perceptions in the image of her own phantasmatic?

The same decade that urged women in the United States to "dress for success" also generated the "butch/femme aesthetic." Not coincidentally, the illustrations used to explain performance theory focused on visual display, calling attention to gestures and bodily adornment rather than other phenomena historically associated with butch/femme, such as gendered divisions of labor and sexual acts. Clothing is more readily subject to individual manipulation (and thus more easily incorporated into theories of performativity) than work hierarchies or other aspects of daily life that must be socially negotiated. If not every lesbian was prepared to become a biker, *chola*, soccer mom, prom queen, or video vamp, she could at least assume the trappings. Or so consumer capitalism seemed to promise.

By now it should be clear that I am not arguing, in reductionist fashion, that people perform gender primarily by manipulating clothing or fashion, as some readers of an earlier, abbreviated version of this essay concluded. Quite the contrary: the particular version of butch/femme that attracted the attention of performance theorists incorporated a culturally and historically specific (if problematic) notion of personhood that was rooted in bourgeois

individualism. Like the worker under capitalism who is formally free to sell her labor (or "free" to die for lack of wages to buy food and shelter), practitioners of this kind of butch/femme are apparently "free" to present gendered representations that they assemble, according to personal taste, from repertoires of commodities. With ties and tunics, heels and haircuts, they freeze and then fragment gender so that it appears not as the product of an oppressive power relation (Man over Woman), but as a cultural resource that can empower without oppressing—a resource utilizable by all, regardless of anatomical differences.

A good number of the women I met located gender and sexuality in traits "possessed" rather than presentation enacted. They understood these perceived traits to be subject to verification not by bank account or social context, but through visual inspection of the body. Commenting on the gendering of a physique that she believed prevented her from passing for straight, Lourdes Alcantara explained, "You can't hide that [your lesbian identity]. It's on your face, in your walking, your eyes, through your gestures. It's all over you." While some women thought they could alter their gendered presentations at will, "like a chameleon," the majority did not. "If I was bald, I'd still look feminine," claimed Vicki Turner. Paula Nevins, a barber with a large lesbian clientele, described the limitations she perceived in being able to the contribute to the gendering her clients desired: "I've gotten some heavy-duty dykes—I mean real masculine, cock-of-the-walk type, bottom-line dykes—that will sit down in my chair, and have the clothes and the attitude to be just the butchest thing in town, and say that they want a haircut and they want it real short, but they don't want to look butch. Well, there's nothing you can do for a person like that. If you're butch, you're butch." Actions and "body language," which many women found more difficult to control than clothing, could also interfere with the desired effect.

Some of the reasons people do not always experience themselves as being in control of gendered performances involve their immersion in social and material relations. The same idealism that makes performance theory so appealing, with its promise of personal/political empowerment, cannot account for the context (including constraints) that leads someone to assemble one type of bodily montage rather than another, the shifts in content and significance of gendered presentations over time, or what a given presentation means to the women who engage in gendering.

At first glance, performance theory would seem to represent the antithesis of an idealist approach: what could be more material than *corporeal* signification, bodies made socially salient through the use of artifacts that are visible to all who care to see? Yet there is no such thing as the "free" play of signification. In a material world, bodies are not passively inscribed by signs; they are inscribed by people who select items of material culture from a restricted range of options and arrange them according to imaginations shaped by historical developments. When a lesbian opens the closet door to put together an outfit for the evening, the size of her paycheck limits the choices she finds available. In a material world, the people fashioning gendered presentations are never identically positioned with respect to relations of power. However carefully crafted a presentation may be, once a woman brings it out into the street, her presentation can be jarred into a different interpretive framework by the teenager who throws a rock at her and calls her "dyke." And in a material world, gendered presentations do not confine themselves to the cognitive tasks of deconstruction. Instead, they extend their appeal to the senses as they beckon gay women into erotic connections.

When performativity does away with the gendered subject, it inadvertently displaces and fetishizes gender by relocating gender in the hair, beads, muscles, trousers, shoes, mascara, fingernails, and "body language" that people draw on to call gender into being through performance. What this tendency to perceive gender as a physical property of possessions—or as a product of the significance culturally *attributed* to possessions—obscures is gender's character as an aspect of social relations.

GOOD TO THINK OR GOOD TO EAT?

Because social relations take shape over time, they entail more than is immediately apparent in the give-and-take of everyday interactions. I now want to look at an equally historicized side of those relations that is crucial for understanding the emergence of the "second wave" of butch/femme: lesbian eroticism. In my description of Prom Nite, I depicted the occasion with an emphasis on the gendering, rather than the eroticization, of lesbian relationships. For all that a reader can tell from this account, the women in the halls outside the auditorium might have been kissing for reasons that had nothing to do with their presentation or attire. Yet in reflecting back upon the conversations and events of that night, I remembered that Rachel Becker worried about ending up a wallflower for multiple reasons. She was concerned that her butch presentation would lack credibility, yes, but she also wanted other women to find her attractive, to dance with her, and perhaps to accompany her home. For Rachel, how she looked remained inseparable from the responses she hoped to receive. As we walking into the Women's Building, what struck all the women in our group was not just the playful atmosphere, but also its "erotic charge."

Most of the lesbians I met in the Bay Area associated gendered performances—both their own and the ones they observed others create—with a perception of themselves as sexual beings. In a setting such as Prom Nite, attraction as well as gendering was the name of the game. Often enough that meant moving beyond a primarily visual orientation to style and appearance in order to engage the other senses of hearing, smell, touch, and (yes) taste. If gender appeared to some lesbians in commodified form as a cultural resource, it had become a resource from which many derived sexual pleasure. When I asked one woman how she would describe butch/femme, her answer situated her experience squarely at the intersection of gender, sexuality, and identity. "It's just who you are and how you like it," she replied.

When the "second wave" of butch/femme began to gather force in the early 1980s, some saw it as a passing fad, while others described it as a return to "cultural roots" derived from an earlier period. By 1990, with "gender fuck" fashion becoming more prevalent and butch/butch and femme/femme couples appearing alongside more "traditional" butch/femme pairs, this "second wave" appeared to many lesbians in San Francisco in a somewhat different light. Even women who had hardly participated in butch/femme started to credit "roles" with bringing sexuality back into lesbian relationships that they perceived as de-eroticized by the almost mandatory androgyny of the 1970s.

Eroticism, like gender, is mediated by "the practices of differently situated and positioned actors within contradictory social relations."[7] In addition to the symbolics of class, race, and age that inform gendered presentations (remember the biker, the *chola*, and the prom queen), how would such differences enter into a revised account of Prom Nite? Just because differences become commodified and incorporated into the aesthetics of butch/femme does not put an end to the ways these differences, when institutionalized, can affect the gendering and eroticizing of relationships. What sorts of questions might break through Prom Nite's insular framework, following social relations not only back through history, but as they connect outward to relations of power in the wider society?

Aesthetics cannot begin to explain why the dance should have attracted a crowd of younger women fascinated with the 1950s; why working-class styles of clothing predominated, apart from the gowns and tuxes linked directly to the prom motif; or why Charlyne Harris insisted that she was preoccupied with more than gender and attraction when she thought about "roles," because every time she asked a white woman to dance, she could be choosing a partner who would type her as butch just because she was black. Performances are negotiated not only in the act, but also in the wake of historical legacies that shape interpretation. Although the meaning of dress and dance, invitation and stance, at the prom was never fixed,

the range of possible interpretations emerged from historically conditioned relations of inequality as well as desire.

What about the power relations embedded in my own presence as a lesbian ethnographer who found herself simultaneously "natived" and "othered," desiring and desired, observing and observed? How to depict my participation? In the Prom Nite narrative I appear as a split subject: marked as the narrating anthropologist and unremarked as "the native" in the pinstriped shirt, the two equally riveted by the vision of a woman in fishnets and gold lamé. Observing, narrating, or theorizing alone cannot trace out the unstable, nonlinear connections that link power to gender and gender to performance, which is to say, to violence, attraction, color, money, and days gone by.

Did the woman who stormed out in the middle of the dance leave for a reason that had anything to do with difference or identity? Was the one busy revving up her motorcycle outside the door as we left climbing aboard a Honda because she couldn't afford a Harley, or was the Honda part of an image she wanted to project? When two women got into their car across the street, was one of them driving because she owned the car, because it was the "right" thing to do as a butch, or because driving and cooking represented her chores for the week?

Butch/femme defies analysis in terms of simple polarities, gendered or otherwise. Like most practices in this society traversed by differences and shot through with hierarchical relations, particular renditions of femme and butch are suffused with aspects of class, race, age, and sexual desire. While butch/femme may supply the "moment of critical reflection" necessary to expose gender as a cultural creation, its radical potential cannot be evaluated apart from particular historical and material contexts.[8] To destabilize is not always to subvert.

If gender cannot be reduced to self-evident identities (Woman or Man), neither can it be conjured away as the compelling but ultimately illusory product of performance. Gender no more resides in gesture or apparel than it lies buried in bodies and psyches. Look beyond the historically specific logic of gender-as-commodity that lends plausibility to the theory of gender-as-performance, and gender studies finds another object. Just outside the circle of the spotlight are inequalities, historical developments, and differences that structure (without determining) the presentations that people variously interpret as masculine or feminine, androgynous or ambiguous, butch or femme. *Social relations* are gendered, not persons or things, and those relations can incorporate pain and oppression as easily as the pleasures of a Prom Nite.

NOTES

1. When the term "gay" appears without qualification, I use it in the inclusive sense to encompass both lesbians and gay men.
2. I conducted the major portion of this fieldwork project, which incorporated both participant observation and fifty-one in-depth interviews, from 1985 to 1986, with follow-up visits in 1987 and 1990.
3. Here and throughout, I have followed the ethnographic custom of using pseudonyms to protect the identities of people encountered and interviewed "in the field."
4. Arlene Stein, "All Dressed Up, But No Place to Go? Style Wars and the New Lesbianism," *Out/Look* 1, no. 4 (1989): 38.
5. Barbara Ponse, *Identities in the Lesbian World: The Social Construction of Self* (Westport, Conn.: Greenwood Press, 1978), 115–117.
6. The phrase is borrowed from Sue-Ellen Case, "Towards a Butch-Femme Aesthetic," *Discourse* 11, no. 1 (1988-89): 65.
7. William Roseberry, *Anthropologies and Histories: Essays in Culture, History, and Political Economy* (New Brunswick: Rutgers University Press, 1989), 10. Although Lillian Faderman correctly notes the centrality of eroticism to the so-called butch/femme revival of the 1980s, she is too quick to reduce the significance of *nouveau* butch/femme to the creation of erotic contrasts ("The Return of Butch and Femme: A Phenomenon in Lesbian Sexuality of the 1980s and 1990s," *Journal of the History of Sexuality* 2, no. 4 [1992]; 578–596).
8. The phrase is Butler's ("Lana's 'Imitation,': Melodramatic Repetition and the Gender Performative," *Genders* 9 (1990):2).

WEIGHTY SUBJECTS
The Biopolitics of the U.S. War on Fat

DISCUSSION QUESTIONS

1. What and who is a "fat subject," according to Greenhalgh?
2. What problems does she see with the "war on fat," especially the use of Body Mass Index (BMI) to measure body fat?
3. What do the three student accounts suggest about the gender, class, and racial effects and dynamics of "fat talk"?

By all accounts, America is in the midst of an "obesity epidemic" of catastrophic proportion, in which rising proportions of the public—now fully two-thirds of adults, and one-third of children and adolescents—are obese or overweight.[1] Although the rate of increase has slowed in recent years, the heavy burden of fat, according to the dominant narrative articulated by government, public health, and media sources, is eroding the nation's health, emptying its coffers, and even depriving the country of fit military recruits. Launched by the U.S. Surgeon General in 2001, the response has been an urgent, nationwide, multisectoral public health campaign to get people—and especially the young, the campaign's main target—to eat more healthfully and to be more active, in an effort to achieve a "normal" Body Mass Index.

The intensified medicalization of the problem of weight since the mid-1990s—the now routine definition of excess weight as a disease, the rapid growth in medical research and news on obesity and overweight, and so on—marks a major cultural shift in Americans' concern about fatness, from "self-control" (or virtue) to "health." No longer are fat people merely "lazy" (and "ugly"); in the current discourse they are also biologically "abnormal," "at risk of disease," and "in need of medical treatment." The medical model has not replaced the moral model of body size, but has built on it in ways that intensify the pressures to be thin. The shift to health as the primary grounds for concern about adipose bodies has led to a dramatic expansion of the social forces seeking to intervene in the

An abridged version of Susan Greenhalgh, 2012. "Weighty Subjects: The Biopolitics of the US War on Fat." Reproduced by permission of the American Anthropological Association and of the author from *American Ethnologist*, Volume 39, Issue 3, Pages 471–487, August 2012. Not for sale or further reproduction. For a longer description of the project and more of the results, see Greenhalgh 2015.

problem and, in turn, an explosion of "fat-talk" in virtually every sphere of life.[2] What started as an urgent public health "call to action" in the early 2000s has now grown into a political, corporate, and broadly cultural war on fat that leaves few domains of life untouched.

I pen this essay from Orange County, California, the wealthy coastal jewel in the crown of the Southern California megaregion (SoCal for short) that is home to 23 million people—fully 61 percent of Californians and some 7.4 percent of all Americans.[3] As any consumer of American popular culture knows, SoCal, with its hyped-up Hollywood celebrity culture and its laid-back OC beach culture, is the epicenter of the cult of the perfect body. For women and girls and, increasingly, for men and boys as well, the thin, toned, "beautiful" or "ripped" body (depending on one's gender) is a central measure of human value and core currency of social success. For such a big and morally and politically freighted part of the world we live in, the issue of corpulence and its control has garnered remarkably little attention from sociocultural anthropologists.[4] For a discipline seeking greater engagement with the contemporary world, however, there are compelling reasons to do so. At least in this corner of the U.S., the war on fat is intensifying already existing cultural anxieties about weight. For those whose biologies refuse to cooperate, it is producing dangerous body practices, tormented selves, and socio-emotional suffering on a vast scale. SoCal is far from typical, but it is important because it represents the cultural cutting edge that, through the power of the Hollywood media, exports its dreams of perfect bodies bringing perfect lives to the rest of the world.

THE "WAR ON FAT" AS BIOPOLITICAL SCIENCE AND GOVERNANCE

I view the war on fat as a biopolitical field of science and governance that has emerged to name, study, measure, and manage the "obesity epidemic"—a newly threatening flaw in the biological and social body of the nation—by remaking overweight and obese subjects into thin, fit proper Americans. Reframing the question of obesity as one of biopolitical governance—that is, a field of politics and governance aimed at administering and optimizing the vital characteristics of human life at individual and, especially, population levels—allows us to move beyond the issue of weight to pose important questions about discourse, subjectivity and, ultimately, power. Focusing on the overweight young people who are its prime target, in this article I examine how the public health, corporate, and cultural war on fat is playing out in the lives of heavyset young people, and with what effects on their bodies, subjectivities, and lives. What, I ask, is the crusade against fat producing, in addition to thin, fit bodies (if, indeed, it is even producing those)?

In the dominant view, the public health campaign is helpfully responding to the problem of rising numbers of hefty Americans by urging them to modify their dietary and exercise behaviors in order to lose weight, thereby avoiding both serious health problems and the heavy stigma associated with being overweight. Based on in-depth research in California, I suggest that the war on fat, far from reducing the number of fat people, is itself producing a large and growing number of self-identified "abnormal" and "irresponsible" "fat subjects" whom it seeks to transform into thin, fit responsible persons. Though not technically fat ("obese") according to the BMI, these weight-obsessed subjects' desperate efforts to lower their weight may actually be endangering their health, a trend with implications for larger issues of social suffering and social justice. As used here, a "fat subject" is not the same as an overweight or fat person. An overweight or fat/obese person is someone with an elevated BMI. A fat subject, by contrast, is someone who may have an only slightly higher than normal weight, but who identifies as fat and takes on the fat subject's characteristics. My argument aligns with the critiques of the fat-acceptance movement, which stress the dangers of weight-loss treatments and the further stigmatization of fat people inherent in the crisis framing (Wann 2009;

Royce 2009). Yet it goes beyond the fat-acceptance scholarship to systematically document the impact of the war on fat on heavy individuals and to frame these effects within a larger analysis of the contemporary biopolitics of the weighty body.[5]

Fat Discourse and Fat Science

To understand this troubling outcome, we need to examine the campaign's effects on discourse and, in turn, subjectivity. My research in SoCal suggests that the noisy public health campaign against fat is producing a veritable epidemic of fat-talk. By fat-talk I mean the everyday communications about weight that circulate in popular culture through conversation, written text, visual images and moving videos.[6] Fat-talk is the conversational component of fat discourse—a complex, internally structured, historically specific body of knowledge that structures how weight and weight-related behavior can be talked about, and that does things, produces effects.

As many have noted, in American culture fat-talk has long been a moralizing discourse in which thinness is deemed a worthy, desirable, and necessary state, and thinness and fatness are associated with traits representing opposite ends of the moral spectrum (from the highly valued self-discipline and self-control, on the one hand, to the moral failings of self-indulgence and lack of self-discipline on the other). Now, however, with the medicalization of weight and the scientization of fat discourse, the discourse on fat is also a scientifically based biopolitical discourse aimed at optimizing a biological dimension of human existence. In this discourse, the science does critically important political work.

Based on the science of weight, today's fat discourse establishes weight-based categories based on the Body Mass Index. In this classification scheme, a BMI of 18.5 to 24.9 is "normal," 25 to 29.9 is "overweight," 30 and higher is "obese," while under 18.5 is "underweight." The BMI discourse is thus both normalizing—specifying an ideal or norm and urging all to normalize their status— and subjectifying, setting out weight-based subject positions into which people are supposed to fit

themselves. Although slender bodies have been a cultural obsession for roughly a century, now overweight and obese people—the main targets of the discourse—are no longer deemed simply unattractive (and morally flawed), they are also "abnormal," "defective," or "flawed" in some essential, biological sense, and in need of remediation. Because fat discourse is a biomedical discourse, the abnormal categories are "diseases," chronic in nature, that must be diagnosed and treated according to the best medical practice, primarily diet and exercise. Thus, fat discourse identifies fat targets to be normalized, and instructs them to follow diet, exercise, and other regimens to reach normal weight and become biologically normal subjects.

As a biodiscourse, fat-talk makes scientific experts (doctors, physical education teachers, and so on) the authorities on body weight and its management. Drawing on the still enormous cultural authority of bioscience and biomedicine among the general public, these experts speak in the name of "the truth" and few challenge their authority. As critics have stressed, the war on fat embeds many assumptions that the scientific community itself considers dubious or controversial, yet embraces as pragmatic compromises in the interests of "doing something about the urgent problem of obesity." Among these areas of scientific uncertainty, three are particularly important here. First is the assumption that the BMI is a good measure of body fat and predictor of future disease. Second is the claim that obesity and overweight are "diseases." Third is the assumption that weight is under individual control, and that virtually everyone can lose weight through diet and exercise. This is not the place to review the science; suffice it to say that a large body of work suggests that each of these premises is deeply problematic.[7] Despite that, the cultural authority of the scientific experts allows them to confine controversies over the science largely to the expert literature, keeping them out of public consciousness. The building of the anti-obesity campaign upon such shaky foundations raises troubling ethical issues, as heavyset people are labeled diseased and insistently urged to lose weight through techniques that do not work for most people, or work at serious risk to people's health. They are in effect asked to do the impossible, and then socially punished for failing.

Making Subjects Fat

Feminist poststructuralist work has explored how bodily selves are shaped through dialogic interaction with social discourses, and how women are more tyrannized by the cultural ideal of the fit, slender, well-managed body than are men (Butler 1990; Bordo 1993; Davis 1995). To understand how fat subjects are being created, we need to examine the social discourses circulating around fatness and how individual subjects are interacting with them. My research suggests that there are two kinds of fat-talk. In the first, biopedagogical fat-talk, the discourse on weight serves to inform people of their weight status ("too fat," "too skinny," etc.) and instruct them on what practices they must adopt to achieve a normative body weight (the term "biopedagogy" comes from Evans et al. 2008). The second is fat abuse, delivered through biobullying of various sorts (the term "fat abuse" comes from Royce 2009; "biobullying" is my term).[8] As cultural historian Amy Farrell shows, in the U.S. today, fat is a mark of shame, a character stigma so discrediting that fat people are often treated as not quite human (2011). Heavy-weight young people are targets of often cruel verbal abuse, and the heavier the child, the greater the abuse (Lumeng et al. 2010; Taylor 2011). These two types of fat-talk have differing effects on subjectivity. I tease these out below.

The process of becoming a fat subject generally unfolds in three analytically distinct (though empirically entwined) steps. A fat subject is born when an above-average-weight young person, often in late grade school or middle school, becomes subject to a growing din of derogatory fat-talk telling her that her weight is excessive and that weight is the identity most crucial to social acceptance. In the second step, her growing self-consciousness and shame about her weight gradually develops into a weight obsession, as efforts to lose weight fail. In the third, as weight struggles come to dominate her life, she gradually takes on the identity of a fat subject and the constellation of emotions, social behaviors, and bodily practices that go with it. Just below, I explore this process of subject-making ethnographically and ask a series of related questions: How do biopedagogical and abusive fat-talk affect subject-making? What are the attributes of a fat subject? Who becomes a fat subject and who resists that identity? Finally, what are the larger consequences of fat subjectivity for young people's health and lives more generally?

THE SOCIAL BODY POLITICS PROJECT

For roughly 15 years (1995–2011) I taught a large course at the University of California, Irvine—located in the very heart of the OC—on the culture and politics of the gendered/raced/classed/sexed body in the U.S. today. In 2010 and 2011, I offered students extra credit for writing an ethnographic essay on how issues of diet, weight, and the BMI play out in the life of a person they know well. Roughly half the class (of 274 in 2010 and 332 in 2011) wrote essays. The majority (three-quarters) wrote auto-ethnographies about their own experiences; the rest wrote about siblings, parents, or close friends. Assigning these essays as a pedagogical tool, I was not prepared for what I would receive. Full of tales of California childhoods dominated—and often devastated—by battles over weight, the essays were eye-opening, disturbing, and, in cases, heartbreaking, to read. Realizing the power of these essays as personal testimony and cultural evidence, I sought IRB approval to use them, and then obtained the permission of each student to use his or her essay in my research.[9] Most were happy to say yes, telling me in emails how writing the essay had provided a positive, even therapeutic and empowering experience for them.

To see how young people become—or, in a few cases, resist becoming—fat subjects, I turn now to the essays of three young Californians who have been labeled "fat" and subjected to fat-talk/fat abuse their whole young lives. These are not of course representative cases, but the stories are ordinary ones, typical of the accounts of the heavier young people whose essays I collected.[10] Until recently, most of the research on the micro-politics of weight focused on white girls. Yet the U.S. is fast becoming a minority-dominant nation.[11] Far from immune, people of non-white ethnicities are just as vulnerable to fat abuse as whites, and the impact on them can be equally if not more devastating, as the achievement of a normative body may be essential to their acceptance into mainstream society. Moreover, it is not just girls and young women whose worlds are full of fat-talk. The research of Nichter (2000) and Taylor (2011) in the southwest suggests that, compared to teenage girls, boys are less closely monitored and criticized for their weight, in part because their self-worth is tied more to their abilities and achievements than to their looks. Yet clearly fat (and skinny) boys are subject to weight abuse. How does this affect them? Nichter found that boys were relatively immune from the feelings of personal failure that girls endured. In Taylor's research boys were hurt by the harsh critiques but, following codes of masculinity, had to "play it cool" and hide the pain. In SoCal fat boys are mercilessly—and perhaps increasingly—teased. How that biobullying affects their sense of self is an important question for study.

I focus here on traditionally silenced, subordinated groups whose struggles with weight have remained largely hidden. I have selected for analysis three non-white young people of diverse cultural backgrounds whose stories are particularly compelling or affecting. All but one grew up in the greater Los Angeles area. One grew up in a financially struggling family, while two were raised in middle-class families.[12]

WEIGHT—A GHOST HAUNTING ME MY ENTIRE LIFE: APRIL'S STORY

April is a 20-year-old African American from the San Fernando Valley of LA. In her auto-ethnography, *she documents a series of life-changing incidents through which she gradually picked up and internalized society's biopedagogical message that for girls and women, a thin body is the ultimate source of happiness.*

Biobullies in School

Weight has affected me [since] I was in elementary school. The two most popular girls in school were one of my best friends and my cousin. My best friend was extremely slender and athletic; she was a White girl with long brown hair and the boys simply adored her nature. My cousin, although chubbier than my friend and Black, experienced early puberty and sported a B-sized chest and curvy hips, and the boys couldn't keep their eyes off her. Where was I in this system of body image, though? I was chubby and flat-chested, with no sensual appeal and a tomboy dressing style— I was nowhere but at the very bottom. Realizing this, I became incredibly depressed and often found myself feeling alone. Despite this, I didn't diet in the beginning. I didn't know what dieting was or that there was a way to not be "ugly." Society's standard punched me in the face, and it hurt.

Growing up and going to middle school, I began to learn more about dieting. My best friend at the time was very big, and I remember her always talking about avoiding certain foods [since] she wanted to lose weight. I always thought she was beautiful; she had large breasts, light skin, beautiful hazel eyes, and a funny personality. However, that image was destroyed when a boy called her a "fat, ugly piece of shit" right in front of me. It was the first time I realized that weight was a huge issue, even for curvaceous girls.

The Warnings of a Concerned Brother

It wasn't long after that that I started getting the critiques from my brother. He constantly told me that I ate too much and that I was going to be a fat girl and that men would throw things at me. I became scared and started dieting. My dieting consisted of starving myself. I would eat a bowl of cereal at

7:00 a.m., then refuse to eat again until I got home about 4:00 p.m. and had dinner. When dinner came around, I would often binge on two large plates because I was so hungry. As a result, my metabolism dropped and I actually ended up gaining weight.

I remember looking in the mirror, gripping the excess fat on my stomach in my hands and imagining ripping it from my body. I imagined blowing all the fat from my nose into a trash can and immediately becoming slender and beautiful. All these fantasies haunted me like a ghost, and my confidence continued to drop as the years drifted into high school.

In high school I hit puberty when I was 14, and started to develop breasts and curves. I entered a dance class and became very active. As if my new body [had] triggered a reaction, boys started asking me out. I never felt more accepted in life than I did at that moment. I continued to diet and dance, dropping to 120 pounds at 5'4" by the time I was 15 [BMI 20.6].

My family and I went to Jamaica that summer. During a boat cruise, one of the Jamaican hosts took me under deck and sexually assaulted me by forcing me to touch his privates. He was supposed to be giving me a foot massage. It was a traumatizing experience. Yet the reaction from my parents—who joked about the massage being my first experience as a woman—told me that seducing men was good, and the only way to do that was to be beautiful. And to be beautiful was to be thin.

High school provided a much more violent experience. One of my best friends started to spread rumors that I was weird, dyke, and White. This caused serious depression and I began to turn to food for comfort. I went from 120 to 135 and fluctuated up to 140 pounds. I often told myself that I would kill myself if I [exceeded] 140, and starved myself every time I got close.

From Self-Starvation to Binging-and-Purging: Weight Loss at Any Cost

When I graduated from high school food became a pleasure. Since I no longer danced, I gained more

weight. During freshman year in college, adjusting to a new lifestyle, I [rose to] 156 pounds by winter quarter—I was fat [BMI 26.8, hardly obese]. At the end of winter quarter, I began to starve myself to lose the weight. I ate once a day at 5:00 p.m. for dinner; usually about a 300-calorie meal. I became very weak, sleeping most of the time when I made it home from school so I would not have to think about the hunger. On the fourth day I didn't eat anything. That night the ambulance was called when I fainted in Starbucks, where I had attempted to get food. My blood sugar was at a dangerously low level and it took about 30 minutes to revitalize it. I can't quite understand why I did it though. I think [perhaps] because my roommates were always so skinny and fit—seeing their perfect bodies tormented me.

Now I stand at about 140 pounds, but am still not satisfied with my weight. Unfortunately, I fear that I may have an eating disorder developing—[some] mixture of starving/binging/purging. Everything in my life has told me that power and happiness come from beauty, and now I feel as if I am conditioned to pursue it. Weight has become a ghost that doesn't leave me no matter what I do. It has haunted me throughout my life.

"WE DON'T LIKE UGLY ASIAN GIRLS": TIFFANY'S HIDDEN STRUGGLE

Tiffany is a 22-year-old Chinese-American from Orange County's Fountain Valley. Unlike April, who experiences the cultural commentary about the body as an informative biopedagogy she must adhere to in order to fit in, Tiffany is the victim of biobullying so vicious it simply crushes her sense of herself as a good, socially worthy person, leaving her vulnerable to others' harsh judgments.

Mean Girls on the Attack

In fifth grade, I was always bullied by the other students and I was never sure why. One day, while

I was waiting in line to get into class, I finally confronted two of the girls who were picking on me. They responded, "Well, we don't like ugly Asian girls with your *hair* and ugly *face*. So you can't be our friend. No one likes you." I was devastated by their words. I asked why they liked this other girl who had the same hair as I did and they responded, "She's cute, and you are *fat and ugly*." I still remember those words; they stuck with me, always in the back of my mind. I never told my mom about what happened; neither did I share this with my sister. I was scared they would laugh at me or even agree with what those girls said.

Going on into middle school, I went on a diet. At that time I did not know what calories were, all I wanted was to not be fat like those girls accused me of. My diet was simple. Since I am Chinese, I would eat rice every evening, one bowl only. I followed that diet for a year. I remember running into [former] school teachers who would comment, "Wow, you have lost a lot of weight! You look so much better." That simple phrase just boosted my confidence. I was so happy that people were noticing that I was losing weight.

Everything ran well in my freshman year in high school until, midway through, my "best friend" came up to me and told me that throughout middle school, one girl whom I considered a "best friend" was just using me, and thought I was a "fat and ugly bitch." It really hurt. That one little statement made it really hard to not look at myself and wonder, "Am I really that ugly? Do I look that fat? What is everyone else thinking right now?" I became very paranoid from then on. I never wore anything tight, I hated clothes that showed the stomach, and I was afraid of the beach. I was so scared of being judged, I was terrified of other people's opinion.

Accusing Eyes All Around

I remember the doctors. I hated to go. My doctors would always look at my weight and say, "Your weight is creeping up, but you are OK still. Just keep exercising." In the last three years it's gotten worse. This year when I went for my annual checkup, my doctor specifically told me, "That one to two pounds may not look like much, but it all adds up." She never said I was fat, but she implied it, which, I felt, was worse. After this incident, I felt my struggles really escalated. I felt like there were accusing eyes around me saying, "You are fat. No one likes fat."

The worst part of this was when those accusations came from home. My mother tried to boost my confidence and tell me that I was still young and anything can happen. It was my little brother and father who really made everything seem like a reality. At the dinner table, my little brother would always chant, "You are fat and ugly. No boy will want you." In the past few months, it has all picked up in pace. Now when my little brother points at me and screams "you're FAT!!," my father says, "He's not wrong." That is crushing. When I think about it, and as I'm typing, I'm trying my best not to cry. It really hurts and it makes me wonder if that is how everyone perceives me. Am I really that fat? Am I that unappealing? Is that why I'm so lonely and have barely any friends?

I'm now a vegetarian and I tell people it's because I love animals. But to be completely honest, it's because of what they have said. Being a vegetarian means I eat much less, feel full much easier, and look healthy while I try to battle with my body image. It seems like I'm following [a well-worn path to] becoming an anorexic. It scares me. I'm just desperate for those comments to disappear, and the only way, it seems, to become unfat is to lose all the weight no matter [what the risk to my health].

ALL THEY CAN SEE IS MY FAT: BINH'S STORY

Binh is a 22-year-old Vietnamese-American from the Silicon Valley city of San Jose. In his essay, Binh charts a long history of fat abuse and encounters with less-than-helpful purveyors of biopedagogical advice. Yet unlike April and Tiffany, who internalize the dominant message about weight and selfhood, Binh sloughs it off, telling a different story about his life.

Mocked in Middle School

During middle school, a combination of my over-weightness and a penguin-like wobble in my walk resulted in mockery by my peers as well as members of my family. My brother and his friends would often walk up to me and call me "fat boy," and tease me endlessly. My mother would hug me and joke, saying "oh, wow, my arms can't reach around you; I can't hug you all the way." It made me sad because I knew I wasn't bothering anyone.

At thirteen years of age, during my period of puberty, I saw that I had gotten taller and my clothes fit better. I was getting more compliments. This brought me joy, but my mentality and fear of looking fat stayed with me.

The Freshman Fifteen: My Worst Fear Comes True

Slowly [but surely], the mentality and fear [receded] in my mind. Before coming home from my first year of college, I gained the [infamous] "Freshman Fifteen." It was not my fault I had to sit on my butt every day to study and all there was to eat was fast food. People from home would often come up to me, poke at my stomach, and tell me how fat I had gotten. The news spread, and I even received comments on pictures on my Facebook, stating how huge I had gotten.

Often when I am depressed or stressed, I find myself eating sweet and junky food because I seek some pleasantness or satisfaction. I felt that I could eat what I wanted because I was upset and it was okay because it was all for making me feel better. The outcome was simply more weight gain and, in turn, more stares and criticism by those close to me.

My mother took my brother and me to see a doctor just for a check-up. I was already afraid the doctor would measure my weight, and he did so as he is required to in a normal [physical] check-up. He told my mother that according to the BMI, I was considered overweight. My mother had not thought so of me until she heard this from the doctor, and since then she has taken every [opportunity] to remind me to exercise and lose weight.

Currently I am living with four other guys who all happen to be some kind of athlete. They always talk about how hard they work out or how much fun they have playing a sport. Unfortunately I don't share their passion. Living with these guys, I often feel like I have to eat in seclusion, or if they're coming into the kitchen I immediately need to hide the food I am about to eat. They often ask me why I don't find the time to exercise. I reply because of my busy schedule but when I do have time I like to spend it relaxing. They often tell me that my way of thinking is weak.

A Stealth Attack on Christmas Day

On the morning of Christmas Day last year, I woke up to find that my family and relatives had all gathered in the kitchen. Groggily yet happily, I walked into the room and greeted everyone. From across the room, I received a friendly smile from my uncle's father-in-law. Naturally, I smiled back, [never guessing] what he was going to say. The old man smiled at me all warmly, and then yelled out to me: "You're fat!" My smiling ceased. I looked at him for five of what were probably the longest seconds in my entire life. My eyes turned to my uncle, who was looking at me already, and laughing wholeheartedly at what his father-in-law had said. Everyone heard it and laughed. I felt that it was the most embarrassing moment of my entire life. I was also very upset because my damn relatives just let me take it.

After that, I just stayed up in my room, except to go on a walk with my uncle and his wife. We walked for a good thirty minutes or so, and he asked me if I was tired. I replied, "[Do you say that] because I'm fat?" "Well, no," [he replied,] "not at all, but clearly you are. I think you need to lose some weight too." I feel like that is all everyone sees and that's all I am. No one in my family cared that I had worked so hard in college, or that I was a big brother figure to their kids, or that I was one of the most, if not the most, responsible and loyal kids in the family. All I was and still am in their eyes is "the fat one of the family."

WEIGHTY SUBJECTS

These essays, and others I have collected, substantiate my argument that the intensified concern about the "obesity epidemic" is producing a parallel epidemic of fat-talk in which both important individuals in the social worlds of young people, as well as the larger media culture actively participate, naming who is fat, ridiculing them, cajoling them to lose weight, and informing them how—as if they did not already know. At once a morality tale about personal irresponsibility, a medical tale about bodily deviance, and a governmental tale about national decline, fat-talk circulates throughout the social body, leaving no one with a few extra pounds immune from its barbs.

Among young Californians I have worked with, the explosion of fat-talk was not creating many fit, trim, healthy Americans.[13] Instead, these accounts suggest, the war on fat—based on poor measures of fatness, faulty assumptions about medical risks, and exaggerated assertions about the ease of weight loss—is producing a new generation of self-identified fat subjects. The two types of fat-talk worked together to transform heavyset youngsters into fat subjects. The biopedagogical fat-talk was productive of new identities and practices. Best illustrated in April's story, the pedagogical fat-talk worked to set out weight-based subject positions, inform people of their status, teach that weight can and must be controlled, and educate people in what practices they must adopt to achieve normative weight. Because of its ubiquity and force, the incessant body-size commentary also taught young people like April that their body weight was an essential component of their personal identity and social acceptability. The fat abuse, by contrast, was destructive because it was experienced as an attack on the self. For Tiffany, especially, fat abuse worked

to erode self-confidence and undermine alternative identities based on other, positive attributes, rendering her vulnerable to the new weight-based subjectivities being thrust on her. In the absence of supportive body-comments from anyone (except her mom), these verbal assaults have worn away Tiffany's self-esteem to the point that she now deeply believes the weight-centric narrative people have imposed on her—that it is her "ugly fat body" that explains why she has so few friends (if indeed she does).

As they struggled with this new socially-imposed identity, these young people developed a shared set of attributes that come together into what we might call fat subjecthood. At least in SoCal, my work suggests, a fat subject has at least four identifying characteristics. First, she sees herself as abject—biologically flawed, morally irresponsible or unworthy, and/or aesthetically unappealing. Second, the fat subject engages in size-appropriate corporeal practices—especially dieting and exercising—in an effort to lose that degrading weight. When those don't work, as they usually don't for people with resistant biologies (which we can assume all these young people have), the self-identified fat subject often takes them to the extremes—self-starvation, binging-and-purging, or (in cases not discussed here) excessive exercise—in a desperate attempt to lose the weight. Though these practices often pose serious dangers to their health (such as lowering metabolism and blood sugar levels, as in April's case) after years of insufferable insults, developing a full-blown eating disorder is seen as the price people like Tiffany believe they must pay to finally rid themselves of that intolerable identity.

A third attribute, common to all three young people, is social withdrawal. Faced with incessant ridicule and social rejection, the fat subject retreats socially, skipping beach parties (Tiffany) or eating in private (Binh), to avoid judgment. Finally, the self-perception of fatness invariably brought emotional suffering—including depression, low self-esteem, and pervasive insecurities—combined with vivid fantasies of radical bodily transformation. For some, brutal social rejection in childhood left them with enduring emotional scars reflected in deep-rooted insecurities and drastic weight-loss practices that had become a way of life.

Labeled "fat" again and again, all were forced into life-consuming identity struggles. The three young people resolved these internal battles in different ways, creating a continuum of subjects that ranged from high to low fat-identification. For April and Tiffany, fat became their dominant (though probably not only) identity. Binh was subject to withering fat abuse, yet he stubbornly refused to follow the bioscript others foisted on him. Binh neither accepts personal responsibility for his heavy weight, nor sees himself as morally or physically abject. Nor does he take up the corporeal practices of the fat subject. Despite the relentless message that he is a bad person for failing to lose weight, Binh resists becoming a fat subject. The differing response appears clearly related to gender. For girls like Tiffany and April, identity and self-worth are closely tied to appearance. Socialized to rely on external acceptance to inform their identity, girls are more vulnerable to others' opinions. For boys, identity and self-worth are measured more in terms of abilities and achievements. Protected by the culture of masculinity, Binh is able to hold onto the notion of himself as a good person with other core identities—a kind cousin and a good student.

At least in this corner of the country, the nationwide campaign to banish obesity and make people healthy seems to be producing anything but thinness, health, and happiness. There are far too many heavyset young Californians whose subjectivities are colonized by the fear of fat, and whose lives are dominated by the efforts of many in their world to get them to shed pounds and be "normal." Instead of studying, engaging in sports, developing a hobby, or building a career, they are obsessed with efforts to lose weight. And in one of the great biopolitical injustices of our time, for most those efforts will surely fail. Buried in the scientific literature—actually, hiding in plain sight, for those who wish to look—is the dismal truth that the world has not yet found a cure for overweight, if "cure" is what is needed. For most people who are biologically prone

to heaviness, there is still no safe, effective way to achieve sustained weight loss. Quite the contrary; the biology of dieting conspires against them to make it almost impossible to achieve long-term weight loss (Sumithran et al. 2011). Far from producing thin, fit, happy young people, the war on fat is producing a generation of tormented selves, heart-rending levels of socio-emotional suffering, and disordered bodily practices that are dangerous to their health.

There is another biopolitical injustice as well, one that is built into our system of corporate capitalism and, indeed, the American way of life. Although I have had little space to devote to big food, food and other corporate entities are critical parts of the biopolitics of the obesity epidemic today. In a striking parallel to the war on tobacco (Benson 2010), in the war on fat, food corporations, which are now trumpeting their social responsibility as producers of "healthy" "diet" foods, continue to manipulate our desires by coming up with ever more biologically rewarding high-fat, -sugar, and -salt junk foods that alter our brain chemistry in ways that lead most of us to crave still more comfort food and some of us to engage in conditioned hypereating (April and Binh illustrate such cravings; for the science, Kessler 2009). Meanwhile, reflecting industry lobbying and prevalent neoliberal ideas about self-governance, public health policies associated with the war on fat focus largely on individual responsibility for weight, not basic industry regulation. Big food emerges as "part of the solution" while large-bodied Americans, who are now deemed "the problem," suffer vicious bullying and diminished lives. A more poignant example of the intimate effects of corporate capitalism can hardly be imagined.

REFERENCES CITED

Benson, Peter. 2010. Tobacco Talk: Reflections on Corporate Power and the Legal Framing of Consumption. *Medical Anthropology Quarterly* 24(4): 500–521.

Bordo, Susan. 1993. *Unbearable Weight: Feminism, Western Culture, and the Body*. Berkeley, CA: University of California Press.

Brewis, Alexandra A. 2011. *Obesity: Cultural and Biocultural Perspectives*. New Brunswick, NJ: Rutgers University Press.

Butler, Judith. 1990. *Gender Trouble: Feminism and the Subversion of Identity*. New York: Routledge.

Chernin, Kim. 1981. *The Obsession: Reflections on the Tyranny of Slenderness*. New York: Harper and Row.

Davis, Kathy. 1995. *Reshaping the Female Body: The Dilemma of Cosmetic Surgery*. New York: Routledge.

Evans, John, Emma Rich, Brian Davies, and Rachel Allwood (eds.). 2008. *Education, Disordered Eating and Obesity Discourse: Fat Fabrications*. London: Routledge.

Farrell, Amy Erdman. 2011. *Fat Shame: Stigma and the Fat Body in American Culture*. New York: NYU Press.

Flegal, Katherine, Margaret D. Carroll, Cynthia L. Ogden, and Lester R. Curtin. 2010. Prevalence and Trends in Obesity Among U.S. Adults, 1999–2008. *Journal of the American Medical Association* 303(3): 235–241.

Frey, William H. 2011. *America's Diverse Future: Initial Glimpses at the U.S. Child Population from the 2010 Census*. Brookings Institute, State of Metropolitan America, no. 29.

Kessler, David A. 2009. *The End of Overeating: Taking Control of the Insatiable American Appetite*. New York: Rodale.

Lumeng, Julie C. et al. 2010. Weight Status as a Predictor of Being Bullied in Third Through Sixth Grades. *Pediatrics* 125(6): 1301–1307.

Nichter, Mimi. 2000. *Fat Talk: What Girls and their Parents Say About Dieting*. Cambridge, MA: Harvard University Press.

Ogden, Cynthia L., Margaret D. Carroll, Lester R. Curtin, Molly M. Lamb, and Katherine M. Flegal. 2010. Prevalence of High Body Mass Index in U.S. Children and Adolescents, 2007–08. *Journal of the American Medical Association* 303(3): 242–249.

Ohrbach, Susie. 1978. *Fat is a Feminist Issue*. London: Arrow.

Pfeifer, Stuart. 2011. Lap-Band has Poor Outcomes, Study Finds. *Los Angeles Times*, 22 March, p. B4.

Rothblum, Esther and Sondra Solovay (eds.) 2009. *The Fat Studies Reader*. New York: NYU Press.

Royce, Tracy. 2009. The Shape of Abuse: Fat Oppression as a Form of Violence Against Women. In Rothblum and Solovay (eds.), *The Fat Studies Reader*. New York: NYU Press. pp. 151–157.

Sumithran, Priya, et al. 2011. Long-term Persistence of Hormonal Adaptations to Weight Loss. *New England Journal of Medicine* 365: 1597–1604.

Taylor, Nicole L. 2011. "Guys, She's Humongous!" Gender and Weight-based Teasing in Adolescence. *Journal of Adolescent Research* 26(2): 178–199.

Wann, Marilyn. 2009. Foreword: Fat Studies—An Invitation to Revolution. In Rothblum and Solovay (eds.), *The Fat Studies Reader*. New York: NYU Press, pp. xi–xxv.

NOTES

1. Data from 2007–08 suggest that the rate of increase in overweight and obesity among U.S. adults is slowing, but the absolute levels remain worryingly high: 33.8 percent of adults were obese, while 34.2 percent were overweight (Flegal et al. 2010). Among children and adolescents aged 2–19, in 2007–08 16.9 percent were obese while another 14.8 percent were overweight (Ogden et al. 2010).

2. In the political sphere, anti-fat legislation aimed at limiting food ads for children, requiring food labeling in restaurants, and so forth, is advancing at the federal and state levels, producing noisy debates over the "nanny state's" right to tell Americans what they should eat and over hefty officials' ability to govern. Corporate interests have been a major force behind the escalation of fat-talk. After profiting handsomely from making Americans fat with its high-sugar, -fat, and -salt "drug foods," big food, along with the pharmaceutical, biotech, fitness, restaurant, and other industries, has figured out how to use a rhetoric of medicine ("it's good for your health") to exploit people's fear of the disease of fat to generate a further $60 billion annually in profits. Building on an already deeply ingrained culture of valorizing thinness and abhorring fatness, the new medically-driven concern with weight loss has also propelled corpulence to the center of our popular culture. The new genre of "Fat TV"—featuring weight-loss reality shows such as "The Biggest Loser" that make the degradation of fat people a media ritual—is only the most conspicuous of these new forms of fat-culture.

3. For this essay, the Southern California region includes San Luis Obispo, Santa Barbara, Ventura, Los Angeles, Orange, San Diego, Kern, San Bernadino, Riverside, and Imperial Counties. The 2012 population numbers come from the U.S. Census Bureau, http://quickfacts.census.gov/qfd/states/06/06059.html.

4. In recent years, medical and biocultural anthropologists have shown a growing interest in

cultural and biocultural aspects of obesity (Nichter 2000; Taylor 2011; Brewis 2011). Yet there is no work that takes the larger governmental, public health, and cultural campaign against fat itself as a point of ethnographic departure. Sociologists of sports and of education have begun to study the biopolitics of the obesity epidemic, though rarely ethnographically. The newly emerging field of fat studies, part of the fat acceptance movement, takes a critical feminist look at the dominant approach to obesity (e.g., Rothblum and Solovay 2009).

5. My arguments also align well with a long history of feminist research on the cult of the slender body (e.g., Ohrbach 1978; Chernin 1981). Most of that research was conducted before today's war on fat was launched.

6. I adopt the term fat talk used by Mimi Nichter (2000), but broaden its scope and link it to the Foucauldian notion of fat discourse.

7. The BMI is a poor measure of fat and predictor of disease. Heavy weights are neither diseases in themselves, nor have consistently been found to predict other disease. Finally, given the significant role of genetics in obesity, it is not surprising that the field of bioscience has not yet found a cure for fatness. Indeed, the literature suggests that for most individuals, there are no safe and reliable ways to achieve long-term weight loss. Diets rarely work, exercise promotes fitness but not weight loss, and diet pills have been associated with serious health problems such as heart attack and stroke. Even surgical solutions—lap band and other bariatric surgeries—pose serious health risks and have poor long-term outcomes (Pfeifer 2011). No wonder the campaign against fat has claimed few successes.

8. This term was suggested to me by Alma Gottlieb.

9. Given the opprobrium heaped on heavy people in our society, for many young people the subject of weight evokes feelings of intense shame and personal failure, feelings too humiliating to share with anyone. Classic anthropological methods—personal interviews, participant observation—are not very effective at eliciting feelings of this sort. For those reasons auto-ethnography is an especially valuable tool in the study of weight.

10. Just over half the essays dealt with problems of overweight young people. The others dealt with the struggles of the obese, underweight, normal, and eating disordered.

11. In 2010 people of color made up 46.5 percent of Americans under 18. In the high-immigrant LA–Long Beach–Santa Ana metropolitan area, non-whites made up an astonishing 79 percent of the youth population (Frey 2011; the figure for California was 73 percent).

12. I have preserved the essays in their original form and language, correcting only spelling and grammatical errors. In a few places, to clarify the meaning, I have changed a word or two or slightly reworked the text. I have also added sub-headings to structure the text. Because of space limitations, for this chapter I have had to substantially edit down the original essays.

13. In the full set of essays, a few heavy-build young people did manage to lose weight through the adoption of drastic diet and/or exercise regimens, but often at some cost to their physical health, and usually at a cost to their overall well-being, as the weight-loss program took over their lives.

2 • *Thaïs Machado-Borges*

MIDDLE-CLASS COMPASSION AND MAN BOOBS

DISCUSSION QUESTIONS

1. Why does Suzana want to help Tião with his "man boobs" by paying for his plastic surgery?
2. How does the Brazilian obsession with bodily appearances and cosmetic surgery reflect and produce social hierarchies of gender and class?

"Man boobs are the nightmare of 65 percent of boys aged 14 to 15," declared one of Brazil's leading newspapers in March 2011. The article, about the increased demand for plastic surgery to remedy the appearance of breasts on young men, quoted a plastic surgeon interviewed on the topic who explained the boob-boom by pointing out that people care about their boys: "There is no reason to let the kids suffer" (FolhaOnline, 2011).[1]

Suzana, a 50-year-old civil servant and the person from whose point of view this story is partially told, couldn't agree more: "Why suffer when plastic surgery could solve it?"

It was a Friday afternoon and she had just had time to get home from her weekly visit to the local hairdresser—buying bread, cheese, and ham on her way. With its newly highlighted strands, her now salt-and-pepper and golden hair was blow-dried and her fingernails were freshly painted red. Suzana announced that she was going to the bus station to pick up Tião. She asked Roberto, her youngest son, if he'd like to go with her. Tião, the young man waiting at the bus station, was 17—one year older than Roberto—and lived in Pilar,

a small village on the southeastern coast of Brazil, where Suzana's family had a summer house.

The income of Tião's family depended a great deal on the summer vacation season, when the arrival of tourists like Suzana and her family increased the population of the village to at least four times its normal size. Tião's father worked on house maintenance. During holidays and vacations, he worked as a plumber and electrician, helping the tourists out with problems. Tião's mother helped the summer families with cooking, cleaning, washing, and other household tasks. During summers and holidays, Tião and his three siblings all worked on the beach. His elder brother and sister waited on customers at one of the several bars along the beach. Tião and a younger brother sold homemade popsicles to sunbathing tourists. They worked every day, from morning to early evening. After his working hours Tião would go to Roberto's home. They would go out to the central avenue, where all the young tourists gathered to party at night.

Roberto was a middle-class boy who hated going to school but was forced to by his mother, Suzana, and his father. They told him repeatedly that if he

A slightly revised version of Thaïs Machado-Borges, 2013. "Middle Class Compassion and Man Boobs." *Anthropology Now* 5(2): 1–9. Reprinted with the kind permission of the author.

didn't finish school he would be nothing. Roberto saw his vacations in Pilar as a kind of paradise on Earth: no school, a beach, and an easy-going atmosphere quite different from the one he experienced daily in the big city where he lived.

So now Tião was coming to Roberto's actual home. Suzana explained to me that he was not just coming to pay her son a visit. Tião was going to have an operation. When I asked if it was something serious, she reassured me:

> No, he's just going to have his chest operated on. You see, he accumulates fat under his breasts, so they're getting bigger than they should be. He was starting to feel embarrassed. I noticed last season, when we'd meet him on the beach. It was so hot but he was always wearing a T-shirt, and he was walking with his shoulders hunched forward and down, as if he wanted to hide something. I commented on that to Roberto, who then told me that Tião was indeed very ashamed, because his flat chest had developed what looked like the breasts of a young teenage girl. When Roberto told me that, I went to talk to Tião and explained to him that this was absolutely common. I told him that both of my sons had already had this problem. I also told him not to worry, and I sat down with his parents to talk about an operation. I really wanted to help them with that.

I wondered then if this really was something common, or if Suzana was just trying to make Tião feel better about his body. Suzana told me, vehemently, "No, really, it's very common. Both Roberto and Paulo [her older son] have had the same problem. They were operated on when they were like 12 or 13."

Suzana's husband reinforced his wife's evidence: "I've got two nephews who had the same problem and they both underwent an operation. It's very complicated for a young man to have this kind of problem, so it's good that one can do something about it."

"But what kind of operation is it?" I asked Suzana. She replied that it was a simple operation done with local anesthesia:

> The procedure doesn't take too long, and afterwards you have to follow almost the same recommendations that women who get a breast reduction do. You have your chest covered with a bandage for a few weeks, and you can't go around waving your arms or carrying heavy things. There are people who have to be operated on twice. Sometimes the breasts reappear a few years after the operation.

DIAGNOSES, CLASS, AND COMPASSION

Gynecomastia, or the excessive development of breasts in men, is the scientific name of what Tião was going to remedy through surgery. The breasts increase in size either due to hormonal alterations causing an accumulation of fat tissue under the nipple area, or due to the use of drugs and steroids. According to a Brazilian medical website,[2] most cases of gynecomastia happen during puberty. This site estimates that up to 65 percent of male adolescents between 14 and 15 years of age present manifestations of gynecomastia. This condition tends to disappear naturally as the adolescents become older, and it is estimated that by the age of 17, only 7 percent of the male population still presents signs of breast development. These numbers increase again with ageing. There are, still according to this same site, different kinds of techniques for operating on developed male breasts. The most common is liposuction.

The information I found in scientific articles and in popular texts about gynecomastia, or "man boobs," in Brazilian print and digital publications raised interesting anthropological questions: What is considered to be a normal male body when approximately 65 percent of male adolescents are said to present manifestations of gynecomastia?

One thing is clear: no matter how common gynecomastia might be, it is described as unwanted and problematic—"the nightmare of 65 percent of boys." Normalcy, to repeat what other social scientists have stated, is not only a neutral description of a common way of being; it is also a representation of an ideal and the endpoint of encouraged transformations.

By establishing gynecomastia as a *common problem* and by providing plastic surgery as an *immediate solution* to it, an ideal norm about how young Brazilian men should look is reinforced, even if in the negative form: men should not have breasts.

One can now wonder: how are these practices of diagnosing and treating "deviating" bodies linked to a Brazilian context of social inequality?

The preoccupation of Brazilians with the body and physical appearance is remarkably palpable and present in contemporary everyday life. This preoccupation is not simply the reflection, at a local level, of a global fixation on bodies and beauty. Brazil, at the end of the 1990s, was the fourth largest consumer of cosmetic products in the world. Brazilians are also one of the largest consumers of diet medicine in the world.[3] During the 1980s Brazil occupied a leading position in the development of certain cosmetic surgical techniques that continue to be practiced today. In fact, far from being a recently established practice, Brazilian cosmetic surgery has a history of more than 150 years. A Brazilian news magazine estimated an increase of 580 percent in the number of plastic surgeries in the country between 1990 and 2000.[4] Every year, since the turn of the 21st century, around half a million Brazilians undergo some kind of plastic surgery. Eighty percent of them are women.[5] Aesthetic preoccupations are also tucked into other medical practices: The percentage of women who underwent Caesarian sections in Brazil amounted to 36.4 percent in 1996—one of the highest rates in the world. Elective Caesarian births are related to socioeconomic class, urbanity, cultural beliefs about birth, pain management, and concerns about sexual function and appearance after birth.[6] As a matter of fact, Suzana has contributed to these statistics: In the course of her life to date, she had undergone three planned C-sections, an eyelid lift, permanent eyelid and eyebrow makeup, and uncountable diets.

Remember that all these practices take place in a country ranked among the top 10 in the world both when it comes to wealth and to unequal income distribution. Within this context of pervasive social inequality and urban insecurity, the body and its appearance are just the right arenas for establishing social hierarchies. Beauty, cleanliness, and other easily naturalized aspects such as tastes, preferences, and feelings work both as ways to maintain and increase social differences, and as means to assert personal value and attain (or aspire to) certain kinds of social visibility.

Indeed, if we return to Suzana's initial diagnosing of Tião's problem, made at the beach, under bright sunlight, we can clearly see interplay between gender and class issues. First, socioeconomic class is manifested in the *lack of* versus *access to* knowledge: Not only did Suzana know what was afflicting Tião (something she assumed his parents did not know/did not notice—in Portuguese "*nem sabiam direito*"[7]), but she also had a medical name for this "condition." Moreover, she knew how middle- and upper-middle-class people treated it, and she had the means to help Tião solve his problem: surgery.

Surgical technology—used in this case to treat gynecomastia—is associated with modern, expensive practices and with particular kinds of consumers: wealthier young men. So Tião traveled from Pilar (a small, peripheral town) to Belo Horizonte (a big city) to go through a surgical procedure that is practiced among middle- and upper-middle-class young men (Suzana's sons had had it; her husband's nephews had had it). Tião's masculinity was not endangered by the diagnosis of gynecomastia because it was going to be *corrected* through a practice that only *privileged* people (in terms of class and in terms of social networks) could afford to have.

Moreover, surgical technology is presented as an *immediate* solution to a physical problem. Situated within a Brazilian context of social inequality, this immediacy in receiving a treatment, in solving a problem, and in not "letting the kids suffer" is also class-bounded.

A class- and gender-inflected economy of compassion is crystallized in Suzana's actions and articulated by the plastic surgeon quoted above. Of course, compassion is not plucked out of thin air.

Consider, for a moment, a snapshot of the historical trajectory of the abnormal or physically deviant body. Brazilian medicine in the colonial and post-colonial period (18th, 19th, and early 20th centuries) was heavily influenced by European trends and ideologies. From being seen as a "monstrosity" in 18th- and 19th- century Europe and met with burlesque curiosity as a living spectacle of the bizarre, the abnormal body was gradually being met, by the end of the 19th century, with another kind of feeling: compassion. Scientific discoveries, and literary and aesthetic expressions were starting by this time to emphasize the *human* (not monstrous) character of abnormal bodies. This trend was reinforced with the advent of the two world wars and the number of mutilated, injured, and deviating bodies of post-war times.

Launched massively, an economy of compassion encouraged individuals to recognize a person, a human being, or an equal beyond physical deviance. Curious gazes once explicitly cast at these bodies were now considered signs of bad, inappropriate behavior. Only medical curiosity was deemed acceptable. Deficiencies and disabilities were to be medically treated and compensated for. The adequate bourgeois feeling towards deviant bodies should be compassion, not curiosity (Courtine 2006).

Compassion, following the work of other social scientists, derives from power relations between people occupying unequal social positions, and it works as a means to express and reinforce these very relations. It has a micro-political capacity as it demarcates borders and social groups.[8]

Compassion should also be contextualized here within a Brazilian historical setting of social inequality: The most frequent way social scientists synthesize structures, values, representations, practices, and institutions of past and present Brazilian society is through a dilemma where universalism and equality clash and fuse with particularism and hierarchy. The heritage of Portuguese colonization (1500–1822) and of centuries of slave traffic and slavery (abolished only in 1888) merged, during the process of the formation of a Brazilian nation in the 19th century, with liberal ideas coming from Europe and the United States.

The country was thus caught in a struggle between a universalistic system of ideas with formal rules and laws that should be applicable to all members of society, and a set of unwritten, naturalized practices centered on personal relationships and hierarchies.

Liberalism's institutional and legal apparatuses were introduced in a slavery-based system, thus establishing "radical freedom for the elites, with no counterpart whatsoever of equality for the rest of the excluded population" (Vaitsman, 2002:39, my translation).

The excluded part of the population could have access to institutions, privileges, or even the legal system only through mediation—that is, through personal relationships with people situated higher up in the social hierarchy. Practices based on alliances—favors, symbolic kinship ties, and client–patron relationships—were and still are mechanisms used to attain mediation.

Contemporary relationships between wealthier and poorer Brazilians are thus also established in contradictory terms: avoidance and dependency; compassion and contempt; affection and servility. Tião, popsicle seller, son of Suzana's house helpers, becomes friends with Roberto, Suzana's son. This friendship is allowed because Suzana sees Tião's parents as honest and hard-working employees. This friendship, moreover, increases Tião's visibility as a *person* in the eyes of Suzana and her family: He is no longer just a poor kid like so many others; he is Roberto's friend. Compassion grows in this web of established asymmetrical alliances.

Even when lazily sunbathing, glass of ice-cold beer in hand, against the noisy background of Brazilian pop music coming from the loudspeakers of competing beach bars, Suzana answers to the calls of this inherited economy of compassion and sees Tião as someone in need of help: Even before it gets struck by the curious gaze of others, Suzana dislocates Tião's body from the hot beach sand and moves it to the air-conditioned privacy of a clinic for cosmetic surgery.

ONCE THE PROCEDURE IS DONE . . . PIECES OF ADVICE AND RECOMMENDATIONS

A few days after he arrived in Belo Horizonte, I invited Suzana's family and Tião to my apartment for a *lanchinho* (an evening snack). Wearing a pair of shorts and a white T-shirt, his pitch-dark hair newly washed, he greeted me with a friendly smile. We talked about several things, but not about the operation. Since he did not bring the subject up, neither did I. However, a day or two later, I was running some errands in Suzana's neighborhood and decided to say hello. I met Tião sitting at the dinner table with its waxed tablecloth. He was bare-chested and had a bandage around his chest.

Tião was talkative, relaxed, and had a good appetite. He made himself a ham, cheese, and burger sandwich (Suzana's evening meal specialty at the time) and topped the combination with *batata-palha* (finely grated fried potatoes). And he said to all of us who were sitting around the table:

> "Oh, God! I'm so relieved now that I've had the procedure! I was nervous about it, but it didn't hurt at all. And now I just feel relieved. I'll have to have this bandage on for a while, and then I'll go back to the doctor to get the stitches taken out."

A beaming Suzana asked Tião if his trip to Belo Horizonte was worthwhile. Tião answered, "Yes! I wasn't feeling OK, you know, having those things . . . I mean, I was used to going bare-chested and I couldn't do that anymore. It was weird." By affirming his recent-but-now-past physical deviancy, Tião is not only showing his awareness of mainstream ideals of masculinity in Brazil but also making sure that all those sitting around the table understood that he stuck to these ideals.

Suzana's rhetorical question can be interpreted in the light of the previously mentioned idea of an economy of compassion. As it was, her effort is recognized by Tião, who confirms through his answer that she was his benefactor and that her gesture made a change in his life.[9] By helping Tião, Suzana

was also, in a sense, reinforcing and maintaining her position as a middle-class woman, a compassionate woman who chooses to help someone by giving him the chance to modify his body.

After one or two more weeks in the big city, Tião was determined to start looking for a job. Suzana commented to me that she had talked to Tião and explained to him that he could stay and try to find a job. But he would also have to study: "Because if you don't study, Tião, you can't progress. So, you stay, work during the day, and study at night. I will help you."

Suzana would talk to Tião's parents and try to explain the situation. "You see," she explained to me, "I like Tião almost as a son. I've known him since he was a little boy. And I want to give him the opportunity to have a better life. A life different from the one he lives in Pilar." Tião's access to a better life, a life with middle-class privileges is not only facilitated, however, but also controlled by his middle-class pseudo-family.[10] As it turns out, Suzana did not hide her dismay when Tião came with a suggestion for a possible job: "I talked to some men who load and unload groceries at the central market, and they told me I could try getting a job there." Probably postponing yet another lecture on desirable aims and ambitions in life, she simply answered, "Yes . . . we'll talk about work possibilities later on."

When Suzana contacted Tião's parents about his moving in with her family in Belo Horizonte, the parents did not agree. Tião's father argued that the family still needed his labor. A few days after his stitches were removed, Tião was sitting on a bus, headed unwillingly back to Pilar.

Anchored to a context of social inequality, Tião's story illustrates the centrality of bodies and physical appearances in Brazilian society. Beyond that, it shows how a compassionate action grown out of established but asymmetric relationships gets reformulated into a practice of diagnosing and treating a "deviating body." In times of wide social inequalities and global anxieties about the body, Tião's story of middle-class compassion and man boobs contributes to understanding some of the mechanisms linking bodies, medical procedures, and social hierarchies.

By looking at the way cosmetic surgeries sculpt bodies, one might be able to chart a kind of map of social space, identifying bodies whose status invites or encourages transformation and flight, and those that constitute the desired direction or endpoint of that flight. By transforming his body, Tião was adapting himself to mainstream ideals about masculinity. His breasted experience confused and embarrassed him: "I wasn't feeling OK, you know, having those things . . . I mean, I was used to going bare-chested and I couldn't do that anymore. It was weird."

Tião's case also shows, through the figure of Suzana, how women participate in the construction and "correction" of male bodies and masculinities.[11] As we've seen, Tião's body is corrected through plastic surgery. This raises some questions left open for debate: Are mothers, sisters, girlfriends, and female employers who came of age during the "Plastic Fantastic" era less reluctant to recommend surgery to the boys they don't want to see suffering? Is this pointing toward a generational shift regarding attitudes toward men as consumers of plastic surgeries?

Orchestrated by a middle-class fairy godmother, Tião's case maps and makes[12] gender and class ideals. His surgery did not transform him into a middle-class young man. However, by undergoing the procedure, Tião experienced middle classness from up close.

Worlds apart from Pilar, he could get a taste of what Pilar's summer tourists do when they are not sunbathing at the beach: after a few days in Belo Horizonte, Tião started wearing his "Pilar clothes" (shorts, sleeveless T-shirts, and flip-flops) only at home and changed to a pair of jeans, a T-shirt, and sneakers whenever he went out. His contacts with Suzana's family, with the hospital staff, with the medical jargon, his physical transformation (and its making it temporarily impossible for him to engage in physical work), and all the other experiences he went through during his four-week stay in Belo Horizonte, crystallize the interplay of bodily practices, compassion, gender, class, and social inequality in contemporary southeastern Brazil.

REFERENCES

Caponi, S. 1999. "A Lógica da compaixão," *Trans/Form/Ação*, 21/22:91–117.

Coelho, M. C. 2010. "Narrativas da violência: A dimensão micropolítica das emoções," *Mana*, 16(2): 265–285.

Connell, R. W. and J. W. Messerschmidt. 2005. Hegemonic Masculinity: Rethinking the Concept. *Gender & Society*, 19(6):829–859.

Courtine, J. J. 2006. Déviances et Dangerosités. In Corbin, A., J. J. Courtine, and G. Vigarello (Eds.). *Histoire du Corps. Vol. 3. Les Mutations du regard. Le XXe siècle*. Paris: Seuil, 201–260.

Durham, D. 2005. Did You Bathe This Morning? Baths and Morality in Botswana. In A. Masquelier (Ed.), *Dirt, Undress, and Difference: Critical Perspectives on the Body's Surface*. Bloomington and Indianapolis: Indiana University Press, pp. 190–212.

Goldstein, D. 2003. *Laughter out of Place. Race, Class, Violence and Sexuality in a Rio Shantytown*. Berkeley: University of California Press.

Romero, M. 1997. Life as the Maid's Daughter: An Exploration of the Everyday Boundaries of Race, Class, and Gender, in M. Romero, P. Hondagneu-Sotelo, and V. Ortiz (Eds.). *Challenging Fronteras: Structuring Latinas and Latino Lives in the U.S.* New York: Routledge, pp. 195–209.

Vaitsman, J. 2002. Desigualdades sociais e duas formas de particularismo na sociedade brasileira. *Cad. Saúde Pública*, 18 (suplemento):37–46.

NOTES

1. *FolhaOnline*, March 21, 2011: http://www1.folha.uol .com.br/folhateen/891667-ter-peitinhos-e-o-pesadelo-de-65-dos-meninos-de-14-e-15-anos.shtml, accessed March 31, 2011.

2. In http://boasaude.uol.com.br, "Ginecomastia," accessed November 15, 2006. These descriptions were corroborated by several websites and articles on the topic. See, for instance: http://www.cirurgia-plastica. com/ginecomastia/; http://www.fitcorpus.com.br/? s=MjM=&p=Mg==&x=NDY=&c=GINECOMAS TIA http://cirurgiaplasticaelo.blogspot.com/2008/09/ ginecomastia-cirurgia-para-retirada-da.html; http://

www.plasticamontenegro.com.br/cirurgias-plasticas/
mamas/ginecomastia-mamas-masculina.htm http://
www.plasticsurgery.org/Patients_and_Consumers/
Procedures/Cosmetic_Procedures/Breast_
Reduction_for_Men.html (for a North American site
on the topic).

3. In: http://www.reuters.com/article/2007/03/01/
us-brazil-drugs-diet-idUSN0121107020070301,
accessed March 28, 2011.

4. *Veja* January 17, 2001, no. 1683. "Brasil, império do
Bisturi."

5. *SBCP* and *Data Folha*, 2009. Cirurgia Plástica no
Brasil. In: http://www2.cirurgiaplastica.org.br/index
.php?option=com_jforms&view=form&id=1&Ite
mid=212, requested on December 2010.

6. In: http://www.suite101.com/content/c-section-rate-
in-brazil-36-of-births-a172360, accessed March 15,
2011.

7. The expression "*nem sabiam direito*" might indicate
that the parents hardly *knew* what was bothering their
son or that they hardly *noticed* that he was bothered.
Its vagueness in meaning might hide implicit middle-
class understandings of poor working-class parents
and their supposed lack of knowledge and lack of
time and energy to spend with their children. For a
discussion on class understandings of childhood in
Brazil, see Goldstein (2003).

8. For more on compassion, emotions and social
inequalities see Caponi (1999) and Coelho (2010).

9. Courtine (2006:468, my translation) observes how
contemporary media, every once in a while, mount
heavy celebrations of medicine's all-embracing power
by indulging viewers and readers with the sighing
feeling of Western compassion toward bodies with
various kinds of deviations. As he puts it, "The South
offers monsters and suffering, the North offers
expertise and compassion, and Federal Express pays
the (patient's) return ticket."

10. For a discussion on class, ethnicity, and affection in
the relationship between domestic workers and their
employers, see Romero (1997).

11. In an essay about the development of research on
masculinities, Connell and Messerschmidt
(2005:848) suggest that "[f]ocusing only in the
activities of men occludes the practices of women in
the construction of gender among men. As is well-
known by life-history research, women are central in
many of the processes constructing masculinities—as
mothers; as school mates; as girlfriends, sexual
partners, and wives; as workers in the gender division
of labor, and so forth."

12. I borrow this expression and reasoning from Durham
(2005:208), when she suggests that the body is "a site
of social making, and not just mapping."

3 • *Aihwa Ong*

THE PRODUCTION OF POSSESSION
Spirits and the Multinational Corporation in Malaysia

DISCUSSION QUESTIONS

1. What are some of the main aspects of dominant Malay gender ideologies? How and why have these been challenged by the migration of young women to urban areas for study and work?
2. How does Ong's explanation of the outbreak of spirit possession among young, female factory workers differ from that of the government, media, and factory managers?
3. What does this account teach us about the role of bodies as sites for the production, regulation, and expression of gender relations? How does attention to power, agency, and structure help us make sense of the situation?

The sanitized environments maintained by multinational corporations in Malaysian "free trade zones"[1] are not immune to sudden spirit attacks on young female workers. Ordinarily quiescent, Malay factory women who are seized by vengeful spirits explode into demonic screaming and rage on the shop floor. Management responses to such unnerving episodes include isolating the possessed workers, pumping them with Valium, and sending them home. Yet a Singapore[2] doctor notes that "a local medicine man can do more good than tranquilizers" (Chew 1978:51). Whatever healing technique used, the cure is never certain, for the Malays consider spirit possession an illness that afflicts the soul (*jiwa*). This paper will explore how the reconstitution of illness, bodies, and consciousness is involved in the deployment of healing practices in multinational factories.

Anthropologists studying spirit possession phenomena have generally linked them to culturally specific forms of conflict management that disguise and yet resolve social tensions within indigenous societies. In contrast, policymakers and professionals see spirit possession episodes as an intrusion of archaic beliefs into the modern setting. These views will be evaluated in the light of spirit possession incidents and the reactions of factory managers and policymakers in Malaysia.

Different forms of spirit possession have been reported in Malay society, and their cultural significance varies with the regional and historical circumstances in which they occurred. In the current changing political economy, new social conditions have brought about spirit possession incidents in modern institutional settings. I believe that the most appropriate way to deal with spirit visitations

Abridged version of Aihwa Ong, 1988. "The Production of Possession: Spirits and the Multinational Corporation in Malaysia." Reproduced by permission of the American Anthropological Association and of the author from *American Ethnologist*, Volume 15, Issue 1, Pages 28–42, February 1988. Not for sale or further reproduction.

in multinational factories is to consider them as part of a "complex negotiation of reality" (Crapanzano 1977:16) by an emergent female industrial workforce. Hailing from peasant villages, these workers can be viewed as neophytes in a double sense: as young female adults and as members of a nascent proletariat. Mary Douglas' ideas about the breaking of taboos and social boundaries (1966) are useful for interpreting spirit possession in terms of what it reveals about the workers' profound sense of status ambiguity and dislocation.

Second, their spirit idiom will be contrasted with the biomedical model to reveal alternative constructions of illness and of social reality in the corporate world. I will then consider the implications of the scientific medical model that converts workers into patients, and the consequences this therapeutic approach holds for mending the souls of the afflicted.

ECONOMIC DEVELOPMENT

As recently as the 1960s, most Malays in Peninsular Malaysia lived in rural *kampung* (villages), engaged in cash cropping or fishing. In 1969, spontaneous outbreaks of racial rioting gave expression to deep-seated resentment over the distribution of power and wealth in this multiethnic society. The Malay-dominated government responded to this crisis by introducing a New Economic Policy intended to "restructure" the political economy. From the early 1970s onward, agricultural and industrialization programs induced the large-scale influx of young rural Malay men and women to enter urban schools and manufacturing plants set up by multinational corporations. Throughout the 1970s, free-trade zones were established to encourage investments by Japanese, American, and European corporations for setting up plants for offshore production. In seeking to cut costs further, these corporations sought young, unmarried women as a source of cheap and easily controlled labor. This selective labor demand, largely met by *kampung* society, produced in a single decade a Malay female

industrial labor force of over 47,000 (Jamilah Ariffin 1980:47). Malay female migrants also crossed the Causeway in the thousands to work in multinational factories based in Singapore.

SPIRIT BELIEFS AND WOMEN IN MALAY CULTURE

Spirit beliefs in rural Malay society, overlaid but existing within Islam, are part of the indigenous worldview woven from strands of animistic cosmology and Javanese, Hindu, and Muslim cultures. In Peninsular Malaysia, the supernatural belief system varies according to the historical and local interactions between folk beliefs and Islamic teachings. Local traditions provide conceptual coherence about causation and well-being to village Malays. Through the centuries, the office of the *bomoh*, or practitioner of folk medicine, has been the major means by which these old traditions of causation, illness, and health have been transmitted. In fulfilling the pragmatic and immediate needs of everyday life, the beliefs and practices are often recast in "Islamic" terms.

I am mainly concerned here with the folk model in Sungai Jawa (a pseudonym), a village based in Kuala Langat district, rural Selangor, where I conducted fieldwork in 1979–80. Since the 1960s, the widespread introduction of Western medical practices and an intensified revitalization of Islam have made spirit beliefs publicly inadmissible. Nevertheless, spirit beliefs and practices are still very much in evidence. Villagers believe that all beings have spiritual essence (*semangat*) but, unlike humans, spirits (*hantu*) are disembodied beings capable of violating the boundaries between the material and supernatural worlds: invisible beings unbounded by human rules, spirits come to represent transgressions of moral boundaries, which are socially defined in the concentric spaces of homestead, village, and jungle. This scheme roughly coincides with Malay concepts of emotional proximity and distance, and the related dimensions of reduced moral responsibility as one moves from the interior space of household, to the intermediate zone of relatives, and on to the external world of strangers (Banks 1983:170–174).

The two main classes of spirits recognized by Malays reflect this interior–exterior social/spatial divide: spirits associated with human beings, and the "free" disembodied forms. In Sungai Jawa, *toyol* are the most common familiar spirits, who steal in order to enrich their masters. Accusations of breeding *toyol* provide the occasion for expressing resentment against economically successful villagers. Birth demons are former human females who died in childbirth and, as *pontianak*, threaten newly born infants and their mothers. Thus, spirit beliefs reflect everyday anxieties about the management of social relations in village society.

It is free spirits that are responsible for attacking people who unknowingly step out of the Malay social order. Free spirits are usually associated with special objects or sites (*keramat*) marking the boundary between human and natural spaces. As the gatekeepers of social boundaries, spirits guard against human transgressions into amoral spaces. Such accidents require the mystical qualities of the *bomoh* to read just spirit relations with the human world.

From Islam, Malays have inherited the belief that men are more endowed with *akal* (reason) than women, who are overly influenced by *hawa nafsu* (human lust). A susceptibility to imbalances in the four humoral elements renders women spiritually weaker than men. Women's *hawa nafsu* nature is believed to make them especially vulnerable to *latah* (episodes during which the victim breaks out into obscene language and compulsive, imitative behavior) and to spirit attacks (spontaneous episodes in which the afflicted one screams, hyperventilates, or falls down in a trance or a raging fit). However, it is Malay spirit beliefs that explain the transgressions whereby women (more likely than men) become possessed by spirits (*kena hantu*). Their spiritual frailty, polluting bodies, and erotic nature make them especially likely to transgress moral space, and therefore permeable by spirits.

Mary Douglas (1966) has noted that taboos operate to control threats to social boundaries. In Malay society, women are hedged in by conventions that keep them out of social roles and spaces dominated by men. Although men are also vulnerable to spirit attacks, women's spiritual, bodily, and social selves are especially offensive to sacred spaces, which they trespass at the risk of inviting spirit attacks.

Spirit victims have traditionally been married women who sometimes become possessed after giving birth for the first time. Childbirth is a dangerous occasion, when rituals are performed in order to keep off evil spirits. As a rite of passage, childbirth is the first traumatic event in the ordinary village woman's life. I visited a young mother who had been possessed by a *hantu*, which the ministrations of two *bomoh* failed to dislodge. She lay on her mat for two months after delivering her first child, uninterested in nursing the baby. Her mother-in-law whispered that she had been "penetrated by the devil." Perhaps, through some unintended action, she had attracted spirit attack and been rendered ritually and sexually impure.

In everyday life, village women are also bound by customs regarding bodily comportment and spatial movements, which operate to keep them within the Malay social order. When they blur the bodily boundaries through the careless disposal of bodily exuviae and effluvia, they put themselves in an ambiguous situation, becoming most vulnerable to spirit penetration.

Until recently, unmarried daughters, most hedged in by village conventions, seem to have been well protected from spirit attack. Nubile girls take special care over the disposal of their cut nails, fallen hair, and menstrual rags, since such materials may fall into ill-wishers' hands and be used for black magic. Menstrual blood is considered dirty and polluting and the substance most likely to offend *keramat* spirits. This concern over bodily boundaries is linked to notions about the vulnerable identity and status of young unmarried women.

Since the early 1970s, when young peasant women began to leave the *kampung* and enter the unknown worlds of urban boarding schools and foreign factories, the incidence of spirit possession seems to have become more common among them than among married women. I maintain that like other cultural forms, spirit possession incidents may acquire new meanings and speak to new experiences in changing arenas of social relations and boundary definitions. In *kampung* society, spirit attacks on married women seem to be associated with their containment in prescribed domestic roles, whereas in modern organizations, spirit victims are young, unmarried women engaged in hitherto alien and male activities. This transition from *kampung* to urban-industrial contexts has cast village girls into an intermediate status that they find unsettling and fraught with danger to themselves and to Malay culture.

SPIRIT VISITATIONS IN MODERN FACTORIES

Multinational factories based in free-trade zones were the favored sites of spirit visitations. An American factory in Sungai Way experienced a large-scale incident in 1978, which involved some 120 operators engaged in assembly work requiring the use of microscopes. The factory had to be shut down for three days, and a *bomoh* was hired to slaughter a goat on the premises. The American director wondered how he was to explain to corporate headquarters that "8,000 hours of production were lost because someone saw a ghost" (Lim 1978:33). A Japanese factory based in Pontian, Kelantan, also experienced a spirit attack on 21 workers in 1980. As they were being taken to ambulances, some victims screamed, "I will kill you! Let me go!" (*New Straits Times*, 26 September, 1980). In Penang, another American factory was disrupted for three consecutive days after 15 women became afflicted by spirit possession. The victims screamed in fury and put up a terrific struggle against restraining male supervisors, shouting "Go away!" (*Sunday Echo*, 27 November, 1978). The afflicted were snatched off the shop floor and given injections of sedatives. Hundreds of frightened female workers were also sent home. A factory personnel officer told reporters:

Some girls started sobbing and screaming hysterically and when it seemed like spreading, the other workers in the production line were immediately ushered out. . . . It is a common belief among workers that the factory is "dirty" and supposed to be haunted by a *datuk*. (Sunday Echo)

Though brief, these reports reveal that spirit possession, believed to be caused by defilement, held the victims in a grip of rage against factory supervisors. Furthermore, the disruptions caused by spirit incidents seem a form of retaliation against the factory supervisors. In what follows, I will draw upon my field research to discuss the complex issues involved in possession imagery and management discourse on spirit incidents in Japanese-owned factories based in Kuala Langat.

THE CRYPTIC LANGUAGE OF POSSESSION

Young, unmarried women in Malay society are expected to be shy, obedient, and deferential, to be observed and not heard. In spirit possession episodes, they speak in other voices that refuse to be silenced. Since the afflicted claim amnesia once they have recovered, we are presented with the task of deciphering covert messages embedded in possession incidents.

Spirit visitations in modern factories with sizable numbers of young Malay female workers engender devil images, which dramatically reveal the contradictions between Malay and scientific ways of apprehending the human condition. In Malay society, what is being negotiated in possession incidents and their aftermath are complex issues dealing with the violation of different moral boundaries, of which gender oppression is but one dimension. What seems clear is that spirit possession provides a traditional way of rebelling against authority without punishment, since victims are not blamed for their predicament. However, the imagery of spirit possession in modern settings is a rebellion against transgressions of indigenous boundaries governing proper human relations and moral justice.

For Malays, the places occupied by evil spirits are nonhuman territories like swamps, jungles, and bodies of water. These amoral domains were kept distant from women's bodies by ideological and physical spatial regulations. The construction of modern buildings, often without regard for Malay concern about moral space, displaces spirits, which take up residence in the toilet tank. Thus, most village women express a horror of the Western-style toilet, which they would avoid if they could.

A few days after the spirit attacks in the Penang-based American factory, I interviewed some of the workers. Without prompting, factory women pointed out that the production floor and canteen areas were "very clean" but factory toilets were "filthy" (*kotor*). A *datuk* haunted the toilet, and workers, in their haste to leave, dropped their soiled pads anywhere. In the Penang factory incident, a worker remembered that a piercing scream from one corner of the shop floor was quickly followed by cries from other benches as women fought against spirits trying to possess them. The incidents had been sparked by *datuk* visions, sometimes headless, gesticulating angrily at the operators. Even after the *bomoh* had been sent for, workers had to be accompanied to the toilet by foremen for fear of being attacked by spirits in the stalls.

In Kuala Langat, my fieldwork elicited similar imagery from the workers in two Japanese factories (code-named ENI and EJI) based in the local free-trade zone. In their drive for attaining high production targets, foremen (both Malay and non-Malay) were very zealous in enforcing regulations that confined workers to the work bench. Operators had to ask for permission to go to the toilet, and were sometimes questioned intrusively about their "female problems." Menstruation was seen by management as deserving no consideration even in a workplace where 85–90 percent of the work force was female. In the EJI plant, foremen sometimes followed workers to the locker room, terrorizing them with their spying. One operator became possessed after screaming that she saw a "hairy leg" when she went to the toilet. A worker from another factory reported:

Workers saw "things" appear when they went to the toilet. Once, when a woman entered the toilet she saw a tall figure licking sanitary napkins ["Modess" supplied in the cabinet]. It had a long tongue, and those sanitary pads . . cannot be used anymore.

As Taussig remarks, the "language" emanating from our bodies expresses the significance of social disease (1980). The above lurid imagery speaks of the women's loss of control over their bodies as well as their lack of control over social relations in the factory. Furthermore, the image of body alienation also reveals intense guilt (and repressed desire), and the felt need to be on guard against violation by the male management staff who, in the form of fearsome predators, may suddenly materialize anywhere in the factory.

Even the prayer room (*surau*), provided on factory premises for the Muslim work force, was not safe from spirit harassment. A woman told me of her aunt's fright in the *surau* at the EJI factory; "She was in the middle of praying when she fainted because she said . . . her head suddenly spun and something pounced on her from behind." As mentioned above, spirit attacks also occurred when women were at the work bench, usually during the "graveyard" shift. An ENI factory operator described one incident which took place in May 1979:

It was the afternoon shift, at about nine o'clock. All was quiet. Suddenly, [the victim] started sobbing, laughed and then shrieked. She flailed at the machine . . . she was violent, she fought as the foreman and technician pulled her away. Altogether, three operators were afflicted. . . . The supervisor and foremen took them to the clinic and told the driver to take them home. . . .

She did not know what had happened . . . she saw a *hantu*, a were-tiger. Only she saw it, and she started screaming. . . . The foremen would not let us talk with her for fear of recurrence. . . . People say that the workplace is haunted by the *hantu* who dwells below. . . . Well, this used to be all jungle, it was a burial ground before the factory was built. The devil disturbs those who have a weak constitution.

Spirit possession episodes then were triggered by black apparitions, which materialized in "liminal" spaces such as toilets, the locker room and the prayer room, places where workers sought refuge from harsh work discipline. These were also rooms periodically checked by male supervisors determined to bring workers back to the work bench. The microscope, which after hours of use becomes an instrument of torture, sometimes disclosed spirits lurking within. Other workers pointed to the effect of the steady hum and the factory pollutants, which permanently disturbed graveyard spirits. Unleashed, these vengeful beings were seen to threaten women for transgressing into the zone between the human and nonhuman world, as well as modern spaces formerly the domain of men. By intruding into hitherto forbidden spaces, Malay women workers experienced anxieties about inviting punishment.

Fatna Sabbah observes that "(t)he invasion by women of economic spaces such as factories and offices . . . is often experienced as erotic aggression in the Muslim context" (1984:17). In Malay culture, men and women in public contact must define the situation in nonsexual terms. It is particularly incumbent upon young women to conduct themselves with circumspection and to diffuse sexual tension. However, the modern factory is an arena constituted by a sexual division of labor and constant male surveillance of nubile women in a close, daily context. In Kuala Langat, young factory women felt themselves placed in a situation in which they unintentionally violated taboos defining social and bodily boundaries. The shop floor culture was also charged with the dangers of sexual harassment by male management staff as part of workaday relations. To combat spirit attacks, the Malay factory women felt a greater need for spiritual vigilance in the factory surroundings. Thus the victim in the ENI factory incident was said to be: "possessed, maybe because she was spiritually weak. She was not spiritually vigilant, so that when she saw the *hantu* she was instantly afraid and screamed. Usually, the *hantu* likes people who are spiritually weak, yes . . . one should guard against

being easily startled, afraid." As Foucault observes, people subjected to the "micro-techniques" of power are induced to regulate themselves (1979). The fear of spirit possession thus created self-regulation on the part of workers, thereby contributing to the intensification of corporate and self-control on the shop floor. Thus, as factory workers, Malay women became alienated not only from the products of their labor but also experienced new forms of psychic alienation. Their intrusion into economic spaces outside the home and village was experienced as moral disorder, symbolized by filth and dangerous sexuality. Some workers called for increased "discipline," others for Islamic classes on factory premises to regulate interactions (including dating) between male and female workers. Thus, spirit imagery gave symbolic configuration to the workers' fear and protest over social conditions in the factories. However, these inchoate signs of moral and social chaos were routinely recast by management into an idiom of sickness.

THE WORKER AS PATIENT

Now I wish to discuss how struggles over the meanings of health are part of workers' social critique of work discipline, and of managers' attempts to extend control over the work force. The management use of workers as "instruments of labor" is paralleled by another set of ideologies, which regards women's bodies as the site of control where gender politics, health, and educational practices intersect.

In the Japanese factories based in Malaysia, management ideology constructs the female body in terms of its biological functionality for, and its anarchic disruption of, production. These ideologies operate to fix women workers in subordinate positions in systems of domination that proliferate in high-tech industries. A Malaysian investment brochure advertises "the oriental girl," for example, as "qualified *by nature and inheritance* to contribute to the efficiency of a bench assembly production line" (FIDA 1975, emphasis added).

This biological rationale for the commodification of women's bodies is part of a pervasive discourse reconceptualizing women for high-tech production requirements. Japanese managers in the free trade zone talk about the "eyesight," "manual dexterity," and "patience" of young women to perform tedious micro-assembly jobs. An engineer put the female nature-technology relationship in a new light: "Our work is designed for females." Within international capitalism, this notion of women's bodies renders them analogous to the status of the computer chips they make. Computer chips, like "oriental girls," are identical, whether produced in Malaysia, Taiwan, or Sri Lanka. For multinational corporations, women are units of much cheap labor power repackaged under the "nimble fingers" label.

The abstract mode of scientific discourse also separates "normal" from "abnormal" workers, that is, those who do not perform according to factory requirements. In the EJI factory, the Malay personnel manager using the biomedical model to locate the sources of spirit possession among workers noted that the first spirit attack occurred five months after the factory began operation in 1976. Thereafter, "we had our counter-measure. I think this is a method of how you give initial education to the workers, how you take care of the medical welfare of the workers. The worker who is weak, comes in without breakfast, lacking sleep, then she will see ghosts!"

In the factory environment, "spirit attacks" (*kena hantu*) was often used interchangeably with "mass hysteria," a term adopted from English language press reports on such incidents. In the manager's view, "hysteria" was a symptom of physical adjustment as the women workers "move from home idleness to factory discipline." This explanation also found favor with some members of the work force. Scientific terms like "*penyakit histeria*" (hysteria sickness), and physiological preconditions formulated by the management, became more acceptable to some workers. One woman remarked, "They say they saw *hantu*, but I don't know. . . . I believe that maybe they . . . when they come to

work, they did not fill their stomachs, they were not full so that they felt hungry. But they were not brave enough to say so." A male technician used more complex concepts, but remained doubtful:

> I think that this [is caused by] a feeling of "complex"—that maybe "inferiority complex" is pressing them down—their spirit, so that this can be called an illness of the spirit, "conflict jiwa," "emotional conflict." Sometimes they see an old man, in black shrouds, they say, in their microscopes, they say . . . . I myself don't know how. They see *hantu* in different places. . . . Some time ago an "emergency" incident like this occurred in a boarding school. The victim fainted. Then she became very strong. . . . It required ten or twenty persons to handle her.

In corporate discourse, physical "facts" that contributed to spirit possession were isolated, while psychological notions were used as explanation and as a technique of manipulation. In ENI factory, a *bomoh* was hired to produce the illusion of exorcism, lulling the workers into a false sense of security. The personnel manager claimed that unlike managers in other Japanese firms who operated on the "basis of feelings," his "psychological approach" helped to prevent recurrent spirit visitations:

> You cannot dispel *kampung* beliefs. Now and then we call the *bomoh* to come, every six months or so, to pray, walk around. Then we take pictures of the *bomoh* in the factory and hang up the pictures. Somehow, the workers seeing these pictures feel safe, [seeing] that the place has been exorcised.

Similarly, whenever a new section of the factory was constructed, the *bomoh* was sent for to sprinkle holy water, thereby assuring workers that the place was rid of ghosts. Regular *bomoh* visits and their photographic images were different ways of defining a social reality, which simultaneously acknowledged and manipulated the workers' fear of spirits.

Medical personnel were also involved in the narrow definition of the causes of spirit incidents on the shop floor. A factory nurse periodically toured the shop floor to offer coffee to tired or drowsy workers. Workers had to work eight-hour shifts six days a week—morning, 6:30 A.M. to 2:30 P.M.; afternoon, 2:30 P.M. to 10:30 P.M.; or night, 10:30 P.M. to 6:30 A.M.—which divided up the 24-hour daily operation of the factories. They were permitted two ten-minute breaks and a half-hour for a meal. Most workers had to change to a different shift every two weeks. This regime allowed little time for workers to recover from their exhaustion between shifts. In addition, overtime was frequently imposed. The shifts also worked against the human, and especially, female cycle; many freshly recruited workers regularly missed their sleep, meals, and menstrual cycles.

Thus, although management pointed to physiological problems as causing spirit attacks, they seldom acknowledged deeper scientific evidence of health hazards in microchip assembly plants. These include the rapid deterioration of eyesight caused by the prolonged use of microscopes in bonding processes. General exposure to strong solvents, acids, and fumes induced headaches, nausea, dizziness, and skin irritation in workers. More toxic substances used for cleaning purposes exposed workers to lead poisoning, kidney failure, and breast cancer. Other materials used in the fabrication of computer chips have been linked to female workers' painful menstruation, their inability to conceive, and repeated miscarriages. Within the plants, unhappy-looking workers were urged to talk over their problems with the "industrial relations assistant." Complaints of "pain in the chest" were interpreted to mean emotional distress, and the worker was ushered into the clinic for medication in order to maintain discipline and a relentless work schedule.

In the EJI factory, the shop floor supervisor admitted, "I think that hysteria is related to the job in some cases." He explained that workers in the microscope sections were usually the ones to *kena hantu*, and thought that perhaps they should not begin work doing those tasks. However, he quickly offered other interpretations that had little to do with work conditions: There was one victim whose broken engagement had incurred her mother's wrath; at work she cried and talked to herself, saying, "I am not to be blamed, not me!" Another worker, seized by possession, screamed, "Send me home, send me home!" Apparently, she indicated, her mother had taken all her earnings. Again, through such psychological readings, the causes of spirit attacks produced in the factories were displaced onto workers and their families.

In corporate discourse, both the biomedical and psychological interpretations of spirit possession defined the affliction as an attribute of individuals rather than stemming from the general social situation. Scientific concepts, pharmaceutical treatment, and behavioral intervention all identified and separated recalcitrant workers from "normal" ones; disruptive workers became patients. According to Parsons, the cosmopolitan medical approach tolerates illness as sanctioned social deviance; however, patients have the duty to get well (1985:146, 149). This attitude implies that those who do not get well cannot be rewarded with "the privileges of being sick" (1985:149). In the ENI factory, the playing out of this logic provided the rationale for dismissing workers who had had two previous experiences of spirit attacks, on the grounds of "security." This policy drew protests from village elders, for whom spirits in the factory were the cause of their daughters' insecurity. The manager agreed verbally with them, but pointed out that these "hysterical, mental types" might hurt themselves when they flailed against the machines, risking electrocution. By appearing to agree with native theory, the management reinterpreted spirit possession as a symbol of flawed character and culture. The sick role was reconceptualized as internally produced by outmoded thought and behavior not adequately adjusted to the demands of factory discipline. The worker-patient could have no claim on management sympathy but would have to bear responsibility for her own cultural deficiency. A woman in

ENI talked sadly about her friend, the victim of spirits and corporate policy:

> At the time the management wanted to throw her out, to end her work, she cried. She did ask to be reinstated, but she has had three [episodes] already . . . . I think that whether it was right or not [to expel her] depends [on the circumstances], because she has already worked here for a long time; now that she has been thrown out she does not know what she can do, you know.

The nonrecognition of social obligations to workers lies at the center of differences in worldview between Malay workers and the foreign management. By treating the signs and symptoms of disease as "things-in-themselves" (Taussig 1980:1), the biomedical model freed managers from any moral debt owed the workers. Furthermore, corporate adoption of spirit idiom stigmatized spirit victims, thereby ruling out any serious consideration of their needs. Afflicted and "normal" workers alike were made to see that spirit possession was nothing but confusion and delusion, which should be abandoned in a rational worldview.

THE WORK OF CULTURE: HYGIENE AND DISPOSSESSION

To what extent can the *bomoh*'s work of culture convert the rage and distress of possessed women in Malaysia into socially shared meanings? As discussed above, the spirit imagery speaks of danger and violation as young Malay women intrude into hitherto forbidden spirit or male domains. Their participation as an industrial force is subconsciously perceived by themselves and their families as a threat to the ordering of Malay culture. Second, their employment as production workers places them directly in the control of male strangers who monitor their every move. These social relations, brought about in the process of industrial capitalism, are experienced as a moral disorder in which workers are alienated from their bodies, the products of their

work, and their own culture. The spirit idiom is therefore a language of protest against these changing social circumstances. A male technician evaluated the stresses they were under; "There is a lot of discipline . . . but when there is too much discipline . . . it is not good. Because of this the operators, with their small wages, will always contest. They often break the machines in ways that are not apparent . . . . Sometimes, they damage the products." Such Luddite actions in stalling production reverse momentarily the arrangement whereby work regimentation controls the human body. However, the workers' resistance is not limited to the technical problem of work organization, but addresses the violation of moral codes. A young woman explained her sense of having been "tricked" into an intolerable work arrangement:

> For instance . . . sometimes . . . they want us to raise production. This is what we sometimes challenge. The workers want fair treatment, as for instance, in relation to wages and other matters. We feel that in this situation there are many [issues] to dispute over with the management . . . . with our wages so low we feel as though we have been tricked or forced.

She demands "justice, because sometimes they exhaust us very much as if they do not think that we too are human beings!"

Spirit possession episodes may be taken as expressions both of fear and of resistance against the multiple violations of moral boundaries in the modern factory. They are acts of rebellion, symbolizing what cannot be spoken directly, calling for a renegotiation of obligations between the management and workers. However, technocrats have turned a deaf ear to such protests, to this moral indictment of their woeful cultural judgments about the dispossessed. By choosing to view possession episodes narrowly as sickness caused by physiological and psychological maladjustment, the management also manipulates the *bomoh* to serve the interests of the factory rather than express the needs of the workers. Both Japanese factories in Kuala Langat have commenced operations in a spate of spirit possession incidents. A year after operations began in the EJI factory, a well-known *bomoh* and his retinue were invited to the factory *surau*, where they read prayers over a basin of "pure water." Those who had been visited by the devil drank from it and washed their faces, a ritual which made them immune to future spirit attacks. The *bomoh* pronounced the *hantu* controlling the factory site "very kind"; he merely showed himself but did not disturb people. A month after the ritual, the spirit attacks resumed, but involving smaller numbers of women (one or two) in each incident. The manager claimed that after the exorcist rites, spirit attacks occurred only once a month.

In an interview, an eyewitness reported what happened after a spirit incident erupted:

> The work section was not shut down, we had to continue working. Whenever it happened, the other workers felt frightened. They were not allowed to look because [the management] feared contagion. They would not permit us to leave. When an incident broke out, we had to move away . . . . At ten o'clock they called the *bomoh* to come . . . because he knew that the *hantu* had already entered the woman's body. He came in and scattered rice flour water all over the area where the incident broke out. He recited prayers over holy water. He sprinkled rice flour water on places touched by the *hantu* . . . The *bomoh* chanted incantations [*jampi jampi*] chasing the *hantu* away. He then gave some medicine to the afflicted . . . . He also entered the clinic [to pronounce) *jampi jampi*.

The primary role of the *bomoh* hired by corporate management was to ritually cleanse the prayer room, shop floor, and even the factory clinic. After appeasing the spirits, he ritually healed the victims, who were viewed as not responsible for their affliction. However, his work did not extend to curing them after they had been given sedatives and sent home. Instead, through his exorcism and incantations, the *bomoh* expressed the Malay understanding of these disturbing events, perhaps impressing the other workers that the factory had been purged of spirits.

However, he failed to convince the management about the need to create a moral space, in Malay terms, on factory premises. Management did not respond to spirit incidents by reconsidering social relationships on the shop floor; instead, they sought to eliminate the afflicted from the work scene. As the ENI factory nurse, an Indian woman, remarked, "It is an experience working with the Japanese. They do not consult women. To tell you the truth, they don't care about the problem except that it goes away."

The work of the *bomoh* was further thwarted by the medicalization of the afflicted. Spirit possession incidents in factories made visible the conflicted women who did not fit the corporate image of "normal" workers. By standing apart from the workaday routine, possessed workers inadvertently exposed themselves to the cold ministrations of modern medicine, rather than the increased social support they sought. Other workers, terrified of being attacked and by the threat of expulsion, kept up a watchful vigilance. This induced self-regulation was reinforced by the scientific gaze of supervisors and nurses, which further enervated the recalcitrant and frustrated those who resisted. A worker observed, "[The possessed] don't remember their experiences. Maybe the *hantu* is still working on their madness, maybe because their experiences have not been stilled, or maybe their souls are not really disturbed. They say there are evil spirits in that place [that is, factory]." In fact, spirit victims maintained a disturbed silence after their "recovery." Neither their families, friends, the *bomoh*, nor I could get them to talk about their experiences.

Spirit possession episodes in different societies have been labeled "mass psychogenic illness" or "epidemic hysteria" in psychological discourse (Colligan, Pennebaker, and Murphy 1982). Different altered states of consciousness, which variously spring from indigenous understanding of social situations, are reinterpreted in cosmopolitan terms considered universally applicable. In multinational factories located overseas, this ethnotherapeutic model (Lutz 1985) is widely applied and made to seem objective and rational. However, we have seen that such scientific knowledge and practices can display a definite prejudice against the people they are intended to restore to well-being in particular cultural contexts. The reinterpretation of spirit possession may therefore be seen as a shift of locus of patriarchal authority from the *bomoh*, sanctioned by indigenous religious beliefs, toward professionals sanctioned by scientific training.

In Third World contexts, cosmopolitan medical concepts and drugs often have an anesthetizing effect, which erases the authentic experiences of the sick. More frequently, the proliferation of positivist scientific meanings also produces a fragmentation of the body, a shattering of social obligations, and a separation of individuals from their own culture. Gramsci (1971) has defined hegemony as a form of ideological domination based on the consent of the dominated, a consent that is secured through the diffusion of the worldview of the dominant class. In Malaysia, medicine has become part of hegemonic discourse, constructing a "modern" outlook by clearing away the nightmarish visions of Malay workers. However, as a technique of both concealment and control, it operates in a more sinister way than native beliefs in demons. Malay factory women may gradually become dispossessed of spirits and their own culture, but they remain profoundly diseased in the "brave new workplace."[3]

REFERENCES

Banks, David J. 1983. Malay Kinship. Philadelphia, PA: ISHI.

Chew, P. K. 1978. How to Handle Hysterical Factory Workers. Occupational Health and Safety 47(2):50–53.

Colligan, Michael, James Pennebaker, and Lawrence Murphy, eds. 1982. Mass Psychogenic Illness: A Social Psychological Analysis. Hillsdale, NJ: Lawrence Erlbaum Associates.

Crapanzano, Vincent. 1977. Introduction. In Case Studies in Spirit Possession. Vincent Crapanzano and Vivian Garrison, eds., pp. 1–40. New York: John Wiley.

Douglas, Mary. 1966. Purity and Danger: An Analysis of Pollution and Taboo. Harmondsworth, England: Penguin.

FIDA (Federal Industrial Development Authority), Malaysia. 1975. Malaysia: The Solid State for Electronics. Kuala Lumpur.

Foucault, Michel. 1979. Discipline and Punish: The Birth of the Prison. Alan Sheridan, trans. New York: Vintage.

Gramsci, Antonio. 1971. Selections from the Prison Notebooks. Quentin Hoare and Geoffrey Nowell Smith, trans. New York: International Publishing.

Howard, Robert. 1985. Brave New Workplace. New York: Viking Books.

Jamilah Ariffin. 1980. Industrial Development in Peninsular Malaysia and Rural-Urban Migration of Women Workers: Impact and Implications. Jurnal Ekonomi Malaysia 1:41–59.

Lim, Linda. 1978. Women Workers in Multinational Corporations: The Case of the Electronics Industry in Malaysia and Singapore. Ann Arbor: Michigan Occasional Papers in Women's Studies, No. 9.

Lutz, Catherine. 1985. Depression and the Translation of Emotional Worlds. In Culture and Depression. Arthur Kleinman and Byron Good, eds., pp. 63–100. Berkeley: University of California Press.

Parsons, Talcott. 1985. Illness and the Role of the Physician: A Sociological Perspective. In Readings from Talcott Parsons. Peter Hamilton, ed., pp. 145–155. New York: Tavistock.

Sabbah, Fatna A. 1984. Woman in the Muslim Unconscious. Mary Jo Lakeland, trans. New York: Pergamon Press.

Taussig, Michael. 1980. Reification and the Consciousness of the Patient. Social Science and Medicine 14B: 3–13.

NOTES

1. "Free trade zones" are fenced-off areas in which multinational corporations are permitted to locate export-processing industries in the host country. These zones are exempt from many taxation and labor regulations that may apply elsewhere in the economy.

2. Singapore is an island state situated south of Peninsular Malaysia. Although separate countries, they share historical roots and many cultural similarities and interests.

3. This phrase is borrowed from Howard's (1985) study of changing work relations occasioned by the introduction of computer technology into offices and industries.

1 · *Casey High*

WARRIORS, HUNTERS, AND BRUCE LEE

Gendered Agency and the Transformation of Masculinity in Amazonia

DISCUSSION QUESTIONS:

1. What were the dominant gender ideologies for Waorani in the past, especially in terms of masculinity and High's concept of "gendered agency"?
2. How have these gender dynamics shaped and been shaped by their encounters and engagement with mass-media images like Bruce Lee and Rambo, changes in warfare and hunting practices, work in urban areas, and other transformations?
3. How does attention to generational differences contribute to our understandings of gender?

INTRODUCTION

In contrast to studies of gender inequality and hegemonic forms of masculinity, ethnographies of Amazonia tend to emphasize a lack of strict gendered hierarchies and pronounced divisions between women and men. Gender differences appear to be secondary to broader questions of personhood, the body, and relations between human and nonhumans in Amazonia, where "the sexual division of labor is not based on a native discriminatory theory that would rank activities on a scale of prestige according to whether they are performed by men or women" (Descola 2001:97). Here anthropologists challenge the very notion that gendered relations can be characterized as a form of hegemonic masculinity, instead framing sociality in terms of non-dominant male and female agencies located in the body (McCallum 2001).[1] Perhaps as a result, Amazonian gender relations have rarely been described through the lens of

An abridged version of Casey High, 2010. "Warriors, Hunters, and Bruce Lee: Gendered Agency and the Transformation of Amazonian Masculinity." Reproduced by permission of the American Anthropological Association and of the author from *American Ethnologist*, Volume 37, Issue 4, Pages 753–770, November 2010. Not for sale or further reproduction.

a critical feminist anthropology. And yet, Amazonia is probably best known for prominent ethnographies in which specific cultural forms of masculine warriorhood take center stage. In Napoleon Chagnon's famous ethnography on Yanomami warfare, *The Fierce People* (Chagnon 1968), and in more recent work on violence in Amazonia, questions about how Amazonian forms of manhood are envisioned and achieved have yet to be fully addressed in terms of anthropological debates about gender and masculinity.

This chapter explores how masculinity is produced and transformed among the Waorani, an indigenous people of Amazonian Ecuador who have been described as an example of both "egalitarian" gender relations and extreme "tribal warfare." I examine how young men negotiate their position within their own communities and in relation to other Ecuadorians in the context of dramatic changes in warfare and hunting practices, engagement with mass-media imagery, and popular stereotypes about Amazonian people. Waorani masculinities can be best understood not only in terms of Amazonian understandings of gendered agency and the body, but also in the context of urban inter-ethnic relations and the new kinds of manhood that these encounters make imaginable. I raise questions about why, in the context of social and economic transformations, emergent masculinities do not necessarily lead to the forms of gender antagonism often described by gender theorists. How, for example, do Waorani men become "engendered" in the context of multiple and contradictory gender discourses? Understanding these processes requires viewing masculinity not as fixed in time, but as produced and remade in a dynamic process of historical transformation (Hodgson 1999). It is precisely in the context of translocal relations that these transformations come into view.

VICTIMS AND KILLERS: IMAGINING THE WAORANI

The Waorani, who today reside in more than thirty villages in Amazonian Ecuador, are best known for their relative isolation and spear-killing raids until mission settlement in the 1960s. While they continue to be viewed in Ecuador as "wild" forest-dwelling Indians, missionary activity, formal education, oil company employment and inter-ethnic marriages place Waorani in direct relations with national and global processes. As local schools, oil camps and migration to frontier cities become part of everyday life for many young Waorani, non-indigenous people and ideas highlight the tensions and intercultural imagination in contemporary masculinities.

Only decades removed from a series of revenge killings that marked relations between Waorani households with fear and hostility during much of the 20th century, the oral histories of violence that elders tell are a striking feature of social memory (High 2009). They often emphasize the victim's point of view, as being victims or "prey" to violence is central to indigenous conceptualizations of personhood and group identity. Until recently Waorani people envisioned their conflicts with "outsiders" (who they call *kowori*) as a relationship of predation, as elders describe how they once feared that all *kowori* people were cannibals intent on killing and eating them. This is part of a broader Waorani logic that locates personhood in the position of the victim or "prey" to outside aggression (Rival 2002). Even as being a victim or "prey" to *kowori* is a generalized expression of Waorani personhood, there are also important gendered dimensions of indigenous cosmology and social life. While Waorani men and women generally have equal social status, gendered differences emerge in the context of violence, as men are seen as susceptible to being overtaken by the non-human desire to kill. A man who is overcome by anger after the death of a kinsman may himself become a predator, leading him to kill enemies or even members of his own household.

Waorani understandings of gender can also be seen in the distinct roles that constitute marriage, which is seen as a productive relationship between women and men closely linked to having children and the collective consumption of food through mutual support. This ideal is voiced at wedding ceremonies where elders sing to remind the couple of their expected roles and can be seen in couvade practices in which men and women are expected to share dietary restrictions during and after pregnancy (Rival 1998). The general absence of spousal abuse or a visible gender hierarchy, coupled with the flexibility and informality of most gendered activities, are part of a wider egalitarian ethos that pervades much of Waorani social and economic life. Whereas women typically reside in their natal homes after marriage and are associated with processes of regeneration and familiarization, a man ideally distances himself from his natal household, eventually to be incorporated into his wife's group.

Waorani understandings of male and female roles in violence and marriage practices point to a native distinction between masculine and feminine agencies in Amazonia, where women are transformers of forest and garden products in the domestic sphere of consanguinity and men are seen to have a predatory role in hunting, warfare and affinal relations (Seymour-Smith 1991, Taylor 1983, Viveiros de Castro 2001). The notion of gendered agency that I adopt, however, refers not just to the gender identities or actual roles of women and men, but also an indigenous theory that attributes distinct capacities and symbolic values to male and female bodies. Emergent forms of Waorani masculinity reveal how specific embodied processes attributed to men and women enable particular capacities and relations, and how these processes change from one generation to the next.

DURANI BAI: HUNTING, KILLING AND MASCULINITY

Understanding contemporary Waorani gender dynamics requires closer attention to the meanings of the expression *durani bai* ("like the ancient ones"). Statements about certain people, practices and objects being *durani bai* are part of an everyday discourse through which young people comment on and identify themselves with previous generations.

It is not uncommon to hear male teenagers using this term to admire elders and ancestors for their perceived autonomy, strength and ability to kill. They also praise as *durani bai* the few "uncontacted"[2] Waorani groups who refuse village settlement and peaceful relations with outsiders, describing them as fearless and able to kill people by throwing spears from long distances. Blowguns, spears, ceramic pots and other locally produced objects are described as *durani bai*, as are traditional group dances and songs. For young men, to be *durani bai* is to assert one's own abilities and achievements in continuity with previous generations.[3]

One practice that is closely linked to the idea of *durani bai* and is seldom observed today is the whipping (*pangi*) of children with a forest vine after peccary (wild pig) hunts. Men and women recall how they suffered painful lashes from their fathers and grandfathers. Elders explain how this made children strong enough to hunt peccaries themselves one day, suggesting that whipping is seen as a way of transmitting knowledge or ability from one person to another. Being subjected to physical beatings not only enables children to acquire the skills of adults, but also reflects a more general Amazonian conceptualization of the "physical creation of social qualities through bodily states" (Fisher 2001:122). Rather than being a form of punishment to correct misbehavior, it reveals an understanding that bodily experiences constitute the acquisition of specific kinds of knowledge and agency. Being whipped by an elder creates a kind of bodily memory that defines the subjective identity of an individual person in relation to ascending generations. It is a kind of social memory that, instead of uniting them in a generalized image of "Waorani people," differentiates people based on their individual experiences. While visible body ornamentation, such as spears, feathers and body paint, establish a certain kind of "social identity" for Waorani youth in certain public contexts, it is the experience of being whipped that is seen to bring about the transformations by which they become able to carry out the tasks exemplified by elders.

Although Waorani elders say they stopped whipping children during the missionary period, this practice continues to have a presence in how Waorani people envision gendered and generational relations. Parents lament that boys and girls today are weaker than previous generations, who they describe as stronger and better able to withstand long treks in the forest. Elders explain that this deficiency is a consequence of children not having been whipped like they themselves were in past times. While the resulting lack of embodied knowledge is said to have affected boys and girls alike, it appears to have had a disproportionate effect on the skills and abilities of young men, who are said to be unable to hunt peccaries with spears because they were not whipped as children. Given the importance placed on peccary hunting and its association with masculinity, it was difficult for me to see why most people abandoned this practice. When asked why he does not whip his children, one senior man commented that young people today cannot withstand the lashes because they eat too much "foreign food" (*kowori kengi*), referring to the rice, noodles, oatmeal and other foods in school lunches. As a result, their arms and legs are too weak and would break from the whipping.

This idea that people, and particularly men, are becoming physically and culturally deficient as a result of changing ritual practices resonates with other Amazonian contexts where men are seen as unable to "actualize their masculine potential" as a result of not experiencing specific bodily transformations (Conklin 2001:155). The problem is not just that men today are failing to fulfill their expected gender roles, but also that they lack specific capacities attributed to previous generations of men. Whereas younger generations are seen as being less "hard" or "strong" than elders, the few remaining "uncontacted" groups are said to have remarkable physical abilities due to their strict diet of "Waorani" foods and because, in contrast to "civilized" Waorani who became Christian and today live in villages, they continue to whip their children. This understanding of how knowledge and agency depend on specific bodily practices

has important consequences for the ways in which young men today envision their own masculinity. The following life histories of men from different generations point to the generational shifts in Waorani masculinities.

Pego is one of the oldest men in his village, having grown up in the decades prior to the arrival of the first missionaries. He was born in the eastern part of the Waorani territory, where his father was killed in a series of revenge killings with other Waorani groups. Pego, who is known for his humor and exciting hunting stories, describes how he was brutally whipped as a child by his senior kin and as a result became an expert hunter of monkeys, birds, and peccaries at an early age. When he was a young man, he married a woman his kinsmen abducted in a raid against an enemy group. In the late 1960s Pego and his wife joined the missionary settlement, where they lived for several years and had four children. In the late 1970s they joined other families to establish a new village, where they have remained intermittently ever since. Pego has voiced to me his frustrations about the noisiness of village life and often goes on hunting trips alone for days or weeks at a time. He has built a hunting lodge about a day's walk away along the bank of a small river, where he receives visits from his children and many grandchildren during school holidays. He also makes extended visits to his ancestral territory to the east, where he enjoys better hunting, visits with relatives, and food gifts from oil companies operating in the area. An old and gregarious man, Pego complains that young men spend too much time in the cities, where their laziness and diet causes them to become "like outsiders." Yet he also asks his grown children to bring him manufactured goods and medicines when they visit urban areas, and is known to block oil roads on Waorani lands with felled trees, demanding that oil workers provide him food and other gifts. When in the village, Pego and his wife live in the home of his oldest son, Wareka.

Pego's relationship with Wareka is generally relaxed and informal. Although Pego is a major provider of game meat to Wareka's large household, he says he prefers to live away from the village and often leaves without consulting his son's family. Wareka, who is in his late thirties, grew up on the mission and later attended a missionary school in the city. As a boy he enjoyed hunting birds and monkeys but has never killed peccaries or other large game. As a teenager he married a woman from a neighboring indigenous group (Quichua) with whom he today has seven children. While his parents' generation consists primarily of monolingual speakers of the Waorani language, Wareka speaks Waorani, Quichua, and Spanish. After working for several oil companies, he was among a group of young men who established the official Waorani political organization in the early 1990s. As a result, he has lived in the regional capital and has been elected to various community offices in his home village. Wareka speaks of his father and other senior kin with admiration, as people who live "like the ancient ones." He praises his father's ability to live on his own in the forest, never failing to return home with meat. On occasions when Wareka is able to provide large amounts of fish, game meat or goods procured in the city, he often compares this to his father's providing monkeys and other meat for his family and neighbors. He explains that he is able to work hard because, as a child, his father whipped him after peccary hunts. Wareka regularly takes his children to visit his parents' distant hunting lodge, where his father joins the young men on fishing trips and enjoys entertaining the children with his storytelling in the evenings.

Dabo, who is twenty-two and unmarried, grew up in the largest Waorani village and is the third oldest of nine siblings. His father grew up on the mission in the 1960s and is today one of the few remaining Waorani active in the local evangelical church. Dabo was among the first Waorani to graduate from the new village high school, speaks Spanish fairly well, and often goes by the name Juan. He is a skilled fisherman and also enjoys dancing to Ecuadorian pop music. Since graduating, Dabo has worked on temporary contracts to clear roads for oil companies. He says that the work, in addition to providing wages, allows him to visit friends in other parts of the Waorani reserve. Dabo also makes frequent visits to the regional capital where he sees relatives, shops for clothes, and occasionally joins friends at local bars and dance clubs. Despite his experience in the city, he says he is uninterested in becoming involved in the Waorani political organization and instead aspires to study business or tourism at a university in the capital. When in his home village he stays with his parents and younger siblings, though he is frequently away for extended periods. Dabo described his father to me as a skilled hunter who, like his ancestors, is able to kill monkeys, peccaries, and other large game. He seldom accompanies his father on hunting trips but occasionally joins him on group peccary hunts near the village, despite never having killed large game himself. At times Dabo insists that he will someday build a longhouse deep in the forest, where he and his older brother will live and hunt "like the ancient ones." At other times he speaks of his desire to become an oil company truck driver and to travel abroad.

The contrasting life experiences of these three men illustrate how the roles and expectations of Waorani men have changed considerably from one generation to the next. While each grew up in different historical contexts, they emphasize a common ideal of autonomy and providing game meat associated with being "*durani bai*." Peccary hunting is today emblematic of a masculinity idealized by young men despite the fact that few have themselves speared peccaries. They show great interest in these hunts and tend to know who has killed a peccary and who has not, much like they know who has killed a human enemy. Whereas most living male elders and ancestors are known to have killed people in warfare, and many of the men who grew up at the mission settlement in the 1960s have speared peccaries (and not people), few young men today have killed animals or people with spears. For teenage and young adult men whose parents converted to Christianity and all but ended the revenge-killing vendettas of preceding generations, peccary hunting has come to be seen as quintessentially *durani bai* practice through which they claim a certain connection with "the ancient ones." In this way, they associate themselves with the assumed strength, endurance and knowledge of older men, even if they admit to not having carried out a number of *durani bai* practices themselves.

VIOLENT IMAGERY AND MASCULINE FANTASY

Of course, peccary hunting and warfare are not the only measure of manhood. To understand the seemingly contradictory ways in which Waorani masculinities are produced requires consideration of the experiences of young men in broader political, economic and intercultural contexts. This is because they spend an increasing amount of time in Ecuador's frontier cities and because mass-media sources are becoming more readily available within Waorani communities. All of this contributes to new masculine fantasies in which Waorani men draw on both popular film imagery and notions of ancestral continuity.

The characters young people see in popular Hollywood films are among the diverse images and practices they describe as *durani bai*. Films have become more accessible in the past decade with the arrival of televisions and video players in Waorani communities, where violent action-adventure movies attract large audiences to the few homes equipped with electric generators. As a result, many young Waorani are as likely as North Americans to be familiar with actors such as Jean-Claude Van Damme, Sylvester Stallone and Jackie Chan.[4] In the early 2000s *Rambo II* was a popular movie among young Waorani men, who were fascinated by imagery of violence in film. After viewing scenes of Rambo killing people in the forests of Southeast Asia, they compared his ability to trick and kill enemies from hidden positions to their own ancestors. While watching a Rambo film, a male teenager explained to me that, upon finishing his studies at the village school, he planned to move to a remote part of the Waorani territory where, like his ancestors and Rambo, he would live "free"

in the forest. Statements like these often emphasized an ideal of independence, as well as a desire to live in traditional longhouses and hunt game with spears and blowguns used by elders.

Bruce Lee and the martial arts are another popular image, particularly for male teenage students. At the time of my fieldwork, they hung Bruce Lee posters and painted Chinese calligraphy copied from the packages of videos onto the inner walls of the school boarding house. Martial arts fighting became so popular that the students' residence was transformed into a martial arts clubhouse. In the household where I lived, a teenager decorated the wall with posters of Bruce Lee, which he placed next to a small wooden spear and a feathered crown. He described these images as "*durani bai*" and explained that his ancestors refused to become "civilized" and live in villages like the Waorani today. He said that, like Bruce Lee, they defended themselves fearlessly against their enemies. Without assuming that young men see in Rambo or Bruce Lee practices that they envision carrying out themselves, the imagery in these films resonates with capacities that young people ascribe to previous generations of men. Much like their parents killing peccaries and their ancestors killing enemies, they represent a form of manhood characterized by autonomy and strength in the face of physical danger.

Whereas male youth elsewhere in the world have seen images like Rambo as "tools for the active construction of their own modernity" to be emulated in actual warfare (Richards 1996:105), young Waorani men emphasize the continuities between Rambo and an idealized form of masculinity associated with their ancestors. This emphasis on generational continuity, however, is itself a product of historical transformation. In various contexts colonialism, missionaries and tourism campaigns have all had a role in the production of masculinities that emphasize "warriorhood" (Hodgson 1999). Young Waorani men, who interact with mestizo Ecuadorians on a regular basis, draw in part on popular imagery of "Amazonian warriors" when they compare themselves to Rambo. Violence in film is attractive to them because it constitutes what gender theorists have described as a "fantasy" of masculine power. The notion of fantasy is useful here in referring to the sense of what kind of person an individual aspires to be and how he or she wants to be seen by others (Moore 1994:66). While voicing plans to engage in specific acts of violence is rare in Waorani communities, Bruce Lee and Rambo embody a fantasy of masculine power that young men both idealize and fail to demonstrate in everyday life. In this context of shifting male roles, masculinity is produced out of multiple, co-existent discourses and images that speak to the widening gap between how gender is constructed culturally and how it is lived in the present.

Just as the imagery of violence that attracts young men differs from the emphasis on victimhood in narratives told by elders, the expression *durani bai* has different connotations for women and men. While for young men, masculinity is associated with the perceived strength, violence and autonomy of their ancestors, women associate themselves more closely with the creation of interiority out of differences. Women at times also make comparisons between violent movie characters and their ancestors, but are less inclined to praise imagery of Rambo and Bruce Lee. This is not because older generations or the past in general are associated exclusively with male practices. While killing people and peccaries is an unambiguous expression of masculine agency, other practices described as *durani bai*, such as the collective consumption of plentiful food and generously hosting visitors, are associated with both men and women.

The ability to provide for visitors in the home and at village-wide feasts, though less exclusively gendered than warfare and hunting, is more closely linked to female agency. The production of manioc beer—a key part of the Waorani diet and an expected feature of visits between households—is clearly demarcated as the realm of women. The transformational power of manioc beer is evident in the Waorani notion that its repeated consumption over time leads to household members sharing a single body. Since the making and serving of manioc beer is one of the few exclusively female activities, women have a special part in the creation of internal consanguinity, just as masculinity is more closely associated with relations of exteriority in which men become detached from the social body, such as warfare and marriage (Rival 2005). Despite the contrasting capacities associated with women and men, adults emphasize the complementarity of male and female activities in marital relations that allow for the production of children and "living well."

Alongside accounts of past violence, the oral histories of Waorani men and women also reach back nostalgically to a past when households invited one another to drink manioc beer together. These events continue today in festivals sponsored by schools or entire villages. In addition to making and serving manioc beer at these events, women sing songs that welcome visitors and emphasize alliance and friendship between the hosts and visiting groups. Whether through providing manioc beer and singing songs for visitors or familiarizing in-marrying husbands into their natal households, women's agency is characterized by the ability to constitute the household group by incorporating and transforming exteriority into interiority. This understanding of gender and agency support the broader assertion from masculinity studies that manhood should be considered in terms of relations between women and men (Brandes 1980; Gutmann 1996). However, rather than asserting masculinity and femininity as gendered oppositions, Waorani men express their gendered agency in relation to previous generations and *kowori* people and images. It is perhaps for this reason that emerging masculinities are not predicated on gendered antagonisms and seldom lead to male violence against women.

URBAN MASCULINITY: GENDER IN CRISIS?

As elsewhere, the gendered experiences of men and women in Amazonia have changed dramatically as indigenous people become increasingly involved in wage labor and the market economy. In these contexts emerging idioms of "modernity" and aspirations to acquire commodities often contribute significantly to gender antagonism and inequality. As men earn cash and prestige through wage labor and urban political leadership, women's roles in agriculture and domestic life are often devalued in relation to the cash income of men. These changes reveal that femininities and masculinities are never fixed, but instead "formed and reformed through interactions with broader historical processes and events" (Hodgson 1999:125).

The experiences of Waorani men have changed considerably in the past few decades, even beyond the transition from warfare to relative peace. Many young men leave their communities to work temporarily for oil companies or at the Waorani political organization in the regional capital. As their expected roles outside the home have transformed from that of killers and hunters to students, oil workers and politicians within just a couple of generations, it appears that the lives of men have changed to a greater degree than those of women. The emphasis many Waorani place today on living in a "community" conveys a stark contrast to stories about young men in the past being trained in spear-killing.

Although women's lives have also changed considerably in the past 50 years, there are few gendered practices associated with previous generations that Waorani women are today unable to carry out. The decrease in inter-group violence has probably expanded the possibilities for feminine agency as a broader range of outsiders are incorporated more readily into kinship relations and household visits in larger villages. While older women lament the difficulty of producing manioc and other garden foods in past times when revenge-killings demanded constant relocation, younger adult women often proudly describe how they serve plentiful amounts of manioc beer to their guests. Even if men's involvement in the wider national economy and indigenous politics has increased women's domestic labor burden, it can equally be said that Waorani men are less successful than women in terms of fulfilling their expected gender roles.

With the growing expectation that boys should attend school, learn Spanish and eventually work for wages, oil development and indigenous political activism have become part of a new masculine ideal for young men. While some men achieve a degree of prestige in these contexts, their roles have changed in ways that reveal their diminishing ability to achieve particular forms of masculinity associated with previous generations. Insofar as women's agency is associated with the creation and expansion of the group, women have become increasingly successful in their expected gendered roles in the decades since mission settlement— a period marked by wider inter-group alliances and rapid population growth.[5] Men, however, even when successful in urban politics and wage labor, are compared in various ways to past generations of killers and successful hunters. Waorani political leaders, who are almost exclusively young men, face criticism from their kin when they fail to satisfy the expectation that they generously provide large amounts of goods obtained from external sources. They are often contrasted to elders and ancestors who are said to have shared game meat for their household and neighbors and come to be seen by their peers as becoming more like "outsiders".

Young men respond to this situation in a number of ways. For the initial generation of Waorani political leaders based in the regional capital, one strategy has been to negotiate contracts with oil companies. One man in his late 20s, who worked at the Waorani political office for several years, explained to me the difficulties of reconciling urban life with the expectations he faces in his home village. He complained that, in contrast to his home community, he needs money to live in the city. He lamented that his low wages make it impossible for him to provide the wealth of manufactured goods that his kin have come to expect of him. Despite having participated in a number of protests against oil development on indigenous lands, he proudly explained to me his role in signing an agreement with an oil company that he hoped would provide school and health supplies to his home community.

While men come to be measured increasingly in terms of the cash and commodity goods they provide for their families through wage labor, this process has not led to the gender antagonism anticipated by theorists who envision an emerging global hegemonic masculinity based on male domination. Spousal abuse remains extremely rare and is criticized by Waorani as a *kowori* practice. Women are not expected to be subordinate to their husbands, nor has female sexuality become commodified or noticeably more restricted. Even as it is generally young men who are elected to leadership positions within the official Waorani political office, women continue to have an active role in voicing their opinions and influencing decisions in local political debates. Conflicts in Waorani communities are very rarely voiced in terms of gender oppositions. Like men, women complain that indigenous leaders are selfish not because they are men, but because they fail to demonstrate the generosity expected of both men and women.

Urban indigenous politics are in part an extension of the Waorani logic that, just as female agency is associated with creating sociality within Waorani communities, relations with "outsiders" involve a specifically masculine form of agency.[6] Rather than having mutually antagonistic gendered roles in their engagement with broader political and economic processes, men and women demonstrate distinct capacities within indigenous Amazonian notions of gendered agency. In the context of recent social transformations, crisis and antagonism are instead expressed primarily in terms of generational differences and inter-ethnic relations that put the masculinity of young men in question. This is not to say that Waorani gender relations are entirely equal, harmonious or unchanging. As we have seen, the roles of men have changed considerably in recent decades, and it remains to be seen whether the forms of manhood produced in ever-expanding Waorani villages and in urban inter-ethnic contexts will lead to a more pronounced gender hierarchy in the future.

Young Waorani men inhabit a world of multiple, contradictory and constantly shifting masculinities (Cornwall and Lindisfarne 1994). They increasingly find themselves in urban contexts where, in the eyes of other Ecuadorians, they embody a specific image of warriorhood. Although they are unable to demonstrate many local *durani bai* practices, in the city these men sometimes embrace their allocated position as "wild Amazonian warriors" in popular imagination. Just as they celebrate stories about peccary hunting, images of Rambo and the idea of superhuman "uncontacted" relatives living "free" in the forest, performing as warriors in front of tourists confers a form of masculinity that is elusive in the villages where they grow up. In these urban settings, the Amazonian warrior becomes yet another element of masculine fantasy for young men who themselves describe their dress and performances as being "like the ancient ones."

Indigenous Amazonian notions of gendered agency are today only part of the lived experiences of Waorani people, especially for men who stay in the regional capital for months or years at a time. Some of them befriend mestizo Ecuadorians and join them in drinking sessions and the male sexual banter familiar to studies of masculinity elsewhere in Latin America. Young Waorani men say that drinking at bars is an important part of being "*amigos*" (friends) with mestizos and other Waorani men in the city, such that urban inter-ethnic relations have become part of "a new collective life of male fraternity" (Knauft 1997:241). These friendships, coupled with popular stereotypes about Waorani violence, have placed young men at the crossroads of contradictory forms of masculinity. Even as leaving one's household was part of becoming a man in previous generations, young Waorani men now find themselves in a position where they must negotiate the demands of their home communities and the expectations of urban Ecuadorian society.

Recent social transformations reveal the tensions and contradictions between indigenous and popular Ecuadorian measures of masculinity. Whereas manhood in Waorani communities is measured in terms of demonstrating autonomy, providing abundantly for one's family and engaging in productive relations with outsiders, urban mestizo masculinity tends to emphasize sexuality, gender hierarchy and solidarity between men through the collective consumption of alcohol. Without attempting to draw an all-encompassing contrast between "egalitarian" Waorani and "patriarchal" mestizos, it is clear that Waorani men are measured differently in urban areas than in their home communities. Increasingly, they fail to satisfy the expectations of manhood in both. While they lack the "hard" bodies that made older men able to hunt with spears, they are also seen as deficient in key aspects of mestizo masculinity. Waorani political leaders, who come from villages where alcohol has only recently become available, are said to be unable to handle social drinking, often ending up belligerently drunk on the streets at night. Even as Waorani folklore performances conform to popular stereotypes, these men often fail to fulfill the expectations of masculinity on the streets of the regional capital, where they are as likely to be accused by mestizos of "losing their culture" when they drink as they are of being anti-social if they don't.

CONCLUSIONS

Anthropological studies of masculinity often evoke the challenges men face when their identities and practices are "out of synch with those regarded as 'traditional'" (Viveros Vigoya 2004:28). In contrast to questions of identity and sexual antagonism that have preoccupied much writing about gender, young Waorani men are involved in a struggle to reconcile urban intercultural relations with idealized forms of manhood associated with previous generations. In specific contexts, such as the village martial arts club and urban "warrior" performances, they are able to emulate the practices they attribute to elders and "the ancient ones." And yet, changing local expectations and new forms of inter-ethnic male fraternity have transformed the ways in which masculine agency is produced and performed. In situations like these, masculine fantasies of power draw simultaneously on multiple gender discourses rooted in indigenous Amazonian

understandings of gendered agency, local oral histories of violence, and global media.

Even as would-be warriors and peccary hunters are today becoming oil workers and urban political leaders, these changes have not led to widespread violence and gender antagonism between men and women. Rather than being fixed in time or entirely egalitarian, Waorani gender dynamics reflect Amazonian understandings of gender and agency that associate women more closely with interiority and men with exteriority. While previous studies of "men as men" demonstrate that masculinity is often constructed and performed in opposition to women, Waorani forms of masculinity are seldom constructed explicitly against or even in reference to femininity. Since masculinities are always a product of historical transformations, it remains to be seen whether intercultural relations and urban migration will lead to more hierarchical gender relations in the future. For Waorani men today, memories of ancestral warriorhood, mestizo Ecuadorians and Bruce Lee are all part of the generational and intercultural relations through which they express their own ways of being men.

BIBLIOGRAPHY

Brandes, Stanley. 1980. *Metaphors of Masculinity: Sex and Status in Andalusian Folklore*. Philadelphia: University of Pennsylvania Press.

Cabodevilla, Miguel Angel. 1999. *Los Huaorani en la Historia del Oriente*. Quito: CICAME.

Chagnon, Napoleon. 1968. *Yanomamö: The Fierce People*. New York: Holt, Rinehart and Winston.

Conklin, Beth. 2001. Women's Blood, Warrior's Blood, and the Conquest of Vitality in Amazonia. In *Gender in Amazonia and Melanesia*. Thomas Gregor and Donald Tuzin (eds.), 141–174. Berkeley: University of California Press.

Cornwall, Andrea and Nancy Lindisfarne 1994. Dislocating Masculinity: Gender, Power and Anthropology. In *Dislocating Masculinity: Comparative Ethnographies*. Andrea Cornwall and Nancy Lindisfarne (eds.), 11–47. London: Routledge.

Descola, Philippe. 2001. The Genres of Gender: Local Models and Global Paradigms in the Comparison of

Amazonia and Melanesia. In *Gender in Amazonia and Melanesia*. Thomas Gregor and Donald Tuzin (eds.), 91–114. Berkeley: University of California Press.

Fisher, William. 2001. Age-Based Genders among the Kayapo. In *Gender in Amazonia and Melanesia*. Thomas Gregor and Donald Tuzin (eds.), 115–140. Berkeley: University of California Press.

Gutmann, Matthew C. 1996. *The Meanings of Macho: Being a Man in Mexico City*. Berkeley: University of California Press.

High, Casey. 2009. Remembering the Auca: Violence and Generational Memory in Amazonian Ecuador. *Journal of the Royal Anthropological Institute* (N.S.) 15: 719–736.

———. 2013. Lost and Found: Contesting isolation and cultivating contact in Amazonian Ecuador. *Hau: Journal of Ethnographic Theory* 3(3): 195–221.

Hodgson, Dorothy L. 1999. "Once Intrepid Warriors": Modernity and the Production of Maasai Masculinities. *Ethnology* 38(2): 121–150.

Knauft, Bruce. 1997. Gender Identity, Political Economy and Modernity in Melanesia and Amazonia. *Journal of the Royal Anthropological Institute* 3(2): 233–259.

McCallum, Cecilia. 2001 *Gender and Sociality in Amazonia: How Real People Are Made*. Oxford: Berg.

Moore, Henrietta L. 1994. *A Passion for Difference: Essays in Anthropology and Gender*. Bloomington: Indiana University Press.

Richards, Paul. 1996. *Fighting for the Rainforest: War, Youth & Resources in Sierra Leone*. Oxford: The International African Institute and James Currey.

Rival, Laura. 1998. Androgenous Parents and Guest Children: The Huaorani Couvade. *Man, Journal of the Royal Anthropological Institute* (N.S.) 4: 619–642.

———. 2002. *Trekking Through History: The Huaorani of Amazonian Ecuador*. New York: Columbia University Press.

———. 2005. The Attachment of the Soul to the Body among the Huaorani of Amazonian Ecuador. *Ethnos* 70(3): 285–310.

Seymour-Smith, Charlotte. 1991. Women Have No Affines and Men No Kin: The Politics of the Jivaroan Gender Relation. *Man* (N.S.) 26(4): 629–649.

Taylor, Ann Christine. 1983. The Marriage Alliance and its Structural Variations among Jivaroan Societies. *Social Science Information* 22(3): 331–353.

Viveiros de Castro, Eduardo. 2001. GUT Feelings about Amazonia: Potential Affinity and the Construction of Sociality. In *Beyond the Visible and the Material: The Amerindianization of Society in the Work of Peter Rivière*. Laura Rival and Neil Whitehead (eds.), 19–44. Oxford: Oxford University Press.

Viveros Vigoya, Mara. 2004. Contemporary Latin American Perspectives on Masculinity. In *Changing Men and Masculinities in Latin America*. Matthew Gutmann (ed.), 27–60. Durham: Duke University Press.

Yost, James. 1981. Twenty Years of Contact: The Mechanisms of Change in Wao (Auca) Culture. In *Cultural Transformations and Ethnicity in Modern Ecuador*. Norman Whitten (ed.), 677–704. Urbana: University of Illinois Press.

NOTES

1. Since indigenous cosmology posits a "unitary human identity" rather than "multiple gender identities inferred from a set of distinct subject positions" (McCallum 2001:165), it appears that social life in Amazonia is not as much about producing women and men as it is about producing bodies and persons.

2. The term "uncontacted" refers to the few mobile groups living in the Waorani reserve who refuse village settlement or contact with outsiders (Cabodevilla 1999, High 2013).

3. My discussion of "young men" refers to a broad category of Waorani males, including teenage students at village schools, as well as married and unmarried men in their mid to late twenties. What is central to this categorization is not exact age or marital status, but the specific generational experiences of men who are compared to the hunting and warfare practices of their elders.

4. Most of these English language films are either dubbed in Spanish or have Spanish subtitles.

5. The total Waorani population has increased from approximately 500 in the 1960s (Yost 1981) to around 2500 today.

6. This is not to dismiss the experiences of Waorani women outside of their home communities. Since the time of my primary fieldwork (2002–2004), the Waorani Women's Organization (AMWAE) has been established in the regional capital, bringing together women to organize the production and sale of Waorani handicrafts in urban areas and abroad.

2 • *Jennifer Johnson-Hanks*

WOMEN ON THE MARKET
Modernity, Marriage, and the Internet in Cameroon

DISCUSSION QUESTIONS

1. Why are women in Cameroon no longer interested in marrying Cameroonian men?
2. What do these women imagine as the ideal characteristics of European men?
3. How has access to the Internet facilitated these new relationships?
4. How do changing gendered ideas and ideals of "love," "honor," "respect," and "marriage" contribute to these dynamics?

Since 1998, thousands of young Cameroonian women have sought European husbands on the Internet. They are not alone: their photographs and self-descriptions appear along those of women from Asia, Eastern Europe, and Latin America. However, their Internet co-presence does not imply a shared construal of romance, marriage, or the Internet itself. Instead, this paper argues that the meaning and motivation of email marriage in the Cameroonian capital Yaoundé derives more from local history than from sexual geopolitics. Cameroonian women are seeking foreign husbands to fulfill local conceptions of proper marriage.

In southern Cameroon, women's respectability has long depended on marriage, but marriage is increasingly a problem. Marriage rates have fallen; the rituals marking the transition to marriage have been altered and reordered; women's expectations of marriage have risen at the same time that men's ability to fulfill even the older, lesser expectations

have declined. And yet, marriage retains its symbolic centrality, and marriage to a European man has come to be viewed by many women as a viable modern substitute—perhaps even the best substitute—for traditional bridewealth marriage. Focusing on the life experiences of a group of young, moderately educated women in Yaoundé, Cameroon, this paper examines the content and reciprocal consequences of marriage and "modernity" through the lens of Beti cultural history.[1]

TRUE MEN AND MODERN HONOR

Young African girl with a very cool nature, 25 years, single without children, nice and kind, of profession: secretary, seeking a serious man of any continent, French or foreign, to establish a loving relationship in view of marriage. If you are not serious, stay away. Thank you.

— "Martine" from Yaoundé, on coeuracoeur.com

An abridged version of Jennifer Johnson-Hanks, 2007. "Women on the Market: Marriage, Consumption and the Internet in Urban Cameroon." Reproduced by permission of the American Anthropological Association and of the author from *American Ethnologist*, Volume 34, Issue 4, Pages 642–658, November 2007. Not for sale or further reproduction.

When certain young women in Yaoundé assert that they must now look abroad to find husbands who are "serious," they are—perhaps paradoxically—drawing on a set of assumptions about marriage, men, and honor that have long local histories. The figure of *l'homme serieux*—the dignified man, honest, calm, and capable—evokes the Beti *mfan mot* or "true man" of a previous era. Prior to the institutionalization of German colonial authority around 1900, there were no political authorities higher than the extended household; as head of that household, the *mfan mot* was not only autonomous, but literally lord of his wives and children.[2] His most important possession was his honor, both pecuniary and as set of embodied dispositions that I have called "self-dominion" (Johnson-Hanks 2006). A threat to his autonomy was taken as an assault on his honor: as Largeau argued over a century ago, "a self-respecting Pahouin [Beti man] does not take orders from anyone" (1901:22). It is important to note here that honor was an element of *male* Beti adulthood, consisting of the right to respect, autonomy, and privacy accorded to the *mfan mot*, and in principle inaccessible to women. In fact, traditional honorability was so strongly male gendered that it entailed a husband's dominion over his wives (Laburthe-Tolra 1981:356). Women could not be said to have honor; Vincent (1976) describes that in their subordination to men, wives were "like sheep."

Over the last century, Beti families have been transformed through the expansion of school, market, church and state. Schemas of honor did not fit these new social conditions, and so, honor stretched. In particular, it stretched to include women. As they became converts, teachers, nurses, and nuns—autonomous actors with self-dominion—women increasingly came to be seen as potential bearers of honor. Because of its relation to the modern institutions of Christianity and formal education, the honor of women is necessarily a modern one, and one that differs somewhat from that of men; nonetheless, it also draws heavily on the honor of the *mfan mot*. Both women's modern honor and the traditional honor of men include

pecuniary and dispositional aspects. With the term "pecuniary," I follow Veblen in referring to the elements of honor related to the control of wealth. In the case of the *mfan mot*, the usage follows Veblen almost exactly: an honorable man achieved his position in part through control over land, women, and children (Veblen 1899:69). Honorable dispositions focused on dominion or control, including self-control and control over others (Laburthe-Tolra 1981:305; Tessman 1913, vol. 2: 241–242).

In the modern honor of women, the relationship between the embodied and pecuniary elements of honor has changed. According to my interlocutors, an honorable woman in contemporary Yaoundé is discreet, sexually restrained, educated, and financially successful. She is proud of herself and her achievements, and respects herself. She is poised, calm, and serious. Perhaps most importantly, she is master of herself—of her desires, gestures, and even emotions. That is, in contrast to many well-known honor systems, a Cameroonian woman's honor is not merely a reflection of that of her husband or lineage, but is something that she claims herself. The self-mastery is achieved through rigorous discipline, especially the disciplines associated with schooling and Catholicism. Waking up at three in the morning to pray and then study for the public exams is not only a method for achieving a good grade, but is also a practice of instilling in the self a set of proper dispositions. Sexuality and sexual self-mastery play important roles in claims to honor; however, it is critical to point out from the beginning that complete sexual abstinence and bridal virginity are not the measure, as they are in the Mediterranean, the Arab world, or in East Africa. Rather, it is wisely managed restraint, good judgment, and self-dominion that matter (Alexandre and Binet 1958:66; Laburthe-Tolra 1981:124).

It is important here to note that the honor of both men and women is related to control over women, but that there is a fundamental difference between the objects of dominion in the two cases. A man must control women and children, but any woman or children will do. For a woman, by contrast, it is her mastery of *herself*—of her *own* desires, reproduction, aspirations, timing, and so forth, that is central to her honorable status.

Like traditional men's honor, the modern honor of women is also pecuniary. As Cole (2004:579) so expertly analyses for the *Jeunes* in Tamatave, here "consumption of consumer goods marks status quite explicitly." As a first approximation, we can think of the social stature that young Beti women ascribe to the woman who earns her own money through clean work, dresses well and in a French style, and is eventually married with a lavish bridewealth or to a European man through Veblen's framework of conspicuous consumption. However, Veblen considers honor as an attribute *only* of men. When women are adorned in luxurious clothing, he argues that they serve only as stand-in consumers for their husbands (1899:171). This aspect of the model is not incidental: men's control over women and women's labor is the basis of class inequality for Veblen, who therefore offers no way to theorize women's financial success or consumption as markers of their *own* honor.

The pecuniary honor of Cameroonian women is contradictory. On the one hand, young women in Yaoundé seek to earn their own money and to be financially independent of their husbands and boyfriends. Similar to the honor of men, the honor of Beti women rests partially on the sovereignty of an independent individual. On the other hand, an honorable woman is elegant and attractive, and fulfills the social expectation that she will be married to a wealthy and generous man. Husbands and boyfriends should buy her clothes, beauty products and—later on—baby supplies. A Beti woman who lacks this care loses the respect of others. Almost every woman I knew in Cameroon in 1998 expressed a commitment to both aspects of modern honor, sometimes in the same conversation. Talking about the respect that accrues to a woman who maintains herself without economic assistance from a man, women said things like:

> I think that it is a question of self-respect first of all [that distinguishes certain women] . . . They are very proud of themselves. They are honorable (*digne*).

And so, because they are proud, they are not dependent. They work, and they love to be financially independent from their husbands.

Or similarly:

> I am going to say how Cameroonians interpret this respectability in women. . . . I think that when a woman is honorable (*digne*) it means first that she restrains her sexual activity, and second that she can earn a living all alone, without waiting for the help of a man.

But just as often, the same women would talk about the honor of being in the care of a man, who gives lavishly on your behalf, particularly at the bridewealth ceremony, who supports you financially and who insures that everyone knows whose wife you are:

> For me, a respectable woman is one who keeps her image clean. When she passes, you know that this person here has to be respected. And then it is good to be [married and therefore] called Madame Such and Such. When someone says, "Here is Madame Such and Such who is passing" you have weight. But when you are unmarried, someone looks and calls you "Miss." Even if you are 50 years old, they can't call you Madame. They call you Madame, but you live with whom? They are going to say Madame Who?

And again:

> A woman who hasn't had bridewealth paid for her in her village, her mother is not respected. Her relatives are not respected. She herself is not happy. So bridewealth, when someone pays bridewealth for a girl before marriage, it is a great joy for the family.

The schemas through which contemporary Cameroonian women think about marriage are largely transposed out of traditional bridewealth marriage, in which men's families give elaborate and costly gifts to the families of the women who will be their brides. To marry correctly, a man must build a house and clear virgin forest to make a field (*esep*) in which to grow pumpkin (*ngwan*) that his wife will prepare into a refined dish called *nam ngwan*. *Nam ngwan* symbolizes conventional bridewealth marriage. Not only is it extremely labor intensive, and sensitive to the skill of the cook, but it also makes explicit the partnership of the man and the woman. For *nam ngwan* to be successful, the labors of the man and woman have to be coordinated and reciprocal: the man clears the field and "plants the seed" while the woman gestates and cooks.

Beti women's honor is internally contradictory: women must be both independent and dependent. And both parts of this contradiction resonate in historical echo chambers—the former as the honor of the *mfan mot*, the latter as the lesser distinction of the proper wife in a bridewealth marriage. When young, educated Beti women say that they hope for a "modern" marriage—by which they mean a marriage that is monogamous, based on love, and eased by financial security—they hope to square the circle of this contradiction. But in addition to the attractions that modern marriage may have, many women argue that modern marriage is the *only* option now, because a proper bridewealth marriage is no longer possible, as the gendered reciprocity based in *esep* and *nam ngwan* has been lost. It is not that young women in Yaoundé want to marry farmers—for the most part they do not—but rather that the gendered exchanges of bridewealth provided an ethical framework for marriage that has not been fully replaced.

WHAT MAKES A GOOD HUSBAND?

My name is Moline and I am 24 years old. . . . I have a modern allure and smile often. Many things interest me: music and reading. I would like to meet someone active. My great desire is to discover France. . . . My skin is the color of chocolate. I speak French fluently. I read it. I write it. I am looking for a man 26 to 45 years old, sincere and honest, elegant and sweet. I like romantic walks and I love family.

— "Moline" from Cameroon, on providence.com

What kind of men do these young women hope to marry? The ideal characteristics for prospective husbands are hybrid, incorporating both dispositional and economic considerations, and both long-standing local and modern elements. Most critically, men should be prosperous, generous, and love their wives sincerely. Prosperity is often equated with global sophistication, modern style and sensibilities. For example, one young woman explained that:

I love [my boyfriend] . . . because he presents himself in front of me like the man I have always dreamed of. Because when I was a little girl I always imagined an ideal boy in my head. I saw him as black, tall, elegant, clean, and intelligent. He is someone who knows how to dress. . . . He knows how to express himself in French, and is not too hypocritical.

Another woman similarly emphasized that fluency in the global language of French made a man attractive, equating men who speak Ewondo with effeminate men, and—by implication—with men bewitched with *tobassi* (lit. "Sit down!", a form of witchcraft whereby a man is made subordinate to a woman):

For me, it is important that he not be too effeminate because I do not like effeminate boys . . . I mean when he has the style of a girl, or when he only speaks Ewondo [instead of French]. And so he must be tall, and not too ugly, but also not too handsome. Because when a man is too handsome it leans toward danger.

The danger lies in the likelihood that the man would not be faithful: a too handsome man could easily entice other women. Men's infidelity is a constant source of concern for young women in Yaoundé, who say that Cameroonian men cannot—or will not—be faithful. Again and again, Beti women whether looking for European husbands on the Internet or married to Beti men explained to me that male infidelity is common, or even inevitable. That does not mean, however, that they do not hope for faithful husbands. To the contrary, fidelity, trust, and "true, true love" vie with economic prosperity as the most important attributes that my informants hoped for in men. For example, one young woman answered my question regarding potential husbands by saying:

> I would like to marry a man who doesn't love other women too much. But that is impossible here in our country. When you have a husband here, you cannot tell yourself that you are the only one. There were others before you, and after you, there will be others still.

Fidelity and generosity come together in many women's explanations of the kind of men they would hope to marry. A man will be trustworthy if, first of all, he truly loves you:

> It is necessary first of all that he loves me as I am. . . . He cannot be the kind of person that is concerned with himself but not with his wife and his children. [He should be] someone who is generous, and someone who perhaps believes, who is a Christian.

In contemporary Cameroon, Christianity is explicitly a sign of the modern and the global, and Christian marriage is assumed to include both the monogamy and interdependence of "modern" marriage. Another high school student had very similar hopes:

> Me, I would like to marry someone I love, first of all. And someone in whom I can find trust. If I find that he could be a good father for my children, and a good husband as well, and also that he contributes for his own family, good. I'll know that he will do the same for me and my children.

Grounded in the logic of bridewealth, a man's commitment to a relationship is often measured in the frequency and extravagance of his gifts. A man who does not give clothes, pocket-money or presents to his female partner thereby indicates that his intentions are not "serious," and that the relationship is unlikely to lead to marriage. If she says with him, it is to the detriment of her own honor.

For 20 years, Cameroon was in economic crisis. Women's expectations of men as marital partners thus rose at the same time as men's ability to meet them declined. Through this period, too, age-specific marriage rates in southern Cameroon fell markedly: data from the Demographic and Health Surveys show that whereas 75% of women born 1940–1944 had married by age 18, only 45% of those born 35 years later had done so.[3] Marriage is postponed more than foregone, and this postponement generally takes the form of waiting to "observe" a boyfriend, to be absolutely certain that he is the right one. It is not union formation, or even cohabitation, that is being postponed, but rather formal marriage. One young woman who had been living with her boyfriend for over a year explained that she was still unsure whether marriage was in their future:

> We tell ourselves that this might [lead to] marriage . . . But you have to first stay together a long time to know his true comportment, to see what he likes and what he doesn't like in order to avoid problems. Because when you realize that he has some faults, you can say no. You can leave. If you don't have children, you are free. . . . But sometimes you can do five years and you do not see too many black spots; so you say "good." If he proposes marriage, you accept.

Why is it so important to know that the man you are choosing is the right one? First because of the rising importance of love in marriage. Surely women in the past loved their husbands and expected to be loved by them; however, love—and particularly fidelity as a sign of love—has taken on new centrality in women's representations of a good marriage. This sentimentalization of marriage has numerous foreign sources, including both *Beverly Hills 90210* and Bible stories. In August of 1996, a priest lamented in his sermon that the men of today no longer love their wives unconditionally as Joseph loved Mary. The mostly female congregation nodded their assent.

But the importance of long observation also comes from the fact that marriage continues to serve a key arena of women's honor. Although many elements of marital honor have been transposed, a durable marriage to the right man remains central. In some ways, it might be argued, marriage is more important now than ever before. Under the traditional marriage system, Beti women were "attributed, from the outset, subordinate and instrumental roles" (Houseman 1988:52). Today, by contrast, women themselves may receive respect for the kinds of modern consumption that accompany a good marriage. That is, marriage rates are declining not because marriage is becoming irrelevant, or because it is less valued than in the past, but rather paradoxically *because* its character matters so deeply for women's status.

INTERNET ROMANCE

For young women in Yaoundé, marriage is a central part of modern honor, pecuniary and dispositional. Unable to find suitable men at home in the context of economic crisis, around the turn of the millennium they turned in large numbers to the Internet. Why and how did this happen? Like so much in contemporary Yaoundé, the emergence of Internet romance demonstrates both continuity with the past and recent innovation. Throughout the early 1990s, a small number of urban women had sought European husbands using airmail catalogs and glossy magazines sent from Europe. In early 1998, the Internet came to Yaoundé. Despite long lines and high prices, it replaced the magazines within a matter of months. Internet access grew rapidly. By 2001, even small quartiers had cybercafés, and the price had fallen from about $10 per hour in 1998 to just about $1.50 per hour. Having an email address, surfing the web, and speaking fluently of chat rooms and listservs increasingly became part of the distinction of educated youth of some means, superceded only partially by the more recent arrival of cell-phones.

In the spring of 1998, there were three Internet access points in Yaoundé: the post office, the Hilton Hotel, and a private venture called Ditof. Each had a distinct character. The Hilton was the most expensive, most comfortable, and frequented primarily by men. The post office was the least private and most gender mixed. Ditof, in a small storefront on one of the main downtown streets, served almost exclusively women. There was only one computer, and most women had to dictate their email messages to an employee who could type. As a result, the line at Ditof was usually long (an hour or more). Yet, few minded, as that time was often productive for the women in search of husbands abroad. Collectively, the assembled women had quite an extensive knowledge of the benefits of alternative portals for posting their messages and of the writing habits of European men. They would read and comment on each other's letters, both received and prepared for sending. One day there was a heated discussion about how to interpret the lyrics of a song that a man has quoted in his letter; another day the topic concerned whether a man who did not want to come to Cameroon to meet his correspondent was seriously looking for marriage or just amusing himself.

The websites that women in Yaoundé use to meet European men differ in their visual presentation but share a basic business model. Without paying, women can post their profiles and men can search them. However, in order to contact any of the women, men must pay the site (on the order of $5 per address in 1998). Men do not have their own profiles on the websites. They send messages to women they find attractive, who may then share their private email address with him. Usually, women would send pictures of themselves (or, occasionally, of their younger sisters), and sometimes they would also ask the men for photographs. Some women had as many as a dozen correspondents at any one time, although most had only one or two.

Many of the women with whom I became acquainted at Ditof were looking for husbands after having been disappointed or deceived by a local partner. Adele explained how she had been living for over three years with a man when she learned that he continued to date other women and give them expensive gifts. Reluctant to leave him, she sought advice from friends and kin. They were unanimous that his behavior would get worse, not better, if they married. So Adele moved out, and decided to try her luck with European men instead. Another woman summarized a common view: "With the men such as we have here [now], marriage is nothing."

Beti women seeking husbands on the Internet use many of the same criteria as they do in seeking local husbands. This is in part because the very reason that many of them have turned to the Internet is that they feel that Cameroonian men can no longer fulfill their part of the marriage bargain. Husbands—local or foreign—should display the traits of modern honor: they should love their wives, have self-control, and contribute generously for the wives and their families. These values appear clearly in some of the personals ads, where women say that they want a man who is *serieux*, meaning both honorable and committed to the relationship. Yolande, for example, gives as "her message to you" the request "if you're not serious, stay away" and lower down she writes that she is, "Seeking a man 28 to 45 years old, serious, respectful, having the [necessary] values for a sincere and lasting relationship for marriage, French-speaking, and living in Europe or America." Similarly, Andze says that she "wish[es] to get in contact with someone serious for strong and durable relationship, marriage." Solange writes "I am searching for a man who is good, serious, strong, responsible, happy, generous. I know that I demand a lot, but that is the man of my dreams. Kisses!" Florence is looking for a "man who is serious, understanding, responsible, intelligent, hard-working. In brief, a man who is good for a serious relationship and even for marriage."

My casual conversations in line for a turn at the computer, and eventually interviews outside of Ditof, with women engaged in the search for husbands further reinforce the interpretation that these women are transposing a set of expectations about gender, honor, and consumption out of local forms of marriage onto their prospective European partners. Echoing both a lavish bridewealth and the gifts that women expect from their local boyfriends, my interlocutors regularly cited financial generosity as a key sign of men's potential as husbands. Very

few men sent money spontaneously, and women developed ways of asking, usually related to specific kinds of expenses: a hospital bill, a funeral, school fees. When asked for money, many men stopped writing, demonstrating that they would not provide their wives with the consumer comforts that modern marriage should bring.

In addition to offering access to a wider range of perhaps more suitable partners, some saw the Internet as providing an excellent means of learning about the true character of a man, so as not be disappointed later. One woman explained that she preferred the Internet to meeting in person because she is shy, but in email, "I can put there what I think about any little thing. And so I can see if he really loves me, because I observe what he writes as a response." This concern about whether men are true in their love is equally important in face-to-face courtship, and indeed is often cited as one of the reasons for delaying marriage. Because the Internet allows all kinds of tests and trials that are not possible in face-to-face courtship, young Beti women hope that Internet romances can progress a little faster. And indeed, much of the correspondence is a kind of testing—trying to put the man into a range of different situations to see how he reacts. Still, drawing on conventional Beti practices of courtship, and especially the importance of a long period of mutual observation, some young women in Yaoundé interpret email romance as a chance to learn the "true face" of prospective partners. In one example, the young man from a suburb of Paris who wrote that he was unemployed probably did not imagine that this admission would become the topic of speculation among a dozen or more women for at least two weeks. Was what he had written true? One interpretation was that he was just a very truthful and transparent person, a good trait, so that even if he was unemployed, he was "serious." A second interpretation was that he was not at all unemployed, but was rather testing his long-distance lover's sincerity and love for him—that is, he was not being honest, but his subterfuge took the form of a recognizable form of "observing" and was not grave. A third reading was that he was actually married, and so did not have any extra money, and was using the false claim of unemployment to justify why he would not behave properly—that is, why he would not send money or gifts on a regular basis. This is precisely the sort of deceit that waiting before you marry is intended to ferret out.

In addition to their concern to find good men, the women who sought husbands from Ditof wanted to consolidate their own claims to honor. The recurrent patterns of life at Ditof itself inscribed on us a certain kind of honorable modernity. The temporality of the mediated conversations—women would print out their messages and prepare replies at home, usually returning a few days or even a week later to send the response—made them formal and stilted, echoing the "measured slowness" of the *mfan mot*. The waiting in line, too, served as a self-disciplining practice, resonant with the waiting women do at church and school and maternity wards, those great institutions of modern subject formation. Beti women put a similar value on waiting *per se* as evidence of female self-dominion and honor in reference to periodic abstinence, also known as the rhythm method (Johnson-Hanks 2002). Women who were too eager or too desperate would not have the patience to wait: by constraining interaction, the Internet both demands and enforces the deliberate, judicious behavior that defines women's modern honor.

Cameroonian women seeking foreign husbands on the Internet are doing something profoundly counterintuitive: using a new, globalizing technology to achieve old, local aims when the old, local methods for achieving those aims no longer suffice. Although the prospect of "modern marriage" emerged in part through globalizing processes—urbanization, the Catholic church, an economic crisis caused by global commodity prices, and transnational flows of people and ideas—it also has deep, cultural roots in the honor of the (male) *mfan mot* and the gendered labor exchange of bridewealth marriage. Although would-be email-order brides from Cameroon appear on the Internet alongside Thai and Russian women, their motivations are distinct. This example points to the continuing importance

of theories of culture as a system, in which even radical change takes place through the transposition and transformation of available cultural categories and practices. Contemporary social life is partly the product of cultural history and social structure. In the seduction of the new, we must not abandon the analytic power of culture and structure.

WORKS CITED

Alexandre, Pierre and Jacques Binet. 1958. *Le Groupe Dit Pahouin (Fang-Boulou-Beti)*. Paris: Institut International Africain.

Cole, Jennifer. 2004. Fresh Contact in Tamatave, Madagascar: Sex, Money, and Intergenerational Transformation. *American Ethnologist* 31(4): 573–588.

Houseman, Michael. 1988. Social Structure Is Where the Hearth Is: A "Woman's Place" in Beti Society. *Africa* 58(1): 51–69.

Johnson-Hanks, Jennifer. 2006. *Uncertain Honor: Modern Motherhood in an African Crisis*. Chicago: University of Chicago Press.

Laburthe-Tolra, Phillipe. 1981. *Les Seigneurs de la Foret: Essai sur le passe historique, l'orginisation sociale et les normes ethiques des anciens Beti du Cameroun*. Paris: Publications de la Sorbonne.

Largeau, V. 1901. *Encyclopédie Pahouine*. Paris: Ernst Laroux.

Tessman, Günther. 1913. *Die Pangwe: Völkerkundliche Monographie eines west-afrikanischen Negerstammes*. Berlin: Ernst Wasmuth.

Veblen, Thornstein. 1899. *The Theory of the Leisure Class*. New York: The Macmillan Company.

NOTES

1. The Beti are the majority ethnic group in the city, and far more so in its hinterlands.
2. The term "Beti" itself means "honorable ones," and it has only in the last century come to refer to an ethnic group, rather than distinguishing free men from slaves (pl. *bolò*). The singular form of Beti, *nti*, serves as the standard translation for "Lord" and today refers only to the Christian God, as in *Nti Zamba wan* (The Lord our God).
3. Author's calculations from Demographic and Health Survey data.

3 • *Mary L. Gray*

NEGOTIATING IDENTITIES/ QUEERING DESIRES

Coming Out Online and the Remediation of the Coming-Out Story

DISCUSSION QUESTIONS

1. How has access to the Internet influenced the gender and sexual identities and experiences of the rural LGBTQ, queer, and questioning youth in the United States studied by Gray?
2. How and why do the stories of these young people challenge dominant narratives about the importance of visibility and "coming out"?
3. What does Gray mean by "queer realness"? How does this concept inform our understandings of these dynamics?

INTRODUCTION

I first started noticing that I was attracted to other girls when I was about 12 or 13. . . . I was over at my friend's house one night joking that I only watched *Baywatch* (my favorite show at the time) for the girls. After I said this, I realized it was true. It wasn't until about a year later, when I got on the Internet and found other people like me that I actually said to myself that I was bisexual. I've always been attracted to both sexes, but I found my true identity on the Internet.

Amy, age 15

Amy, a white teenager living in Central Kentucky, cited the discovery of an Internet forum for lesbian, gay, bi, trans, queer (LGBTQ) and questioning young people as a defining moment in understanding her own bisexual identity.[1] She found that online representations of LGBTQ lives seemed more pivotal to her articulation of identity than fictionalized LGBT narratives, such as *Baywatch*'s campy queer subtexts or *Queer as Folk* and *Will and Grace*'s out and proud gay and lesbian characters. Media visibility seem a natural step in the progression for full rights and equal citizenship. Sociologist and feminist scholar Suzanna Walters (2001) convincingly argues, however, that LGBTQ visibility in the media means we are more widely seen but not necessarily better known. That is not to say that images of LGBTQ characters in popular media didn't inform (and fuel) the queering of Amy's desires. But the narratives of authenticity that she found online, reading coming out stories from teens both in her state and living worlds away, following news bulletins posted to the National Gay and Lesbian Task Force and PlanetOut websites, and outlets for buying rainbow flags, jewelry, pride rings, and stickers, stood out for her; they

An abridged version of Mary Gray, 2009. "Negotiating Identities/Queering Desires: Coming Out Online and the Remediation of the Coming-Out Story." *Journal of Computer-Mediated Communication* 14: 1162–1189. Adapted by the author with permission of John Wiley and Sons.

provided the grammar for a bisexual identity she eventually claimed as her own.

Drawing on a 19-month ethnographic study of digital media use among rural LGBTQ, queer and questioning youth in the United States, this essay explores how rural young people weave media-generated source materials into their identity work, particularly as they master the politics of visibility's master narrative event: "coming out."[2] I argue that, in rural contexts, Internet-based texts offer materials for the labor of parsing out and responding to the expectations of LGBTQ visibility. Engaging these online representations as a genre infuses them with what I refer to throughout this essay as *queer realness*.[3] Instead of focusing on the aesthetic codes or features of the texts themselves, I apply media scholar Jason Mittell's practice of analyzing themes and patterns that surface across media texts, the audience members' experiences of those texts, and industry practices that consistently produce and recycle these themes and patterns (Mittell, 2001, p. 19).

Rural LGBTQ-identifying youth come to see themselves in terms made familiar through the narrative repetition of self-discovery and coming out found in this genre. As such, these digitally produced texts circulate the politics of LGBTQ identity and visibility as a hegemonic grammar for the articulation of identity. How much rural youth absorb and rework these identity categories turns on each young person's material conditions, cultural context, and history. The accounts rural youth gave me of their reckoning with these genres highlight the recalcitrance of social categories like race, class, and kinship norms that trouble what we might uncritically attribute to the powers of the Internet.

Online representations, from non-commercial, youth-spun websites to subscription-based personal ads on for-profit media properties like PlanetOut and Gay.com, provide rural young people with materials for crafting what it means to "come out" as LGBTQ or questioning in rural contexts. Case studies of rural sexualities and genders offer fresh vantage points to consider the links between larger structural issues, such as statewide social service funding and regional race and class relations, media representations, and day-to-day processes of individual presentations and negotiations of identity. From this perspective, identities index complicated dialogues—re-circulations of coming out narratives most notably—that increasingly involve digitally-mediated renderings of LGBTQ identities complete with particular ways to dress, look, and speak.

QUEERING THE EFFECTS OF MEDIA VISIBILITY

Films, television characters, press accounts of social movements, AIDS reporting, plays, books, and the Internet are where most stories of queer desires transpire. These representations translate queer desires into LGBTQ-specific identities and give them a proper locale, typically the city. As such, media are the primary site of production for social knowledge of LGBTQ identities. It is where most people, including those who will come to identify as LGBTQ, first see or get to know LGBTQ people. In other words, media circulate the social grammar, appearance, and sites of LGBTQ-ness. Yet, mass media consistently narrate rural LGBTQ identities as out of place, necessarily estranged from "authentic" (urban) queerness. These images teach rural youth to look anywhere but homeward for LGBTQ identities.

I borrow the notion of "in situ" from the archeological study of material artifacts to assess how rural queer youth contend with dismissive representations of their lives.[4] This approach requires radically de-centering media and tracing the layers of socioeconomic status, race relations, and location that make media engagements meaningful. Additionally, I investigate rural queer youth identities as performative, socially mediated moments of being and becoming—the collective labor of crafting, articulating, and pushing the boundaries of identities. I argue that rural youth do the collective labor of identity work differently than their urban counterparts not because rural queer youth have it inherently harder but because they confront different heteronormative/homophobic burdens and different identifications with the commercially mediated identities available to them. As a result, they bear the weight of a politics of visibility that, I argue, was built for city living.

IMAGINED TERRAIN OF ONLINE QUEERNESS

Most of the working poor to lower middle-class youth I interviewed shared their computers with family members. And with the high cost of extending Internet to all homes, cable and digital subscriber line (DSL) services are still largely unavailable or priced beyond reach for many in rural Appalachia.[5] This speaks to the importance of considering not just the availability of new media to rural queer and questioning youth but also the limits of that access for a range of reasons. For example, rural youth involved in this study had universal access to the Internet through computers available at their schools. Their state governments had invested heavily in school-based access through federal grants. But these grants also included some of the most sophisticated web-monitoring and filtering software available. Even when young people reported being able to circumvent the filtering software they did so at great risk as their passcodes for accessing school computers logged their browsing, email, and chat exchanges. And, regardless of issues of access, youth must continually search for queer representations of realness as the Internet is always changing, constantly displacing reliable locations for the kinds of reflections of realness they seek.

QUEER REALNESS

What distinguishes and clusters Internet-based personals, search engine results, coming out stories, and chat rooms as genres of queer realness is that they provide moments of storytelling that transform how rural youth think and talk about their identities. Rural youth used the Internet, particularly engagements with youth-spun web sites and personal ads on commercial media properties like Gay.com, to confirm the existence of queerness beyond their locales and strategize about how to bring that queerness home to roost.

For example, Darrin, a gay-identifying 17-year-old from an agricultural town of 6,100 people, sees web sites, like the commercial portal, PlanetOut.com, as, "a place to feel at least somewhat at home." He adds, "but then I have to figure out how to make that home here too, you know? Chat rooms give me a place to go when I don't feel I can connect to others where I am." PlanetOut, like other commercial sites that cater to community-specific niche markets, prominently promotes community areas and rotates spotlighted personal profiles along with designated message boards and chat rooms targeting youth, women, men, and a range of sexual and gender identities.[6]

Sarah, a 17-year-old from a town of 12,000 along the Ohio River separating Indiana and Kentucky, liked "reading things from Betty DeGeneres [mother of lesbian comedian Ellen DeGeneres] on PlanetOut . . . using their experiences as possibilities" for her life. Sarah, like most of the youth I met, didn't voice a strong desire to escape from rural Kentucky. In part her plans to stay put were because of her close ties with family. But she, like several other youth I interviewed, also had no funds to leave her hometown and no educational training or particularly marketable job skills to make moving anything but a frightening prospect. Instead, she wanted to refashion her local circumstances with the help of what she discovered online. As I discuss elsewhere, "family" represents a social safety net that is otherwise absent from the public infrastructure of impoverished rural communities (Gray 2009). Because this ethnographic study focused on youth who hadn't run away or been kicked out of their homes, what I learned about the conditions for queering identity and publics in rural communities came from young people who either did not want to leave their small towns or could not muster the means to do so.

Justin, another 15-year-old questioning youth from a small Kentucky town (4,500) on the Kentucky–Ohio border, describes his research this way:

> When I first got the Internet, my main goal was . . . I was about 13, I guess . . . of course, pornography 'cause I heard boys at school talking about it. When I first started, I would go lookin' for main places and they would have lesbians and gays in separate categories. Finally, I realized they [lesbians and gays] had their own [websites]. I had to search. It really was work. It was really, really hard to get onto these websites 'cause some of them had a block, and you'd have to hunt around for the ones that were free. Sometimes, you'd wait for a picture to download for 5 minutes! I was risking getting caught so I wanted to find something I really wanted to see!

The Internet presented both opportunities and challenges to Justin's research agenda. It required him to weigh his desires against the risk of exposure. He balanced the covertness and patience needed to find queer realness—primarily on personal listings on gay and lesbian-specific web sites—with his need to view something he could not see in his daily life.

Josh also talks about the Internet as a means to explore his new community:

> I was so uneducated about the gay life. I knew almost nothing. I mean like, gay terminology. People on the Internet would use something and I'd be like, "What is that?" I didn't know. I didn't have a computer at home. I mean, I knew about a few things from other friends but most of them were, like things, you know, like how to act in a bar. Well, this is a dry county and we don't have any bars. And I don't think there's much in the Western Kentucky area where I'm from for gay people.

Josh doesn't attribute his ignorance of gay life to his rural surroundings. Indeed, Josh is no more "ignorant" than any young person steeped in the heteronormative world that shapes our lives. He recognizes that local places and people can provide some of the references he craves, but he also knows his lack of Internet access limits his ability to connect with them. Josh continues:

> Online you're able to meet a lot more people than you are off-line. You may get five people at a Tri-State meeting [regional LGBTQ advocacy agency] one day and they may know two other people, so there's like 15 there. Online, I can talk to maybe 20 GLBT people in an hour! Since I live in a small town, where I know very few gay people, it gives me a sense that the gay community is small but when you get on the Internet you realize the gay community is everywhere and it's huge!

Rural youth use genres of queer realness to symbolize and actualize their connections to a larger network of gays, lesbians, bisexuals, and transpeople. They also use these media engagements with genres of queer realness to bring their performances home, anchor them locally, and transform them into experiences of self/senses of identity that can and do happen to youth "just like them."

Some young people seamlessly integrate genres of queer realness into their construction of identity but this is not always the case. To incorporate genres of queer realness into an imagined sense of self, youth must traverse a dense terrain of other social realities. They must weigh how doable or desirable such realness is. Disrupting (or queering) the norm stands out in rural communities where the audience is oriented towards presumptions of familiarity and claiming queerness isn't just "different," it's decidedly urban and white.

THE CASE OF BRANDON: NEGOTIATING QUEER REALNESS AND RURAL RACISM

Brandon and I emailed several times about his desire to share his story of growing up as an African-American in rural Central Kentucky. Brandon is a self-effacing, yet confident, first-year student at a small college a few hours from his hometown. After graduating from a Catholic high school in a town of 5,000, he had become a respected leader on campus and was particularly known for his work as the president of the campus's Black Student Caucus.

Brandon and I talked for nearly an hour about the organizing he did around race issues at his high school. He laughed loudly but his voice belied exasperation as he recalled those early leadership experiences. "Any black student at my high school knew that they were representing black with a capital 'B.' . . . We were coming from two or three counties from around the region but when we got to school, we became an instant community . . . I used to joke with my best friend, Lana, that we were the NAACP, BET, and NBA all rolled into one!"

Few people knew of Brandon's same-sex desires other than a young man on campus he had dated briefly and a smattering of friends he knew through online chat rooms and instant messaging. He had come out as bisexual to his friends in the Black Student Caucus only two weeks earlier.

I asked Brandon how his student activism and political organizing affected his sexual feelings and identity. He gathered his thoughts and said:

> I've known for some time that I was attracted to both males and females . . . since probably sophomore year in high school . . . [long pause] . . . but, I guess . . . well, I felt like I had to choose between being Black, I had to be either an African-American student leader or labeled the "gay guy" and I saw what happened to kids labeled "gay" . . . I don't think I could have handled being rejected by other black kids. Being black was more important to me.

Brandon wondered aloud whether the pressure he felt to appear heterosexual would have been tempered if he'd attended a more racially diverse high school. His high school was in one of the few, non-urban areas of Kentucky with a sizeable, visible, and well-established African-American middle class.[7] The rural communities surrounding Brandon's are typical of the racial makeup of Kentucky's many counties, which are 90%–96% white, the legacy of ethnic cleansing and "Sundown" laws at the turn of the 20th century.

Brandon felt his white and Black friends accepted him because of his middle-class upbringing, which as he said, "put them all in the same kinds of clothes, neighborhoods, and high school classes." But when it came to opening up about his attraction to boys, he kept his feelings confined to a small circle of friends he talked to exclusively online:

> High school was a continuous battle between self-recognition or self-destruction. . . . It was a constant thing. . . . I realized that graduating from college, making achievements, all of that might not matter if people found out I was attracted to guys. So that was the sad part—why try to do good things if it wouldn't "count" 'cause I liked males? I think that was the reaction that most people in my life—family and friends—would have had. I wasn't courageous enough at that point to, like some of the people that I knew, to just go against the grain and come out. I think it was an ostracizing reaction for me to have, but it helped me survive this far.

One way to interpret Brandon's discomfort with disclosing more about his sexuality is that he sees it as a potential threat to affirmation as a Black leader at school and his closeness with family and friends. Brandon does not possess the unequivocal self-acceptance and "sense of integrity and entitlement" that sociologist Steven Seidman defines as the "post-closeted gay sensibility" of today's gay youth identity (Seidman, 2002, p. 75). But Brandon's relationship to a bisexual identity is more complicated.

Seidman suggests that in this unprecedented age of gay visibility most gay Americans "live outside the social framework of the closet" (Seidman, 2002, p. 9). But as anthropologist Martin Manalansan argues, gay identity in the United States is "founded on a kind of individuation that is separate from familial and kin bonds and obligations" and "predicated on the use of verbal language as the medium in which selfhood can be expressed" (Manalansan, 2003, p. 23). Brandon's struggle is as much with expectations of distance between gay identity and family or strong claims to an identity that might be seen as "competing" with his racial identity as with heterosexism writ large.

Brandon must reconcile the demands of distancing that Manalansan describes as fundamental to U.S. gay identity and the need to maintain family ties and recognition as a local African-American leader. Seidman suggests that the identity negotiations Brandon confronts are exceptions to the rule attributable to the challenges individuals face when they must synthesize sexual identities and racial or other core identities (Seidman, 2002, p. 43). But this is hardly a small number of individuals raising the question: why are those who privilege gay visibility valorized as "beyond the closet" and youth of color, rural young people, and other individuals with core identities vying for recognition seen as in denial or not doing their part for LGBTQ rights? For rural youth, particularly rural youth of color like Brandon, the politics of LGBTQ visibility do not provide greater access to unequivocal pleasures of acceptance and identification because they simultaneously devalue the necessities—and pleasures—of familiarity and other identity priorities.

Brandon expressed ambivalence about coming out to his friends and family but did find solace and a way to negotiate the expectations of visibility through what he called his "gay outlet":

The summer before my junior year, I got work as a station assistant at our local public radio station. The computer I worked on had Internet access, no filters like the computers at school, which I wouldn't have touched with a 10-foot pole! So one night, I don't even know what I typed in; I just found chat rooms with guys looking to hook up with other guys. But I also found websites about political stuff . . . there was a whole world of people talking about being bisexual . . . well, not as many people talking about that but at least I could see places that were for people like me . . . this was my gay outlet . . . I could read personals, stories about people my age telling their parents about their feelings . . . I could even find rooms for chatting with people living near my hometown!

For Brandon, reading online personals and coming-out stories was a way to experience what coming out to his parents might feel like at a time when his ability to talk about his bisexuality seemed incompatible with his identity as a young, progressive African-American student leader in rural Kentucky. Ironically, his online explorations reinforced the racial reality of his daily life:

You know, no matter how many times I went into the Kentucky chat rooms on Gay.com or looked at [online] personals, I never once saw another black kid my age living in my area . . . I didn't find anything for Black kids anywhere! Maybe that says more about my computer skills? [laughs] . . . All of the personals I read either said they were white guys looking for white guys or race didn't matter . . . but it matters a lot to me!

Youth, like Brandon, use new media to temporarily patch the incongruence or alienation between their sexual desires and other social worlds. They must reckon this mending, however, with the resources locally available to continue their identity work. Brandon's "gay outlets" attended to parts of his experiences of identity. These engagements with genres of queer realness also reminded him that while "gay outlets" could offer the promise of connection with others "like him," these others would necessarily reproduce the segregation and racism of his surroundings.

THE CASE OF JOHN W.: NEGOTIATING GAY IDENTITY AND QUEER DESIRE

John W. generously made room for us to sit down by clearing away stacks of sheet music and leftover coffee cups from his weathered, plaid couch. He offered a quick apology for the apartment's disarray. "Sorry, the dudes I live with are kind of pigs."

John W.'s tattoos and facial piercings together with the safety pins holding his jeans together fit the moniker of "progressive punk rocker" he proudly claimed. He had recently declared himself "gay" but he wasn't sure if that identity resonated deeply with him.

A 19-year-old white middle class college student, John W. grew up in a factory town of 10,000 and prided himself on being one of the "edgy kids." He continues to commute on weekends from the college he attends to his hometown. Of his high school, he says, "There really weren't too many different kinds of kids. There were the jocks, which I tried to be. There were the smart kids and a few African American kids." John W. grew up in a strict Catholic household where sexual desires were not discussed. He recalls memories from as early as 5 years old when he realized that tying himself to his backyard swing set and hanging from its bars sexually excited him. "I really didn't know what bondage was at that point. Sometimes I even say that maybe my sexual attraction is more towards bondage than male or female." He found friends early on with whom he could share and act out some of these desires: "I don't know if the other cliques got into a little bit more of the alternative lifestyle of having sex or doing sexual things than my group of friends. I would probably think that my group of people was more apt to doing things a little bit different because we were different in the first place." In describing his forays into sexual play, John W. continued:

> I had this friend; I think he's straight. But he would come over, and we would get drunk. We just started tying each other up. I was between 15 and 16. One time we were at his house and we were looking at a Playboy and then there was like a couple pictures in the back of some guys lifting weights, and he was like, "Do you like that?" "Yeah." He asked me if he could do me up the butt, so I was like, "Okay, sure." As soon as he came and pulled out, he was like, "What have I done? I can't do this again." I haven't talked to him in a while. We didn't leave on bad terms. That's just when I started wondering if maybe I was gay.

John W. singles out his move to a midsized college town and subsequent access to the internet as the means through which he acquired what he described as the language for his innate desires:

> In high school, I didn't really have too much access to the Internet because it was newer at the time and slower and, of course, all the school computers had software trackers and filters on them. We didn't have a computer at home either. When I came to college, my sophomore year I got a computer, so I had instant access to the Internet. Before I had a computer I didn't have any sense of what I'd find online. I just typed in so many things on the computer and just learned about what to type in, what to find. I think with Gay.com I probably just typed in www.gay.com, like randomly, and found that this was the access to all the perverts like me. That's when I started learning about bondage and the terms, what BDSM was and S&M, and I just, I can't remember how I started looking for groups.

Web sites were critical to John W.'s process of naming his desires but they also played an important part in his search for local belonging in communities of practice organized around his new identity:

> Three or four years ago you'd have a hard time finding something to do with leather or bondage or whatever around here, but now about every weekend there's a party. So the Internet has allowed all that to come forth. . . . Before I met my boyfriend [at the campus LGBTQ group], I was actively involved with a BDSM bondage group that met in South Central Kentucky area. I would travel and play around with male and females—mostly safe sex. I was actively involved with that group.

For John W., claiming a gay identity was a means towards a more salient identity. As he notes, "I have to emphasize that my sexual interests are a big part of who I am, and my attraction for men . . . I don't know. I'm not all that sure that I feel gay like the other guys I meet who are gay. Like my current boyfriend, he's really gay, wants to settle down with one other guy and isn't into bondage at all." When asked how he was different from other gay men his age, John W. responded that from reading websites and negotiating his current relationship he had the sense that being gay came packaged with a set of expectations, such as monogamy and normality "like working at a regular job and settling down."

As John W. saw it, "bondage just comes with a desire to play with other people. I'm not just out to have sex. I'm fulfilling this internal need." Identifying as "gay" made it easier for him to find other men with whom to have the intimacy and sexual connection he desired even if a gay identity did not squarely fit his sense of self and his range of desires:

> Gay.com really isn't that great for me because a lot of people aren't into bondage. But I go to the "Kentucky" chat room because you know that you're probably going to find somebody near you. A lot of people will travel two or three hours to meet somebody. You can't just like hit on a guy on campus 'cause you don't know. I can find people on campus that I would have maybe one-night stands, but I really didn't have fun because there was no bondage. If I didn't have access to computers, I don't know what I would do.

The web sites and online communities John W. finds don't confirm an identity for him. Rather, he picks up definitions to pragmatically serve his sexual desires. This process of sorting through the available terms led to his identity as a young gay man. But his gay identity is an approximation. He has ambivalence with the category "gay" but he finds utility in it. Digital representations of what it means to be "gay" have been undeniably vital to Brandon's sexuality. But they also underscore the frustration of what philosopher Kenneth Burke long ago noted, "to define or determine a thing is to mark its boundaries" (Burke, 1969, p. 24).

CONCLUSION

Until recently, Brandon felt his bisexuality was incommensurate with his racial identity. John W. questions whether his identification with bondage fits with his understanding of "gay." Presuming that rural youth in the United States are isolated from LGBTQ identity formation, from the processes that can queer one's normative sense of self, ignores how identities settle on our skin. The politics of LGBTQ visibility compel Brandon and John W. to put sexual identity ahead of their familial, racial, and queer desires. But, Brandon and John W. teach us that we need to change our perception of the closet as an open or shut door. Closets are, in part, shaped by the "compulsory heterosexuality" that structures our everyday interactions (Rich 1980). Culturally, we all work under the assumption that individuals are heterosexual (and "male" or "female") until "proven" otherwise. Rural communities' material dependencies on structures of familiarity and the value placed on conformity as a sign of solidarity intensify the visibility of compulsory heterosexuality's hegemonic sexual and gender norms. Brandon's experience of what is commonly referred to as "the closet" challenges Seidman's assertions of or hopes for an America beyond the closet as long as we hitch a generic and universalizing logic of visibility to queer difference.

Like most teens, Brandon and John W. grew up with gay visibility readily available in the media. They knew what "gay" meant but it was an identity category otherwise conspicuously unfamiliar to and popularly depicted as out of place in his rural surroundings. Both Brandon and John W. searched for identities online that would lend authenticity to their own desires but that they could also experience locally. But the ascribed expectations of visibility and normative sexual mores that Brandon and John W. associated with the genre of queer realness that they found online conflicted with the obligations that already deeply engrossed them locally. The genre of "gay" available to them as a commodity through online coming-out narratives and personal ads provided partial relief to their search for realness. However, the packaging of gay identity's "auxiliary characteristics," those hegemonic behaviors and affective dispositions represented as integral to the status role of "gay" read as incommensurate with other pieces of their sense of self (Brekhus 2003). Their rural locales did not present them with options to tune out this dissonance. This is not a case of the Internet opening netherworlds of desire and identification unavailable in the everyday lives of rural queer youth. Instead Brandon and John W.'s engagements with genres of queer realness demonstrate the dialectical production of modern LGBTQ identities that, by definition, draw on narratives driven by a politics of visibility.

Narratives of isolation reflect the ascendancy and dominance of a self-discovery/disclosure paradigm that structures not only LGBTQ lives but also modern notions of how identities work. What we call "the closet" springs from the idea that identities are waiting to be discovered. Authenticity hinges on erasing the traces of others from our work to become who we "really" are. To leave the traces of social interaction visible is to compromise our claims to authenticity and self-determination (Giddens, 1992, p. 185). Genres that queer realness simultaneously expand and consolidate the possibilities of identity by prompting youth to rework the unmarked categories of heterosexual, male, and female; embrace their burgeoning non-normative desires; and then re-articulate LGBTQ identities as "real," "natural," "unmediated," and "authentic." In this sense, identity, even the most intimate, personal senses of self, can be explored as deeply social and highly mediated no matter who we are or where we live.

REFERENCES CITED

Brekhus, W. (2003). *Peacocks, chameleons, centaurs: gay suburbia and the grammar of social identity.* Chicago: University of Chicago Press.

Burke, K. (1969). *A grammar of motives.* Berkeley, CA: University of California Press.

Giddens, A. (1992). *The transformation of intimacy: sexuality, love, and eroticism in modern societies.* Stanford, CA: Stanford University Press.

Gray, M. L. (2009). *Out in the country: youth, media, and queer visibility in rural America.* New York: New York University Press.

Halberstam, J. (2005). *In a queer time and place: transgender bodies, subcultural lives.* New York: New York University Press.

Manalansan, M. F. (2003). *Global divas: Filipino gay men in the diaspora.* Durham: Duke University Press.

Mittell, J. (Spring 2001). A cultural approach to television genre theory. *Cinema Journal, 40*(3), 3–24.

Rich, A. (1980). Compulsory heterosexuality and lesbian existence. *Signs: Journal of Women in Culture and Society, 5*, 631–660.

Seidman, S. (2002). *Beyond the closet: the transformation of gay and lesbian life.* New York: Routledge.

Walters, S. D. (2001). *All the rage: the story of gay visibility in America.* Chicago: University of Chicago Press.

NOTES

1. The inclusion of "queer" and "questioning" in the name of the forum Amy found online was not an anomaly. Several of the most commonly cited youth-specific websites and discussion forums referenced queer and questioning if not in their titles then in their Frequently Asked Questions (FAQ). Arguably these terms, typically left undefined, operated as umbrella terms or placeholders for a spectrum of sexual and gender identities and practices that these sites and their offline counterparts meant to include. While queer and questioning challenge heteronormative structures of teenage life in multiple ways they can also operate as stabilizing identity categories. I use "queer" throughout this essay to signal my own desire to consider how a moniker that de-naturalizes norms associated with sexual and gender identities might also paradoxically operate as an identity category. In most cases, the youth involved in this study did not primarily identify as queer but used it as casual slang or a term of endearment for each other and a broader imagined community.

2. Fieldwork for this project took place between September 2001 and April 2003, and several short follow-up trips in the summers of 2004 and 2005. Thirty-four young people, ages 14–24 years old, provided most of the interview materials while a broader group of youth allowed me access to participation and observation of their day-to-day lives. I anchored my research in several small towns and rural communities, most with populations between 900 and as large as 15,000 found in what is referred to by the U.S. Census and Appalachian Regional Commission as the Central Appalachian Region.

3. I draw on J. Jack Halberstam's prescient definition of realness which, as Halberstam asserts, is "not exactly performance, not exactly an imitation; it is the way that people, minorities, excluded from the domain of the real, appropriate the real and its effects" (Halberstam, 2005, p. 51).

4. Archaeologists use this phrase to describe an artifact at the point of its unearthing or sighting, one that is still embedded in a deposit suggesting its age and cultural context. Although similar to media ethnographies of audience reception, my approach radically de-centers media as the focus of study. Instead of examining audiences' reactions to specific programs or websites, I attempt to map the relationship between rural young people's experiences of a cluster of media engagements and a milieu that is constitutive of its meaning.

5. ConnectKentucky, "Internet and Broadband Use in Kentucky: Statewide Results from the 2005 County Level Technology Assessment Study" available at www.connectkentucky.org.

6. PlanetOut and Gay.com merged in 2001.

7. To respect Brandon's request for confidentiality, I do not specify the town or region in which he grew up. However, he does live in one of several communities where race relations have long been addressed by a powerful though small community of African-Americans in coalition with White civil rights and labor organizers.

PART THREE

Gendered Negotiations

Although all of the readings have looked at gender as a negotiated, contested, and dynamic process, the topics in this section focus on these negotiations in three distinct but intertwined domains: at home, at work, and in the context of state policies and practices. Gender ideas and politics are central to the very constitution of these domains. Moreover, changing gendered dynamics in one domain shape and are shaped by the gender dynamics in another. Nonetheless, it is useful to explore how some of the distinctions between them—of affect, power, intimacy, inequality, and more—influence the form and content of these negotiations.

10. *Gender at Home:* These readings examine changing gender dynamics in the home. What are the gendered expectations for "husbands" and "wives"? How are these relations and responsibilities shaped not just by gender, but also by "race," class, culture, and generation? How do these ideas of masculinity and femininity change as a result of new economic opportunities, class mobility, access to reproductive technologies, and more? Richard A. Schroeder offers a nuanced analysis of the tactics used by men and women in a Gambian village to (re)negotiate their "conjugal contract" in light of marked economic changes that have made women the primary income earners in their families. Riché J. Daniel Barnes explores how middle-class African-American mothers in Atlanta negotiate the conflicts between (racially based) mothering strategies that trained them to be independent and their own

(class-based) desires and possibilities to be more available to their families. Matthew C. Gutmann analyzes how prevalent ideas of masculinity, especially men's "natural" sexual desires and practices, inform debates and decisions between men and women (and medical practitioners) in Oaxaca, Mexico, about whether or not men should get vasectomies.

11. *Gender at Work:* These readings investigate how gender shapes and is shaped by different kinds of work and work sites, with attention to the changing structures of capitalism. Carla Freeman examines how and why young women have been recruited as ideal workers in the "pink collar" data-entry business in Barbados, and how these women experience and express their new gendered and classed identities. Gracia Clark explores the relationship among concepts of work, gender, and parenting among Asante people in Ghana. A key concept is what she calls "economic motherhood," whereby a "good" Asante mother is expected to earn money outside the home to support her children, rather than stay home to care for them. Carrie M. Lane analyzes how structural changes in work and cultural shifts in the meanings of career, masculinity, and marriage have shaped the experience of job loss and unemployment for some middle-class workers in the U.S. technology industry.

12. *Gendered States:* These readings explore how certain gendered ideas (such as women as "mothers of the nation") are produced and challenged in the formation and reproduction of nations, the structures and policies of states, and the creation of certain kinds of "citizens." Aihwa Ong examines how ideas of "appropriate" gender roles, family formations, and women's appearance, work, and sexuality become the sites of intervention and, eventually, struggle between the state and Islamic revival movements in Malaysia. Lesley Gill analyzes how the Bolivian state uses compulsory military service to try to instill a dominant form of masculinity among long-marginalized indigenous men that privileges conformity and compliance with military values (of aggression, obedience, and discipline), transforms them into a specific kind of Bolivian "citizen," and tries to "civilize" them. Sara L. Friedman explores how state regulations and intimate relationships have become intertwined in a region of China where the reluctance of new brides to live with or have sex with their husbands has provoked repeated state reform campaigns since the establishment of China's socialist regime in 1949.

1 • *Richard A. Schroeder*

"GONE TO THEIR SECOND HUSBANDS"

Marital Metaphors and Conjugal Contracts in The Gambia's Female Garden Sector

DISCUSSION QUESTIONS

1. What were key principles of the "conjugal contract" in the community in The Gambia studied by Schroeder? How and why did the "conjugal contract" change?
2. How did men and women use the phrase "second husbands" differently to communicate their opinions of women's time-consuming labor in their gardens?
3. Describe some of the tactics that men and women used to renegotiate their household financial obligations in light of the changes in their ability to make money.

INTRODUCTION

Since the mid-1970s, the response of Gambian women to prolonged rainfall deficits, IMF/World Bank-mandated austerity measures and opportunities created by gender-equity oriented development expenditures has been to greatly intensify commercial vegetable and fruit production. Although the phenomenon of a female cash crop system is perhaps not quite so anomalous as was once assumed, The Gambia's garden boom is one of the more dramatic cases on record. Indeed, hundreds of women's communal gardens along the Gambia River Basin have replaced the male peanut crop as the primary source of cash income in many areas. Between forty-five and eighty per cent of

An abridged version of Richard A. Schroeder, 1996. "Gone to their Second Husbands": Marital Metaphors and Conjugal Contracts in The Gambia's Female Garden Sector." *Canadian Journal of African Studies* 30(1): 69–87. Adapted by the author with permission from Taylor and Francis. See Schroeder (1999) for the full case study.

the women in highly productive horticultural enclaves in The Gambia's North Bank Division now earn more cash than their husbands (Schroeder, 1999), this despite significant market constraints and intense competition for land, water and labor resources (Schroeder, 1993, 1995, 1999; Schroeder and Suryanata, 1996).

One of the offshoots of the surge in female incomes and intense demands on female labor produced by the boom has been an escalation of gender politics centered on the reworking of what Whitehead once called the "conjugal contract" (Whitehead, 1981). Focusing on several Mandinka-speaking communities along the northern border with Senegal, I outline two phases of political engagement between gardeners and their husbands below. The first phase, comprising the early years of the garden boom, was characterized by a some-times bitter war of words. Men frequently claimed that gardens dominated their wives' lives to such a degree that the plots themselves had become the women's "second husbands." Returning the charge, their wives replied, in effect, that they may as well be married to their gardens: the financial crisis of the early 1980's had so undermined male cash crop production, and by extension, husbands' contributions to household finances, that gardens were often women's only means of financial support during this period.

As the boom has intensified, so, too, have intra-household politics. The focus of conflict in the second phase—which extends into the mid-1990's—is related to the use of cash crop income and the amount of time gardeners allocate to their complex horticultural enterprises. These struggles mirror the image several authors have painted of "non-pooling" households in Africa (e.g. Guyer and Peters, 1987), except that Gambian women enter budgetary negotiations holding the economic upper hand. I document below the wide range of tactics gardeners and their husbands have used to try and control household budgets. Generally speaking, I have found that women in garden districts have assumed greater budgetary responsibilities, including an increasingly obligatory transfer of cash to their husbands from garden proceeds. I argue below that while this outcome appears in some respects as a capitulation on the part of gardeners, it can also be read as strategic and symbolic deference designed to purchase the freedom of movement and social interaction that garden production and marketing entail. I contend that garden incomes have indeed won for women significant autonomy and new measures of power and prestige.

DEVELOPMENT IDEOLOGY AND FEMALE HORTICULTURAL PRODUCTION

The basic rationale for prioritizing horticulture over other development objectives in The Gambia was developed under the auspices of so-called Women in Development (WID) programs following the 1975 UN Declaration of the International Decade of Women. These projects have been characterized by a strong underlying ideological conviction that women are motivated in their economic activities in ways that differ fundamentally from men. Put simply, women are characterized as being more attuned to the "bread and butter" issues of food and family welfare than men; and they are considered better parents because they are seen to be more responsible providers (Whitehead, 1981). In this sense, donor funding for women's horticultural projects was simply a logical, direct and cost-effective strategy for making investments "pay off" in terms of family well-being.

In the context of the mid-1980's, this rationale dove-tailed neatly with the mandate to intervene to save "starving African children" that emerged in the wake of the devastating famines that swept the region. The combined effect was a sharp upsurge in international aid, which targeted with increasing specificity drought prone areas (the Sahel, the Horn), agricultural development and female producers. The enactment of WID strategies in The Gambia consequently translated directly into hundreds of grants to women's garden groups for barbed wire, tools, hybrid vegetable seed and well-digging costs.

Significantly, this investment pattern fed into a dramatic intensification of the demand for women's agricultural labor. The garden boom marks a fundamental shift away from predominantly rain-fed agriculture toward ground–water-based irrigated production. Not only has this forced gardeners to mobilize for a second full production season with the cessation of seasonal rains, but high evapotranspiration rates during the dry season gardening period also necessitate a rigorous watering schedule. Gardeners hand irrigate their crops twice daily—in the morning and evening when evapotranspiration rates are lower due to cooler temperatures. These tasks can take up to six hours a day depending on the distance between village and garden sites and the extent of an individual gardener's holdings.

MAPPING MARITAL METAPHORS

During the first phase of the boom, the routine absence of women from family living compounds was widely criticized. Husbands claimed that no good would ever come from the gardens, and that women should stop neglecting their marital responsibilities. A key complaint stemmed from the fact that women were no longer available to greet guests properly. As one male informant put it: "Presently you are here talking to me but my wives are not here. They are not doing what is obligatory. If you had found them here, they would have given you water to drink, and perhaps you would need to wash as well. I am now doing . . . what they are supposed to do."[1]

Indeed, the work regime followed by women, extolled by developers as the embodiment of positive maternal values, very quickly became imbued with meanings associated with a failure to meet marital obligations. As one women described the situation: "Some men, when they are asked about their wives, they will say, 'She is no longer my wife; she has a new husband.'" The phrase, "She's gone to her husband's" (Mandinka: "*a taata a ke ya*"), was widely used by men to indicate that their wives

were not at home but working in their gardens instead. This shorthand marked women's neglect of responsibilities, misplaced priorities, decentered obligations, shirked duties; it demonized gardeners as bad wives.

When asked directly to interpret the garden-as-husband metaphor, men and women in the garden districts offered two distinct readings. One interpretation, common among men, reflects the frustrations they confront in the garden boom: to wit, gardens dominate women's lives to such a degree that their husbands hardly see them anymore on a day-to-day basis. According to this interpretation, gardens have supplanted husbands' wishes as the primary ordering force in a woman's workday. Vegetable growers "greet" (*saama*) their gardens (and not their husbands) when they water their vegetables first thing in the morning;[2] they spend their days "at the side of" their gardens; and they bring their gardens water at dusk, i.e. at precisely the time when a man might expect his bath water to be delivered. Consequently, gardeners' marriage partners find themselves increasingly without companionship, and forced, by default, to assume new domestic labor responsibilities. This is especially true of older men who have been economically marginalized due to age or ill health, and who spend a great deal of time within the spatial confines of the family compound or its immediate vicinity. Early in the boom, the loss of these "prestige services" caused a great deal of bitter resentment.

By contrast, women's interpretations of the garden-as-husband metaphor emphasize the importance of garden earnings in meeting household budgetary obligations. For them, gardens have, for all practical purposes, replaced husbands as the principal source of cash for subsistence and other forms of consumption ("Women are doing what men *should* be doing"). Somewhat sardonically, they maintain that women may just as well be married to their gardens. One grower underscored the point dramatically by asserting that not just her garden, but the *well bucket* she used to irrigate her vegetables was her husband, because everything she owned came from it: "This [indicating her dress];

this [her shoes]; this [her earrings]; this [miming the food she put into her mouth]; and this [clutching her breast to indicate the food she fed her children, her voice rising in mock rage]—they all come from this bucket! That's why this bucket [and the garden] is my husband!!"

Clearly the Mandinka marriage system has been under significant strain due to the changes accompanying the push toward commercialization. Equally apparent is the fact that the hard fought rhetorical struggle in which men and women have mapped marital meanings onto garden spaces has as its object the right to occupy the moral high ground in the broader battle over the conjugal contract.

RAISING THE STAKES

In the first phase of conflict brought on by the boom, men openly expressed their resentment in pointed references to female shirking and selfishness. Their feelings were also made plain in actions taken by a small minority who forbade their wives to garden, or agitated at the village level to have gardening banned altogether (Schroeder and Watts, 1991). In the second phase, many men dropped their oppositional rhetoric and became more generally supportive as they began exploring ways to benefit personally from the garden boom.

The key to vegetable growers' success in winning over their husbands lay in their strategic deployment of garden incomes. Rural Gambian households were under significant economic stress in the late 1970's and early 1980's when the boom was initiated. Given the poor market conditions facing the male cash crop sector at the time, many men were forced into what might be called *legitimate default* vis-à-vis their customary obligations to feed or otherwise provision their families. Survey data show that both senior members of garden work units and women working on their own have taken on many economic responsibilities that were traditionally ascribed to men. Fifty-six per cent of the women in my sample, for example, claimed to have purchased

at least one bag of rice in 1991 for their families.[3] The great majority buy all of their own (95%), and their children's (84%), clothing, and most of the furnishings for their own houses.[4] Large numbers absorb ceremonial costs, such as the purchase of feast day clothing (80%), or the provision of animals for religious sacrifice.[5] Many pay their children's school expenses. And, in a handful of cases, gardeners claim to have been responsible for major or unusual expenditures such as the roofing of family compounds, the provision of loans for purchasing draught animals and farming equipment, or payment of the house tax. Indeed, several male informants stated unequivocally that, were it not for garden incomes, many of the marriages in the village would simply fail on non-support grounds.

One category of income expenditure by North Bank gardeners has been especially important in gaining men's support for gardening. Of the women sampled, thirty-eight per cent reported undertaking some measure of direct support of their husbands via cash gifts; typically dispersed in small, regular amounts, they occasionally amounted to much greater sums. These unilateral gestures stem from the desire of gardeners to promote harmony, to overcome resentment, to encourage their husbands to relax control over their (the wives') labor; in short, cash gifts are used to buy goodwill.

In this regard, the effect of the gifts has been quite decisive:

Today no one would say 'a taata a ke ya' ['she's gone to her husband's'] . . . Every man who is in this village whose wife is engaged in this garden work, the benefit of the produce goes to him first before the wife can even enjoy her share of it. That is why those statements they used to say would not be heard now. . . . In fact some men among us, if it were not for this garden work, their marriages would not last. Because their [own economic] efforts cannot carry one wife, much less two or three, or even four. Women can [now] support themselves. They will buy beds, mattresses, cupboards, rice . . . from the produce of these gardens. . . . In fact I can comfortably say that gardening generates a greater benefit than the peanut crop that we [men] cultivate. Before you offer any help to people farming groundnuts, it is better you help people doing gardening, because we are using gardening to survive.

—*Gardener's husband*

The impression left by this comment is that the choices women have made with regard to the disposition of their garden incomes, some motivated by compassion and others of a more strategic nature, have met their mark. There is a third possible interpretation of these actions, however. According to some male informants, the disposition of women's garden incomes may not be such a clear-cut matter of *choice*. They pointed out that men also actively pursue opportunities to gain access to their wives' money. In other words, the cash gifts and in-kind contributions women make to their families may be construed as a *taking* by men. This proposition requires closer inspection.

THE PRICE OF AUTONOMY

Open admissions by men that they consciously engage in maneuvers to gain access to their wives' garden incomes are understandably quite rare. Those who did divulge information on this topic stressed the difficulty of generalizing about the strategies they were describing, and felt it important to emphasize that men only engaged in such practices when they knew that their wives could afford to share their assets. These caveats notwithstanding, the data shed a great deal of light on the process of negotiation and mutual accommodation precipitated by the boom.

The first set of strategies can loosely be described as loan-seeking. It consists of several different circumstances under which men ask their wives for money, each with its own degree of commitment toward eventual repayment, and its own threat of reprisal should the funds not be forthcoming. The simplest scenario involves asking for a loan with no intention whatsoever of repayment. In this case, the crucial consideration for the husband is how much

to request. If he aims too high, his request may not be granted because his wife can legitimately say she does not have the means. Also, if she does give him a larger sum, she is much more likely to either insist upon repayment, or refuse to grant him an additional loan in the future should he fail to make restitution. The ideal, then, is to ask for a substantial amount, in order to make the request (and its attendant loss of face) worthwhile, but to keep the request small enough so that the eventual financial loss can be absorbed or effectively written off by the woman without retribution. Informants indicated that a request for the equivalent of US$10–15— slightly less than an average week's net earnings— would be a reasonable amount in most cases.

After defaulting more than once on repayment, or upon encountering resistance from his wife, a man might ask an intermediary to request the loan on his behalf. There are actually two or three different scenarios under which this might occur. In one, the man's wife realizes that the third party is acting as a surrogate. She nonetheless participates in the transaction willingly, since she knows that, in the event of default, she can at least pursue the matter through the traditional court system. That option would not necessarily be available to her in the case of her husband's *direct* default, given the prevailing (and often erroneous) assumption that money exchanged between marriage partners would inevitably provide some form of joint family benefit.

A second case of loan-seeking via intermediary typically takes place when the wife is not aware that the loan is actually intended for her husband. This option presents itself when the husband has already exhausted his other more straightforward prospects, or in the event he is simply too ashamed to ask his wife for cash directly. Since the wife has no knowledge of the fact that her husband will be the end beneficiary of the loan, it retains the advantages of the first form of "indirect" loan: she more willingly acquiesces to terms because third party loans are more enforceable than direct loans between marriage partners. Moreover, from the husband's perspective, his prestige is not sacrificed in the process. In practice, however, the husband must still meet the terms set by his surrogate for repayment.

A third variation on the strategy of loan-seeking via intermediary occurs when a third party, typically a junior family member, or even a child, first approaches the *husband* for a loan. In this situation, the man refers the would-be loan recipient to one of his wives. ("Presently if any child asks his/her father to buy anything for him/her, he will say to that child, 'Go to your mother'.") It is worth noting that it does not matter if the husband has cash of his own at the time of the request, or not. Indeed, if he *does* have cash on hand, his objective in diverting the loan request may well be to protect his personal assets and shift the loan burden onto his wife's shoulders.

Another more casual ploy rounds out the gamut of loan-seeking behaviors. This centers on the regular battle between husbands and wives over everyday petty cash expenditures, or what I will refer to collectively as "fish money." These involve cash outlays for meat, fish, cooking oil, sugar, condiments, matches, candles, flashlight batteries, laundry soap; in short, all the basic recurrent expenditures of everyday life in rural Gambia. Typically, the woman (or a small child sent on her behalf) will mention to her husband as he is about to leave for the morning that she needs money to buy fish so she can cook lunch. This is sometimes done deliberately in front of guests if she wants to embarrass him for some reason. He will complain that he has no money and ask her to "help" him (*maakoi*) with a small loan, or forestall her request until later, and then not return until lunch has already been cooked.[6]

A woman's failure to provide a loan or pick up everyday expenses can result in a variety of sanctions being imposed upon her. Most common are the quarrels men initiate with their wives in order to raise the stakes in money matters. According to my informants, the pretext for picking a fight should be carefully selected. The incident should not occur immediately after the loan request has been denied; nor should it occur so long after the request that the connection is obscured altogether. According

to one hypothetical scenario, the husband decides to return home unannounced from a firewood cutting expedition, or a hard day of work on the family's fields. He arrives at a time when he knows his wife is either in her garden, or has yet to draw the evening water supply from the town tap. He then demands to know why there is no bath water waiting for him, complaining: "I came from the farm very tired and dirty, and this woman wouldn't even help me with bath water!" With women routinely absent from family compounds, and cutting corners in order to juggle competing demands on their labor, finding an opportunity to exert such leverage is a simple matter. Men are now in a position to selectively invoke the abrogation of any number of traditional norms governing marriage relationships. The message, in any event, is quite clear: women who do not comply with requests for cash and acquiesce in the niceties of the loan-seeking charade will pay different sort of price. The number of shouting matches does not have to be terribly high before this point sinks in.

To be sure, the tactics men use to alienate garden income need not necessarily poison social relations in this manner. Indeed, informants produced a short list of strategies with the opposite effect, which they placed under the general heading of "sweetness" (*diya*). In the first hypothetical circumstance, the man is exceedingly nice to his wife—what might be called in English, "buttering her up." He may support her positions in public discussion, or even advocate on her behalf on matters of substance having to do with her garden.[7] Alternatively, he may offer material support by (1) contributing labor; (2) lending her his donkey cart;[8] or (3) providing a small cash loan. He thus places himself on secure footing with his wife in order to benefit from her good graces when she makes her decisions regarding the distribution of her financial assets. The final set of strategies employed by men seeking to control their wives' money entails decisions over the disposition of their own cash crop returns. I have already alluded to the fact that men routinely default on the financial obligations they are expected to fulfill. Much of this behavior can justifiably be attributed to the generalized economic hardship that has accompanied the economic trends of the 1980's. Above and beyond such "legitimate" default circumstances, however, are steps taken by men to *deliberately* default on their responsibilities. This they accomplish by quickly disposing of their own cash assets before the exigencies of everyday life ("fish money," third-party loans) absorb them.

The key consideration for men in such circumstances is to choose an investment target that meets with the tacit approval of his wife or wives. Examples of expenditures that would be fully sanctioned would include: the purchase of corrugated zinc pan or concrete for a construction project on the family living quarters; acquisition of a horse or donkey or additional animal traction equipment for farming purposes; or payment of costs associated with ceremonial occasions such as circumcisions or dependents' marriages. Likewise, investment in a seasonal petty trading venture would be largely beyond reproach on the grounds that some joint benefit could potentially be derived from the income generated by the husband's entrepreneurial efforts. Far less welcome would be the purchase of luxury items such as a new radio, fancier furniture for the husband's personal living quarters, or expensive clothing, or, perhaps, spending money on other women. A wife's reaction in the latter case is highly contingent, however. A middle-aged woman without a co-wife may not object strongly to her husband paying the bride price necessary to take a second wife, for example, since she stands to benefit from sharing her domestic workload. However, when the husband already has more than one wife, and his money from groundnut sales or salary payments provides little or no apparent joint benefit to the family unit, the assumption may well be that he is squandering his money on gifts to girlfriends, perhaps the most illegitimate expenditure of all. This and other deliberate default practices are not only frowned upon by women, but are actively resisted, as the next section demonstrates.

BUYING POWER

While men often seek to shift the balance of economic power in the household (back) in their favor, they are not in a position to leverage their wives' consumption choices at will. Indeed, there is considerable evidence that women are firmly resolved to protect their interests, as the following quote demonstrates:

> Our husbands stopped buying soap, oil, rice . . . We provide all these things. Obviously our marriages would change. We do all this work while our husbands lie around home doing nothing. Whenever we return from gardening, we still have to do all the cooking, and all our husbands can say is, "Isn't dinner ready yet?" And then they start to shout at us. Remember, this is after we have already spent the whole day at the garden working. . . . A husband who has nothing to give to his wife—if that wife gets something from her own labor, she will surely find it more difficult to listen to him. We women are only afraid of God the Almighty. Otherwise we wouldn't marry men at all. We would have left them by themselves. . . . Men are always instructing us, you better do this or that for me, while they sit at the *bantaba* [the neighborhood meeting place] all day doing nothing. They describe us as foolish, but we are not, and we will not listen to them.
>
> —*North Bank gardener*

Women use several different strategies to protect their cash incomes. The most basic approach for a woman is to prevent her husband from ever knowing how much cash she has on hand in the first place. This requires that she adopt a "false face" of sorts within the family compound, as though she were not engaged in a complex year-round production system involving perhaps a dozen different crops, grown in three or four sometimes far-flung locations, each generating its own seasonal pattern of income. In order to create and maintain this fiction, women rarely discuss garden matters with, or in the presence of, their husbands. This resolute silence stands in sharp contrast to the running discussion and debates women engage in along the footpaths to and from, and in, the gardens themselves. A veritable stream of information concerning prices available at the different North Bank market outlets (*lumoolu*) is exchanged as women move about and tend to their crops.

Many gardeners hide their income through use of intermediaries to carry produce to market on their behalf. Survey results show that well over half of the women in my research sample rely at least occasionally on someone else to carry produce to market for them. Others ship produce to market directly from garden sites. In this way, their husbands are prevented from actually seeing the produce assembled in one place, an opportunity that would allow them to develop a clearer sense of how much their wives actually earn. Women also sequester their savings so that their husbands cannot easily access them. This they accomplish in a literal sense by wearing money belts on a regular basis. With respect to larger cash sums, the money is commonly given to older female relatives or trusted neighbors for management and safekeeping. In one village, for example, gardeners have opened up savings accounts with a local shopkeeper. Parallel records are kept by the shopkeeper and a trusted local civil servant, each tracking the running balances on individual accounts. Assets are thus protected from seizure by the merchant, who is held accountable by the civil servant. At the same time, the shopkeeper pays no interest and is free to use the cash to capitalize his business or engage in money-lending. In exchange, women benefit from keeping their assets relatively liquid without exposing the extent of their accumulation to husbands directly.

Even with such diversionary tactics in force, the peak of the marketing season almost inevitably brings with it increased "loan-seeking" behavior on the part of men. Consequently, the second major area of attention for women concerns controlling the terms under which loan agreements are undertaken. Thus, if a woman's husband repeatedly defaults on a loan she may choose to stop granting him loans altogether. Alternatively, she can wait for, or insist upon, the intervention of a third party to the loan transaction. In the relatively rare event that this fails to generate the desired outcome of a reasonable repayment rate, the woman may choose to go the risky route of public disclosure. Airing the dirty laundry of intra-marital finances is a virtual invitation to divorce; the messiness of such a scandal would also almost certainly damage the woman's reputation along with her husband's. Such a course may, nonetheless, be preferable to enduring the repeated predatory demands of a greedy husband. Adopting a different strategy, the woman may opt to strategically pre-empt her husband's loan requests by giving him a cash gift before he even asks for money. Such gifts amount to an attempt to carry out an increasingly obligatory transfer of assets under terms the women themselves control: rather than suffer the whims of their husbands, women determine both the amount and the timing of the gift, thus inoculating themselves against unexpected and exorbitant loan requests, which can run the risk of disrupting personal plans at inopportune moments.

Finally, when all else fails, women simply opt for the same solution widely employed by their husbands—they tie up their cash assets by spending them as quickly as they receive them:

> What happens is, some men would like their wives to loan them some money out of their garden sales. Many times women will grant the requests, but most of them will never be refunded. So women gradually limit, or refuse, credit to their husbands. We have a new tactic: when we go to market [with our produce], we simply spend all our money on things that we need, and come home with no money at all to avoid the loan requests altogether.
>
> —*North Bank gardener*

Among the items women buy under such circumstances are dowry items for their daughters such as dishes or pieces of cloth. While some of the men interviewed bitterly criticized their wives for assembling overly lavish trousseaus for their daughters, this tactic may simply be a woman's response to her husband's own profligate spending habits. In cases where deliberate default is mutual, the family's financial security is obviously placed in jeopardy, and the marriage itself rests on quite shaky ground.

CONCLUSION

The Gambia's garden boom has clearly produced dramatic changes in the normative expectations and practices of marital partners in the country's garden districts. In the context of climate change, new foreign investment patterns and structural economic adjustment, the growth of a female cash crop sector has virtually inverted the economic fortunes of rural Mandinka men and women. As a partial consequence, men have withdrawn key financial support from their families. At the same time, the rigors of a double crop (rainy/dry season) rice and vegetable production regime have forced women to either default on, or otherwise finesse, a variety of domestic labor obligations. In short, both men and women have responded to the garden boom in ways that have led to a significant reconfiguration of customary marriage practices.

Verbal sparring between marriage partners has played a prominent role in the negotiations that have accompanied those changes. The wielding of marital metaphors as weapons in a battle to seize and/or regain the moral high ground has resulted in something of a stand-off: men have used the garden-as-husband metaphor to force their wives to transfer control of at least a portion of their assets or face continued verbal assault. Women gardeners have appropriated the metaphor to underscore the perpetual failure of their husbands to provide for their families, and have won for themselves considerable freedom to go about their gardening tasks unimpeded. In short, the garden-as-husband metaphor encapsulates the mutual default of *both* marriage partners on certain customary responsibilities.

Generalizing on societies with "a pronounced division into male and female spheres," Jane Guyer notes that "the specialization [of budgetary responsibilities] is never complete; it oscillates according to

each sex's ability to cope with its own sphere, and its ability to tap into the other or to shift the responsibilities" (Guyer, 1988: 171–72). The "ability to cope" in rural Gambia is directly tied to the capacity of individuals to earn cash incomes, and thereby to the respective fortunes of the separate crop production systems. These fortunes can vary widely by household; they may also hinge on factors such as climate and international market perturbations that are well beyond local control. By contrast, the "ability to tap into" another sphere or "shift responsibilities" is directly related to the localized power dynamics that have taken shape in the garden districts. These have to do with moral economic forces, strategies of deception and the tactics of marital negotiation concerning property, income and power relations.

Since "coping" strategies and ruses designed to shift responsibilities are in play at all times, it becomes extremely difficult, from an analytical standpoint, to prise the two apart. Negotiations over cash transfers between men and women become—quite literally—give and take situations. Loans are loans until men stop paying them. Then they either become "cash gifts," as described above, or the source of more serious struggles, which may lead to divorce. By a similar token, gardens are "husbands" that control women's labor, until they become "husbands" that provide food for women's families. Such ambiguity inflects a final reading of women's "autonomy" in the context of the garden boom. While there is evidence that acts of accommodation undertaken by women on the North Bank have softened the rhetorical stance their husbands once took against gardening, the achievement of this accommodation plateau has not alleviated the pressure on women entirely. They must still meet a rigorous set of competing obligations: not only must they contend with the domestic financial squeeze engineered by their husbands, but they do so under the pressure of surplus extraction from vegetable traders and truck drivers, who largely control the terms of trade for their produce. This double bind is exacerbated in drought years when the irrigated vegetable crop becomes the only bastion against generalized food shortage and extreme economic hardship.

The price of autonomy notwithstanding, women in The Gambia's garden districts have succeeded in producing a striking new social landscape. By embracing the challenges of the garden boom, they are in a position to carefully extricate themselves from some of the more onerous demands of marital obligations. Indeed, in a very real sense, they have won for themselves "second husbands" by rewriting the rules governing the conjugal contract. Thus the product of lengthy intra-household negotiations brought on by the garden boom has not been the simple reproduction of patriarchal privilege and prestige; it has been a new, carefully crafted autonomy that carries with it obligations and considerable social freedoms.

REFERENCES

Guyer, J. 1988. "Dynamic Approaches to Domestic Budgeting: Cases and Methods from Africa." In *A Home Divided: Women and Income in the Third World*, eds. Daisy Dwyer and Judith Bruce, 155–172. Stanford, CA: Stanford University Press.

———— and P. Peters, eds. 1987. "Special Issue: Conceptualizing the Household: Theory and Policy in Africa." *Development and Change* 18 (2).

Schroeder, R. 1993. "Shady Practice: Gender and the Political Ecology of Resource Stabilization in Gambian Garden/Orchards." *Economic Geography* 69 (4): 349–365.

————. 1995. "Contradictions Along the Commodity Road to Environmental Stabilization: Foresting Gambian Gardens." *Antipode* 27 (4): 325–342.

————. 1999. *Shady Practices: Agroforestry and Gender Politics in The Gambia.* Berkeley: University of California Press.

———— and K. Suryanata. 1996. "Gender and Class Power in Agroforestry: Case Studies from Indonesia and West Africa." In *Liberation Ecology: The Political Ecology of Development,* eds. R. Peet and M. Watts. London: Routledge.

———— and M. Watts. 1991. "Struggling over Strategies, Fighting over Food: Adjusting to Food Commercialization among Mandinka Peasants in The Gambia." In *Research in Rural Sociology and Development: Vol. 5, Household Strategies,* eds. H. Schwarzweller and D. Clay, 45–72. Greenwich, CT: JAI Press.

Whitehead, A. 1981. "'I'm Hungry Mum': The Politics of Domestic Budgeting." In *Of Marriage and the Market,* eds. K. Young, C. Wolkowitz and R. McCullagh, 88–111. London: CSE Books.

NOTES

1. At least one North Bank community banned gardening altogether in the mid-1980's because of the irritation men felt at losing this highly symbolic service from their wives (Schroeder and Watts, 1991).

2. It is a traditional sign of deference for a woman to go to her husband's sleeping quarters first thing in the morning and greet him with a curtsey before going about her daily affairs. This is especially the case when a large age differential exists between marital partners. Women interviewed on this topic admitted that garden work sometimes interferes with this practice—"Yes, it's true because a man may go [to the mosque] for dawn prayers and continue on some errands in the village. Before he comes back home, the wife may leave for the garden without seeing him." In most cases, however, women go out of their way to continue performing this highly symbolic gesture. A pattern of shift work between women and their daughters has even evolved to accommodate this and other similar expectations, and thus preserve marital harmony (Schroeder, 1999).

3. This is a substantial contribution. Prices for rice ranged in the neighborhood of US$27 per bag on the North Bank in 1991. By comparison, the annual rural per capita income is roughly US$200 and the average income for gardeners in my research sample is US$150.

4. Husbands and wives commonly occupy separate living quarters. Women sleep with their husbands on a rotational basis with other co-wives; typically a rotation lasts for two days and nights, during which time the wife "on-duty" also cooks and cleans for her husband.

5. In an informal survey conducted in 1989 of mostly well-to-do gardeners, eight of 35 women surveyed had purchased the ram or goat for that year's major Islamic feast day of *Tabaski* (*Id ul Kabir*).

6. These sorts of domestic budgetary battles did not originate with the garden boom; nor are they unique to The Gambia (cf. Guyer, 1988).

7. For example, some men have been instrumental in helping their wives negotiate access to land.

8. The loan of a donkey or ox cart is not an insignificant gesture. Since men control virtually all animal traction resources in The Gambia, vegetable growers would otherwise be forced to carry hundreds of kilos of produce by head pan a kilometer or more to the village. Many women without the benefit of "*diya*" do so anyway.

2 · *Riché J. Daniel Barnes*

BLACK WOMEN HAVE ALWAYS WORKED
Is There A Work-Family Conflict Among the Black Middle Class?

DISCUSSION QUESTIONS

1. What is the "work–family" conflict experienced by the African-American women interviewed by Barnes? Why is their conflict distinct from, for example, that of white middle-class women?
2. What historical practices and processes have produced the enduring image of "the strong black woman"?
3. How do race and class shape their ideologies of motherhood, gender strategies, and negotiations of the demands of career and family?

INTRODUCTION

"I was raised to be independent. I did not know who would be there for me and so it was very important for me to have my own money and my own everything. Depending on my husband now is so contrary to how I think of myself I sometimes think I need to go back to work just to make sure he knows I am making a contribution."

Gail, a married mother of two, and former Chief Operating Officer, who became a stay-at-home mom after she had her first child, discussed what many African American[1] career women who have what has been called a "work and family conflict" navigate. Rather than having a conflict between being working moms and mothers, African American college-educated career women negotiate a conflict between mothering strategies that train them to be independent alongside their desire to be available to their families. Using narratives like Gail's collected through qualitative interviews, observations and family life histories, this chapter challenges the notion of work and family conflict for African American, middle-class families and explores how African American mothers conceptualize and respond to this perceived conflict. While African American and white middle-class mothers have similar options, including part-time, full-time, and flex-time work, and staying home, this chapter draws attention to a persistent distinction between black and white middle-class families that is rooted in separate work and family histories. This chapter focuses on four African American mothers who participated in the larger study. These women, Gail, Nancy, Marilyn and Cara,[2] made changes to

An abridged version of Riché J. Daniel Barnes, 2008. "Black Women Have Always Worked: Is There a Work-Family Conflict among the Black Middle-Class?" In E.R. Rudd and Lara Descartes, eds., *The Changing Landscape of Work and Family in the American Middle Class.* Lanham: Lexington Books, pps. 189–209. All rights reserved. Reprinted with the kind permission of the author and of the publisher.

their work and family practices based on perceived "work and family conflicts." They found that the real conflict was in how to negotiate expectations for educational and professional achievement while responding to very real concerns for the survival of black marriages and families.[3]

BLACK WOMEN HAVE ALWAYS WORKED: A BRIEF HISTORY

Since the first African woman arrived in America during slavery, black women have always worked; and in those years, black men and women labored side by side without wages. Even after the abolition of slavery, and following the Industrial Revolution, black men's wages were so low they needed their wives' and domestic partners' earnings to support their families. At the start of the Industrial Revolution, white men were encouraged to move from an agricultural economy to a manufacturing economy through employment in factories and mills. Some white women entered the industrial workforce as well—typically in gender-segregated industries—and they often stopped working outside the home after marriage. This departure of white women from the formal labor economy was largely influenced by a Victorian ethic of "true womanhood," predicated on ideals of "respectability" and "domesticity" (Lerner 2005).[4] Poor whites, immigrants, and recently freed blacks aspired to this ethic, as it represented a higher station in life, even if their families could not afford it.

The conditions for most industrial workers (primarily men) were poor. They often worked long hours for low wages. The circumstances were even worse for African Americans, as racial discrimination made it difficult for them to find and retain jobs. Both men and women in black households were forced to be primarily low-wage, full-time workers. As a result, pursuing the "cult of domesticity" posed an economic conundrum since black women's wages were necessary. In response the black community developed a tradition of viewing black women's professional work as a contribution to community uplift.

Decades before the feminist movement, African American professional women were "having it all and doing it all," and encouraging others to do the same (Shaw 1996, Landry 2000). Rather than suggesting stay-at-home motherhood, this model placed the educational achievements and professional employment of black women as central to "uplifting" the black race. The uplift movement was particularly important to the success of black communities following Reconstruction and prior to the Civil Rights Movement. Its focus was on education as a means to social, political, and economic equality. Consequently, the first black female professionals pushed themselves to excel and transcend their meager backgrounds. Their success made black women's achievement outside of the home, while simultaneously raising families an expectation that has continued into the present day (Higginbotham 1993).

The maternally oriented structure of the black family, erroneously labeled matriarchal, is another legacy of African American family history that is important for middle-class African American mothers today. This structure is reflected in that most of the African American women in this study, regardless of their parents' marital status, were trained to view their children and careers as their first priority. Some of the maternal orientation is cultural since many parts of pre-colonial West Africa were historically matri-focal. However, African American families continued to be matri-focal as a result of the structural and economic constraints created through the legacies of slavery and racial discrimination.

The African American family has been extensively researched and critiqued, but African American mothers have been largely undertheorized outside of the mass perceptions of the "matriarch," "welfare queen," and hypersexualized "jezebel" (Harris-Perry 2011, Collins 1991). The history of black women at home is also fraught with stereotypic images. One common perception is that of a black unwed mother, on welfare, with several children, and limited parenting skills. Additionally, issues of class bias are evident in the literature, as black middle-class women may self-identify as "stay-at-home mothers," and black single mothers on public assistance may not (West 2003). Indeed, media representations of welfare mothers are typically depicted as black, whereas stay-at-home mothers are most often portrayed as white (West 2003).

RACE, CLASS, AND MOTHERHOOD IN ATLANTA, GA: ETHNOGRAPHIC METHODS AND CONTEXT

This chapter is based upon three years of anthropological research in Atlanta, Georgia, with married, "professional women"[5] with at least one child under the age of six. My research included ethnographic observations of three formal support groups (one white American and two African American) for women who self-identify as "stay-at-home moms"; semi-structured life histories of twenty-three African American stay-at-home and full-time working mothers and their husbands; and twenty-three couple/family histories, including contextualized genealogy charts. The women were contacted through two stay-at-home mothers' support groups and a private school in Southwest Fulton County, where a majority of the parents are married, college graduates, and African American. These women, who live primarily in a zip code recorded by the census as ninety-eight percent black, reported a median income of $151,000.

Due to Atlanta's unique racial history, a sizable black middle class has been a staple of the city since the Civil War. African American citizens have long held powerful positions in city and county government, including the first African American mayor of a major city in 1973 and, in 2001, the first African American female mayor of a major city. A relationship between the city's white business elite and black public officials kept Atlanta from following the hostile racial path of its neighbors during the Civil Rights Movement. At the same time the city developed middle- and upper-class black upscale, affluent neighborhoods

separate and apart from middle- and upper-class whites (Bayor 2000).

At the beginning of my research, each of the women was a member of formal stay-at-home mother support group, which I observed for several months. Later, they each stopped their memberships and either attended intermittently or formed informal groups with others. One woman was a part-time employee for most of her mothering years but over time made modifications to her schedule based on the needs of her family. Each of the women's stories illustrates common themes that I found during my fieldwork. These include: persistent images that negatively portray black men and build distrust within black male–female relationships; the contemporary socio-economic and cultural crises within black communities (especially "ghetto culture" that pervasively represents blacks, particularly black youth, in the media); and the "strong black woman" model of African American motherhood that provides guidelines for mothers and children but leaves marriage a dream often deferred.

REFRAMING THE MYTH OF THE STRONG BLACK WOMAN

From slavery, to the Great Migration, to contemporary structural inequities within the black community, there has been limited reliance on the presence of men. For black mothers, teaching their daughters to be "strong black women" has been about ensuring their daughter's survival. Black mothers have traditionally felt that they must maintain a delicate balance of preparing their daughters to survive within interlocking structures of race, class, and gender oppression, while also rejecting and transcending these structures.

The model of the strong black woman was what sustained many of these women through college, graduate school, and professional training; often while enduring racism and sexism. However, researchers are beginning to understand that the myth of the "strong black woman" can be detrimental to African American women and their families because it expects them to single-handedly take on numerous issues within their families and communities with minimal support (Harris-Perry 2011, Morgan 1999). Gail spoke at length about the effects this strategy for survival had on her perception of herself and her desire for a marital relationship. Gail, the oldest of five children from St. Louis, Missouri said, "I could not wait to get out of there [St. Louis]. I never thought I would be married, have kids, or even think about being at home with them." She was thirty-five, and pregnant with her second child—a girl—her first was a boy. Gail had been married for three years and had left her career as a Chief Operating Officer for a small firm and became a stay-at-home mother. She and I talked extensively over several months as I shadowed her during her daily routines. Her husband was an accounting executive at a major corporation headquartered in Atlanta and they lived in a quiet subdivision in South Fulton County.

When I asked Gail how she decided become a stay-at-home mom, which she had not planned to do, she explained that she was laid off just after she became pregnant with her first child. She and her husband decided that they would wait until the baby was eighteen months old before she returned to work. After eighteen months, neither Gail nor her husband were ready for her to go back to work. They decided that she would stay home indefinitely, as long as they could afford it. While at home, Gail tried her hand at several home-based businesses (medical billing, property management, and staffing local election campaigns), and she also earned her property manager's license.

When I asked Gail how she would describe herself, she said as a "part-time worker" and "full-time stay-at-home mom"— titles she never thought she would have. Prior to meeting her husband, Gail's perception of marriage and motherhood was largely negative. She always knew she would be successful, but she was raised in a working-class family where her mother's full-time job prevented her from spending much time with her children. And although Gail was raised in a two-parent

home, her stepfather and mother had a rocky relationship. "There just weren't any good models of how to do marriage and family," she concluded. The only other married person Gail knew was an aunt, whom she described as a religious zealot who explained marriage as being submissive to a man. Gail said, "While I understand what it means now, as a kid I did not get it and I knew I did not want what she had." In fact, Gail admitted that she was "totally against getting married," and when she did marry, being a stay-at-home mother was not part of that equation.

All the women I talked to expressed similar sentiments. They all valued being independent and being able to take care of themselves; children were often a family expectation; and marriage was something families wanted but did not expect. The seeming pessimism around marriage and family is well founded. According to recent reports, only one-third of black children have two parents living in the home (Page and Huff Stevens 2004). Reports by the National Urban League and others suggest that once one takes into consideration incarceration, drug abuse, and unemployment, the number of marriageable black men to marriageable black women is a stark one man for every two women (Banks 2011, Davis et al. 1997). Additionally, the divorce rate among African American couples has risen sharply: two-thirds of all black marriages end in divorce, and by the time they are sixteen, two-thirds of all black children will experience the break-up of their parents' marriage (U.S. Bureau of the Census 1991). These facts, coupled with economic policies focused on the advancement of women in education and career development, and social services that have historically focused on mothers and children, mean that black women are raised to assume that at some point they may have to support their families and therefore must learn to depend upon themselves.

Nancy invited me to one of the support group's weekly meetings. This group claimed as its mission a Christian, biblically-focused, support network for women who were transitioning from professional careers to being stay-at-home mothers. This was uncharted territory for many of these women, who had left their professional careers behind to be full-time parents. Many of these women's mothers managed full-time work and family obligations (often as single parents), and thus encouraged their daughters to excel in education, careers, and marriage so they could have a better life. However, these women represented a growing number of African American women who are choosing to stay at home with their children. Consequently, they found themselves in an ambiguous position, trying to decipher how to do the right thing, with few clear models for success.

This uncertainty was reflected in the women's discussions. At one meeting seven women were present: a doctor, a fundraising manager for a national non-profit research center, a hotel management executive, two teachers, a small business owner, and a cosmetologist. All of the women were college graduates, some had advanced degrees, and they were all married and considered themselves stay-at-home moms. Following the opening pleasantries, and an update on families and careers, the meeting began with the topic for the day. The group leader (a member who volunteered to lead) began the meeting with the topic "friendship." This bible-based group used the Old Testament narrative of Ruth and Naomi, and their intergenerational friendship, as the basis for their discussion. The conversation quickly turned to a personal discussion of the relationships the women had with their mothers-in-law, which in turn moved to the fragile relationships some of them had with their mothers. They discussed how they had been raised to think of family life in one particular way, but were working hard in their own marriages and as mothers to be different. Nancy, a former physician with three children, said she struggled with both of her parents' expectations for her career alongside her desire to be a good wife and mother.

> It's like my mom does not want me to be happy or she thinks I am an idiot. She thinks my husband is taking advantage of me or something because I try to be the type of wife God wants me to be and she

does not understand that . . . to her it is about being in charge with my dad . . . for me it is about being submissive and letting my husband do what he needs to do for our family and supporting him.

Many of the women could relate to Nancy's comment. They suggested that there were generational differences in how they and their mothers understood their roles as parents and wives and explained that those differences were rooted in the expectation that they would be independent black women—able to take care of themselves and their children—first and foremost. Correspondingly each of the women discussed their predicaments as daughters of "strong black women" who expected them to be independent. As Gail revealed, that focus on independence often made black women believe they should not desire or plan to get married.

MAKING BLACK MARRIAGE AND FAMILY WORK

Despite the "baggage" that weighs down black couples, many hope that marriage and family can work and are willing to try both. In an attempt to cultivate positive relationships, women like Marilyn and Nancy reveal how different the work and family conflict is for black women than what is often depicted in contemporary narratives of family formation.

Marilyn reported that she was raised to be an independent career woman. As a result she said she was ambiguous about marriage and family until she met her husband. "I never daydreamed about my wedding day or what my husband and kids would be like," she said. But then she met her husband. "We had been dating for a couple of years, I loved him and he asked so it seemed like a good time to get married. Then a few years later it seemed like a good time to start having kids." But Marilyn and her husband separated after their seventh year of marriage. Marilyn attributed their separation to having too much "I" and "me" in their relationship. She notes: "I was going through a point where

I was redefining who I was and we hit a point where he did not connect with me at all . . . Too much 'I' and 'me' makes it hard on a marriage."

Marilyn was a very achievement-oriented woman. Before reducing her hours as an account executive for a national health insurance firm, she also managed her church bookstore, served as moderator for several women's groups, volunteered as a class parent at her children's school, and dabbled in an at-home marketing firm. Working part-time for her insurance firm eight to ten hours per week, Marilyn continued the same "extra-curricular" activities. "The only difference is I get seven hours of sleep per night instead of five and we are not rushing around as much," she said. Marilyn's three children were in school, ranging from pre-school to fifth grade. She kept a tight grip on their activities and time management and at one point served as president of the Parent Teacher Association (PTA), as well as soccer coach and team parent for her children, alongside her husband.

Nancy, a former doctor of internal medicine, was born in Waco, Texas to a sixteen-year-old mother and an eighteen-year-old father. Unsure of their future, her parents separated, but later reunited and married when Nancy was seven. Nancy was raised by her maternal and paternal grandmothers while her mother worked as a nurse. Although her parents stayed together, and had three more children, their relationship was rocky. Nancy said she did not want a marriage like theirs. But instead of opposing marriage, like Gail, or being ambivalent to it like Marilyn, Nancy hoped for a better partnership.

At the time of this study, Nancy was thirty-six, and the mother of three children under the age of four. She did not self-identify as a stay-at-home mother, although she was the primary caretaker. When I asked Nancy how she identified she was unsure, but knew she did not identify with women who "sat at home and ate bon-bons." "I am too busy to be a stay-at-home mom!" Nancy exclaimed. Her husband, a former attorney, owned a home-building company, and they lived in a gentrifying Atlanta neighborhood near Turner Stadium.

When Nancy first left the medical profession, her family was supportive. However, when one

year turned into three, the women in her family decided Nancy had been home long enough: "I can remember being home for Christmas and I was taking care of the kids and it was difficult because the baby was really small. My grandmother walked by and said, "I don't know why you doing all that, they ain't gonna appreciate it." Nancy continued:

> It hurt a lot when she said that and I decided that, even though I appreciated my mother and my grandmothers and all that they had done for me, I did not want to raise my family the way they had raised theirs and I battle with that every day.

Nancy did not fall into the category of having been raised by a strong, black, single mother as both her grandparents and parents were married. However, she had watched both her grandmother and mother struggle with their husbands. "There is no love," said Nancy. "I mean there is. I know my grandmother loved my grandfather and my mother loves my father but you cannot see their love in how they interact and how they treat their husbands. There is no respect. I do not want that kind of relationship with my husband." Even though Nancy critiqued her mother and grandmother, she realized that the interaction they had with their husbands was related to the ideals of strength they had to assume to maintain their families. Nancy was taught this same strength when she saw how hard her mother worked to earn her nursing license. It was Nancy's mother and grandmother who provided the encouragement and funding for her to become a doctor, and she knew that was the type of strength that she was expected to exhibit. For African American professional women, such as Nancy, many feel their worth as black women is deeply connected to the strength of their mothers.[6]

Nancy articulated a purposeful position of building a "healthy marriage and family," in which the needs of her family, and particularly her husband, were foremost. She saw this as a way to break a seemingly multi-generational cycle of low marriage and high divorce rates. What Nancy called for in her decision to leave her medical career to support her husband and care for her children was a shift in the black community from an emphasis on career and individual achievement to family centeredness. Instead, Nancy and the other women in this study saw the work and family conflict through a new ideology of black motherhood, which teaches independence, individuality, and a focus on black women's roles as community leaders, mothers, and professionals, but less frequently as wives.

Likewise when asked if they were raised by their parents (or guardians) to be more career women, wives, or equal parts both, each of the women in this study responded that they were raised to be career women and most felt they had not been prepared to be wives. The tenuous male-female relationships in the black community have created a conundrum in which black women are raised to "take care of themselves," with the understanding that children are a blessing, but husbands often are not. While women, particularly middle-class women, continue to be encouraged to marry, these "mother-wit"[7] cultural cues often disrupt marriage by suggesting that marriage will not last.

Overall, the women in this study made it to the altar, yet they were learning that lasting marriages were built on negotiation. These women had to negotiate larger societal expectations that they would contribute to the rising divorce rate and make another female-headed, single-parent, household. They also contended with centuries-old stereotypes about black men (they will leave, will not work, and will cheat), and they had to maintain their own independence—never depending on a man—if they wanted to be strong black women and good mothers. The question was increasingly; at what cost?

ENCULTURATING MIDDLE-CLASS BLACKNESS

Their class position and their relationship with work placed these women in a position where they were faced with the challenge of remaining an integral part of the black community while simultaneously mediating many of the seemingly negative influences associated with blackness. Correspondingly, there were costs to these mothers associated with reformulating black families and their focus on sustaining their families, especially in the arena of gender equity. When asked to categorize household tasks by the person responsible for completing them, all the women in the study stated that they completed more of the tasks than their husbands. While they were dissatisfied with how much of the responsibility was their own, when asked if and what they would change, none of the women suggested their husbands do more but indicated instead that they would like to outsource more. At first glance, this position seems like a return to what has been termed neo-traditional gender roles, but a conversation with another woman in the study suggests other identity formulations may be materializing. Cara, a thirty-six-year-old mother of three and former school psychologist turned real estate investor, relayed that when people learned she worked from home, her children attended preschool, and she employed a housekeeper they would ask, "What do you do all day?" Cara responded, "White women have been doing it for years . . . When I think of black womanhood I think struggle and I don't want to live like that."

While Cara pushed against normative expectations of black women, her sensibilities were ruffled. For black women, hiring help is mired in social dictates that are not easily overcome. Many are daughters or granddaughters of domestic workers, nannies, or washer women, and they find hiring women to do similar tasks synonymous with hiring their own kin. They are also well aware of the history of the exploitation of black women's labor and understand that women who provide productive labor for one household are typically unable to afford household services for their own families.

CONCLUSION: BLACK AND MIDDLE-CLASS MOTHERHOOD

The cultural memory around African American, male–female relationships has long held that they are fragile and susceptible to the forces of racism, sexism, and classism, in ways that other ethnic groups are not. This knowledge has motivated African Americans to bolster their families through the use of support systems such as the church, extended family, and governmental assistance. A folk culture arose that understood, articulated, and disseminated the belief that African American women could and most likely would, at some point, experience being a single mother and with that "fact" firmly set in place, African American women must be able to take care of themselves and their children.

It is within this context and this cultural memory that the women in this study found themselves juxtaposed between an educational and family of origin background that thoroughly prepared them to be professionals and mothers, often at the expense of marriage, and an upper- middle class social location that expected and often demanded stable, two-parent homes. For Nancy and Gail it meant ignoring the advice of mothers and grandmothers who cautioned them "not to depend on a man," or otherwise exhibit "laziness." They both saw what that type of attitude did to their parents' marriages and knew they wanted different marriages, unions that were both intact and happy.

While Gail and Nancy dealt most specifically with the contradictions inherent in their desires to be good wives and mothers and their educational, professional, and family background, Marilyn grappled with reformulating her identity as a high-achieving corporate woman to nurture her family, taking a reduction in hours in Marilyn's case.

It was Cara who provided the most telling depiction of the ambiguities inherent in these women's lives as each and every one of the women in the study made some reference to being a strong black woman, an independent woman, or a woman who could take care of herself and her children. The mythic view of the strong black woman has been passed down within families and communities. Its origins are in African tribal customs and in the capitalistic nature of the slave trade, which designated black men and women as perfect chattel. The title, although a badge of honor, has dictated through cultural memory that black women must be able

to do it all. However, what is carried forth along with the apparent strength of the black woman is the constant sense of struggle. While these women want to be responsible to their communities, their families, and themselves, often choosing to live in racially segregated, black, middle-class neighborhoods, they also want a bit of reprieve, a "lighter" way of life, wherein they are not constantly called upon to carry the weight of the black family on their backs. The women in this study were working to build strong marriages, however, this framework often meant rejecting the good advice of mothers, grandmothers, sisters, aunts, and friends, who traditionally have been the people African American women depended on when the men were not around. It was difficult to turn away from the cultural models they had always known and that they identified with and built their futures on. But these women recognized that the framework in which African American women were taught to expect to be alone, while praying not to be, was bad for their well-being. While it was not an easy statement to make, and may have felt like betrayal, Cara and the other women in this study were beginning to assert, "I don't want to live like that. We shouldn't have to."

In academic and popular press publications, placing husbands and children before personal career and professional goals has been termed neo-traditional (e.g. Gerson 1985). However, for African American, middle-class women, although taking care of family has always been a priority, it was not at the expense of a professional role, but in tandem with it. These African American women experienced a conflict between career and family that results in them reducing their employment hours, changing their professions, and becoming stay-at-home moms. However, these choices are not a result of the reasons the scholarship suggests. The literature, concerned mostly with white couples, talks about the demands and inequities of the workplace, and the inequalities inherent in the gendered division of labor. The women in this study, however, were reformulating their identities as they turned away from the icon of the "strong black woman" and built up one of the "strong black family."

BIBLIOGRAPHY

Banks, Richard. 2011. *Is marriage for white people? How the African American marriage decline affects everyone.* New York: Random House Press.

Bayor, Ronald. 2000. *Race and the shaping of twentieth-century Atlanta.* Chapel Hill, NC: University of North Carolina Press.

Collins, Patricia Hill. 1991. *Black feminist thought: Knowledge, consciousness, and the politics of empowerment.* New York: Routledge.

Davis, Larry, Shirley Emerson, and James Herbert Williams. 1997. Black dating professionals' perceptions of equity, satisfaction power, romantic alternatives and ideals. *Journal of Black Psychology* 23: 148–164.

Gerson, Kathleen. 1985. *Hard choices: How women decide about work, career, and motherhood.* Berkeley, CA: University of California Press.

Harris-Perry, Melissa. 2011. *Sister citizen: Shame, stereotypes, and black women in America.* New Haven: Yale University Press.

Higginbotham, Evelyn. 1993. *Righteous discontent: The women's movement in the black Baptist church, 1880–1920.* Cambridge: Harvard University Press.

Kinnon, Joy Bennett. 1997. Mother wit: Words of wisdom from black women. *Ebony Magazine,* March. http://findarticles.com/p/articles/mi_m1077/is_n5_v52/ai_19201537

Landry, Bart. 2000. *Black working wives: Pioneers of the American family revolution.* Berkeley, CA: University of California Press.

Lerner, Gerda. 2005. *The majority finds its past: Placing women in history.* Chapel Hill, NC: University of North Carolina Press.

Morgan, Joan. 1999. *When chickenheads come home to roost: My life as a hip-hop feminist.* New York: Simon and Schuster.

Page, Marianne E., and Ann Huff Stevens. 2004. The economic consequences of absent parents. *Journal of Human Resources* 39: 80–107.

Shaw, Stephanie. 1996. *What a woman ought to be and to do: Black professional women workers during the Jim Crow era.* Chicago: University of Chicago Press.

Stack, Carol. 1974. *All our kin: Strategies for survival in a black community.* New York: Harper & Row.

Sudarkasa, Niara. 1997. *Strength of our mothers: African and African American women and families.* Trenton, NJ: Africa World Press.

U.S. Bureau of the Census. 1991. *Population profile of the United States.* Current Population Reports, Special Studies, Series P-23, No. 173. Washington, DC: Government Printing Office.

West, Laurel Parker. 2003. *Welfare queens, working mothers, and soccer moms: The socio-political construction of state child-care policy.* PhD diss., Emory University. http://wwwlib.umi.com/dissertations/fullcit/3103824

NOTES

1. "Black" and "African American" were used interchangeably by the study participants to refer to their racial/ethnic identity. I use them both here in keeping with their self-identification and to signal their ethnic location as descendants of American slavery.

2. Gail, Nancy, Marilyn, and Cara are pseudonyms used to protect the identities of the study participants.

3. This analysis does not aim to dispute the usefulness of the phrase "work and family conflict," but rather it shows how the phrase operates within a different meaning system for African American middle-class mothers, and, therefore, is understood and articulated differently even when the work and family practices are the same.

4. The Victorian model of womanhood dictated that "respectable" women refrain from working outside the home. This model, also termed the "cult of domesticity," was espoused by the land-owning ruling class and carried into less well-off communities.

5. The term "professional women" is herein defined as women holding, or having previously held, a corporate executive or professional position and/or having an advanced degree.

6. "Strength of their mothers" refers to the book penned by Niara Sudarkasa, *Strength of Our Mothers* (1997), in which she discusses the strength African American women have had to demonstrate from slavery to the present to preserve their families.

7. According to Joy Bennett Kinnon, "mother wit" is referred to in the dictionary as simply "common sense." In black history, the word usage began in the seventeenth century. Thus the word was born and distilled in the brutality of slavery and has survived to enter the new millennium. It was a code word then, and is still a code word for the knowledge you must have to survive. Kinnon states, "It is, as author Toni Morrison says, 'a knowing so deep' that the lesson has been instilled and distilled to its essence. Collectively these words are a gift—from your own mother, or anyone's mother. They are wise words for life's journey" (1997).

3 • *Matthew C. Gutmann*

SCORING MEN
Vasectomies, Gender Relations, and Male Sexuality in Oaxaca

DISCUSSION QUESTIONS

1. What are some of the dominant ideas or "folk beliefs" about male sexuality in Oaxaca? How are these ideas and beliefs similar or different to the realities of men's sexual practices and desires?
2. How do gender, sexuality, reproduction, and power inform the negotiations between men and women about whether or not men should have vasectomies?
3. What are the roles of doctors and friends in these discussions and decisions?

INTRODUCTION

This paper discusses why some men in Oaxaca, Mexico, get vasectomies and what this decision has to do with negotiations between men and women there about birth control and sexuality. Through this research I explore broader issues relating to men's sexuality, including normative assumptions about men's "natural" sexual desires and practices. Clearly numerous issues influence and determine a man's decision to get this permanent form of contraception, including cultural, historical, physiological, commercial and individual factors. A key issue that emerged in the course of a larger study on men's reproductive health and sexuality in Oaxaca is how cultural folk beliefs about supposed male sex drives influence men's decisions about birth control. Conventional wisdom among medical practitioners as well as the men who get vasectomies treats male sexuality as naturalized, as both a fixed entity and as something entirely distinct from female sexuality (see Gutmann 2003). The social beliefs and mores regarding male sexuality are therefore medicalized, transformed into a physiological truism.

What occurs locally in Oaxaca is, of course, also governed by global events. In the case of men choosing to get a vasectomy, this decision takes place at a time when highly effective forms of birth control for women have become widely available throughout the world, and in fact there has developed what Colombian anthropologist Mara Viveros Vigoya (2002:328)—referring to modern forms of birth control—calls a *cultura anticonceptiva femenina* (a female contraceptive culture). Nowhere on earth do men participate in contraception in larger numbers than women; in most locations the percentage of men using male forms of birth control is a tiny fraction of women employing other methods.

An abridged version of Matthew C. Gutmann, 2005. "Scoring Men: Vasectomies and the Totemic Illusion of Male Sexuality in Oaxaca." *Culture, Medicine and Psychiatry* 29: 79–101. With kind permission of Springer Science+Business Media and of the author.

Indeed, one striking feature of decision-making about birth control in Oaxaca is the fact that the number of vasectomies performed there has never been large. Through 2000, according to official statistics, 3,105 men had undergone a vasectomy in Oaxaca (INEGI 2000:265), out of a population in the state of over three million men and women. The procedure itself is unknown to most people in the region, and irrelevant to all but a few who express familiarity with the term. Figures on male sterilization in Mexico overall hover slightly above one percent of the adult male population; by way of contrast, figures for China and the United States, for example, are 10 and 14 percent respectively. The rate of female sterilization in Mexico is around 28 percent (country figures on sterilization are from EngenderHealth 2002). Thus the number of men who participate in birth control by getting sterilized is relatively low in Mexico, including Oaxaca, both in comparison with other countries and with women in this area.

Understanding why some men in Oaxaca do opt for this form of birth control is not dependent upon the numbers or percentages of those involved. At the outset it is nonetheless worth mentioning two possible factors influencing men's decisions about sterilization that ultimately were less in evidence than originally anticipated. First, because the vast majority of people in Mexico are Catholic, it could be argued that men who choose to get a vasectomy must deliberately reject Church doctrine forbidding the use of artificial contraception and sterilization of any kind. Yet not only do the vast majority of women in heterosexual relationships in Mexico use some kind of birth control—in 1970, the fertility rate in Mexico was 6.5, whereas in 2002 it was 2.8—but, tellingly, the issue of Catholic strictures in this realm rarely arose in the course of dozens of interviews with men and women from this admittedly self-selected group.

Second, there is also a culturalist explanation that attempts to explain what men in Oaxaca who are thinking about the operation must overcome. In fact, this cultural rationale is sometimes used to explain why there are lower numbers of men getting vasectomies in Mexico compared to men in certain other countries and to women in Mexico itself: supposedly there are differences between "macho" and "non-macho" cultures, as if those men who do get sterilized in Oaxaca might somehow be acting in a manner unrepresentative of their macho culture. In addition to the fact that "macho" means different things to men and women of different ages (see Gutmann 2006), such a line of reasoning skirts the larger context of decision-making about birth control in Oaxaca. Building on Viveros's notion of a female contraceptive culture, it is of great significance that there are few modern forms of artificial birth control designed for men. This circumstance is not unique to men in Oaxaca. Therefore the problem of how to understand men's participation in birth control, such as by choosing to get a vasectomy in Oaxaca, is governed by the cultures of global pharmaceutical companies and basic research on male hormones (see Oudshoorn 2003) as much as by specifically local gender identities and relations of inequality (e.g., "machismo").

Among the truly salient local factors influencing decision-making about vasectomies in Oaxaca is a set of folk beliefs shared by health care specialists and the population at large concerning male sexual practices and urges, beliefs whose basis in fact extends no further than their wide acceptance in society. Among health care practitioners, for example, the main source of certain foundational beliefs about male sexuality in Oaxaca and Mexico continues to be prosaic sentiment represented as scientific knowledge that serves as the starting point in reproductive health care efforts. These beliefs include the penchants of adolescent males for sexual self-gratification, the equation of male sexuality with uncontrollable urges, and the presumption that many men are having extra-marital affairs. Sexuality is understood both popularly and in the medical community as a process of psychosocial compulsions and restrictions, in which ostensibly male sexual desires, needs and satisfactions are given a naturalized and thoroughly gendered character.

Vasectomy is not inherently a good or bad form of contraception, reproductive health policy, or means to promote equality between men and women. Throughout the world vasectomy has been employed by certain individuals, institutions, and governments to encourage the expansion of sexual rights and obligations and by others to further eugenicist and neocolonialist goals. As important as it is to study men's reproductive health and sexuality in local historical context, scholarship in this area is, unfortunately, scarce. To date, many anthropological studies on reproduction have also focused on women (see Browner 2000; Ginsburg and Rapp 1995); the present study seeks to provide new information about the "missing" players in the reproductive process.

PERSONNEL AND PLACES IN THE OAXACA STUDY

This study of heterosexual couples was conducted in Oaxaca de Juárez, a metropolitan area of around 500,000 people located in a mountain region 300 miles south of the Mexican capital. Approximately half the population of the state, totaling over 3 million people, self-identifies as belonging to one or another indigenous group (the largest being Zapotec and Mixtec). According to nearly all indices, living standards in the state of Oaxaca are among the lowest in Mexico, especially in the countryside. My ethnographic fieldwork in Oaxaca City in 2001–2002 was carried out in two vasectomy clinics, the state-run AIDS clinic, and in the Ethnobotanical Garden of Oaxaca where I worked as a laborer clipping cactus and digging ditches for planting and irrigation.

I observed 22 vasectomies in three different clinics and I interviewed dozens of other men and women in clinic corridors. Interestingly, both ethnographic fieldwork with dozens of men and archival research on files for hundreds of other men in this project show that men who decide to get vasectomies are not clearly distinguished by any particular demographic features related to age, income, education, or being of particular ethnic groups.[1] I also watched three tubal ligations to witness what I had been told was a dramatically more

serious surgery. As performed in Oaxaca's public clinics, there can be no doubt about this.

My opening line at the outset of a vasectomy—as I stood near the man's head, introduced myself and described the purpose of my presence in the procedure and asked permission to attend the operation—was, "Well, they did this to me six years ago. Of course, I wasn't paying much attention to the details of the operation at that time." Before long, owing primarily to the lack of surgical nurses in one clinic (Centro Urbano #38) and to the somewhat taciturn nature of the doctors operating in another (Clínica #1), I was integrated into the procedure in various ways.[2] Primarily I was used by the doctors as an emotional anesthesiologist to soothe the men's nerves.[3] Other times I was asked to hold upside down a bottle of the liquid anesthetic lidocaine in order for a doctor to extract more into a needle and thus further numb the man's scrotum.

I shared stories with the men as to pain I suffered after my own surgery, vaguely discussed mutual concerns regarding sexual performance post facto, and once was asked to photograph an operation. It was the doctors who initially asked me to take the photos. When I raised the idea timidly with the patient, a gas station attendant named Alberto, he smiled broadly, enthusiastically agreed to allow me to shoot pictures of his genitals in the procedure, and asked me to drop by copies at his PEMEX workplace on the north side of the city.

The challenge of distinguishing between what people say and what they might mean is important here. In recounting the comments of men and women who shared their views and experiences on vasectomy, some of the women I interviewed identified their husbands as the real decision-makers. Yet, like Rayna Rapp, who studied women's decision-making surrounding amniocentesis in New York City, I too "often wondered whether I was witnessing male dominance or female invocation of a classic manly privilege" (2000:99–100). Of particular interest to me were interactions akin to what Rapp calls gender scripts that "revealed healthy doses of female manipulation." Decision-making about vasectomies in Oaxaca, as with amniocentesis in New York, indicates "a complex choreography of domination, manipulation, negotiation, and, sometimes, resistance in the gender tales women tell about their decisions." This tension between what people say for public consumption and hints at ulterior motives and hidden rationales necessarily undergirds much of the analysis to follow.

VASECTOMIES TO SHARE SUFFERING

Whether men who opt for vasectomies express demonstrably more egalitarian relationships with their wives, and whether they say they are prompted to make this decision by persuasive women is relevant to tracing patterns of decision-making among men with respect to reproductive health and sexuality. Indeed, in several case histories we find what can be termed an initiating-catalytic role of women in these couples and a group of men who are willing to attend to the desires and demands of women; in other words, men who hardly fit the model of emblematic patriarch (see Gutmann 1997). It is not uncommon for women themselves to make the appointments for their husbands to get *la operación*, as many refer to it.

At the same time, although the decision has most direct bearing on the reproductive and sexual relationship between men and women, many men also recount that it was another man or group of men who convinced them to seek the operation. Many men told me about their discussions with male friends, coworkers, and relatives as to what would happen during and following the procedure. And interviewing men during *la operación*, I occasionally mentioned that I had checked with my brother-in-law beforehand to relieve my own concerns.

Marcos was a man whom I interviewed during his vasectomy and later in his home. After driving a taxi for thirteen years in his native Mexico City,

Marcos had recently followed his wife and moved in with her family in Oaxaca. He had also spent a year in Las Vegas trying to recoup finances after an extended illness of his father. When asked about the decision-making process prior to his vasectomy, after returning from Nevada, Marcos related:

> Right, more than anything, it wasn't a discussion, it was . . . in our case when she and I talked about it, she told me, "What do you think about it if I get the operation?" So I told her, "Well, whatever you want, babe, but I can get an operation, too." And she says, "You would do it?" I say, "Yeah, yeah, I would do it, because, yeah, you've already suffered in one way or another with the kids, in childbirth, so there's nothing wrong with them operating on me."

When I asked Marcos if he considered himself in any sense unusual or unique in comparison to other men who relied entirely on their wives to "take care of themselves" in terms of contraception, and why other men might be like this, Marcos replied, "It's the ideas we Mexicans have. We have ideas that are a bit macho. And if I say 'we have' it's because sometimes I have these ideas, too. We don't appreciate that women really suffer in childbirth with our children. And all that idiosyncrasy about, 'Mothers are self-sacrificing women.'"

Juan used a specific term when describing the negotiations preceding his vasectomy: his intention was "try to help my wife a little in family planning." She had always reacted poorly to pills and injections. As to why more men did not follow his example, Juan also, like others, thought there might be something peculiar to Mexican men: "Here in Mexico I think that because of the . . . ummm . . . how to put it . . . the machismo, men think that having a vasectomy will put an end to everything and that you won't have . . . relations any more. Well, what do I know?" He offered a pragmatic explanation as well: as soon as his wife learned about vasectomies she was done with trying the other methods. The next man in line for the operation nodded in agreement. That is what had happened to him, too.

Rogelio is a 29-year-old fireman with two children. After using an IUD for six years, Rogelio told me, his wife was delighted about his decision to get a vasectomy. And, he emphasized, it had been *his* decision alone to get *la cortadita* (the little cut). Her enthusiasm was an important factor in his decision—"Just think what it's like to have kids!" When I asked Rogelio what would happen if he and his wife some day decided they wanted another child, his answer was simple, "We'll adopt." But even more decisive it seemed was the role of his best friend, also a fireman, who told him, "Get with it!" Rogelio estimated that 10–12 men at work had had vasectomies in the year or two since a health care promoter named Orvil from the state-run AIDS clinic, COESIDA, gave the men a talk on safe sex practices. Men who have had vasectomies and others who are receptive to the possibility of getting sterilized are utilized by health promoters like Orvil to induce more men to get *la operación.*

Miguel is 32 years old and went to school through eighth grade and has two children. At the time of our talk, he made plywood in a local factory. When I asked whether he and his wife had used condoms he told me, "For about three days." Like other men, Miguel told me that neither he nor his wife liked condoms. And, like others, he gave two reasons: one, *"no se siente lo mismo"* (you don't feel the same), and two, "because of machismo." When I pressed Miguel to explain the connection between machismo and not liking condoms, like other men he was unable to further analyze his views. But he did insist that he wanted to "be different than most men," and that this was a key motivation behind his decision to get a vasectomy: *"Hay que ser comprensivo con las mujeres"* (You've got to be understanding with women), he counseled me. At this, Dra Serret, the female specialist in vasectomies at Clinic #1, commented, *"¡Qué bueno que ha decidido cooperar!"* (It's great you've decided to support your wife).

Suffering was also on the mind of Marcelo, 29 years old and the father of three children, who worked as a policeman on the outskirts of the city, near the famous archeological ruins of Monte Albán. He recounted to me that his wife was the one who prompted him to get sterilized, with the admonition, *"Te toca un poco sufrir"* (It's your turn to suffer a little).

Talking with Esteban, yet another bus driver who had a vasectomy, and his wife one afternoon under an awning of their house near the Río Atoyac that runs through Oaxaca City, it was made clear to me that Andrea's medical condition had made sterilization a most pressing issue. "The doctor told me that it was strongly recommended I not get pregnant again," his wife said. Besides, Esteban added, they already had three children. They thought seriously about Andrea getting her tubes tied, Esteban recounted:

> It's just that she was really bad off then. I said, "I'm going to have to take care of you, I am going to have to be waiting on you if they tie your tubes. They're going to operate on you, they're going to cut you. It would be better not," I told her, "it would be better if they did it to me." Because I didn't want her to go through with it. I, well, the truth is that I love her a lot, no? So I don't want her to suffer.

Esteban's sister later praised his decision, "Well, I congratulate you, little brother, because you are rare among men." Friends of his were not as inspired by his vasectomy. When Esteban encountered another driver at the big Central market, he explained that he was not working because he had "a little surgery: they gave me a vasectomy." "Don't jerk me around!" his companion taunted him. "And now?" "Everything's fine," Esteban responded. But his friend seemed skeptical. "The hell you're really fine?" he quizzed Esteban. "Yeah, I went into the clinic walking and I left the clinic walking. It was no big deal. It's a slight cut [*una cortadita*], maybe half a centimeter. That's all they do. *No hay problema.*"

Empathic responses to women's suffering and desire to share spouses' pain are clearly motivations involved in some men's decision to get sterilized. At the same time, the influence and authority of friends who had already had the operation was often described by the men I interviewed in Oaxaca as the deciding factor for many men. They checked with their friends about pain, turnaround time until they could return to marital liaisons, and residual effects on their sexual desires and performance from the procedure. There were a few men who expressed complete lack of concern as to potential "side effects" from the surgery, like impotency or at least diminished sexual *apetito*, but they were in a distinct minority. Good information about vasectomies was rarely readily accessible, and several men explained that only because they had been so determined were they able to ultimately obtain correct information about vasectomies and secure an appointment for the surgery. All in all if there is one thing that characterizes most of the men I interviewed as to why they opted for vasectomies it would be their expression of sympathy for women's suffering in the past and their desire to have the women avoid such suffering in the future, either through another unwanted and potentially harmful pregnancy or through a tubal ligation. Yet these were not the only reasons men chose to sterilize themselves.

AFFAIRS AND DOUBLE-STERILIZATIONS

Despite such concerns on the part of most men I came to know through the vasectomy clinics in Oaxaca, and the real empathy and generosity demonstrated by men and women upon arriving at difficult decisions such as sterilization, the picture presented thus far is not complete. Indeed there is another set of reasons men offer for getting vasectomies that also reveals much about underlying patterns of gender relations and inequalities in a variety of ways.

In fieldwork, I encountered cases of men who had received vasectomies, despite the fact that their wives had earlier had tubal ligations. Here I discuss the case of one such man.

I met Alejandro's wife and son outside the room where the vasectomies take place at the Centro de Salud #1 in downtown Oaxaca City. Alejandro was out pacing the sidewalk, while Mercedes and their child held Alejandro's place as second in line for the four vasectomies scheduled that morning. Alejandro entered the building just before 8:30 A.M., when he had been told to return. He was whisked quickly into the changing anteroom, then onto a padded table used for the operation. Assuming my by-now standard position up at the patient's head, Alejandro and I began talking as the doctors prepped him down below.

The nurse interrupted me by asking Alejandro to fill in a standard epidemiological survey:

"Age?" "40."

"Marital status? "Married."

"Children?" "Two."

"Reason for having a vasectomy?" "I don't want any more children."

"Previous birth control?" Alejandro paused, finally answering, "None."

A few days later I talked with Alejandro and his wife, Mercedes, in their living room. He was still a bit sore from the operation, but back at work and brushing off the after-effects of the procedure. I asked why he decided to get a vasectomy. Mercedes responded instead, "We'd been talking about it for eight years. Ever since our son was born."

Alejandro said he had delayed so long mainly because he was worried about "mistreating" his body with the vasectomy. But, he insisted, when he finally determined he would go ahead with the procedure, "It was my idea. I decided to do it. I did it to satisfy her, not because I am going to '*dejar hijos regados*' (sprinkle children around). Because she's already had her tubes tied, so . . . well . . . "

"Oh, yeah?" I exclaimed in surprise when I realized that this meant that they both had been sterilized. "Then why . . . ?"

"To please me," Mercedes agreed with tenderness.

"Why was this important to you?" I pressed her.

"Better to avoid surprises" (*más vale prevenir sorpresas*).

"So I don't go around sprinkling children everywhere, that's what she says," Alejandro added somewhat defiantly.

"Mexican men are like that, just like that," Mercedes concluded, as if little else was necessary to explain the couple's double-sterilization.

When I encountered her a couple of months later at Clinic #1, where she had come for a consultation of her own, Olivia again repeated the phrase *"más vale prevenir sorpresas"* (better to avoid surprises) though added that she did not think he was actually running around on her (*saliendo*) at the time.

In another case of a man getting a vasectomy despite the fact his wife already had a tubal ligation, he just shrugged when asked to explain the double-sterilization method of birth control. The female doctor operating on the man suggested it might just be a precaution, because there is always the risk of *fallas* (mistakes), even with drastic surgery like tubal ligation. The male doctor speculated aloud that it might be more related to the man's occupation as a bus driver, and nudged the man as he noted how many girlfriends of drivers are said to be found waiting at the end of many bus lines.

Even well-intentioned doctors and others who are in the forefront of promoting vasectomies as a simple, effective, and egalitarian form of birth control, and whose message is that vasectomies should become more common than tubal ligations, make reference to "culture" as what is holding people in Mexico back in general, including in promoting egalitarian forms of reproductive health. One doctor expressed dismay that Mexican women are simply more used to suffering physically, and Mexican men are afraid of "mutilating themselves" and therefore do not want doctors to "cut a thing" on their bodies.

And not surprisingly, perhaps, even men who describe the decision-making process prior to their sterilizations as equitable and aimed at sharing contraceptive burdens acknowledge with a wink the sexual urges that supposedly come preloaded in male bodies. Marcos, the taxi driver from Mexico City who had recently relocated to Oaxaca, insisted that he and his wife talked, and as long as his wife satisfied him sexually, there was no need for him to seek (male) release elsewhere: "In a relationship, when one person leaves home 'well fed,' there's no point in looking for food anywhere else. No, I've got food at home. Why should I go looking for more?"

SHARING RESPONSIBILITY FOR CONTRACEPTION

Throughout the world today, debates are unfolding in families and public institutions regarding men's shared responsibility for sexual behavior and improving women's and men's reproductive health. Since international conferences in the mid-1990s on gender and development in Cairo and Beijing, the official policy of government agencies and NGOs around the world has been to encourage men's involvement in birth control and safe sex as part of the effort to promote the right of women and men to regulate their fertility and to have sexual relations free from fear of unwanted pregnancy or disease. Yet little headway has been made in achieving real gender equity and men's participation in this realm (see Chant and Gutmann 2000). Until we better understand the actual sexual and reproductive lives of men and women, such projects will continue to flounder.

On the more intimate level of families and households, for example, we know too little about how women and men discuss, debate, and decide on sexual behavior and make reproductive decisions and how changing affective relations between men and women in turn alter cultural values concerning reproductive health and sexuality. In order to better understand decision-making processes in couples regarding birth control it is important to include men in studies of contraceptive aspects of reproductive health. There is a host of "outside" factors—from the media to the church to public health institutions and campaigns—that influence the wrangling within couples over such decisions. Determining the impact on men and women of cultural preconceptions in the medical community, for instance, with respect to male sexuality, is crucial to chart how people are pressured to adapt to one kind of sexual behavior or another.

The relationship between globalizing and localizing factors—sexual commodification, ethnic coding, and migratory circuits of information, disease, and novel practices—in governing negotiations over men's reproductive health and sexuality is only now emerging as a significant field of study and with respect to vasectomy and male contraception is still largely terra incognita. Recent scholarship on gender in Mexico and Latin America has demonstrated the relationship of engendered power identities and inequalities to culture change (e.g. Núñez Noriega 2014). In line with these studies, what is most salient in the present investigation is an emphasis on viewing inequality as the *basis* of change. For example: the relationship that women have to men's sexuality and negotiations regarding birth control; how to understand men's role in reproduction and why they are only just beginning to be included in studies and public health efforts concerning reproductive health; and the realities of birth control: what role biology, culture, and politics have in determining which forms of birth control exist, are utilized, and are developed.

Regarding the matter of choice and whether health practitioners are practicing bad faith medicine, cultural assumptions about men's reproductive health and sexuality often unintentionally sway men against opting for vasectomies. Given that Mexico in the twenty-first century is completely dependent on the products of foreign pharmaceutical companies, virtually the only other options available to men who wish to play an active role in birth control are condoms, withdrawal, or the rhythm method. There are branches of these companies in Mexico, but usually these are simply the local sales force. Occasionally there is a clinical trial carried out in Mexico, yet then, too, the trials are for products already developed elsewhere.

There are few doctors in Oaxaca who know how to perform vasectomies. There is widespread ignorance as to what the procedure entails. In the absence of temporary forms of male contraceptives other than the condom, women will continue to take overwhelming responsibility for birth control. In the absence of widespread information including public campaigns regarding vasectomy, it is unlikely that the numbers will grow of men in Oaxaca who choose sterilization. How else may one open the debate on the relationship between vasectomy, procreation, and machismo?

Even if small in scale, several campaigns in Oaxaca have been aimed at simply involving men in the sphere of reproduction, and have sought results primarily in the form of participation of one kind or another in family planning programs. Yet these approaches have repeatedly failed in any but short-term bursts because they have not even attempted to resolve underlying causes of male reticence to use birth control. General inequalities, including in the sphere of reproductive health and sexuality, have remained concealed, and therefore unchallenged.

Because there are today in Oaxaca no widely available forms of male contraception based on manipulating male hormones, we might casually assume that no method can be found because of factors inherent in some special culture of men there, which in turn is believed grounded in male physiology. We could casually assume this. But if we did we would be missing the larger picture.

BIBLIOGRAPHY

Browner, Carole. 2000. Situating Women's Reproductive Activities. American Anthropologist 102(4):773–88.

Chant, Sylvia, and Matthew C. Gutmann. 2000. Mainstreaming Men into Gender and Development: Debates, Reflections, and Experiences. Oxford: Oxfam.

EngenderHealth. 2002. Contraceptive Sterilization: Global Issues and Trends. New York.

Ginsburg, Faye D., and Rayna Rapp. 1995. Conceiving the New World Order. *In* Conceiving the New World Order: The Global Politics of Reproduction. Faye D. Ginsburg and Rayna Rapp, eds., pp. 1–17. Berkeley: University of California Press.

Gutmann, Matthew C.. 1997. The Ethnographic (G) Ambit: Women and the Negotiation of Masculinity in Mexico City. American Ethnologist 24(4):833–55.

———. 2003. Discarding Manly Dichotomies in Latin America. *In* Changing Men and Masculinities in Latin America. Matthew C. Gutmann, ed., pp. 1–26. Durham, NC: Duke University Press.

———. 2006 (1996). The Meanings of Macho: Being a Man in Mexico City. Second edition. Berkeley: University of California Press.

INEGI. 2000. Anuario Estadístico del Estado de Oaxaca, Edición 2000. Tomo I. Mexico City: INEGI.

Núñez Noriega, Guillermo. 2014. Just Between Us: An Ethnography of Male Identity and Intimacy in Rural Communities of Northern Mexico. Tucson: University of Arizona Press.

Oudshoorn, Nelly. 2003. The Male Pill: A Biography of a Technology in the Making. Durham, NC: Duke University Press.

Viveros Vigoya, Mara. 2002. De quebradores y cumplidores: Sobre hombres, masculinidades y relaciones de género en Colombia. Bogotá: Universidad Nacional de Colombia.

NOTES

1. I interviewed dozens of men before, after, and during their vasectomies. Initial contact took place in clinics. With several men I followed up with visits to their homes, where I would talk with both the man and his wife for several hours. With some men contact continued after the two interviews; with most, this was it. Demographically, perhaps the only outstanding characteristic is that men who sought sterilization reported already having as many children as they wanted. While they had income and education levels slightly higher than the state average, far more impressive was the range of these levels.

2. I conducted the bulk of this research in two clinics. One, the Centro de Salud Urbano #1, is operated by the Ministry of Health, which is supposed to provide health care services for the rural and urban poor in the Oaxaca City metropolitan area. The other clinic, the Unidad Médica Familiar #38, is part of the Mexican Institute for Social Security, which officially serves workers in the formal private sector of the economy.

3. The doctors who performed vasectomies in Centro #1 were both originally from Oaxaca and had received their medical training, including in this procedure, there. One of the doctors at the Unidad #38 was from Mexico City (where he went to medical school) and the other was from Oaxaca and was finishing her residency there. In Centro #1, one of the doctors was a man and the other a woman, and there was a female nurse generally present throughout the procedure. In Unidad #38 one of the doctors was a man, the other a woman, and nurses were rarely present.

DESIGNING WOMEN
Corporate Discipline and Barbados's Off-Shore Pink-Collar Sector

DISCUSSION QUESTIONS

1. What gender ideologies shape the belief of Data Air and other corporations that young women in Barbados are "better suited" for data-entry positions? How do these ideologies accord with gendered ideas and practices in Barbados?
2. What is the "pink-collar" sector? How does this sector reflect and produce ideas of gender and class?
3. Why do dress and appearance become key sites for asserting corporate control and discipline? Why do women "consent" to demands that they dress "professionally"? How are ideas of power, agency, and structure useful for analyzing this issue?

THE OFF-SHORE OFFICE AS SCENE FOR RESEARCH

The bright yellow awning-shaded tables of Chefette are crowded with young Bajan women animated in their lunchtime conversation; their colorful and fashionable dress turns the heads of passersby. Within moments, the fast-food tables empty and the high-heeled workers of Data Air[1] escape the midday Caribbean sun, hurrying back to the air-conditioned hum of the "open office." These women represent vast changes in international labor patterns and technology. Their lives have suddenly become intertwined with service workers in such disparate places as Ireland, the Dominican Republic, Mauritius, and the United States, as the information age signals the virtual collapse of national boundaries and labor and capital become increasingly globalized.

An abridged version of Carla Freeman, 1993. "Designing Women: Corporate Discipline and Barbados's Off-shore Pink-Collar Sector." Reproduced by permission of the American Anthropological Association and of the author from *Cultural Anthropology*, Volume 8, Issue 2, Pages 169–186, May 1993. Not for sale or further reproduction. See Freeman (2000) for the full study.

On the data-entry floor of this off-shore information processing facility, more than 100 women sit at clustered computer stations, entering data from some 300,000 ticket stubs from one airline's 2,000 daily flights. One floor below, an equal number of women work as "approvers," entering data from medical claims sent for processing by one of the largest insurance companies in the United States. This expanding company alone hires close to 1,000 Barbadian workers—almost all of whom are young women. Their fingers fly and the frenetic clicking of keys fills a vast and chilly room as Walkman-wearing women work eight-hour shifts at video display terminals—constantly monitored for productivity and accuracy—typing to the latest dub, calypso, or easy-listening station. The muffled clatter of keys creates a sort of white noise, and the green glow of a sea of computer screens lends an Orwellian aura to the tropical setting outside.

Data Air and Multitext Corporation are both foreign-owned off-shore companies (American and British). Both set up shop in Barbados in the mid-1980s, and are managed almost entirely by Bajans. The move from the American Southwest to Barbados has saved Data Air's parent company roughly 35% on its data-entry costs, in addition to the profits made from its expansion into insurance claims processing for one of America's largest firms. From the Barbadian standpoint, this company provides close to a thousand jobs, and its Bajan general manager anticipates that a recent expansion will generate significant foreign exchange, desperately needed in the face of new structural adjustment measures.

Located under the general umbrella of manufacturing, and marking the latest version of high-tech rationalization of the labor process, the expansion of this new off-shore industry represents a massive international commodification of information, including everything from academic texts and airline tickets, to pornographic novels, scientific articles, and literary classics. New satellite technology facilitates fast and relatively inexpensive transmission of information between "offices" all over the world, connecting "core" and "periphery"

within and between nations. These information-based enterprises closely model their traditional manufacturing counterparts, and what looks like clerical work (generally considered white-collar "head" work) begins more closely to resemble low-skilled, highly rationalized assembly-line work in corporate garb.

Recent studies have addressed the ways in which the global economy, with its vast movements of capital, labor, and changing technology, is radically reshaping people's (and particularly women's) lives. Traditional boundaries and spatial relations have suddenly blurred as capital, labor, and relations of production and consumption are conflating as borders vanish altogether.

Although international movements of people, goods, culture, and ideologies are hardly new historical phenomena in the West Indies, the current character and scale of these processes are arguably distinct. As these newly incorporated pink-collar workers so clearly reveal, "natives" (and this is particularly evident within the Caribbean) travel between the global north and south in increasing numbers, as imported goods and ideologies—from religion to electronic media—circulate freely. Information, and the processors of that information, zoom between countries in these internationalized relations of production. At Data Air, employees are rewarded for exceptional production rates with "thank you cards" in the form of travel vouchers for trips to other Caribbean islands, Canada, or the United States. Women purchase clothes, jewelry, and household goods from abroad, both for their own consumption and for marketing back home in an active and diverse informal sector.

While work processes are increasingly fragmented and deskilled, in the case of office work these processes produce a gendered working class. Clerical jobs are often believed to constitute middle-class "mental" or "non-manual" work. However, new "office" contexts (with a one-to-one boss:secretary ratio at one extreme and vast data-processing pools at the other) force us to look more closely at the organization of labor process. Informatics in the form of high-volume information processing—with its low skill level, low pay, and repetitive, fragmented nature—more closely resembles the labor of factory work than traditional office work.

Some feminist analyses of automation argue that, although increased office-computerization reduces some areas of boss–secretary exploitation, it simultaneously enables other forms of control and oppression (Barker and Downing 1980). Rosemary Pringle suggests that the decline in status of clerical work in the 1950s and '60s compromised the feminized status of clerical workers as "ladies"—they were consigned to a mass category of "girls" (1989, 193). In Barbados, I would argue that *both* processes are taking place together; creating a new class fraction of distinctly feminine subjects. The notion of "pink-collar" workers here implies these simultaneous processes of feminization and proletarianization.

WOMAN AS "BETTER SUITED": REINVENTION OF A FAMILIAR MYTH

One development officer who specializes in off-shore information processing in Barbados offered a familiar explanation for why women workers are preferred for this work. It was not deliberate selection, he said, but the nature of the production process, as well as the educational and cultural climate.

> Women tend to do light assembly work which involves sitting and manipulating fine objects. Some persons claim that men don't have that good coordination . . . I don't know how true that is, but . . . some people claim that. I think it might more be a matter of aptitude—and aptitude is probably cultivated by your society and so on. A man is seen in movies and in real life doing things, moving and so on. A man is never seen sitting . . . sitting especially on a line manipulating fine things. And he may not have had the practice, because in terms of practice, women have had practice manipulating needles and doing fine intricate things, embroidery or cake icing, or being more delicate. And also they have

smaller hands, so if you're going to manipulate fine things the physical structure may have some impact. Whatever the reason is, it so happens that women tend to do data entry, garments, electronic assembly, and men tend to do heavier type work. As for the reasons, I wouldn't try to imagine.

This development officer resorts both to a biological rationale that women's passive, patient, and dexterous nature makes them best suited for sedentary, monotonous, and meticulous work, and to the liberal position of choice—that women do these jobs because they have the requisite skills and exercise individual free will. He vacillates between the "nature" and "culture" rationales for the selection of women, but overall, implies that these patterns are obvious, and bear little comment, far less challenge.

From management through rank-and-file data-entry clerks, such "commonsense" explanations abound: women perform these jobs because they are simply "better suited" for the work. One of the few male employees in a non-typing job at Data Air explained,

> I never really thought about one of the keying jobs. I probably think my fingers are too big for the keyboard. To me, a lady would handle that a lot better than a gentleman . . . 'cause . . . the touch a lady has, it would be much more comfortable to her. And I personally am the type of guy that likes to be moving around—active—I mean lifting things and that kind of thing.

In Barbados, as elsewhere, girls traditionally learn typing in school, not boys. It's not surprising then that it is women who apply to data-processing jobs. A certain tautology pervades this logic and effaces the underlying cultural ideologies surrounding gender-based occupational categories. Notably, in the sister plant of Data Air in the Dominican Republic, the work force (performing virtually identical jobs) is roughly half male and half female, a majority of whom hold postsecondary technical degrees.

A Data Air personnel assistant conducting recruitment interviews shed light on the large numbers of young (often single) mothers hired. The six women she interviewed one day ranged in age from 18 to 22, and *all* had children. Although she sympathetically "wondered how they manage it all," she added, "in the long run they [mothers] make the best workers . . . They have better family values and a greater sense of responsibility" than others, who are "too flashy" and "in there just for their paychecks." The implication here is that single mothers work harder and exhibit greater commitment to their jobs.

In the data-entry industry, two contradictory profiles of "ideal" workers underlie management's preference for women workers. The young single woman is the quintessential off-shore worker: a "daughter" enjoying the independence that comes from earning a wage, and contributing a nonessential income to the household. The alternative stereotype is of the "older" woman, a *mother* who is both the backbone of her family and a dependable employee. One of these "older" women described this generational divide:

> Now I'm 25. When I came here I was 18 . . . one of the youngest in my department . . . Down here, although the age difference is only about 5–7 years apart, I think it is very noticeable. When I came here I was working for BDS$187.50 (US$ 93.75 biweekly). That is one figure I will never forget. How many of these people do you think are going to work for that? What they are making now is considerably more than what I was making then, but they don't think it's enough. I know people that even resign from here and just went home and sat down because they didn't think that coming in here and working for that salary made it worthwhile . . . they don't really stick it out . . . I think that generation now are different . . . they don't take the same hassles that we have in our day. They're less tolerant. Most of these people in here was born in the '70s and I was born in the '60s. I think if you want you could call it a generation gap . . . they haven't seen this company transformed and maybe they don't feel a part of it, but we that were here saw the progress.

Contrary to other global contexts, the old guard of Data Air are a significant presence, often favored over younger "school leavers" in the Barbados-based data-entry industry.

CORPORATE DISCIPLINE IN THE OPEN OFFICE

A number of elements distinguish the new information-processing enterprises from the off-shore assembly plants that preceded them, from the labor process itself to technological surveillance and the ideologies shaping an ideal feminine work force. Although the garment and electronic industries have also targeted young Third World women, the particular methods of control and surveillance fostered by computer technology lend a new dimension to "corporate discipline." Using a video display terminal (VDT) every employee can be electronically observed continually; her productivity can be measured; and she need never be engaged in face-to-face contact. The computer is not only a primary attraction for women to this job, but it represents a tool of convenience that evaluates the worker as well.

Michel Foucault described early processes of industrial management as "laying the groundwork for a new kind of society, a 'disciplinary society,' one in which bodily discipline, regulation and surveillance are taken for granted" (in Zuboff 1988, 319). The phenomenon of VDT workers in the information industry is, even in its clean and "cool appearance," a haunting reminder of Jeremy Bentham's 18th-century panopticon that Foucault analyzed as a form of control. Managers' and supervisors' glass-enclosed offices surround the data-entry floor while workers, susceptible to their gaze, focus on the VDT screens. Additionally, as I will show, workers behave in proscribed ways even when not under direct surveillance by management, and regulate each other's approach to work.

Focusing on hardware alone ignores the processes by which technology is mediated through a host of other social practices such as language and dress—critical to feminist labor studies. Technological transformations are integrally bound up in forms of supervision as well as in the general—and gendered—expectation that clerical workers conform to so-called traditional female stereotypes (e.g., that they be pleasant, courteous, well groomed, and cheerful).

Dress is a key realm through which discipline and control are enacted and enforced in this new "clerical" enclave. One corporate officer proudly proclaimed that the information-processing industry offers a work environment on a par with that of other *offices*. "Women are expected to dress professionally here," he said. "This is not a production mentality like jeans and tee shirts." Women stated that "you can tell by the way [a woman] looks" whether she is going to work at one of the nearby garment factories or in data entry. Although they note little difference in pay between the two, data entry is considered a step above garment factories. Vividly illustrating this point was the expression of disbelief and even indignation when some data processors learned of a fellow worker who quit her job as a keyer to work at a piece rate in a neighboring cigar factory.

Discussing her job in this information enclave, buzzing with the sound of computer keys and "plenty of gossip," one young woman explained how "professionalism" is maintained:

> They had to talk to one or two people in there already about the way that they dress, but I never had to be spoken to like that. You should dress in a place like that not like if you're going to a party or a disco or going to town . . . [you should] dress as if you are working at an office . . . 'cause some people don't really look at it as being an office. But if they were working in an office they would dress a certain way, so I think that if you think that way about working at an office, think that way about working at Multitext and dress to suit the occasion.

In the arena of the "open office," dress and fashion are not only forms of invisible labor and powerful metaphors of corporate discipline but also key to individual expression and pleasure. Data Air's employee-produced newsletter clearly connects dress, corporate ideals and cultural values:

> What you wear is really who you are and how you feel about yourself.
>
> Clothing sends a message, a statement to others about you.
>
> Clothing can whisper stability and high moral standards, or it can shout rebellion and discontent. It can serve as a form of identification.
>
> Supervisors are concerned about the way you dress; for them it is more than an issue of personal taste. They want you to send the right message, one that projects you as a balanced, responsible person.
>
> Ladies, before you select what to wear, you must decide whether the clothing is suitable for work. Materials that are so revealing should be reserved for the bedroom. Stop and think about the impression you are giving to onlookers; and it matters not whether you are on the night or day shift. You are dressing for work!
>
> Deodorants! What you wear with what you wear! People won't notice how neatly and appropriately dressed you are if they're gasping for fresh air when you're in the same room!

Despite the fact that this service job is behind the scenes, off-shore data entry operators are expected to present themselves as though they are serving a client face-to-face. The enticing appeal of the slick, air-conditioned "open office" and the dress codes go a long way in persuading workers of the "professional" nature of their jobs. The contradictions between their factory wages and fancy titles, such as "material controller," and "instructor specialist," heighten the ambiguities.

When women compare their present "professional" jobs in data entry to those in other industries (in terms of status, monetary reward, job mobility), some said that they could be making more money working as domestic or agricultural workers, and that their wages are comparable to those in a garment or electronics factory. Many have held these jobs but would rather be in data entry because of the job setting and the "cool" look of the place. The manager-owner of one of the smaller, local data-entry operations explained:

> When you see a group of the young ladies, like the ones from Data Air, you can see that they're much better dressed than the ones from the assembly plant. That's my observation. They're probably not getting paid much better but their work environment is a cleaner one, a purer one, and they in fact live out that environment . . . The Data Air office is very plush, so the young ladies working in there perceive that they are working in an office and they dress like it and they live like it. It's a very interesting phenomenon—it only got started when the data entry business got started—this new breed of office-type workers. They equate themselves with . . . clerical staff in an office and they carry themselves in that way.

Women acknowledge exploitative production quotas, labor practices, and what one called the "we say and you do" attitude, however, their pride at working in a "professional enterprise" (whether real or imagined) quells some of these frustrations and, in the face of rising unemployment and economic uncertainty, assists in maintaining very low attrition rates (2%). For example, although excessive discipline is an often-mentioned complaint (along with pay and favoritism), it is also cited as a contributing factor to the workplace professionalism integral to an "office" environment.

One woman described, on the one hand, the company's obsessive concern for time and order—a half-hour lunch, constant monitoring, and "rules and regulations on everything under the sun"— and complained, on the other hand, that many "new girls don't understand the importance of a serious professional approach" to their jobs. They talk instead of working and dress casually in "short short skirts and off-the-shoulder tops or rolled-up pant legs and flat shoes." Peer pressure both contradicts and supports corporate prescriptions: groups of workers voice complaints to management about bathroom conditions or excessive overtime, and at the next moment tease and harass a fellow worker

for her "inappropriate" clothes or her "unmannerly" work habits.

Like multinationals in other parts of the world, these high-tech enterprises have shrewdly tapped into a strong Barbadian concern with appearance and have turned this set of cultural values to the advantage of international capital by encouraging workers to identify with a well-defined corporate image. Corporate ideologies about femininity and work, and disciplinary measures that subtly enforce them, contribute to pink-collar workers' pride as "professional" workers. Dress as a manifestation of corporate discipline becomes interwoven with the pervasive and conservative Barbadian ethic that places great emphasis on grooming and deportment.

Feminists have long debated fashion: is it a "part of empty consumerism, or is it a site of struggle symbolized in dress codes? Does it muffle the self, or create it?" (Wilson 1990:231). I would argue that dress becomes an arena in which local (class-based) and international corporate values are simultaneously contested and consented to. As Wilson convincingly states, the puritanical position that construes consumer culture as an opiate, "duping the masses into a state of false consciousness," ignores the complexities of women's decision making and the pleasures derived from fashion. Women's experimentation with clothes reveals an aesthetic inventiveness that can be interpreted either as conformity to international corporate consumer culture or as enhancing their exploration of alternative subjectivities. Women of all ranks refer to their enjoyment and expenditure in clothes, as well as to the "pressure to dress hard" and the rampant gossip and teasing to which they are subject when their hairstyles and clothes fail to conform. One woman expressed her contradictory sense of the dress question in the following way:

> Our policy is governed by a dress code . . . We are not a factory. We call ourselves an "open office" and if you were working in an office, you wouldn't go in a jean skirt or jean pants or short skirts. You would dress as if you were an executive. That's what we

expect our persons to do. Now when we realize that our people are not dressing the way we think they should, we speak with them; we have even gone as far as to ask persons to go back home and change because their attire was not properly suited for the work atmosphere. And we instill that in our people, so by practice and counseling, we have reached the stage where people recognize us for the way we look. They usually say we work for a lot of money [she laughs]. It's not that, but you're governed by a particular code you have to adhere to—you are being watched. And not only that but, because there are so many young persons, they usually talk about you if you don't look good. They say "how could you come in here looking like that?" and they want to keep the image up, and certainly as a manager, I wouldn't like to think that my people are coming in here and looking better than me [laughs again]. So you want to dress a certain way to be in line with them, because they do speak about you.

Even as a manager, she describes a sense of surveillance—from below. Recently, and independently, work groups within these vast data-processing facilities have designed and commissioned needleworkers to make them uniforms—brightly colored skirt suits and dresses with distinctive matching scarves and pocket handkerchiefs. Women are proud of this symbol of professional status that is comparable to airline workers and bank tellers, yet presents an economical way of adhering to the style protocol.

Whereas the Malaysian factory women in Ong's work (1987) are reputed in their local contexts to be "loose" and "modern" for having adopted Western-style clothes, the Barbadian women are often reputed to look well-off, and even showy, their dress obscuring the reality of their low-skilled, low-paid, tedious work. In the tradition of Boserup (1970), Lim (1985) asserts that women working in multinational factories gain independence through exposure to the modernity of urban free-trade zones. Indeed, the relative prestige associated with being one of "the Data Air family," along with the promise of independence (amorphous as it may be) and fewer jobs in the context of structural adjustment

measures, seem to effectively convince many of the young women that they are fortunate to be where they are.

Yet many of the women testified that their motivations for working in the industry extended beyond basic economic necessity. Some emphasized "getting out," dressing up and "being a working woman" among friends in addition to earning a wage and contributing to a household economy. In Barbados, and the Caribbean in general, women's wage work has a long history, and female independence is considered high relative to other parts of the developing world (Barrow 1986). Not one of the 85 women I interviewed indicated that her job created turbulence within her family. Most reported that their families were pleased with their contribution to the household economy and the sense of responsibility and prestige associated with a full-time job using a computer. No one described being pressured or prohibited from taking a data-entry job, as has been widely noted in Mexico and Malaysia (Beneria and Roldan 1987; Ong 1987).

Women's own statements about work are complex and often contradictory. Some say that sitting at a computer for eight hours every day is "easy" or "cool" compared to other jobs that "have you on your feet all day" (e.g., shop assistant or garment assembly worker). Others, however, describe being "chained" to the machine. They express enormous frustration and annoyance at being treated like "school girls" with rules and regulations, and time constraints. They resent being surrounded by so many other "girls," where "every day is the same," and, perhaps worst of all, with "nowhere to go from there."

At both Data Air and Multitext Corporation, incidents of computer-based theft or sabotage reveal ingenuity on the part of the workers as well as an unexpected sort of mastery over a fragmented and apparently sealed system. In each case, individual keyers figured out ways of "tricking the computer" by copying disks or hitting particular keys in such a way as to achieve exceptional speed and accuracy reports and effectively double their paychecks in the process. When the scandals were uncovered, management at both companies was forced to "tighten security" either by reorganizing the distribution of work to ensure greater control or investing in an entirely new computer system. Even under exceedingly close technological supervision, workers have discovered high-tech loopholes that, if even for a short time and in the form of theft, enable them to gain an element of control over their labor.

WOMAN'S BODY: SITE/SIGHT OF CORPORATE DISCIPLINE AND STYLE

I have alluded to a distinctive "corporate style" that underlies the relations of production in the off-shore information-processing industry, and that plays a significant role in the constitution of the Barbadian off-shore data processor in ways that set her apart from other enclave workers (i.e., garment and electronics workers). Elements of ergonomic design that turn a factory shell into an "open office," along with an identifiable fashion statement become bound up in the overall labor process through a notion of corporate "style."

Corporate style molds discipline as well as ideologies. The "smart, professional" dress code reinforces several contradictory messages and subjectivities. When asked to account for the reputation of Data Air workers as exceptionally well-dressed, many said that Bajan women simply love to dress. Therefore, even though they acknowledge the company's strict dress code, they locate the distinguishing mark of the "Data Air girls" in themselves—their own cultural practices and values. The lines are thus blurred between corporate control, worker consent and complicity in presenting themselves as the company prescribes, amid broader cultural mores regarding dress and fashion.

The "well-dressed" reputation of the Bajan processors is accompanied by outsiders' assumptions that they must be making good salaries to afford such expensive-looking wardrobes. Thus, the notion of "professional style" is a powerful

expression of a particular corporate ideology and discipline that runs through the labor process as well (Freeman 2000).

Along with the other aspects of decor and ergonomic design—the framed floral prints in the offices, the muted colors of the walls and carpeting, the high-tech look of the computer work stations with their swivel chairs and divided desk spaces, the soft lighting and air conditioning—the women's presentation of themselves as professional workers sets this off-shore industry strikingly apart from others whose labor processes are remarkably similar. If dress is a form of corporate discipline lending itself to a certain work ethic, many women willingly consent to this demand, claiming it as part of their own cultural identity and individual expression.

Many women clearly like their jobs and express great loyalty toward their employers. Several repeated lines resonating from Data Air's corporate "mission:" "We're like one big family," and "We're all in it together." Despite the fact that they work for a foreign company and have witnessed (and/or personally experienced) the sudden flight of similar off-shore companies, most seem to have a surprising degree of faith in the company's commitment to them and to Barbados.

Women's consent to corporate guidelines does not necessarily imply that they are simply duped by a monolithic corporate construction of a feminine worker; rather, it emphasizes the complex and contradictory nature of their positions as workers and women. As revealed in the development officer's quotation above, the focus on women's "inherent" sense of responsibility, manual dexterity, patience conceals very real measures of control within the workplace and reinforces a sexual division of labor that consistently places women in low-skilled, low-paid, dead-end jobs.

As automated technologies replace the need for a vast data-entry arena off-shore, some companies have again shifted operations closer to their North American or European home offices. Increasingly companies are poised to move into more specialized off-shore computer based arenas (e.g., software design, computer graphics, data-based research, animated video production services, computer-aided design [CAD]). The massive growth of Business Process Outsourcing, including the call centers in India and many other countries including Barbados, represents the next wave of globalized informatics. Developing and industrialized nations alike scramble to come to terms with the labor and technological demands that will enable them to win other such potentially lucrative contracts. Barbados has responded to these impending changes, in part, by advancing higher value added services to the off-shore sector and endorsing the neoliberal call for self-employment and *entrepreneurialism* (Freeman 2014). Within the informatics realm, the shifts promise higher-skilled jobs for more-educated people and pose important questions in light of the gendered face of those industries that preceded them. Enrollments at the University of the West Indies, like universities all over the world, are increasingly dominated by young women prompting public outcry about boys and men in crisis. However, as informatics work becomes increasingly skilled, the work force appears to assume a more masculine profile. Will we witness a reversal of the feminization of informatics? Will the pleasures as well as the pressures be transformed? These are among the complex questions posed with the growth of immaterial labor and the rise of services in the 21st century.

REFERENCES CITED

Barker, Jane, and Hazel Downing. 1980. "Word Processing and the Transformation of the Patriarchal Relations of Control in the Office." *Capital and Class* 10:64–99.

Barrow, Christine. 1986. "Autonomy, Equality and Women in Barbados." Paper presented at the 11th Annual Caribbean Studies Association Meeting, Caracas, Venezuela.

Beneria, Lourdes, and Martha Roldan. 1987. *The Crossroads of Gender: Industrial Homework, Subcontracting and Household Dynamics in Mexico City.* Chicago: University of Chicago Press.

Boserup, Esther. 1970. *Women's Role in Economic Development.* New York: St. Martin's Press.

Freeman, Carla. 2000. *High Tech and High Heels in the Global Economy: Women, Work and Pink Collar Identities in the Caribbean.* Durham: Duke University Press.

———. 2014. *Entrepreneurial Selves: Neoliberal Respectability and the Making of a Caribbean Middle Class.* Durham: Duke University Press.

Lim, Linda. 1985. *Women Workers in the Multinational Enterprises in Developing Countries.* Geneva: International Labor Organization.

Ong, Aihwa. 1987. *Spirits of Resistance and Capitalist Discipline: Factory Women in Malaysia.* Albany: SUNY Press.

Pringle, Rosemary. 1989. *Secretaries Talk: Sexuality, Power and Work.* New York: Verso.

Wilson, Elizabeth. 1990. "The Postmodern Chameleon." *New Left Review* 180 (March/April): 187–190.

Zuboff, Shoshana. 1988. *In the Age of the Smart Machine: The Future of Work and Power.* New York: Basic Books.

NOTE

1. The names of companies and individuals have been changed.

2 · *Gracia Clark*

MOTHERING, WORK, AND GENDER IN URBAN ASANTE IDEOLOGY AND PRACTICE

DISCUSSION QUESTIONS

1. How does the concept of "economic motherhood" explain the ideals and expectations of Asante women as mothers?
2. What are the different economic, political, and social responsibilities of men and women as spouses, parents, siblings, and workers among Asante? How does the fact that Asante are matrilineal influence these responsibilities?

Motherhood is central to female gender ideals for the Asante people of Ghana, West Africa, as in many cultural systems. They consider parenthood an essential element of both male and female gender and of personhood in the deepest sense. Neither men nor women can be fully gendered, one way or the other, and become whole persons, without biological children. In order to be a fully adult human being, a person must have descendants. A person who voluntarily refuses or neglects to have children counts as a kind of suicide, since this rules out the final stage of life, as an ancestor. Motherhood and fatherhood both have culturally defined biological, social, spiritual, and emotional aspects, and both have consequences for a person's work life.

Exploring the relationship among Asante concepts of work, gender, and parenting sheds light on Western assumptions about the conflicted working mother, the source of so much controversy in the United States today. Asante market traders work at least as long hours as the double day faced by U.S. working mothers, but without the same supposed guilt. The good, self-sacrificing Asante mother does not stay home with her children, but goes out working hard for them. Asante culture links motherhood tightly with work in unselfish maternal devotion, opposing them conceptually to marriage and sexuality, considered more individualistic and potentially self-indulgent. Asante single and working mothers still confront the practical dilemmas of their material situation, but without the additional burdens of stigma, recrimination, and frankly hostile public policies. Public hostility to their trading work has not been lacking in recent history, but it draws on conflicts rooted in marriage, not motherhood (Clark 1988).

An abridged version of Gracia Clark. 1999. "Mothering, Work and Gender in Urban Asante Ideology and Practice." Reproduced by permission of the American Anthropological Association and of the author from *American Anthropologist*, Volume 101, Issue 4, Pages 717–729, December 1999. Not for sale or further reproduction.

Asante is one of the matrilineal Akan cultures predominating in the south of Ghana (West Africa), where most of its wealthiest and historically most powerful areas lie. Akans comprise about two-thirds of the multiethnic national population, and Asante culture dominates in Ashanti Region and its capital, Kumasi. As elsewhere, Asante naturalize their own culturally constructed elements of motherhood into biological imperatives, linked to naturalized elements of other matrilineal relations. The moral principle that both men and women should give absolute priority to their matrilineal kin, not their spouses, is strongly held by urban as well as rural residents, and across class lines. In this matrilineal society, the structural importance of maternal ancestry makes it an ineradicable part of personal identity.

The fundamental Asante kinship unit, the *abusua*, comprises the adult descendants of one grandmother: her children, her daughters' children, and her granddaughters' children. These minimal lineage units link mothers with children and also uterine brothers and sisters as the closest categories of kin. As long as the oldest set of siblings remains active elders, they should confer about funerals, inheritance, succession to leadership, and other important decisions. Abusua members live together in inherited or rented housing when possible, and exchange many kinds of assistance on a negotiated basis. Asante kinship ideals endorse a very high degree of flexibility and negotiability in the content, if not the fact, of kinship.

The Asante gender framework still sets up specific tensions between work and motherhood, but these focus on the financial demands of motherhood rather than the labor demands of childcare. Mothers considered many market and home occupations incompatible with childcare, but found arranging for child minders relatively unproblematic. Most children experience the physical intimacy of childcare with siblings and other relatives, and delegating primary childcare is not seen as a threat to maternal–child bonding. By contrast, delegating cooking, even to a husband's own daughters, is seen as easily weakening and endangering the marital relationship (Clark 1989). The sharp time conflict

between work and personal cooking sets up a structural tension between work and marriage that is located between motherhood and marriage within the female gender ideal, a tension that Asante consider natural and inevitable (Clark 1989).

In urban gender relations, often with male strangers not already classified as brother or husband, broader economic and sexual tensions feed into contested claims to public respect. Adult women are expected to be assertive in their relations to lineage brothers and sons, deferring no more to their senior uncles than these men do. The ideal of female deference and gentleness exists but applies mainly to younger wives in their interactions with older husbands. While trading in the market, the same women may behave quite aggressively, conforming to another accepted gender stereotype of market women. Western nuclear family ideals Ghanaians encounter in church, school, and official life complicate rather than resolve these contradictions. Many are devout Christians, yet the marital admonition "til death do you part" pales beside the eternal bond between matrilineal ancestors and their descendants.

During a wide geographic and temporal range of fieldwork situations, I checked whether urban traders varied significantly from other Asante populations on major gender and kinship issues. On home visits, social occasions, and village trips, I discussed them with non-trading kin and neighbors. Development project work also provided a basis for relationships with farmers and food processors in small towns and villages. A remarkably consistent master narrative of the ideal responsibilities of kin and spouses showed up across these diverse situations, as did the acceptance of individual renegotiation. Although expectations of actual practice varied sharply with location, class, and other situational factors, the flashpoints triggering especially intense negotiation or conflict also showed strong continuity.

Perhaps it was predictable that women traders, even in such a uniquely large city market, fall within the Asante mainstream on family values. Census records list trading as the occupation of 70–80% of the women resident in southern Ghana's larger cities and as extremely common for rural women as well. The extensive scholarly literature on the Asante and closely related Akan groups, including ethnographic work since 1923, extends this confirmation of the expected range of values and practices to other places and times (Abu 1983; Rattray 1923). For example, the percentage of married women not living with their husbands in the 1979 market survey fell within the 40% range reported by Fortes for two small Asante towns in the 1940s (Fortes 1949). His informants also explained their residence choices and dilemmas in terms repeated in my interviews.

MOTHERING CHILDREN

Asante women explain their financial obligations to feed their children as the dominant bond of motherhood in everyday life. Women in the archetypal women's occupations of rural food farming and urban trading can feed their children directly with their produce, but those in other jobs nonetheless say they work to look after their children. Several traders mentioned that they did not need to settle down and work seriously until they began having children to look after. The subsistence or commercial farming of Asante village women is likewise considered work, not homemaking.

Asante ideals and practices underline the importance of enacting motherhood through economic support as a continuation of childbirth itself. Pregnancy and childbirth are essential parts of motherhood, painful and risky ones that make birth mothers irreplaceable and entitled to unconditional support. They naturalize tight mother/child bonding into an inevitable biological response that should last through life. The biological event of childbirth establishes a culturally undeniable debt to the mother for her pain and blood and the invaluable gift of life. This debt can never be repaid or canceled, but must be honored by passing it on to one's own children. But these relatively brief initial biological stages are fruitless, in the final analysis, without the capacity to complete the process by raising the baby to adulthood.

Successful reproduction means producing someone "to replace yourself," as a functioning Asante adult with children. Biological motherhood remains a key responsibility, but one that logically or naturally mandates income-generating work rather than personal responsibility for childcare. Both daily survival and social sponsorship require financial investments that many women must struggle hard to provide, and whose outcome is as uncertain as pregnancy. Women who were describing their trading careers to me in 1994 and 1995 used the phrase "and that's how I had Kwame, Abenaa, and Kofi" about specific kinds of work they did, actually using the same word *wo* used for birth and conception. The Twi phrase "*Saa na mewo Kwame*" merges, without exactly conflating, the physical and economic processes of creating and raising children.

Asante ideology endorses economic responsibility as the emotional heart of motherhood as well as its practical bottom line. In the absolute bond between mother and child, the conditionality and renegotiability so conspicuous in the fluid relations between Asante kin and spouses are supposedly absent. Children's loyalty to their mothers is explicitly rooted in the economic merging or fusion expected and experienced in this relationship alone. Mothers' hard work supporting the family is the dominant image in the powerful child attachment that remains into adulthood.

The popular song "Sweet Mother" expresses this sentiment with the common proverb: "When I don't eat, she doesn't eat." It resonates strongly at the literal level; if she had food you would also be eating it. Sharing food shortage is far from a trivial issue for the many mothers facing chronic financial crisis. At the metaphorical level, the phrase also evokes complete emotional identification, sharing your worries and sorrows. For Asante, persons grieving at a close relative's funeral or facing some other upsetting situation show strong feelings by not wanting to eat, while others refrain out of respect for those feelings.

An Asante mother does accept the responsibility to make sure that her children are well cared for, but she does not feel that a mother would care for her children better than another attentive, capable relative of reasonable age might. One mother explained that "no one will sit and listen to a child cry," so anyone around will see that they have water, food and shelter, but "no one will work for them like I do." Her devotion to her children, far from making her feel ambivalent about working, drove her to work harder and longer. Taking time off work to raise children seems almost a contradiction in terms. Providing adequate economic support is in fact more difficult and problematic, given most mothers' life circumstances, than providing childcare and a good moral example.

The weak relation between physical childcare and maternal child bonding is the more remarkable because childcare is considered the basis for warm emotional ties to other relatives. It is recognized as creating special bonds between a baby and its primary caretakers, most often older sisters. Men and women both recognize a special debt to "the sister who carried me on her back," even compared to other siblings. The physical intimacy of childcare establishes warm loyalty to men as well as to women, reflecting Asante boys' and men's noticeable willingness to carry around and play with infants and toddlers, as well as older children. In 1995, adult children used "I peed on his knee" as their formulaic reason for supporting fathers in old age, referring to the bodily intimacy of infancy as the epitome of fatherhood.

The maternal bond normally does strengthen throughout childhood, maintained as a live relationship through continual interaction. Domestic work by growing children seems to intensify Asante bonding more than domestic work by mothers. One mother explained her painful and continuing grief for the death of a daughter at age seven or eight by describing how the girl had been so helpful around the house, compared to babies she had lost at younger ages. Children are also fostered out, especially to grandparents, aunts, and cousins, to provide childcare, cook, and run errands for elders. They also move in with kin or non-kin when they cannot be cared for at home, or for vocational training or educational opportunities. In these cases, it is the children's work (domestic or income-generating) that generates the bonding.

MALE PARENTS

The stereotype of economic and emotional merging between mother and child is invoked so powerfully for mothers that, by implication, fathers, uncles, or siblings may not show the same degree of concern. Their support is more conditional and variable, like relations between other relatives and between spouses. Maternal and paternal uncles represent valued alternative sources of financial support and moral guidance, even when the father is still alive. According to matrilineal principles, the mother's brother is as much her reproductive partner as her husband. In a structural sense this uncle is the male mother, like the father's sister is the female father. Male financial responsibility for children can thus be spread over several individuals, forming a range of potential substitute or supplementary fathers.

Financial support in childhood or young adulthood is important in bonding children to fathers and male kin, as with mothers. In order to claim paternity publicly, the biological father should participate in the baby's naming ceremony by presenting a cloth and other gifts that at least symbolically support the mother during her resting period after birth. Children often solicit school fees and other important support in person, so that fathers who consistently refuse or disown their children face old age with little reciprocation.

Fatherhood does have a more absolute spiritual aspect, from the precolonial *ntoro* affiliation passed on from father to child. Just as the blood of childbirth shows the shared blood, or *mogya,* of the matrilineage, or *abusua,* so a person's bones (white like semen) serve as the biological referent for the paternal *ntoro* spirit. Without a close relationship with the father, a child lacks the protection of the father's *ntoro* spirit. This is said to be especially important for the health of very young children whose own *ntoro* spirit has not yet grown strong. That spiritual affiliation is not transferable to other male sponsors, except to a father's full brothers, who have the same one. Asantes usually confirmed this metaphysical link, but Christian belief also lent strong spiritual reinforcement to fatherhood, by analogy to God the Father.

Asante women are severely criticized for putting the interests of marriage and husband before those of their children, which would be both immoral and stupid. Individual men as husbands cannot and should not be relied upon, because of circumstances beyond their control as well as possibly unsuspected moral failings. Added to the legitimate prior claims of their matrilineal kin are the ever-present dangers of death, illness, divorce or polygyny, any one of which might abruptly end their financial support of wife and children. After remarrying in middle age, men can and often do beget a new set of children who may displace the first wife and her children emotionally and financially. This specter also weakens children's confidence in a father's absolute commitment to them. A mother's excessive attachment to her husband implies self-indulgence in sexual gratification or vanity almost as obvious as adultery.

Friends and relatives described cases where men or women put their spouses first as scandalous. These doting spouses were judged immature and unnatural, raising questions about possible witchcraft. They provide a stereotypical example of witchcraft, in much the same way as a middle-aged U.S. man still living with his mother suggests psychological problems. A woman who ignored this common knowledge was considered either below normal intelligence or an irresponsible mother, because she was not taking the most ordinary precaution

The practical and moral issues here merge in the popular proverb "you can get a new husband, but not a new brother." I often heard it repeated, in the male or female version, to explain the priority Asante give to matrikin. Women expect their brothers to remain loyal, since lineage continuity depends on the sister's children. When one elderly woman wanted to express her close relationship with a sweetheart of her youth, she said "we were like twins," that is, brother and sisters. Armah puts

it more poetically, but just as forcefully: "A father is only a husband, and husbands come and go; they are passing winds bearing seed. They change, they disappear entirely, and they are replaced. An uncle remains" (Armah 1970:139).

PRAISES AND INSULTS ACROSS THE GENDER FRONTIER

The concept of economic motherhood also facilitates applying to men the praiseword given good mothers, *obaatan*, conventionally translated as nursing mother. Literally, the Twi word refers to the period of seclusion after childbirth, ideally forty days. The woman, *obaa*, stays inside the compound near the hearth, *otan*, keeping herself and the new baby warm and protected while she recovers from birth, until the baby's outdooring ceremony. It makes no verbal reference to nursing, although the mother would certainly be nursing her baby then and for about a year to come. She also is more likely to take full physical care of the baby during this period, since she has already suspended her usual work schedule to rest. Nonetheless, speakers knowing English invariably used the English term nursing mother to translate it, and those who did not speak English pantomimed holding a baby to their breast, for instance when I asked, "Did you just say your father was a real nursing mother?" Both terms make biological and domestic references to childbirth, cooking and childcare, but none to paid work.

The most common use of the word *obaatan*, on the other hand, refers not to that seclusion or rest period but to what follows, when the mother has returned to work with renewed motivation. Several proverbs that apply to both men and women contrast the home with the street. The stereotypical *obaatan* was hard at work, just as she should be, in the street, the market, or even on the road. People usually spoke of new mothers at home with the phrase *wawo foforo*, literally "she has newly given birth."

Asante apparently saw nothing odd about using the word *obaatan* for a man, if he showed the appropriate qualities. I even heard the Christian God called an *obaatan paa* in public prayer without raising an eyebrow in a fairly conservative audience. The conceptual contrast between fatherhood and motherhood is rigid enough to remain consistent even when used across gender lines. When fathers show the devotion associated with motherhood they are praised as good mothers, not fathers. One young woman described her father as a very good man and, in the next breath, as an *obaatan paa*. He proved his unusual level of love and concern, not by staying home like a U.S. "househusband," but by his eagerness to provide for all of his children's needs as soon as he heard of them. His children by both wives enjoyed the same willing financial support; none of the usual nagging for school fees here. This *obaatan* behavior made him more, not less, of a father.

Paradoxically, the conceptual separation between work, framed in economic motherhood, and sexuality, framed within marriage, enables positive work attributes to cross with some ease from women to men and vice versa, without implying deviant sexual behavior or gender identification. Fathers who devote their income gladly to their children, or mothers who manage to accumulate capital, are freely called motherly men or manly women.

In Asante, the male gender ideal most often transferred from men to women is the positive capacity for economic self-aggrandizement. A mother's breadwinner role compels her to work but also drains away the income she needs to save in order to accumulate capital. This mirrors the transfer of economic motherhood from mother to father and likewise leaves behind the specifically sexual or biological content of the original term. The phrase *obaa barima,* which could be translated as "manly or brave woman," uses the word *obarima,* that refers to young male bravery and strength but is also the most polite positive way of referring to sexual virility. The sexual conduct of an *obaa barima* was not suspect, although her subservience to her husband might be reduced. In the same way, the nursing-mother father was no less male in the positive senses of sexual and business competence.

The market women I heard called *obaa barima* in 1979 and 1994 were those who had achieved the level of financial success and economic independence considered essential for men, not those showing unusual physical strength, bravery, or sexual prowess. The Asante image of womanly beauty already includes more strength than in Western beauty ideals, consonant with historic female responsibilities for farming, so physically strong women did not attract particular comment. One market woman was known as unusually loud and aggressive in personal interactions, even by market standards, but people called her "rough," not *obaa barima.*

The separation kept between sexuality and economic activity in parenthood contradicts their close linkage in the relations of marriage. If praises often define gender in terms of the economic sphere, negatively gendered insults also indicate strong connections between sexual and economic power. Both men and women who shirk their financial responsibilities as husbands or mothers receive sexually charged insults.

Ama Ata Aidoo reveals the linkage succinctly, if sarcastically, with this categorical statement: "In Ghanaian society, women themselves believe that only two types of their species suffer—the sterile, that is those incapable of bearing children—and the foolish. And by the foolish, they refer to the woman who depends solely on her husband for sustenance" (Aidoo 1970:x). The force of her judgment depends partly on understanding the implied sexual insult behind the Twi word translated as *fool* (*kwasea*). It is a very common insult, but a strong one, especially when aimed at a man, as it often is. It carries a strong connotation of sexual impotence, one of the most damaging accusations for a man and the most visible form of sterility. In this one sentence, therefore, Aidoo associates and equates voluntary female economic impotence with both female reproductive impotence and male sexual impotence, both presumably involuntary.

Even stronger male insults continue this conflation of economic and sexual inadequacy, often translated for me in conversations as the "useless" husband. He literally may be a person who does nothing, *oyehweeni,* or even worse, an empty person, *onipa hunu.* I was told that this last phrase was so terrible that a woman would never use it in her husband's hearing without expecting both violence and divorce to result. These insults also carry sexual and biological connotations not explicit in the words themselves.

GENDERED WORK AND PROPERTY

The gendered category for Asante is capital accumulation, not income-generating work. *Obaatan adjuma,* or nursing-mother work, is defined not by its location, at home, or its occupational content, light or otherwise feminine, but by its purpose, single-minded devotion to the child. Because of this purpose, nursing-mother work absolutely has to provide a steady, reliable daily income to feed the children, the more urgently after she stopped actually nursing. The priority placed on low risk meant such work is also likely to employ a low level of capital and give a relatively low rate of return, even on that small investment.

A real man, or *obarima paa* (by which most Asantes would imply an Asante man), should aspire beyond nursing-mother work to a more lucrative occupation that enables him to accumulate. A real woman aspires beyond this also, but there is less expectation that she will succeed. Some women traders did manage to build houses or accumulate other property, but many others bemoaned their inability to leave such *gyapaadee,* or inheritance, for their children.

Asante values encourage and celebrate the achievement of wealth by women as well as men, but they assume that men, on average, will have more. This affects lineage relations as well as marital relations. A popular proverb says "men bring money to the lineage, and women bring children." When lineages assess contributions per capita for funerals, court costs or other joint expenses, each woman owes half of what a man owes. People justify this differential burden by explaining how children limit women's earning capacity. They mention the constant drain of spending money on the children, not the time constraint of caring for them, as the factor that restricts women's business growth and limits their income. The ideal division of financial responsibilities between mothers and fathers makes mothers responsible for daily subsistence. Fathers pay for major items such as school fees or new houses, which come later in the children's lives and can be done without if necessary.

The nursing-mother work a woman does helps her husband to accumulate faster because the woman uses her own income or farm produce to feed his children and himself. The husband can then use his income and any possible inheritance for reinvestment in property that remains his, not subject to routine subsistence demands. This dynamic is sharply visible in cocoa farming areas, where women's farms are fewer and smaller, but applies equally to urban commercial enterprises (Mikell 1989; Okali 1983). Women's access to this kind of food subsidy is rarer. They can establish a stable accumulative dynamic if they begin early enough in life, often before marriage, and can still rely on their mothers for free food. These fortunate and energetic young women may later have enough capital that its derived income can continue accumulating after their children enter school and begin to require serious investment in school fees.

The ambivalent relationship between motherhood and work lies in this competition for income. Motherhood demands work, but also constrains it, not through the demands of childcare or other domestic work, but through a financial demand for daily income that can preclude capital accumulation. At the same time, the most devoted mother needs to carefully balance the immediate needs of her children against their long-term interests, since she also knows that her own accumulation is the best way to provide long-term security for them and higher levels of schooling in the future. An avowed motive of taking care of their children provides a cloak of respectability for women's wealth and even greed. Higher aspirations for their education, reaching to university education abroad, can justify almost infinite accumulation. Children's financial security is an extension of their mothers', whereas men's accumulation is more likely to compete with child support both in the short term, as personal aggrandizement, and in the long term, through matrilineal inheritance by a brother or nephew.

MARKET MOTHERS

Asante see market trading as compatible with motherhood financially because it provides frequent, regular income, but so do other occupations. A long-standing line of ethnographic commentary proposes a specific compatibility between the labor processes of childcare and small-scale trading, based on the predominance of women in local trading in many parts of Africa, Asia, and Latin America. McCall, Brown, and Mintz all classified local trading as inherently "women's work" because women could easily take care of their children at the same time (Brown 1970; McCall 1956; Mintz 1971). Their analyses claimed that trading, like other predominantly female work, was safer, more interruptible, and had more flexible scheduling than male-dominated, long-distance trading or other predominantly male tasks like felling forest trees.

Kumasi traders' comments while watching children in the central market in the 1970s, along with the childcare decisions they reported in the sample survey and life histories, showed quite a different evaluation of the compatibility of trading with childcare. Unlike these ethnographers, they did not find market trading particularly safe, interruptible, or flexible. They considered the work environment in the central market very unsafe, especially for younger children. Mothers went to considerable lengths to leave young children at home with other caretakers, even if these had to bring nursing infants to the market for feedings several times a day. Women recognized these risks even when they felt forced to bring their children to the market with them. Childcare conflicts might not keep poorer traders home from the market entirely, but they might well hamper their attempts to build stable, growing businesses.

Women traders did not find their work easy to carry out with children present, nor as interruptible as analysts had. They complained that children's cries for food and attention were disruptive during bargaining sessions, especially at the busy times of day when they made most of their income. The more prosperous women traders were wholesalers, who found these conflicts more absolute. Passing trucks and carts piled with goods made the open wholesale yards and crowded wholesale lines dangerous even for older children of six or nine years, who were sent away. Established or aspiring wholesalers had to spend most of their working day in these locations, reliably available to the steady customers essential to their business success. Many retailers had to visit these areas daily to buy supplies. They often needed to come in the early morning, just when children were getting ready for school, in order to get the best prices and compete successfully.

Childcare conflicted less with trading, not because most traders brought their children to work, but because it was relatively unproblematic to arrange for childcare at home. Unlike cooking, delegating childcare did not pose risks of alienation of affections, and the skills involved were considered even simpler than cooking. A young daughter or sister would be particularly reliable because of her kinship sentiments toward the baby, but unrelated maids were perfectly capable if less motivated. Asante residential patterns are flexible, with several options for supporting extra dependents at home who can take care of the children before the eldest is old enough to care for the others.

Careful attention to the life cycle timing of the peak trading years reveals a similar fast track for young women more fortunately placed in their families. Unlike men, who sometimes do domestic chores before marriage but expect to rely on their wives later, young women can often rely on their female kin for assistance early and expect more personal involvement after they marry. It is important to accumulate early, when their first child or two can still be cared for by their younger sisters. By the time ambitious young women outgrow this arrangement, they should have enough capital to support extra dependents of their own for child-care and still maintain or increase their earning capacity for when their children start school. This faster career path requires self-discipline because the immediate cash needs of their infant children are still minor, and gifts from boyfriends and new husbands may be sufficient to meet them.

Occasionally women did speak of having to restrict or change their trading activities because of childcare problems, but this was in unusual circumstances. One trader who traveled in the 1920s through the remote Upper Region with her husband remarked in the 1970s that it was so difficult to find Twi-speaking maids there then that she moved back to Kumasi after she had several children. Another elderly woman recalled stopping her hawking activities and staying home to prepare cooked food for sale after her mother died. She said she had to take care of many younger siblings and did not make enough money to support a maid. This woman then had trouble accumulating enough capital to delegate care of her own children when they arrived. Childcare problems can thus result from an income crunch, as well as cause it.

CONCLUSION

Tracing the thread of gender through these various arenas of Asante life, each with its own dynamic of contestation, reveals an intricate web of contradiction and confirmation at each intersection of arenas. The balance of competing demands from marriage and motherhood, or from investment in children or business, continually shifts at the individual and societal levels in response to internal dynamics as well as external economic and ideological pressures. The constant renegotiation of all these gendered ideals and practices, far from indicating their weakness or imminent disappearance, signals that they remain valuable sociocultural assets that give powerful leverage still needed to meet new challenges in contemporary life. Among Asante, this renegotiation process need not even be much disguised, since cultural norms endorse it as an inevitable and desirable fact of life.

It seems even more remarkable that the mandate for Asante mothers to earn cash incomes has been so thoroughly internalized and naturalized when it represents a pattern that has changed dramatically within living memory. The oldest women narrators born in villages explained that rural women were expected to provide foodstuffs from their own farms and rely on their husbands for cash purchases in the early decades of this century. Elderly women reported in 1995 that Kumasi husbands during the same period provided a subsistence subsidy to their wives. They normally contributed enough daily food money to their wives that married women expected to save out of it for personal items like headscarves and for trading capital. In Kumasi, already an urban capital, many married women then did not feel obliged to work, and felt none of the stigma of idleness commonly expressed today. The small numbers in this early cohort of women traders allowed them to enjoy a windfall of high profit levels as young adults, which helped them start the businesses that still sustain them.

Female predominance in market trading also results from a transition still barely within living memory. In the 1910s and 1920s, men moved out of trading into the more lucrative new occupations of cocoa farming, government employment, and skilled trades (Clark 1994). Massive urban growth and rural commercialization expanded marketplace trading opportunities, but kept ordinary traders' incomes relatively low. This new gender division of labor was naturalized so rapidly that by 1978 men were ridiculed for trying to buy foodstuffs in Kumasi's central market, let alone trade in them. As inflation and devaluation shrank employment and incomes in male sectors through the 1980s and 1990s, the few men who returned to trade in foodstuffs were discussed as gender deviants.

The preeminence of economic issues for Asante in many of these contestations reminds analysts that sexuality is not always the most salient aspect of gender practices or ideas. Anthropologists have frequently pointed out instances where economic, political, or ritual relations can be firmly gendered without necessary implications for sexual practice or identity (Amadiume 1987; Strathern 1980). As in Asante, this detachment from sexuality facilitates the transfer of gendered attributes or statuses from men to women and vice versa. Third World feminists have also repeatedly criticized the reliance on sexuality to indicate femininity and liberation alike, linking it to hypersexualization of contemporary Western media and commercial life, starting as early as 1972 (Davis 1989).

For Asante the importance of economic factors in gender applies to parenting and trading relations that express and conform to expected majority gender roles, as well as to deviance (positive or negative). Without devaluing sexuality for women or men, the economic performance of gender appears more central and more notable. In the case of urban Asante, economic mothering also takes precedence in the daily lives of ordinary biological mothers, whether single or married. The economic implications of mothering become a central aspect of gender, whether in the lineage, marriage, or workplace, for better or for worse.

Competing loyalties in both matrilineal and marital relations find their most consistent expression in decisions about financial support. Hostility and distrust between men and women focus on economic relations more openly than on sexual relations, so that financial tensions bear a displaced sexual charge (Clark 1989). Praises and insults about gender conformity and deviance often feature economic performance, although they are far from silent on sexual performance.

The sharp differentiation between the respect and authority a woman enjoys as a mother and an elder in her matrilineage and the deference expected of her as a wife is maintained more easily when these relations are performed with different people and often in different houses. In the intimacy of a small village, men and women who meet will usually already know whether they should treat each other as siblings, spouses, and so on.

Urban settings bring encounters with men who are not already classified as husband, son, or brother, making gender more impersonal and less relational, like other aspects of urban life.

Gender in urban Asante today is becoming a more abstract and standardized category, within which such contradictions are more problematic. When women and men meet as strangers or in an occupational context, even when both are Asante, the question of which set of norms will govern their interaction becomes important for negotiating the power balance between them. Women brandish their motherhood as the essence of their female identity, but it is also precisely what pushes them beyond the limits of wifely femininity creating new points of contestation about what model will prevail.

The marketplace, an archetypal urban location, regularly brings men and women together, not as individuals in a known relationship, but as members of predominantly male and predominantly female groups contesting tense economic issues. I heard both maternal and wifely models invoked in Kumasi Central Market, by men and by women, when predominantly male soldiers and officials confronted predominantly female market traders. Market elders complained in 1979 that soldiers "treat us like children when we are old enough to be their mothers." Between strangers, the metaphor of husband and wife, the archetypal non-kin, may seem more appropriate. After all, a tax collector is "somebody's husband," if not yours. This ambiguity puts not only public deference and sexual harassment at issue, but also the legitimacy of high female incomes and economic ambitions, since these are anchored in motherhood, not in wifehood.

The Asante experience also suggests that cultural endorsement of economic mothering and consensus about the structure of negotiation among competing claims from motherhood, wifehood, and trading do not eliminate significant material and ideological conflict. Instead, gender issues play a key role in structuring other arenas of conflict. Despite the hegemony of Akan family patterns within Ghana, and the flexibility and negotiability those norms endorse, bitter public and private conflict is all too frequent over how to fulfill the three central, conventional gender roles of wife, mother, and trader. Teasing out the gendered connections between arenas of conflict distinct from sexuality, marriage, and child rearing (the intimate core of much gender analysis), turns out to be an essential step for understanding either the overall configuration of gender or the course of political and economic conflicts. Internal structural tensions, in this case between wifehood and motherhood, sharpen under pressure from local and international economic crisis. In return, tensions over family loyalties intensify national conflicts over commercial policy and wealth differences (Clark 1988).

REFERENCES CITED

Abu, Katherine Church. 1983 The Separateness of Spouses: Conjugal Resources in an Ashanti Town. *In* Female and Male in West Africa. Christine Oppong, ed. pp. 156–168. London: George Allen and Unwin.

Aidoo, Ama Ata. 1970. No Sweetness Here. London: Longman.

Amadiume, Ifi. 1987. Male Daughters, Female Husbands. London: Zed Press.

Armah, Ayi Kwei. 1970. Fragments. Boston: Houghton Mifflin.

Brown, Judith K. 1970. A Note on the Division of Labor By Sex. American Anthropologist 72:1073.

Clark, Gracia. 1989. Money, Sex and Cooking: Manipulation of the Paid/ Unpaid Boundary by Asante Market Women. *In* The Economy of Consumption. B. Orlove and H. Rutz, eds. pp. 323–348. Monographs in Economic Anthropology No. 6, Society for Economic Anthropology. Lanham, MD: University Press of America.

———. 1994. Onions Are My Husband: Survival and Accumulation by West African Market Women. Chicago: University of Chicago Press.

Clark, Gracia, ed. 1988. Traders vs. the State. Boulder, CO: Westview.

Davis, Angela. 1989. Women, Culture and Politics. New York: Random House.

Fortes, Meyer. 1949. Time and Social Structure: An Asante Case Study. *In* Social Structure. Meyer Fortes, ed. pp. 154–184. London: Oxford University Press.

McCall, Daniel. 1956. Family and Women in the Gold Coast. PhD Dissertation, Department of Anthropology, Columbia University.

Mikell, Gwendolyn. 1989. Cocoa and Chaos in Ghana. New York: Paragon House.

Mintz, Sidney. 1971. Men, Women and Trade. Comparative Studies in Society and History 13:247.

Okali, Christine. 1983. Cocoa and Kinship in Ghana. London: Kegan Paul.

Rattray, R. S. 1923. Ashanti. Oxford: Clarendon Press.

Strathern, Marilyn. 1980. No Nature, No Culture: The Hagen Case. In Nature, Culture and Gender. Carol MacCormack and Marilyn Strathern, eds. pp. 174–221. Cambridge: Cambridge University Press.

3 • *Carrie M. Lane*

MAN ENOUGH TO LET MY WIFE SUPPORT ME

Gender and Unemployment Among Middle-Class U.S. Tech Workers

DISCUSSION QUESTIONS

1. Why, according to Lane, does losing a job and even extended unemployment no longer produce a "crisis of masculinity" among the male U.S. tech workers in Texas whom she interviews?
2. In contrast, why is job loss now experienced as a "crisis" by female tech workers?
3. What do the interviews reveal about changing ideas of gender, marriage, and work in the United States?

> [The unemployed man] experiences a sense of deep frustration because in his own eyes he fails to fulfill what is the central duty of his life, the very touchstone of his manhood—the role of family provider.
>
> —Mirra Komarovsky, *The Unemployed Man and His Family* (1940)

> Downward mobility strikes at the heart of the "masculine ideal" for the American middle class. When the man of the house has failed at the task that most clearly defines his role, he suffers a loss of identity as a man. When this is coupled with the admirable efforts of a wife to salvage the situation by going out to work, the man's response may be intensified feelings of impotence and rage culminating in abuse.
>
> —Katherine Newman, *Falling from Grace* (1988)

> I make a badass crème brûlée. I made cookies this morning. I've been doing a lot of June Cleaver type things at home. The Mrs. likes it because, like, I made beef ribs last week. I seriously made cookies the other day. Chocolate chip with four kinds of chips that she took in to the office . . . [Being

An abridged version of Carrie M. Lane, 2009. "Man Enough to Let My Wife Support Me: How Changing Models of Career and Gender are Reshaping the Experience of Unemployment." Reproduced by permission of the American Anthropological Association and of the author from *American Ethnologist*, Volume 36, Issue 4, Pages 681–692, November 2009. Not for sale or further reproduction. For the full study, see Lane 2012.

unemployed is] not the end of the world. I think Americans probably identify too much of their self-worth with what they do for a living. And that's
too bad.

—Interview with Craig Murray, unemployed U.S.
technology worker, 2002

As the first two quotations above demonstrate, studies of unemployment throughout the last century have consistently equated job loss and unemployment with a crisis of masculinity that prompts depression, frustration, self-blame, and self-doubt in jobless men. More recent research confirms that the expectation that men should succeed at work and support their families has by no means disappeared in the contemporary United States (see, e.g., Potuchek 1997; Townsend 2002). Yet the final quotation above, and similar accounts from other unemployed middle-class high-technology workers, complicates the framing of unemployment as inherently devastating and emasculating. As I demonstrate in this article, structural changes around work and cultural shifts in the meanings of career, manhood, and marriage have transformed the experience of job loss and unemployment for some middle-class U.S. workers, both men and women. Together, these shifts, and how they play out in the lives and minds of individual workers, necessitate a rethinking of the relationships between job loss, unemployment, and personal and professional crisis.

This article is based on four years of ethnographic fieldwork among unemployed technology workers in Dallas, Texas, including open-ended interviews and participant-observation.[1] Most of the research took place between 2001 and 2004, when Dallas, like many other U.S. cities, was experiencing waves of layoffs centered in the high-technology fields of telecommunications, computing, and Internet-related businesses. As I spoke with out-of-work tech professionals, in their homes, at coffee shops, and at various networking events, I was surprised to hear them express a relatively upbeat and accepting attitude toward their layoffs and, for

some, prolonged unemployment. The job seekers I spoke with were not happy about having lost their jobs; they worried about money, chafed at the insulting lack of response to their e-mailed resumes, and missed making use of their professional skills. Yet, in our discussions, these workers quickly made it clear that the loss of a job, frustrating as it might be, was not an unexpected or unprecedented event in their professional lives. Many had been laid off before, some multiple times, and most had come of professional age long after mass layoffs had become an expected if unwelcome feature of the U.S. labor market. Few had expected to spend the rest of their working lives with their former employers, and so job change was not so much an aberration in the careers they had imagined as an expected component of them. Indeed, for these workers, the very idea of pursuing job security and satisfaction through long-term employment at a single company seemed outmoded and naive, not to mention tantamount to professional suicide.

The social contract of employment in which corporate employers reward loyalty and hard work with job security, steady pay, and a shot at upward mobility was never a reality for the majority of U.S. workers. Yet, at one point in the postwar United States, elite, educated, white males expected to live out their professional lives ensconced in the security of long-term corporate employment. That era, today's tech workers insist, is long gone and unlikely to return, regardless of whether one celebrates or laments its demise. In place of long-term job security, they say, a less predictable, more protean model of employment exists, in which employees themselves assume responsibility for managing their careers. According to this philosophy of work, which I refer to as "career management," each individual must conceptualize him- or herself as an independent contractor, regardless of whether his or her current work situation is full-time, part-time, contract, consulting, volunteer, or no job at all.[2] For "career managers," as adherents to this philosophy are called, job change is not only expected but also necessary, and retraining, networking, and job seeking are permanent aspects of a well-managed career. For them, job security is born not of steady employment at a single company but of constant vigilance, flexibility, and employability.

Critics have aptly noted that maintaining an image of oneself as a flexible, self-reliant entrepreneur, particularly in the face of a tight labor market and obvious power disparities between employer and employee, is itself a form of labor, and an exhausting one at that (Kunda and Van Maanen 1999). Workers who embrace insecure employment as a means of achieving autonomy are, in fact, doing exactly what corporations would prefer that they do, namely, take pride in their work while on the job and not make a fuss when their "contract" ends. It would be inaccurate and overly simplistic, though, to characterize career managers as unwitting dupes of corporate capitalism. Career managers are well aware that it was employers, not employees, who initially reneged on the promises of the social contract of employment by engaging in frequent and widespread layoffs, even in times of high profits. Despite this, tech workers still tend to frame career management as a means of retaliating against, or at least protecting oneself from, disloyal, self-interested employers.

Project manager Mike Barnard, for instance, lost his job when the telecommunications company at which he worked disbanded his entire department in late September 2001. Like many tech workers who lost their jobs soon before or after the terrorist attacks of September 11, that event loomed large in his explanation of both his layoff and the unwelcoming labor market he has encountered since. Yet sitting across from me at a Starbucks in an upscale Dallas shopping center, Mike, who had just turned 50, was less interested in looking back at the events that prompted his layoff than in looking ahead to the kind of future he believed all workers will one day face.

> We're not going to go back to the 60s or 70s or whatever in terms of the job market, so I think people are going to have to start changing their view on their jobs. . . . You need to be able to look at your job now as temporary and evolving. . . . Look at yourself as an independent contractor, more as an independent contractor and less as an employee. Think of what it is that you can offer as opposed to [asking,] "What do you want me to do?" . . . Going out and looking for a job, it's a sucker's game. You'll keep it as long as they want to let you have it. That's easy to say. A lot of people are more than happy to go and do the nine-to-five gig and go home and not worry about it but they are liable to be a victim. They will be victimized because they allow themselves to be.

For Mike and the many job seekers who echo his perspective, job change—voluntary or not—is an expected and even necessary part of professional development. When each job is simply one in a long string of temporary positions, rather than the foundation on which professional identity depends, losing a single job, although rarely easy, is not the personal or professional crisis it would be for an employee who expected to spend the rest of his or her career with one employer. Juxtaposing the savvy, self-sufficient career manager and the naive, dependent corporate victim provides jobless workers like Mike with a narrative that celebrates rather than stigmatizes their unsteady employment records. It associates job loss not with failure but with self-reliance and a willingness to rise to the occasion, both traits that soften the allegedly emasculating effects of unemployment.

Although career managers seldom acknowledge this, managing one's own career and withstanding prolonged financial and professional uncertainty can be a pricey and precarious endeavor, one that is not equally tenable for all Americans. All but one job seeker in my study had a bachelor's degree; some held advanced degrees in fields such as engineering, physics, computer science, and business administration. Their pre-layoff annual incomes ranged from approximately $40,000 to $100,000, with a few high-end outliers among former executives. Solidly positioned in the middle and upper classes, these job seekers have access to financial and professional resources rarely available to people in less profitable fields, including savings and retirement accounts, easy access to credit, and strong extended networks of employed friends, former colleagues, and professional associates on whom they rely in their job search.

Many job seekers also rely heavily on another, less obvious resource—the working spouse or partner. Over the last half century, the rising cost of living has coincided with the dismantling of barriers against married middle-class women's workforce participation to create a situation in which most middle-class U.S. households either need or prefer to have two full-time incomes. Just over half of laid-off tech workers in the greater Dallas area had a working spouse at the time of their job loss, which corresponds closely to the nation as a whole, in which more than half of all married couples include two full-time earners (North Texas Technology Council 2003). The working spouse and the financial safety net she or he represents complicate the model of the self-reliant career manager, as the ideal of complete independence must be reconciled with the reality of financial dependence on another person.

On a sunny fall day in 2004 I met Ed Donnelly for breakfast at a café in a used-book store just east of Dallas. Ed, 58 at the time of that interview, is a slight, intense man with piercing blue eyes and a quick laugh. I had interviewed Ed two years earlier after meeting him at an early-morning networking event for unemployed tech workers. In our first interview, he told me about being laid off from his job as a computer programmer at a major telecommunications company on the Thursday before September 11, 2001. Since then, Ed had taken a part-time job at a gardening supply store to pass the time and earn some money while he retrained in a more in-demand field of programming. When we met again more than two years later, Ed was still in the midst of what he called his "personal remake,"

accumulating certifications in new programming fields while working part-time.

In the meantime, Ed said, his family was managing pretty well financially. They had paid off their mortgage, which eased their financial responsibilities considerably, and had not had to cut too deeply into their savings. His wife, also a software programmer, had been laid off around the same time Ed was, but she quickly found a new position and the couple and their teenaged son were getting by on her salary, supplemented by Ed's part-time income. Ed told me, "[My wife] has gotten a pretty decent job, so she is basically the breadwinner in the family and I am struggling to pay my share of the expenses. And unlike a lot of guys I don't have a problem with me having the lower income."

At that moment it occurred to me that a lot of the men I had met and spoken with over the preceding few years had uttered similar statements. Many were in situations similar to Ed's, and they too were quick to praise their spouses for their support, both financial and emotional, and to reference the partnership ideal at the core of their marriages.

Will Ericsson, a technology executive laid off from the defense firm where he had worked for 22 years, mentioned numerous times how fortunate he was to have an employed spouse:

> I've been fortunate that my physical needs have been taken care of [by my wife's income and our savings]. I see that others tend to panic when they start to see that money running out. So people need to know that this is how long I've got and this is how long I need to take [to find a job]. . . . Mine can take as long as it needs to take. Not everybody has that luxury. And I recognize that as a luxury.[3]

Craig Murray, a 41-year-old website developer, was not only grateful for his wife's support, he reveled in his (admittedly temporary) transformation into a stay-at-home spouse. With his stylish but casual clothing and funky black-rimmed glasses, Craig, who I quoted at the start of this article, was something of a poster boy for the irreverent high-tech style of the time. His job loss in the first weeks of 2002 came as no surprise to him, as his employer had already held multiple rounds of layoffs. It did surprise him, however, when his usually high blood pressure immediately dropped 15 points. Craig was not sure what sort of job he wanted to find, but he knew he wanted something less stressful and more fulfilling than his previous position. In the meantime—and perhaps for the long term—he was pursuing various short-term freelance positions while his wife's steadier income as an accountant paid the majority of their bills. He was perfectly comfortable, even gleeful doing "June Cleaver type things at home." Clearly, Craig was not fixated on achieving the role of male breadwinner, or even equal co-earner, and neither were Ed and Will, although they were somewhat less exuberant about it.

Craig and his wife did not have children, nor did Will. Yet nearly two-thirds of the men I spoke with who were married or lived with female partners did have children, as did more than a third of female interviewees with husbands or live-in male partners.[4] Young, highly educated couples without children are far more likely than other couples to embrace the ideal of "co-breadwinning," in which neither spouse's job is seen as the primary source of income or the more important career (Potuchek 1997), which explains in part why the educated, middle-class tech workers in this study are more comfortable relying on spousal income than are other workers. It also begs the question of whether and how parenthood, and fatherhood in particular, shapes job seekers' attitudes toward unemployment and relying on a spouse's income.

I first met Alex Brodsky at a networking happy hour for high-tech executives in October 2001. At that event, Alex kept our table captivated with stories of the comically awful demise of the Internet consulting firm from which he had been laid off and that was now being sued by numerous former employees (although Alex was not one of them). Alex was neither surprised nor particularly disappointed by his layoff, as the office had become a miserable place in the months leading up to it, but his job loss left his family—which included his wife Hannah, a schoolteacher, and their young daughter Ella—in

a difficult financial position. And yet, Alex told me more than a year after his layoff, his family was stronger than ever.

> They key to [handling the discouragement of prolonged unemployment] is my marriage. I've got a very, very strong marriage and a little kid who no matter what you do that day, no matter what's happened that day, you can't look at a little one like that and be pissed off. She doesn't care that you feel like a schmuck. She doesn't care that you've had a bad day. When she sees you at the end of the day she runs up to you and screams "Daddy" and you forget all the rest of it. I've been married ten years now as of March. This isn't my first time being unemployed. . . . And again that's put a big burden on her [Hannah]. She supported me through that. That's the key to it. She has taken on incredible burdens to help me to do the things that I need to do. Not to her complete detriment to the point that she completely loses [her] identity, but knowing that we're both working towards something. I'm doing my part, she's doing her part.

His part, he clarified, consisted primarily of caring for Ella and the household during the day while Hannah worked and waiting tables in the evening to help pay the bills. Together, he and Hannah had decided he would not accept the first full-time tech job that came along but would, instead, wait for a position that matched his skills and interests.[5] Until then, they agreed, Hannah's teaching salary would continue to be the family's primary support, and Alex would retain his role as manager of the "second shift" of domestic work and child care.

Alex rejects the ideal that a man's primary contribution to his family must be in the form of a monthly paycheck. He believes he does his part in supporting the family by caring for his daughter, keeping up with the laundry, and waiting tables part-time. He is therefore comfortable with his wife serving as the family's primary earner while he manages the house and Ella's care, an arrangement he sees as an effective division of labor for the time being. Within marriages conceived as egalitarian partnerships, then, the ideal of self-sufficiency can be reconceptualized as "couple self-sufficiency" (Townsend 2002:10), in which getting by as part of a couple, rather than as an individual breadwinner, is the yardstick by which one's success is measured.

As I explained at the start of this article, the experiences and attitudes of the men I describe represent a significant shift from the attitudes of unemployed men as documented in previous studies of white-collar unemployment. As Alex's experience illustrates, when one's identity as a man is no longer yoked so tightly to employment, it makes sense that a disruption like job loss might be experienced in a more complicated, less emasculating way.

The very notion of what it means to be a man is, of course, always in flux. As historian Gail Bederman argues, alleged crises of masculinity are simply part of the "constant contradiction, change, and renegotiation" (1995:11) inherent in the ongoing ideological process through which gender is experienced and understood. The ideal of the male breadwinner has been shifting for decades, a casualty of increasingly insecure employment, rising numbers of working women, and a feminist movement that privileges female independence, male sensitivity, and egalitarian households (Newman 1988: 117–119). Thus while the masculine ideal that associates manly success with steady paid employment and providing for one's family still has a strong influence on how the American man sees himself and how he is seen by others, as my research indicates, middle-class men who have lost their jobs now have alternative standards of masculinity, and alternative models of professional success, toward which they can turn.

Just as career management reframes job loss within a different narrative of professional success, job seekers' conceptualization of marriage and self-sufficiency reframes the experience of relying on a spouse's income. Believing that marriage is a partnership and that men should respect and support their wives' professional achievements—along with the twin assumption that employed middle-class women should be comfortable assuming the role of primary breadwinner—allows unemployed men to reconceptualize relying on a partner's income, at least temporarily, as evidence of their masculinity, rather than a challenge to it.

The belief that job loss and unemployment provoke crises of masculinity in middle-class men is often paired with the assumption that it does not provoke similar crises for working women (of any class), who are generally believed to ground their identity and sense of self-worth primarily in emotional connections that transpire outside the world of paid employment. One might expect, then, that as men ground their identity less fundamentally in paid employment, their reactions to job loss will start to more closely resemble women's experiences. Yet my own research found that, although the stigma and stress faced by unemployed middle-class men seem to be lessening, the opposite might be said for middle-class women.

In four years of fieldwork and more than 100 interviews, few people cried while discussing their unemployment with me. Of those who did, two were women, and neither cried about losing her job or about the challenges of finding work in a tight labor market. Instead, they cried about how unemployment was affecting their relationships with their male partners, and both blamed themselves for the difficulties they faced.

Natalie Lawson, a website manager in her early thirties, loved her job at a high-profile Internet consulting firm. Hers was a tight-knit office with a fun, lively culture despite the hard work and long hours. When the company announced its first layoffs, Natalie was rattled by the departure of close friends and colleagues but still hoped to stay with the company for at least a few more years. By the time she was laid off half a year later, survivor's guilt and an evaporating workload had her actually looking forward to leaving the company she once adored.

Natalie immediately found a contract position at the software company where her boyfriend Daniel worked. Between her severance pay and the contract job, she was able to make her mortgage payments, but when we met in April of 2002, the two-month contract position had ended and she was about to start dipping into her savings.

I've got a nice amount of savings, I just don't like going into it. So, movies stopped, going out to dinner stopped. Just little extras. I'm very good at spending nothing. . . . I think the biggest hit has been entertainment. My boyfriend loves to do all that stuff. It's kind of hard sometimes because he'll go, "Oh, let's go to the climbing gym." And it's just kind of an extra that I shouldn't be doing now. [So I say] "Let's go jogging." . . . He takes me to the movies here and there, which is great, but I'm not really one to actually love someone paying for me all the time.

She described her boyfriend as incredibly supportive and encouraging of her job search efforts, but Natalie was concerned about the effect her unemployment was having on their relationship. Now that she had so much free time, she found herself relying on her boyfriend in ways that were new to them both:

I've probably become a little bit clingy with my boyfriend because I have so much time on my hands. [I'll say] "Oh, just take tomorrow off," "Come home for lunch, I'll cook for you." Which I would do normally but it's coming from a different place now. . . . I'm doing a lot of things for my boyfriend, which is nice. Actually I kind of enjoy doing things for him. We've had talks about me feeling at times that I don't offer as much because I'm kind of, and it's not money-wise, it's just that I don't feel like I'm extremely successful as a person right now. [Natalie begins to cry] I'm sure that affects my feelings of insecurity around him.

Relying more on a spouse or partner was, for some male job seekers, a badge of their forward-thinking attitudes to marriage and gender roles. For Natalie, despite her financial independence, relying more on Daniel made her feel uncomfortably needy. Even though she was doing more for Daniel in terms of caretaking than she had when she was employed, Natalie felt that she did not "offer as much" to him because, as someone who was not employed as a professional, she was, in her own eyes, not successful as a person.

Like Natalie's, Erica Roth's fears about how her job loss had affected her relationship provide an interesting contrast to accounts of male job seekers. Erica lost her job at an international tech company in the beginning of 2002, just two months before we met for our first interview. She had been laid off once before, and although that layoff was more financially challenging—at the time, her husband was in graduate school and she provided the couple's entire income—this one was proving more stressful for Erica. Like the male job seekers described above, Erica was quick to express her good fortune at having a working spouse, but her comments reveal a more complicated mix of gratitude and guilt.

At first, [my husband] was very, very good because unfortunately it was really challenging for us that it was totally unexpected for me to lose my job. . . . The hospital that he was working for, their company bought out another hospital. So the two are going to merge and . . . he inherited [responsibility for] the other hospital, which was three times the size of his operation. . . . And he's working twelve- to fourteen-hour days. If I hadn't lost my job, he would have had the flexibility of taking a severance package and it would have been very easy for him to find another job being in the field that he is. But since I lost my job, he didn't feel he had the leverage. So he's in a very stressful situation. . . . And I think he thought that based on my contacts and everything else I'd be able to land a job really quick and it hasn't been that way. And so I think it's starting to dawn on him that it's going to be a much rougher road than he originally thought. And then the stress of his own job. So it's starting to be very challenging.

When asked how she and her husband had been handling that stress, Erica began to cry. Still crying, she said, "I try not to overreact to what he says, because he has every right to react that way. And I did put him in a bad situation." Wiping away her tears, Erica repeated, "It could be a lot worse. I'm lucky. I'm in a better position than a lot of people." Yet Erica felt guilty that her job loss created a situation in which her husband no longer felt he had the option to leave a stressful and unsatisfying job. Rather than framing the couple's current situation as a simple reversal of the time when her husband was in school and she was the sole earner, Erica instead saw her current failure to contribute financially as placing an unfair burden on her husband. She blamed herself for "put[ting] him in a bad situation," even though she had no control over her layoff, the tight job market, or the recent changes in her husband's job satisfaction. The emotional cushion that couple self-sufficiency offers to job-seeking men like Alex was absent for Erica. Instead, she saw her obligation to contribute financially as independent of her husband's employment status.

Natalie's and Erica's feelings of dwindling self-worth and insecurity mirror, in many respects, those of male managers in earlier decades, far more so than did the comments of their male peers. Whereas the grounding of masculinity in secure employment has weakened for middle-class men in recent decades, for women like Natalie and Erica, professional identity and self-worth have become more closely intertwined, at least with regard to their role in personal relationships. In the past, researchers have presumed that women are less disturbed by job loss because they place such value on their personal relationships. Yet for Erica and Natalie, it is exactly because their relationships matter so much to them that they are so distraught about being unemployed. Women are not simply inheriting the identity-crisis model of unemployment now that men have shed it; job loss is, indeed, a crisis for these women, but it is a crisis with decidedly nuanced and gender-specific roots and implications.

It is not surprising that job loss is discomfiting for women who came of age in a world in which paid labor is expected of educated, middle-class women (at least until childbirth). Indeed, for many middle-class women, it is the decision not to work for pay that has become the culturally fraught one, tapping into broader cultural debates over feminism and the family. For a man to accept a wife's support suggests an open-minded, nonsexist attitude toward changing gender roles and women's professional achievements. Craig Murray can pride himself on the homemade cookies he sends to work with his wife, and Ed Donnelly can pronounce himself more enlightened than "those other guys" who might balk at living off a wife's income. For Natalie, however, the opposite is true. Cooking more for her partner during her now-ample spare time actually undermines her sense of self-worth, making her feel less accomplished, less progressive, and, potentially, less attractive.

Shifting narratives of career, gender, and marriage have apparently had a more buoyant effect on married men's experience of unemployment than on married women's. The situation is not so simple that one can proclaim men the winners and women the losers in these newly negotiated models of work and family. Neither dual-earner couples nor career management have entirely paved over the pitfalls and pressures of job loss for middle- and upper-class U.S. men, but they have certainly shifted the landscape—cultural, professional, and economic—on which men face those challenges. It is clear, for instance, that the financial pressures of unemployment are lessened for both men and women by the presence of a working spouse, despite dramatic gender differences in how they respond to that support.

The implications of the cultural shifts under discussion here extend far beyond the lives of individual workers and professional communities. Those same second incomes that ease the financial and emotional hardships of unemployment also soften any backlash that might be directed against the labor system and market economy that created these hardships in the first place. The sustaining income of a working spouse obscures, for instance, the extent to which public and private programs intended to protect unemployed workers have failed to do so. Absent a working spouse, the inadequacy of the current systems of unemployment benefits, health insurance, workers' rights legislation, government-funded job training and employment programs, severance and pension payments, and affordable child care would be far more visible and perhaps more likely to garner national attention. Instead, the burdens of a volatile and increasingly global labor market, an ailing economy, and the disappearance of corporate welfare have been quietly transferred onto the shoulders of the dual-earner family.

Yet, rather than conceptualizing those responsibilities as a burden, most tech workers draw on the self-empowering philosophy of career management to frame them, instead, as evidence of their own autonomy and self-reliance. That philosophy is itself a product of labor market realities, namely, the demise of the social contract of employment, and it addresses the victimhood and depression experienced by previous generations of unemployed men. Lack of anger at "the system"—the corporations, government policies, and labor market that shape tech workers' experiences of work and the lack thereof—is not a side effect of the philosophy of career management. It is, instead, both a symptom of and a remedy, albeit a partial and imperfect one, for the failure of that system to protect and provide for individuals and their families.

REFERENCES CITED

Bederman, Gail. 1995. *Manliness and Civilization: A Cultural History of Gender and Race in the United States, 1880–1917.* Chicago: University of Chicago Press.

Bolles, Richard. 1972. *What Color Is Your Parachute?* Berkeley, CA: Ten Speed Press.

Hall, Douglas T. 1976. *Careers in Organization.* Glenview, IL: Scott, Foresman.

Komarovsky, Mirra. 1940. *The Unemployed Man and His Family.* New York: Dryden Press.

Kunda, Gideon, and John Van Maanen. 1999. Changing Scripts at Work: Managers and Professionals. *Annals of the American Academy of Political and Social Science* 561:64–80.

Lane, Carrie. 2009. Man Enough to Let My Wife Support Me: How Changing Models of Career and Gender Are Reshaping the Experience of Unemployment. *American Ethnologist* 36(4):681–92.

———. 2012. *A Company of One: Insecurity, Independence, and the New World of White-Collar Unemployment.* Ithaca: ILR Press.

Newman, Katherine. 1988. *Falling from Grace: Downward Mobility in the Age of Affluence.* New York: Free Press.

North Texas Technology Council (NTTC). 2003. Research Report: The Effects of Layoffs in the North Texas Region. Electronic document, http://www.literatecats.com/nttc2/survey2, accessed June 22, 2009.

Potuchek, Jean L. 1997. *Who Supports the Family? Gender and Breadwinning in Dual-Earner Marriages.* Stanford: Stanford University Press.

Sarason, Seymour. 1977. *Work, Aging, and Social Change: Professionals and the One Life-One Career Imperative.* New York: Free Press.

Townsend, Nicholas. 2002. *The Package Deal: Marriage, Work and Fatherhood in Men's Lives.* Philadelphia: Temple University Press.

NOTES

1. I engaged in participant-observation at events intended for unemployed professionals, including job fairs, job search training sessions, professional meetings, and organized networking groups for the unemployed. In addition to meeting and speaking with more than 400 job seekers, I conducted open-ended interviews with 75 unemployed tech workers, many of whom I met with repeatedly over a four-year period. Interviews ranged from one to four hours each. Approximately 70 percent of interviewees were male; more than 80 percent were white. No interviewees were in long-term lesbian or gay partnerships at the time of their interview. All quotations attributed to job seekers are excerpted from interview transcripts; all names used herein are pseudonyms. I also interviewed a small number of recruiters, career counselors, professional and networking event leaders, and spouses or partners of job seekers.

2. The central tenets of career management were first outlined by management experts in the 1970s (e.g., Bolles 1972; Hall 1976; Sarason 1977).

3. Will ultimately searched for 13 months before he landed an executive position at another Dallas-area defense company.

4. Roughly one-quarter of male job seekers and over 40 percent of female job seekers were single at the time of the interviews.

5. One year later, Alex landed a full-time position at a major online retailer that he describes as a "perfect fit." Ella then began day care, and the couple then returned to a more equal division of child care and domestic work in the evenings when both are at home.

1 · Aihwa Ong

STATE VERSUS ISLAM

Malay Families, Women's Bodies, and the Body Politic in Malaysia

DISCUSSION QUESTIONS

1. What were gender relations like in Sungwai Jawa before the Malaysian state began to implement its New Economic Policy in the 1970s?
2. What kinds of changes did the government promote to "modernize" Malays? What were the effects of these interventions on Malay gender relations?
3. What kinds of gender ideals and relations were promoted by the Islamic revival movement? How did class, rural versus urban location, and other factors shape how these Islamic ideals were received and experienced by women and men?
4. Why did the state and the Islamic movement try to influence such "intimate" domains as family formations, reproduction, and women's work, appearance, and sexuality?

Competing images of the Malay woman and family are key elements in the social construction of modern Malaysian society. This article examines the social effects of recent state policies and Islamic revivalism as they negotiate different models of Malay womanhood and kinship. My analysis looks at the ways in which "women" and "the family" have been defined and redefined in concepts, policies, and practices circulated by the state and by resurgent Islam. Challenging prevailing views, I argue that Islamic revivalism reveals itself to be an ideology of the middle class brought into being by state policies. Furthermore, I argue that struggles between state power and revivalist Islam over the changing body politic seem fundamentally to depend on controlling the definition of Malay womanhood and the family.

An abridged version of Aihwa Ong, 1990. "State versus Islam: Malay Families, Women's Bodies, and the Body Politic in Malaysia." Reproduced by permission of the American Anthropological Association and of the author from *American Ethnologist,* Volume 17, Issue 2, Pages 258–276, May 1990. Not for sale or further reproduction.

Since independence in 1957, the Malaysian government, led by the United Malays National Organization (UMNO) party, has been based on a careful demographic balancing of the "races" (*bangsa*): Malays, who are all Muslim, and the predominantly non-Muslim Chinese and Indians. Statistics measuring the relative size of the three "races" and providing evidence of their relative poverty and wealth have been a critical part of modern Malaysian politics and racial consciousness. In 1969, racial riots protesting the poverty of Malays, the majority of whom were peasants, forced a rapid adjustment in relations between the state and the races. This was to be effected by a New Economic Policy (NEP) designed to "eradicate poverty" and end ethnic identification with economic role. The immediate effects of the NEP were, first, to bring the rural Malay population more directly under state administration, and, second, to integrate them more fully into the industrializing capitalist economy. Social policy was elaborated to ensure the health and security of Malays, now legally defined as *bumiputera,* or "sons-of-the-soil." Most critically, the NEP was to provide a new racial balance-sheet: by 1990, *bumiputera* were to control 30 percent of equity capital in the country, up from 2.4 percent in 1970 (Government of Malaysia 1976:86–89).

A new state ideology (the *Rukunegara),* spelled out in a series of Five-Year Plans, produced a view of modern Malay society in which the *bumiputera* were to become capitalists, professionals, and workers, modern citizens who were to know themselves primarily in terms of their claims to national wealth. An expansion of state policies to remake the peasantry along these lines gradually increased class differentiation in Malay village (*kampung*) society and stimulated the urban migration of young women and men. This crisis of the peasantry, rooted in men's loss of land and of control over female sexuality, became inseparable from a crisis in Malay cultural identity. *Kampung* notions of kinship, conjugal rights, and gender were increasingly subjected to the operation of state policies.

KINSHIP, GENDER, AND COMMUNITY AMONG MALAY PEASANTS

Local conditions and the historical interactions of custom (*adat*) with Islam have shaped Malay beliefs and practices concerning kinship, residence, and property. Although men traditionally enjoyed prerogatives in religion and property, women were neither confined to the household nor totally dependent on men for economic survival. Malay society is often cited as an example of a Muslim society that permitted relatively egalitarian relations between the sexes, compared, say, with the rigid gender segregation found in Bangladesh. However, in the postindependence period, forces linked to economic development and Islamic revivalism have undermined the *adat* emphasis on bilaterality while strengthening Islamic tenets that increase male control over domestic resources.

In 1979 and 1980, I conducted fieldwork in Sungai Jawa, a village in Kuala Langat. Among the villagers, the sexual division of labor and emphasis on bilateral kin somewhat attenuated the patrilateral bias of Islamic law. Both men and women tapped rubber and tended coffee trees in their holdings. Until the early 1970s, only *kampung* men sought migrant work; a few women, usually divorcees or widows, were compelled to earn wages outside the village as rubber tappers or domestic servants. In recent years, however, population growth and land scarcity have affected gender relations and peasant householding. The *adat* practice of awarding equal land shares to sons and daughters has been superseded by the Islamic Shafi'i law dictating that daughters be given half-shares. Female-owned plots too small to be farmed separately are now often bought up by brothers. This emphasis on male inheritance has led to a situation in which most farms are constituted by the husband's property.

Malays throughout the Peninsula (excluding the matrilineal Minangkabau) prefer nuclear households to more complex domestic arrangements. In Sungai Jawa (pseudonym), Selangor, 80 percent of the 242 households I surveyed were nuclear units. Despite important day-to-day relations between kin and neighbor, the founding of a *rumah tangga*—a "house served by a single staircase"—was considered essential to male adulthood. A married man compelled to reside with his parents would consider his status diminished. *Adat* required the father to give his son the property for establishing a new household upon marriage. Once the head of his own household, a man was free from parental claims on his labor and earnings. A married man working on his father's land would expect to be paid like any other hired help.

Second, independent householding by a man made clear his sexual rights in his wife and authority over his daughters. This fact was brought home to me when I first sought residence in Sungai Jawa. Since I am an ethnic Chinese woman, villagers advised me against setting up a separate household. Elsewhere, single female nurses and teachers who wished to live in villages stayed in government quarters, their status and reputation protected. As a researcher, however, I did not have such a clearly specified role or this sort of official supervision. If I were to rent a house on my own, I would be perceived as a woman eminently seducible by village men. I was kindly invited to lodge with a household, but on the condition that I take the role of an adopted daughter, thus dispelling suspicions that I might be a mistress to men in the family.

In the Malay village, gender differentiation was commonly expressed not in terms of biological makeup but in terms of morality. A basic aspect of a man's role was guardianship—of his sister's, wife's, and daughter's virtue. By extension, all village men were responsible for the moral status of all village women. This code of morality was often explained in terms of men's greater rationality and self-control (*akal*) and women's greater susceptibility to animalistic lust (*nafsu*). Islamic emphasis on female chastity imposed restrictions more rigorously on unmarried women (called *anak dara,* or virgins) than on unmarried youths, although promiscuity in either sex was criticized. Young girls were required to be bashful and modest, but the

Islamic emphasis on *aurat* ("nakedness" that should be covered) did not, until recently, extend to covering girls' hair (an erotic feature), which they wore loose or plaited. Everyday wear was loose-fitting long tunics over sarongs (*baju kurong*). Before the recent wave of outmigration for wage work and higher education, adolescent daughters were expected to stay close to home and to keep a circumspect distance from kinsmen. An important role of young men was to prevent their sisters from interacting with men, a practice that compromised their virtue.

Adat defined adult womanhood in other ways, but always within the Islamic construction of their relation to men. In everyday life, married women could move freely in tending to their cash-crop gardens or engaging in petty trade. They were not, however, supposed to sit in coffee shops or to seek male company. Women were the ones who maintained kin and neighborly relations through sharing resources, information, childcare, and the work of preparing feasts. *Keluarga,* the word often rendered as "family" in English, were open-ended kindred circles maintained by female kin between village households. In their own homes, married women customarily held the purse-strings, despite Islamic emphasis on men's keeping and handling money. Most important, women's special knowledge and skills were used in cooking, child birth, health care, and intensification of sexual pleasure. Women's *adat* knowledge included the art of preserving sexual attractiveness to retain their husbands' interest. Married women wore their hair in buns, but on special occasions they dressed up in close-fitting, semitransparent jackets (*kebaya*) and batik sarongs. A lacy shawl (*selendang*) draped loosely over the head and shoulders could be used as a sunscreen and, occasionally, as a means of flirtation.

Emphasizing sexual charms, married women's clothing was in sharp contrast to the modest attire required of unmarried girls. Because sexually experienced and not legally subordinated to any man, previously married women, whether widows or divorcees (called by the same term, *janda*), were considered both vulnerable and dangerous. *Janda* were frequently suspected of trying to steal husbands. The virginity code and sanctions against adultery permitted sex only between spouses. This does not prevent premarital or extramarital sex, but the Islamic ban on *khalwat* (illicit sex outside wedlock) made having affairs a risky business.

Just as control of his wife's sexuality defined a man's adult status, regulating the activities of unmarried women-virgins and *janda* defined the collective identity of *kampung* men. In Sungai Jawa, young men, with the implicit backing of Islamic elders, kept a watch on couples carrying on illicit affairs. If "caught wet" (*tangkap basah*) and found to be unmarried, a couple would be compelled to marry as soon as possible. If either party were already married, the man would be beaten as a warning to other would-be adulterers. Sometimes the Islamic court would impose fines or even imprisonment, but villagers preferred to police and punish sexual misconduct themselves, as part of their role in safeguarding morality and protecting the boundaries between Malays and non-Malays. Thus, youths would be more ferocious in their attacks if the paramour were an outsider or non-Malay man.

In *kampung* society, then, Islamic law defined a man's identity in terms of his ability to prepare his sons for independent householding, to control the sexuality of his wife and daughters, and to provide all economic support for his household. However, *adat* practices and kindred relations provided women a measure of autonomy and influence in everyday life that prevented a rigid observation of male authority. In recent years, state policies and capitalist relations have created conditions that make the regulation of female sexuality a major issue. The possibilities for interracial liaisons created by the interweaving of Malay and non-Malay worlds have been perceived as a threat to Malay male rights and as a dangerous blurring of boundaries between Muslim and non-Muslim groups. As we shall see, control over female sexuality has been made a focus of the resulting efforts to strengthen male authority, reinforce group boundaries, and ensure the cultural survival of the Malay community undergoing "modernization."

STATE INTERVENTIONS: MAKING THE MODERN MALAY FAMILY

Capitalist Development and Outmigration

Among the complex effects of the NEP was an improvement in living conditions in the *kampung* coupled with a reduction in the ability of most peasants to support their children by farming. In my survey of 242 households, a quarter were landless or owned only their house lot. Sixty-one percent had access to farms under 2.5 acres, a size just adequate for supporting a family of four. About 65 percent of the household heads (mainly men) were working as day laborers or migrant workers, reflecting a movement out of cash-cropping into the wage economy. With land fragmentation, rising land costs, and an increasing reliance on wage employment, many village men found themselves unable to pass property on to their children for making a *kampung* livelihood. In Sungai Jawa, many fathers did not have enough land left for their sons. In fact, they were beginning to depend on children's wages to augment the household budget.

Meanwhile, welfare policies seemed to prepare *kampung* children for different places in the wider economy. In Kuala Langat, a coeducational high school and a free trade zone were set up. The best students were creamed off through nationally certified examinations and sent to urban schools and colleges or to overseas universities on state scholarships. Like *kampung* youth throughout the country, those high school graduates left in Sungai Jawa rejected farming as a way of life. Many youths preferred to remain unemployed, waiting for a plum job as office-boy in some government agency. With the NEP, the outmigration of young *kampung* men and, increasingly, women for higher education and wage work became an irreversible process, dramatically changing parent–child and gender relations.

Family Planning

As in many developing countries, family planning in Malaysia was informed by the postwar World

Bank prescription of increasing agricultural development while reducing family size. Concerned that family policy could be construed as interference in Malay husbands' rights, officials packaged family planning as a "health programme," emphasizing nutrition and well-being while strategically pushing fertility control. Family planning ideology promoted a model based on the Western conjugal family, using the term *keluarga* (kindred) to designate a "nuclear family" made up of a working father, housewife, and dependent children. A pamphlet promoting contraceptives depicted family problems caused by a tired and irritable wife burdened with housework and childcare. She was portrayed as inadequate to her husband's needs. Village women were urged to take the Pill in order to spare their husbands "inconveniences." But in suggesting that the Pill could improve husband–wife relations, the program overlooked the value placed on female fecundity and its reflection of the husband's virility.

Not surprisingly, village men actively resisted family planning, using the health services of the "maternity and children's" clinic in Sungai Jawa to attain the highest birthrate in the district. Nevertheless, the ideology of family planning increased tensions between husbands and wives. In Sungai Jawa and, I suspect, most villages, the Pill was the main contraceptive provided by government clinics. Villagers noted that women taking the Pill complained of headaches, a "bloated" appearance, and a lethargy that made them "too lazy to work." Some husbands even threatened that if their wives got sick from the Pill, they would be refused help. Male hostility to family planning was so strong that men rejected contraceptives even when they were poor and could barely support large families. A 27-year-old mother of six children under 15 was seven months pregnant when I met her; she had wanted to go on the Pill after the fourth child but her husband, a laborer, had refused her permission. She said that most women had children because their husbands wished it, even though women themselves did not desire many children (although they did feel some concern about having children for old-age security).

Family planning challenged *kampung* men's exclusive rights to their wives' sexuality. In addition, the men feared that contraceptives might embolden women to dissent from their husbands' wishes. Villagers and religious leaders often used Islam, citing the Hadith (an authorized compilation of the Prophet's words, deeds, and exemplary practices) to criticize family planning as "killing the fetus." In the villagers' daily conversations, the distinctions between miscarriage, abortion, and contraception were often blurred. An imam told me that the Koran allowed abortion when the mother's health was endangered or the family could not possibly support another child, but, as the above example illustrates, husbands rejected contraception even in such cases.

Since family planning was considered anti-Islam, those who used contraceptives had reason to conceal their decision. The Sungai Jawa clinic kept records on 97 family planning couples, showing that 70 percent of the husbands were wage workers. Most of the wives were between 14 and 28 years old. I was told that perhaps 20 or more young couples bought their own contraceptives rather than get them free at the clinic. The factory women whom I interviewed said they did not intend to have more than four children. Young couples who depended mainly or exclusively on wage income had begun to talk about children in terms of "costs." Besides creating more expenses, children required help with their schoolwork so that they could later compete for white-collar jobs.

Whatever the local effects of the family planning program, most Malays viewed the family planning ideology as ultimately a threat to their national survival. Although teachers and other state servants might be practicing contraception in private, in public they loudly proclaimed the practice contrary to Islam. Moreover, family planning conflicted in practice with state policies encouraging Malays to have many children as one way of increasing wealth and ensuring the success of the race. Civil servants warned that if contraception were widely adopted, Malays would lose their voting power vis-à-vis the other races. Modern concepts and practices concerning health and sex thus challenged male conjugal rights and moral authority over women. And not only did family planning challenge male rights, but it threatened racial power as well.

The Deployment of Female Labor in Free Trade Zones

As welfare policy tried to manage the bodily care and reproduction of peasant Malays, social engineering redistributed the younger generations in new locations scattered throughout the wider society. Throughout the 1970s, state intervention in the peasant sector generated a steady influx of Malays into cities, a rising number of them young women. Tens of thousands of female migrants collected in urban free trade zones, working in labor-intensive subsidiaries of transnational corporations. These corporations had established electronics firms, garment factories, and other light manufacturing plants in the special zones, where they were legally required to have a 30 percent *bumiputera* representation in their work force. By the late 1970s, some 80,000 *kampung* girls between the ages of 16 and the mid-twenties had been transformed into industrial laborers (Jamilah 1980). The industrialization strategy, originally focused on creating a Malay male working class, found itself producing an increasingly female industrial force, largely because of the manufacturing demand for cheaper (female) labor.

This army of working daughters introduced another line of division into the Malay household. In Sungai Jawa, the local free trade zone turned village girls into factory operators. Many peasants eagerly sent their daughters off to earn income to be put toward household expenses. Most working daughters were induced to hand over part of their paychecks, especially when brothers proved reluctant to share their own earnings, were unemployed, or were attending school. Daughters' wages paid for consumer durables and house renovations that broadcast the new wealth of *kampung* families. Not unexpectedly, working daughters strengthened the influence of mothers in the household: since it would be shameful for fathers to ask help from daughters, mothers extracted the earnings. Village men found themselves unable to fulfill their duties as fathers and husbands. Some felt humiliated that they depended on daughters' wages and could not keep them at home, their virtue protected.

Nationwide, as thousands of peasant girls descended on cities and free trade zones, they came into competition with their male peers. For young men, sisters became an easily tapped source of cash, but as would-be wives working women transgressed the wider arena of male power. So long as unmarried girls were confined to the *kampung* milieu, men's superiority in experience and knowledge could remain unchallenged. Now, young women too were acquiring experience in market situations, situations where they could mingle freely with men. Furthermore, the new class of female workers and college students induced in their male peers a widespread fear of female competition in the changing society.

For the first time in Malay history, a large number of nubile women had the money and social freedom to experiment with a newly awakened sense of self. Many came to define themselves, through work experiences and market choices, as not materially or even morally dependent on parents and kinsmen. Factory women could now save for their weddings, instead of receiving money from their parents, and could therefore choose their own husbands. The increasing number of brides who were wage-earners produced a trend toward larger wedding outlays by grooms for feasting and for outfitting the bride and the new household. In the changing *kampung* society, young men and women found themselves dependent on the labor market and the state, rather than on their parents, as they negotiated the path toward adulthood. Young women, however, came to bear special moral burdens for realizing the image of a modern Malay society.

Work Ethics, Women's Duties, and the Modern Family

In the early 1980s, the state introduced a "Look East" policy to enforce discipline in modern institutions. The presumed "communal spirit" of Japanese enterprises was presented as in keeping with Islamic kinship values. Whereas health policy pushed a nuclear family ideal, industrial ideology promoted a patrilineal "family welfare" model said to reflect *keluarga* stress on mutual obligations and loyalty. In the Kuala Langat free trade zone, a company motto proclaimed its goal to be

> to create one big family,
> to train workers,
> to increase loyalty to company,
> country and fellow workers.

Despite this corporate "philosophy," many factory women felt manipulated and harassed by male supervisors whom they were urged to consider as family elders. To some workers, management was implacably the other ("aliens"): it did not speak their language, was not Muslim, profited from their labor, and sometimes treated them as though they were not "human beings." Among operators, only fellow workers were considered "siblings" (*saudara saudari*). Despite factory-induced competition among operators, workers in the same section would help each other and look out for new recruits, as one would for one's *keluarga*. Such mutual dependence, of course, unintentionally reinforced self-regulation, commitment, and discipline among workers—the goals of the "one big family" ideology.

The "poverty eradication" program also promoted new concepts of female duty, based on the Western notion of family as a privatized unit of obligations and exclusion. In the Fifth Malaysia Plan, women were seen as key to improving the lot of "low-income households." Rural women were blamed for not being hard-working and for their presumed lack of response to "modern practices" and "new opportunities" for improving the well-being of their families. Officials dictated a series of tasks women could undertake to improve the health and wealth of their families. Peasant mothers were instructed to ignore "customary" practices in preparing their children for "a progressive society"; they were called upon to raise children with values such as "efficiency" and "self-reliance" (Government

of Malaysia 1986:83–84). A government program called KEMAS ("tidy up") instructed village women in home economics and handicrafts. The new housewife requirements echoed the slogan "Clean, Efficient, and Trustworthy" proclaimed in factories with largely female work forces. Official discourse on the modern family thus defined women's modern roles: as working daughters who could pull their families out of "backwardness" and as housewives (*seri-rumah*) who could inculcate "progressive" values in their children. This privileging of the mother–child relationship reflected the Western family model while ignoring the central role of the Muslim father.

Through various NEP programs, then, the ideology of a modern Malay society unintentionally undermined the source of customary male power. Welfare policies progressively defined a privatized domestic sphere and women's responsibilities in it. This family model seemed to undermine male conjugal and paternity rights while supporting a more assertive role for women at home. Second, the emphasis on *bumiputera* rights greatly raised the expectations of young people without eliminating their sense of uncertainty in the multiethnic society to which they were channeled as students, wage workers, professionals, and unemployed youths. Their cultural dislocation was compounded by the changing sexual division of labor and the new freedoms of daughters, wives, female students, and female workers. Moral confusion over the proper roles of men and women and the boundaries between public and domestic, Muslim and non-Muslim worlds produced a crisis of national identity.

ISLAMIC REVIVALISM: ENGENDERING THE *UMMA*

In the 1970s, diverse Islamic revivalist groups, collectively referred to as the *dakwa* (proselytizing) movement, began to develop among the *kampung*-born and educated Malays who had emerged as a new social force under the NEP. Here, I will focus on the major group, ABIM (*Angkatan Belia Islam*

Malaysia or Islamic Youth Movement of Malaysia), which rose to national prominence through the 1970s, at its height numbering some 30,000 members and innumerable sympathizers. Besides its size, it drew on the largest cohort of young Malays to have benefited from mass literacy. They differed from earlier generations of revivalists in that they emphasized a direct engagement with holy texts (the Sunnah, Hadith, and Koran), bypassing the received wisdom of traditional religious leaders (*ulama*). ABIM members and supporters were mainly young men and women who, hailing from villages like Sungai Jawa, had migrated into cities for wage employment and higher education. Despite the *bumiputera* rhetoric, they had been made aware of the gulf between them and the older Malay elites who had come to power under British tutelage. Students sent on scholarships to universities in London, Cairo, and Islamabad were exposed to the various strands of Islamic resurgence abroad. Upon returning home, many became *dakwa* leaders who railed against the decadent lifestyle of nouveaux-riches Malays, with their pursuit of glittering acquisitions and sensual pleasures and their blithe disregard of Islam.

ABIM's search for an Islamic revivalist identity was an assault on a hegemonic construction of *bumiputera*-hood that did not address the cultural problems of Malays living in a secular, multiethnic world. The recovery of the *umma* (social and religious community) became a central goal in dealing with the breakdowns in social boundaries that had traditionally defined Malay group identity. Through *dakwa* activities, ABIM members aimed to awaken a "broader religious consciousness" among Muslims (Nagata 1984:81–82). *Dakwa* attacks on capitalism focused on its spawning choices and practices "based not on divine morality but on sensuality and as such not according to truth and justice" (Anwar Ibrahim, quoted in Mohammad 1981:1046). The "truth" that Islamic revivalists sought was to be found in an *umma* that would infuse the community as well as the government with revitalized Islamic values (Muhammad Kamal 1987). By insisting on a stricter adherence to the *umma*, the *dakwa* was urging a more gender-stratified social system than existed in Malay society.

For Malay revivalists, the *umma* had been unmade by the influx of women into modern schools and offices; a new "sacred architecture" of sexuality (Mernissi 1987: xvi) had to be created, through everyday practices inventing "Islamic" traditions that would redraw boundaries between Malay men and women, Muslims and non-Muslims. Almost overnight, large numbers of university students, young workers, and even professionals began to enact—in prayer, diet, clothing, and social life—religious practices borrowed from Islamic history, Middle Eastern societies, and South Asian cults.

In Sungai Jawa, villagers felt a general anxiety about the ways in which state policies and secularization had weakened male authority over young women. Parents were torn between wanting their daughters to work and being concerned about keeping their status honorable. With independent earnings, women's agency, formerly channeled through legal superiors (parents, husbands), came to express individual interests in consumption and in dating. Factory women took to wearing revealing Western outfits (such as mini-skirts) and bright makeup. This "sarong-to-jeans movement" was seen as a license for permissiveness that overturned *kampung* norms of maidenly decorum. In the factories, nubile women were daily supervised by men, many non-Malays—an arrangement that seemed to mock Malay male authority. Worse, some working women began to date non-Malay men, breaking village norms of sexual and religious segregation. Women who were unrestrained (*bebas*) by family guidance in relations with men were derided as being no longer Malay (*bukan Melayu*). Villagers viewed this development of an autonomous female agency as a weakening of male control and of the boundaries between Malays and non-Malays.

The religious response to women's assertiveness was exemplified in a speech given at a village celebration of Prophet Mohammad's Birthday in 1979. A young scholar complained that the modern ills afflicting Malays included drug-taking, excessive watching of television, and communism. Islamic societies were weak not because Islam was weak, but because Muslims were weak human beings who succumbed to their baser nature (*nafsu*). He elaborated this theme by saying that women's roles as mothers and wives had to be strengthened according to Islamic tenets. When a student at Al-Azhar, Cairo, he had the opportunity to observe the great respect children showed their mothers in societies where Islam was an overwhelming force in everyday life. He urged villagers to raise their children with great respect for authority. And, while all Muslims should obey Islamic laws and respect their elders, women should first and foremost serve their husbands. He then raised the vision of factory women "letting themselves" be cheated by men, thus "damaging themselves." Wage work was presented as dishonorable, inducing women to indulge their indiscriminate passions. He continued by saying that a woman's sensual nature was acceptable only if (his hands sculpting the air to suggest a curvaceous body) her sexual allure was reserved for her husband's pleasure. He ended by calling on village women to emulate the Prophet's wife, Katijah. This call for a strengthening of the Malay race required women to adhere to a stricter Islamic version of male authority and of women's roles as mothers and wives.

In thus defining a new *umma*, ABIM and other *dakwa* groups invented practices harking back to a mythic, homogeneous Islamic past, while rejecting their Malay–Muslim cultural heritage. This Arabization of Malay society depended in large part on implementing a rigid separation between male public roles and female domestic ones, a separation quite contrary to indigenous arrangements. A new, radical separation of Malay women and men, Muslims and non-Muslims, was created in public life, primarily by inscribing this spatialization of power on women's bodies.

WOMEN'S AGENCY AND THE FEMALE BODY

In Malaysia, women displayed a range of responses, both to modernization and to Islamic revivalism

that cannot be reduced to "resistance," a term implying only oppositional tactics. Here, I suggest that among Malay women, agency in terms of autonomy or adherence to interests not independently conceived differed according to class. Whereas working-class women tended to operate as agents in their own self-interest, middle-class women were significantly swayed by the spirit of Islamic resurgence.

It would be erroneous to assume that state policies unambiguously provided Malay women with conditions for employment and individual security. Land scarcity, widespread female wage labor, and secularization in many cases reduced men's customary obligation to be the sole supporters of their families. Furthermore, the trend toward female wage employment made all Malay women vulnerable to a reduction or even withdrawal of their husbands' support. At an UMNO Women's meeting, wives of the rural elite complained that government promotion of the "housewife" did not guarantee women economic support. Leaders reminded village women of their responsibilities for the educational success of their children and the preservation of the UMNO heritage for their grandchildren. However, some women noted that men viewed their wives as having rights only in housework and childcare, with no claim on their husbands' salaries. Invoking the Islamic marriage contract, members proposed that mutual respect and intimacy within marriage would be improved if the state could guarantee that "housewives" would be paid an "allowance" drawn from their husbands' salaries.

For unmarried women, the impact of modernizing forces has been greater and more disorienting, especially among the first large generation of Malay university women. Many have found refuge in the *dakwa* movement. On the campus of the University of Malaya, at least 60 percent of the students showed some commitment to *dakwa* in the early 1980s (Zainah 1987:33). Whereas ABIM men wore Western shirts and pants, *dakwa* women put on the *mini-telekung*, a cloth that tightly frames the face and covers the head, hair and chest, considered parts of the *aurat* ("nakedness") that Islam requires women to conceal. This headcloth was usually worn with the customary *baju kurung*. Some women also donned long black robes (*hijab*), socks, gloves, and face-veils, denoting a full purdah (*parda*) historically alien to Malay culture.

Students walking around in full purdah were a source of irritation to government officials worried that "Arabic" robes would scare off foreign investors. In fact, *dakwa* groups were critical of the kind of cultural colonialization promoted by the market, media, and foreign corporations. A female *dakwa* lecturer assailed working women for adopting the consumerist "feminine false consciousness" promoted by factory culture (Amriah 1989). As a male revivalist remarked, "I feel that secularism is the biggest threat to the Muslim *umma*" (Zainah 1987:76). *Dakwa* groups sought to provide networks and daily support for Malay women disoriented by the consumerism of modern life.

ABIM recruitment of women was not only a resistance to capitalist culture, but also a reorienting of women's agency for rebuilding Malay–Muslim identity. State policies had "liberated" women for campuses and the marketplace, but could not offer protection against new selfdoubts and social anxieties among women and men. Released from the guidance and protection of their kin, many young women were compelled to act as "individuals" representing their own interests in the wider society. Furthermore, Malay society for the first time confronted the problem of a large group of unmarried young women, whose unregulated sexuality was seen as symbolic of social disorder. The *dakwa* obsession with women's "modesty" in "male" and multiethnic spaces was reflected in their insistence that women cover themselves. Women's bodily containment was key to the envisaged order that would contain those social forces unleashed by state policies and the capitalist economy. The *mini-telekung* and long robes marked off the female body as an enclosed, "pregnant" space, symbolic of the boundaries drawn around Malay society, and the male authority within it.

Such dramatic reversals from their brief exposure to personal liberation were more evident among female university students than among blue-collar women. Campuses were the seats of the most intensive *dakwa* campaigns to cover the female body and maintain sexual and ethnic segregation. Women were discouraged from participating in sports that displayed too much of their naked limbs. A University of Malaya ban on the *mini-telekung* in lecture halls failed to deter many female students from covering their heads. Even female lecturers who rejected the *dakwa* prescription felt sufficiently intimidated to wear headscarves and avoid Western-style clothing.

The following two examples illustrate the centrality of sexuality to female students' struggles between autonomy and group identity. One student, who favored leotards and disco dancing, was repeatedly chastised by *dakwa* members over a period of two years. One day her boyfriend urged her to don the *mini-telekung* because, he said, it would help him resist her sexual appeal. When she finally complied, *dakwa* women immediately embraced and salaamed to her (Zainah 1987:64–67). In another case, a student confided that when she first came to the university she had worn "mini-skirts and low-cut clothes." She had mixed with Chinese students and attended campus "cultural" events, but not religious ones. One day she received a letter, signed "servant of Allah," accusing her of having sinned by befriending Chinese infidels, who would lead her astray. Just for not covering her head, she would burn in hell (Zainah 1987:60). As these cases indicate, ABIM recruits were often women who had tasted individual "freedom" but, subjected to pressure and even outright threats, later found security and acceptance in Islamic revivalism. By donning *dakwa* outfits, they could negotiate the urban milieu without being insulted by men. The *dakwa* robes registered the multiple effects of cultural disorientation, protest, and intimidation, enfolding them into a moral community.

Furthermore, university women experienced conflict between the demands of individualistic competition in modern education and the job market, on the one hand, and their hopes of being married, on the other. Although most had *kampung* roots, university women were seen by men as direct competitors for higher-status jobs, and thus more serious threats than factory women to male class privileges. For *dakwa* members, women in the modern economy, the "modern family" ideology, and the "housewife" ideal were all threats to male authority at home and in the public sphere. ABIM members insisted that women's first duties were to their husbands and that wives should obey their husbands just as all Muslims should obey Allah. The insistence on obedient wives seemed an appropriate ideology for the urban middle class, among whom divorce has lately declined, possibly because of women's fear of the economic and social losses it would entail. (Working-class women still experienced high rates of divorce [Azizah 1987:109–110].) Very few factory women adopted *dakwa* in the village, *dakwa* robes were considered the mark of the educated woman—although many did believe that the intensified religious environment provided them protection against sexual and social abuse in the wider society (Ong 1987:181–193). Furthermore, the nurturing and "self-sacrificing" role of women as mothers, stressed in both state and revivalist discourses, was more easily realized by middle-class women, who did not need to earn a living. ABIM members frequently invoked the Koranic phrase "paradise lies beneath mothers' feet" (Nagata 1984:100), celebrating women's primary responsibility to instill Islamic values in their children. Women were also urged to spread Islamic values among their female friends. In *dakwa* discourse, the redirection of women's agency from labor force to moral force tapped the visceral and spiritual unease of upwardly aspiring women filled with ambivalence about careers and the solitude of modern life.

Thus, although a substantial number of its members were engaged in a genuine spiritual quest, the *dakwa* movement also reflected discontent with changing gender roles and the declining force of male authority in the middle-class family. The above reading helps to explain the apparently paradoxical fact that many young women who had benefited from state education policies found the *dakwa* call so appealing. In *dakwa* visions, women are all married and fulfilled. As wives and mothers, they play central roles in rebuilding and preserving Malay society as part of the larger Islamic family (Anwar 1986:5). Islamic revivalism reminds women of their moral capacity to construct and preserve the imagined Malay community. In the university survey, most of the women interviewed considered themselves to be "first and foremost Muslims," arguing that "nowadays, there is only one tradition—that is, Islamic tradition." They saw Islam as a "more comprehensive value system" than Malay customs, one more fit to guide them in an era of rapid change. Some insisted on being reidentified, saying, "I am Muslim rather than Malay" (Narli 1981:132–133). This religious nationalism, potentially radical in politics but conservative in sex roles, is the ideology of an emergent middle class. By means of a complex system of intimidation and persuasion, women have been reconciled to their retreat from the modern economy and compensated with the honor due devout Muslim mothers. Furthermore, by wearing their *dakwa* outfits, women have proclaimed the impossibility of interethnic liaisons or marriages, thereby stemming any potential loss in progeny to the Malay race, a numerically small majority in Malaysia. *Dakwa* women have thus asserted Malay singularity against Malaysian multiculturalism, at the same time partaking of the aura cast by the global Islamic florescence.

THE NEW FAMILY POLICY AND BODY POLITIC

This powerful Islamic claim on women's moral agency was met by the state's launching an Islamization campaign of its own. In 1983, the government co-opted the charismatic ABIM leader Anwar Ibrahim and set up special Islamic institutions for banking, education, and missionizing programs. More rigorous efforts were made to punish Muslims who broke religious rules forbidding gambling, drinking, and sex out of wedlock. On television, Islamic programs promoted an image of an "ideal mother" who would put her husband and children before anything else.

This religious showcasing of state institutions set the stage for a new "family development" policy. In 1984, the government proclaimed that the labor needs of rapid capitalist development required the population to grow from 14 to 70 million over the next hundred years (Government of Malaysia 1984:21–22). Although there was widespread skepticism about the possibility of attaining the goal, the new family policy found support even among Malays disaffected from the UMNO-led government. First, there was no mention of intended ethnic composition, but it was patently clear that only population growth among Malays would be encouraged. Second, in producing a discourse on "family development," the state appropriated *dakwa* themes of defining and empowering Malays in relation to non-Malay communities. Third, the "pro-natalist program" (Stivens 1987) diffused male Malay fears of female domination in the labor force while accommodating the *dakwa* insistence on women's primary role as mothers. The Prime Minister was quoted as saying that women whose husbands could afford it should stay home to raise families of at least five children (Chee 1988:166). Thus, in its official discourse the state regained control over the definition of the domestic domain, earning moral and even Islamic legitimacy in the process.

The Malaysian case illustrates that in modernizing societies, "women" and "the family" enter into the social construction of national politics. Regulating Malay women is central to two intertwined processes also found in other societies:

1. The social construction of gender and the family is always class-specific in its effects.

2. Among emergent middle classes, conservative ideologies concerned with preserving and extending class privileges link the privatization of female sexuality to the maintenance of male authority, social order, and the body politic.

Thus, despite differences over the issue of economic development, both renewalist Islam and the secular state have manipulated women's status to mediate changing relationships between female and male, private and public, "the family" and the body politic. The consequence of this struggle of capitalist state versus Islamic *umma* has been an intensification of gender inequality in Malay society. These hegemonic and counterhegemonic visions are both consistent with the Malay middle-class emphasis on women as domesticated producers of the racial stock. Rather than seeing the agency of middle-class women in terms of mere resistance or passivity, I have argued that it has been shaped by the intersections of their own self-interests with group identity. By yielding to religious and class forces and by working to protect the integrity of their bodies, families, and the body politic, women have found new ways of belonging in a changing Malaysia.

REFERENCES CITED

Amriah, Buang. 1989. Development and Factory Women—Negative Perceptions from a Malaysian Source Area. Paper presented at the Commonwealth Geographical Bureau Workshop on Gender and Development, University of Newcastle, April 16–21.

Anwar, Ibrahim. 1986. Development, Values and Changing Political Ideas. Sojourn 1(1):1–7.

Azizah, Kassim. 1987, Women and Divorce among the Urban Malays. *In* Women in Malaysia. Hing Ai Yun, Nik Safiah Karim, and Rokiah Talib, eds. pp. 94–112. Petaling Jaya, Malaysia: Pelanduk Publications.

Chee Heng Leng. 1988. Babies to Order: Recent Population Policies in Malaysia and Singapore. *In* Structures of Patriarchy: The State, the Community and the Household. Bina Agarwal, ed. pp. 164–174. London: Zed Books Ltd.

Government of Malaysia. 1976. Third Malaysia Plan, 1976–1980. Kuala Lumpur: Government Printing Press.

———. 1984 Mid-Term Review of the Fourth Malaysia Plan, 1981–1985. Kuala Lumpur: Government Printing Press.

———. 1986 Fifth Malaysia Plan, 1986–1990. Kuala Lumpur: Government Printing Press.

Jamilah, Ariffin. 1980. Industrial Development in Peninsular Malaysia and Rural-Urban Migration of Women Workers: Impact and Implications. Jurnal Ekonomi Malaysia 1:41–59.

Mernissi, Fatima. 1987. Beyond the Veil: Male–Female Dynamics in Modern Muslim Society. Rev. Ed. Bloomington: Indiana University Press.

Mohammad Abu Bakar. 1981. Islamic Revivalism and the Political Process in Malaysia. Asian Survey 21:1040–1059.

Muhammad Kamal Hassan. 1987. The Response of Muslim Youth Organizations to Political Change: HMI in Indonesia and ABIM in Malaysia. *In* Islam and the Political Economy of Meaning. William R. Roff, ed. pp. 180–196. Berkeley: University of California Press.

Nagata, Judith. 1984. The Reflowering of Malaysian Islam. Vancouver: University of British Columbia Press.

Narli, Ayse Nilufer. 1981. Development, Malay Women, and Islam in Malaysia: Emerging Contradictions. Kajian Malaysia 2:123–141.

Ong, Aihwa. 1987. Spirits of Resistance and Capitalist Discipline: Factory Women in Malaysia. Albany: State University of New York Press.

Stivens, Maila. 1987. Family and State in Malaysian Industrialization: The Case of Rembau, Negri Sembilan, Malaysia. *In* Women, State, and Ideology. Haleh Afshar, ed. pp. 89–110. Albany: State University of New York Press.

Zainah Anwar. 1987. Islamic Revivalism in Malaysia. Petaling Jaya, Malaysia: Pelanduk Publications.

2 • *Lesley Gill*

CREATING CITIZENS, MAKING MEN
The Military and Masculinity in Bolivia

DISCUSSION QUESTIONS

1. What kind of masculinity does the Bolivian state try to create through its military training? Why? What practices does the military use to do this?
2. How and why do indigenous men adopt this form of "militarized masculinity," even though the military and state have a long history of oppressing them?
3. How do concepts of power, agency, structure, and intersectionality help us to analyze this case?

In Bolivia, young male military conscripts come from the most powerless sectors of society: Quechua, Aymara, and Guarani peasant communities and poor urban neighborhoods. Like recruits from impoverished ethnic groups and working classes elsewhere (Gibson 1986; Zeitlin et al. 1973), they are the foot soldiers who risk death in warfare to a greater degree than members of dominant social groups and frequently suffer emotional abuse at the hands of commanding officers. Their rural communities, mining camps, and urban neighborhoods have also long experienced repression in the military's fight against "internal enemies." Why, then, are these young men frequently eager to serve? And why do many experience social pressure from friends, family members, and their communities to enlist?

There is no simple answer to these questions; the reasons are both straightforward and complex. On the one hand, military service is a legal obligation for all able-bodied Bolivian men, and it is understood as a prerequisite for many forms of urban employment. Perhaps more important, young men may acquiesce to military service because Bolivia, unlike Peru and various Central American countries, has not been mired in bloody warfare for over a generation. On the other hand, compulsory military service facilitates more ambivalent processes: even as the state attempts to create "citizens" out of "Indians" and "men" out of "boys," conscripts simultaneously lay claim to militarized conceptions of masculinity to advance their own agendas. They advance a positive sense of subaltern masculinity tied to beliefs about bravery, competence, and patriotic duty. They do so to earn respect from women (mothers, wives, sisters, and girlfriends) and male peers, both as defenders of the nation and, more

An abridged version of Lesley Gill, 1997. Creating Citizens, Making Men: The Military and Masculinity in Bolivia. Reproduced by permission of the American Anthropological Association and of the author from *Cultural Anthropology*, Volume 12, Issue 4, Pages 527–550, November 1997. Not for sale or further reproduction.

broadly, as strong, responsible male citizens who can make decisions and lead others.

Military service is one of the most important prerequisites for the development of successful subaltern manhood, because it signifies rights to power and citizenship and supposedly instills the courage that a man needs to confront life's daily challenges. Through the experience of military service, men assert a dignified sense of masculinity that serves as a counterpoint to the degradation experienced from more dominant males and an economic system that assigns them to the least desirable occupations. Military service thus enables them to challenge their exclusion from full participation in Bolivian society and to contest more genteel notions of masculinity associated with upper-class males who avoid military service altogether.

Yet self-affirmation and the legitimate desire for respect are also inextricably tied to ongoing patterns of collusion with hegemonic uses and representations of subaltern men and bound to evolving relationships of inequality among subjugated peoples. Conscripts collude with hyper-aggressive notions of masculinity that demean women, "weaker" men, and civilians in general, and that conjoin maleness with citizenship. They further assert an imposed falsehood: soldiers like themselves defend the interests of *all* Bolivians from an array of internal and external threats. By so doing, they aggravate the estrangement between men and women, and deepen their alienation from their class peers and the history of indigenous peoples in Bolivia.

This article examines these contradictions. It explores how men, through compulsory military service, shape a positive sense of masculine identity that is, nevertheless, linked to collusion with their own subordination and tied to other gendered patterns of social degradation. To understand this process, I consider how notions of masculinity are constructed in a field of unequal power relationships. My analysis scrutinizes the interplay between masculinity and power by probing the ways that material constraints and beliefs about gender lead subaltern men to participate in a state institution

that contributes to the continuing oppression of dominated peoples. It also examines how the armed forces approach the task of creating male soldiers who subscribe to a particular notion of masculinity, and the ways that class, ethnic, and regional tensions threaten this totalizing project.

I argue that the state, through the institution of the armed forces, conjoins key concepts of masculinity and beliefs about citizenship that are claimed by many of the poor as they simultaneously accommodate to domination and assert their own interests vis-à-vis each other and the dominant society. Other notions of masculinity and, of course, all notions of femininity are ignored, ridiculed, or marginalized. Conscripts thus become "men" and "citizens" in very contradictory ways, as they are used and represented in different ways by the military. Military service both differentiates them from elite white males and incorporates them into society. Military conscripts also become differentiated from their female class peers and men who have not done military service. The ensuing ruptures that emerge among the poor from these patterns of differentiation and incorporation undermine attempts to shape understandings of masculinity, femininity, and citizenship that can be used to fundamentally transform relations of domination, rather than simply contest some of them. The discussion draws on interviews with men and women from the urban neighborhoods of El Alto, a sprawling, 14,000-foot-high satellite city of 400,000 people that surrounds part of La Paz, the Bolivian capital, and several Aymara communities on the periphery of La Paz.[1]

It is important to understand the broad historical contours within which militarism, masculinity, and citizenship became conjoined. Following the mobilization of indigenous men in the Chaco War (1932–1935), which created a new sense of national identity among them, the Cold War and the 1952 Bolivian national revolution furthered the identification of masculinity and citizenship with military service. The Cold War moved the U.S. government to finance the expansion of Latin American militaries, and the influx of U.S. military aid to Bolivia permitted the incorporation of thousands of young men into the armed forces every year. This was consistent with the project of the post-1952 Bolivian state, which, in accord with its enduring rhetoric of populist nationalism, utilized compulsory military service as a tool for constructing a homogeneous national community and "civilizing" the male masses.

CREATING CITIZEN SOLDIERS

The efforts of militaries to instill civic consciousness among persons marginalized by their states are a persistent theme in the experiences of diverse countries (e.g. Enloe 1980). In Bolivia, a key aspect of basic training and the formation of male citizens is that recruits experience the military as omnipotent and omniscient. Young inductees are incorporated into an institution in which every aspect of their lives becomes controlled and regimented, and their ties to the broader society are cut off or severely restricted. To become a man and a soldier, it is essential that recruits be separated from home, especially the care and influence of their mothers, and that they move to being under the control of older, unrelated males. The military then strives to subordinate their individuality to the identity of the male group and instill rigid conformity and compliance to military values.

Basic training is a gendered process of moral regulation in which the armed forces define the parameters of appropriate male behavior and link masculinity and citizenship to the successful completion of military service; indeed, military obligations are linked as closely to civic duty as to the actual practice of warfare. Militarized male Bolivians are created by the imposition of acceptable forms of masculinity that prize aggressivity, male camaraderie, discipline, autonomy, and obedience to authority. As certain forms of individual and collective identification are stamped with the official seal of approval, others are denied legitimate expression. This is a process that depends on the acceptance of young men and is reinforced by their simultaneous brutalization, an aspect of the "civilizing" experience that is central to military training and much anticipated by prospective recruits. It requires an enormous amount of power and must overcome deep regional and ethnic cleavages.

At present, calls for military recruits are issued twice a year, at which time young men of the appropriate age are required to present themselves at designated induction centers. Conscripts are then sorted into groups and sent to various installations around Bolivia. The military tries to mix men from different parts of the country in the same barracks in order to break down strong regional sentiments. In addition to the more abstract purpose of creating male citizens who identify as "Bolivian," rather than as Aymara, lowlanders, and so forth, this policy also has a direct, practical rationale: conscripts, it is believed, are more likely to shoot "subversives" if they do not come from the same regional or ethnic background.

The first three months of military service are dedicated to basic training, in which new recruits engage in endless drills and marching. They are also taught how to use weapons and are prepared to fight. During this period, troops suffer the abuse of commanding officers and the dominance of a more experienced group of conscripts known as the *antiguos,* or old-timers, who have entered the service six months earlier. The newcomers are verbally and even physically castigated for violations of military discipline, misunderstanding commands, and not carrying out required exercises. They are referred to as *sarna,* or mange, by their superiors. Militarized masculinity is shaped in these contexts through the symbolic debasement of women and homosexuals: recruits are called *putas* (whores), *maricones* (faggots), *senoritas* (little ladies), and other gendered insults. Punishment for an infraction of the rules may entail dressing as a woman and parading around the base, or, as one ex-conscript described, sleeping naked with another man in a physical embrace.

Closely tied to this rigid hierarchy is an ideology of male equality and bonding. This ideology pervades basic training and conflates combat preparedness with beliefs about masculinity: troops share the same food and living accommodations, wear the same uniforms, display identical shaved heads, conform to the same rigid codes of behavior, and are trained for war, the ultimate test of their manhood. They are taught to rely only on themselves and each other and to distrust civilians, who are considered weak, incompetent, and lacking the discipline and responsibility of a uniformed soldier. As one ex-recruit described the experience to me,

> You learn how to survive in the barracks, because there is no help from your family. You only get help from yourself and those who live with you. It's a really beautiful experience, because you are isolated with others [men] who become even more than your brothers because they share everything with you. The guy who is beside you is more important than your own family.

Indeed, the strong, self-reliant man who works together with other men is the desired product of this training.

Male bonding and camaraderie are heightened as recruits encounter "the enemy" in actual confrontations or, more likely, in mock skirmishes and exercises. However, class, regional, and ethnic divisions are reproduced in the barracks and threaten to undermine the military's totalizing project, even as conscripts encounter "enemies," bond with each other, and experience overwhelming pressure to conform to military values. Although recruits from diverse regional backgrounds are mixed together, informants consistently recount that high school graduates, who are more likely to be urban-born and fluent Spanish speakers, stand a better chance of remaining on urban bases, while peasants are routed to much more onerous rural and frontier postings. Moreover, peasants often experience greater difficulty in understanding orders and lessons, which are conducted entirely in Spanish, and they must therefore endure more abuse from commanding officers and the old-timers. They are also less likely to be chosen for advanced instruction after the initial period of basic training draws to a close, and are frequently destined to labor on arduous civic action programs, such as clearing ditches

and making roads. Some are even put to work in the homes of commanding officers.

Some men, in fact, find military service intolerable and may even go to the extreme of deserting, which undermines the military's omnipotent self-representation and, not surprisingly, is viewed as treasonous. Felix Chuquimia recounted to me how his commanding officers on a lowland base obliged him and other highland conscripts to beat a paceño deserter who had been captured and returned. In another instance, according to Chuquimia, two deserters were dressed as women:

> The officials forced them to trot around the base carrying their [unloaded] guns, bricks, and old tires. They had to shout, "I'm a woman, not a man." One of them even fainted a couple of times and we [the troops] were ordered to throw water on them. If we did not obey, the officials would punish us. This is what happens to people for deserting. You just have to endure.

In this instance, traitors were identified with women by commanding officers. By involving highland conscripts in their punishment, these lowland-born officers not only made them accomplices but also reinforced a militarized male identity closely linked to patriotic duty and separated from specific regional and ethnic identifications.

SISSIES AND "NEW CITIZENS": SUFFERING FOR MANHOOD

A complex array of pressures and motivations prompt young Bolivian men from La Paz and its surrounding hinterland to enlist in the armed forces every year. For some young men, the military offers the possibility of adventure and an opportunity to visit other parts of the country; for others, it is a way of obtaining food and clothing in a time of need. According to the military itself, service provides recruits with opportunities to learn electrical, mechanical, and carpentry skills, yet only one of the men interviewed for this article mentioned the acquisition of useful skills for civilian life. Although the reasons have varied over time, two primary explanations for responding to the military's biannual calls for men stand out among former soldiers: (1) the importance of the *libreta militar* (military booklet), which documents the successful completion of military duty, for key transactions with the state and for obtaining work in urban factories and businesses, and (2) the desire to validate themselves as men in the eyes of families, peers, and communities. Establishing themselves as men requires the competence necessary to support themselves and a family amidst considerable economic adversity, and to participate in community positions of authority.

Obtaining the military booklet is not a concern for middle- and upper-class young men who wish to avoid military service. Once past the age of 23, when an individual is no longer eligible for service, a man may pay a fee to obtain equivalent documentation. The cost, in recent years, has varied between $200 and $500, which is prohibitive for men from poor peasant and urban backgrounds, since they typically earn only a few dollars for an entire day's labor.

For subaltern men, military service is the only practical means of acquiring the military booklet, which is quite literally a prerequisite for citizenship. Only with this document can a man register with the state and acquire a national identity card. The libreta is also indispensable for other key relationships with the state, such as obtaining a passport, a job in a government agency, or a degree from the state university. Similarly, military documentation is essential for obtaining employment in many of the businesses and factories of urban La Paz, where employers use it to guarantee themselves a disciplined, Spanish-speaking labor force.

The military booklet is thus part of the "civilizing process" through which young men are symbolically incorporated into the nation and the capitalist discipline of the labor process. Furthermore, with the collusion of their commanding officers, recruits may use the booklet as a way to change their Indian surnames to Spanish ones. But while it symbolically creates citizens, the booklet also facilitates the converse: the categorization of "aliens" within the boundaries of the state, a designation that is all too close to the lived experiences of poor men.

The subtle and overt forms of violence associated with processes of exclusion and incorporation are illustrated by former tin miner Raul Gutierrez. When interviewed, Gutierrez recognized the importance of the military booklet for the professional aspirations of his son, whom he has sent off to boot camp even though Gutierrez hates the army and is frightened by the sight of soldiers. Gutierrez had survived a horrific army massacre in the Caracoles tin mine after the 1980 military coup d'état of General Luis Garcia Meza, and intolerable working conditions subsequently forced him and his family to move to La Paz's poor satellite city, El Alto, to search for other work. However, Gutierrez recognizes the importance of military documentation. "It's an indispensable document," he says. "My sons are going to be professionals some day, and they will be asked for their military booklets." Indeed, the military's continuing regulation of society in the present and Gutierrez's hopes of a professional future for his son virtually require a passive stance toward the military repression that he has experienced in the past. The military domination of Bolivian society has, in this way, reshaped aspects of social life.

For many young men, the importance of establishing their manhood is also a central reason for military service. They believe that service is indispensable to becoming responsible, disciplined men who are capable of making decisions, heading a family, and commanding others. As Felix Mamani, a rural immigrant who resides in El Alto, told me,

> In the countryside, people think that you are a coward if you don't go to the barracks; that is, they think you're like a woman. The community pushes young men toward military service, and [we] have to go in order not to be faggots. It's a question of manliness.

Peasant recruits who return to highland Aymara communities are referred to as *machaq ciudadano,* or, literally, "new citizen," and if domestic resources permit, their returns are celebrated with eating, drinking, and dancing. Rolando Cusicanqui, a 26-year-old immigrant from the Lake Titicaca region, understood a machaq ciudadano to be someone who is "able to be fully involved in society and participate with adults. Someone who is considered to be a responsible person and who can fully take part in a series of events, meetings and so forth." Similarly, when Fernando Huanca falsified his birth certificate in 1974 to enter the military under the legal age requirement, it was because he had heard about the "new citizens" and wanted to be one himself. According to Fernando,

> I was born in Igachi and grew up an orphan. When I was 15 or 16 years old, the other boys always acted like they were better than me. Seeing the way that they behaved, I thought, I'm also a man. I'm also *gente* [someone]. What difference is there between someone who goes to the barracks and one who does not? I wanted to understand this. I'd heard about new citizens, and for the pride [of being a new citizen], I enlisted.

In the immigrant neighborhoods of La Paz, the connections between manhood and citizenship are equally evident, if somewhat more diffuse. Military service is not so directly linked to the assumption of community positions of authority, but young men still hope to earn the respect of families and peers by participating in a rite of passage that is understood as a prerequisite for full male adulthood and a duty of every good Bolivian man. They also hope to obtain the documentation necessary for permanent positions in a factory, business, or state agency and thus escape from the poverty and insecurity of the informal economy. Francisco Perez recalls the mockery of his high school peers, who claimed he was not man enough to bear the rigors of military life. Francisco, a self-described loner, says that these taunts stimulated a flood of self-doubt and that this, in part, moved him to enlist. He remembers that after completing the obligatory year in the military, his father, who had always encouraged him to enlist, began to treat

him very differently. "You've been to the barracks," Francisco remembers his father saying. "Now you are a man and can do what you want with your life. You can marry or do anything that you please." Like Francisco, other informants recount how their families prohibited them from consuming alcoholic beverages prior to military service and how this prohibition was invariably lifted upon their return home.

Key to the transformation of these young men is the experience of suffering. Suffering is not only something that they anticipate before enlisting but also an experience that, when safely in the past, is constantly embellished and reinvented, as ex-soldiers represent themselves to others and assert claims within evolving social relationships. Given the myriad ways in which these young men and their families suffer every day of their lives with poor health, low wages, bad harvests, and racism, it is shocking to listen to them boast of their transformative experiences of hardship, which must be understood as part of a desperate and painful search for dignity and self-worth.

Rufino Amaya, for example, dreamed of and eventually received a posting on a distant frontier base in the tropical lowlands, where living conditions were particularly harsh. The isolation of the base meant that during weekend leaves he could not visit friends and family members, and he frequently did not have enough to eat because commanding officers were selling troop rations for personal profit. The food shortages prompted him to work as an agricultural laborer during leaves so that he could buy bread and other basic necessities, even though working for civilians was strictly forbidden by the military and considered a punishable offense. Yet, as Amaya told me,

> The person who goes to the barracks, especially from the highlands, suffers a lot during the year, but those who do not serve never experience what corporal punishment is like and are more or less semi-men. [People in my community] criticize the ones who serve nearby. They say that they've just been to the kitchen.

Amaya went on to describe how highland men like himself were better suited for the rigorous tests of military manhood.

> [In my group] we were 161 paceños and 80 *orientales* [residents of the eastern lowlands]. The orientales were very weak and when things got rough, they started deserting. But the *colla* [highlander] man— as they call us—deserts very little, because he is able to endure any kind of hard work.

Informants related similar accounts to me over and over. One individual even likened the Aymara propensity for military service and allegedly superior soldiering abilities to their history as a "warlike people."

We can recognize a number of self-destructive beliefs in these assertions: suffering is a prerequisite for manhood; poor people like themselves can tolerate suffering more than others; and Aymara have special abilities for warfare. To make these claims is to participate in the production of a dominant fiction. It is to create a virtue out of suffering, a condition imposed on the Aymara by both the military and, more generally, the form that class and ethnic domination takes in Bolivia. It is also to link extreme suffering in the military with an exalted form of manhood and to thereby deny the very real daily suffering of women and other men who cannot or will not participate in the rituals of militarized masculinity. Finally, it is to misconstrue Aymara history, a history in which warfare was integral to the process of Incan and particularly European domination, but which has little to do with any essential Aymara characteristics.

At this point, we must explore in greater depth the way that militarism and men's experiences in the military shape ongoing social relationships in their home communities and neighborhoods. How, specifically, do militarized notions of masculinity inform the relationships between male peers, between men and women, and between subaltern men and male members of the white, middle and upper classes? And how, too, are these beliefs sustained in the context of inequality?

CONTENDING WITH MILITARISM IN DAILY LIFE

Recruits never become true citizens after completing military service and returning to civilian life. The realization of their continuing marginalization leaves many men feeling disillusioned and questioning the point of having dedicated a year of their lives to the armed forces. In most cases, they are no better prepared for a job than before entering the military, and the few decent jobs that remain in La Paz, after years of economic crisis, restructuring, and state retrenchment, cannot possible accommodate everyone. Young men typically return to their impoverished villages or seek a livelihood as gardeners, chauffeurs, part-time construction workers, and vendors in the urban informal economy and in low-paid positions in the state bureaucracy, such as policemen. Thus excluded from the economic rewards of the dominant society, they remain ineluctably "Indian" in its eyes, and some, not surprisingly, conclude that the entire experience was an enormous waste of time.

In addition, all subaltern men do not develop identical relationships to militarism, nor do they understand it the same way. The experience of military service, once safely in the past, assumes different meanings for them in the context of changing social relationships in the present. Felix Amaya, for his part, understands the military very differently today as a university student and former socialist party member than he did 13 years ago as a teenage army recruit fresh from the countryside. "Look," he told me,

> peasants in civilian life understand who the army defends. I went to the barracks with a lot of expectations. I thought that afterwards I would easily get a job [in the city], and I thought that people in the city would respect me. But it wasn't that way . . . Everything was false. It was then that I realized that the army just protects the bourgeoisie, but that was only after I got out.

In failing to meet the expectations of Amaya and other recruits like him, the military has trained a potential source of opposition. Yet the nature of the opposition is ambiguous. Military service, as mentioned above, is key to acquiring certain kinds of urban jobs that provide a modicum of economic security. It is also important for participating in the male world of formal community politics, taking part in discussions and decisions, establishing a family, and being perceived by others as a leader. The suffering, male camaraderie, and discipline that supposedly made them male citizens in the first place are not easily cast aside, because they help to ratify these forms of male empowerment, which exclude women and those subaltern men who have not passed through the armed forces. This is an affirmation of male citizenship, albeit of a subordinate form, within the broader context of Bolivian society.

Military experience also provides ammunition for the construction of masculinity and the assertion of male power in other settings. It is typically part of the repartee of all-male social gatherings, such as weekend drinking parties, where male solidarity and competition are closely combined. Exaggerated tales of suffering, hyperbolic anecdotes of bravery in the face of fear, and inflated accounts of cleverness when confronted by abusive superiors shape the male bonding that occurs amidst the music blaring from cassette players, commentaries on daily life, and invitations to drink. Yet this bantering and one-upmanship can easily move from friendly jousting to violent competition, and thus becomes a form of domination and ranking among men. They also, of course, exclude women, who in these gatherings usually hover in the background, awaiting a summons to bring the next round of beer.

The competence and citizenship equated with postmilitary manhood are also used by former conscripts to assert their dignity and claim respect from more powerful middle- and upper-class males. The latter view military service as a waste of time that can be more usefully spent studying, and they fear the prospect of serving with Indian and lower-class men in a context where military hierarchies theoretically take precedence over class and ethnic ones. Some even view the soldiers' claims to manhood as presumptuous. One individual, for

example, criticized the peasant practice of requiring military service for male marriage partners because it was, he claimed, based on mistaken beliefs about how men acquire a sense of responsibility. Ex-soldiers are highly critical of these men, whom they view as unpatriotic sissies. One scoffed to me that

> They're mamas' boys. They come from a different social class than we do, and their form of thinking and reasoning is so distinct that they forget about their patriotic duty. They are much more individualistic [than we are]; they forget about the nation so that they can be totally independent. The upper class only thinks about its future and its social position and generally not about the country and what could happen one day.

This man and others like him were particularly critical when, in early 1995, a public scandal enveloped a high-ranking government official who had falsified his military booklet to avoid service. Sixty-year-old Rufino Teja, for example, was absolutely disgusted. "These parliamentarians," he sneered,

> say that they are the fathers of the country, but they are the first ones to avoid the barracks. These little gentlemen wouldn't know where to shoot. They always come from privileged families. They're mamas' boys. They can fix anything with money, but then they fill these government positions and demand that everyone else obey the law. They should be removed from their jobs and obliged to serve in the military at their age.

Tejar's remarks that these men claim to be "the fathers of the country" suggest something of the paternalism and the denigration that shapes the reality of actual encounters between men of different classes. It is as waiters, gardeners, chauffeurs, shoe shiners, handymen, and janitors that indigenous and poor urban men typically meet white males of the upper class. These structurally subordinate positions require them to display deference, subordination, and humility. They are not only demeaning, but also place men in relationships to more powerful males that are analogous to those of women in male–female relationships. Because they cannot command the labor power of others and they possess none of the wealth necessary to embellish an elegant lifestyle and control, provide for, and protect women, lower-class men and men from subordinate ethnic groups experience greater difficulty backing up their claims of personal power and sexual potency than their class and ethnic superiors. Moreover, the class privileges of the latter enable them to develop a well-mannered, dignified, and controlled masculinity; one that is contrasted with the behavior of poor men, who, depending on the context, may either be labeled as weak and ineffectual *or* condemned for impulsive and irrational outbursts of violence.

Thus in certain contexts many poor urban and peasant men have considerable difficulty cultivating and defending a positive image of themselves as men vis-à-vis more dominant males. Surviving the trials and tribulations of military service is one way in which they can affirm their masculine power and rights to citizenship. In the absence of recruits from the upper echelons of Bolivian society, subaltern men can claim the experience of compulsory military service as strictly their own and use it as a weapon in their ongoing struggles for respect and dignity in a society that routinely denies them both.

We should, however, view their assertions with caution since subordinate and dominant notions of masculinity degrade women and are premised, in large part, on the ability of men to control and dominate women. Given this, we might expect to find women in highland Aymara communities and the poor urban neighborhoods of El Alto considerably less enthusiastic about military service than their male family members. Some evidence does exist to support such a view. Mothers commonly recall their tears and the deep sadness with which they dispatched their sons to the barracks; they also remember the fears that their sons would be abused in the armed forces and return permanently disabled. Yet these women hope that completing military service and obtaining the requisite

documentation will ensure a more prosperous future for their sons, and indeed, a mother struggling too hard to withhold her son from the military might be seen as depriving him of the chance to attain full male adulthood.

Women whose sons have no prospects of upward mobility provide the most enthusiastic support for compulsory military service. Many of these women, like men, believe that military training and discipline will produce responsible, mature adult males, and they have ample reasons to want this to occur. Poor women are frequently disappointed by men who are unable or unwilling to support their families, who spend hard-earned cash on drink, cigarettes, and other women, and who are physically abusive. Military service, they hope, will develop men into reliable, serious adults and serve as a guarantee to women and their male relatives that a prospective husband will fulfill his social and economic responsibilities to the domestic unit.

These women are suspicious of men who have not done military service. A street vendor in El Alto, for example, disparagingly describes a 40-year-old male acquaintance who never served. "He gets occasional jobs that don't pay well, but he can't go to work in a factory [because he doesn't have his military booklet]," she explains. "This is where irresponsibility comes from. The military booklet structures one's future and encourages responsibility." She went onto discuss how women who get stuck with such men have to work more outside the home to support their families.

Following military service, men may in fact become more responsible, that is, dedicated to family and home. Rufino Perez, for example, told me that he "saw things more seriously" after returning from the barracks.

I wasn't the same prankster that I had been before. My friends noted this and so did my family. In my community, when one arrives from the barracks, people give you more responsibilities because you are now one among adults. I was no longer juvenile and assumed these responsibilities myself. I was another member of society.

Yet men's relationships to militarism do not always bring positive benefits for the women whom they encounter in civilian life. The experiences of Arminda Mamani illustrate how the expectations of women are frequently left unfulfilled. Arminda Mamani is a 45-year-old divorcee with two sons. Born into a family of artisans in a small, provincial town, she moved to La Paz in 1970 and currently works as a secretary. Mamani's two sons have lived without a father in the home for most of their lives, and she has always encouraged them to pursue respect and economic security through higher education instead of going into the military. She views the military as a waste of time and does not want her sons to associate with "Indians" in the barracks. Her views, however, are strongly opposed by her ex-husband, his female relatives, and his six brothers. This side of the family maintains a strong tradition of male military service and constantly chides Mamani's eldest son, Sergio, for failing to enlist. Sergio, for his part, is content with his decision not to serve. He not only has his mother's full support but has, indeed, found a new sense of dignity as the first member of his family to attend university.

Despite her success with Sergio, Mamani was frustrated with a younger son, Pancho, who became a juvenile delinquent in high school; he constantly skipped classes, stole household items and sold them on the street, and argued incessantly with his mother. "Every year that he was in school," Mamani said, "I told him that if he didn't study and behave better, I was going to send him to the barracks." She finally carried out the threat and successfully appealed to an acquaintance with military connections to have the boy sent as far away as possible. She was backed up by her sisters, who, like Mamani, viewed the barracks as a reform school for problem boys. Pancho spent a year in the army on the lowland frontier but, according to Mamani, returned worse than he had departed. "When he returned," she said,

> I realized that it had not done him any good, and he was not reformed. The only thing that he acquired was his military booklet, but he was even more obnoxious than before. He thought that he had more

rights, because now he was a man, an adult, and could therefore do whatever he felt like. Just because he had his military booklet, he thought he could arrive home at whatever time he pleased and get drunk whenever he wished. He told me that I wasn't a good mother because I didn't give a party when he returned like all the others [families].

The disappointment that Arminda Mamani feels about her son's sojourn in the military is not uncommon. Indeed, the high level of domestic violence in El Alto, where two major military bases are located, suggests that many men are not living up to women's expectations. Although domestic violence is far too complex a phenomenon to be reduced to the effects of militarization on men, it is indicative of the strains that poverty and another decade of "lost development" are placing on men and women, as well as the misogyny inherent in military training.

CONCLUSION

The large-scale militarization of masculinity in Bolivia is the legacy of the Cold War and the fervor with which the U.S. government financed the expansion of the armed forces to preserve and defend a status quo antithetical to the interests of the majority of Bolivian citizens. It is also the inheritance of the 1952 revolution and the populist nationalism that prioritized the transformation of "Indians" into "citizens" who nevertheless continue to be excluded from the political and economic rewards of Bolivian society. Although this process takes place in a number of arenas, the military is where the dynamic interplay between masculinity, citizenship, and power is most evident.

Those poor urban and rural young men who embrace military service do so because it offers them the opportunity of crafting a positive sense of themselves as men and as Bolivians in a society where they are routinely demeaned and excluded; indeed, military service, especially the rigors of boot camp, provides them with an arena for serving the nation that they have increasingly claimed as their own. But even as these men engage dominant institutions in order to assert their dignity and establish their self-worth, they are not only used by the military in ways that have nothing to do with improving the lot of peasants and poor urban dwellers, but they also assert a number of imposed beliefs about themselves and their relationships to others. Such beliefs not only degrade women and nonmilitary men, but also injure those men who are the objects of conscription and grant legitimacy to a patriarchal state.

As understandings of masculinity and citizenship have become intertwined with military service, poor women remain marginalized. There is no state institution that links femininity to citizenship and provides a vehicle for female empowerment, even of a subordinate form; indeed, as young men carry out military service, their female peers are likely to undergo a different kind of trial as domestic workers in the homes of well-to-do urban families. The experiences of humiliation, suffering, and insecurity endured by these women are never recognized as empowering. Rather, they are viewed by men, and society in general, as personal affairs that unfold in the privacy of a home.

Separating the construction of gender from militarism is not an easy task. Conceptions of masculinity, femininity, and citizenship that enable men—and women—to resist the state's demand for military service are continually undermined by the contradictory processes of incorporation and differentiation that disrupt the social relations of subaltern peoples. Even as men and women are brutalized by the military in their neighborhoods, communities, and the military barracks, they must engage the armed forces to cope with their own poverty and social marginalization. Resolving the ensuing contradictions in the future will depend on how people perceive their life circumstances as well as their capacity to change them.

REFERENCES CITED

Enloe, Cynthia. 1980. Ethnic Soldiers: State Security in Divided Societies. Athens, GA: University of Georgia Press.

Gibson, James William. 1986. The Perfect War: Technowar in Vietnam. New York: Atlantic Monthly Press.

Zeitlin, Maurice, K. A. Luttennan, and J. W. Russell. 1973. Death in Vietnam: Class, Poverty, and the Risks of War. Politics and Society 3(3): 313–328.

NOTE

1. This article emerged from a research project conducted over an eight-month period between June 1994 and May 1995 on the relationship between nongovernmental organizations, the state, and popular organizations in La Paz. It draws on wide-ranging conversations with a large network of informants that I developed for that project and on focused interviews with 30 ex-soldiers from rural Aymara communities and poor neighborhoods in La Paz and El Alto. The men completed their military service between 1952 and 1994 and represented approximately equal numbers of urban- and rural-born individuals. Throughout this article, I use pseudonyms for the names of people I interviewed or spoke with during my field research in Bolivia.

3 • Sara L. Friedman

THE INTIMACY OF STATE POWER
Marriage, Liberation, and Socialist Subjects in Southeastern China

DISCUSSION QUESTIONS

1. Why was the new socialist regime in China concerned about marriage practices in Huidong?
2. How did the state try to change these practices?
3. How and why did young people in the 1990s aspire to "cultivate feelings" in their intimate relationships? How was this different from state efforts encouraging them to "build feelings" in marriage?

> In the modern era, marriage has become the central legitimating institution
> by which the state regulates and permeates people's most intimate lives.
>
> —Michael Warner, 1999

Marriage, Michael Warner (1999) asserts in his critique of gay marriage advocacy in the contemporary United States, is anything but neutral or benign, a simple choice or right. Instead, he contends, marriage is an institution that links personal desires with state goals. In this article, I examine how state regulations and intimate relationships have become intertwined over the past half century in a region of China where new brides' reluctance to live or have sex with their husbands has provoked repeated state reform campaigns since the establishment of China's socialist regime in 1949. My goals in analyzing this relationship between state power and intimate life are twofold: one, to show how socialist rule developed through campaigns to transform women's conjugal experiences and desires; and two, to probe the limits of this state project and its unintended consequences.

THE PROBLEM OF EASTERN HUI'AN COUNTY

Hui'an County lies halfway along the coast of China's southeastern Fujian Province, directly across from Taiwan. Over the years that I have been visiting the region, I have witnessed its passage from a remote, marginalized coastline to a flourishing site of industry and tourism. Deeply rutted dirt roads have slowly given way to paved highways; dark, squat buildings have been replaced by modern, multistoried homes and businesses; and carefully tended fields have gradually yielded to cavernous, dimly lit stone-carving factories—the new economic motor of the region.

Eastern Hui'an (Huidong) was historically quite poor, with an economy based primarily on fishing and the few crops that could be grown by

An abridged version of Sara Friedman, 2005. The intimacy of state power: Marriage, liberation, and socialist subjects in southeastern China. Reproduced by permission of the American Anthropological Association and of the author from *American Ethnologist*, Volume 32, Issue 2, Pages 312–327, May 2005. Not for sale or further reproduction.

women in the sandy soil of the coast. By the time I began research in the township of Chongwu in the mid-1990s, however, market reforms introduced by the national government over a decade earlier were beginning to expand this narrow economic universe. Township officials had seized on the opportunity to mechanize a local stone-carving industry and develop what would become a burgeoning export sector. The dusty factories dotting the landscape offer lucrative employment to both young women and men, creating a work environment in which young people can meet and socialize casually. Together with the rise of consumerism and the emphasis on individual needs and self-fulfillment that have emerged with market reforms, the stone-carving industry has dramatically altered the contours of community life. A growing range of new consumer establishments complement the industry's mixed-sex workplaces and foster a vibrant youth culture funded by access to wage income.

It was not Huidong's long-standing poverty or its current wave of prosperity that markedly distinguished the region from its surrounding areas, however. Instead, it was the distinctive nature of local marriage practices (known as extended postmarital natal residence), coupled with unique styles of female dress and the power of all-female networks. In most rural Han communities, new brides moved to their husband's home immediately on marrying, at which point they effectively transferred their obligations and allegiances to their conjugal families. Huidong women, by contrast, did not reside with their husbands after marriage. Several days after the wedding, they returned to live with their natal families and made only periodic visits to their conjugal homes, usually when summoned by a mother-in-law or sister-in-law. During this period of postmarital separation, wives were considered part of their birth families: they labored for and contributed wages to them and were included in natal family rituals and ancestral worship. Because women were not expected to live permanently with their husbands

until they bore a child, most young wives sought to maintain the freedom of natal residence by shunning conjugal visits to avoid sexual relations and the pregnancy that might result.

Well into the last decade of the 20th century, married women in the Huidong village of Shanlin continued to reside with their parents prior to bearing their first child.[1] Through the early 1990s, most marriages in the community were arranged by parents or matchmakers and often took place when both parties were still in their teens, well below the legal marriage age. Moreover, women faced ridicule and condemnation from female peers and other villagers if they displayed an inclination to spend the night or live with their husbands in their early married years. Not surprisingly, I found that throughout most of the 20th century, Shanlin couples typically lived apart for at least four to six years after marriage.

These practices might have attracted less concern if, after China's socialist revolution in 1949, eastern Hui'an residents had been identified as members of one of China's many national minorities. Instead, they were classified by the socialist regime (and they defined themselves) as Han, the majority ethnic group. As official members of the national majority, Huidong villagers were expected to pursue ways of life that reflected their "civilized" status within a new socialist evolutionary hierarchy, distinguishing them from minorities whose customs were initially protected by the party-state. Because Huidong marriage patterns, together with women's dress styles and same-sex social networks, resembled those of certain minority groups, however, local women came to occupy an anomalous position within this socialist hierarchy, one that was simultaneously Han and, yet, not quite Han. Accordingly, women's intimate lives became subject to intense state scrutiny as reformers struggled to remake them as liberated Han socialist citizens. In other words, Han civility and socialist liberation were tied to the practice of a form of conjugal intimacy that was radically at odds with existing Huidong marriage customs.

MARITAL REFORM AS STATE CIVILIZATIONAL PROJECT

Why were the marriages of its citizens of such grave concern to China's new socialist regime? In all political systems, marriages are inherently public as well as private affairs; they link the individual, the community, and the state in a common bond, enabling states to use marriage and family policies to promote their own visions of citizenship and national belonging (Borneman 1992; Cott 2000; Kendall 1996). Certainly Maoist state reformers in the 1950s and 1960s were closely attuned to this public face of marriage, for it was clearly articulated in the specific meanings attributed to marriage under state socialism. Influenced by the 19th-century anthropologist Lewis Henry Morgan, the new regime correlated marriage customs and family organization with progressive stages of societal evolution, making marriage central to a national project of building a socialist civilization.

This approach to marriage as a marker of development was further premised on the belief that, with the proper influence, groups could transform how they married and move up the evolutionary ladder toward full socialist liberation. Reformers drew inspiration from Morgan's model as they encountered unusual marriage practices in eastern Hui'an, classifying local women as evolutionary oddities mired in a backward, feudal developmental stage. Under the auspices of the 1950 Marriage Law, outside work teams and local cadres in eastern Hui'an set out to eradicate the oppressive vestiges of this feudal marriage system and replace them with civilized socialist marriages. Focused on eliminating arranged marriages, instilling an ethos of free choice in marital decision making, enforcing the legal marriage age and marital registration, and encouraging wives to reside with and labor for their husbands immediately after their wedding, Marriage Law campaigns made marital reform integral to societal transformation in eastern Hui'an. Their purpose was not simply the liberation of women or the undermining of patrilineal kin groups (although

these were not insignificant goals); rather, marriage reforms also aimed to fashion appropriately liberated socialist women who would create the new socialist nation.

Despite repeated campaigns during the height of Marriage Law implementation in the 1950s and renewed efforts a decade later, marital reforms often foundered in the face of Huidong women's commitment to local customs and entrenched patterns of conjugal avoidance. Many Shanlin residents who married in the first decades after 1949 claimed that the Marriage Law's emphasis on marital freedom and self-determination had little impact on parental matchmaking traditions; at most, they recalled, a young person was shown a picture of his or her future spouse or allowed a brief meeting and then given the nominal right to refuse the match. Because many villages in the region were dominated by a single surname group, customary prohibitions on same-surname marriage made it difficult for youths to meet eligible marriage partners or freely choose their own spouse, and most women were forced to marry out of their natal villages into other communities in the region. All of these factors created conditions that made young wives unwilling to live with their conjugal families.

By the mid- to late 1950s, moreover, Marriage Law campaigns were rapidly giving way to efforts to collectivize the rural economy, engendering new pressures that also undermined effective marital reform. In eastern Hui'an, the collectivization of fishing, farming, and manual labor reinforced gender-distinct labor patterns, separating young women and men in their daily tasks and sending them away from their home villages for months or even years at a time. As a result, the number of occasions on which young wives would or could visit their husbands diminished significantly, in turn perpetuating their postmarital natal residence and, in some cases, further lengthening periods of conjugal separation.

Because reform campaigns failed to overturn many of these underlying conditions, they ultimately produced few changes in local marital practice. They were more successful, however, in mobilizing an array of propaganda tools to redefine the larger significance of marriage itself, incorporating conjugality into a national effort to build a productive, liberated socialist society. Propaganda folk songs and campaign rhetoric proclaimed that socialist marriages were not to be confined by shyness, reluctance, or shame—all ostensibly products of oppressive social relations and the repressed consciousness of subjugated women—but were to build, instead, on openly acknowledged "feelings" (*ganqing*). Here, reformers were appropriating a standard term for feeling or sentiment and imbuing it with newly politicized content, making it available to the project of socialist construction. Folk songs promulgated throughout Huidong in the 1950s and 1960s urged couples to "build feelings" (*jianli ganqing*) for one another, a collective endeavor that would improve family harmony and enhance productivity. These efforts to eradicate postmarital separation and to "build feelings," in other words, were also oriented toward creating a productive society liberated from the bonds of feudal family and economic forces.

In this manner, Maoist reformers in the 1950s and 1960s appeared committed to fostering intimacy in Huidong marriages. The image of conjugal intimacy conveyed by campaign propaganda, however, distanced spouses from the experiential aspects of marriage itself and oriented them toward more abstract collective ideals. I see use of the term *building* as an intentional discursive choice that made human relations into components of a larger productive apparatus. This mechanistic approach to marriage reform treated "feelings" as the nuts and bolts of a productive relationship. Villagers were supposed to assemble those components in the proper order to create a liberated socialist marriage. To do so, however, they had to identify with the project of marital reform and forge a connection between ideals of socialist liberation and their own marital desires.

In the end, the limited achievements of Maoist reform campaigns confirmed that creating this connection was not so simple. Neither was the meaning of female liberation itself so straightforward.

Reformers hastily condemned women's postmarital natal residence as a feudal remnant that sapped society's productive power and encouraged scores of young women to take their own lives. Hence, they failed to consider why women remained so committed to the practice and ignored its empowering potential—the way it gave women time to adjust to new, frightening, and at times abusive experiences as new wives and enabled them to preserve what they viewed as the freedom of natal residence. Instead, reformers emphasized the needs of husbands, who, so they argued, turned to dissolute habits like visiting prostitutes and gambling in the face of "abnormal" conjugal relations. Reaffirming their commitment to patrilocal living arrangements, reformers contended that wives belonged in their husbands' homes, often employing simple rhetorical conventions like use of the verb to return (*hui*) to describe a married woman's residence shift. Only when she resided with her husband, seemingly, could China's new socialist woman display her properly twinned commitment to building a civilized socialist marriage and creating a productive social order. Thus, marital reforms during the Maoist period aspired to wed gendered visions of the liberated socialist subject to state civilizational and developmental goals, embedding conjugal intimacy in a national project of socialist construction.

"REFORM AND OPENING" IN THE POST-MAO ERA

Despite reformers' efforts to define the new socialist woman as one who established feelings and intimacy with her husband, Huidong women generally failed to identify with this ideal or to change their marriage practices accordingly. As a result, Shanlin residents who married in the 1980s, the first decade of post-Mao market reforms, painted a picture of conjugal relationships strikingly similar to those of their elders. Young people were still acquiescing to matches arranged by parents, often when they were mere children, frequently to people with whom they had never spoken or whom they had only glimpsed from afar. Marriage at ages 15 and 16 was not uncommon for women in the 1980s; in fact, market reforms enabled village families to accumulate the resources needed to marry off their children, and many did so at increasingly younger ages, well below the new legal standard of 20 for women and 22 for men enshrined in the 1980 Marriage Law. Conjugal intimacy continued to be thwarted by the lengthy postmarital separations that remained the norm in Shanlin. Of the 120 Shanlin marriages I documented for the period 1977–89, 36 percent of the couples did not reside together until four to six years after marriage, 29 percent waited seven to nine years, and 6 percent lived apart for ten years or more. Only 17 percent of women who married during this period moved in with their husbands within three years of marrying.

Once again, however, the Maoist regime's efforts to redefine marriage had not completely failed, for like state actors elsewhere, reformers had been somewhat successful in introducing a shared language that shaped the debates over marital practice that took place in ensuing decades. Well into the 1990s, when terms such as "comrade" and "class struggle" had generally been dismissed as anachronistic, Shanlin men and women continued to weave this official discourse into their own speech, at once to condemn customs long attacked by socialist reformers and to shore up local standards of respectable femininity. They depicted extended natal-residence marriage and its practitioners as feudal and backward, criticized wives' reluctance to live with their husbands as a product of "closed" or "fettered" thinking, and often ridiculed young women hesitant to visit their husbands or socialize with non-kin men, describing them in local dialect as *pai se*—ashamed, embarrassed, or shy. When I asked villagers who wed in the 1980s to recount for me their own marital experiences, I was struck by the widespread use of these expressions both as a form of critique and as a description of expected behaviors, even among those much too young to have personally experienced the high socialist campaigns that introduced this rhetoric. Put simply, then, residents continued to represent themselves and their practices through the conceptual frameworks established by the post-1949 leadership.

At the same time, this official discourse did not always retain a direct connection to its original goals. The marital recollections of Siuden, a slight yet feisty Shanlin native, provide a good example of how villagers adapted a state discourse of marital behavior to portray their own experiences. When I met Siuden in 1995, she was living in a rented home in the older section of the village, together with her husband of nine years and their three children. Dissatisfied with their living situation and her husband's inability to provide for the family, she relished recounting for me the fear she had experienced as a seventeen-year-old on her wedding night when she first encountered her husband: "I was sitting on the bed and refused to face him, turned away. It was night, the doors were all closed. I didn't know him at all." Having married a man from her own village did not make Siuden any more comfortable with her husband, and she avoided him as best she could: "If I went to the harbor and ran into him, my heart would begin to beat fast and pound. I was scared to death. If he was with a group of men, I would run away as fast as I could." "In those days," she continued, "it was like that. Everyone was afraid, everyone was *pai se.*"

The intertwining of fear, shame, and avoidance in Siuden's narrative is precisely what earlier reform campaigns had sought to replace with liberated thinking and a norm of conjugal intimacy. And yet for Siuden, such sentiments were not simply reflections of feudal consciousness, as was so often claimed by outside work teams and local cadres; they were literally embodied—something Siuden emphasized when she slammed shut the door of her house to re-create for me the physical shock of fear and isolation she experienced on her wedding night. For women of Siuden's generation as well as their elders, these dispositions constituted a way of acting in the world that was expected of young Shanlin wives: fleeing at first sight of an approaching mother-in-law, performing the bare minimum of required tasks in one's conjugal home and then escaping at the earliest possible moment, or spending the entire night of a conjugal visit standing against a wall or sitting in a chair, refusing to get into bed with a strange husband. The normalizing force of such expectations had continued throughout the Maoist decades, undermining state efforts to liberate women from ostensibly oppressive marriage practices and introduce new modes of conjugal intimacy. Even when Shanlin women used the language of such reforms in the 1990s, moreover, they rarely expressed a commitment to the original goals of Maoist campaigns. In fact, as in Siuden's case, expressions of fear and embarrassment might just as readily express discontent with one's husband and his ability to support the family.

Not all villagers, however, reacted the same way to community expectations of shyness and avoidance on the part of new wives. By the 1980s, socialist ideals of liberated marriage were becoming interlaced with a discourse of marital desires and intimacy influenced by the rapidly commodified and individualistic environment of the market-reform era. The post-Mao regime's emphasis on progress and openness was inspiring not only economic development and international trade but also the flowering of personal needs and desires in emerging patterns of courtship and marriage. In Shanlin, young men were the first to seize on this convergence, dissatisfied as many of them were with the lack of intimacy in existing marital practices.

Zinzai married in 1984 at age 19 to a Shanlin woman two years his junior, his marriage arranged by a matchmaker and the auspicious wedding date selected by his father during Zinzai's absence from the village. The couple met for the first time on their wedding day. Despite his wife's reluctance to join him in bed or even look him in the face, Zinzai maintained that he sought to persuade her of his good intentions on the rare occasions after the wedding when she did acquiesce to conjugal visits. As he recounted his experience of these visits for me during a series of interviews in the winter of 1997, he vividly depicted how his wife had shivered through the cold night as she stood alone to avoid joining him in bed, portraying her as a feudal young wife whose shyness and fear of physical

contact were difficult for him to accept. Zinzai was upset by his wife's distance: "I was so angry that I didn't want to pay any attention to her. I called out to her with good intentions, not with any ulterior motives, nothing. But in those days, no one's thinking was open, village women weren't open-minded. They all were afraid of being ashamed or embarrassed [*gnia pai se*]."

In Zinzai's account, openness functions as the antithesis of feudal dispositions marked by shame, embarrassment, and fear. A wife who was open would have been willing to sleep with her husband during conjugal visits, and she would have accompanied him in public, perhaps attending a movie playing at the village theater or traveling with him to visit one of the cities along the coast. Although this discourse of openness was circulating in Huidong villages by the 1980s, it was rarely coupled with changes in actual marital practice, as Siuden's and Zinzai's accounts make abundantly clear. Like the state-sponsored reforms of earlier decades, the "reform and opening" policies ushered in by the post-Mao leadership in the 1980s initially failed to produce significant changes in how Shanlin couples married. A Lan, Zinzai's wife, listening carefully to her husband's depiction of her as a young bride, grew indignant at his expectation that she could have acted differently: "In those days, who did things like that?" she retorted. The outrage in her voice confirmed that ideals of openness introduced with market reforms were not enough to convince women such as A Lan to adopt new conjugal practices. The marital changes that I witnessed a decade later resulted from the convergence of those ideals with both new leisure activities and state policies to control population growth.

OPEN MARRIAGES

In the mid-1990s, Shanlin marriages suddenly began to resemble the liberated marriages advocated by socialist reformers 30 to 40 years prior. Both young women and men emphasized "being open" as part of enacting patterns of courtship and marriage they deemed appropriate for the more liberal society ushered in with stone-carving factories and an increasingly vibrant market economy. For post-Mao youth, this conjugal intimacy was not oriented toward earlier state goals of socialist liberation and heightened productivity, but ideals of heterosexual compatibility and attraction that dovetailed with newly integrated industrial workplaces and an expanding realm of leisure activities. These new aims produced striking changes in how young people socialized with one another, how they fostered intimacy in their marriages, and how they defined themselves as open and progressive. As A Lan continued her tirade against her husband, she contrasted the marital norms of her generation with those of youth in the 1990s, concluding, "It wasn't like nowadays. Now they go all over the place even before marriage, they stay in hotels together."

The changes in courtship and marriage that sparked A Lan's outburst are indeed striking when one compares them with long-standing patterns of conjugal avoidance in Shanlin. In contrast to young wives (and often husbands) who did not dare to speak directly to their spouses, much less eat or venture out in public with them, young couples in the 1990s were developing relationships based on feelings, choice, and shared activities. Many young people argued that the most important thing to look for in a marital relationship was the existence of feelings between the two people, again the sentiment earlier reformers had argued was critical to the establishment of a liberated socialist marriage based on conjugal intimacy. Whereas Mao-era officials had urged an older generation of Shanlin residents to "build feelings" in their marriages, youth in the mid-1990s instead aspired to "cultivate feelings." "Cultivation" (*peiyang*) presumed devotion to the relationship itself, a bond between two people that was developed over time through familiarity and mutual understanding. Whereas "building" had mechanistically incorporated marriage into a larger productive project premised on a couple's laboring together, "cultivating" refocused young people's attention on creating a more personal form of conjugal intimacy

through engaging in leisure activities such as strolling together along the beach, visiting restaurants and singing karaoke, or taking trips to nearby cities. This was a conjugal intimacy that seemed free of parental and community intervention—one that, at first glance, also appeared detached from collective goals and state regulatory policies.

For young Shanlin women like A Ping, cultivating feelings was essential to newly emerging marital ambitions. A Ping was originally forced into an arranged marriage by her parents and grandparents when she was 16, during a period when cadres generally ignored underage marriages and families tended to marry their children young. A mere 20 years old when we met in 1996, A Ping was still childless and, therefore, she continued to reside with her birth family. When I asked her to describe her relationship with her husband, A Ping admitted that she did not know him very well because he had been away for much of their marriage, fishing for tuna on his father's deep-sea boat. She had tried to cultivate feelings in their relationship despite his frequent absences, but the arranged nature of their match left her with a deep sense of bitterness.

A Ping also attributed her marital unhappiness to her contentious relationship with her mother-in-law, who, she claimed, treated her as an outsider and frequently demeaned her and her family in public. In that first year we spent together, A Ping's regular run-ins with her mother-in-law intensified her desire for a divorce, but her parents would not permit her to initiate the divorce request, for to do so would cost the family too much in compensation money.[2] During a late-night talk one cold winter evening when I stayed over at her home, A Ping summed up her mood of despair: "So now I just have to wait; nothing will change until my husband returns [from fishing overseas]. We are really hurt by this arranged marriage, and so young. I just want to find someone with whom I can get along, someone I can talk to."

More important than a supportive mother-in-law, A Ping frequently argued, was the presence of feelings between spouses, something that had to be cultivated over time through regular interaction and hence was lacking in her own marriage. By cultivating feelings even in arranged marriages, Shanlin youth sought to redefine their conjugal bonds to more closely approximate the ideal of an open, progressive marital relationship. Like A Ping, they could never actually realize that ideal, however, because by agreeing to an arranged match they had given up another of its widely recognized preconditions, free spousal choice. Although choosing one's own spouse had been a major plank in the marriage-reform campaigns of the 1950s and 1960s, only in the mid-1990s were young people beginning to realize these ideals of marital freedom beyond initial efforts to cultivate feelings. Inspired by popular media images of romantic love and emboldened by a new culture of mixed-sex socializing emerging from industrial workplaces, growing numbers broke off childhood engagements arranged by parents or divorced unsuitable spouses. These trends were bolstered by renewed government enforcement of the legal marriage age, which gave youths more time to seek marriage partners on their own initiative or to become acquainted with a potential spouse introduced by parents or kin.[3]

In A Ping's case, this new youth culture produced both empowering possibilities and additional hurdles in her efforts to transform her arranged marriage. Like many young people in the mid-1990s, A Ping socialized in mixed-sex groups and visited the new leisure sites that had emerged with the stone-carving industry. Although she was married, her continued natal residence and her husband's extended absence from the village enabled her to create a social life fairly similar to that of her unmarried peers. Yet unlike those peers, A Ping faced disapproving comments from her in-laws who complained about the young men who stopped by her village shop each evening or about her outings to restaurants and karaoke parlors. A Ping sought to mitigate their criticisms by defending her own propriety, to the point of adopting a more modest approach to conjugal visits. Rather than initiate those visits herself, as most young wives did by the mid-1990s, A Ping chose instead to wait for her mother- or sister-in-law to summon

her. That her mother-in-law did call for her reflects the older woman's own commitment to a pattern of conjugal visiting premised on an earlier norm of reluctant brides, one that was rapidly disappearing in the community.

Despite A Ping's efforts at conciliation, when her husband returned to the village in 1997, he bowed to pressure from his mother and suddenly informed A Ping that he wanted a divorce. Divorce negotiations quickly deteriorated into open hostility between the couple's families, leaving A Ping in a liminal state somewhere between being married and single. Under constant surveillance during the year it took to settle the divorce, A Ping proclaimed to me when I saw her the following summer that the next time she married, it would be to someone who lived far away from such prying eyes. In 1999, when she finally wrote to tell me that she had found a new boyfriend among her coworkers at a local stone-carving factory, I was not surprised to learn that he hailed from Chongwu, the township seat, and not from Shanlin. Emphasizing again the role of feelings and choice in her decision to make him her partner, A Ping explained, "Two or three coworkers pursued me, but I didn't accept them. My boyfriend pursued me for a long time and treated me very well. He is very sincere about feelings, so I chose him."

THE REGULATORY STATE

To foster a new breed of socialist citizen fit for the demands of a market economy, officials once again focused their attention on marriage as a key productive and reproductive nexus joining individual desires to state efforts to cultivate a quality citizenry. Population policies that strictly limited the number of children a couple may bear have been an important feature of this state agenda. In the early to mid-1990s, local cadres in Shanlin began registering all marriages and closely monitoring couples' ages, all as part of accomplishing the goals of late marriage and childbearing deemed critical to successful population control. Although periodic attempts to limit births had been made in previous years, only with a new policy push in 1994 did township and village leaders effectively link marriage regulation to the project of controlling the fertility of Shanlin women.

No longer able to ignore bureaucratic requirements and marry their children when they pleased, as had A Ping's parents, Shanlin residents soon faced a long list of marriage registration procedures that enabled officials to extend their reach over both individuals and society more generally.[4] Yet if one focuses exclusively on the ways such registration has made Huidong society legible to the current government, one misses other, equally important consequences of that process. By enforcing the legal marriage age and registration procedures, officials provided village youth with the time and recognition needed to reshape their marital experiences. Young people argued that delaying marriage until they reached the legal age empowered them to cultivate feelings and establish compatibility with potential spouses, both cornerstones of the conjugal intimacy heralded by the early socialist regime. Furthermore, the legal recognition provided by official registration emboldened many couples to travel beyond the village borders, staying at hotels in the county seat or nearby cities, the very behavior that so outraged A Lan, Zinzai's wife.

Although registered couples were legally married in the eyes of the state, they lacked the societal recognition bestowed by a wedding ceremony. In local dialect, legal registration was identified simply as "becoming engaged" (*ding hun*), a stage distinct from marriage (*giat hun*), as marked by the appropriate wedding ritual and the social passage it performed. The strict enforcement of marital registration was beginning to redefine this distinction, however, such that the marriage process bore less and less resemblance to earlier social and ritual forms. For instance, not long after A Ping wrote to me in 1999, she and her boyfriend registered their marriage at the township government office and A Ping began living with him and his family. Bypassing earlier engagement rituals associated with arranged matches, the couple engaged in forms of behavior conventionally associated with marriage,

including spending the night together. Before their relationship was socially acknowledged by a wedding ceremony, moreover, A Ping was already pregnant with their first child.

Whereas some women such as A Ping took up permanent residence in their conjugal home before their wedding, others simply adapted the practice of periodic conjugal visits to fit the new stage of the marriage process created by official registration. As a consequence, young women were becoming pregnant and shifting residence much sooner than their predecessors, and even those marrying for the first time were often pregnant by their wedding day. Village elders generally countenanced these new practices precisely because they increased the likelihood of earlier pregnancy and coresidence. The growing acceptance of such trends was reflected in the fact that of the 15 couples whose first marriages I recorded for the period 1994–97 (when the legal age and marital registration were strictly enforced), a little over half had had a child and moved in together within three years of their wedding.

Renewed official preoccupation with marriage has also inspired transformations in the concept of intimacy itself, producing unexpected consequences for both young women and local officials. The private conjugal intimacy that market forces have fostered is now interwoven with a form of public intimacy in which women's wombs and reproductive potential are subject to strict government monitoring. Put another way, although for young people conjugal intimacy is directed inward toward the marital relationship itself and their own desires (as opposed to national goals of socialist construction), this intimacy is simultaneously enabled by, and in turn supports, a new collective project of producing a properly disciplined and high-quality population. Young women are closely attuned to these powerful linkages between intimacy and state regulation as they incorporate the regulatory effects of population policies into their own marital calculations. When I returned to Shanlin in 2002, I found that although A Ping was no longer content with her second marriage, she was reluctant to end it for fear that she would be unable to remarry. Her concern was not with future spousal compatibility or affection, as in her previous marital decisions, but with her already having borne a child (and a son at that), making her reproductive future subject to the whims of state policy and her own desirability as a wife thereby uncertain.

At the same time that intensified state regulation appears to limit the emancipatory potential of conjugal intimacy, however, it also enables the expansion of intimate relationships beyond a narrow marital sphere. The social and sexual behaviors made possible by the enforcement of marriage registration have begun to take on a life of their own in Shanlin. As officials and older villagers gradually accepted the practice of conjugal visits and public socializing once a couple had registered with the government, those practices began to spread to couples too young to register, whose sexual activity fell outside the regulatory purview of the state. By the late 1990s, growing numbers of young women and men were forming relationships prior to reaching the legal marriage age, not all of which culminated in marriage. Even when those relationships involved sexual intimacy, local cadres had no recourse for controlling or even monitoring the fertility of the women involved, precisely because state policies focused exclusively on reproduction within marriage (Friedman 2000). Only if an underage woman became pregnant would officials intervene. Thus, despite expanding bureaucratic control over villagers' intimate lives, new state efforts to regulate marriage (and, through it, fertility) have produced a range of unintended consequences. Some of these potentially undermine the regulatory aims of the population policy, whereas others call into question the purely personal nature of new ideals of sexual and conjugal intimacy.

CONCLUSION

In eastern Hui'an, young people's ability and desire to forge marriages based on feelings and free choice emerged not from the reformist campaigns of high socialism that introduced this particular model of conjugal intimacy but from the largely unintended consequences of a more recent meeting of market forces with new population control policies. It is this latter convergence—including bureaucratic interventions aimed at controlling fertility and marriage, a market economy, mixed-sex work and leisure activities, and a general atmosphere of societal openness—that has created an environment in which marital intimacy has flourished with broad social acceptance. From this perspective, neither state-sponsored reforms nor market forces alone have been able to produce lasting changes in intimate life in eastern Hui'an.

The recent convergence of state regulatory policies with market forces in eastern Hui'an has also generated a series of contradictory effects that undermine a simple model of official repression or youth liberation. Although state surveillance of young women's bodies, sexual behavior, and marriages enables local officials to enter personal lives in unprecedented ways, it also inspires new sexual ideals and intimate relationships that appear to threaten both the reach of official regulation and national efforts to contain population growth. The methods adopted by village youth for creating these intimate relationships are themselves fueled by the fruits of market reforms—wage income and mixed-sex workplaces— inspiring forms of consumption and leisure activities that conflict with the productivist orientation of a regime committed to building a socialist civilization founded on a high-quality population. Given these inherent conflicts, the experiences and desires of young women and men in eastern Hui'an will continue to be inflected by an ongoing struggle over the very meaning and consequences of marriage and intimate attachments.

Modern state power works internally as well as externally, shaping subjectivity and desire along with monitoring borders, imposing taxes, and enforcing laws. Only recently, however, have scholars begun to explore the connections between state power and intimacy, and the role of intimate attachments in creating ideal citizen-subjects. Studies of family, marriage, and courtship in capitalist societies tend to emphasize economic factors as the source of changes in these domains, whereas similar inquiries in the socialist world often highlight the role of state policies and official actors. By integrating these two approaches, this article shows how both market and state forces call on individuals to become new kinds of citizens through transforming intimate life. In so doing, it also proposes a broader conception of intimacy—one shaped as much from without as from within—as a basis for understanding how and why official actors across different state systems have aspired to mold their citizens' most intimate acts and desires.

REFERENCES CITED

Borneman, John. 1992. *Belonging in the Two Berlins: Kin, State, Nation.* Cambridge: Cambridge University Press.

Cott, Nancy F. 2000. *Public Vows: A History of Marriage and the Nation.* Cambridge, MA: Harvard University Press.

Kendall, Laurel. 1996. *Getting Married in Korea: Of Gender, Morality, and Modernity.* Berkeley: University of California Press.

Warner, Michael. 1999. *The Trouble with Normal: Sex, Politics, and the Ethics of Queer Life.* New York: Free Press.

NOTES

1. Shanlin is a pseudonym for the village where I conducted research for 18 months in 1995–97, and again in the summers of 1998, 2000, and 2002. All personal names used in this article are also pseudonyms.
2. Village practice required that the initiator of the divorce compensate the other party.
3. By 1994, Shanlin women's average age at first marriage had jumped to 22 years (with that for men equivalent or a few years older).
4. First, parents had to confirm that their child had in fact reached the legal marriage age, now determined by precise birth dates, rather than the traditional age reckoning system. Once age was established, the couple had their photo taken together, another key element of marriage registration established in principle as early as the 1950s. Armed with a document from the village government attesting to their residence and ages, the engagement photo, and a sum of money, the couple then set off for the township or county government. There the woman underwent an ultrasound exam to determine whether or not she was pregnant. Once cleared, the couple was given a marriage license and a birth permission certificate, both necessary if they were to be permitted to have a child.

PART FOUR

Gender Matters

The topics in this section demonstrate the continuing importance of taking gender seriously as a category of analysis and insight by analyzing how and why gender matters to understanding an array of contemporary topics.

13. *Global Connections of Life, Labor, and Love:* As many of the readings have discussed, people around the world are deeply, if unevenly, connected to one another. Many move (or flee) across national boundaries in search of work, security, intimacy, and other goals. These readings apply a gendered analysis to the study of these global circuits of mobility, connection, and dispossession. Lieba Faier examines how love is made meaningful through global processes and the roles it plays in migrants' efforts to craft new gendered and sexualized subjectivities. She does so through a study of the relationships between Filipina women working in hostess bars in rural Japan and their Japanese husbands. Deborah A. Boehm explores how males and females present, perform, and negotiate their gendered selves and gendered relationships through and as a result of the migration of primarily Mexican men to the United States in search of work. Louisa Schein looks at the gendered and sexualized ways in which Hmong migrants in the United States imagine their homelands (and their relationship to their homelands) in the video dramas they produce, watch, and engage.

14. *Structures of Violence:* These readings analyze how gender shapes the experience and expression of violence and trauma, whether in the form of intimate partner violence, military conflicts, or gender-based violence. They move beyond simplistic renditions of men as the agents of violence and women as their victims to examine such phenomena as domestic violence between women, the involvement of states as perpetrators of violence, and the ambivalent position of certain people as both victims and victimizers. Krista Van Vleet traces how ideas of gender, power, and kinship produce regular occurrences of domestic violence between women and their mothers-in-law in the Bolivian Andes, as well as between husbands and wives. Kimberly Theidon explores how a gender analysis (especially of the strong links among weapons, masculinities, and violence) is necessary to understand the possibilities, limits, and experiences of disarmament, demobilization, and reintegration (DDR) programs for former combatants in Colombia. Lynn Stephen examines the gendered and ethnic patterns of militarization and torture against indigenous people in southern Mexico.

15. *Politics of Human Rights and Humanitarian Interventions:* "Human rights" has become the dominant international legal framework for assessing and challenging injustices throughout the world. Many activists in the Global North and Global South have drawn on the rhetoric of human rights to design and deploy programs to address gender-based violence and "improve" the lives of others. These readings examine the gendered assumptions, consequences, and politics of such efforts. They explore how assumptions about "gender" and "culture" can be used to perpetuate hierarchies of power between and among international activists/donors and "local" people and obscure the specific contexts and histories that produce the injustices. Elora Halim Chowdhury traces shifts in the gendered ideas and objectives of a campaign against acid violence launched by a local feminist advocacy group in Bangladesh as international donors become involved. Dorothy L. Hodgson explores the politics of international and national campaigns against "female genital mutilation" (FGM) in Tanzania to analyze the tensions among culture, power, and human rights. Sharon Abramowitz and Mary H. Moran examine how local communities in postconflict Liberia engage and challenge international efforts to define and address "gender-based violence" in ways that ignore their situations, histories, and perspectives.

1 · *Lieba Faier*

FILIPINA MIGRANTS IN RURAL JAPAN AND THEIR PROFESSIONS OF LOVE

DISCUSSION QUESTIONS

1. How and why do Filipina women use the language of love not only to describe their relationships to their Japanese husbands, but to "craft lives and selves"?
2. How does love reflect and shape the gendered dimensions of broader transnational processes such as migration, work, and capitalism?
3. What do we learn from this article about agency, power, structure, and culture?

Jōdan <u>lang</u> [Just joking]. I love my husband."[1]

Tisya's comment surprised me. Only minutes before, she had suggested that she had married her Japanese husband Kato-*san* because of fear of Japan's new immigration law.[2] Kato-san had been Tisya's customer at a Filipina hostess bar in Central Kiso, the region of depopulated mountain towns and villages in southwestern Nagano prefecture where I had been conducting fieldwork.[3] When

she first told Kato-san that she was pregnant, he had asked if she wanted to marry him just to secure a visa. At the time, a spousal visa was one of two types of visas (a six-month entertainer visa [*kōgyō biza*] being the other) under which Filipina women without postsecondary educations could legally work full-time in Japan, Tisya had run away from her third legal contract on an entertainer visa five years earlier. I asked if Kato-san was still concerned

An abridged version of Lieba Faier, 2007. Filipina migrants in rural Japan and their professions of love. Reproduced by permission of the American Anthropological Association and of the author from *American Ethnologist*, Volume 34, Issue 1, Pages 148–162, February 2007. Not for sale or further reproduction.

about her reasons for marrying. "Only in the beginning," she responded. "Not any more. I love my husband."

In professing love for her husband, Tisya was not alone among the Filipina migrants I had met. Many women married to local Japanese men made similar assertions, frequently in English—what they identified as an elite "global language"—and often in the context of discussing the difficulties and vulnerabilities of their lives in Japan. I also heard women assert their love for their husbands in the presence of other Filipina women; some women even attested to other Filipina women's love for their respective spouses. Most of these women— upward of 90 percent of the 65 who had married Japanese men in the region—had met their husbands while working as "hostesses" or "companions" in Filipina hostess bars.[4] Although Filipina migrants working in hostess bars are not legally permitted to have sexual relations with customers (and many do not), they are clearly paid to "love" these men. Why, then, did the women I met in Nagano place such emphasis on the special love they felt for their husbands? What was the significance of love in their lives?

Here, I explore how love came to have meaning for Filipina migrants in Japan through the transnationalities of their daily lives. I examine love as a term of global self-making: a language *and* a set of conditions through which these women articulated globally recognizable forms of agency and subjectivity within transnational relations of power. I argue that, when professing love for their husbands, Filipina women in Central Kiso were claiming a sense of humanity, countering stigmas associated with bar work and articulating themselves as cosmopolitan, modern, and moral women who had emotional interiority. In addition, I suggest that, by enabling these women to craft moral senses of self in their married lives, love facilitated their commitments to financially supporting their families in the Philippines and to becoming new citizen-subjects in Japan. Love was significant for them both because it engaged globally translatable languages of cosmopolitan personhood and

because it made the transnational ties of their lives possible.

My analysis is based on ethnographic fieldwork conducted between September 1998 and August 2000, primarily in rural Nagano but also during three trips to metropolitan Manila and surrounding Philippine provinces. It is also informed by work I did between 1995 and 1997 with an NGO in Tokyo that assists Filipina and Filipino migrants throughout Japan. I became acquainted with some Filipina women in Central Kiso through my involvement with this NGO. I also met women through a local-government-sponsored Japanese-language class for foreign wives in the area. Throughout my fieldwork, I attended government-sponsored events for Filipina wives as well as prayer meetings and social gatherings that women organized for themselves. I regularly visited women's homes and the bars in which they worked, and I lived with three Filipina–Japanese families in the region. I also returned to the Philippines with three women to visit their families there.

LOVE IN GLOBAL ENCOUNTER

By focusing on love as a key term through which Filipina migrants in rural Japan craft lives and selves, I foreground the affective dimensions of contemporary transnational processes. Although many recent studies have illustrated the roles that global flows of people, capital, and media play in the formation of new identities and cultural forms, few have seriously considered the intimate and affective terms through which the transnational is lived.

I build on two bodies of literature. First, over the past two decades, feminist anthropologists, ethnopsychologists, and other scholars have demonstrated that sentiments such as love are socially constructed (e.g. Abu-Lughod 1986; Lutz 1988, 1990; Lynch 1990). This work challenges notions that emotion is rooted in either universal biological processes or autonomous ideologies and focuses on how sentiments are discursively produced within sociocultural practices and processes. Because these studies have aimed to illustrate the cultural variation and specificity of emotional experience, they have tended to focus on the construction of sentiment in discrete and bounded "cultures" or "societies." Here I show how sentiments are produced at sites of global encounter in which different "cultures" come together and remake each other.

Second, I build on the work of feminist scholars who have argued for attention to how intimacy and desire figure in global processes (e.g. Brennan 2004; Constable 2003; Manalansan 2003; Tadiar 2004). Although these scholars have asked whether love is compromised or commodified under global capitalism, they have not considered how intimate and cultural meanings of love are produced through transnational practices or the roles that they play in transnational subject-making processes. I therefore consider what scholars can learn from the multiple and sometimes contradictory ways that love figures in Filipina migrants' transnational daily lives and presentations of self. Doing so can help us look beyond empowerment–resistance models of globalization and enable us to better understand the ways that power works in transnational processes by producing unequally situated gendered and sexualized subjects.

I restrict my discussion below to the ways that love was performed, professed, and made meaningful by Filipina women I knew in rural Nagano, not to defining whether, how, or to what degree they "actually" felt it. I prefer to leave open the question of whether Filipina women in Central Kiso "really" loved their husbands and, thus, the possibility that different women understood their relationships in different ways at different moments. Rather, I explore the conditions of possibility for, and introduced by, love in these women's lives. I focus on love as a cultural discourse and a self-making term, part of those "techniques of the self" (Foucault 1990:10–11)—those "intentional and involuntary actions" (Foucault 1990:10)—through which women not only established and conformed to rules of conduct but also sought to transform themselves and their lives through their global encounters.

FILIPINA HOSTESS BARS AND THE TRANSNATIONAL LABOR OF LOVE

Most Filipina women in Central Kiso came from poor communities in the Philippines, often from Manila and its surrounding provinces; few of them had postsecondary educations; none were eligible for working visas other than entertainer visas. Hostess bars offered the women opportunities to go Japan as migrant laborers and enabled Filipina migrants to meet their husbands. Yet every woman with whom I spoke insisted that she had not planned to marry a Japanese man when she went abroad to work; they had had boyfriends in the Philippines at the time and plans to return home. All the women maintained that they had gone abroad for financial reasons, primarily to help their families. Hostess bars shaped the ways that Filipina migrants learned to relate to Japanese men, the forms of intimacy that developed between members of these groups, and the ways these women came to understand their relationships with Japanese men in terms of love.

Relationships between Filipina migrants and rural Japanese men in Central Kiso were influenced by the capitalist organization of the women's work in hostess bars. Filipina women were expected both to serve and entertain customers and to perform "emotional labor" (Hochschild 2003b:7), to convince men that they cared for them and were having a good time so that the men would patronize the bars and increase their tabs.[5] Many Filipina hostess bars also instituted quota systems—"drink back," "request," and *dōhan* quotas—that offered financial incentives and penalties, not unlike commissions, for getting men to, respectively, order a certain number of drinks, request the women's presence at their tables, and arrange to take them on "dates." Because of these quotas, Filipina migrants had strong incentives to encourage customers to remain and spend money at their bars.

Women were also under financial pressure to get customers to like them so that these men would request their presence and take them on dates. Such endeavors frequently involved spending extended time with customers and developing intimate relationships with them. Women described how they learned to attend to these men, remembering details of their lives as well as their favorite drinks and songs. They would slow dance, flirt, and cuddle with them. Such efforts were not limited to the space of the clubs. Women (even those who were married and continued to work in bars) would call their customers on their cell phones, sometimes repeatedly over the course of a single afternoon. They would flatter these men in Japanese, saying how much they liked them and how they missed them when the men did not visit the bar. In this sense, being "loving"—a practice of affection, caretaking, and careful attention—was a key component of the women's labor in hostess clubs.

Filipina women in Central Kiso were aware that their employers and customers expected them to be attentive and loving. They also knew that many rural Japanese men came to local hostess bars to meet girlfriends and wives. According to local residents, young Japanese women no longer are willing to live in rural areas and do not consider rural Japanese men, particularly those in construction or other blue-collar jobs, desirable marriage partners; Japanese women want to live in cities and marry white-collar workers. In Central Kiso, hostess bars—which almost exclusively employed women from the Philippines—were places in which rural Japanese men were not only able to "feel like men" but they could also feel like adult, cosmopolitan, wealthy, and modern "Japanese" men, in part by meeting Filipina women they could flirt with, date, and even marry.[6]

PLEASURES AND POSSIBILITIES OF LOVE

The possibility that a male customer could be looking for a serious relationship enabled Filipina women working in these bars to interpret their interactions with these men outside the framework of "hostess" and "customer" and to reframe their interactions in terms of romance and even love.

Women perceived that going to Japan as an "entertainer" could be glamorous and exciting. First, because of Japan's restrictive visa laws, Filipina migrants who entered on entertainer visas were hired as cultural performers after extensive training, an examination and an audition. Second, as entertainers, they had historical links to an elite and glamorous tradition of cultural dance performance in the Philippines. Third, many women applied to go to Japan after witnessing the success of other migrants who built large new homes or purchased dyipnis (jeepneys) or sari sari (general) stores. They were impressed by the consumer items and glamorous appearance of women who had worked in Japan and "become beautiful." Fourth, Filipina women described being treated like celebrities when they were recruited and trained. They often received cash advances after signing their contracts, which they used to shop for clothes and makeup to take abroad. According to their training manual: "The honor, glamour, and privilege of this profession are only for those who can be considered as talented and beautiful according to standards of show business" (Esguerra 1994:42).

The allure of an exciting life of a celebrity not only informed their decisions to sign up to go to Japan but also shaped the ways women made sense of their encounters with their Japanese male customers. Many spoke with pride of the attentions they garnered from customers and of their abilities to attract and manage these men. Tessie described the "technique" that she and other hostesses would use to get customers to take them on dōhan. According to Tessie, the women would tell their customers, "Oh, I want to buy such and such, do you know where I can find it?" The customers would then offer to take the women shopping. The men not only wound up buying the women whatever they wanted but also took them out to dinner and then to the club.

Some women who had grown up in strict Catholic homes or who did not have money or time to care for their appearance in the Philippines enjoyed receiving attention from men with the means to take them out on dates and buy them gifts. Women boasted of being the "number one request" in the bars in which they worked, attesting to their popularity and desirability. Many women also spoke with amusement about the customers who vied for their affection and who wanted to marry them. Some also spoke with confidence of the strategies they had developed for deflecting the advances of *sukebei* (lecherous men) while still cultivating their business.

FINDING LOVE IN A HOSTESS BAR

Women's descriptions of the pleasures they found in receiving attentions from customers were heightened in discussions of the men they had decided to marry—and whom they professed to love. Many women told dramatic and romantic love stories about their courtships, speaking of their love for their husbands as something that had developed unexpectedly while they worked in bars, the result of either their husbands' romantic courtship or love at first sight.

Tessie, for example, stressed the attentiveness and generosity of the man she decided to marry. She confessed that she had not "liked" Yoshimoto-san when he first began courting her. Her feelings for her future husband had grown, she said, because she felt that he was *majime* (serious): He had a steady job, he did not drink heavily, he was not lecherous or pushy, and he took marriage, and her, seriously. She boasted that he came to see her every night, requesting her at his table and lavishing her with attention, At the time, Tessie explained, she also had a boyfriend in the Philippines. She was frustrated, however, because he had not proposed marriage and did not have a job that would enable him to support a family. Her feelings for Yoshimoto-san developed, and when he proposed marriage, she said yes.

Many Filipina women I knew in Central Kiso related stories similar to Tessie's: how they had grown to love husbands they met while working as entertainers. These women similarly described the excitement of their courtships, of going to restaurants or for drives, and of being called and visited regularly by their future spouses. Some women offered even more dramatic examples than Tessie of the surprise of love they had discovered in hostess bars. Pilar's eyes sparkled as she described her reaction when her husband, a customer at the bar where she had worked, first caught her eye. "Ooh, I like that guy," she had thought to herself. She explained that her feelings had been reciprocated and her husband had also felt—What was the English word? she queried—"*hitome bore*" (love at first sight).

Indeed, several Filipina women in Central Kiso told me that they had felt "love at first sight" with their future husbands. Sharyn, for example, explained that she had decided that her husband was her "type" the minute he walked into her club. She reenacted the first time she saw him, demonstrating how, tall and handsome, he had strolled into the bar with his jacket slung over his shoulder. To meet her husband, Sharyn had circumvented the rules of the club, which usually permit only customers to select which women will serve them, and had arranged to sit at his table when the hostess he had requested was busy with other clients.

Insofar as women's love stories stressed their agency in their marriages, these narratives presented the women as individual, modern, and glamorous subjects free to form intimate and romantic relationships regardless of financial, familial, or other concerns. Tessie, for example, stressed that she had chosen to marry her husband, preferring him over both a Filipino boyfriend and several other Japanese men. Others, like Sharyn, described how they had gone after the men they married. These women's stories focused on personal factors (he was my type; he visited me every day), rendering unimportant the context of the bars in which their relationships developed or the women's employment in the bars at all. Such stories stand in stark contrast to the women's discussions of their motivations in coming to Japan, which focused on the poverty of their lives in the Philippines and their desires to help their families abroad. The courtship stories women told were stories about women who were so desirable that men would go to great lengths to win them over and about lovers who were meant to be together—and who were free to acknowledge and respond to the call of fate.

THE GLOBAL STAGE OF LOVE

One might understand these love stories as self-conscious claims of belonging to a modern world and universal humanity defined both by the ability to love as a free, self-governing subject and by the competencies in cosmopolitan languages (like English and "romance") that these stories demonstrated. One day I asked Ruby why she thought Japanese men found Filipinas attractive. She responded to my query without missing a beat: "Malambing kami [We're affectionate], very loving." Ruby then compared Filipina women with Japanese women, who, she explained, were not affectionate at all.

Several Filipina women, and some Filipino men, whom I met in both Japan and the Philippines explained their own and others' attitudes toward or behaviors in their marriages and intimate relationships by saying, "We Filipinos [sic] are very romantic." Such claims can also be found widely in Philippine popular culture. For example, in 2001, a Social Weather Station survey concluded, "Filipinos More Romantic than Americans." National newspapers in the Philippines have also been known to invoke "Filipinos' romantic culture" (Malaya Entertainment 2004).

One might, then, read women's assertions that "Filipinos [sic] are very romantic" as claims that they are fully—even paradigmatically—modern. Indeed, these assertions suggest that when it comes to being romantic and loving, people from the Philippines can both hold their own on a global stage and participate in a "universal" humanity. Such claims were manifest not only in the stories that Filipina women told me about dating the men

they married but also in the women's extravagant weddings, which they viewed as culminations of their courtships. For instance, Tessie boasted that she had married Yoshimoto-san in a choreographed ceremony held at a church in the Philippines. Yoshimoto-san had paid for the wedding and for the professionally produced photo album that documented the event. Later, as Tessie and I looked through her wedding album together, I asked her about the elaborate matching gowns and dress clothes worn by her wedding party. In English (a language in which she was not confidently fluent but that she wanted to practice that evening), she explained that her husband had purchased her bridal party's clothing and even bought outfits for her guests. She then bragged that her wedding dress had cost P45,000 (at the time, more than $1,000). Now she regretted spending so much, she said. "But that's every girl's dream," she explained knowingly, "to be a bride, the 'Wedding Day.'"

MANAGING THE *JAPAYUKI* STIGMA

Through their encounters with men they met in hostess bars, not only were Filipina migrants able to accumulate capital, buy consumer items, and send money to their families in the Philippines but they also articulated identities as successful business-people and desirable, modern, and cosmopolitan women. In this way, hostess bars provided Filipina migrants both entry and socialization into glamorous, exciting, capitalist worlds. "Love" figured centrally in these processes. Love was part of both the emotional labor women performed in these bars and the pride and the pleasures they found in their employment. In this sense, love was more than a strategic display of emotion (Brennan 2004) or a form of "deep acting" (Hochschild 2003a) for these women. *Love* was also a term for claiming selfhood and asserting belonging in a modern, global world.

Yet just as these women's professions of love enabled them to craft senses of self, their stories must also be understood in the contexts of negative perceptions of the women's work in bars and of their relationships with their husbands after their marriages. Bar work also stigmatized these women. Because of the relationships between Filipina migration to Japan and Japanese sex tourism to the Philippines, Filipina women who go to Japan on entertainer visas are widely perceived as prostitutes in both countries and disparaged as *japayuki* or *japayukisan*. When I began my fieldwork, my Japanese landlady cautioned me against associating with Filipina migrants. She explained that these women must be poor, desperate, shallow, and immodest—to work in bars. When I tried to protest, she asserted that her parents would never have let her take such a job, even if they had been reduced to the direst of circumstances. People in the Philippines shared similar perceptions. For example, the Filipino uncle and nieces of a woman living in Central Kiso explained (as one of this woman's nieces put it), "The reputation of japayukis here is not very good: They are thought of as prostitutes." So pervasive in Japan was the association of Filipina women with sex work that most Filipina migrants found their lives affected by it.

As a result, all the Filipina women I knew in Central Kiso were extremely self-conscious of the stigma attached to working as an entertainer, and these concerns sometimes overshadowed the pleasures they found in their employment. Elsie told me that, as a Catholic, she believed she was committing a sin by working in hostess bars because she was "entertaining men." One day while we sat around playing cards before the bar opened, she and several other women working at the club explained that they were "embarrassed in front of God" to do such work. "But it is O.K. to work in a place like this if you have a good reason," Elsie added. She and the others agreed among themselves that one could justify working in a club if one did not do so for selfish purposes, that is, just for personal gain or to buy expensive things. Elsie maintained that more than 50 percent of her salary went to her family in the Philippines.

The stigma associated with bar work, especially the notion that Filipina women would do anything for money, also attached to these women's marriages. Many Central Kiso residents told me that Filipina women married Japanese men for instrumental reasons, particularly so that they could escape the poverty of the Philippines and live in a wealthier country. Similarly, in the Philippines, the uncle of one Filipina woman living in Central Kiso explained, "Most [Filipina 'entertainers'] go to Japan because they want to marry a rich Japanese."

Filipina women I knew sometimes challenged these perceptions by explaining that their married lives in Japan, like their employment in hostess bars, were part of the "sacrifice" they were making to help their families abroad or their children in Japan. Cora described her life in Japan in terms of "trials," suggesting that, following Jesus, she too suffered for a greater good. Married women went to great lengths to demonstrate their selflessness. Most regularly sent large amounts of money and gifts to their families in the Philippines. When women returned home for visits, they brought large boxes of goods ranging from television sets to packages of instant ramen to distribute among friends and family. Through consumption, display, and gift exchange, Filipina migrants demonstrated their commitments to their families abroad and reinforced the idea that they had not gone to Japan simply for selfish economic interests.

Claiming that one loved one's husband, then, was another important way that Filipina women responded to the stigma attached to both their work in hostess bars and their marriages. This point was made clear to me in an exchange I had with a woman named Girlie, who was unmarried and working without papers at a Filipina hostess bar in Central Kiso. We had been talking about Irma, Girlie's mamasan at Club Ilo Ilo, and Irma's gregarious husband, Sato-san, who owned the bar Irma managed. Girlie explained that their situation was unusual: Whereas many Filipina women married to Japanese men have to "adjust to Japanese ways," in this case, it was Sato-san "who has to adjust to

Filipino culture." She pointed out that Irma cooked mostly Filipino meals.

"How did Irma and her husband meet?" I asked. Girlie replied that they had met a few years earlier when Irma was working at a bar in town. Sato-san was 23 years older than Irma, she added. He was once divorced and had two daughters Irma's age. "But they're in love," Girlie maintained, "Other people can't necessarily understand that, but they are." "It seems that many Filipina women in Japan marry men who are notably older than they are," I observed. "Yes," Girlie replied, "it is common." But this did not mean that the women marry the men simply for visas or for financial gain, she maintained. "Filipinas can't do that . . . just marry a man for financial reasons. They're not so cold. They love their husbands."

Girlie's assertion that Filipina women "love their husbands" was an explicit challenge to the stigma attached to these women's marriages. In making such a claim, Girlie delineated two types of people: those who were cold and calculating and those who were loving and decent. She suggested that loving one's husband was a measure of both morality and humanity—of an emotional interiority evidenced by love. For Filipina migrants in Central Kiso, all of whom were raised Christian and the overwhelming majority of whom were Catholic, love was both how a woman lived as a good Catholic and how she maintained (to herself and to others, in a language translatable in the Philippines, if not through significant portions of the world) that she had an emotional interiority—in short, that she was both moral and fully human. In this light, love offered women not only the pleasures that might be found in working at hostess bars but also a means of managing the perils, including the stigma, of their lives in Japan.

Cherie, who was married to a Japanese man in Tokyo, stated on several occasions that she was "nakahiya" (ashamed, embarrassed) by the idea that a Filipina would get married just for a visa. This seemed to her an insult to the "sacrament of marriage." Cherie's assertion was clearly shaped by Catholic ideas about gender, love, and marriage circulating in the Philippines. If one believes marriage to be a sacrament and a life commitment based on love, one has little choice but to try to find a way to love one's spouse. Nevertheless, Cherie's comment also suggests that these women's professions of love for their husbands can be conditionally understood in a sense parallel to the ways that Tagalogs historically understood confession through pre-Christian notions of "hiya," shame or disgrace, and its relationship to "loob," an "inner loc[us] of will, feeling, and action" (Tadiar 2004:235).

Vicente Rafael explains that 17th- and 18th-century Spanish missionaries tried to use the notion of "loob" as an equivalent of a subjective locus of love, sorrow, conscience, and repentance in their efforts to teach lowland Tagalogs to confess and repent (Rafael 1988:91–109). However, Rafael argues, the missionaries were only partly successful in circumscribing the indigenous concept of loob in Western terms of subjectivity. Instead, Tagalogs made sense of confession through pre-Christian relations of reciprocity, and specifically, the notion of "utang na loob," an unsettleable debt of gratitude. Consequently, Tagalogs participated in Catholic confessional practices not as guilty and repentant subjects but to avoid the shock of hiya, the shame that comes from one's failure to bargain with a contracted creditor (one to whom an utang na loob is owed) through symbolic gestures of respect and repayment (Rafael 1988).

Although the meanings of such terms have clearly changed over time, and not all Filipina women in the Central Kiso were Tagalog, one might reread the women's assertions that they loved their husbands as articulations of a form of selfhood that was not necessarily identical to the Western free, individualistic self that scholars have elsewhere associated with romantic love (Ahearn 2001; Giddens 1992). Rather, as I further suggest below, we might understand their claims as symbolic gestures of respect and repayment made in an effort to avoid the hiya that comes from failing to bargain with a creditor to whom an unsettleable debt of gratitude (i.e., utang na loob) is owed.

MAINTAINING TRANSNATIONAL TIES

As wives and mothers of Japanese, my interlocutors were instructed by their husbands, in-laws, neighbors, and community members to do things "the Japanese way." For example, they were expected to learn to speak Japanese, to prepare and eat Japanese foods, and to interact with neighbors in prescribed manners. Because spousal visas were temporary visas issued for periods ranging from six months to three years, the women faced considerable pressure to comply with their Japanese husbands' and families' desires. Some women lamented that their husbands were now *tsumetai*, cold and unaffectionate, and did not sufficiently share in the household division of labor. Tessie cautioned me against marrying a Japanese man, telling me that Filipino men were more thoughtful and romantic. Tessie and others expressed wonder at how they had found themselves living in rural Nagano, and they sometimes discussed their desires to leave their husbands and return to the Philippines.

Despite these dissatisfactions, women like Tessie also expressed feelings of indebtedness to their husbands and found pleasures in their married lives. One evening, Cora, Tessie, Ana, and I were sitting at the big country-style oak table in Tessie's kitchen when Malou arrived and shared photographs of the house she had recently built for her mother in the Philippines. The other women expressed envy, both that Malou's husband permitted her to return to the Philippines so frequently and that he allowed her to continue to work in a bar where she made considerably more money than they did in their waged labor in factories or doing piecework at home. Malou rarely spoke English, but that evening she dramatically announced, "My husband is the best! I love my husband! I love-love-love my husband!"

Like Malou, Tessie also claimed that she was "lucky"—an English word some used to suggest that they had navigated the vulnerabilities of their lives by choosing their husbands wisely. Unlike most Filipinas' Japanese husbands, Yoshimoto-san was one of the few who had a white-collar job. Tessie was proud of her elegant house and that her husband took her to the nicest restaurants in town. But perhaps more important, Tessie maintained, Yoshimoto-san really listened to her and attended to her needs and desires. She explained, for example, that he permitted her to do waged labor (factory labor and piece work) so that she could send money to her family in the Philippines, and he even helped her complete her piece work when she was tired or busy. He sometimes assisted with child care and housework and he supported her commitment to activist activities, including mobilizing Filipina women in the area to work for their rights. He also generously allowed her undocumented friends and relatives to live at their home rent free, sometimes for several months.

Like Tessie, other women spoke with pride of their husbands' ability to support them and take them shopping, drive them to church, permit them to attend Filipino potlucks or prayer meetings, or let them do things, even small things like preparing meals, the "Filipino way." For many of these women, their love for their husbands was tied, in measurable ways, to the way he treated them, and in particular, to actions that inspired appreciation or gratitude: Love was linked to a man's ability to financially and emotionally support his wife; to the small, daily kindnesses he showed her; and perhaps, above all, to the degree to which he supported her desire to send money to, and visit, her family abroad. Thus, when women asserted that they loved their husbands, they gestured to forms of intimacy and subjectivity that enabled the transnationalities of their lives. They suggested that love was not only a product of their migration to Japan but also of their ability to maintain their ties to the Philippines. In this regard, however, these women's assertions of love were not simply claims of the freedom and pleasures they enjoyed through these transnationalities. They were also efforts at managing the debts incurred through them and concessions to the stigmas and hardships these women faced.

LOVE MAKES THE WORLD GO 'ROUND

I have illustrated how the meaning and force of love in the lives of Filipina migrants in rural Nagano were tied to these women's positioning within global relations of power. *Love* was a key, if contradictory, term through which Filipina migrants in Central Kiso crafted senses of self as they carried out and made sense of their transnational daily lives. Love enabled these women to claim both globally translatable senses of modern personhood and a sense of humanity in the face of their work in hostess bars. Love also made the transnational ties of their lives—and their accumulation strategies—possible. Women who did not "love" their customers did not meet their quotas or get new work contracts; and if a woman could not "love" her husband, because, for example, he was abusive or would not let her send money home, she was constrained in her ability to support her family abroad. Love was an integral part of what enabled Filipina migrants to work in Japan on entertainer visas and what encouraged them to remain in Japan after those visas expired.

Discussions of the lives of Filipina migrants in Japan, and, more generally, of women who work in sex industries or meet their husbands through marriage mediators, often center on whether these women have come to their jobs and their marriages of their own accord or whether they were "trafficked." Behind many of these debates lie questions of love and human rights: Are these women free to love, that is, to choose their sexual partners freely on the basis of love, and, if not, in what ways are their human rights being violated? However, the stories and experiences of Filipina migrants in rural Nagano illustrate that love is much more than a matter of freedom. *Love* is a powerful condition of these women's transnational lives, a term of global self-making that is made meaningful through and that enables their transnational everyday practices.

In recent years, scholars have worked to understand how new forms of identity and subjectivity have emerged through contemporary global processes. These scholars have considered how a variety of factors—global capitalist flows, travel and migration, a global imagination, new technologies like the Internet, the circulation of cultural and media forms, and language practices and ideologies—are transforming the ways people craft identities and senses of self in a transnational world. Here, I illustrate how attention to the affective terms of global processes can promote understanding not only of the constraints and possibilities through which new transnational subjectivities are taking shape but also of the ways that transnational practices themselves are made possible by sentiments such as love and the gendered and sexualized subjectivities they enable.

REFERENCES CITED

Abu-Lughod, Lila. 1986. Veiled Sentiments: Honor and Poetry in a Bedouin Society. Berkeley: University of California Press.

Ahearn, Laura M. 2001. Invitations to Love: Literacy, Love Letters, and Social Change in Nepal. Ann Arbor: University of Michigan Press.

Brennan, Denise. 2002. Selling Sex for Visas: Sex Tourism as a Stepping-Stone to International Migration. *In* Global Woman: Nannies, Maids, and Sex Workers in the New Economy. Barbara Ehrenreich and Arlie Russell Hochschild, eds. Pp. 154–168. New York: Metropolitan Books.

———. 2004. What's Love Got to Do with It? Transnational Desires and Sex Tourism in the Dominican Republic. Durham, NC: Duke University Press.

Constable, Nicole. 2003. Romance on a Global Stage: Pen Pals, Virtual Ethnography, and "Mail Order" Marriages. Berkeley: University of California Press.

Esguerra, Lawrence A. 1994. Philchime Career Manual for Overseas Performing Artists. Manila: Philchime.

Foucault, Michel. 1990. The History of Sexuality, vol. 2: The Use of Pleasure. Robert Hurley, trans. New York: Vintage Books.

Giddens, Anthony. 1992. The Transformation of Intimacy: Sexuality, Love and Eroticism in Modern Societies. Stanford: Stanford University Press.

Hochschild, Arlie Russell. 2003a. The Commercialization of Intimate Life: Notes from Home and Work. Berkeley: University of California Press.

———. 2003b. The Managed Heart: Commercialization of Human Feeling. Berkeley: University of California Press.

Lutz, Catherine A.1988. Unnatural Emotions: Everyday Sentiments on a Micronesian Atoll and Their Challenges to Western Studies. Chicago: University of Chicago Press.

———. 1990 Engendered Emotion: Gender, Power, and the Rhetoric of Emotional Control in American Discourse. *In* Language and the Politics of Emotion. Lila Abu-Lughod and Catherine A. Lutz, eds. Pp. 69–91. Cambridge: Cambridge University Press.

Lynch, Owen M., ed. 1990. Divine Passions: The Social Construction of Emotion in India. Berkeley: University of California Press.

Manalansan, Martin F. 2003 Global Divas: Filipino Gay Men in the Diaspora. Durham, NC: Duke University Press.

Rafael, Vicente L. 1988. Contracting Colonialism: Tagalog and Christian Conversion in Tagalog Society under Early Spanish Rule. Quezon City, Philippines: Ateneo de Manila University.

Tadiar, Neferti Xina. 2004. Fantasy Production: Sexual Economies and Other Philippine Consequences for the New World Order. Quezon City, Philippines: Ateneo de Manila Press.

NOTES

1. Words or phrases in Japanese are *italicized*; those in Tagalog are <u>underlined</u>. For Japanese words that are now widely used in the Philippines, I use <u>*both*</u>. If words within quotation marks are not italicized or underlined, they were said in English.

2. *San* is a respect suffix added to Japanese surnames and terms of address. Following Japanese convention, I refer to Filipina women's husbands by their last names and the suffix *-san*. I refer to the women, however, by their first names because this is how they requested that I address them.

3. A Filipina hostess bar is a bar that employs Filipina women to clean and care for the bar, serve drinks, entertain customers (usually by talking, flirting, and dancing with them and singing karaoke), encourage customers to return and spend money, and sometimes go on dates with customers.

4. While I conducted research in Central Kiso, at any one time, between 10 and 15 Filipina bars were open for business in the main towns in the region (which had a combined population, not including the outlying villages, of about 15,000). In 1999, there were 191 Filipina women registered in Kiso County (almost exclusively in the central region), including the 60 women married to Japanese men. Those women who had not met their husbands in bars were introduced to their spouses through marriage mediators, friends, relatives, or other work or social arrangements.

5. According to Hochschild, emotional labor is "the management of feeling to create a publicly observable facial and bodily display" (2003a:7).

6. Some men actually went to such bars expressly to find brides. Tessie shared that, after witnessing the success of her marriage, her husband's brother had started patronizing a local bar because "he's looking for a Filipina to marry."

2 • *Deborah A. Boehm*

"NOW I AM A MAN AND A WOMAN!"
Gendered Moves and Migrations in a Transnational Mexican Community

DISCUSSION QUESTIONS

1. How is gender central to the process and experience of migration for these Mexican men and women?
2. How do "gendered migrations" produce "gendered moves"?
3. Does male migration "liberate" women? Why or why not?

On a hot, dusty spring afternoon in San Marcos, Rosa sat on her concrete living room floor, with her daughter and two of her sons, sorting through beans in preparation for planting. Their hands moved quickly, building a mound of lime green while separating out some shriveled beans and tossing them aside. As she worked, Rosa recounted how her life had changed since her husband had gone to the United States three years earlier. "I take care of the fields, our animals . . . I'm currently painting our house. I have to do all the work my husband used to do. And, I'm still responsible for everything I did before—cooking, cleaning, caring for the children." She sighed and looked up at me from the growing pile of beans. "It's a lot of work, isn't it?" I nodded, and we sat in silence as she reflected on her life. Then she smiled, threw back her head and laughed out loud, "Now I am a man *and* a woman!"

Rosa's declaration reflects gendered migrations—that is, transnational movement with a decidedly gendered dimension—and what I call gendered moves, or the transformation of gender subjectivities.

Highlighting the multiple ways in which males and females present, perform, and negotiate gendered selves through and as a result of migration, I argue that gender is fundamental to who migrates and why, if and when they do so, and how and where they cross the U.S.–Mexico border. This process is dialectical—gendered selves shape migration and transnational movement transforms gender identities.

This discussion emerges from a study of the intersection of gender, family, and nation among transnational Mexicans with ties to San Marcos, a small rural community in the state of San Luis Potosí, Mexico, and Albuquerque, New Mexico, U.S.A. Incorporating qualitative ethnographic methods, the research has included longitudinal fieldwork in multiple sites where members of the network are situated. Transnational movement is rarely linear: migration from south to north and from north to south is common and takes the form of seasonal migration, travel between the two countries, trips for rituals or special events, short and extended stays in either country, and settling for years in both Mexico and the United States.

An abridged version of Deborah A. Boehm, 2008. "'Now I am a Man *and* a Woman!': Gendered Moves and Migrations in a Transnational Mexican Community." *Latin American Perspectives, 35* (1): 16–30. Adapted by the author with Permission of SAGE Publications.

Recognizing that the line that divides migration and immigration is difficult to establish, I use these terms interchangeably and draw on research that challenges the conceptualization of migration as a predictable or uniform process.

My work underscores the need to make a gendered and feminist analysis central to theories of transnationalism and the study of (im)migration. I employ a feminist frame to study the lives of women and girls, but also men and boys. My analysis considers the shifting and fluid nature of gender performances and constructions. Gender is made (Ortner 1996), crafted (Kondo 1990), performed (Butler 1989). Indeed, "gender is fluid over time [and] . . . within different social situations" (Stephen 1991, 253) and masculinity and femininity "are gender categories whose precise meanings constantly shift, transform into each other, and ultimately make themselves into whole new entities" (Gutmann, 1996, 21). Here, the focus is flexibility and mutability, particularly the many ways in which shifting gender subjectivities are linked to migration.

The study of gender constructions in a transnational context interrogates previous research about the benefits of migration for females. Scholars have suggested that migration—because it can destabilize rigid gender roles—is generally positive for women. This project builds on and also complicates this view. Migration results in a complex interplay between men and women—a series of negotiations through which women are exercising increased power in some circumstances but also facing the reassertion of male dominance. Similarly, men practice new forms of control as they simultaneously experience loss and are subjected to power imbalances in the United States. While the specifics of gendered migrations may vary regionally throughout Mexico and within different global flows, a framework that prioritizes gender can be expanded to other cases, and many of the patterns outlined below may be present in different migration contexts. Research that closely examines interactions between men and women enriches understandings of the lived experiences of both male and female migrants.

Beyond the benefits to gender and women's studies, placing research about gender subjectivities at the core of migration studies can also provide a more sophisticated understanding of global migrations. Indeed, immigration research without a fully integrated study of the intimate workings of gender provides only an eclipsed view of transnational movement. As Patricia Pessar (1999) has argued, there is a need to "engender" transnational studies and theories. Not only will such research more accurately reflect transnational processes, but it will also demonstrate that gender and family are inextricably tied to transnationalism itself.

GENDERED MIGRATIONS, GENDERED MOVES

Gendered migrations can be traced historically and currently through multiple intersecting and overlapping political, economic, and familial relationships. Mexican (im)migration to the United States has been fraught with ambiguities, primarily due to a series of conflicting U.S. immigration policies and practices: systematic labor recruitment beginning in the 1800s, the massive repatriation of Mexican nationals in the 1920s and 1930s, the Bracero program (1942–1964), "Operation Wetback" (1954), contradictory legislation such as the Immigration Reform and Control Act (IRCA) of 1986 and the Illegal Immigration Reform and Individual Responsibility Act (IIRIRA) of 1996, and, most recently, post-9/11 border "security" acts. U.S.–Mexico transnationalism reflects a profound imbalance of power—in relation to capital, according to political influence, and along lines of race/ethnicity and gender—that plays out in the everyday lives of transnational migrants.

Masculinized migration has been driven by economic necessity and has developed over generations. The Bracero program (1942–1964) played a fundamental role in shaping present gendered migrations. Through this program, the U.S. state contracted with male laborers, initiating a pattern of predominantly male migration from multiple regions throughout Mexico that persists today. The gendering of migration continued under IRCA, which allowed individuals who could document continuous residency in the United States to legalize their status, secure U.S. residency, and, if they desired, seek naturalization as U.S. citizens. Of particular relevance are the Special Agricultural Worker provisions (SAW I and II) that provided amnesty specifically for agricultural laborers. Notably, the majority of agricultural workers and virtually all individuals from San Marcos who received amnesty through IRCA were male.

The amnesty provided by IRCA was impacted by an earlier piece of legislation, the Immigration and Nationality Act of 1965. This legislation altered U.S. immigration policy by establishing family reunification—rather than national-origin quotas—as the central criterion for immigration and naturalization. The dialectic of the Immigration and Nationality Act and IRCA has had a powerful impact on transnational Mexican families: once family members were able to legalize their status, they could begin the process of petitioning for additional family members. The two laws operating together established a pattern of Mexican males' petitioning for female spouses and routinized male-led migration.

Because of the gendered history of migration, gender subjectivities often play out through the restriction of female movement. At the same time, male migrations are both territorial and emblematic of the relative flexibility of masculinity: physical and figurative movement often characterizes the experience of boys and men. The actions of transnational migrants as gendered subjects defy a simple dichotomy of regulated females and liberated males—for example, men's actions are controlled by the U.S. state, and many women in the rancho exercise unprecedented independence. However, gendered migration patterns directly inform the construction of gendered selves, and gender identities continue to guide transnational movement.

Gendered moves are characterized by the many negotiations, controls, conflicts, alliances, strategies, and maneuvers that coincide to construct gender subjectivities in a transnational space. Masculinity is both reconstituted and compromised by migration to the United States, which, in turn, simultaneously liberates and puts new controls on women, redefining what it means to be a woman. Because men are expected to migrate, the masculinity of those who do not go north is called into question. Paradoxically, men may have their masculinity stripped from them as they leave behind their role as farmers to work in low-wage jobs in the United States. Meanwhile, women who stay in Mexico face new burdens alongside increased freedoms: still responsible for domestic chores and childcare, they take on tasks that were previously understood as the sphere of men, such as farming and managing finances. The lives of women living in the United States are also transformed: they may perform wage labor for the first time, and their roles in the family are notably altered. Rosa's assertion—"Now I am a man *and* a woman!"—underscores that gendered migrations are always gendered moves.

MASCULINITIES AND THE SHIFTING STATUS OF MEN

Transnational movement impacts what it means to be a man, what is appropriate masculine behavior, and how men are judged in both sending and receiving communities. Even men who have never been to the United States are affected significantly by migration and the individuals who do go. No longer able to support their families as they have in the past, men go to the United States to fulfill their role as providers, or stay in Mexico and are reminded of how their work in the *milpas* cannot financially maintain a household. Increasingly, to be a man, one must migrate.

One afternoon in front of the elementary school, Aida told me about her husband's experience with migration. Aida and Ramón married when they were twenty years old, and went to live in the home of Ramón's family. Aida was soon pregnant, and the young couple prepared to become parents.

Meanwhile, Ramón's father, Gabriel, became increasingly concerned about Ramón's ability to support his wife and baby. Gabriel took Ramón aside, and told him that the time had come for him to migrate to the United States to work and earn money for his new family. Gabriel told Ramón sternly: "If you don't go to the United States, you are not a man." Ramón shared his plans with Aida, but she protested—she did not want him to go, especially with their first child arriving in just a few months. Despite the fact that Aida was opposed to him going, Ramón left that same day for the United States. Financial need, his father's wishes, and social pressures "to be a man" by going to the other side were more powerful than his wife's desire that he stay.

The centrality of migration in the construction of masculinity was also expressed at a wedding ceremony that joined Martín and Alejandra. On a warm, spring day, more than 100 people were packed in the town's small chapel for the long-awaited event. Martín had been in the United States for the past four years, sending money to Alejandra so they could build the home they would live in together. Now the home was built and the young couple was finally getting married. During the ceremony, the priest talked about how Martín was a "good man," a hard worker who knew how to make sacrifices. In fact, explained the priest, he had spent years in the United States earning money. He had shown that he could provide for his wife, and that he would make an honorable husband. The priest's description of Martín was glowing—this marriage, he told family and friends, would grow and flourish.

These examples show that the creation of masculinity is strongly tied to migration. Paradoxically, in this community, migration simultaneously is equated with masculinity and calls it into question: if going to the United States is a primary path to manhood, there are profound implications for men who stay in Mexico. For men who do not migrate, masculinities are often expressed through exaggerated performances of manliness. While "real men" migrate, men who do not go to the United States

may need to prove themselves through hyper-presentations of male identity, arguably a kind of compensation for not fulfilling the expected role of migrating to financially support family. Men in Mexico often put on exaggerated displays of masculinity—including "jokes" about control over women, bouts of drinking, violence against partners and children, fights with other men, and even shootings—in large part because masculinities are undergoing such change.

For males, migration is characterized by deep ambivalence. "I can't wait to go!" Benito proclaimed one afternoon, grinning broadly. Seventeen-year-old Benito was dressed up, about to drive to a dance in a nearby rancho. As he leaned against his family's truck, he told me about the detailed plans for his first migration to the United States:

> I leave for the border tomorrow with my cousins. We'll go to Juárez, and then on to Albuquerque. There are so many opportunities for me there. I'll have a good job in a restaurant, there are great clubs for listening to music, I may even buy a truck of my own. . . . I am so excited. I know I won't be able to sleep at all tonight!

Several months later, I saw Benito in Albuquerque, at the home of his aunt and uncle, where he was living until he could afford an apartment of his own. It was after 8 p.m. when he arrived. He walked through the door, greeted me, and collapsed on the sofa. "I'm exhausted," he sighed. "I work all the time. . . . I miss my family. Please tell me the news from the rancho." After we talked about people back in Mexico, I asked Benito if Albuquerque was what he had expected. "It is very different from home. It is a fine place to live, but lonely, and very different from the rancho. I think of home often."

When men from the rancho go north, they often find employment in the service sector, typically busing tables, preparing food, or washing dishes at restaurants. This is a significant shift for men coming from rural Mexico, where they essentially work for themselves, managing their farm. Such changes result in a loss of autonomy and a kind of erosion of masculinity as it is defined in men's home communities. As men go from being farmers who work for themselves, to laborers who work for others, they are stripped of their masculinity, and arguably, femininized. Paradoxically, migration enables a man to enact masculinity through labor that supports his family, and yet migrating to the United States means living under the control of the nation-state and being employed in low-wage, often exploitative service-sector work—a particularly demasculinizing endeavor and one that threatens male power.

As such, rather than experiencing migration as an empowering process, men are often disappointed when they arrive in the United States and respond with new performances of masculinity. Felix first came to the United States in the early 1980s, working seasonally in agriculture in Texas and Washington state. Because he was undocumented, each crossing into Texas was uncertain, and yet he did so numerous times. Eventually, he was able to establish U.S. residency through IRCA, but he has chosen not to settle in the United States. Although he is eligible to apply for residency for his family, his wife and three children still live in the rancho. Felix often makes the trip north to work at odd jobs, but he returns to Mexico several times a year to plant and harvest beans. Felix's identity as a man is strikingly distinct when he is in each country, and his experience illustrates the dramatically different positions of men in Mexico and the United States. Felix told me that he is unwilling to bring his family north because he does not approve of many "American" ideals and he does not want his children raised here. He also recognizes his tenuous masculinity in the United States: by maintaining his life in Mexico, he is protecting his power within the family, his status within the community, and ultimately, his identity as a Mexican man.

While Felix's U.S. legal status protects his masculinity within Mexico, men's documented status can also redefine and reshape masculinity in the United States. Enrique exemplifies emergent formations of masculinity linked to U.S. legal status among transnationals. Although he has four brothers, Enrique was the first to naturalize as a U.S. citizen, and so he is the *de facto* patriarch of his transnational family. Since several of his siblings are undocumented, Enrique is responsible for many of the duties that other male family members are unable to carry out because of their insecure position within the United States. Enrique is currently petitioning for family members to acquire residency, including his parents and several siblings. He works in a higher-paying job than many others from his hometown, and he was recently promoted to an assistant manager position at the restaurant where he is employed. He is able to travel back and forth between Mexico and the United States easily—and for less money since he does not have to hire a *coyote*—and so it is Enrique who goes to Mexico when there is an ill relative or help needed on the family farm. In the United States, Enrique frequently meets family and friends at the border and facilitates their border crossings. He houses family and community members, and helps them find employment. He is well respected within the community as a successful migrant, and as a good man.

This is a new form of masculinity that is being ushered in with transnational movement: paradoxically, a man is better able to provide for his family in Mexico when he has U.S. residency or U.S. citizenship. A man with documents, unlike men who are undocumented, has increased privilege within the United States. While there are some women who gain "legal" status in the United States, they almost always do so through their relationship with a male partner, or perhaps a father or brother, and so the power of "legalization" is closely linked to masculinity. A primary factor is that it is primarily men who have been in a position to legalize their status first within the family because of the amnesty through IRCA. Intersecting with the U.S. immigrant status of men and women, power is redistributed according to an already well-established gender hierarchy, one in which male power is strong and pervasive.

WOMEN'S CHANGING ROLES IN THE FACE OF (IM)MIGRATION

With large numbers of men away in the United States, women, who were once responsible for exclusively domestic work, are increasingly taking on roles that were previously performed by men, such as attending school meetings, managing household finances, supervising labor in the family farm, and overseeing home construction and renovation projects. The growing number of female-headed households in the rancho are resulting in emergent constructions of womanhood. As men migrate to the United States, they must relinquish some of their power within the family; however, men do not easily let go of control over their wives and children. Far from passive, women are central players in the construction of gender, both reproducing previous gender roles and creating alternative ones. New forms of gender relations and subjectivities surface, and challenge previous ideals of what it means to be a woman.

Celia is a woman in her late twenties with two young sons. Her husband, Miguel, has been in the United States for over three years. Her day-to-day life is vastly different from that of women of the previous generation, or that of her neighbors whose husbands have not migrated. She has notable independence: she owns a truck that she drives to neighboring towns for family visits or to Zacatecas in order to withdraw money that Miguel sends for the family. She manages the family finances and oversees her sons' schooling. For several years, she supervised the building of her family's home. She and Miguel speak by telephone often, and although Celia does consult with her husband about important family decisions, she recognizes her increased autonomy. As she explained, "My life changes when Miguel is here." Celia told me that when her husband is in the rancho he expects her to work constantly: she has to wake up early to clean the house and prepare elaborate meals. Celia said that when she is alone she lightens up on domestic chores—for example, she prepares simple food for her sons and if she doesn't feel like making the bed, she will not do so.

Some women on the rancho are experiencing more independence than ever before. Left alone when their husbands go to the United States, women are now responsible for a wide range of roles. Femininities are in flux: today, there are multiple ways to be a woman. However, these new expressions of femininity are often contested, and women face challenges as they create new gender subjectivities. The shift in the position of women is a complex negotiation involving both the erosion and the reconstitution of male power.

According to some feminists, women's expanding roles lead to new freedoms (see Pessar 1999 for discussion). Certainly, growing responsibility within the family is changing the place of females vis-à-vis males and within the community as a whole. But how liberated are women as a result of immigration? As women gain independence, they are also facing new struggles and newly configured male power. The "double day" takes on new meaning as women are responsible for a range of gender roles. As one woman told me, it is very difficult to be "*una mujer sola* [a woman on her own]" in the rancho. In addition to the stress of increased responsibilities, women face further challenges: newly constituted male dominance and gendered power inequalities, domestic violence, and abandonment by their husbands.

Cristina, one of the rancho's elementary school teachers, described the changes she has seen in families because of migration. She explained that men still control, or attempt to control, their wives from thousands of miles away. Husbands maintain a type of long-distance or transnational male dominance through male family members, budget management, phone calls, threats, and "*chismes* [gossip]." Men may ask a son or brother to step in as a surrogate head-of-household, or husbands may telephone incessantly and question wives about their whereabouts. Men also solicit the assistance of other men in town to keep an eye on their partners and to report to them about what female family members have been doing. Finally, men exert control by not sending money for family support or by threatening to leave their wives for another woman—a threat that is actualized in many partnerships.

Women living in the United States are also subjected to emergent formations of male control, and often they, too, do not find themselves "liberated" in the ways that some theorists might speculate. They continue to live under the daily control of a male head-of-household. Additionally, rather than freeing women, work outside the home is likely to be an increased burden, particularly because men are not compensating by taking on more of what has previously been labeled "women's work." Finally, migration disrupts strong female networks; groups of friends and family members play a central role in the daily lives of women in Mexico but can be difficult to sustain in the United States.

When women migrate to the United States, they may find themselves under the watch of men in ways they were not in Mexico. Most of the time, they migrate with males, and then live with partners or perhaps brothers and other male relatives. It is very rare for women to migrate alone and even more so for them to live on their own once they have arrived. In the United States, men have significant control over women's actions, complicating notions that migrations inevitably lead to gender egalitarianism. If men with legal status in the United States embody emergent masculinities and new forms of male power, women who are undocumented are perhaps the most vulnerable, underscoring the importance of considering the gendered aspects of the construct of "illegality" (De Genova 2002) in the United States.

The experiences of Lupe illustrate this point. Lupe lived in San Marcos for several years while her husband, Antonio, was working and living in Albuquerque. When it became clear that Antonio, who is undocumented, would not be returning to the rancho anytime soon, he arranged for a *coyota* to bring Lupe and their three youngest children to New Mexico. I met Lupe in San Marcos when she was living without her husband. Community members characterized Lupe as an opinionated, somewhat feisty, woman who did not acquiesce

to others. She was often the focus of complaints from her neighbors—she always played music loudly from her house, people said, and without her husband in town she seemed to have license to do whatever she wished. When I visited Lupe in Albuquerque, however, I was struck by the dramatic change in her demeanor and way of life. After migrating without documents, she was living in what was previously an all-male apartment where she was expected to cook and clean for not only her husband, but also for her brother-in-law and two other men from San Marcos. She told me that she felt very lonely, that she hardly ever left the house, and that she very much missed Mexico. Men who migrate often bring women to care for them and perform domestic duties, and as a result previous ideas of masculinity are typically reasserted. In fact, one of the motivations for men to bring their families to the United States is that they are able to reestablish themselves as head of household and benefit from the privilege that comes with the position.

But women do not passively submit to new forms of male control and exaggerated performances of masculinity. Instead, they repeatedly challenge such demonstrations of male power, especially through critiques of men. In kitchens, at family celebrations, or on shopping trips, women provide their own assessment of the workings of power in their lives. Some of the strongest female critiques are expressed through humor at all-female gatherings. I attended several events in both countries in which women presented such candid commentary about male control. In these settings, the jokes centered on a reversal of gendered (and often sexual) power and/or the deflation of male domination. For example, at a baby shower, there was a constant stream of sexual jokes, most of which described an extremely large phallus not as a symbol of power but as a source of embarrassment for men.

Males re-create masculinities in the United States, and women who migrate face new and persistent forms of male control. Through migration, however, women exercise flexible and diverse roles and redefine what it means to be a woman even as they are subjected to ongoing male dominance. Teresa, a woman living in Albuquerque, has a life that is quite distinct from her previous life in Mexico. Before migrating, she was constantly in her home doing domestic chores and she and her family struggled because they had so little money. Today, she works full-time for a corporate cleaning business and is responsible for many public interactions—with her children's teachers and doctors, the family's immigration attorney, bank tellers, and her realtor, among others. But while she finds herself in spheres that are entirely new for her and in charge of important family business, she is still the one who must do everything in the home. Her teenage daughters help with the load, but her husband and son do not. Teresa tells me that she is exhausted. Although she still vividly recalls the difficulties she faced as a woman before coming to the United States, she often dreams of returning to Mexico.

Migration scholars have argued that global migrations can lead to more balanced power relations between men and women, especially through women's work outside the home and the resulting power within partnerships and families (e.g., Grasmuck and Pessar 1991). My research has similarly uncovered ways in which women's changing roles push the boundaries of gender ideologies. However, the ethnographic study of gendered moves can also emphasize changes that are taking place—and, importantly, not taking place—among men and how migration fosters previous and new forms of male dominance and male privilege.

Sofía, a woman living in the rancho, told me that men continue to valorize agricultural work while diminishing the importance of work done by women. She explained that today women do both "women's work" and "men's work," and so she asked, "Why can't men help with cleaning and caring for the children?" Such changes to male lifestyles are very slowly coming about in the rancho, and perhaps only slightly more so in the United States. For example, when men live in all-male apartments in the United States, they will take turns cooking for one another and some (typically

younger) women in Mexico scoff when their migrant husbands return to the rancho and expect to be waited on; however, men essentially never cook when they return to Mexico or if their wives join them in the United States. Although women are challenging gendered norms and reshaping gender subjectivities, it seems unlikely that gender parity will emerge from within multiple systems that perpetuate such strongly gendered relations of power.

Like men, women face a gendered dilemma whether they are in Mexico or in the United States and whether they are living with or without male partners, fathers, or brothers. In this conundrum, women are subjected to existing and emergent masculinities and patriarchies in both places and neither setting offers egalitarian gender relations. And yet, in the context of transnational migration, females do challenge male power, question rigid gender ideologies, and experience transformations in their everyday lives. The boundaries that limit their actions are not fixed, and transnational movement is reshaping gender identities among both women and men.

GENDER SHIFTS

Through the interplay of gendered migrations and gendered moves, notions of appropriate gender roles are shifting. Transnational movement, cultural ideologies, the workings of global capital, and the persistence of the nation-state are resulting in a range of new gendered subjectivities: emergent forms of male power and strategies through which women assert themselves, as well as newly defined masculinities and femininities. These are transitions that "happen unevenly" (Hondagneu-Sotelo 1994, 193). Gender is created through contradictory processes: masculinity is both reasserted and compromised because of migration between Mexico and the United States, and this, in turn, simultaneously frees and constrains women.

Shifting gender subjectivities problematize conclusions from previous research on changing gender roles and transborder movement. While theorists have often understood migration to be a path toward gender equity, my research complicates such models, demonstrating the starts and stops, new manifestations of power imbalances between men and women as well as changes that provide alternatives to gendered expressions. Such findings also suggest that some of the most potent challenges to confining gender constructions will come from those who are marginalized. Males who do not migrate and do not easily fulfill notions of "a good Mexican man" and females who migrate often and are criticized for transgressing community norms are well positioned to be key players in destabilizing rigid gender ideals and effecting change in their families and communities.

As anthropologist Gail Mummert (1994, 207) reminds us, "Changes do not flow in a unilinear fashion, as in an elegant model, from female subservience to emancipation." As gender dynamics change with transnational movement, women will increasingly call on men to do their part even while facing intensified or emergent male power moves. Similarly, men will exercise gendered power and control as they construct new forms of masculinity that support family and community members in the process of migration. The creation and reconstitution of gendered selves is a complex and uneven process characterized by control, contention, acceptance, and contestation.

Never static, gender subjectivities are constantly evolving and shifting through what transnational feminists have called the "interminable project of production and reproduction" (Alarcón, Kaplan, and Moallem 1999, 8). Like transnational migration itself, gender identities are characterized by flexibility, movement, and transformation. Masculinities and femininities will continue to change as transnational Mexicans participate in the constant and complex negotiation of gendered migrations and gendered moves.

REFERENCES CITED

Alarcón, Norma, Caren Kaplan, and Minoo Moallem. 1999. "Introduction: Between Woman and Nation." In *Between Woman and Nation: Nationalisms, Transnational Feminisms, and the State*, edited by Caren Kaplan, Norma Alarcón, and Minoo Moallem, 1–16. Durham: Duke University Press.

Butler, Judith. 1989. *Gender Trouble: Feminism and the Subversion of Identity*. New York: Routledge.

De Genova, Nicholas P. 2002 "Migrant 'illegality' and deportability in everyday life." *Annual Review of Anthropology* 31: 419–447.

Grasmuck, Sherri and Patricia R. Pessar. 1991. *Between Two Islands: Dominican International Migration*. Los Angeles: University of California Press.

Gutmann, Matthew. 1996. *The Meanings of Macho: Being a Man in Mexico City*. Berkeley: University of California Press.

Hondagneu-Sotelo, Pierrette. 1994. *Gendered Transitions: Mexican Experiences of Immigration*. Berkeley: University of California Press.

Kondo, Dorinne K. 1990. *Crafting Selves: Power, Gender, and Discourses of Identity in a Japanese Workplace*. Chicago: University of Chicago Press.

Mummert, Gail. 1994. "From Metate to *Despate:* Rural Mexican Women's Salaried Labor and the Redefinition of Gendered Spaces and Roles." In *Women of the Mexican Countryside, 1850–1990*, edited by Heather Fowler-Salamini and Mary Kay Vaughan, 192–209. Tucson: University of Arizona Press.

Ortner, Sherry B. 1996. *Making Gender: The Politics and Erotics of Culture*. Boston: Beacon Press.

Pessar, Patricia. 1999. "Engendering Migration Studies: the Case of New Immigrants in the United States." *American Behavioral Scientist* 42: 577–600.

Stephen, Lynn. 1991. *Zapotec Women*. Austin: University of Texas Press.

3 • *Louisa Schein*

HOMELAND BEAUTY
Transnational Longing and Hmong American Video

DISCUSSION QUESTIONS

1. How does the movie Dr. Tom reflect the "male gaze" of Hmong-American men?
2. What is the moral message of the movie? How is this message gendered?
3. Why is Schein's "ethnotextual" approach an insightful way to understand how the meanings of videos like Dr. Tom are produced, circulated, and consumed?

Since 1975, Hmong highlanders from Laos have been arriving in the West after the withdrawal of the United States from intervention in the Vietnam War. Those Hmong who became refugees had assisted the CIA in a covert anti-communist effort within Laos; the failure of this effort necessitated political exile, especially for those who had served as guerillas. Minorities in their homelands, they had dwelled on the high mountain slopes, practicing swidden agriculture, speaking Hmong language, retaining distinctive styles of dress and a highly elaborated religiocultural system.[1] Through their alliance with the U.S., they had hoped in vain to gain a greater measure of political self-determination within Laos.[2] Instead, perhaps 200,000 to 300,000 Hmong now reside in various localities across the United States as well as France, Australia, Canada and French Guyana. It was with haste and regret that they left their homes and, for many of the middle and elder generations, their longing for the Asian agrarian lifestyles they have lost remained alive.

For some Hmong, who have attained U.S. citizenship and a degree of economic security, this longing has taken the form of nostalgia touring—to Laos, Thailand, China, even Vietnam—in search of connectedness to the lives from which they were so abruptly severed. Hmong American voyages to Asia may be family visits, tours, business trips or a combination; in the case of some men, Asian sojourns have involved sexual trysts, longer-term relationships, or marriages with homeland Hmong women. Liaisons of varying duration, between Hmong men from the West and co-ethnic women in Asia, have become the micropractices that constitute an increasingly gendered structure of relations with a feminized homeland.

My problematic here concerns media practices in and around an eroticized homeland. Dozens of the primarily male Hmong travelers to Asia are

An abridged version of Louisa Schein, 2004. "Homeland Beauty: Transnational Longing and Hmong American Video." *The Journal of Asian Studies* 63 (2): 433–463. Reprinted with permission of Cambridge University Press and of the author.

involved in the production of videos that constitute diverse representations of the lands they call home. These videos, shot, edited and marketed all by Hmong, take their place in the context of a huge Hmong media scene in which hundreds of newspapers, magazines, audio cassettes, CDs, music videos, videotapes and DVDs are produced and sold, all within the Hmong market. Videos are in Hmong language and made by a range of amateur and semi-professional producers, many of whom have established companies with names such as Hmong World Productions, Asia Video Productions, Vang's International Video Productions, and ST Universal Video. Produced almost exclusively in the United States, they are marketed at Hmong ethnic festivals, through Asian groceries and video shops, and by mail order domestically and abroad.

Media production appears to be especially voluminous in the Hmong diasporic community, as compared to other groups dispersed in the West; this is possibly because, for Hmong, there is no national media in their own language which they might import and consume as do, say, South Asians in the consumption of Bollywood videos. Among the large volume of videos are dramas, martial arts and action thrillers, documentaries of important events, performance or music videos of singing and dancing, historical reconstructions, and Asian feature films dubbed into Hmong. A moderate proportion concern Asian homeland sites—Laos, birthplace of almost all Hmong Americans and locus of the Secret War, Thailand, where Hmong sojourned in refugee camps, and China, a mythologized land of origins in the mountains of southwest China where filmmakers encounter their ethnic counterparts, the Miao.[3] Several genres regularly appear on the market: narrated travelogues on the order of homemade tourism videos, stories and folktales enacted in "traditional" homeland sites, historical reconstructions and tracings of migration routes, dramatic re-stagings of war and flight, martial arts action stories, contemporary (melo) dramas concerning Asian lives, documents of festivals, pageants and other events, and an avalanche of music videos.

Hmong who watch videos of their co-ethnics in other parts of the world come to think of themselves as ever more unified across distances not only of space but also of dialect, costume style, form of livelihood and other diacritics of cultural identity. There is great emotional investment in these newly forged unities, but they are unities which are produced only in defiance of the global asymmetries that structure the Hmong diaspora. It is Hmong Americans who are the bearers of camcorders positioning those in Asia as earthbound peasants, objects of pleasure under their gaze; and it is in the leisurely moments of urban lives that Hmong Americans watch the spectacle of rural life and agricultural labor in Asian mountains.[4] As for the actual relations of video production, not only are Hmong Americans producers and directors, they also, in a kind of offshore, "flexible" approach to production (Ong 1997:62–66), involve many Asian Hmong in their enterprises, hiring crews and actors on site in Thailand or Laos. Hmong entrepreneurs also buy the rights to feature films out of Hong Kong, Thailand, China or even India and dub them into Hmong language, subcontracting the translation and voiceover work to co-ethnics in Asia since labor costs are so much lower.

SUBJECT FORMATION AND ETHNOTEXTUAL READING

This article is about reading the video texts of Hmong diaspora to the West and conceiving of videos and other media as *imbricated* with migrant subjectivities. I will argue that the gendered structure of transnational relations is not separable from the forms of representation that Hmong consume. Beyond gender, we enter the more elusive domain of erotics—of structures of desire that suffuse Hmong video and other media, potentially inciting longings around the homeland that are sexual and/or sexualized.

My project has included multi-site ethnographic work on production, distribution, and consumption of Hmong videos in the context of other processes of Hmong transnational cultural production.[5] In the course of research, I interviewed producers, performers and scriptwriters about their visions and their particular production practices and occasionally observed them at work on set. In a method I call "itinerant" ethnography, I followed the products, visiting stores, periodic festivals, video companies and other sites where videos were sold. I shopped alongside Hmong customers as participant observer. I conversed with audience members and I watched videos with them in their homes. I took the videos home as well, and watched them through my own eye.

I perform here what I call an *ethnotextual* approach to the contents of the videos. I watch and interpret through my ethnographic entanglement with those whose subject positions allow a more seamless identification with the films. I pursue intertextual interpretations, charting the unspoken dialogues between different video genres, and locating them in wider cultural significations. Forms of folklore, textures of festival and costume, modes of homeland representation—all factor in to understanding video meanings, as do conversation upon informal conversation. I read, for instance, the saturation of Hmong homeland nostalgia with eroticism as tied to the recalling of a disappearing sexual culture—a cherished part of what is ambivalently recalled about the lands called home. The potential for lands distanced through exile to become sites for recuperated passions produces a reconfigured structure of intimacy; to get at this we turn to media, which promises both multisensory stimulation and narrative closure. So I too watch videos and in the course of my acts of viewing my own desiring subjectivity is also implicated. My moments of pleasure are cross-cut with critical perceptions, sharpening my awareness of the politics of my white American woman's eye as it is cast upon these texts and images. Ethnotextual reading, then, means reading alongside and as an interlocutor for Hmong viewers; it connotes an anthropologist's encounter with culturally embedded materials and regards the particularity of *my*

locations as constituted by my long-term engagement with *Hmong* particularities.

ASIAN WOMEN AND THE SEMIOTICS OF THE (HMONG) MALE GAZE

For those Hmong men from the West who form liaisons with co-ethnics in Asia, their economic power translates into the social power to court, bed, and wed very young homeland women anxious for economic support for their families or an opportunity to immigrate for themselves. Resonant with the time-honored East–West practice of picture, catalogue and mail-order brides, regimes of video representation picture such voiceless and powerless women as objects of a cruising type of gaze that surveys unwitting faces singled out by the framing power of the camera lens. *China Part 3* (1995), which follows the visit of a delegation of Hmong American men to a festival of their co-ethnics in China's Yunnan province, like many Hmong-made travelogue/documentaries, is lavishly ornamented with women—usually in ethnic costume, often portrayed in bashful close-ups of their faces. In the opening sequence, which surveys the content of the film in thirty-some brief clips, fully half of the shots are of women. Intercut with such festival scenes as pans of the crowd, bullfighting, pole-climbing, and inaugural ribbon-cutting are shot after shot of women dancing, women walking or riding busses to festival, women accompanying the Hmong Americans, women watching from the audience, and women as disembodied faces, unknowingly submitted to the intrusion of the zoom, surveyed one by one like commodities in a catalogue.

That literal cruising is part of the content of such videos is indicated by scenes of requesting young women's clan names—a first consideration of clan-exogamous Hmong when identifying potential partners. For Hmong anywhere in the world, sharing a surname means that marriage is taboo and sex is considered incestuous. In another video, three rural young women are arrayed on a hilltop, colorfully dressed before a backdrop of panoramic scenery. The cameraman asks: "Will you sing a song for me to take back to America to find you a man?" And then: "Are you girls still young and unmarried?"[6]

The girl who is apparently the eldest, but still appearing to be in her mid-teens at most, utters: "Yes, we don't have 'it' yet."

"Thank you very much," he replies. The camera hesitates, zooms in on the face of the speaker, then pans to the other two girls. They smile awkwardly and smooth their skirts and aprons self-consciously. The cameraman, now self-appointed matchmaker, narrates: "These are three of our Hmong girls. They are going to sing and I'm going to record a couple songs to take back to our men in America." He chuckles audibly, then asks one of them the key question:

"What clan are you?"
"Zhou clan," the eldest offers.

Then they proceed to sing, not knowing where to cast their eyes. They appear disoriented at the staging of what, in face-to-face courtship, would have been a dialogue, but now has been rendered as a one-way self-marketing opportunity. They communicate, but in codes not of their own making to audiences not visible to them.

The bulk of Hmong video, then, is embedded within a masculinist discourse, reflected in the eye of the privileged migrant's camera, that has affinities with time-honored codes of orientalist representation of the East as feminine, sexually exotic, available, and seductive (Said 1978). By troping women as homeland, dreamed of and longed after, differences of economic location and social power can be elided in favor of a repeated rehearsal of loss-quenching reunion.

HOMELAND TRAFFIC AS TEXT

Beyond the literal documents of available Asian women, another Hmong genre in which the dream of homeland women figures centrally is that of the dramatic story in which the pains of transnational asymmetry meld with the emotional-erotic fulfillment attained by Hmong American men. It was in a Hmong-run beauty salon in Fresno that I first heard of the then two-part drama formally titled *Yuav Tos Txog Hnub Twg* (1995), colloquially referred to as *Dr. Tom*. In the months after its release, the work was almost universally touted by Hmong Americans as the most popular Hmong video in the U.S. market.[7] Shot in Thailand on the spur of the moment with a shoestring budget and an improvised script, the blockbuster was the creation of Ga Moua. Spending only $2,000, Moua assembled local relatives and Thai acquaintances to concoct a poignant plot, with a believable cast of characters, enacting a scenario that would make Hmong viewers think twice.

Set in a refugee camp near the Mekong River, the opening scenes of the original *Dr. Tom* feature a beautiful young woman, Nkauj Iab, who is just falling in love with her childhood friend, Tub Nus, a foster brother who has been raised in her family since his parents met a terrible death at the hands of a gang of Thai predators as they crossed the Mekong out of Laos. He has grown up to be an exemplary son and brother, his first appearance one in which he offers to help as she prepares a meal, the next one in which he discovers her pushing a heavy cart and valiantly falls in beside her to alleviate the weight of her labor—a courtship idiom that recurs both in Hmong custom and in myriad videos.

Soon the neophyte lovers leave the cart and stray off the road. They walk by a river, lean against trees, sit on rocks, all the while exchanging the kind of tentative dialogues conventional to Hmong courtship. She queries, "There are a lot of girls in the camp, do you have a friend?" "It's not time yet; when I do, you'll be the first to know!" "You have to tell me or I'll be angry at you," she retorts. "Just wait til the time comes." She feigns a huff and walks away, requiring him to pursue her to the foot of a giant tree where she keeps her back turned. "Are you mad at me?" he asks, communicating everything by daring to place a hand tentatively on her shoulder. "I've had someone in mind for a while now," he adds, "but I'm poor and I still live with your family. So I can't tell anyone. And I don't know if she is going to love me back. Do *you* have a friend?" She too is coy, "Yes, but I can't tell you." "C'mon!" "When *you* tell *me* . . ."

Recurrent close-ups of Nkauj Iab's face allow the viewer to indulge in the sensuality of her beauty while the story line encourages watching her with longing through her new lover's eyes. She epitomizes desirability in a highly recognizable form of Hmong femininity. She wears her long black tresses flowing down her back, her eyebrows are plucked and her lips glossed for the camera. Her face and her figure are rounded and healthy, betraying none of the hunger and physical stress of camp life. Her Thai-style sarong—stock dress for Hmong women once they left Laos—insures that her gait will be mincing and controlled. She speaks in a soft and exceptionally high voice, redolent with the vulnerability of youth, and coyly averts her eyes, feigning bashfulness, even as she is the one to initiate a confession of their blossoming emotions. Her vulnerability will turn to victimhood at the hands of a man more positioned to exploit his socioeconomic advantage, but for the moment what is staged is a passionate intimation of reciprocal feelings.

The next scenes emphasize that the brother-turned-boyfriend is diligent and strong. He chops wood with great force and then is shown walking away from their house telling someone he is going to do wage labor for the Thais. This honest physicality sets up the contrast that will mark the entry of his counterpart, Dr. Tom. As the boyfriend heads off to his toil, the scene cuts abruptly to an approaching airplane, producing a menacing roar and glinting against the blue sky. The next scene features a violent thunder and lightning storm, ominous with gusty wind and torrents of rain. Nkauj Iab watches from her doorstep, sheltered by the thatched roof.

The rain ceases and a car approaches, honking brashly. We have not seen Tom yet; he has been ensconced in two forms of transportation that are unavailable to the camp refugees who do everything on foot, exposed to the elements. The car stops and the camera focuses on the unpaved earth outside the passenger door where an ornately patterned cowboy boot descends slowly and touches ground. The camera pans up Tom's body to reveal quintessential Americana: blue jeans, a large camcorder draped on the shoulder, a white shirt, a black tailored blazer, an oversized necktie printed with sexy images of Marilyn Monroe, dark shades and slicked-back hair. He is stocky, clearly not a regular physical laborer, and not particularly handsome. In the life of the *Dr. Tom* series, the protagonist, played by director Ga Moua himself, will become known for his silly clothes, contrived to impress ignorant Hmong in Asia, but fully recognizable as utterly lacking in style to amused Hmong American audiences.

There is a moment of silence, then Tom's commanding voice is heard, just before his face is finally revealed: "Mmmmm, so this is Thailand. . . . Just as the heart desires." With drama, the heavy drumbeat of a Hmong rock song winds up as Tom begins his pretentious swagger toward the camp. The song pauses for a moment as he meets his sidekick, Jerry, a local and the comic fool in the story, who promptly performs his subordinate status by relieving Tom of all his weighty baggage, leaving Tom to walk freely in ungainly American strides while displaying his technological potency by talking on a cellular phone. Later, he convenes a publicity event at the camp primary school, giving away supplies to schoolchildren who stand in long lines and are coached to say "thank you" to Dr. Tom from America.

In the next scene, Tom's touristy videotaping is arrested by Jerry's introduction of Nkauj Iab in the marketplace. Immediately struck by her, he arranges to visit her at home, commenting to Jerry, "Oooh, are girls in Thailand pretty!" Later, he approaches her house, now dressed down with sneakers and no tie. He sneaks a shot of her mother embroidering at the doorstep, then asks to see Nkauj Iab. Waiting outside, Tom perches awkwardly on a very low stool, removes his shades to shoot a quick nostalgic clip of the traditional embroidery sitting in its basket, then painstakingly repositions his sunglasses and vainly smoothes down his hair. He has become a self-conscious suitor. Nkauj Iab emerges from the house, smiling and friendly. As we have learned in an earlier scene of a dinner conversation, she wants very much to go to America, but she does not yet realize what Tom's scheme is for her . . .

NOSTALGIA AND THE MEDIATED FANTASY OF RECOVERY

Nkauj Iab epitomizes a recuperated Hmong femininity, one that is seen as threatened by the Americanization of Hmong migrant women. As such it can be read as normative, a critique of westernization. The rituals of courtship, where men wooed and loved very young and innocently beautiful girls, come to constitute a quintessential facet of culture that is imperiled by flight to the United States. If diasporic loss is irremediable, then, not so in the fantasy world of narrative videos. Regardless of the Hmong wife he already has in America, and despite his dubious moral fiber, Tom will vanquish Tub Nus in winning the hand of Nkauj Iab. He begins negotiations immediately, seducing her family with promises of money and migration opportunities. Mother, grandmother, and eventually father abandon their promise to Tub Nus's dying parents: instead of looking out for Tub Nus's welfare, they choose the economic comfort garnered by making Tom kin. Nkauj Iab resists vociferously, but she has become a gendered pawn in a dealmaking that far exceeds her feelings. The video features a traditional wedding in which male elders seal her fate.

As for Tom, he has procured a few nights of bliss in bed with his new wife, nights only enhanced by her initial reluctance and her eventual surrender to his embrace. His pleasure is short-lived, however, for his economic stature is a fraud. In desperation, he steals away from a street restaurant where he is entertaining Nkauj Iab to furtively call his wife in America hoping that she'll wire him more cash. His request is met with ire, as his wife barks that he has absconded with their family's welfare money. Tom's facade has crumbled and he will have to skulk home or face discovery.

How can the script avoid restaging the paradigmatic loss of homeland that was so excruciating the first time? A surprising scene occurs just as Tom bids farewell to his bride, concealing from her that his money has run out. Having consummated their marriage and lived as husband and wife for a brief time, they sit close together on a bench and when Tom moves to embrace his bride with one arm, she does not resist. In her most purringly submissive voice, she suddenly expresses longing for Tom, proclaiming regret that she had not loved him sooner. She now does not know how she can wait through his impending absence. The scenario is irresolvably ambiguous. Does Nkauj Iab make this proclamation in calculated anticipation of her husband's departure, as a strategy for insuring that he comes back for her? Or have her feelings actually undergone a dramatic shift?

INTERPRETIVE DEBATES

The diverse readings that Hmong audiences offered of this scene confirm its ambiguity. Several different Hmong recounted to me a basic principle of Hmong sexual culture: Such a turnaround—from adamant rejection of the man's advances to an ardent love—can be considered the product of the conjugal bed, of the desires awakened in formerly innocent women. "She loves him now because she was virgin. Now that she's married him, she has to love him," says a grandfather in his fifties. A mother of grown daughters, on a visit from Thailand to see in-laws, emphasizes pragmatics: "She has no choice: since she has to go with him, she loves him." Not all women expressed unqualified belief in this tenet, however, but dismissed it as an ideological position of those who would enjoin women to accept their arranged matrimonial fates: "Hmong *say*," a thirty-something professional Hmong woman noted cynically, "that once a woman sleeps with a man she will love him for life!"

If we take Nkauj Iab's professed longing as literal, that she has indeed come to love Tom, we can read in this plot development the male migrant sensibility of the text. Nkauj Iab's reciproca tion of Tom's desire can be seen as metonymic for the successful recovery of the homeland, that object of nostalgia whose actual recovery would be just as incredible as the turnaround in Nkauj Iab's feelings. Never simply about sexual adventuring or marital conquest, the fantasy requires a woman/homeland who loves back, for if she doesn't there is no salve to that persistent and painful sense of loss that haunts refugee stories.

SEDUCTIVE EMIGRATION

Further reading illuminates a complementary longing—of Nkauj Iab to leave the refugee camp and migrate to America. Tom metaphorizes this object of desire. He has become the seducer, and the effectiveness of his conquest is based not on his provocation of bodily desire but on his proffering of migrant opportunity. Tom's entire presentation—his slick attire, his charitable handouts at the school, his descriptions of his transnational business, and his flashing around of cash—has been geared to convincing Hmong in the camp that he does in fact stand for this possibility. Moreover, she now wants him physically as an effect of this fragile edifice which is crumbling underneath him: "I have to go, but I'll hurry up and file papers to come and get you," he promises, disingenuously. And then, as if acknowledging that the wait will be interminable, for he has neither the resources nor the marital status to legally bring her to the U.S., he adds, "When I'm gone, please be patient." The video ends, tragically: each day Nkauj Iab waits in vain for a letter from chimeric Tom.

According to the script of *Dr. Tom,* then, it is not that Tom *is* American, but how he *plays* American, that has seduced Nkauj Iab. Much of what avid Hmong audiences consume is the power of seduction itself which is, in Baudrillard's words, "found in the strategy and mastery of appearances, as opposed to the power of being and of the real" (Baudrillard 1999:133). That the text is in crucial ways about the power of appearances is emphasized in a comic relief scene in which Tom coaches sidekick Jerry how to "do like Hmong Americans do" to win girls over. Tom gets Jerry to don cowboy boots, a blazer, and finally his own sunglasses. "Why is it so dark?" asks Jerry, with emblematic homeland inexperience. "Girls like dark glasses," explains Tom. "So that the girls' fathers can't see you, too!" jokes Jerry. After he is dressed, Jerry slicks back his hair in front of the mirror, "Ooohh, so handsome! This time they're going to die in my hands!" But Jerry's artifice is penetrable, not seductive at all, and he instead plays the hapless local buffoon unable to seduce any girls.

MORAL AMBIGUITY AND MEDIA'S MULTIVALENCE

The figure of Tom, in the end, represents a deeply ambivalent heroic masculinity. The script revels in his prowess at playing a big shot with almost unbridled access to women, but at the same time it heaps derision upon him for his duplicitous, self-seeking ethos. The overt text must affirm this censure or risk being intolerable to the imagining of Hmong global solidarity. Indeed, the more didactic *Part II* reveals the gradual demise of the evil-doing Dr. Tom, as director Ga Moua, by his account, adjusted to the demands of audiences who wanted to see justice done. Tub Nus makes it to America and goes to look up "Dr." Tom, who turns out to be nothing but a janitor in a white American doctor's office. Meanwhile, Tom deceives his first wife into believing he wants to make a new beginning and she takes him to her uncle for a loan to start a farm. He immediately absconds back to Thailand where he discovers that his homeland wife has learned of his lies, abandoned her marriage to him and returned to her original boyfriend. Her parents curse him mercilessly. Foiled, but now desperate for a homeland tryst, Tom tries in vain to impress many other women, all of whom let him know that they are no longer to be duped by men from America.

Humiliated, he returns home, where he vents his frustration violently on his Hmong American wife. She in turn reports him for domestic abuse, and he ends up, in a dramatic climax, hunted down in his home by white and black cops and carted off to jail.

Clearly, *Dr. Tom* works as a pedagogical text, warning Hmong men of the perils of straying into the temptations of homeland relationships and cautioning Hmong women in Asia of the risks of succumbing to a con. It chastises marital infidelity, and portrays Tom as doubly economically exploitative: he both makes off with his wife's meager welfare income, and flaunts it among refugee poor to coerce a reluctant family into marrying their daughter off to him. At this level, the story could not be more didactic and, indeed, director Ga Moua espoused this intention when I asked him why he had made these films on what, at the time, was an unprecedented theme that proved to be highly subversive to Hmong American men. "I wanted them to stop doing it! They should be shamed!" he exclaimed with passion. Hmong American audiences also analyze the film as conveying a useful politico-moral message. Deeply concerned, Hmong viewers I spoke with envisioned a social impact for the film. "The movie warns men about what they shouldn't do when they go to Thailand or Laos," was an interpretation voiced commonly by women and men. That the message of *Dr. Tom* continues to retain a doubleness—of a suggestive potential combined with a moral reprehension—is an artifact of media's polysemic character.

In some ways, then, what happens in *Part III* (1999) could be read as an attempt to come to terms with that doubleness of *Parts I and II*. Emerging from jail, Tom is told by a friend that his U.S. wife has had multiple affairs, giving him an excuse to return to Thailand for a third time. But Tom is now much detested by people in Thailand. They accuse him of all the crimes of Hmong migrant malehood: "You Hmong Americans are always saying you are the top leader; how do we know who's really the one?" Over and over again they ask what he's going to do for Thailand. Amidst his mounting disgrace, a friend suggests that he go to Laos. There his artifice

is gradually restored. Tom travels, on more and more primitive types of transportation, to a village remote enough that he can find a bride even more traditional, pictured humbly working in the fields, wearing full-blown traditional Hmong highland costume rather than the Thai-style lowland attire in which Nkauj Iab had been outfitted. He consummates the marriage through an orchestrated traditional abduction, right from the girl's doorstep, which her parents acknowledge as legitimate. His conquest complete, however, he continues womanizing. The new wife's family persuades her to come home and abandon the marriage. Miffed, he steals back the motorcycle he had bought her and, once again, gets in trouble with the law.

Now arrested and jailed in Laos, he calls upon his U.S. wife. Unbeknownst to Tom, the audience has been privy to her having an extended affair with a "Dr. Tony," a real Hmong doctor. Upon hearing Tom's pleas to revive their relationship, however, she dutifully bails Tom out. He comes home to Fresno, and sheepishly makes a repentant speech: "Honey [in English], let's put the past behind us and reconcile. I promise you that from now on I will be your beloved husband and not go to Laos or Thailand ever again." In the closing scene, they are pictured walking arm in arm at the Fresno Hmong New Year festival, she in full traditional costume, smiling into each other's eyes as if nothing had ever happened.

Part III condenses the issues of clashing marriage and sexual mores: That matrimony remains Tom's objective, despite a wife at home, opens up the issue of the moral standing of polygyny. While monogamy is now the norm, ardently supported by most Hmong in the West, the memory of Laos as a place where polygyny was permitted, even prestigious, remains alive, the stuff of fantasy for some, of critique for others, and of recuperative practice for still others.

WOMEN'S MIRTH AND THE PROBLEM OF AUDIENCE

Dr. Tom's complexity of meanings reverberates through its reception. In discussing *Part III*, director Ga Moua recounts that he designed the ending that he did because people were too depressed by the first two videos. "I wanted to make the audiences happy," he explains, aware that the finale was of dubious credibility. Women, the majority audience for the *Dr. Tom* series and other such narrative films, were especially attuned. What kind of pleasures might women derive from consuming such videos again and again? Most often, what they described was the pleasure of laughing at Tom, his horrible wardrobe, his buffoonery. In a kind of gendered laughter, a laughter of inversion, they made Tom an object of fascinating mirth, his masculine power fragile, threatened and ultimately untenable, premised as it is on his web of lies and falsities.

Meanwhile, the lure of the melodrama, the poignancy of tragedy, and the sensual pleasure of viewing nostalgic homeland scenes in films such as *Dr. Tom* cannot be underplayed in women's consumption. Women, too, remember the lost courtships of their youth, and are subject to the visceral incitements of Nkauj Iab's beauty and to the titillations of unconfessed love. As with the romance readers described by cultural studies critic Janice Radway, women simultaneously consumed these texts *both* for "emotional gratification" (1984:212) and out of "dissatisfaction, longing and protest" (1984:214).

Despite her victimized fate, Nkauj Iab is not portrayed as entirely lacking in subjectivity, agency, or sexuality. In a scene just before she is wed to Dr. Tom, she seeks out her boyfriend alone in his room. They lament their tragic fate, but he, ever filial, assures her that it is the right thing to do for the good of her family. Then, in a remarkable assertion of female sexual agency, she rises to undress, beginning to remove her jacket while proclaiming that if they are to part she wants first to give him "that which is most precious to me"—a euphemism for her virginity.

Hmong women with whom I've discussed this scene find it implausible in the extreme. They are astounded that an unmarried woman should be pictured risking her social standing by initiating sex. And they are cynically amused that the boyfriend should not seize on this irresistible opportunity. Nonetheless, the tender crafting of the boyfriend—as orphaned, loyal, humble, and moral—holds out for another version of manhood, one full of heart and upright in society. This rival form of masculinity opens up a hopeful domain for contestation over how Hmong men should conduct themselves under new transnational conditions and at differing locations in the globalizing Hmong social structure.

CONCLUSIONS

As we've seen, refugees and other diasporics, or at least some of them, are active cultural producers. What they make are texts infused with meanings, images, loss and longing that are imbricated with subjectivities. By this I mean at least two things: first, in the consumption of media, people may develop social imaginaries and senses of community and identity that are supralocal—*even when they are not mobile themselves.* Conversely, media production and circulation can themselves *generate* certain forms of transnational mobility and new types of transnational relations.

Importantly, then, media is never only about meanings harbored within texts, but also about myriad social effects, in relations of production and reception as well. And precisely because of the polysemic character of media, we must bring complex, ethnotextual readings to them. Methodologically this involves engagement with producers and audience members who occupy diverse subject positions and who receive the contents of media from divergent viewing perspectives. It means attending to intertextual references and to dialogues between audiences and producers as members of a community. Finally it means imagining that such media as Hmong homeland videos might be plural in meanings, containing not only didacticism and pedagogy, but also incitement and eroticism, that they engage the senses as well as moral sensibilities.

The Hmong diaspora, like many others, must be differentiated along gender lines. Men are socially positioned to quest for home through actually returning and pursuing homeland liaisons (although only a small proportion actually do it); women are situated as purveying moral censure for such practices. Although nostalgic Hmong women are also returnees to Asia—as kin, as travelers and as businesspeople—they are rarely located in the dynamics of erotic interchanges in which men are chronically implicated regardless of their individual actions. At the transnational scale, gender binary has taken on a new valence as homeland becomes the quested after feminine and sex becomes a subject of male fantasy from far away.

VIDEOGRAPHY

China, Part 3. Su Thao. ST Universal Video. 1995. VHS.

Death in Thailand. Va-Megn Thoj. C.H.A.T Television Productions, Frogtown Media Productions. 2002. VHS.

Yuav Tos Txog Hnub Twg (How Long Until the Day I Am Waiting For?). Ga Moua. Ntsa Iab. 1995. VHS.

Yuav Tos Txog Hnub Twg (How Long Until the Day I Am Waiting For?): Dr. Tom II. Ga Moua. Ntsa Iab. 1997. VHS.

Yuav Tos Txog Hnub Twg (How Long Until the Day I Am Waiting For?): Dr. Tom III. Ga Moua. Ntsa Iab. 1999. VHS.

REFERENCES

Adams, Nina S. and Alfred W. McCoy, eds. 1970. Laos: War and Revolution. New York: Harper Colophon Books.

Baudrillard, Jean. 1999. Revenge of the Crystal: Selected Writings on the Modern Object and Its Destiny: 1968–1983. London: Pluto Press.

Cooper, Robert. 1984. Resource Scarcity and the Hmong Response: Patterns of Settlement and Economy in Transition. Singapore: Singapore University Press.

Dommen, Arthur J. 1971. Conflict in Laos: The Politics of Neutralization, rev. ed. New York: Praeger Publishers.

Geddes, W.R. 1976. Migrants of the Mountains: The Cultural Ecology of the Blue Miao (Hmong Njua) of Thailand. Oxford: Clarendon Press.

Gunn, Geoffrey C. 1990. Rebellion in Laos: Peasants and Politics in a Colonial Backwater. Boulder, CO: Westview Press.

Hamilton-Merritt, Jane. 1993. Tragic Mountains: The Hmong, the Americans, and the Secret Wars for Laos, 1942–1992. Bloomington: Indiana University Press.

LeBar, Frank M. and Adrienne Suddard. 1960. Laos: Its People, Its Society, Its Culture. New Haven: Human Relations Area Files.

Lee, Gar Yia. 1981. The Effects of Development Measures on the Socio-Economy of the White Hmong. PhD. Diss., University of Sydney.

Lee, Gary Y. 1982. Minority Policies and the Hmong. In Contemporary Laos: Studies in the Politics and Society of the Lao People's Democratic Republic. Martin Stuart-Fox, ed. New York: St. Martin's Press.

Lemoine, Jacques. 1972. Un Village Hmong Vert du Haut Laos: Milieu Technique et Organisation Sociale. Paris: Centre Nationale de la Recherche Scientifique.

Ong, Aihwa. 1997. The Gender and Labor Politics of Postmodernity. In The Politics of Culture in the Shadow of Capital. Lisa Lowe and David Lloyd, eds. Pp. 61–97. Durham, NC: Duke University Press.

Radway, Janice A. 1984. Reading the Romance: Women, Patriarchy, and Popular Literature. Chapel Hill: University of North Carolina Press.

Said, Edward. 1978. Orientalism. New York: Vintage Books.

Schein, Louisa. 1999. Diaspora Politics, Homeland Erotics and the Materializing of Memory. Positions: East Asia Cultures Critique 7(3): 697–729.

———. 2000. Minority Rules: The Miao and the Feminine in China's Cultural Politics. Durham, NC: Duke University Press.

———. 2002. Mapping Hmong Media in Diasporic Space. In Media Worlds: Anthropology on New Terrain. Faye D. Ginsburg, Lila Abu-Lughod and Brian Larkin, eds. Pp. 229–244. Berkeley: University of California Press.

Stuart-Fox, Martin. 1986. Laos: Politics, Economics and Society. London: Frances Printer Publishers.

Tapp, Nicholas. 1989. Sovereignty and Rebellion: The White Hmong of Northern Thailand. Singapore: Oxford University Press.

———. 2003. The Hmong of China: Context, Agency, and the Imaginary. Boston: Brill Academic Publishers, Inc.

Yang Dao. 1993. Hmong at the Turning Point. Minneapolis: WorldBridge Associates.

NOTES

1. For classic ethnographic treatments of Hmong history, religion, culture, and economic development in Southeast Asia see Cooper (1984), Geddes (1976), Lee (1981), Lemoine (1972), and Tapp (1989). An important recent addition is Tapp's (2003) study of Hmong in China.

2. For historical treatments from differing political standpoints on the Hmong as minorities in Laos and their relations to Lao, French colonists and Americans, see Lee (1982), LeBar and Suddard (1960), Stuart-Fox (1986), Gunn (1990), Dommen (1985), Adams and McCoy (1970), and Hamilton-Merrit (1993). For an analysis by a French-trained Hmong-Lao intellectual, see Yang (1993).

3. The term Miao has a long history of various usages to denote non-Han peoples in China. In the Maoist era, the term was stabilized to refer officially to a large umbrella category, the fifth largest minority in China, within which researchers included several subgroups, including the people that call themselves "Hmong." For the purposes of this article, the Miao term appears when I refer to Hmong co-ethnics in China. Although readily adopted by many in China, the term remains highly contested outside the mainland. For more detailed discussion of the politics of ethnonyms, see Schein (2000b:xi–xiv, 35–67).

4. There has been a gradually increasing circulation of Hmong American videos within Hmong communities in Thailand and even Laos, however these are particular, sometimes more town or urban, communities with greater resources; it is far from the norm for villagers in Asia to have VCR or DVD player access.

5. Research effectively spans more than two decades since I began working with Hmong refugees in Providence, R.I. in 1979. Primarily in the years since 1995, I have attended events and conducted interviews and participant observation during short-term visits to multiple U.S. cities, including Fresno, CA, Minneapolis-St. Paul, MN, Washington, D.C., Philadelphia, PA, Wausau and Milwaukee, WI, Providence, RI, Detroit, MI, and others.

6. All translations are a result of collaborations with Hmong native speakers. For translation assistance I would especially like to thank Nouzong Ly, Ly Chong Thong Jalao, Doualy Thao, Yuepheng Xiong, KaYing Yang, Long Yang, Yang Teng, Ga Moua, and Doua Thor.

7. I purchased the video and each sequel up to #9 as they came out, widely distributed through ethnic groceries, festivals and by the director's mail order business. I have watched it dozens of times and in multiple contexts, with Hmong men and women of all ages, in Hmong communities in California, the Midwest, Philadelphia and in my own living room. I have also watched many parts with director Ga Moua. In many instances, watching the video together was also accompanied by extended group and individual discussions of key elements of the story and images.

THE INTIMACIES OF POWER
Rethinking Violence and Affinity in the Bolivian Andes

DISCUSSION QUESTIONS

1. Why do mothers-in-law hit their daughters-in-law and husbands hit their wives in Sullk'ata, Bolivia?
2. How does attention to gender, difference, power, and kinship help us understand these patterns of domestic violence?
3. How do people justify, explain, or "normalize" violence between family members?

Michelle Rosaldo pointed out several years ago that too often scholars assume to "know just what . . . it means to be a parent, sibling, spouse, or child" (1980:408–409). She challenged anthropologists and feminists alike to examine closely the intricacies of kinship relationships, not only the intimacies but the hierarchies as well, and to "ask how varying relationships within the home might influence relationships outside it" (Rosaldo 1980:408–409). Inspired by her words as well as those of the women of the highland Andean region of Sullk'ata, Bolivia, I trace kinship relationships through various events of domestic violence that occurred during my field research in 1995 and 1996. Almost every instance of physical abuse that I know about from

that period involves affines, or in-laws. Violence erupted between women and their husbands, mothers-in-law, and sisters-in-law (especially their husbands' brothers' wives). The violence between husbands and wives is more frequent, and more readily acknowledged by Sullk'atas, than violence among women affines. Nonetheless, many women in Sullk'ata recount stories of the violence of their mothers-in-law. The unequal relationship of power between *swiras* (mothers-in-law) and *qhachunis* (daughters-in-law) is not unique to Sullk'ata. Anthropologists have noted the subordinate position of qhachunis in other regions of Bolivia and elsewhere in the Andes (e.g. de la Cadena 1995; Harvey 1994; Weismantel 1988). Although scholars have closely

An abridged version of Krista Van Vleet, 2002. The intimacies of power: rethinking violence and affinity in the Bolivian Andes. Reproduced by permission of the American Anthropological Association and of the author from *American Ethnologist*, Volume 29, Issue 3, Pages 567–601, August 2002. Not for sale or further reproduction.

examined conflict between spouses in the Andes (e.g. Harris 1994), they have directed little attention to the violence among women affines or the overlapping discourses that sustain asymmetries of power among affines, both women and men. I explore relationships of intimacy and power among affines in order to expand understandings of domestic violence and kinship in Sullk'ata, and more generally.

Analyzing domestic violence in terms of the complexities of kinship, particularly affinal relationships, illuminates the ways that moments of violence are shaped by multiple aspects of identity and power.[1] In societies organized by kinship, marriage is an arena in which relationships of inequality, such as sexuality, ethnicity, gender, age, and class, mutually constitute each other. Thus, I incorporate gender as a category of difference but do not base my analysis of domestic violence solely on gender hierarchy because affinity is both a category of identity and a trajectory of power that influences relationships among variously positioned individuals and groups in Sullk'ata. I focus on the ways in which discourses and practices of relatedness and violence between husbands and wives and among mothers- and daughters-in-law unevenly overlay each other, creating a context in which intimate violence occurs and is normalized.[2]

Moreover, analyzing kinship in terms of asymmetries of power, including instances of physical conflict, reinvigorates anthropological interpretations of kinship and gender in the region. Attention to domestic violence forefronts the material and emotional ways that individuals are intimately involved with each other and the negotiated aspects of "relatedness" (Carsten 2000). Focusing on Sullk'ata women as perpetrators as well as victims of violence who are caught up in webs of broader relationships requires acknowledgement of differences in positionality within households and communities. Bringing together these strands of analysis demonstrates that ultimately neither kinship nor violence may be understood outside of the lived relationships of individuals that are at once structured by multiple trajectories of power

(variously claimed and contested) and are embedded in, yet at times transgress, the intimacies and ideally sociable sentiments of home.

The violence between kin in Sullk'ata is part of a pattern of domestic violence that occurs among individuals of virtually all social classes, ethnicities, genders, sexual orientations, and ages. Far from a suggestion that domestic violence is an issue exclusive to a particular socioeconomic status or ethnic minority in Bolivia, my attention to this particular ethnographic context emerges from my research experiences. I base my discussion on 18 months of field research with primarily Quechua-speaking peasants who live in six small dispersed communities in a rural region of the Andes called Sullk'ata (Province of Chayanta, Department of Potosí). In Sullk'ata, marriage is based upon ideals of gender opposition and complementarity rather than on ideals of love or companionship.[3] Moreover, marriage embeds individuals in a broad network of kinship relationships and obligations, including exchanges of labor and patterns of market and subsistence production, that unevenly affect individuals of different genders and generations. I present it in hopes of generating and extending analyses of the multiple contexts in which violence occurs and the ways that relationships of power are differently constituted and contested in the everyday lives of individuals, both kin and non-kin, in the Andes.

THE CASE OF CLAUDINA AND HER DAUGHTER-IN-LAW[4]

One of the first instances of violence between affines that I heard about was between a mother-in-law and daughter-in-law. I did not witness the incident, but my comadre Ilena did. She told me about it that evening as I sat preparing a meal with her. At the time, I had been living with Ilena and her family for over six months, cooking and eating evening meals with them, often assisting with agricultural labor, and accompanying Ilena to community work projects and fiestas. Claudina, a swira, was in her late fifties, and she and her husband had just sponsored one of the largest and most financially demanding fiestas in the community. Their children, all married adults, had arrived with their families to help with the preparations and to celebrate the fiesta, which took place over the course of a week. On the final day of the fiesta, Claudina accused her qhachuni of failing to collect eggs or assist with cooking that day's midday meal. Angry and drunk, Claudina hit her daughter-in-law in the eye.

Claudina's explanation for hitting her daughter-in-law—that she had failed to cook—is the most common explanation given for a woman being hit, whether by her husband or her mother-in-law. Cooking and serving food, the primary task of a married woman, indexes not only gender identity, but also adulthood and specific kinship relationships with other household members. Cooking may be understood as a locus of power indicating women's control of the consumption and distribution of subsistence products. However, more than one woman may live in any particular household. Married couples traditionally live together in the household of the husband's parents for the initial two to five years of marriage. While she lives with her in-laws, a woman is compelled to work for her swira: herding sheep, cooking over an open fire, washing clothes in the stream, and assisting with the harvesting and planting of potatoes, fava beans, and corn. Although the mother-in-law typically serves the food, emphasizing her role in allocating household resources, the daughter-in-law demonstrates her proficiency, obedience, and care for the sustenance of the household by cooking. Even after a qhachuni has moved out of the household of her husband's parents, she is still bound by obligations to her mother-in-law and may be hit by her.

The daughter-in-law's position within a network of relationships shifts over the course of time, however, altering the ways in which relationships among mothers- and daughters-in-law, husbands and wives, and mothers and sons are negotiated. In this case, Claudina's daughter-in-law and son were no longer living in Claudina's household. The daughter-in-law was already well established as a *warmi* (adult woman and wife) with six children of her own (one

of whom was soon to be married), a household in another community, and extensive labor exchange relationships in both communities. When Claudina's son heard about the conflict that day, he supported his wife rather than his mother in the dispute. The daughter-in-law and son returned home with their children the next morning. Five months later when I asked Claudina about the incident, they had not yet returned to visit, refusing to come even for Carnival when people throughout Bolivia return home to celebrate and bless their natal communities.

LOCAL DISCOURSES OF VIOLENCE AND AFFINITY

The ways in which women negotiate potentially violent situations or react to the physical abuse of an affine vary according to the contingencies of the situation, the histories of individuals, and the more general social and historical contexts in which violence takes place. Sullk'ata women, like others in the Andes and elsewhere, may challenge the abuse of their affines, as did Claudina's daughter-in-law, by lamenting and complaining about affinal violence to other women in everyday gossip or during fiestas or more formally to local and state authorities. Women may fight back physically or more commonly inflict pain through other means as in Weismantel's (1988:181–182) description of a woman who offered bowl after bowl of food to her abusive husband, who was obliged to eat in spite of his hangover. A Sullk'ata woman may simply leave her in-laws and return home to her parents, especially if her marriage has not yet been formalized by a civil or religious wedding ceremony; however, most women do not have the financial, material, or emotional resources to live alone.[5]

Yet in their talk about particular events of abuse, Sullk'atas also silence more far-reaching deliberations about violence. Both men and women normalize affinal violence by pointing out the drunken state of the abuser or by claiming that violence is "just custom" (*kustumbrilla*, or *costumbre*, Sp.). Both women and men joke and make innuendoes

linking violence, heterosexuality, and sexual reproduction, marking the violence of spouses. In this
section, I trace the overlapping discourses about
domestic violence introducing a double distinction
between the unevenness of normalizing and marking violence and the variabilities of women's power
and vulnerability. Attention to the crosscutting
axes of these discourses indicates the complexities
of the lives, relationships, and stories of women
who clearly suffer from abuse but are not simply
powerless in relation to their affines.

Normalizing and Contesting the Violence of Affines

In Sullk'ata, both men and women normalize affinal violence by pointing out the drunken state of
the abuser. When Claudina told me her version of
the story months after she had hit her daughter-
in-law, she reiterated how drunk she had been at
the time. Quechua speakers conceive of drunkenness as an altered state, similar to a dream state,
and believe that people cannot be held responsible
for their actions when they are drunk. In some instances, the disclaimer of drunkenness does not go
uncontested; however, all of the violence among affines in Sullk'ata that I know of occurred during
ritual contexts in which people were drunk.

The discourse of drunkenness is also intertwined with a discourse of custom through which
violence is simultaneously publicly disclosed and
pushed to the margins of public attention. At
times, the normalization of violence through talk
of custom is implicit, as when Ilena told me about
the incident of violence between Claudina and
her qhachuni. She said that she regretted the incident had ever occurred: Ilena had work exchange
relationships with both women involved in the
dispute. She did not directly criticize Claudina's
actions, however. Instead, she recounted stories of
her own mother-in-law's violence, and ended with:
"I suffered badly. I lived there for 5 years, and I had
to do everything."

"Did you and your swira get mad at each other?"
I asked.

"Yes," she said.
"What did your husband do?"
"He went back to his mother. He should have
been with me. She really hated me." Here, Ilena
positions Claudina's actions within a more general
context of affinal relationships. Especially older
women told me stories of their swiras and the difficult years that they endured living in the households
of their in-laws. Although women emphasized the
painfulness of their experiences, they did not suggest that their experiences were exceptional.

At times, the discourse of custom is far more
explicit. One afternoon when people were gathered at Ilena's house celebrating the fiesta Carnival,
Máxima came over to me where I sat amidst several
other women and said tearfully, "My husband hit
me . . . Am I still black on the side of my face?" Her
left eye was red around the edges and the side of her
face by her temple was purple and black, though
the skin wasn't broken. "When are you going to
Sucre?" she asked me. "I want to go to the city. I
will tell my sons what he did. He kicked me." She
confessed that she had no one else to tell. I had
become close to Máxima, a grandmother of almost
70 years, and her extended family over the past several months, and was deeply troubled by her story.
I agreed to travel with her and glanced to Máxima's
comadre, Roberta (who was sitting right next to
us), to gauge her response. Her head was turned
in the other direction though I thought she could
hear Máxima quite plainly.

"You have to understand it is the custom here,"
said Roberta when I asked her later that evening
if she'd heard what Máxima had said. "It's the
custom. When men are drunk they scold and hit
their women."

"Does [your husband] hit you?"
"Yes," she said. "It's the same with [my husband]."
Roberta's explicit statement to me that a husband's abuse is custom challenged me to acknowledge that Sullk'atas have proper and improper
ways of doing and talking about violence, as well
as accepted ways of being in relationships with
kin and non-kin.[6] Affinal violence is custom when
people are drunk, as Roberta states, but violence

between affines is decidedly *not* customary when people are sober.[7] Although criticism of an affine's actions and expressions of pain may be intertwined with the details of personal circumstances, the general notion that affines may use violence is rarely challenged by Sullk'atas. Sullk'atas recognize that some individuals are more inclined to violence than others, but the more pervasive notion is that violence is associated with particular states (such as drunkenness) and positionalities (such as affinity).

Sexuality and Violence: Marking the Violence of Husbands

Additionally, Sullk'ata women tend to emphasize the violence of their husbands more than the violence of their women affines. The underscoring of spousal conflict may indicate the greater frequency of abuse by husbands or the greater potential for a spouse's violence to inflict harm, whether because of his physical strength or the social and economic consequences that ensue. Although either a woman or man may dissolve a partnership with relative ease early in the relationship, separation is infrequent after a series of rituals and the birth of children. While the intensity and significance of the relationship between a husband and wife tends to increase over time, that between a mother- and daughter-in-law tends to lessen as a woman establishes her own household.

Just as significant, Sullk'atas have access to a greater range of public discourses giving voice to men's violence against women. For instance, in the story-telling, joking, and sexual innuendo that occurs among same-gender groups in Sullk'ata, men and women attach affinal as well as sexual meanings to eating (*mikhuy*) and cooking (*wayk'uy*). As they tease each other, men ask, "Does your wife cook well?" or say to a married but childless man, "Your wife doesn't know how to cook." Cooking is not just about sex but about sexual reproduction in the context of marriage; from this perspective, a husband may also imply that his wife has failed to uphold the sexual and reproductive obligations of affinity when he alleges that she has not cooked for him.

I have also heard women using the verb *to hit* (*maqay*) in suggestive joking. One of the first times I was asked if my husband hit me, I was carrying water with a group of women in order to prepare corn beer for a wedding. I answered seriously, "No, he doesn't."

Another woman, feigning surprise, exclaimed, "Your husband doesn't hit you? Mine does!" to the uproarious laughter of the other women.

That women at once talk and cry about the pain of physical violence inflicted on them by their husbands and joke about the sexuality of hitting, and the violence of sex, points to a complicated relationship between sexuality, affinity, and violence in Sullk'ata. Yet, violence between native Andean spouses is also easily stereotyped. Phrases linking physical violence and love, such as "The more you hit me, the more I love you," (*Más me pegas, más te quiero,* Sp.), are commonly used by urban Spanish speakers to disparage Quechua-speaking campesinos. Of course, assumptions of racial or ethnic otherness obscure the lived realities and complexities of Sullk'ata relationships of gender, sexuality, and affinity.

Likewise, in media representations and development discourses in Bolivia, men's violence against women is emphasized, based on national and transnational ideologies of gender hierarchy that do not take account of local categories of power. In late December 1995, former President Gonzalo Sanchez de Lozada signed Bolivia's Law Against Family Violence (*Ley contra Violencia Familiar*). The law was advertised for months, broadcast in Quechua and Aymara from the regional radio station. One announcement began with a woman screaming and crying and a man yelling in the background. Moments later, the calm (male) voice of a doctor, superimposed upon the drama, states: "I have seen many women come to the clinic with injuries from domestic violence. Now with the Law against Family Violence, women are protected." According to the text of the law, *any* family member, male or female, adult or child, is protected against the abuse of another family or household member (as long as the abuse is reported within 24 hours). These announcements partially obscured the extent of the law's protective power by representing domestic violence as a man's abuse of a woman and by leaving implicit from whom a woman is protected.

The explicit emphasis on gender difference and sexuality in these discourses blurs the significance of affinity to the emergence of violence between spouses and simultaneously conceals the violence that occurs among women in Sullk'ata. Yet women's emphasis on the violence of *husbands* as opposed to other men indicates that affinity is a significant aspect of this violence. For Sullk'atas, a husband occupies a unique positionality; not any man may hit a woman. Violence is rare between unrelated men and women, and relationships characterized by gender difference but not affinity (for example, adult brothers and sisters or comadres and compadres) are marked more by an exaggerated politeness than by violence or aggression. The relationship of affinity between spouses is indicated by the violence itself, as Harvey (1994:84–85) has argued, and by the layers of jokes, folktales, and narratives of personal experiences that support acceptable explanations of violence. The similar justifications given by husbands and mothers-in-law for hitting a woman and the overlapping discourses of drunkenness and custom that normalize affinal violence suggest that gender difference is not a sufficient category of analysis for domestic violence in the region. The relationship between affines is inflected by gendered and racialized asymmetries of power, but affinity is also a category of power and shapes hierarchies among individuals.

SWIRAS AND QHACHUNIS: READING AFFINITY AMONG WOMEN

Thus, further analysis of kinship relationships, in particular relationships among women affines, is necessary to understand the power hierarchies that structure those relationships and the ways in which violence emerges among kin in Sullk'ata. I highlight the relationship between qhachunis and swiras, particularly the asymmetrical exchanges of food and labor through which a qhachuni is integrated into her in-laws' family and the uneven efforts that women undertake to uphold ideals of affection and respect. This further demonstrates the salience of *differences among women* for understanding kinship and illuminates *affinity* as an ethnographic and analytical category necessary to understanding domestic violence in the Andes.

Kinship relationships are forged between a qhachuni and her affines through the same practices—feeding, eating, and working together—that create relatedness among parents and children (Van Vleet 2008). When she marries, a woman moves away from the network of kin with whom she grew up, the familiar pantheon of sacred places, and the material sources through which her body developed. She typically moves into the house of her husband's parents and begins a long process of becoming integrated into his family. Feeding a child is the primary means through which parents symbolically and materially produce relatedness and love and nurturing. Feeding children also establishes hierarchy within the household. In distinction to exchanges of food and labor among adults, in which the return of reciprocal food and labor is expected, kinship between parents and children is the result of "having been fed by others whom one does not oneself feed" (Harvey 1998:75, my translation). Children are dependent on their parents until they establish productive relationships in the community. They are expected to work for their parents and to respect and obey their parents and older siblings. A qhachuni is similarly positioned as a child who is morally obligated to work because she is fed.

Moreover, a swira is the main locus of integration for a qhachuni into her husband's household and community; a young married woman may initially spend far more time with her swira than with her husband. Because of a gender division of labor, a qhachuni accompanies her swira and works for her. A swira makes the most labor demands of her qhachuani, yet the structure of the affinal relationship means that the swira does not reciprocate the time and effort extended by her qhachuni. Through her facility in the kitchen, her willingness to work, her respect for her mother-in-law's authority, and her ability to be sociable and lively, a new daughter-in-law is expected to win the approval and good will of her mother-in-law. Simultaneously, a qhachuni is engaged in the process of becoming an adult, a process which demands her labor be directed outside the household of her in-laws so that she can establish other productive and exchange relationships in the community.

Because the practices that forge bonds of relatedness also manifest the hierarchies between them, swiras and qhachunis navigate ambivalences of affection and authority in their daily interactions. Qhachunis may directly challenge the asymmetrical nature of their labor relationships and the legitimacy of their swira's claims to authority, or use of physical force, by pointing out the fact that the swira is not "true kin" (*parientes legítimos*, Sp.). A qhachuni may contest the asymmetry of her relationship with her mother-in-law by drawing on national and transnational discourses of class and ethnicity and modernity (that emphasize the relative status of speaking Spanish, earning money, being educated, buying consumer goods, and living in the city).[8] Some qhachunis simply refuse to live with their swiras for more than a few months after marriage; others bring attention to their ambiguous position by lamenting their aloneness in times of distress. Most gradually consolidate a position relative to their swiras by securing their relationships with husbands, establishing bonds with their children, and developing more egalitarian labor exchange relationships with other women.

In the Andes, successful kinship relationships are relationships where a hierarchy remains intact, where respect is given to the appropriate individuals (Harvey1994:69). Because the material and affective ties of relatedness are initially tenuous among affines, verbal conflict and outbursts of violence may be triggered as individuals attempt to resolve ambiguities of hierarchy and establish harmonious kinship relationships. Women also recognize that in

their affines' community they have little recourse; there is no one, really, to protect their interests. A mother-in-law's abuse may be checked by her son (as in the case of Claudina's daughter-in-law), or a husband's abuse may be lessened by the presence and intervention of his parents (Harvey 1994:77) or his wife's bothers (Harris 1994:54). Whether or not a husband or swira or brother will support a woman is not clear-cut, and often shaped by the contingencies of situation and the histories of relationships among various individuals. Thus, women in Sullk'ata, swiras and qhachunis, draw on personal experiences and local and national discourses to establish bonds of intimacy and negotiate interpersonal relations at the same time that their talk and actions reproduce hierarchies and normalize conflict among kin, especially along the trajectory of affinity.

CONCLUSION: REFLECTING ON VIOLENCE AND KINSHIP

Attention to the discourses and practices around the violence of affines in Sullk'ata demonstrates that gender discourses and hierarchies alone do not adequately explain the ways that domestic violence ensues. Although gender hierarchy is not an inconsequential aspect of domestic violence in the Andes, kinship obligations and ambiguities of hierarchy and affect significantly shape the ways in which relationships are negotiated and create the conditions for the emergence of violence among individuals. Moreover, examining the violence among women who are related through affinity highlights the ways that domestic violence, which is largely gendered in public discourses and practices, also develops in relationships among same-gendered individuals. Thus the violence among women, though not as frequently acknowledged as violence between husbands and wives, is crucial to a more general understanding of domestic violence in the Andes.

Analyzing violence through the lens of affinity shifts both the meanings and general underpinnings of violence another way. By locating conflict in a network of negotiated yet hierarchical relationships among kin, both violence and kinship may be understood as extending beyond the walls of a singular household, affecting and affected by wider relationships of power. Husbands and wives, mothers- and daughters-in-law, and others who may or may not reside in the same household, are bound by the obligations, opportunities, and expectations of affinity, and kinship more generally. From this perspective, a narrow definition of domestic violence that only incorporates violence between married couples, or those individuals living within the same household, obscures the instances of violence among women affines, the particular histories of events, and the discourses of power that make violence possible in Sullk'ata. Rather than existing in a distinct category (something other than domestic violence), violence between affines in Sullk'ata requires more complicated and expansive notions of both "the domestic" and "domestic violence."

Assumptions about who may be a perpetrator or victim of domestic violence, what actions constitute domestic violence, and whether violence is acceptable or not are intimately tied to unequal relations of power. Expanding the boundaries of the domestic might enable more integrative interpretations of domestic violence that occurs within and across generations, in Sullk'ata and elsewhere. In many localities, legal definitions of domestic abuse incorporate notions of heterosexuality and residency into the formalization of who is protected from whom. Institutions and individuals may see only certain abuses as legitimate, influencing how abuse might be interpreted against wider asymmetries and limiting who might claim harm or gain assistance. The varying constraints under which women and men live, the material, social, and political options that they may access or mobilize, and the ways in which differently positioned individuals may interpret a law in a context of multiple asymmetries of power are significant to an understanding of violence on the ground, yet these contingencies may be obscured by hegemonic discourses on violence.

Conversely, integrating physical violence and interpersonal conflict, as well as social and affective intimacy, into ethnographic accounts of kinship works against the tendency to reduce the strategic interactions and practices of individuals to static structures. Kinship is lived in and through bodies and subjectivities, in the everyday interactions of individuals. Attention to relationships between mothers- and daughters-in-law in Sullk'ata contributes to defining the parameters of relatedness in Sullk'ata. Further attention to the ways siblings and sisters-in-law, mothers- and daughters-in-law, parents and children, and husbands and wives interact with each other, and through these interactions deploy and transform the intimacies and hierarchies of everyday life is required. For not only are power hierarchies constantly reproduced in the interactions of individuals, but also the specific experiences of individuals, the histories of interaction between them, and the situational contexts in which they encounter each other are significant to how relatedness and conflict are played out and interpreted.

Finally, comparing the violence among women affines in Sullk'ata further demonstrates that gender relations and hierarchies are not just about the differences between homogeneous categories of men and women. Gender also extends to the relationships, practices, and interactions that constitute differences *among* men and differences *among* women such that distinctive identities and positions of power are embedded in specific contexts. Women contend with the obligations, unequal exchanges, and ambiguities of affect in affinity as mothers-, sisters- and daughters-in-law. Yet both gender and affinity are experienced and negotiated in different ways depending on age and generation, relationship with spouse, access to resources such as wage work and education, and other factors. Just as gender is not necessarily the only, or the primary, axis of inequality that structures a woman's life at any particular moment, affinity is not the only or necessarily the primary category that shapes the identity and experiences of power asymmetry among affines. Attention to relationships among women and relationships among men may, thus, be fundamental to understanding the ways that power is deployed between women and men in other contexts as well as in Sullk'ata.

Violence in Sullk'ata is culturally embedded and reflects interpersonal negotiations for positioning and power in the context of multiple structured inequalities. In spite of the seemingly universal nature of domestic violence, violence like kinship requires complex and locally relevant modes of interpretation and understanding. In this article, I have broadened the focus on domestic violence to incorporate the webs of power within which women and men find themselves or through which they might actively seek to alter their circumstances. I have brought attention to kinship as lived by people who are sometimes in pain and through relationships that are sometimes fraught with uncertainties. These networks of relationships, and the individual interactions that are implicated, shape events and the ways that interlocutors, including anthropologists, may interpret kinship or violence as lived interactions. Thus, to understand violence and kinship, and to understand the place of each in dynamic relationships that converge in the domestic arena yet extend beyond it, requires detailed analysis of spoken and unspoken meanings, the micropolitics of interactions, and historical structurings of power in particular places at specific moments in time.

REFERENCES CITED

Carsten, Janet, ed. 2000. Cultures of Relatedness: New Approaches to the Study of Kinship. Cambridge, UK: Cambridge University Press.

de la Cadena, Marisol. 1995. "Women are more Indian": Ethnicity and Gender in a Community near Cuzco. In Ethnicity, Markets and Migration in the Andes: At the Crossroads of History and Anthropology. Brooke Larson and Olivia Harris, eds. Pp. 329–348. Durham, NC: Duke University Press.

Harris, Olivia. 1994. Condor and Bull: The Ambiguities of Masculinity in Northern Potosí. In Sex and Violence: Issues in Representation and Experience. Penelope Harvey and Peter Gow, eds. Pp. 40–65. New York: Routledge.

Harvey, Penelope. 1994. Domestic Violence in the Andes. In Sex and Violence: Issues in Representation and Experience. Penelope Harvey and Peter Gow, eds. Pp. 66–89. New York: Routledge.

Rosaldo, Michelle. 1980. The Use and Abuse of Anthropology: Reflections on Feminism and Cross-Cultural Understanding. Signs 5(3):389–417.

Valderrama Fernández, Ricardo, and Carmen Escalante Gutiérrez. 1997. Ser mujer: Warmi kay—La mujer en la cultura andina. In Más allá del silencio: Fronteras de género en los Andes. Vol. 1. Denise Arnold, ed. Pp. 153–170. La Paz, Bolivia: Centre for Indigenous America Studies and Exchange/Instituto de Lengua y Cultura Aymara.

Van Vleet, Krista. 2002. The Intimacies of Power: Rethinking Violence and Affinity in the Bolivian Andes. American Ethnologist 29 (3): 567–601.

———. 2008. Performing Kinship: Narrative, Gender, and the Intimacies of Power in the Andes. Austin: University of Texas Press.

Weismantel, Mary J. 1988. Food, Gender, and Poverty in the Ecuadorian Andes. Philadelphia: University of Pennsylvania Press.

NOTES

1. My emphasis on affinity does not seek to supplant scholarship that has emphasized gender as a category of analysis of domestic violence and men's violence against women as both symptom and foundation of gender hierarchy. However, collapsing relationships of affinity into a notion of gender opposition weakens the analytic force of affinity and confines gender as an analytic category to a binary opposition between homogeneous categories of men and women.
2. The original article (Van Vleet 2002) includes analysis of conflicts between women and their sisters-in-law as well as their husbands and mothers-in-law.
3. Complementarity emphasizes married partners as ideally equal and opposite parts of a whole. This symbolic ideal is linked to the gender division of labor so that women and men take on different kinds of labor within households and communities.
4. This and all subsequent names are pseudonyms.
5. Even in the shadow of an event, an affine's violence may seem less problematic than living without that person or cut off from the network of encompassing relationships of kinship in Sullk'ata. Women may not be prepared to denounce their abusers: they may not have alternative places to live or means of economic and emotional support, conceive of life outside of

marriage as a viable possibility, or trust the adequacy of the protection of the state. Women may face gendered, racial and class stereotypes, and language, literacy, and financial barriers if they turn to state authorities.

6. At the time, Roberta's display of indifference surprised me though it reflects the more typical Sullk'ata reaction to physical violence in the context of drinking. The disjunctures between my attitude and those of my Sullk'ata companions also reflects the ways my own deep-seated cultural assumptions—about love in marriage and the stigma associated with being a victim of abuse—became entangled with their very different sets of assumptions and material conditions through the contingencies of fieldwork.

7. The one incident of violence that I heard of between a husband and wife that occurred when both were sober was met with horrified exclamations and discussion of the man's improper upbringing.

8. Of course, a swira may also reverse national discourses of ethnicity and class that stigmatize native Andeans, and instead disparage a qhachuni who is "beautiful" and "white," who does not know how to work or to be sociable with other women (Valderrama et al. 1997:167).

2 • *Kimberly Theidon*

RECONSTRUCTING MASCULINITIES
The Disarmament, Demobilization, and Reintegration of Former Combatants in Colombia

DISCUSSION QUESTIONS

1. Why did men join the guerillas and paramilitary groups? How does the "war mask" reflect the "militarized masculinity" they have learned?
2. How does the prevalence of violence in Colombia (re)shape relations between men and women?
3. How does attention to gender, especially the production of "militarized masculinities," provide a more nuanced understanding of the challenges of the DDR and transitional justice programs in Colombia analyzed by Theidon?

INTRODUCTION

A key component of peace processes and post-conflict reconstruction is the disarmament, demobilization and reintegration (DDR) of ex-combatants. According to the World Bank, in 2005, over one million former combatants were participating in DDR programs in some twenty countries around the world. Traditional approaches to DDR have focused almost exclusively on military and security objectives, which has resulted in these programs being developed in relative isolation from the growing field of transitional justice and its concerns with historical clarification, justice, reparations and reconciliation. Similarly, evaluations of DDR programs have tended to be technocratic exercises concerned with tallying the number of weapons collected and combatants enrolled. By reducing

DDR to "dismantling the machinery of war," these programs have failed to adequately consider how to move beyond demobilizing combatants to facilitating social reconstruction and coexistence.[1]

Drawing upon my ongoing research with former combatants in Colombia, I want to extend these arguments. I am convinced that successful reintegration not only requires fusing the processes and goals of disarmament, demobilization and reintegration programs with transitional justice measures, but that both DDR and transitional justice require a gender analysis that includes an examination of the salient links between weapons, masculinities and violence in specific historical contexts. Constructing certain forms of masculinity is not incidental to militarism: rather, it is essential to its maintenance. Militarism requires a sustaining gender ideology as much as it does guns and bullets.

An abridged version of Kimberly Theidon, 2009. "Reconstructing Masculinities: The Disarmament, Demobilization, and Reintegration of Former Combatants in Colombia." *Human Rights Quarterly* 31:1 (2008), 1–34. © 2009, The Johns Hopkins University Press. Abridged by the author and reprinted with permission of Johns Hopkins University Press.

And yet, what has it meant to "add gender" to disarmament, demobilization and reintegration programs? In gender hearings, gender units and gender-sensitive truth commissions, "adding gender" is policy-speak for "adding women." The powerful insights that gender studies might offer to our theoretical and practical understanding of war, peace and post-conflict reconstruction is limited by reducing gender to a synonym for women. Consequently, men and masculinities are left largely unexplored, reminding us that "Research on men is as old as scholarship itself, but a focus on masculinity, or men as explicitly gendered individuals, is relatively recent."[2]

What might it mean to "add gender" to DDR and transitional justice processes if one defined gender to include men and masculinities, thus making these forms of identity explicitly visible and a focus of research and intervention? My research in Colombia has been driven in part by a desire to understand how violent forms of masculinity are forged and sustained, and how DDR programs might more effectively "disarm masculinity" following armed conflict. I am interested in militarized masculinity—that fusion of certain practices and images of maleness with the use of weapons, the exercise of violence, and the performance of an aggressive and frequently misogynist masculinity. While I do not deny the diversity that exists within the group of former combatants with whom I work, neither can I deny the hegemonic masculinity these men have in common.

This article focuses on a cultural and political economy of militarized masculinity, addressing how little access these former combatants have to civilian symbols of masculine prestige. I analyze the "technique du corps" that produce the body and bearing of a soldier among men whose bodily capital may be their only marketable asset. In considering the practices used to produce violent masculinities, I explore the role of both men and women in constructing masculinities, underscoring the relational aspects of all gendered identities. I conclude by considering how one might "add gender" to the DDR program in Colombia as one

important step toward successful reintegration, peace-building, and sustainable social change.

COLOMBIA: A "PRE POST-CONFLICT" COUNTRY

Colombia's civil war is the lengthiest armed conflict in the western hemisphere. What began forty-two years ago as a war waged by Marxist revolutionaries against an exclusive political system has devolved into a bloody struggle over resources: military, paramilitary, guerillas, domestic elites and multinational actors vie for control of this resource-rich country. In the struggle, all groups have committed serious human rights violations. The vast majority of the war casualties are unarmed civilians, and the escalating violence and fear for one's life have prompted massive internal and cross-border displacement.[3] In addition, thousands more have been kidnapped, disappeared, tortured and forcefully recruited by illegally armed groups, among other grave violations of fundamental rights. In sum, the war in Colombia has resulted in a humanitarian crisis provoking international concern, as various armed groups commit serious human rights violations and demonstrate their disregard for international humanitarian law.

Among the armed groups that are of particular interest to our discussion of demobilization processes are the Fuerzas Armadas Revolucionarias de Colombia (FARC), the Ejército de Liberación Nacional (ELN) and the Auto-Defensas Unidas de Colombia (AUC), commonly referred to as the paramilitaries. Although promoted as "self-defense committees" founded to protect local communities against the guerrillas, they came to assume greater responsibility in state-organized "search and destroy" operations seeking to eliminate the guerrillas. The use of paramilitaries as auxiliary forces assumed a central place in the government's counterinsurgency plan. It was the fusion of paramilitary organizations and drug trafficking that gave rise to the phenomenon known as *paramilitarismo*—the transformation of paramilitary groups into an economic, social, and political force—an institution—that has infiltrated Colombian society. For some, *paramilitarismo* is a policy of state terrorism, while for others it is the response of desperate citizens confronted with guerrilla abuses due to an absent state.[4]

DISARMAMENT, DEMOBILIZATION AND REINTEGRATION: COLOMBIA'S SERIAL SEARCH FOR PEACE

In the glossary of post-conflict reconstruction and peace building, three terms are omnipresent: disarmament, demobilization and reintegration. According to the United Nations Department of Peacekeeping Operations, *disarmament* consists of the collection, control and elimination of small arms, ammunition, explosives, and light and heavy weapons from the combatants and, depending upon the circumstances, the civilian population. *Demobilization* is the process in which armed organizations (which may consist of government or opposition forces, or simply armed factions) decrease in size or are dismantled as one component of a broad transformation from a state of war to a state of peace. *Reintegration* consists of those measures directed toward ex-combatants that seek to strengthen the capacity of these individuals and their families to achieve social and economic reintegration in society. Reintegration programs may include economic assistance or some other form of monetary compensation, as well as technical or professional training or instruction in other productive activities.[5]

In its traditional formulation—and implementation—DDR was squarely located within a military or security framework. This focus failed to give sufficient consideration to the host communities, and to the need to consider local, cultural or gendered conceptions of what constitutes the rehabilitation and re-socialization of ex-combatants. The UN underscores the deficiency of reintegration efforts and insists on "the need for measures to be conducted

in consultation and collaboration with all members of the community and stakeholders engaged in the community, and that [DDR programs] make use of locally-appropriate development incentives."[6]

By the presidential elections of 2002, an increasing number of Colombians demanded change. The debacle of past peace processes readied many sectors of Colombian society for someone who would take a "heavy-handed" approach to the violence, such as President Alvaro Uribe, who cautiously explored the possibility of negotiating with the paramilitaries, while simultaneously promising to rein in the guerrillas. In August 2002, the government began negotiations with the paramilitaries. The Uribe government promoted the demobilization of individual combatants from all armed groups, and began negotiations for the collective demobilization of the AUC. The signing of the *Santa Fe de Ralito I* agreement marked the beginning of formal talks between the AUC-linked paramilitary groups and the government and included the demobilization of all combatants by the end of 2005. The negotiations also obligated the AUC to suspend its lethal activities and maintain the unilateral ceasefire, as well as aid the government in its anti drug-trafficking efforts.[7] Since 2002, 30,151 AUC combatants have collectively demobilized, and almost 10,000 combatants from the FARC, ELN and certain paramilitary bloques have individually demobilized.

METHODS

Since January 2005 I have been conducting anthropological research on the individual and collective demobilization programs. The first stage of the project included in-depth interviews with demobilized combatants in order to determine where to focus my case studies. To date my research assistant and I have interviewed 137 male and 33 female ex-combatants from the AUC, the FARC and the ELN. In methodological terms, I believe the utility of questionnaires is limited when studying sensitive topics and subjective processes in a climate of great distrust. I have opted to complement semi-structured interviews with a sustained presence, and to converse and observe rather than limit myself to formal interviews. I have used an ethnographic approach in the hope of moving beyond the black and white of statistics to explore the grey zone that characterizes the complex realities of a fratricidal war.

IN SEARCH OF RESPECT[8]

I had my first conversation with a member of the paramilitaries in the summer of 2001, several years before the demobilization process began. A friend from the Diócesis of Apartadó knew I was interested in speaking with members of the AUC, and mentioned that Vladimiro, a childhood friend, had joined and might be willing to speak with me.

Throughout the course of our three-hour conversation, Vladimiro inspired both revulsion and pity. He had completed his obligatory year of military service and found himself discharged to join the swelling population of the unemployed. After spending a few months unemployed, he decided to respond to a recruiting poster for the AUC displayed on the wall of his local store. I had to ask him to say this again, stunned that the allegedly illegal paramilitaries actually recruited via flyers at a local store. "Oh yeah, they even have a website where you can go on and read all about the AUCs."

In the midst of staggering unemployment, Vladimiro signed on at 450,000 pesos a month—roughly $225 in a country where minimum wage was scarcely more than $100. He kept returning to this theme, telling me repeatedly that there was no work in Apartadó. However, now that he had joined the paramilitaries, *Everyone treats me with respect, It's not like it was before.* When I walk down the street, people move out of my way. Now I can send my mom 350,000 pesos a month—she's doing all right now. I even saved up and bought my mom a house."

At the paramilitary's "educational camp," he reviewed weapons, learned to interrogate, learned how to kill, and learned about human rights. My eyebrows rose in disbelief: "Human rights? They taught you about human rights?"

"Yeah," he nodded. "They told us that when we're going to kill everyone in a village, we need to kill them one by one over a period of a few days. If we kill everyone all at once, they call it a massacre and we have problems with human rights." I could not hold back a grimace. He leaned forward: "We were forced to take very drastic action. An order is an order."

About two hours into our conversation—after he had explained that it was necessary to "finish off everyone, because if one guerilla falls, there are five more behind him just waiting to kill you"—he paused and began telling me about the cold side of the mountains, the lack of food, and the close friend who died at his side. "A tear escaped me when I saw him die. I risk my life for 450,000 pesos a month. Friends die and you can't do anything."

I had been so focused on Vladimiro that I had only looked away when my tape recorder clicked at the end of each cassette. Somehow I now turned toward my friend Jefferson who was slumped on the bed, holding his head between his slender hands. I think he had been sitting that way for some time, and he remained in that position until I finished talking with Vladimiro. After Vladimiro left, Jefferson shook his head. "I've known him since we were kids. We used to play soccer together—we went to the same school. We grew up together."

One component of the political and cultural economy of violent masculinities that interests me is the complex motivations these men had for joining the armed groups in which they fought. Social mobility is one such motivation. The absolute majority of these men come from poor backgrounds: for some of the young men, joining the guerrilla meant they had food, a gun, and a uniform. For those who joined the paramilitaries, the above benefits were supplemented with a monthly wage. In the complex scenario of violence that characterizes Colombia, cycling through an armed group is a rite of passage for many young men. In a context of generalized violence, the proliferation of criminal networks, a limited legal labor market, and a cultural economy that fuses weapons, masculinity and power, grabbing a gun is not necessarily an aberration.

Indeed, for members of the poorest social classes, a pervasive "gun culture" blurs the line between combat zone and homefront. In our conversations with demobilized combatants, we made a point of asking why they had joined. For ex-combatants from the FARC or ELN, the primary reasons given for joining were: via an acquaintance who convinced the person to join (21%); because they lived in a zone controlled by an armed group and entering the ranks was quasi-"natural" (36%); recruited by force or threat (9%); or economic motivations (9%). With ex-combatants of the AUC, their principal reasons for joining were: via an acquaintance who convinced the person to join (29%); because they lived in a zone under paramilitary control and joining was "just what you did" (17%); recruited by force or threat (14%); or economic motivations (27%). If we combine "lived in a zone controlled by an armed group" with "entered via an acquaintance," we see that these young people grew up in contexts in which alternatives to war were almost invisible.

It is also worth noting that these former combatants live with images of a "militarized masculinity"—both the men and the women. One goal of the DDR process should be "demilitarizing" the models of masculinity that these men and women have, particularly when these men have so little access to civilian symbols of masculine prestige, such as education, legal income, or decent housing. I emphasize both the men and the women because this militarized masculinity is part of a performance, and the audience is comprised not only of the other men, but also the young women who seek out these *gran hombres* (big men) as desirable partners in an economy of war.

GENDERING SECURITY

I am not the first researcher to argue that justice and security are "private goods" in Colombia; clearly the state has failed miserably in both areas. However, in addition to the privatization of security, I want to consider how security itself is gendered and with what consequences. As I would learn during my years of research, the level of sexual violence in those communities was staggering. Thus I began to question whose security and at what price? Communal agreements implied certain sexual agreements, and security was a gendered good. In some communities with which I worked, sex became commodified as women began selling sex. Far more common, however, was rape. Communal "security" worked in contradictory ways. Guns—and the men who use them—are both a threat *and* a source of security in a highly violent environment.

Many of the former combatants with whom I work fear reprisals from members of their group who are still active. Moreover, these former combatants do not just fear for themselves: they fear reprisals against the loved ones they are committed to protecting. Revenge for the death of family members was another motivation in the life histories of these men, and retribution figures strongly in their conceptions of justice. Laying down their weapons presents many of these young men with a conundrum: surrender their guns and trust the police to protect them, and in turn determine how they will protect their families in the event that armed actors come looking for them. While some of the former combatants stoically accepted the possibility of their own deaths, they were not as stoic when considering possible murder of partners, parents, or children. As I was frequently told, "I was trained for this, but they weren't. If someone comes looking for me, I'll defend my family—they don't have any training for this sort of shit."

Security is one reason that women seek these men out. In 2007, during one of my visits to the *comunas* in Medellín, I spent the afternoon talking with a group of former combatants, their mothers, and their girlfriends, none of whom carried a weapon.

I was able to talk with some of the young men alone as we stood in the middle of a small park they were building for their children. I asked them if they felt safe. One young man nodded and answered on behalf of the group. "We have protection at home. We keep some protection in the house just in case something happens."

Guns in the house for protection. The irony warrants further comment. "Family" is one of the primary reasons these former combatants demobilized. Family draws them back, yet it may also become another site of violence. Being a "good man" includes protecting and providing for one's family; thus, setting down one's weapon may be emasculating in several senses. So they hide their guns in the house "just in case."

However, the fantasy of family frequently conflicts with the reality of returning to one's partner and children, contributing to a "domestication of violence" following war. One enduring impact of the militarization of daily life and the forging of militarized masculinities is an increase in domestic violence, a phenomenon noted in many postconflict settings. Thus the "public" security these men provide may force women to accept a great deal of abuse in their personal lives. Indeed, one constant concern among the staff I interviewed at the DDR shelters was how to address the high level of domestic violence that occurs. Certainly this will require structural changes—for example, a state that can fulfill its obligation in terms of providing security and justice, a viable legal labor market, and poverty reduction—but it will also require changes in the hegemonic masculinity these men perform and the women desire.

"YOUR OWN BODY BETRAYS YOU"

In addition to carrying a weapon and strutting around like a "big man," militarized masculinity has other important components. With very few exceptions, each interview begins with the "war mask," their "paramilitary face," a face that explicitly seeks to inspire terror in others, and is one tenacious trace of their participation in an armed group. However, the war face is certainly not limited to the paramilitaries. As a former member of the FARC told me during a conversation outside of Bogotá, "It's an expression of machismo." I assumed this was something unconscious, the result of being surrounded by other combatants. It was

Mario, however, who explained how they are trained to use their bodies because "It's the body itself that can betray you."

"Mario, there is something that really strikes me. It's how you learn to look at people . . . you sometimes start to do it with me, no? It's sort of funny—so many years learning how because your survival might depend on being harder than the next guy. You were telling me how you learn to use your body, your face . . . wait—you're doing it again right now."

"A defiant look?"

"Exactly. The war face."

"Yeah, because I remember the police stopping me so many times in the street. They kept asking me if I was a soldier. I said no, but they would keep insisting—asking if I had done my service . . . If the enemy grabs me and is interviewing me, I have to show firmness. Let's say a military guy is interviewing me, a military psychologist is sitting across from me—he'll play a lot with my *mirada* [look]. I have to show him firmness in my look—they trained me for that when I was out there [in the FARC]. For example, I received that kind of training—they teach you this. The first thing you are going to do when you greet a soldier [*un militar*] is give him a firm look. You never lower your eyes because if you lower your eyes he's going to immediately wonder what you're hiding . . . So they [FARC] teach you how to look, how to use your face. I had to deal with this so many times."

"This is so interesting. I didn't know you learned this—So they really teach you how to look, how to hold your body?"

He nodded. "In the intelligence courses—that's where they teach you these things. If you have to deal with a member of the military, get it into your head that you are not a guerrilla but a soldier. So you learn that and with practice you learn. So when you are seated with a military psychologist—well, they really study bodily expression, no? So you really get trained in this. I know that from the first moment you need to know how to defend yourself. You have to know how to express yourself, and they train you for that."

Once again his face changed. All animation drained from his face and the mask appeared again.

"Oh Mario—that face is back!"

He shook his head. "So many times I give myself away by that. I mean now—I give myself away . . . It's just that you receive so much training *and se mentaliza tanto en eso, realmente hasta usted se convence de las mentiras* [they 'mentalize' you in that really, until you are convinced by the lies]. But it's so difficult later for you to remake yourself in civil society."

"I hadn't thought about that, but it makes sense."

"Of course. Physical ability is when you realize—lots of people get fingered for that. Oh, you've got to be careful when they train you how to march. They call that *orden cerrado*, and it's whether you turn out to the left or the right. In the army, in the police, they always turn and stamp with the right foot. In the guerrilla, the FARC, it's with the left. So you—you're just a *muchacho* maybe and don't even know what's going on. They keep giving you the order, over and over. If you turn left—'Ah, he's not military'."

"So that must be why you told me the body itself can betray a person?" Mario nodded. "It betrays you because it's mechanized. Your body is mechanized."

"Mario, can someone learn to lose this? I mean, so the person demobilizes. Can they unlearn the things they were trained to do?"

"Sure, but they need to start. Therapy will always be a part of it. It's a huge therapy, working. But yeah, you have to leave behind the traces, return to being a civilian. And it's practice—it's daily life."

I have come to think of these muchachos I have interviewed as "untouchables": they have learned to be hard and impenetrable, both physically and emotionally. However, what served them well as combatants does not translate well into civilian life. In militarizing themselves they have also attempted to limit the range of emotions to those best suited to the combat zone. Emotions, of course, are also gendered, and gaining access to a wider range of emotions is also a component of demilitarizing

these men. One way to open up space for alternative masculinities to emerge is by assisting these men in accessing a full range or emotions beyond those that made them "combat ready." I am convinced that one reason these former combatants have been so willing to speak with me is that they can "let down their guard," at least for a few hours. Thus an important component of the reintegration process must include corporeal and sentimental re-education.

And once again, I think of the women. How might we resignify what it means to be "*verraco*"— virile and desirable? The following conversation provides some ideas of the challenges to doing so, and perhaps some ideas of where one might begin.

I had a long conversation with a former combatant from the FARC who was staying at a shelter in Medellín. I had asked him about the role of women in the guerrilla, and he thought for a moment before responding.

"In the group, a woman—well, she's practically not a woman, because she's just one more combatant. I mean, the women do the same work—it's not as though it's individualized like the women are more delicate so they can't do this or that—everyone's equal. So women lose their femininity and . . . well, it's like in the society in general—not just out there. Men are really *machista* with women, always exploiting them sexually. Part of it's the man's fault, part of it's the woman's because the women '*se relajan*' ['get relaxed,' as in loosening up their morals] out there [in the group]. The guys are thinking about women a lot because every guerrillero wants to get himself a '*socia*' to be with him, sleep with him, you know. And so the women—well, the women really become prostitutes because they start out . . . first with one guy in one bed, then the next night another one, another night another bed. When their *compañero* is on a mission, they get together with someone else— that's how it happens."

"But Mario—tell me something. Do the women get together with men to protect themselves? I ask because some of the women have told me they look at, say, the *commandante* and think to themselves that there is a man who can protect her from the rest of them. So there's a kind of logic to it. I don't know, but I wonder if that is part of it?"

Mario nodded his head emphatically. "Inside [the group], well, that's another role that society has sold us on. Society has filled women's heads with the idea that they're the weaker sex."

"Hmmm, that is the message, isn't it?"

"Yeah," he replied. "But look—this isn't just in the guerrilla. You see this everywhere in the barrios. Let's say a guy has a motorcycle, a gun—that's the guy the girls are looking for. Now, let's take the guy who goes out every day, he takes his lunch with him, he goes to work and from work he goes back home. Maybe he even finds the time to study. Ah! That guy is a joke, a fool! He's not like the guy who walks up and down with his gun, rides around on his motorcycle. The women like that guy—he's got power and can take care of her."

"I think you're right, Mario. That's part of what needs to change because the women also participate in all of this."

"Yeah. Absolutely! You can't just lay the blame on the men or on the women—they're both guilty here."

In his analysis of gender and war, Goldstein notes that women often actively participate in facilitating men's militarized masculinity.[9] Mario eloquently demonstrates how this works both in the guerrilla and in the low-income barrios in which these men and women live and provides insight into the gendered double standard that belies the guerrillas' discourse of equality. Former combatants from the FARC and ELN—both men and women—would frequently begin by assuring me that everyone is treated equally in the armed group, and then proceed to give innumerable examples of gender bias. Female ex-combatants spoke at length about forced abortions, sexual harassment, and other forms of gender discrimination they had experienced and witnessed. Similarly, male ex-combatants would assure me that equality was the norm, and then proceed to discuss how their female comrades had been sexually promiscuous.

Thus "adding gender" to DDR programs should include examining the stereotypes that former combatants articulate and that DDR programs may unintentionally perpetuate about men and women, masculinity and femininity. In the shelters and *fincas* I visited, staff told me the "women are more problematic," referring to the female ex-combatants. They were described as emotionally needy, disruptive, sexually promiscuous, and prone to fighting. While I do think women may well have *different* problems than the male ex-combatants, but I am not convinced they are "more problematic" per se! The figure of the "combatant" has been so over-determined that gender has simply been shoved into the background. To be a combatant was to be male and thus "gender" was not an issue. I turn now to a discussion of how DDR programs might benefit from making masculinities visible and thus more amenable to discussion and transformation.

"ADDING GENDER" TO DDR: RECONSTRUCTING MASCULINITIES

The need for structural reforms in Colombia is clear, and those reforms are admittedly beyond the mandate of a DDR program, or transitional justice in its narrow "transition to liberal democracy" guise. However, this does not mean that nothing can be done, nor that the material always trumps the ideological or cultural, (mis)understood as separate realms. Thus my recommendations focus on what could be incorporated into the existing DDR program. The incentives to remain a "civilian" will need to include a combination of economic benefits and a change in attitudes. I think there are several ways to approach the attitudinal issue, moving between the individual, the family, the broader community and the Colombia state.

As I previously mentioned, family was a key theme in the conversations I have had with these former combatants. Despite the contradictions, the (perhaps idealized) image of *la familia* could be a point of departure for discussing new ways of caring for, providing for, and protecting loved ones.

Being around to participate in raising one's children and seeing them grow into adulthood is a powerful incentive. At one of the collective demobilization ceremonies in Apartadó, when small children went running across the soccer field to throw their arms around the men standing in rows before piles of discarded weapons, I heard several of the children say, "Papa, stay with me and don't ever go back to *el monte*." Family offers a key incentive to remain a civilian, but it must be a site in which the DDR program intervenes to script new possibilities.

Unfortunately, the DDR program perpetuates gender stereotypes. Where there are "*nucleos familiares*," I watched the mealtime routines and daily interaction. It is the women who prepare the meals and care for the children while the men participate in the various program requirements—which include educational and vocational training, thus reinforcing a patriarchal "family unit" with marked, gendered division of labor. Additionally, the designated beneficiary of the program is the demobilized combatant; should he or she repeatedly fail to abide by the rules of the DDR program, they can be expelled and their monthly stipend terminated. This is a powerful disincentive for battered partners to report abuse; a female partner who is financially dependent on a former combatant may find herself forced to choose between his monthly allowance or another beating. This is just one of many examples of the ways in which DDR programs, as they are currently designed, fail to consider the unintended consequences of their policies and remain remarkably gender blind.

Additionally, most of these men were not taught how to be loving partners or fathers. Several commented to me how difficult it was to suddenly find themselves living with crying babies and female partners who want more than the *socia* role. The idealized image of family may contrast sharply with the reality of living together, and the tensions this provokes frequently turn violent. These men and their families would benefit from family counseling that examines the violent patterns of interaction these men have learned, situating that violent

behavior within broader structures of inequality that include not only gender but also class, ethnicity and race.

These suggestions will require additional training for the staff in the DDR program. Many of the people staffing the program share a similar background with the men and women enrolled in the DDR process, and at times I was uncertain who was staff and who was a former combatant. While this background allows them to establish credibility with the former combatants, they may well share the same sort of gendered double standard that is one of the problems that must be addressed. Working on "gender issues" requires increasing awareness of how gendered relations involved power differentials that may not change simply because male combatants lay down their weapons.

Additionally, the shelters, *fincas* and CROs are heteronormative environments in which the men continue to "jockey" for position. Part of this jockeying includes aggressive male behavior and a continued devaluation of characteristics considered "feminine." Where is there "refuge" from the hegemonic masculinity they have learned? Most telling was a conversation in Medellín with an ex-combatant from the FARC. The young man did not want me to tape anything or even take notes. We spoke for about an hour before I could tell he was working himself up to reveal a big secret. And what was it? Not the training, killing, combat—no, his big secret was that he was gay and that he could not let anyone know. "They don't put up with that in the group—no way. And here?" He laughed bitterly and rolled his eyes. Thus, opening space for alternative masculinities is something the DDR program could do.

Moreover, I recall Jefferson, the young man who brought his paramilitary friend to speak with me. Where are the young men who are not involved in violence? They practice an alternative masculinity, and it would be important to find out how they have managed to do so. Did Jefferson's involvement in an active diocese of the Catholic Church allow him to construct and maintain a non-violent identity? Where are the other social spaces in which violence is not a central component in the construction of manhood? How might the DDR program make these young men and their non-violent options more visible, valued and desirable?

CONCLUSIONS

I began by suggesting that both DDR programs and transitional justice initiatives could benefit from exploring the ways in which militarized men are produced and militarized masculinities performed. This exploration could in turn inform strategies designed to actively reconstruct what it means to be a man in particular historical and social contexts. As Butler has argued, gender is not only a social construct, but a performance as well—less a state of being than a process of becoming.[10] This process is continuous, disrupting the linear, teleological narratives of both DDR and the field of transitional justice.

Addressing violent masculinities should be a key concern when "adding gender" to these interventions. A focus on violent masculinities could in turn bring into focus the daily forms of violence that escape the limited time frame of a "transition," and extend our scope of concern to the forms of violence that fall outside what is narrowly defined as "political." These daily forms of harm—what I refer to as the "post-violence violence" that characterizes periods euphemistically labelled post-conflict—have been located "outside" the standard transitional justice framework. Yet, these forms of violence that escalate dramatically in the wake of war, and the failure to dismantle the gender regimes that were forged in conflict settings allows them to remain woefully intact during times of "peace." Security itself is a gendered good. For the millions of girls and women who reap so little from the proverbial "peace dividend," transforming boys and men could help separate out violence from masculinity, security from wielding a gun or seeking out a man who does.

It is an anthropological maxim that masculinities and femininities are culturally constructed and variable. I foreground that here: what is constructed can be transformed. This will require an interdisciplinary approach that brings the tools of psychology, political science, anthropology and economics to bear in analyzing locally and regionally salient notions of gender and violence. Transforming the hegemonic, militarized masculinities that characterize these former combatants could help further the goals of both DDR and transitional justice processes. By doing so, "adding gender" might contribute to building peace on both the battlefield and the homefront.

NOTES

1. Amnesty Int'l, The Paramilitaries in Medellín: Demobilization or Legalization? Ai Index: Amr 23/019/2005 2 (2005).
2. Scott Coltrane, Theorizing Masculinities in Contemporary Social Science. In Theorizing Masculinities 41 (Harry Brod and Michael Kaufman, eds., 1994).
3. Charles Berquist et al., eds. Violence in Colombia, 1990–2001: Waging War and Practicing Peace (2001).
4. Daniel Jaramillo García-Peña, La Relación Del Estado Colombiano Con El Fenómeno Paramillitar: Por El Esclarecimiento Histórico, 59 Análisis Político (2005) [author's translation].
5. United Nations Department of Peacekeeping Operations, Disarmament, Demobilization And Reintegration of Ex-Combatants in a Peacekeeping Environment: Principles and Guidelines (1999).
6. United Nations Integrated Disarmament, Demobilization and Reintegration Standards, Ii.2.4 (2006).
7. Amnesty Int'l, Supra Note 2, at 8.
8. I borrow this title from Philippe Bourgois' book on street culture, drug dealing and masculinity in East Harlem. See Philippe Bourgois, In Search of Respect: Selling Crack in El Barrio (1995).
9. Joshua S. Goldstein, War and Gender: How Gender Shapes the War System and Vice Versa (2001), 306.
10. Judith Butler, Gender Trouble: Feminism and the Subversion of Identity (1990).

3 • *Lynn Stephen*

THE CONSTRUCTION OF INDIGENOUS SUSPECTS

Militarization and the Gendered and Ethnic Dynamics of Human Rights Abuses in Southern Mexico

DISCUSSION QUESTIONS

1. How does Stephen's ethnography help her to analyze the gendered and ethnic patterns of militarization and torture in southern Mexico?
2. How is gender central to the perpetration of this violence by the military and its experience by indigenous people?

INTRODUCTION

Analyses of political change in Mexico offer an enthusiastic assessment of the country's transition to democracy through permitting political opposition and through the strength and variety of social movements that have come to be known as civil society. My own research reveals a fundamental contradiction in Mexico's transition to democracy: a political opening accompanied by increased militarization of Mexican society and accompanying human rights abuses. I use the tools of ethnography to analyze the gendered and ethnic patterns of militarization and torture in southern Mexico. Such patterns replay gendered and sexual stereotypes of indigenous men and women as captured in national myth and vision.

In the low-intensity war being carried on in southern Mexico, the militarization of communities and the arrest and torture of indigenous people and their construction as guerrilla suspects operate through figurations of gender and indigenous ethnicity. The scripts of current militarization indirectly replay crucial colonial and postcolonial tropes such as that of La Malinche (who served as translator for Cortéz) and the Virgen of Guadalupe (Patron Saint of Mexico). Since the arrival in 1519 of Cortes and his troops in what is now Mexico, the subjugation of indigenous identity, the feminization of indigenous men through domination by other men, and the conquest of indigenous women and men through sexual assault and coercion have been standard practices of militarization. The empowerment and accompanying masculinization of

An abridged version of Lynn Stephen, 1999. "The Construction of Indigenous Suspects: Militarization and the Gendered and Ethnic Dynamics of Human Rights Abuses in Southern Mexico." Reproduced by permission of the American Anthropological Association and of the author from *American Ethnologist*, Volume 26, Issue 4, Pages 822–842, November 1999. Not for sale or further reproduction.

military and paramilitary men through feminiza-tion and sexualization of their victims is, unfortu-nately, a common colonial and postcolonial theme. What makes such continuing practices in Mexico interesting in the 21st century is not only their perseverance through the last 500 years, but their continued existence in a modern state that publicly maintains it has made the transition to a democ-racy and has become a multi-cultural nation.

The militarization of Mexican society through the integration of police and army units has had its counterpart in the emergence of armed gue-rilla movements. The Popular Revolutionary Army (EPR) first appeared in June 1996, in Aguas Blan-cas, Guerrero, one year after 17 peasant activists were gunned down in the same spot by state police. During 1996, 1997, and 1998, the EPR carried out a series of coordinated armed attacks against the Mexican Army and public security forces in the states of Guerrero, Oaxaca, Puebla, Mexico, Tabasco, and Mexico City. The other major move-ment is the Zapatista Army of National Liberation (EZLN), which made its debut on January 1, 1994, on the first day of the implementation of the North American Free Trade Agreement (NAFTA). The EZLN engaged in 12-day armed conflict with the Mexican military and then pushed for national leg-islation which would promote a broad set of indig-enous rights. When these efforts failed to produce real political and economic power for indigenous communities, the EZLN focused instead on estab-lishing autonomous communities in Chiapas with locally and regionally controlled systems of gover-nance, justice, education, health, and farming. As indigenous peoples in Oaxaca and Chiapas pushed for rights, their territories were militarized.

Increasingly, integrated operations carried out by various police units and the Mexican army combine what are often called "drug searches" with counter-insurgency. In such operations, profiles are developed of those suspected of participating in armed illegal activity. In the two case studies of militarization and human rights abuses in Oaxaca and Chiapas (below), the suspects are primarily indigenous men and women suspected of partici-pating in either the EZLN or the EPR.

MILITARIZATION AND HUMAN RIGHTS ABUSES IN OAXACA AND CHIAPAS

The most important aspect of the militarization of Mexican society has been the concentration of federal, state, and local police forces under the command of the army. In regions like southern Oaxaca and eastern Chiapas, a strategy of low-intensity war has emerged as the dominant model. The long-term engagement of the Mexican army in Chiapas, Oaxaca, and elsewhere has required the introduction of other forms of military control. In many parts of Chiapas where the army regularly carried out patrols on road networks they had built or improved, the Public Security Police now op-erates. The Public Security Police use army vehi-cles, weapons, and tactics but have blue uniforms instead of green. The extension of the domains of Public Security Police and Federal Judicial Police as well as their integration with the army has al-lowed for increased military coverage. This permits the army to concentrate operations in the most inaccessible parts of Chiapas and Oaxaca, usually by establishing permanent residence in rural indig-enous communities.

With roadblocks and permanent bases the army has established itself geographically in cen-tral spaces as a large and public presence. These permanent and mobile roadblocks force people to incorporate the army and police into their daily geographies of work and travel. The army has also established its presence through daily local patrols that pass through communities, on their perim-eters, and in people's fields. Moreover, the army has established barracks that are within the boundar-ies of communities, often taking over community lands without permission.

The primary targets of these strategies of mili-tarization are indigenous communities in Chiapas and Oaxaca. The fundamental result of the militarization of these regions is that local indigenous communities are forced to adjust to the lifestyles and consumption habits of thousands of young Mexican men in the army and police living in their midst. Perhaps of greater importance is the self-censorship and fear that has become part of people's lives. And then there are the hard-core human rights abuses including assassinations, kidnappings, torture, rape, and illegal detentions.

THE GENDERED AND ETHNIC DIMENSIONS OF MILITARIZATION AND HUMAN RIGHTS ABUSES

In the section that follows, I will draw on examples from Tzotzil, Tzeltal, and Tojolabal communities sympathetic to the Zapatistas and testimonies of prisoners from the Zapotec region of Loxicha in Oaxaca to discuss the gendered and ethnic patterns of human rights abuses that go hand-in-hand with the militarization of southern Mexico. My information from Chiapas stems from personal interviews I carried out during my fieldwork and those conducted by human rights and humanitarian aid delegations in which I participated. In Oaxaca, the basis of my analysis are the written testimonies of political prisoners and others who were illegally detained.

In cases investigated by Human Rights Watch/ Americas (1997) in Chiapas and documented by local human rights organizations in Oaxaca (Brigada Pro Derechos Humanos Observadores Por La Paz 1997), a majority (but not all) of the victims of torture, illegal detention, assassination, and disappearance are men. The particular patterns of torture and detention of men documented in both states often include asphyxiation with wet towels (held over people's noses while their mouths are blocked); the forcing of carbonated water into nasal passages (sometimes in combination with chile powder); asphyxiation with plastic bags; electric shocks to the testicles, nipples, and other parts of the body; severe beating with a variety of implements including hoses, rifles, and sticks; ramming people's bodies against walls; sleep and food deprivation; and a lack of sanitary facilities forcing people to urinate and defecate in their cells. A variety of psychological tortures are also documented in individual testimonies and in documents referred to above, including threats of death by shooting, threats of being thrown out of helicopters and airplanes into the ocean, deliberate exposure to the cries of others under torture, and threats to kill, injure, and sexually violate family members. In addition, the ethnic identity of indigenous men is often a point of emphasis in their detention and torture.

Women are detained, but less frequently. The primary means of terror used against women is rape, gang rape, and the threat of rape. The ethnic identity of indigenous women is also used as a part of their belittlement in the process of threats, rapes, and attempted rapes through racially charged remarks.

Case One: The Zapotec Men of Loxicha

The following section draws on testimonials given by 37 Zapotec men from ten different communities in the municipality of San Agustin Loxicha. These men were detained, tortured, and incarcerated in 1996 and 1997. They were part of a group of 150 charged with federal crimes and imprisoned for up to 30 years. In 2013, seven were still jailed. Most of these testimonies were tape recorded by human rights workers from several Oaxacan human rights organizations in February 1997. They were recorded in the Ixcotel prison in Oaxaca as well as in the communities of La Sirena and Loma Bonita in the municipio of San Agustin Loxicha. The tapes were transcribed. A few of the testimonies were written by prisoners.

The analysis that follows is based on the written transcripts and testimonies. Organizations from Oaxaca that participated in collecting the testimonies are the Regional Center for Human Rights Bartolomé Carraso (BARCA), The Center for Human Rights Flor y Canto, and the Center for Human Rights Siete Príncipes. These organizations also participate in a larger coalition titled Brigada Pro Derechos Humanos Observadores Por La Paz (Brigade for Human Rights, Observers for Peace). I have changed the names of those who provided testimonies to protect their identities.

A close reading of the testimonial statements given by Zapotec men from the municipio of San Agustin Loxicha reveals several significant aspects of their treatment related to their gendered and ethnic identities. In reading these texts I made four observations. First, many of the Loxicha men who testified about their experiences were removed from their homes while their wives and children were present; in many cases, these family members were also threatened. Second, five of the men received sexually linked tortures, and others received threats that their wives and children would be sexually violated. Third, more than half of the men were monolingual in the Zapotec language and unable to understand most of the charges made against them or conversations held between their captors during their torture and detention. All were forced to sign blank pieces of paper that later appeared as signed confessions in Spanish despite obvious evidence of monolingualism and illiteracy. Fourth, the indigenous ethnic identities of many were belittled in the process of their detention, torture, and imprisonment as racial insults were yelled at them.

The violent methods used to remove men forcibly from their homes were designed to intimidate their families and to emphasize their incapacity as men to protect their families against the superior force of the men representing the state. The raids were carried out by integrated teams composed of several different federal and state police units along with the Mexican army. Those most consistently mentioned in the testimonies are the Federal Judicial Police (los Judiciales). Los Judiciales dress in black, carry machine guns, and are known to specialize in brute force and torture.

Many of the detentions described by Zapotec men occurred at four o'clock in the morning when they were asleep at home with their families.

Consider the testimony of Mario Lopez Fuentes, who is 38 years old and was detained in November 1996:

> At four o'clock in the morning they arrived at my house, surprising us. They forced the door open and fired their guns just a few centimeters from where my children were sleeping. They pushed me out of bed practically naked (except for my underwear) and kicked me in the butt. They then kicked me in the back and stomped repeatedly on my left foot. . . . At this moment I saw that a lot of cars had arrived and were moving toward the center of the community. They were ordered to throw me on the floor. After this they threw me handcuffed into a truck and continued to slap, punch, and kick me. They told me that I had guns in my house, things I don't even know about. I told them that I was barely able to get enough money together to feed my family. (Brigada Pro Derechos Humanos 1997:12–13)

The violent removal of Mario from his home, naked except for his underwear, and the firing of shots at his children is an explicitly gendered and sexual message. His nakedness sexualizes him and makes him vulnerable in a community where all adults keep their bodies covered at all times in public. He was feminized in front of his family because of his inability to protect his children from the gunshots of the judicial police. The constant physical punishment he describes at the hands of judicial police also serves to reinforce his powerlessness and the superior masculinity of judicial police.

The entire process of detention, torture, judicial hearings, and incarceration described in the testimonies of Zapotec men emphasizes their vulnerability as men. Constant physical punishment was augmented by electric shocks to the testicles in four cases and perhaps in more (reporting is probably low, given the difficulty of bringing up this subject with the strangers recording their testimonies). The application of electric shock to the testicles is not only a physical torture, but also is a gendered and sexual torture emphasizing the control judicial police have over their indigenous prisoners who are *agarrados por los cojones* (grabbed by the balls). Judicial police thus control the key symbolic and biological manifestation of the detained men's masculinity and sexuality. Once de-masculinized, they become feminine equivalents, or genderless.

The treatment of Zapotec prisoners involved the feminization of men and thereby their symbolic subordination as men to other men. It also involves the sexualization of men through enforced passivity. Indigenous Zapotec prisoners who are suspected of being members of the EPR and are interrogated primarily by Federal Judicial Police who come from Mexico City to carry out such work are clearly positioned in a relationship of subordination—not only through their de-masculinization, but through the symbolic sexual control held over them by the police. As seen below, masculine control of Zapotec men by Federal Judicial Police is reinforced through the use of Spanish.

In two of the cases where men described being tortured with electrical shocks, they were also threatened with the sexual violation of their wives and children, indicating an additional gendered dimension to their horrific treatment. De-masculinized and sexualized through their physical torture, this process is symbolically extended by putting them in the equivalent position of a cuckold (who has no rights over his wife) and is so lowly that his wife and children can be sexually violated. The testimony of Fransisco Pérez Luna, who was detained in San Agustin Loxicha in November 1996, provides a startling example of this intertwined physical and psychological assault:

> Then they threw me into another truck where there were other people from my community. They drove us toward San Bartolome Loxicha and there they took me to an abandoned area where they took all of my clothes of. They bound my hands and feet and threw me on the floor. They covered my mouth with a wet towel and began to force dirty water into my mouth and nose at the same time that they administered electric shocks to my testicles and other private parts of my body that are very sensitive. They

told me that they had already raped my wife and children and that they had carried all of this out on the order of the State Attorney. When I heard all this I was stricken with great sadness. (Brigada Pro Derechos Humanos 1997:13–14)

Fransisco's testimony pulls together multiple levels of gendered and sexualized violence in which physical, psychological, and social masculinity are simultaneously assaulted—ultimately by the authoritarian power of the Oaxacan State Attorney's office, or so he was told. His great sadness seems to stem not just from his treatment, but from the statement (true or not) that this treatment was being carried out in the name of the state government, a formidable force. Fransisco ends his testimony by stating from prison, "I have been in this prison since they arrested me. They have accused me of crimes I didn't carry out. I was simply carrying out my duties as a local judge in my community" (Brigada Pro Derechos Humanos 1997:14). His role as a local indigenous authority is his defense in response to the accusations of another authority and sphere of influence.

The naked lines of unequal power and authority revealed in the detention, torture, and imprisonment of rural men from San Agustin Loxicha at the hands of Federal Judicial Police and the army are further intensified by the active highlighting and insulting of their indigenous identity through language. Many of the men detained were monolingual in Zapotec and remained unclear about the accusations against them and the questions used in their interrogations under torture. The automatic use of Spanish as the language of interrogation immediately renders Zapotec invisible and useless—a non-language. In the hands of the Federal Judicial Police, Spanish becomes another weapon of control as the "suspects" are seen not even to have the capacity or right to speak because they are suspected of being subversives.

According to the testimonies and interviews carried out with human rights workers representing the prisoners from Loxicha, no efforts were made to provide translators or to ascertain whether the prisoners had any level of comprehension of Spanish. The response of one detained man is echoed by many: "Because we don't speak Spanish, the most we could do was to give our names. They asked me a lot of things, but what were they saying?" (Brigada Pro Derechos Humanos 1997:8). One bilingual man reported, "There were various people among us who didn't speak Spanish and couldn't respond to the questions. I tried to help one of them, but the judicial police told me, 'Quiet. We aren't asking you, stupid'" (Brigada Pro Derechos Humanos 1997:6). Ultimately the act of translation became irrelevant as the Federal Judicial Police created words for all of the detained, tortured, and imprisoned men. All of the men's testimonies mention that they were forced to sign blank pieces of paper and were later presented with confessions (written in perfect Spanish) they had supposedly signed, a violent supplanting of their indigenous tongue and identity for a manufactured identity in Spanish words not their own.

The final way in which the Spanish language became a weapon wielded against the prisoners was through racial slurs. In six of the 37 testimonies, there is mention of derogatory remarks made by Federal Judicial Police in reference to ethnicity. Luis Lopez, a 36-year-old bilingual teacher, recalled in his testimony, "As we were getting on the plane to be taken to Oaxaca, they told us, 'You filthy Indians, you all smell like shit, you assholes'" (Brigada Pro Derechos Humanos 1997:6). Manuel Ramirez Mendoza, detained in Oaxaca City, reported specific mention of his Zapotec origins, stating, "They discriminated against me because of my race and made fun of my Zapotec language" (Brigada Pro Derechos Humanos 1997:21).

Thus the feminization and sexualization of Zapotec men by Federal Judicial Police was further reinforced by their racist commentary throughout torture and interrogation sessions and the silencing of many through the linguistic exclusion of Zapotec and the supplanting of false testimony

in Spanish. Ironically, even in telling their stories to human rights workers, these indigenous men were reminded again of their marginal position for they had to use translators to make themselves understood.

Case Two: Rape and Threatened Rape of Women in the Conflict Zone of Chiapas

In Chiapas, rape and the threat of rape have been deployed as both physical and symbolic violence to discourage women from ongoing participation in community and regional forms of organization. As seen in the discussion below, women in Chiapas are quite clear that they (not men) are the targets of rape precisely because of the specific nature of their political activity. Rape confirms their importance as effective political actors.

Women who engage in activities that are seen as disobeying government authority are cast in the role of symbolic whore by police, government security forces, and soldiers. When women take over public spaces and engage in behavior that is viewed as inappropriate for their gender or ethnicity, they are treated with suspicion. In Chiapas, they become suspected members of the EZLN.

One of the hallmarks of public demonstrations in support of the EZLN is the high level of women's participation. The armed battalions of the EZLN itself are estimated to be about 30 percent women. Civilian women who support the Zapatistas actively confront and attempt to drive the military out of their communities. They also gather in large numbers to resist men from paramilitary groups who are attempting to terrorize their communities. For example, when the Mexican military invaded communities held by the EZLN in February 1995, women took active roles in driving them out. They have also represented their communities' defense efforts to the press and the media. On several occasions, Tojolabal women, EZLN supporters from La Realidad, have told me about how they drove the military outside of the boundaries of the community and how they continue to monitor their activities. Lucía told me her version in June 1996:

> The army arrived on the ninth of February in 1995. We withdrew to our ejido lands behind the town. Then the army came again. They said, "We have come for peace." But that isn't true. We drove them out of town. We got together a group of women and shouted at them, "Get out. Get out of here! We are in charge here, not you. Go back to your barracks. Don't come here to frighten the women." . . . We kept on screaming this. This is still going on. They come here all the time. We have coffee groves where we can't go to work alone because they are there. We have to constantly be on the lookout for them because we never know when they will try to take advantage of us.

Women like Lucía are clearly stepping over the boundary of acceptable female behavior in the face of a military invasion. The fact that Lucía is indigenous Tojolabal adds another dimension to her challenge. Defiant acts such as shouting at the army until they leave the community work sharply against the stereotypical image of indigenous women. Through their actions, women such as Lucía are redefining historical images of indigenous women.

The actual rape of women and the continuously implied threat of rape is perhaps the greatest tool of terror used against women in the militarized zones of Chiapas as well as in the city of San Cristóbal. Many NGOs supporting indigenous women in the countryside have made their home bases in San Cristóbal, often bringing indigenous women into the city for program-related activities or to live. The virtual occupation of most Zapatista communities by army encampments has resulted in a situation in which women are afraid to leave their communities to gather firewood or go to the fields, for fear of rape and sexual harassment. Women in La Realidad told me of how their piles of firewood, left by the road, were stolen by soldiers. They also related how soldiers undressed them with their eyes and told them to be careful if they were out alone. The

detention and rape of four Tzeltal women at an army checkpoint in Altamirano in 1994, the rape of three nurses in San Andres in 1995, and other acts of violence committed against women by soldiers have made rape and sexual harassment tools of war in Chiapas.

Nuns I spoke with at the San Carlos hospital in Altamirano presented other evidence of rape. San Carlos was one of the best sites for gathering information on human rights abuses in the region because many of the victims and their families came to the clinic. They often arrived from long distances because they felt safe there and trusted the doctors and nurses. The sisters have run the hospital since 1976. Sister Marina provided an interesting response to a question about rape during a 1997 discussion:

> Lynn: Do you have women who report rape here at the hospital? What do you know about accusations of rape by the military in the region?
>
> Marina: What happens to women who are raped? They don't report it. It is very difficult to get women to talk about it. But in the past two months we have had something happen here which is quite unusual. We have had two cases of a mother and father who came in when the woman was giving birth. Afterwards, they tell us that they don't want the child. The women won't even look at them. This is very strange behavior. People here love their children to pieces. When these mothers tell me, "I don't even want to look at the child, take it away," then I have to wonder.

Women in army-occupied communities and those who work with them in health projects stated that it was highly unusual for women to report being raped by soldiers for fear of retaliation. Within militarized communities in Chiapas, the daily comings and goings of everyone in the community are closely monitored. People reported to me that when they left their communities to go to larger towns such as Altamirano, they were asked at checkpoints where they were going, with whom they were speaking, and when they would return.

But more than actual rape, the threat of rape and the psychological control that is exerted over communities through a male army presence is probably the strongest weapon used against indigenous women. The physical presence of the army is augmented through their surveillance tactics, which include intimidating patrols through communities with video cameras. On several occasions, I witnessed such patrols in La Realidad. At about nine o'clock in the morning, just when the sun is beginning to heat up the mud, a very slow-moving caravan of about sixteen humvees moves through La Realidad. Most of the people hide in their houses peering through the windows and doors. A few people continue their activities, ignoring the army's presence. Machine guns are mounted on top of the humvees and about four to eight soldiers sit in each vehicle. While one soldier stands behind the machine gun, another one or two in each vehicle are snapping photographs with still cameras while others are videotaping. The faces of the soldiers holding the still cameras and the video cameras are not visible. They appear as human machines mounted on the humvees, filming all that comes into their line of sight. They extend a very slow, deliberate, and intimidating gaze over the community. They travel at about two miles per hour and slow to a standstill periodically in their sojourn in the village. When they stop, everyone stops moving and is frozen in their tracks. In about fifteen minutes, they have passed through the two-block town. People come out of their houses to resume work and to complain about the military presence. Some break the tension by joking about whether or not they were really taking pictures. "They would have to spend thousands and thousands of pesos on all their film and pictures of La Realidad." Others talk about the army being able to watch them on video even when they are not driving their humvees through the town. Such a suggestion leaves a chilly pall over conversations.

The effect is quite striking over the long term. While men, women, and children in La Realidad became accustomed to the videotaping and picture-taking, they internalized it as a constant violation. Women in the town talked about "always being watched" and the "eyes of the army being everywhere." That sense of always being watched, of never being alone, has had a profound effect on women in militarized zones of Chiapas. It has heightened the constant fear of rape and harassment and creates high levels of intimidation that isolates women within their communities or homes.

Threats of rape and other forms of violence were also perpetrated against women sympathetic to the Zapatistas. Two women from a weaving cooperative located in San Cristobal, also sympathetic to the Zapatistas, were brutally attacked in two different incidents and threatened with rape. Gabriela Lopez, a young Chamula women who is part of the staff at Jolom Mayatik, told of attacks against her in the streets of San Cristobal in January and February 1997:

On the last day of January this year, some men approached us as we were coming home from a workshop. We were just walking down the street. They jumped on us, beating us and kicking. There was a whole group of them. We rested for ten days, hurting, trying to recover. Then again on the sixth of February we were confronted by more men on Chiapa de Corzo Street. They parked their car and six men got out. They followed us and then grabbed us saying, "You are whores. We know you sleep around with men, you know what sex is. Let's see if you want to be Zapatistas now. Let's see who will win. You are just whores on the street." Everyone on the street was listening. Imagine how we felt.

After this happened, we decided we had to move. Now I live with my family in San Cristobal. They all live here now. . . . Soon after, these men came to where I was living with my family. They came looking for me. My family told them, "We don't know where she is." Then they pulled out a knife and attacked and threatened my family.

Gabriela has been working in the cooperative for many years and has carefully considered her role as a woman leader and its consequences in terms of both her family and herself as an individual.

She and other women in the cooperative have analyzed the violence carried out against them and talk about it as directed specifically against them as women engaged in struggle. The women in Jolom Mayatik have become accustomed to living with their fear, but acknowledge that the constant threat of rape and physical violence takes a toll on them after years of intimidating actions.

CONCLUSION

Militarization of indigenous regions of southern Mexico acknowledges the importance of regional cultural and political challenges to the legitimacy of the Mexican state. Oaxaca and Chiapas are the centers of strong regional indigenous and peasant organizations which operate at a national level. The heart of these movements is outside the formal political arena of electoral politics. In part because these movements offer new political forms that move the contestation for political power outside of the electoral arena, they have attracted and sustained the attention of the Mexican government.

The gendered and ethnic dimensions of human rights abuses associated with high levels of militarization in Chiapas and Oaxaca reflect, in part, the cultural and ideological perspectives of those in the occupying forces of the army, Federal Judicial Police, and Public Security Police.

These in turn are rooted in the processes of military conquest, Catholic conversion, and the mestizoization of Mexico during and since the colonial period. National stereotypes of indigenous peoples written into the myth and vision of Mexican history continue to be played out in contemporary strategies of conquest and militarization. These include tactics aimed specifically at stripping indigenous men of their masculinity, sexualizing them, and reducing them to feminine sexual equivalents on the part of male Federal Judicial Police agents. The casting of Tzotzil, Tzeltal, and Tojolabal women as whore-like Malinches, as an element of sexual disciplining, suggests the importance of national myths in the self-legitimating ideology underlying the behavior of men in the army and police toward women. National gendered myths are part of the cultural scripts of rape.

In Chiapas, the active and public involvement of women in repelling military invasions of community lands and in others who threaten their communities and families has made indigenous women particular targets of threats and abuses. Nevertheless, women in Zapatista communities, in weaving co-ops, and in nongovernmental organizations continue their work and take active stances against the military and others who try to intimidate them. They have publicly denounced the threats against them in the press and have continued to pressure the State Prosecutor's office to find and prosecute those carrying out the threats. By taking such a politically active stance both because of and in spite of personal danger, they are redefining indigenous femininity—they are neither active collaborators (Malinche) nor passive asexual victims (Virgin de Guadalupe).

The resistance of indigenous women and men in Chiapas and efforts on the part of Zapotec and other indigenous peoples in Oaxaca to take control of their own governments is part of a coordinated national effort on the part of indigenous organizations and communities to redefine their place in the Mexican nation. This challenge involves local cultural, legal, and social forms that rework top-down nationalism and create a sense of local nations. Bringing nationalism down to the local level and coupling it with self-determination offers an alternative to the marginalized position of many indigenous communities in Mexican history, in national and regional politics, and in economic development schemes. The tools of ethnography can be put to powerful use in exposing how dominant representations create categories of people susceptible to political violence, "suspects" who become victims of human rights abuses. By doing so, anthropologists align their own tools with those of the men and women who also draw strength from their own parallel projects of resistance and analysis.

REFERENCES CITED

Brigada Pro Derechos Humanos Observadores Por La Paz. 1997. Testimonios escritos y verbales de los presos de Loxicha. Proporcionados por habitantes de las Comunidades de La Sirena, Loma Bonita, Loxicha, el día 21 de Febrero, y por los presos (CERESO Ixcotel) el día 22 de Febrero, 1997 Oaxaca City: BARCA/ Regional Center for Human Rights "Bartolomé Carraso."

Human Rights Watch/Americas. 1997. Implausible Deniability: State Responsibility for Rural Violence in Mexico. New York: Human Rights Watch.

1 · *Elora Halim Chowdhury*

FEMINIST NEGOTIATIONS
Contesting Narratives of the Campaign Against Acid Violence in Bangladesh

DISCUSSION QUESTIONS

1. What were the objectives and strategies of the initial campaign against acid violence started by Naripokkho?
2. How did these objectives and strategies change with the involvement of international donors?
3. Why does gender "matter" in understanding and analyzing these shifts?

Acid attacks against women have been increasingly reported in Bangladesh since the early 1980s. Acid attacks involve the splashing of acid (car battery or sulfuric acid) on the face and/or body of victims. The rise in acid attacks needs to be understood not only in relation to existing gender inequality but also within complex and shifting socio-economic, political and cultural processes as they intersect with neoliberal development policies and globalization. Because women are considered bearers of tradition and honor, it is on their bodies that contestations over gender, ownership and power are

played out. Both physical and emotional scars are permanent. Social reintegration is difficult, and victims are often isolated or rejected by their families and communities. In the mid-1990s, a campaign against acid violence was started in Bangladesh by Naripokkho, a Dhaka-based feminist advocacy organization, later expanding to include international players. By addressing the tensions between the competing visions of local women activists and international donor agencies regarding social transformation and women's empowerment, this essay examines the consequences of international aid

An abridged version of Elora Halim Chowdhury, 2005. "Feminist Negotiations: Contesting Narratives of the Campaign against Acid Violence in Bangladesh." *Meridians: feminism, race, transnationalism* 6 (1): 163–192. Reprinted with the kind permission of the author and of the publisher.

and nongovernmental organizations (NGOs) in redefining the relationship among women, gendered violence, and the state.

Acid attacks against both men and women have a long history in Bangladesh and elsewhere in the world and must be understood in the larger context of socioeconomic, political, and cultural transitions. Following the 1971 War of Independence, Bangladesh witnessed a decline in agriculture-based economy and a growth in landlessness, landless laborers, and unemployment. Naila Kabeer (2000) has linked the intrusion of market relations into the employment of labor with setting in motion the gradual dissolution of older forms of family organization among landless peasants and the erosion of traditional support systems. The intensified competition in the rural economy produced diversification of livelihoods and migration to urban areas leading to a more monetized economy. There were inevitable gender implications for the changes in economy and society as women became more mobile as they were integrated in "income generating" activities. The transition from subsistence to monetized economy contributed to a visible and sizable female labor force and a significant shift from long-established norms of female seclusion in Bangladesh. Women's increasing participation in the labor force in some cases compromised the traditional obligations of men toward women. It was commonly perceived that women were taking jobs and the natural role of primary breadwinner from men.

Feminist researchers have posited that hostile attitudes and reactions toward women's emerging visibility, particularly in the context of increasing male socioeconomic disempowerment, often manifest in male-initiated abuses against women. Dina Siddiqi (1991) noted that women's movement into previously male-dominated public spheres may have broken the norms of female seclusion but has also redefined these norms to take on new significance in the context of globalization and wage labor. Strict disciplinary measures and surveillance continue to govern female behavior both in and outside of work-spaces. This emergent new

order in Bangladesh has been accompanied by systematic violence against women as exemplified in the steady increase in numbers of fatwa,[1] rape, acid attacks, murder, battery, and trafficking (Ain O Salish Kendro 2001). While reported incidents of acid attacks in the past five years have ranged from 150 to 450 cases per year, reports of other forms of violence, with the exception of fatwas, have been consistently higher (Ain O Salish Kendro 2001, statistics 1999–2003). A study by Women for Women, a Dhaka-based feminist research group, reveals that women acid victims are often characterized in their community as women who are "wayward and disobedient" (*udhyoto meye*) (H. Akhter and S. Nahar 2003). In a changing gendered social order, acid throwing against women and girls has to be seen within the larger trend of women's oppression with the reasons for attacks overwhelmingly cited as marital, family, and land disputes; refusal to pay dowry; or rejection of romantic advances and marriage proposals (Islam 2004).

In this context, Naripokkho developed an issue-based campaign during 1995–2003[2] focused on acid violence against women. Scholars of transnational organizing have emphasized the importance of complex relationships within networks that include local women's groups, international donor agencies, and the state. While these networks may be held together by a perceived shared commitment, odds over fundamental issues of agenda and strategy often lead feminists to deradicalize their own agendas in order to receive funding (e.g. Basu 2000). This happened in the acid campaign when a donor-driven intervention shifted its radical vision of structural change and women's empowerment into a neoliberal one of incremental change and individual transformation.

These dynamics can be illuminated through the three consecutive stages of Bangladesh's anti-acid campaign. From 1995–1998, members and staff of Naripokkho began devising a campaign to transform incidences of acid attacks into a public issue. From 1998–1999, the success of the Naripokkho actions led to a diversification of actors engaged with the campaign, expanding and changing its scope with unintended consequences. Finally, from 1999–2003, the Acid Survivors Foundation (ASF) gradually took over the role of the consolidated service-providing agency to assist acid violence survivors and witnessed the gradual dissolution of Naripokkho's involvement with the campaign.

NARIPOKKHO LAUNCHES ACID VIOLENCE AS AN ISSUE

Naripokkho, literally meaning pro-women, is a membership-based women's advocacy organization founded in 1983 (Naripokkho 2002). Its members collectively seek the advancement of women's rights and entitlements and encourage resistance against violence, discrimination, and injustice. Their activities include advocacy campaigns, research, discussions, cultural events, and lobbying on issues of gender justice. In 1995, when Naripokkho activists embarked on their work on acid violence, no systematic study or records existed to document incidents of acid throwing on women and girls in Bangladesh. Bristi Chowdhury, then an intern at Naripokkho, said, "Acid violence was not yet a buzzword [in the mid-1990s]" (B. Chowdhury 2003). Chowdhury (2003) has described the initial phase of campaign building necessary to create a public discourse on acid violence. Strategies included: data collection; creating and maintaining a "violence logbook"; meeting with and providing support to victims of acid attacks and their families; and developing a network of allies such as journalists, activists, philanthropists, medical and legal professionals, and international donors. The emergent network produced a campaign, whose principal strategy was the internationalization of a domestic issue, thereby reinforcing voices of local women activists while affecting national policy priorities. Chandra Talpade Mohanty (2003) described how internationalization of the women's movement shifted earlier discourses of "sisterhood is global" to the "human rights" arena in the mid-1990s as a result of United Nations (UN) conferences on women (249). Naripokkho hoped to leverage this issue into the arena of international women's rights and affect policy changes on the national front. Nasreen Haq said, "The focus on acid burns is part of an overall campaign on Violence Against Women, which draws on the government's mandate to address specific forms of violence articulated in the 1995 UN Beijing Conference on Women and the Program of Action of the International Conference on Population and Development (ICPD) in 1994" (1996).

As a result of the efforts of Naripokkho activists in the mid-1990s, there emerged a network of young girls and women who had endured acid violence. In April 1997, amid the escalating phenomenon of acid throwing in Bangladesh, Naripokkho activists organized a three-day workshop with a group of teenaged survivors. The purpose was to present in a public forum the phenomenon of acid throwing as a form of gendered violence; to point out the gaps in the service-providing institutions; to mobilize local, national, and international actors to take action; and to promote solidarity and visibility of survivors whose economic and social lives had been affected as a result of the acid attacks. Naripokkho's approach was motivated by the belief that the experiences of the survivors should be central to the shaping of the campaign and its objectives and that the survivors should be the leaders of the campaign.

The successful expansion of the acid campaign hinged on Naripokkho's extensive network and grounding within a national women's movement. Save the Children, UK, offered the use of their conference room for the workshop sessions. Women's Voluntary Association donated their guesthouse to host the girls and their families and Naripokkho staff put them up in their own homes. UNICEF provided transportation. The UN Women's Association hosted a presentation and donated funds. Naripokkho members contacted the Law and Home Ministries and set up meetings. Another member of Naripokkho, a gender advisor at the Danish International Development Agency (DANIDA) who at the time was collaborating with the Bangladeshi government on a project called the Multisectoral Project on Violence against Women, emphasized the importance of the integration of the campaign into this larger project. Negotiations with Gonoshastho Kendro (GK), a national NGO providing affordable healthcare to the poor, led to an alliance envisioning the development of a burn center. The only existing center at the time was located at Dhaka Medical College Hospital (DMCH) with a mere eight-bed capacity.[3]

The workshop featured sessions where participants developed strong relationships with one another and their families. Separate sessions were held with family members, particularly the mothers of the young women, who were the primary caregivers in the long recovery process. These emotionally charged sessions enabled the formation of solidarity among women, a critical feature of the emergent Naripokkho campaign. Bristi Chowdhury wrote in a report of the workshop:

> [W]hen all the harrowing stories were being told, no amount of logical thought could stop the tears. When I cried Rina [a survivor] held my hand tightly the way I had held hers when she had cried in DMCH [where the survivors recuperated in the burns unit and Naripokkho staff regularly visited them] and Bina [another survivor] cradled my head like I had cradled hers. Even now I don't know if I was right to cry, maybe I should have remained strong so that they could feel that they could lean on me. (1997, 15)

During the workshop, acid survivors and their family members were encouraged to map out their future plans, their visions of social justice, and recommendations of adequate services for victims of violence. The sessions reflected an attempt to create an imaginative space for the girls—for instance through painting and storytelling—to express their feelings and develop friendships. Naripokkho activists provided a supportive space for the young survivors to develop confidence to confront the consequent isolation and ostracism following acid attacks. Bristi Chowdhury described one particular event:

> [S]urvivors, mothers and Naripokkho staff and volunteers from the "Theater Center" went to Shongshod

Bhaban, the Parliament Building. Shongshod Bhaban is a place for boys to ogle girls and girls to more subtly ogle boys, it is a place for married couples to go openly and for unmarried couples to go covertly, but essentially it is a place for couples. Many people told us that we must either be mad or inhumanely insensitive to take a group of girls whose outside appearance was, to say the least, shocking, to this place and what is more on a Friday when the place is literally swarming. (1997, 16)

Naripokkho activists believed in reclaiming the public space and social lives of the young girls that gendered abuse so methodically denied. Bristi Chowdhury continued:

> We got out of the microbuses slightly apprehensive, but Nasreen [the campaign coordinator] covered her own apprehension by taking control of the situation and telling us to hold hands so that we were in one long line, then we sang, even those like me, who are tone deaf, sang. We started with "We shall overcome/Amra korbo joy" and went on to many more. We took over Shongshod that day! We were all standing on the steps singing and of course a large crowd of male oglers had gathered to watch the freak show (or at least that's what we thought), when one young man pushed his way to the front and asked if we would let him sing us a song, we were all very dubious about this thinking that perhaps he would make fun of them or something of the sort, but he proved us to be a bunch of paranoid cynics. He sang beautifully. All he wanted to do was have fun with us not at us; maybe he even wanted to show his solidarity with us. We had been worried that everyone would treat the girls as freaks and for a while the oglers did treat them as freaks but after a while they stopped having fun at our expense and began to have fun with us. (1997, 16)

Nasreen Haq emphasized that the Naripokkho workshop brought together a group of girls who as a result of the acid attacks had been deprived of living their adolescence. The session at the Parliament House was intended to reclaim not only the public spaces and social lives of young women but also their lost youth (N. Haq 2003). Bristi Chowdhury's report showcased such youthful activities:

> . . . at one point we were playing a game where you have to chase a person around in a circle and if you catch them before they get back to their place in the circle they are out, the audience were cheering us as in "ey taratari, dhorlo dhorlo" [hey quick quick she's going to catch you] and so on. It was fantastic; these guys [the public] were with us. (1997, 16)

The visibility of the survivors became a key strategy in the anti–acid violence campaign in order to challenge the enforced isolation of the survivors (Del Franco 1999). The sessions designed to encourage the survivors to talk about their futures gave them a sense of community and prepared them to collectively make a statement to state representatives, journalists, doctors, lawyers, and police officers in a public forum called Face-to-Face with Acid Survivors. The girls spoke at length about the long process of recovery and the inadequate services in the country's one burn unit, the financial strain on their families pursuing medical and legal redress, and their inability to continue with their education or meaningful employment due to lack of finances, trauma and isolation, and the loss of physical ability to see and to hear as a result of the acid attack. Moreover, the girls talked about the corrupt and ineffective judicial system, which, in spite of rhetorically offering services, systematically discriminated against them.

The workshop was a turning point for the acid campaign. For the first time Bangladeshi civil servants and international donor community came face-to-face with young Bangladeshi women who had endured acid attacks. Naripokkho's efforts had broken through a wall of official denial and trivialization of this phenomenon. Achieving this breakthrough launched acid violence against women in Bangladesh as an issue that needed instant and systematic attention from the state, the media, donors, and the medicolegal establishments. The conference also attracted the attention of the international media. Bristi Chowdhury recalled, "Money started to come in. A member of the royal family of Jordan

sent a large sum upon reading an article in *Marie Claire* . . . A plastic surgeon from India was invited to Gonoshastho by its director to develop a national project to train local medical staff in caring for burns patients. Simultaneously there were offers from medical professionals in Spain and Italy. The work took on a life of its own" (B. Chowdhury 2003).

At the same time, strengthened by the supportive feminist space of Naripokkho and the growing network, the young survivors began to participate more fully in the campaign. Survivors Bina Akhter and Nurun Nahar were hired to do research and networking. They continued developing a nationwide network with other survivors by visiting them at DMCH and in their homes as well as encouraging them to speak in public to organize information drives on the issue. Nasreen Haq said in an interview, "Bina Akhter was critically involved in handling the press, in developing a network, etc. In her we saw a whole spectrum unfold of victim to survivor to activist. Right in front of us. This is what we had dreamed of " (N. Haq 2003). Bina Akhter went on to become one of the most prominent leaders of the acid campaign. UNICEF nominated her to participate in the 1998 Amnesty International Young Leaders Forum.

The workshop allowed survivors to share experiences with one another as a collective, enabling recognition of their experiences as political and transformative. Such visibility is particularly important in the case of acid violence because it challenges the motivation behind the crime, which is to force women into isolation and to end their social lives. Naripokkho's intervention set in motion the subsequent entrance of key actors in the continuing development of the campaign. It was continuous with the organization's participation in a larger movement against women's oppression.

THE UNICEF INTERVENTION

The second stage of the acid campaign, from 1997–1999, marked the diversification and internationalization of the campaign. During this time I was part of a consulting team that UNICEF hired to conduct background research on existing services for survivors of acid violence in Bangladesh as part of the broader objective of setting up the Acid Survivors Foundation (ASF). The 1997 acid workshop, in addition to mobilizing NGOs, the government, the media, and the medical and legal professionals, also stirred the interest of international donor agencies, namely UNICEF-Bangladesh. Over a series of strategic meetings Naripokkho activists pressured UNICEF staff to recognize the relevance of the campaign to their own institutional agenda. Following a host of reports by CNN, the BBC, *Marie Claire* and *Ms.* magazines, and Oprah Winfrey, offers of assistance streamed in steadily to Naripokkho. The executive director of UNICEF personally traveled to the Dhaka office to meet with acid survivors and asked the Dhaka office to take on the issue. Furthermore, the British High Commission set up an inquiry and put at its head a British expatriate who later became the first executive director of the ASF.

One of the first programs UNICEF supported was bringing in a team of experts from the United States specializing in Eye Movement Desensitization Reprocessing (EMDR), which at the time was an experimental therapy designed to treat victims of natural disasters, conflict, and war. While I am not qualified to comment on the effectiveness of such treatments for survivors of acid violence, I would like to point out that the decision to involve EMDR specialists was made without discussion with partners in Naripokkho or the survivors themselves. While therapy appears to be an obvious necessity for victims of trauma, in the Bangladeshi context counseling is practiced in different, more informal settings. Safia Azim, a professor of psychology at Dhaka University and member of Naripokkho, has suggested that alternate forms of "therapy" in Bangladesh would be more appropriate given that there is not a "culture of therapy" per se. Instead of putting local professionals through costly training in EMDR, a better course of action, according to Azim, would be to bring in trained counselors to teach at Dhaka University and build capacity locally (Azim 1998).

UNICEF's "quick fix" strategy was not only limited to the endorsement of EMDR; it spilled onto other areas of campaign building. For instance, midway through the consultancy, the consulting team was instructed to set aside research on existing services and instead focus on interviewing five hundred survivors of acid violence around the country to develop a database of information on their needs and lay the groundwork for program development. While it was a worthy proposal, the practicalities of developing a network of five hundred far-flung survivors within one month were unrealistic given the time and resource parameters of the consultancy. Moreover, such groundwork, albeit in a smaller scale, already existed due to the early research that Naripokkho activists had conducted. Honor Ford-Smith (1997) has talked about the tendency of aid agencies in developing countries to fund short-term projects that would produce quick and measurable results. She asks, "Measurable by whom?" And, "By whose standards?" Smith goes on, "Essentially, agencies wanted to know that their funding criteria had been met. The people who were presumably being served had little input in evaluating the achievements of the project; they had even less say in establishing the criteria for evaluation" (232). Finding "500 acid-burnt girls" and providing them with rehabilitative care would satisfy the funder's criteria of offering measurable solutions. While UNICEF broadened the scope of the campaign and opened up access to resources previously unavailable, at the same time it led to the loss of Naripokkho's earlier survivor-centered strategy. The eventual process that lead to the creation of the ASF was a combination of Naripokkho's efforts in conceptualizing acid violence as a national and international issue along with the UN headquarters' decision to act on what by the late 1990s an international audience had begun to perceive to be a violation of women's human rights.

THE CONSOLIDATION OF THE ASF

In 1999, at the time of its creation, the ASF ostensibly became the coordinating organization to provide services for acid survivors. UNICEF's establishment of an umbrella organization such as the ASF has to be commended, and UNICEF draws kudos because with the exception of the donors, an Italian NGO and the British High Commission, the remaining eight members of the board of trustees are prominent Bangladeshi nationals and NGO representatives. Over the years it has made important headway in the campaign. One of its most noteworthy achievements was to lobby with the government to pass new and more stringent laws, namely the Acid Crime Prevention Law 2002 and Acid Control Law 2002 to prosecute perpetrators of acid violence and more effectively criminalize the sale of corrosive substances without license. With the institutionalization of the anti–acid violence campaign into the ASF, resources came primarily from Western donors such as UNICEF and the Canadian International Development Agency (CIDA), but not without strings attached or without ramifications for the shape of the campaign. In her study of women organizing in contemporary Russia, Valerie Sperling (1999) has noted that although foreign-based aid can provide crucial support for social movement organizing in developing countries, it can exacerbate divisiveness within and between national and local groups as well as influence the priorities and agenda of these groups (220). The ASF strategically co-opted Naripokkho's strategy, albeit in rhetoric only, of placing survivors and their experiences at the center of their programs. However, considerable contradictions exist in the ASF's rhetoric and its actual practices.

When the ASF was first founded, it primarily provided medical and rehabilitative services. It had a thirty-five-bed nursing center and shelter home, Thikana House, as well as a surgical center, Jibon Tara, named after a woman who had died of an acid attack. Over the years it has developed legal, research, and most recently prevention units that work together in assisting survivors along the recovery process. John Morrison, the first executive director of the ASF, said at its founding that efforts must be made to make acid survivors into "productive and effective citizens of the country" (1999). The ASF's primary objective is "[t]o provide ongoing assistance in the treatment, rehabilitation and reintegration into society of survivors of acid violence by identifying and improving existing services and to also work to prevent further acid throwing attacks." The mission of the ASF is "[t]o aid the recovery of acid violence survivors to a condition as near as possible to that of their premature situation by providing treatment, rehabilitation, counseling and other support during their reintegration into society and afterwards" (Acid Survivors Foundation 2002). To facilitate the reintegration of survivors into society by returning them to a "condition as near as possible to that of their premature situation" seems a gross injustice in representing the process a survivor experiences post–acid attack, for rarely is a "return" possible, even in the most insignificant of ways. Through the ASF's rehabilitation unit survivors are routinely "reintegrated" into clerical and service positions or set up with microbusiness ventures. This model relies on social and neoclassical economic development programs which assume "women need to be helped to develop their potential so that they can solve their problems themselves" (Schild 2002, 185). It is not clear, however, whether women's insertion in the productive machinery of the state, namely as active economic agents, translates into the meaningful participation that gender-sensitive programs envision. Veronica Schild (2002), using a term used by Marguerite Berger, chief of the Women and Development Unit at the Inter-American Bank, calls the women who are the subjects of such development ventures "reluctant entrepreneurs" or women who participate in the income-generating and skills-training economic development programs out of a lack of other alternatives. The development industry reconfigures these reluctant entrepreneurs as "empowered clients" who are viewed as capable of enhancing their lives through judicious, responsible choices. Schild characterizes this shift as exemplary of new ways of governing subordinate populations. Bristi Chowdhury's research has noted that most survivors wanted to continue their education or find meaningful employment, both of which were often impossible because of the social stigma against and public rejection of women victims (B. Chowdhury 1997).

Nicoletta Del Franco (1999) has observed that the main activities of the ASF were giving financial and medical help to some survivors. She has characterized the role of the ASF in 1999 as a "savior giving new hope and life" to survivors whose needs are interpreted mainly in terms of welfare (Del Franco 1999, 5). This approach continues to stigmatize acid survivors as "victims deprived forever of their main roles as mothers and wives" (12). Thus the ASF provided services to integrate survivors into development programs without disrupting gender inequities or confronting systemic and institutional gender discriminatory practices and values contributing to gendered abuse. As Schild has said, "Indeed, in the present context, this rights-based agenda, as implemented in practice, seems to be more a tool for a hierarchical and exclusionary project of social integration which is functional to the 'modernization' restructuring project more generally, than it is a means for enabling the meaningful citizenship of the majority of poor women" (2002, 198). The welfare discourse, says Del Franco (1999), lacks a long-term vision because it does not recognize the need for change of the social system. It targets in a piecemeal manner a specific group of women and thus isolates and depoliticizes the issue at hand. In this way, acid survivors are pathologized as victims in need of rehabilitation and reintegration into society. "Meaningful citizenship" would emerge from development programs that ensured survivors economic and social access to services and resources and power to self-determine their choices, and simultaneously to question the hierarchical structures and institutions that allow gendered abuse.

One cannot underestimate the services that an umbrella organization such as the Acid Survivors Foundation can provide. The creation of such a coordinated body of services reflects the achievement of the evolving campaign against acid violence in Bangladesh. In 2003 the ASF underwent some changes in their approach, which now involves survivors in shaping programs geared to serve them. This change in part can be attributed to the recruitment of several key staff of Naripokkho who had been involved in the anti–acid violence campaign

in the mid-1990s. Some of the noteworthy developments within the ASF include collaborating with national NGOs such as Bangladesh Rural Action Committee to disseminate educational materials on gendered violence and to monitor progress of survivors nationwide; conducting research in various districts on existing legal aid services; lobbying with the government, leading to drafting and passing new laws against acid throwing and selling, and setting up a National Acid Council and Special Tribunal to oversee speedy investigation of cases and swift trial processing; and providing improved medical care and reconstructive surgery to survivors. One of the most creative programs that the ASF is developing includes community-based focus groups to raise awareness at the grassroots level across the nation. Two particularly innovative strategies have involved training survivors to perform their stories. These traveling theater productions have challenged societal perceptions of acid victims and encouraged women's articulation of their own stories. Following such a performance, a group of youth in the community had spontaneously painted a mural expressing resistance to acid throwing. Such grassroots efforts have the potential to mobilize participation across diverse social groups. Although commendable, as the head of the ASF prevention unit, Mahbuba Huq, reports, such innovative organizing efforts remain sporadic and marginal to the foundation's mainstream activities due to a lack of sustained funding and focus (M. Huq 2003).

Despite these changes, there is no indication of actual survivor participation in the decision-making process. The self-validating progress narrative of the ASF does not allow for women to be seen as complex subjects in agency and in struggle. Rather than promoting empowerment, they entrap recipients within discourses of victimization. While one cannot disparage the assistance that survivor Promila Shabdakor acquired from the ASF in getting her life together after the acid attack, simple narratives such as "I did not want to live. ASF inspired me to look at my child and family. Please all of you pray for me to sustain" (Acid Survivors Foundation 2003) do not show the array of roles and activities that constitute Promila Shabdakor. Acid survivors like Promila are reinscribed as a socially marginalized woman in need of help from an organization such as the ASF, who in turn, is validated for its benevolence. This narrative creates a divide between "false overstated images of victimized and empowered womanhood, which negate each other" (Mohanty 2003, 248). Perhaps the future of the campaign lies in the rejuvenation of its initial broader movement-based agenda, which would require building and strengthening careful alliances with diverse social groups such as local grassroots communities with a vision to transform women's meaningful participation as full citizens in social, political, and economic aspects of society.

WORKS CITED

Acid Survivors Foundation. 2002. "Introduction." Accessed 10 September, 2002. http://www.acidsurvivors.org/

Acid Survivors Foundation. 2003. *Annual Report*. Dhaka, Bangladesh: ASF.

Ain O Salish Kendro. 2001. "Human Rights Report." Accessed 21 December 2004. http://www.askbd.org/.

Akhter, Halima, and Shamsun Nahar. 2003. *A Study on Acid Violence in Mymensingh*. Dhaka, Bangladesh: Women for Women Report.

Azim, Safia. Personal Interview. 15 June 1998.

Basu, Amrita. 2000. "Globalization of the Local/ Localization of the Global: Mapping Transnational Women's Movements." *Meridians* 1(1): 68–84.

Chowdhury, Bristi. 1997. *Burning Passions: A Study of Acid Violence in Bangladesh*. Dhaka, Bangladesh: Naripokkho.

———. Personal Interview. 7 March 2003.

Del Franco, Nicoletta. 1999. "Changing Gender Relations and New Forms of Violence: Acid Throwing against Women in Bangladesh and the NGO Response." Master's Thesis. IDS: University of Sussex.

Ford-Smith, Honor. 1997. "Ring Ding in a Tight Corner: Sistren, Collective Democracy, and the Organization of Cultural Production." In *Feminist Genealogies, Colonial Legacies, Democratic Futures*, ed. M. Jacqui Alexander, and Chandra Talpade Mohanty, 213–58. New York: Routledge.

Haq, Nasreen. Personal Interview. 10 October 1996.

———. Personal Interview. 11 April 2003.

Huq, Mahbuba. Personal Interview. 14 April 2003.

Islam, Kajalie Shehereen. 2004. "Campaigning against Crime." *Star Weekend Magazine* 4 (2 July): 2.

Kabeer, Naila. 2000. *The Power to Choose: Bangladeshi Women and Labour Market Decisions in London and Dhaka*. London: Verso.

Mohanty, Chandra Talpade 2003. *Feminism without Borders: Decolonizing Theory, Practicing* Solidarity. Durham, N.C.: Duke University Press.

Morrison, John. 1999. "All They Need is Social Commitment to Peaceful Life." *The Daily Star* (Dhaka). 23 July.

Naripokkho. 2002. Accessed 10 September. http://www.naripokkho.org.

Schild, Veronica. 2002. "Engendering the New Social Citizenship in Chile: NGOs and Social Provisioning under Neo-liberalism." In *Gender Justice, Development, and Rights*, ed. Maxine Molyneux and Shahra Razavi, 170–203. London: Oxford University Press.

Shehabuddin, Elora. 2002. "Contesting the Illicit: Gender and the Politics of Fatwas in Bangladesh." In *Gender, Politics, and Islam*, ed. Therese Saliba, Carolyn Allen, and Judith Howard, 201–34. Chicago: University of Chicago Press.

Siddiqi, Dina. 1991. "Discipline and Protect: Women Factory Workers in Bangladesh." *Grassroots* 2: 42–49.

Sperling, Valerie. 1999. *Organizing Women in Contemporary Russia: Engendering Transition*. Cambridge: Cambridge University Press.

NOTES

1. In Islamic legal context *fatwa* means clarification of an ambiguous point or opinion of a jurist. In recent decades impoverished women in Bangladesh have been the targets of fatwas—edicts punishing women for transgressing patriarchal codes of behavior—by elite men of their communities. In addition, NGO offices and schools offering development and literacy programs for rural women have been targets. Cases include stoning and whipping of women and setting fire to NGO offices and schools. See Shehabuddin (2002).

2. During these years I studied the campaign activities first as a journalist, second as a consultant with UNICEF-Bangladesh, and third as an independent researcher.

3. Although a burns center at GK did not eventually materialize, following Naripokkho's workshop on acid violence the government of Bangladesh undertook a project to build a fifty-bed burn center on the premises of the state-sponsored Dhaka Medical College Hospital.

2 • *Dorothy L. Hodgson*

"THESE ARE NOT OUR PRIORITIES"

Maasai Women, Human Rights, and the Problem of Culture

DISCUSSION QUESTIONS

1. What are the economic and political priorities of Maasai people and their organizations?
2. Why do international and national activists ignore these priorities?
3. How do different ideas of gender and culture shape the struggles between local activists and national/international activists and donors?
4. Why does Hodgson argue that the problem is one of power, not culture?

"MWEDO urged to step up fight against female genital mutilation," read the headline of the *Arusha Times*, a weekly newspaper in northern Tanzania (Aug. 19–26, 2006). Since Tanzania made female genital modification (FGM)[1] illegal in 1998, there have been constant articles in the English and Swahili language press outlining the dangers of FGM, announcing yet another campaign to stop it, praising the successful eradication efforts of local, national and international women's organizations, and lamenting the stubborn persistence of the practice among certain ethnic groups, most notably Maasai.[2] So as one of the two main non-governmental organizations (NGOs) working with Maasai women, it seemed only natural (to the national press and most Tanzanians) that MWEDO (which stands for the Maasai Women's Development Organization) would join the fight to eradicate FGM. But the fact that MWEDO was being "urged" suggests that the organization was somehow slow or reluctant to get involved in the FGM campaigns. And, indeed, it was. Most Maasai women leaders, including the

leaders of MWEDO, have tried to resist demands to focus their efforts and resources on eradicating FGM, insisting instead on the need to address a different set of priorities and human rights—namely, economic and political empowerment.

The differences between the agendas of MWEDO and those of the dominant Tanzanian society (who Maasai call "Swahili"), including prominent national and transnational women's organizations, on the matter of FGM point to larger tensions over culture, power and human rights. As international campaigns to end the practice of FGM have shifted from framing the practice as a health concern to a human rights violation in order to justify their interventions (Shell-Duncan 2008), they have broadened and intensified the pressure on "grassroots" organizations like MWEDO to join forces. Moreover, both the health and human rights frameworks have downplayed the history and complicated cultural and social meanings of the practice for societies like Maasai, condemning FGM outright as a "traditional oppressive

An abridged version of Dorothy L. Hodgson, 2011. "These are not our Priorities: Maasai Women, Human Rights, and the Problem of Culture." In Dorothy L. Hodgson, ed. *Gender and Culture at the Limit of Rights*. Philadelphia: University of Pennsylvania Press, pps. 138–157.

practice," a "harmful cultural practice," and, now, a form of violence against women (cf. Hernlund & Shell-Duncan 2007). This chapter explores the history, objectives, agendas and practices of MWEDO in order to analyze the consequences, or "perils and pitfalls" (Shell-Duncan 2008), of the international anti-FGM campaign and the larger "problem of culture" for the agendas and struggles of Maasai women leaders, activists, and community members, especially now that FGM has been reframed as a human rights issue. My purpose is not to explore the practice and meaning of FGM for Maasai women and men, which I have done elsewhere (Hodgson 2001, 2005), nor to trace the history of campaigns against FGM (Boyle 2002) or for "women's rights as human rights" (Merry 2006, Hodgson 2003).

Exploring the consequences of the reframing of FGM as a human rights issue for the lives of African women is important for several reasons. The chapter contributes to a growing body of feminist scholarship that explores the limits of a human rights approach to gender justice (e.g. Hodgson 2011b). Clearly the inclusion of women's rights as human rights has helped women throughout the world challenge oppressions of various kinds. But such rights-based approaches to justice, with their assumptions about the privileging of the individual and power of secular law, often make it difficult to recognize and address the structural causes and context of gender injustice such as the dismantling of health care, education and other social services as well as the deepening impoverishment produced by the adoption and implementation of neoliberal policies and practices. Moreover, "culture" is often depicted as an obstacle to "progress," thereby, at times, undermining women's power and autonomy by ignoring cultural practices and beliefs that serve to empower women while stigmatizing others, like FGM, that are often central to rites of passage or ritual transformations. But, as the chapter will show, the "problem of culture" is really a problem of power—of the continued assumption by many Euro-American donors and activists, and, increasingly, by African elites, that they can speak for (rather than listen to) rural, poorly educated women or even well-educated African women who are deemed culturally "other." Even if we acknowledge the interconnection of all rights (including economic, political, cultural), the question still remains as to who decides which rights to pursue at any given time.

TOWARD EQUAL RIGHTS FOR WOMEN: MWEDO

Maasai Women Development Organization (MWEDO) was registered as an NGO in 2000 "to work towards the empowerment of disadvantaged Maasai women economically, politically, culturally and socially through implementing activities in capacity building, advocacy, and promotion of human rights within the Maasai community" (MWEDO 2005:6). In 2006, MWEDO described its primary program areas as human rights and advocacy, household economic empowerment, public services development, and cultural citizenship. Work was conducted by a staff of five from a central office in the regional headquarters of Arusha through over 35 village-based membership groups spread throughout four of the five so-called "pastoralist districts" (Monduli, Simanjiro, Kiteto, Ngorongoro and Longido).

One of the founders and the first Executive Director, Ndinini Kimesera ole Sikar, is an educated Maasai woman who was taken from her rural Maasai homestead as a small child to live with her uncle in the large city of Dar es Salaam for health reasons. As a result, she was educated and easily assimilated into the guiding norms of urban, elite, "Swahili" society, yet maintained strong ties with her rural base. After secondary school, she studied finance and then worked as a banker for several years before marrying an older Maasai man, moving to Arusha, and helping to start MWEDO.

I first met Ndinini at the United Nations in New York in 2004, at the annual meeting of the UN Permanent Forum on Indigenous Issues (UN

Permanent Forum). She was browsing through a table of pamphlets and posters outside the main assembly room, dressed in a stunning rendition of customary Maasai dress, with a long beaded skirt and cloak, headdress and jewelry. I approached her and greeted her in Maa, which at once surprised and pleased her. We spoke for a while, then continued to meet and talk throughout the week-long session. We discussed many things, including news about mutual friends in Tanzania, her unusual life as one of the few well-educated Maasai women, MWEDO's work, and current policy debates in Tanzania. At the time, Ndinini felt very drawn to "indigenous rights" as a useful frame for pursuing Maasai political struggles; "it allows everyone to work together to pressure the Tanzanian state without making it an 'ethnic' or 'tribal' issue."

Ndinini has continued to be involved in the international indigenous rights movement (including attendance at the 2007 UN Permanent Forum). As evidenced by MWEDO's program in "cultural citizenship"[3] and use of the Maa language in workshops and meetings (despite government injunctions that only Swahili be used in such venues), she seeks to promote and protect Maasai culture and language in the face of radical social and economic changes. But her primary concern is with the political and economic empowerment of women. According to one MWEDO document:

> MWEDO was initiated in 1999 by three Maasai women inspired by the government efforts towards achievement of the goal of sustainable and equitable human development. But the patriarchal relations, attitudes and practices between men and women and between elders and young in Maasailand prevent these efforts. The women realized the need for doing something to support the government's efforts in transforming and operationalising a qualitative shift in Maasai land and national development so that gender equality is recognized in Maasailand. (MWEDO 2005:4)

As the cover of a MWEDO brochure states, beneath a picture of a group of seated Maasai women:

"women have equal rights within the society" (MWEDO nd).

The creation of MWEDO and other local pastoralist women's NGOs is timely, given the increasingly dire situation of pastoralists in general and pastoralist women in particular. As a nation, Tanzania has not only embraced the Millennium Development Goals, but set out an even more ambitious set of goals in two key policy documents: Tanzania Vision 2025 (which outlines a "new economic and social vision for Tanzania," including good, quality lives for all; good governance; and a competitive, neoliberal economy); and MKUKUTA (the latest Poverty Reduction Strategy Proposal). Although both discuss the need to direct resources and thought toward overcoming pervasive economic inequalities among Tanzanians, neither addresses the specific social, cultural, or economic needs of pastoralists, who currently number over 1,000,000 out of a population of over 34 million (including Maasai, Sukuma and Barabaig). Moreover, the strong neoliberal assumptions and goals of both documents, and recent related sectoral policy initiatives, suggest a bleak outlook for pastoralists as their land, livestock and livelihoods come under increasing threat from national and international economic interests. Under pressure from the World Bank, IMF, and northern countries to meet global demands for increased competition, the Tanzanian government has privatized key industries, revised land regulations to encourage the sale and alienation of land, promoted large-scale commercial agriculture, expanded the highly profitable wildlife tourism and big-game hunting sectors, instituted service fees for healthcare (primary school fees were instituted then revoked), withdrawn support for education and other social services, and encouraged pastoralists to replace transhumant pastoralism with more "productive" and less "environmentally harmful" modes of livestock "farming" (as opposed to "herding"), such as ranches. As a result, there has been increased alienation of pastoralist lands (especially drought and dry season grazing land), competition for water sources and other livestock-related resources, decline in the use of health facilities, and increased impoverishment (Hodgson 2001, 2011a). As pastoralism becomes less economically viable, growing numbers of pastoralist men have left their homesteads to seek work as miners or guards and laborers in towns like Arusha and Dar es Salaam (May and Ikayo 2007).

Pastoralist women are often now the *de facto* heads of household, although their increased workloads and responsibilities are rarely matched by increased rights and decision-making control. Historical evidence suggests that Maasai gender relations were complementary: each gender-age category had distinct roles, responsibilities and rights, all of which had to be accomplished successfully for their households and homesteads to prosper. As such, in addition to childcare, cooking, and other domestic duties, adult women shared use and access rights to family herds with their husbands, travelled widely to barter livestock products for food and other household goods, managed disputes among women and influenced the political decisions of male leaders, and were recognized as the moral authorities (Hodgson 2001, 2005). Over the past hundred years or so, however, as resources like land and livestock have become commoditized; men have been targeted as political leaders, household "heads" and livestock "owners" by first colonial then postcolonial authorities; and women's moral authority and spiritual significance have been dismissed; pastoralist women have occupied increasingly vulnerable and dependent positions in their households and homesteads. They now hold only limited rights to livestock, lack inheritance rights and significant decision-making power, and have few ways to earn cash. Yet they are increasingly responsible for feeding and caring for their children, including paying any school fees or health-care costs. Very few are literate or speak Swahili, the national language.[4]

The precarious position of pastoralist families, especially pastoralist women and girls, has been exacerbated by the disproportionate impact of neoliberal economic policies on pastoralists' access to quality education and health services, among other sectors. In 2000, for example, while 78% of children were enrolled in primary school nationally, only 8% of eligible children were enrolled in Monduli District, a large district comprised of mainly pastoralist Maasai. Moreover, the ratio of boys to girls in primary school in 2005 was 222 boys for every 100 girls in Monduli District, as compared to the national average of 98 boys to 100 girls (MWEDO 2006:7; URT 2006). The discrepancy when attendance and completion data is considered is even more marked: in Simanjiro District in 2003, there were a total of 2,759 boys and 2,115 girls enrolled in Standard I, as compared to only 729 boys and 527 girls in Standard VII—a dramatic decline suggesting a completion rate of approximately 26% (Simanjiro District Report 2005: Table 38). In terms of secondary school, pass rates on the national exams are much lower in the pastoralist districts than the national average of 22%, and the stark lack of secondary schools within pastoralist districts (in 2005 there were two in Simanjiro, two in Kiteto, four in Monduli, and four in Ngorongoro as compared to 22 in neighboring Arumeru District, which is densely populated with settled farmers) means that the few pastoralist children who pass the exam and obtain secondary school placements must attend boarding schools far from home.

Health indicators in pastoralist districts are severely underreported, in part because they do not include deaths outside of health facilities. Traditional birth attendants assist about 90% of deliveries, and few report maternal or infant deaths to health centers (Simanjiro District Report 2005). Moreover, Mother-Child Health (MCH) clinics are not offered at all health facilities, decreasing the likelihood of referrals and routine data collection. The recent introduction of fees for health services (except for MCH clinics, which are supposed to be free) and escalating costs of medicines have created further barriers to healthcare for poor pastoralist women and their children, who must often ask their husbands for money. Even those who try to use the health system in pastoralist districts face innumerable challenges and frustrations, including absent doctors, cancelled clinics, and lack of medicines. Many women must still travel long distances for more than rudimentary healthcare, such as in difficult pregnancies and deliveries, further contributing to maternal and infant mortality.

The top causes of morbidity and mortality in pastoralist districts are malaria, pneumonia, diarrhea, and tuberculosis. While the national average in 2004 for under-five mortality and maternal mortality was 126 children per 1,000 births and 1,500 per 100,000 respectively, research and experience suggests that these figures are substantially higher (but seriously underreported) in pastoralist districts.[5] Pastoralists are at a significant disadvantage because of their remote, dispersed locations. For example, in 2007 there was only one health facility per 780 square kilometers in Ngorongoro District, as compared to one per 31 square kilometers in Arumeru District (Arusha Regional Commissioners Office 2009). Even today, there is a notable lack of health centers and hospitals, with only three serving the five pastoralist districts. These difficulties are further magnified by the poor roads and lack of reliable transportation within these districts.

To date, MWEDO has pursued three primary strategies to promote women's empowerment and equality in the context of their increasingly difficult lives. First and foremost, MWEDO has worked to strengthen the economic capacity, income and autonomy of women through providing small start-up grants for group income-generating projects and training on how to keep accounts, run small businesses, and market their products. Many MWEDO groups, like those in Longido and Kimokowa, have used the money to start projects that produce beaded jewelry, ornaments, and other items for the tourist market. Others have purchased goats and even cattle to raise and then sell for a profit. These projects are not without their problems (especially how to market beaded crafts to transient tourists in a flooded domestic and international market), but Maasai women, as discussed below, have clamored to get involved.

Secondly, MWEDO has supported the education of pastoralist girls in secondary school and beyond through the provision of full financial support for tuition, room, board, and other needs, including a year of "pre-form I" training[6] where necessary. In 2005, they supported 45 girls who were selected by committees from all of the "pastoralist" districts. Funds have come from donors but also Maasai community members; MWEDO has met with community members and leaders, both men and women, to convince them of the need to educate Maasai girls and encourage them to contribute to the Pastoralist Girls Education Fund. In 2005, they organized a huge community-based fund-raising campaign for the Education Fund involving *ilaigwenak* (leaders of male age-sets), women leaders, politicians and others. By August 2006, they had received over 6 million shillings (approx. $5,000) in contributions and pledges.

Finally, MWEDO has conducted workshops and awareness-raising sessions on aspects of women's rights. In 2005, these included a large, USAID-sponsored workshop on human rights and democracy designed to educate women about their legal and political rights (in preparation for the 2005 national presidential and parliamentary elections); a series of workshops about HIV/AIDs (which MWEDO framed as a women's right issue, as in their right to know how to protect their own bodies and decide who would be their sexual partner); and numerous training sessions with different member groups on land rights, livestock policies, legal rights (including marriage, divorce, inheritance), and other relevant economic and political issues. Workshop participants were primarily uneducated Maasai women from rural areas, ranging from elderly grandmothers to young, nursing mothers.

Focus group discussions, individual interviews, and informal conversations with MWEDO members in 2005 and 2006 suggest that they enthusiastically support MWEDO's initiatives. As one older woman explained to me, "before we stayed home and waited for men, we were dependent on them for everything. But now we go out and support ourselves." "In the past," another woman interjected, "women had no cattle, but now we do." Older women were also avid supporters of providing secondary education to their daughters. "Papers have gotten heavy," noted a delegate to the 2006 MWEDO Annual General Meeting, "we can't understand them. Pastoralist women are far behind. We need education and MWEDO has helped." Or as another commented, "I really want girls to study. In the past they were married/sold off [*kuozwa*] and then some returned home because their husbands had no property. Then they became burdens to their fathers. But now they can support themselves." When one of the male delegates to the Annual General Meeting suggested that MWEDO also fund the education of Maasai boys, "Nanyore," a younger female member of the MWEDO Board of Directors replied:

> MWEDO does not discriminate against boys. But because of the history of discrimination against girls, it has decided to help girls. We women are mothers of both girls and boys. But if a father has cattle, he uses it to educate boys. That is why Munka, Brown and others are here [referring to older Maasai men who were members of the Board of Directors]. Why are there no older educated women here? The money MWEDO is given is for educating Maasai girls. We would encourage men to start their own education fund—you have the money and ability, but we'll work with you.

Nanyore has herself benefited from MWEDO's education initiatives. As the fifth of six wives of an older man, mother of four, with only a primary school education, she decided several years ago that she was finished having children and wanted more education, including learning English, leadership, and computer skills so that she could work with an NGO. Moreover, disgusted with the poor performance of local political leaders, she decided to compete in the election for ward councilor—and won. She is now a respected politician and community leader who carefully navigates the demands of her husband and family and her ambitions for economic security and personal advancement.

In interviews conducted throughout Maasai areas with women (both MWEDO members and non-members), they expressed the same urgent needs: hunger, poverty, lack of clean accessible water, and, for many, lack of functioning, affordable health facilities. (Men echoed many of the same needs in my interviews with them.) No one mentioned FGM, polygyny, or even arranged marriage as priorities for change. The issue of "culture" was, however, raised at the Annual General Meeting in a fierce debate about cultural authenticity, exploitation, and protection. One woman described an incident in which a donor group visited, took a lot of pictures, and claimed they would help—but never followed through. Several women and men discussed the issue of Maasai clothing—how other ethnic groups wore it at weddings and such, or even to make claims to donors that they were indeed Maasai. But when, for example, Maasai men wore shirts and pants, they were accused of no longer being Maasai. "I am wearing a t-shirt," proclaimed a younger man, "does that make me not Maasai?" Only one woman raised the issue of FGM: "What about the problem of circumcision [*kutahiri*]? It is part of our culture, but the government says don't do it. What do we do now?" No one responded, but many shook their heads, and several muttered about the recent vehemence of government sponsored anti-FGM campaigns.

WHOSE PRIORITIES?

Ironically, although MWEDO propounds a fairly typical agenda of political and economic initiatives to support women's empowerment in which cultural issues are in the background, donors and mainstream feminist groups in Tanzania foreground Maasai "culture" in their interactions and assessments of MWEDO's work. Two examples suffice. The first involves MWEDO's relationship with one of their main international donors, which has an office in Dar es Salaam. During my year of research with MWEDO in 2005–6, representatives from the donor group visited the MWEDO offices constantly, usually with little notice and official visitors in tow. MWEDO workers, in turn, were expected to suddenly drop their work to escort the donors and visitors to visit some of the Maasai women's groups. Ndinini and other MWEDO staff made phone calls to members of the group, begged women like Nanyore to ask the women to gather, purchased gifts for the women to give the visitors, organized transport and food, and so forth. Inevitably, the same women's groups were visited every time, because they were only an hour from Arusha and easily accessible by a tarmac road. During the visit, the women would dance and sing, give the visitors gifts, and pose patiently for the many, many pictures that were taken.

Although Ndinini was grateful for the substantial support that MWEDO received from the donor, she confided in me that she sometimes wondered about the "real" reasons for their support:

> I am not sure if we are just cultural tourism for them. I looked at their website the other day, and there is a big picture of one of their visits to Longido. I am worried that they are just interested in MWEDO because of the nice pictures of Maasai. But we want to get something out of them. We gave them a proposal for maternal health, but they were not interested. They asked us to prepare a proposal on family planning, but we weren't interested. They wanted to encourage Maasai women to take birth control pills! Can you imagine!?! But what women need is food, health services, education and income—not pills! [The donor] is very heavy-handed!

My interviews with some of the donor staff confirmed Ndinini's suspicions. When asked why they worked with MWEDO, one senior expatriate man quipped, "they make good photo-ops [opportunities]!"

But it is not just white expatriates who romanticize and exoticize Maasai women, treating them as photo-ops to be seen and admired, but not to be listened to. Many Tanzanians do the same. In September 2005, Merry (a staff person from MWEDO), Nanyore, and three other MWEDO group members traveled to Dar es Salaam to participate in the biannual "Gender Festival" organized by the Tanzanian Gender Networking Programme (TGNP) and the Feminism Activist Coalition (FemAct), two prominent Tanzanian feminist organizations, on the topic of "Gender, Democracy and Development: Popular Struggles for an Alternative and Better World." For four days, over 2,000 women and men from grassroots organizations, civil society organizations, development groups, government, academia, and overseas participated in plenary sessions, workshops, and performances related to the theme. In addition, there was a large exhibition featuring booths of craft vendors, activist organizations, bookstores and more. The MWEDO members ran a small booth on the fringes of the exhibition to sell beaded jewelry and crafts produced by member groups. Generally, an older *koko* (grandmother) and younger woman staffed the booth most of the time, in part because they barely spoke or understood Swahili (much less English), the dominant languages of the Gender Festival sessions. A third Maasai woman who had attended secondary school in Kenya, and so was quite fluent in Swahili and English, also stayed with them. Nanyore and Merry, however, browsed the other exhibitions, attended some plenary and workshop sessions, and occasionally helped at the booth. Merry also presented a brief description of MWEDO's efforts to educate pastoralist girls at a workshop on "popular struggles over education." I spent the days sitting with the women in the booth, accompanying Merry and Nanyore to sessions and meals, and helping Merry prepare and type up her presentation.

From the first day, it was clear that the presence of the MWEDO women and booth created quite a stir among other Tanzanians. Many men and women tried on the jewelry, belts, and shirts to see how they looked, modeling to the exclamations and admiration of their friends (far fewer bought anything). (By the last day, several neighboring vendors were visibly upset, complaining about why "the Maasai" received all of the attention. "Why don't they take pictures of us?") Nanyore, in particular, was the focus of much attention, as she aggressively tried to sell the jewelry ("oh, you look terrific!") or proudly strode her slim, almost seven-foot frame through the crowds. On the days that she dressed in Maasai clothes, she was thronged by men and women who wanted to have their picture taken with her, to the point where I suggested, only half-jokingly, that she start charging them for the photos. "Are you really Maasai?" asked one woman. "Yes, original!" she responded. "See how my ears are pierced?" (pointing to the holes on both the lower lobe and upper ear). When she stood up to ask a question (about why there were not more women members of parliament, ministers and government officials in attendance) at one of the plenary sessions, she was mobbed by photographers and participants taking pictures with their own cameras.

But the problem of culture was more than just a performance or display of difference. On the third day, Nanyore wore an elegant dress and modest gold jewelry, enjoying a respite from the constant attention of her admirers. Together with Merry, we attended a workshop on "African Feminism: Theories and Discourses of Resistance." At one point in the discussion, a Tanzanian woman reminded everyone that they should "remember the problem of culture. For example, among Maasai, where I have done research, women have no rights, they are forced to marry instead of go to school, and are forced to undergo female genital mutilation. Men can sleep around, while women can't." Merry and Nanyore just rolled their eyes at me, but neither responded. Afterwards, I asked them if they agreed with the woman. "No," Nanyore replied, "it is not that simple. And the problem is that it is always Maasai who are given as the example of cultural oppression, but they never think about their own cultural oppression." Perhaps more importantly, "challenging polygyny [which was also raised in the discussion as a sign of women's oppression] and female cutting *are not our priorities*." Instead,

she listed land rights, livestock, hunger, poverty, and education as the more important issues to be addressed.

DEBATING CULTURE AND DEVELOPMENT

So what does the story of MWEDO, and its relationship to donors, Tanzanian society, and mainstream Tanzanian women's organizations tell us about the role of culture and power in current debates about gender and development? Nanyore's comment, "[these] are not our priorities," gets to the crux of the problem. While she, Ndinini and other Maasai activists may be concerned about FGM, polygyny, and other cultural practices, they are far more alarmed by the increasing impoverishment, lack of rights, and marginalization of Maasai women. What they find troubling is that dominant society in Tanzania, including the main feminist organizations, does not seem to listen to, recognize or support their priorities. Instead, these groups continue to condemn and even criminalize Maasai for one specific cultural practice—FGM—and use its presence or absence as a measure of Maasai progress and "modernity."[7] Their attacks on Maasai cultural practices echo repeated campaigns (like "Operation Dress Up" in the late 1960s) by colonial and postcolonial governments (and several religious denominations) to forcibly change other seemingly "primitive" aspects of Maasai "culture" such as their attire, jewelry, and use of ochre on their skins (Hodgson 2001, 2005; Schneider 2006).

Maanda, a Maasai activist who heads the Pastoralist Women's Council (PWC), the other large Maasai women's NGO in Tanzania, told me a story about how the issue of FGM radically changed her relationship with another well-known feminist NGO in Tanzania, Tanzania Media Women's Association (TAMWA). TAMWA had helped to support Maanda when she fled her village as a young woman to pursue further education rather than marry against her will. She also worked for them for a few years in community outreach. But when, several years later, TAMWA asked Maanda and PWC to collaborate in their national anti-FGM campaign, Maanda refused. "I told them it was not my priority, it would block my work." In response, "the woman in TAMWA just told me, 'you won't work against it because you are just an uneducated woman.'" Maanda even refused an offer of over $150,000 from a German donor "because I was not willing to work and campaign against the practice." Instead, "I believe that it should be dealt with indirectly, by educating girls so that they can make their own decisions."

Moreover, like Ndinini and other educated Maasai women activists, she argues that any effort should be toward seeking alternatives to the modification, which is only one small part of a long series of ceremonies and celebrations that ritually transform a Maasai girl into a Maasai woman. As she argues, "it is about cultural survival. You can change the cutting, but you need to keep the ceremony, it is important." And in fact, in several Maasai communities the cutting of the clitoris is being replaced by a small, "ceremonial" cut on the inside of the thigh (Hodgson 2001:241–249). But in other communities, fierce condemnation and government criminalization of the practice is making it more secretive, and pushing some parents to "cut" their girls at younger and younger ages, before they can be discovered—which creates new problems about the status of these girl-women with regards to marriage, sex and pregnancy.

Maanda, Ndinini and other educated Maasai women activists' stance on FGM is both pragmatic and political. It is pragmatic in the sense that they recognize that their constituents—rural, largely uneducated Maasai women—have more pressing priorities, such as ensuring the present and future survival and security of their families in increasingly difficult circumstances. Moreover, they believe that the only way the practice will change is indirectly, through the education of girls (and boys). But their position is also political; it is intended to confront and challenge the structural power of TGNP, FemAct, TAMWA and other Tanzanian and international women's groups who

continue to "speak for" Maasai and other indigenous women, rather than listen to, learn from, and work with them.

Conflicting ideas of "culture" and the role of "culture" in "development" are central to these tensions. Most Tanzanians, especially Tanzanian feminists, view "culture" as equivalent to "tradition," a predominantly negative set of static practices that they believe have oppressed women and obstructed their progress toward equality and development. Yet their fascination with Maasai clothes, jewelry and women suggests an acceptance, even an embrace, of culture as display and performance. Unfortunately for organizations like MWEDO and Maasai women like Nanyore, the result is that they figure more as "photo-ops" than protagonists struggling for political and economic empowerment.

In contrast, Maasai activists and their constituents view culture as dynamic, contested, and often the site of female power and authority. As such, they often disaggregate "culture" by applying a gender analysis to foreground "positive" practices (that is, those that are empowering for women) such as spiritual healing and dispute "negative cultural practices" (which they see as disempowering) like domestic violence. Moreover, they make clear that the problems they face today are not inherent to their "cultures" and "traditions," but the product of broader political and economic forces such as colonialism, missionary evangelization, capitalist industry, the privatization of land and other natural resources, population pressures and HIV/AIDs that are depriving them of their lands and livelihoods and seriously eroding their rights. Even domestic violence and the "culture of patriarchy" are understood as historically produced, linked to and articulated with conflict, violence and patriarchal orders occurring nationally, regionally and internationally.

But the tensions also reveal different ideas about "gender" and "gender equality." Several Maasai women, in conversations with me, explained that while they wanted "equality" vis-à-vis Maasai men and all Tanzanians in terms of rights to control and inherit property and resources and access to health, education and other social services, they were not necessarily seeking "equality" in terms of "women taking men's roles and men taking women's roles." Instead, as Mary Simat, a Kenyan Maasai activist, stated at the UN Permanent Forum in 2004, "The key principle should be the *complementarity* of gender." Many Maasai women, in other words, are seeking equality in terms of rights but not necessarily roles; most would be content to pursue their historical responsibilities caring from young and sick animals, managing milk processing and distribution, trading, cooking, caring for children, and so on if the related rights and respect that used to accompany these roles were restored. But they also recognize that years of political and economic changes have undermined such possibilities, imposing new regimes of cash, commodities, private property, and wage labor that require new ways of being and surviving.

Thus they confront the mainstream international women's movement with a more radical perspective on individual rights that recognizes how political-economic structures like capitalism, neoliberalism, or what some have called "the New World Order" produce structural obstacles to the free exercise of such rights, so that the promotion of individual rights may at best mask and at worst perpetuate and aggravate these systemic inequalities and imperial relations. They also show how some of these seemingly universal, acultural rights are in fact inherently "culture-bound," with their naturalized assumptions about individual agency, liberal ideas of gender equality, and the inherent values and specific visions of modernity and progress. Moreover, several examples in this chapter illustrate how the national and international women's movement itself, in its practices and policies toward Maasai women, has been complicit at times with imperialist "recolonization." If these organizations really cared about the health and well-being of Maasai women, why not support them in addressing the economic and political causes of disease, hunger and insecurity? And if they really cared about the human rights of Maasai women, why not support the economic and political rights that Maasai women are seeking to obtain? Although they face

tremendous struggles in their daily lives, Maasai women are hardly the ignorant "beasts of burden" shackled to tradition or the docile embodiment or exhibitors of culture that some have assumed. Their current struggles should encourage us to consider more nuanced, dynamic understandings of the relation of culture, power and rights in the context of history and socio-economic change.

REFERENCES CITED

Arusha Regional Commissioner's Office. 2009. Online source for assorted data on health, education and other areas. http://www.arusha.go.tz, accessed 14 May 2009.

Boyle, Elizabeth Heger. 2002. *Female Genital Cutting: Cultural Conflict in the Global Community*. Baltimore: The Johns Hopkins University Press.

Hernlund, Ylva and Bettina Shell-Duncan, eds. 2007. *Transcultural Bodies: Female Genital Cutting in Global Context*. New Brunswick: Rutgers University Press.

Hodgson, Dorothy L. 2001. *Once Intrepid Warriors: Gender, Ethnicity and the Cultural Politics of Maasai Development*. Bloomington: Indiana University Press.

———. 2003. "Women's Rights as Human Rights: Women in Law and Development in Africa." *Africa Today* 49(2):1–26.

———. 2005. *The Church of Women: Gendered Encounters between Maasai and Missionaries*. Bloomington: Indiana University Press.

———.2011a. *Being Maasai, Becoming Indigenous: Postcolonial Politics in a Neoliberal World*. Bloomington: Indiana University Press.

———.ed., 2011b. *Gender and Culture at the Limit of Rights*. Philadelphia: University of Pennsylvania Press.

Maasai Women Development Organization (MWEDO). nd. One-page glossy brochure describing "programs and activities."

———. 2005. "Five Year Strategic Plan 2005–2009." 23 pp.

———. 2006. "Baseline Survey on Pastoralists Education in 3 Districts of Monduli, Kiteto and Simanjiro." Prepared by FAIDA BDS Co. Ltd. Photocopy in author's possession.

May, Ann and Frances Ndipapa Ole Ikayo. 2007. "Wearing Ilkarash: Narratives of Image, Identity and Change Among Maasai Labour Migrants in Tanzania." *Development and Change* 38(2):275–298.

Merry, Sally Engle. 2006. *Human Rights and Gender Violence: Translating International Law into Local Justice.* Chicago: University of Chicago Press.

Schneider, Leander. 2006. "The Maasai's New Clothes: A Developmentalist Modernity and its Exclusions." *Africa Today* 53(1):100–131.

Shell-Duncan, Bettina. 2008. "From Health to Human Rights: Female Genital Cutting and the Politics of Intervention." *American Anthropologist* 110(2):225–236.

Sikar, Ndinini Kimesera and Dorothy L. Hodgson. 2006. "In the Shadow of the MDGs: Pastoralist Women and Children in Tanzania." Special issue of *Indigenous Affairs* on "Africa and the Millennium Development Goals," 1/06:30–37.

Simanjiro District Report. 2005. Photocopy of sections in author's possession.

United Republic of Tanzania (URT). 2006. Millennium Development Goals, United Republic of Tanzania. Progress Report 2006. Ministry of Planning, Economy and Empowerment. Available online at http://www.tz.undp.org/docs/MDGprogressreport.pdf, accessed 14 February 2007.

NOTES

1. As anyone familiar with the scholarly and activist debates over female genital modification knows, there is a politics to the very naming of the practice. Following Kratz (2007), I choose to use the politically neutral term "modification" instead of "mutilation" or "cutting." As a scholar seeking to understand how and why the practice occurs, its role within the social and ritual lives of men and women, and the meaning of the practice to all involved, I believe that the term "modification" enables understanding rather than immediate condemnation. Moreover, the phrase "female genital modification" complicates the too-easy north–south divide by including consideration of such increasingly common cosmetic surgical procedures in the global north as labiaplasty (reduction of "large" labias) and vaginoplasty ("tightening" and "rejuvenating" of vaginas), and clitoral unhooding. For more information on these procedures, see, for example, www.labiaplastysurgeon.com (accessed September 22, 2008).

2. The titles of recent headlines include: "Communities urged to shun FGM," "Dangers of FGM in childbirth," "The crime that is FGM," "Anti-FGM rally to mark Zero Tolerance Day," "How secure are Tanzanian girls from FGM today?"

3. In the brochure, "cultural citizenship" is described as follows: "The program presents overwhelming evidence, carefully documented and organized events of Maasai culture, and shows its potential validity and usefulness; example that of indigenous knowledge and its utility to human development. Likewise, the 'Arts' that is going beyond the Opera house or gallery. It is meant to encourage cultural mapping in development and provision of opportunities without hindering the good traditions and people of their culture."

4. The previous two paragraphs are drawn from Sikar & Hodgson (2006:31–32).

5. From "At a Glance: Tanzania, United Republic of." UNICEF table of statistics. Available online at http://www.unicef.org/infobycountry/Tanzania_statistics.html, accessed January 19, 2006.

6. Pre-Form I training is a year of intensive remedial instruction in English, Swahili, math and other subjects to prepare for the secondary school placement exams that determine which students can attend the much less expensive government secondary schools.

7. Among Western feminists, of course, polygyny is also condemned, but such debates have little public space in a country like Tanzania where Muslims constitute over one third of the population.

3 • *Sharon Abramowitz and Mary H. Moran*

INTERNATIONAL HUMAN RIGHTS, GENDER-BASED VIOLENCE, AND LOCAL DISCOURSES OF ABUSE IN POSTCONFLICT LIBERIA

A Problem of "Culture"?

DISCUSSION QUESTIONS

1. How is gender-based violence (GBV) defined in national and international laws and by NGO activists? What kinds of practices are considered as examples of GBV?
2. How and why do these legal definitions differ from the perspectives and priorities of local women in postconflict Liberia?
3. How do different ideas about culture, gender, and power shape the interactions between Liberian communities and national and international NGO workers?

GBV INTERVENTION, CHAPTER 1

One steamy afternoon in 2008, a white four-wheel-drive vehicle with tinted windows drove into a rural community in the Liberian interior. The village was located close to a regional capital near a central highway and as a result it was a popular destination for donors, journalists, and other visitors seeking out "real culture" and traditional ways of life in postwar Liberia. The truck carried three foreigners: a historian, an anthropologist, and a lawyer. All were white women invited by a prominent human rights NGO to study gender-based violence. They were accompanied by the NGO's Liberian staff and by a local youth organization that the NGO funded to run gender-based violence workshops for rural residents. None of the foreign visitors, including the anthropologist, spoke the local language.

At the thatch-roofed "palava hut" in the center of town, it took some time in this presentation-fatigued community to round up a group of adults willing to be interrupted from their daily chores before an audience of a hundred people was collected. Because this was a "gender" event, older women were seated on benches in the front while the men—including the town chief—sat off to one side. The three

An abridged version of Sharon Abramowitz and Mary H. Moran, 2012. International Human Rights, Gender-Based Violence, and Local Discourses of Abuse in Postconflict Liberia: A Problem of "Culture"? *African Studies Review* 55 (2): 119–146. Copyright © 2012 African Studies Association. Reprinted with the permission of Cambridge University Press and of the authors.

foreigners were seated behind a small table in front, facing the audience. The anthropologist expected to find customary kola nuts and drinks; but when none appeared, she wondered if this lack of hospitality was due to postwar poverty. She was also concerned because the visitors had brought no gifts for their hosts.

This event transpired in a small village in the center of a small West African country, Liberia, which was recovering from a civil war that lasted from 1990 to 2003. Although many questions can be asked of this scene, we are concerned with the following: how did a small town in the interior of Liberia become the focus of an internationally renowned human rights organization? What did the NGO hope to achieve by sending three academics thousands of miles to this location to observe a humanitarian intervention to end gender-based violence? How were the visit and the "gender" event interpreted by the community members? Most importantly, what assumptions did the local and global participants bring with them about gender and violence, and what implications did that have for the success of gender-based violence interventions in Liberian communities?

In this article, we examine the microdynamics of humanitarian-sponsored gender-based violence (GBV) interventions in postconflict Liberia and the discourses surrounding GBV at the local, national, and international levels. We analyze how gender, violence, laws, and norms articulate with global discourses about human rights in local contexts of implementation. We present a set of "intersecting texts" documenting GBV activities in post-war Liberia, drawn from the fieldwork experiences of the authors, and incorporating historical and contextual analysis. Our intention is to juxtapose ethnographic "chapters" with a streaming analysis that highlights how local populations have the capacity to powerfully contest global forms of humanitarian intervention through redefinition, displays of conflict, argumentation, and ultimately nonparticipation. To protect our informants, we have disguised their identities and the locations of these events.

GENDER AND VIOLENCE IN THE LIBERIAN CONTEXT

Humanitarian aid organizations working in postconflict settings across Africa carry into their engagements with local populations certain preconceived notions about postconflict recovery, development, and peace-building. Many believe that the "state of crisis" both requires and makes possible certain forms of intervention (see Moran 2010). In Liberia specifically, humanitarian workers carried into their encounters preconceived notions about the meaning of culture and the role of "African tradition" as a determinant of gender-based violence, and of human behavior more generally. Yet many of these well-intentioned outsiders know little about the specific history of the country or the social institutions that had regulated life in Liberia before the war.

Located on the Atlantic coast, Liberia has historically been enmeshed in complex and violent regional networks of trade, colonialism, and postcolonial nation-building. In the seventeenth and eighteenth centuries, the small-scale chiefdoms and confederacies of the Guinea Coast or Mano River region experienced frequent conflicts over land, trading partnerships, and the right of small communities to act autonomously. Local institutions existed for addressing violence between spouses, neighbors, in-laws, and all those who shared in the embedded relationships of daily life. Patrilineal descent and virilocal residence were the institutional structures that grounded an ideology of male dominance and female subordination, but women held a crucial role in food production, and were also able to organize collective responses to unjust treatment that served as a check on the authority of men (Moran 1989, 1990). In the rural "traditional" sector, women were widely recognized as breadwinners and their economic contribution was valued and celebrated. Women held institutionalized authority roles in local political structures, ranging from the Sande society hierarchy in the northwest to the classic "dual sex" political offices in the southeast (Okonjo 1976, Bledsoe 1980,

Moran 1990, 2006). These cultural apparatuses allowed some women to rise to positions of community and regional leadership, but even "ordinary" women had authority within their kin groups and households as mothers, sisters, and aunts; and as they aged, they commanded the labor and respect of younger kin, both male and female. Although many indigenous communities would have insisted that men and women were not "equal," these communities also provided spaces for women to speak and act freely, and recognized women's accusations of unjust and abusive treatment. Rape and other sexual crimes were neither tolerated nor ignored; sanctions against sexual violence were documented by observers from as early as the mid-nineteenth century (Abramowitz 2014).

In the early 19th century, Liberia became the site of an experiment in resettling enslaved populations of African descent. Free black Americans, freed slaves, and Africans taken from impounded slave ships created a vibrant creole community in a series of small coastal cities, which declared themselves an independent republic in 1847. For much of its early existence, Liberia was little more than a loose assemblage of coastal cities where the Americo-Liberian settler elite dominated the political and economic structures. Following World War II, an economic boom in rubber and iron ore drew many indigenous Liberians into urban centers, the market economy and emerging modern cultural forms. The contrast between settler wealth and privilege and indigenous exclusion became stark. Through the 1970s, students, labor unions, and an active press demanded greater political openness and transparency, and an end to the single-party rule that had lasted for decades. A military coup in 1980 brought to power young enlisted men of indigenous background and began a process of creating politicized ethnic groups out of "tribes" that had been defined by governmental administrative units.

In contrast with the indigenous conception of women as breadwinners, the settler Liberian ideology that existed in urban society throughout the 20th century held that the ideal woman should be economically dependent upon her husband and that political and domestic authority fell "naturally" to the man. Derived from the nineteenth-century middle class and missionary tradition and reinforced through Christian churches, it resembled essentialist Victorian gender constructions of the "modern" West. Paradoxically, "freeing" women from their roles as agricultural producers made them more dependent on their husbands, and thus more vulnerable to domestic abuse. Yet, due to the small size of the coastal elite, some women attained high degrees of Western education and achieved prominent positions in government, business, and international institutions like the United Nations. Before the outbreak of civil war, Liberian women ran households, managed their own businesses, traveled unaccompanied without fear, and wielded political and economic authority. It is not surprising that Liberia's first post-war president, Ellen Johnson Sirleaf, is also the first women to be elected president of an African country, but she had also served as a cabinet secretary in the 1970s.

But the late 1970s and 1980s brought a coup d'état, political instability, and increasing political conflict and violence to Liberia. With the central government unraveling by 1990 and refugees streaming into neighboring countries, the Economic Community of West African States (ECOWAS) sent a military force to intervene. From 1990 to 1997, a stalemate existed between ECOWAS peacekeeping forces, a series of transitional governments based in the capital, Monrovia, and several rebel groups that had taken over the majority of the country. Porous regional frontiers and valuable resources like diamonds and timber contributed to the escalation of conflict across the region, drawing the neighboring countries of Sierra Leone and Guinea into the fighting. After a brief peace, Charles Taylor, a notorious rebel leader, won a presidential election in 1997, and rival warlords returned to battle as the territory outside Monrovia fell under the control of several armed factions. Estimates of civilian death ranged as high as two hundred thousand, and more than half the population of about three million was displaced.

Liberians lived in a state of insecurity, without a functioning legal, criminal justice, or military system from 1990 to 2003. During this time, the Liberian and Sierra Leonean wars attracted international attention for their shocking displays of state collapse, violence against civilians, and sexual abuse. A 2005 survey of more than 1600 women found that over 90 percent reported being subjected to some form of sexual abuse during the conflict (Hodson 2007:7). The kidnapping of young women by competing armed factions and their imprisonment in relations of sexual servitude, the forced conscription of young boys and girls into service as child soldiers, and the rise of militarized femme fatales like Black Diamond and Jewel Taylor captured the world's imagination. Throughout the conflict, humanitarian NGOs provided Liberians with food, medicine, shelter, and social services including gender-based violence counseling and and human rights education.

The war came to its conclusion in 2003, and plans were made to relocate half of the country's population back to long abandoned homes, communities, and cities with little remaining infrastructure, destroyed institutions, and weakened networks. Liberia was materially and socially devastated, and statutory and customary law had uncertain legal authority due to a long series of political and legal manipulations implemented by recent Liberian presidents in order to consolidate power. With a weak transitional government in place, and statutory law in dispute, the administration of security was managed through a partnership between the Liberian government and the United Nations Mission in Liberia (UNMIL).

Quickly, in the context of what was effectively an extra-legal space, the international community and women's organizations like the Association of Female Lawyers of Liberia (AFELL) pressured the parliament to pass new GBV legislation, including a 2003 law that defined women's property rights in marriage and divorce and prohibited husbands from demanding compulsory labor from their wives or directing them to have illicit sexual intercourse with another man. A 2005 law punished first-degree rape (specifically, gang rape) with life imprisonment, and second-degree rape with a ten-year prison sentence. Along with the international community, organizations like AFELL saw "traditional" institutions such as bridewealth and patrilineal inheritance as impediments to full citizenship for women, and they were convinced that they were acting with the tacit consent of uneducated indigenous women. Some rural women, however, thought that the new laws' emphasis on *wives* undermined their positions elsewhere; for example, as sisters within patrilineal descent groups.

In addition to new national legislation, other GBV interventions were implemented under the legal authority of U.N. Security Council Resolution 1509 (2003), which passed on to Liberia the jurisdiction for the implementation of UN Security Council Resolution 1325 on "Women, Peace and Security" (2000). These mandates included the following three priorities: (1) women should be included at all levels of decision-making, (2) gender perspectives must be integrated into all aspects of peace-building to mitigate the impact of conflict upon women, and (3) women should be protected from violence during and after conflict. Significant efforts were made to implement Resolutions 1509 and 1325 in Liberia. Many women were given senior positions in the government, and the Ministry of Gender and Development amassed great power and resources. Additionally, the United Nations Mission in Liberia (UNMIL) trained police officers, staff, and legal advocates on GBV issues, and the UN created a formal humanitarian coordination system to monitor GBV activities.

Most GBV activity, however, took place through the services and training programs of international NGOs. These well-documented interventions included the provision of shelters for abused women, training for local leaders on GBV issues, training for police and military personnel about GBV enforcement, training and matériel for rape kits to local clinics, and the provision of trained psychosocial counselors for victims of domestic abuse and rape. Their goal, as they moved through the country providing community-based education programs, was to transform local social norms and values regarding gender and to decrease violence across Liberian society.

GBV INTERVENTION, CHAPTER 2

In the center of the hut, a clear space was left for the workshop performance. The presenters—a Liberian youth group of men and women in their twenties—put on a play illustrating the proper postwar response to domestic violence. In the scene they performed, a woman saw her husband off to work and was then called away to assist a friend with a problem. The husband returned to find his wife not at home; jealous and angry, he waited for her to return, and then beat her savagely. The acting was exceedingly realistic and the audience participated actively, laughing and whooping along with the action. The play ended with another man breaking up the domestic dispute by explaining that the law of the land forbids such violence. A man must not beat his wife because doing so violates her human rights. It is a crime that must be answered for in court, and it is the duty of the police to arrest the offender and begin criminal proceedings. His injunction to the audience was clear: "A woman who has been beaten should report her husband to the police, and the town chief, himself a government official, should assist her in bringing criminal charges." At the play's conclusion, the actors invited the audience to discuss what they had seen and to ask questions they might have about the rule of law in the new, postconflict Liberia.

In humanitarian efforts to combat gender-based violence, the definition of GBV is foundational to the purpose and scope of GBV interventions. In 2005 a transnational initiative called the Inter-Agency Standing Committee (IASC) on Gender-Based Violence brought together NGOs, UN agencies, and experts to issue guidelines for GBV activities in humanitarian contexts. They defined GBV through a complex definition that includes

both abstract principles and detailed practices. Included in the definition are three core statements: (1) a statement of principle coupled with a statement of legal protection, (2) a statement of scope, and (3) a non-exhaustive list of examples of gender-based violence (IASC 2005):

> [Statement of Principle] Gender-Based Violence is an umbrella term for any harmful act that is perpetrated against a person's will, and that is based on socially ascribed (gender) differences between males and females. Acts of GBV violate a number of universal human rights protected by international instruments and conventions.
>
> [Statement of Scope] Many—but not all—forms of GBV are illegal and criminal acts in national laws and policies. Around the world, GBV has a greater impact on women and girls than on men and boys. The term "gender-based violence" is often used interchangeably with the term "violence against women." The term "gender-based violence" highlights the gender dimension of these types of acts; in other words, the relationship between females' subordinate status in society and their increased vulnerability to violence. It is important to note, however, that men and boys may also be victims of gender-based violence, especially sexual violence.
>
> [Specific Examples] The nature and extent of specific types of GBV vary across cultures, countries, and regions. Examples include: (1) sexual violence, including sexual exploitation/abuse and forced prostitution, (2) domestic violence; (3) trafficking, (4) forced/early marriage, and (5) harmful traditional practices such as female genital mutilation, honor killings, widow inheritance, and others. (IASC 2005)

The statement of principle is remarkably broad and potentially sensitive to cultural nuance. The statement of scope expands the statement of principle to ensure that practitioners recognize that acts of GBV may or may not be defined as illegal or criminal, and that the defining nature of these acts involves the subordinate status of women. The third statement, the list of examples of GBV acts, includes a narrowly defined range of crimes including rape, sexual exploitation, domestic violence, trafficking, forced or early marriages, and "harmful traditional practices."

This definition is grounded in the global legal framework of human rights: a framework with the capacity to embrace both universal standards and local relevance, and creates many new opportunities for activism in transitional contexts. But in Liberia, GBV has come to be understood and addressed within an extremely constrained set of specific parameters. Under UNMIL's Gender Coordination Committee the categories of GBV that are emphasized—sexual violence, domestic violence, forced or early marriages, and harmful traditional practices like female circumcision—were the focus of most outreach and education efforts. Unfortunately, this meant that GBV-related NGO interventions targeted a narrow range of violent behaviors and outcomes, but excluded other issues like women's health, economic rights, and girls' and women's access to educational and economic opportunities.

GBV INTERVENTION, CHAPTER 3

As the play and the subsequent discussion went on in the local language, NGO staff translated for the three visitors. Very quickly, it became apparent that the audience was directing urgent questions to the three white women watching at the front, who sat uneasily in what had become a sort of tribunal. One by one, women rose from their seats to describe actual (rather than hypothetical) cases of what they considered to be gender-based violence. They complained that men in the audience were perpetrators, and they bemoaned the unwillingness of their village chief to hear cases and bring the culprits to justice.

What was the remedy, they demanded, for the case of a man who had supposedly divorced his wife and left her without support for their children, yet kept coming "home" late at night, demanding sex? Did she have to satisfy him? No, said the lawyer,

definitively; if he forced her, it was rape, and she should go to the police or to the U.N. peacekeeping authorities, and prosecute him to the full extent of the law. What about men who fathered children and refused to support them? According to the lawyer, such situations, while unfortunate, were "not GBV" and therefore not relevant to this discussion.

Yet the Liberian women kept returning to the issue of financial support, arguing that most of the quarrels leading to one form of violence or another stemmed from the desperate economic situation. How could anyone know, they demanded, what type of offense was appropriate to bring to the police and what was not?

NGOs had defined their agendas without reference to local populations' definitions of gender subordination, exploitation, and abuse, and in response, Liberians demanded that the visible representatives of the NGOs speak to their own priorities, uncertainties, and real-life needs. The NGO-supported Liberian youth group had offered a global definition of gendered oppression in their drama by focusing on an incident of domestic abuse, and advocating for contacting local authorities—police, or village elders or chiefs. Community residents, however, had their own concerns about gender subordination which were quite different from those portrayed, and they made their concerns known. The women speaking focused on forms of structural and social violence that were associated with unclear gender roles and responsibilities, such as ambiguous sexual obligations and nonpayment of material contributions to the family unit. They believed that these conflicts caused the subsequent acts of physical violence with which the NGOs seemed to be obsessed. From the perspective of the townspeople, if NGOs could help them sort out their basic social and structural norms, obligations, and roles, violence would decline. Women who sought protection from male violence but wished to keep their households intact and men who struggled with high unemployment and women who were challenging their authority were all in a limbo of social and legal ambiguity.

From an NGO perspective, however, the violent act itself was the principal source of concern, and the "root cause" of this violence was the inherently unequal relationship between men and women sanctioned by "tradition." While aware of the post-conflict economic and structural issues that was leading to family and community disarray, NGOs treated these problems as "confounders" of the postconflict situation over which they had little control. Instead, they focused on gender-bias, patriarchy, and "tradition" as the source of GBV.

GBV INTERVENTION, CHAPTER 4

The community had heard about changes in the national law regarding rape, the rights of children, and other "human rights." They understood that the national legislature, under the previous government, had passed a new inheritance law regulating the property rights of spouses under both statutory and customary marriages and that this new law was intended to give women greater access to productive resources. They knew they were not supposed to "take the law into their own hands" and that the end of the war had resulted in a return to "the rule of law," but the laws themselves seemed to be changing rapidly around them. Information campaigns seemed to be contradictory, on the one hand, emphasizing the punitive nature of the new laws, like maximum sentences for rape, while on the other emphasizing the possibilities for egalitarian access to authentic justice afforded by the new court system. Furthermore, the police and courts were located in the regional center or the national capital. Only those with cash to spare for taxis, court fees, and other costs could think of bringing criminal or civil charges. Yet, with more and more areas of personal relations falling under criminal statutes, people were very worried about their potential liability for not reporting something to the police. If all the neighbors heard the man who banged on the door at midnight, demanding sex with his ex-wife, were they all complicit in the "rape"? What were the limits of the chief's authority under the new legal regime, in determining whether or not the couple was "really" married or divorced?

The anthropologist by this time had come to suspect that the arrangement of the seating and furniture had been designed to create the simulacrum of a courtroom all along. Both the men and women of this community wanted answers to their legal questions, and they were anxious to make use of any resources that happened to blunder into their town. As the questions mounted, they began to outstrip the ability of the visiting lawyer to answer, although she had carefully reviewed Liberia's prewar legal codes and postwar transitional justice plan. The three foreign observers, suddenly turned "judges," had no way to fit most of the cases brought before them as examples of gender-based violence into the legal framework defined by universal human rights conventions.

The meeting ended on a dramatic note when the complaints began to single out the town chief as responsible for not taking cases to the next administrative level. The town chief replied by chastising the women for giving the visitors a bad impression of the town as a whole. He was in the middle of his speech when the elder women sitting in the front row of benches rose as a group, turned their backs on him, and walked out of the palava hut, followed by the young women who had provided most of the specific complaints. This was a rather stunning moment because the team of visitors had been hearing for the entire week that the root cause of gender-based violence in Liberia was the "traditional" oppression of women and their status as "property" under the law. Indeed, just that morning at the oldest and most elite private college in the country, they had heard these aspects of "culture" cited by well-dressed women students. After the exit of these supposedly powerless and uneducated rural women, the workshop broke up, "in confusion" as one member of the Liberian NGO staff put it. The men, including the town chief, went off laughing to cover their embarrassment while the visitors scrambled, with relief, back into their air-conditioned vehicle.

For Liberian village residents, the NGO's message was an opening parry in a complex local negotiation that sought to open a broader forum for dispute resolution. In Liberia's history, legal entities had existed to resolve matters now seen as contributing to widespread GBV. Informal dispute-settlement procedures known in prewar communities as "house palavers," or moot courts (Gibbs 1963) had operated under the authority of elders to negotiate and define the obligations of domestic partners. Gibbs described the efficiency of the formal courts run by Poro-sanctioned chiefs, but he also noted "the [statutory] court is particularly inept at settling [the] numerous matrimonial disputes because its harsh tone tends to drive spouses farther apart rather than to reconcile them" (1963:2–3). The less formal moot court, run by senior kinsmen of both parties, was the preferred means of settling domestic disputes, including those involving abuse and violence.

Recent legal changes, however, created tremendous uncertainties for both men and women about the meanings of kinship, marriage, and property rights, as well as the conditions of social and governmental control, and proposed NGO solutions were consistently unsatisfactory. Wartime displacements left many Liberians without any means of proving rights to land, either through traditional mechanisms or registered deeds, and women's access to productive resources has been seriously threatened. The close timing of the two GBV-oriented legislative acts (the "Rape Law" and the "Inheritance Law") as well as the extensive publicity and educational campaigns raised serious fears for many men and women, and misinformation abounded. Communities were either deploying traditional mechanisms of dispute resolution secretly or illegitimately, or they had become afraid to use the moot court structure in the new post-war regulatory environment.

Scenes like the women's walkout were explained by NGO workers with one of two statements: "The problem is the culture," or "The problem is noncompliance." When NGO staff members complained about community noncompliance, they often expressed frustration with local leaders for participating in trainings, accepting the financial support of NGOs, and then failing to follow through with enforcement after the NGO's departure. The training of village elders, chiefs, teachers, and religious leaders through workshops was a major form of GBV intervention. At workshops, leaders were trained in the international definitions of GBV, lectured about gender oppression, told about human rights, and informed of the types of behaviors that constitute violations. Trainings conclude with appeals to community leaders to take the lead in stopping gender-based violence in their communities. Continuing incidents are then be attributed to "tradition," or the "savagery," "illiteracy," "traditionalism," and "backwardness" of the local partners, and recall "long discredited but still powerful stereotypes about passive, powerless, 'other' women" (Hodgson 2011:5). Local "culture" is always the source of the problem.

From the local community's perspective, the NGOs have their priorities confused. Community members agree that the illegitimate use of force related to relations of gender subordination is unacceptable, and must be addressed. Their concern, however, is with the failure of dispute resolution at the community level, rather than the specific *act* of violence. The "problem" is not patriarchy, it is the illegitimate use of force. Where NGOs see violent behaviors, Liberians see ambiguous and undetermined gender roles and structural uncertainty; where NGOs see "tradition," Liberians see the absence of the force of *both* tradition *and* governance in their lives.

But there is a positive side to the tremendous uncertainty observed here. These dynamics are working to pry open a discursive space for the postconflict renegotiation of gender roles and relationships. Moreover, the long-term implications of these changes for foundational social relations on the local level are utterly undetermined. The NGOs appear to be urging women to embrace their identity as Liberian *citizens*—that is, autonomous, bounded, rights-bearing individuals—at a moment when everyone understands that the state is still too fragile and resource poor to guarantee those rights (see Hodgson 2011). Women's rights as members of kin-based domestic groups have been weakened by the war, and there is considerable moral uncertainty about just what men and women owe to each other. As in postwar Sierra Leone, women exposed to violence were failed in equal measure by the international community and by their own society, which proved unable to sustain intergenerational traditions: "rural men and women, and parents and children, no longer really know what to expect from each other. This is . . . exciting, as it opens up new possibilities and creates new ways in which to be a woman or a man. At the same time it is distressing, as this fluidity in some cases delegitimizes traditional knowledge and authority" (Coulter 2009:251–52).

GBV INTERVENTION, CHAPTER 5

A few months later, on a hot summer day in the U.S. South, in a cool conference room, expatriate anthropologists, lawyers, NGO officers, and Liberian activists, government officials, and NGO workers met to discuss gender-based violence and the rule of law in Liberia. The conference opened with presentations from the anthropologists, who uniformly agreed that gender-based violence was not a core cultural feature of Liberian society. They concurred that the space of violence that currently existed was a product of specific historical formations that could be successfully challenged on local terms. Then the next panel began to speak.

One after another, regally dressed Liberian women rose from their seats to argue that "the problem was the culture." Speaking of Liberian men and women, they said—one after another—"it's our tradition that has made us this way." "It's our tradition that makes people do these bad things." The anthropologists argued. The lawyers responded. The air grew tense. Finally, one Liberian activist rose from her seat and said, "What are we doing. The problem is the MEN!"

Most expatriate NGO workers in Liberia are unaware of the history of gender relations in the country and of the daily realities in which men and women negotiate their responsibilities in the present moment, but the same cannot be said of the elite Liberian women who sat at the table. NGO workers may not understand how their own presence shapes the political economy of postconflict spaces and asserts a powerful, but indirect, influence over permissible discourses in those spaces, but the opening statements of the Liberian women attendees highlight these effects.

In a class-based discourse that has historical antecedents in ethnic and class divisions in Liberian society, Liberian women leaders are now at the forefront of the culturalist message; they decry the tradition of Liberian patriarchy, they assert that gender violence is deeply rooted in Liberian culture, and they advocate for the annulling of cultural norms in order to advance the status of women. They are supported in their efforts by academic research and by global NGO discourses, but they risk abandoning the historical legacy of Liberian women in authority, and dismissing local historical expressions of gender equity and protection.

As NGOs create new moral and material economies in the post-conflict Liberian sphere, a new class of Liberian women leaders has emerged who share the belief that international NGO GBV activities are legitimate, that globally circulated "GBV best practices" are, in fact, best, and that the problem is the culture . . . as though Liberian culture is static and primordial. NGO workers and Liberian feminist activists are equally unable to hear alternatives.

GENDER-BASED VIOLENCE IN THE VERNACULAR

At the core of this narrative is the problem of whether or not there is a fundamental "incommensurability" (Povinelli 2002) between global discourses about gender-based violence and local understandings of gender, power, violence, and moral behavior in postconflict Liberian life.

Povinelli used the term "incommensurable" to describe the clash of fundamentally different worldviews within the structure of a legal framework that posits itself as universal. The Liberian GBV experience shows how incommensurable the universal human rights approach and local vernacular interpretations of justice, protection, and obligation really can be. While both Liberian populations and NGOs share the goals of justice, rights, and equity, their respective theories regarding the specific causes of violence, the meanings of infractions, the expectations of the justice process, and meaningful consequences differ so fundamentally that they are almost mutually unintelligible. While all parties may wish for gender justice, NGOs' silence on the matter of a father's nonpayment of children's school fees, or local uncertainties about questions of sexual access to one's spouse, mean that GBV interventions are fundamentally ambivalent when applied to real relationships.

In Levitt and Merry's (2011) work on "vernacularization," or the active creation of human rights by civil society group at the local level, they identified three strategies, all of which use international human rights language as "discursive and aspirational resources" even when they lack the "authority provided by formal law" (92). These are (1) emphasizing women's rights, (2) integrating sexual minorities, and (3) linking the core concepts of human rights discourse to locally appropriate ideas and practices in new institutional settings (2011:91–2). But we contend that this "vernacularization" of human rights discourses about gender-based violence to locally specific contexts is not unidirectional; it is bidirectional, or "dialogic" (see Abramowitz 2010, 2014).

The chapters presented here demonstrate how local populations assert power and authority over the cultural narrative about gender violence that is being ascribed to them. They also show how local communities have the ability to derail the most basic of GBV initiatives through challenges to their legitimacy and authority. NGOs, too, exist in a specific cultural space—the space of international development and human rights discourses—which

attempts to integrate cultural sensitivity into programming while maintaining that local "cultures" are the "root causes" of gender-based violence. Unfortunately, as the parties with the most power in the dialogue, NGOs are wedded to the notion that "culture" is intrinsically oppositional to the full inclusion of women into human rights discourse. Liberian communities, for their part, retain actual power through passive tolerance, nonimplementation, nonattendance, or noncompliance.

CONCLUSION

We believe that it is imperative to integrate culture into GBV initiatives in postconflict contexts by adapting universal principles to local conditions and translating them into local idioms. But this process, we wish to emphasize, will be effective only if both sides of the encounter take into account the concerns of local actors, and the limited capacities of international organizations. In postconflict situations where there is great deal of uncertainty about legal codes, transitional justice mechanisms, and dispute settlement in general, the attempts of ordinary people to maintain or recreate social relationships should be supported, rather than threatened, by GBV interventions.

On a positive note, the encounter between NGO activists and Liberian populations has created new discursive and social spaces of possibility and action. While Liberian women are not shy to assert themselves and challenge the authority or competence of their "traditional" leaders, the notion of "traditional culture" as an impediment to gender equity has taken hold—especially among Liberian women who work closely with the international NGO community. Still, in order to avert the further disempowerment and destabilization of local "traditional" cultures in the aftermath of conflicts, humanitarian interventions in postconflict African societies must take seriously local African attempts to define, address, and resolve the problems of GBV in their own terms. NGOs must integrate more complex ideas of "culture" into their programmatic operations than currently circulate in humanitarian discourse in order to build locally relevant frameworks for intervention. GBV initiatives must be "living" initiatives that can "hear" local problems, "see" local strategies for resolution, and "think" actively about the best forms of engagement for local contexts before committing to specific tactics for intervention. They must be aware of, and sensitive to, the underlying currents of social conflict within communities and societies, and recognize the dynamic nature of gender roles as they take shape in postconflict contexts.

REFERENCES CITED

Abramowitz, Sharon. 2010. "Trauma and Humanitarian Translation in Liberia: The Tale of Open Mole." *Culture, Medicine, and Psychiatry* 34: 353–79.

———. 2014. *Searching for Normal in the Wake of the Liberian War.* University of Pennsylvania Press.

Bledsoe, Caroline. 1980. *Women and Marriage in Kpelle Society.* Stanford: Stanford University Press.

Coulter, Chris. 2009. *Bush Wives and Girl Soldiers: Women's Lives through War and Peace in Sierra Leone.* Ithaca, N.Y.: Cornell University Press.

Gibbs, James. 1963. "The Kpelle Moot: A Therapeutic Model of the Informal Settlement of Disputes." *Africa: Journal of the International African Institute* 33: 1–11.

Hodson, Igor. 2007. *UNMIL: International Engagement in Addressing Violence against Women.* London: ActionAid.

Hodgson, Dorothy, ed. 2011. *Gender and Culture at the Limits of Rights.* Philadelphia: University of Pennsylvania Press.

Inter-Agency Standing Committee (IASC). 2005. *Guidelines on Gender-Based Violence Interventions in Humanitarian Settings: Focusing on Prevention of and Response to Sexual Violence in Emergencies* (Field Test Version). Geneva: Inter-Agency Standing Committee.

Levitt, Peggy, and Sally Merry. 2009. "Vernacularization on the Ground: Local Uses of Global Women's Rights in Peru, China, India, and the United States." *Global Networks* 9(4): 441–61.

Moran, Mary H. 1989. "Collective Action and the Representation of African Women: A Liberian Case Study." *Feminist Studies* 15: 443–60.

———. 1990. *Civilized Women: Gender and Prestige in Southeastern Liberia.* Ithaca, N.Y.: Cornell University Press.

———. 2006. *Liberia: The Violence of Democracy.* Philadelphia: University of Pennsylvania Press.

———. 2010. "Gender, Militarism, and Peace-Building: Projects of the Postconflict Moment." *Annual Review of Anthropology* 39: 261–74.

Okonjo, Kamene. 1976. "The Dual Sex Political System in Operation: Igbo Women and Community Politics in Midwestern Nigeria." In *Women in Africa,* edited by Nancy Hafkin and Edna G. Bay, 45–58. Stanford, Calif.: Stanford University Press.

Povinelli, Elizabeth A. 2002. *The Cunning of Recognition: Indigenous Alterities and the Making of Australian Multiculturalism.* Durham, N.C.: Duke University Press.

Author Bios

SHARON ABRAMOWITZ is an assistant professor of Anthropology and African Studies at the University of Florida. She researches violence, gender, and health in West Africa.

LILA ABU-LUGHOD teaches anthropology and gender studies at Columbia University. Her first book was *Veiled Sentiments* and her most recent is *Do Muslim Women Need Saving?*

RICHÉ J. DANIEL BARNES is Cultural Anthropologist in the Africana Studies Department at Smith College and author of *Raising the Race: Black Career Women Redefine Marriage, Motherhood, and Community.*

DEBORAH A. BOEHM is Associate Professor of Anthropology and Women's Studies/Gender, Race, and Identity at the University of Nevada, Reno.

DEBORAH CAMERON is Professor of Language and Communication at the University of Oxford, UK.

ELIZABETH CHIN is a Professor in the MFA program Media Design Practices/Field at the Art Center College of Design. Her book *Purchasing Power* (Minnesota 2001) was a finalist for the C. Wright Mills Award.

ELORA HALIM CHOWDHURY is an Associate Professor of Women's and Gender Studies at the University of Massachusetts Boston. Her research and teaching interests include transnational feminism, gender violence, human rights, narrative and advocacy.

GRACIA CLARK is Professor Emerita at Indiana University at Bloomington. She has published *Onions Are My Husband* (1994), *Asante Market Women* (2010), three edited volumes, and a web gallery *Everyday Islam in Kumasi.*

SHELLEE COLEN is an anthropologist with an abiding interest in gender, race, and class in a global context. She has taught at university and in worker education and other programs.

DAISY DEOMAMPO is assistant professor of anthropology at Fordham University. She specializes in medical anthropology, science and technology studies, and global health.

LIEBA FAIER is Associate Professor in the Geography Department at the University of California, Los Angeles. Her Ph.D. is in Anthropology and Women's Studies.

CARLA FREEMAN is Professor of Women's, Gender & Sexuality Studies and Senior Associate Dean of Faculty in the College of Arts and Sciences at Emory University.

SARA L. FRIEDMAN teaches Anthropology and Gender Studies at Indiana University. She recently co-edited *Wives, Husbands, and Lovers: Marriage and Sexuality in Hong Kong, Taiwan, and Urban China.*

LESLEY GILL teaches anthropology at Vanderbilt University. Her research focuses on issues of gender, class, political violence, and human rights in Latin America.

MARY L. GRAY is a Senior Researcher at Microsoft Research and maintains an appointment as an Associate Professor in the Media School at Indiana University.

SUSAN GREENHALGH is Professor of Anthropology and Fairbank Professor of Chinese Society at Harvard University. She has explored the workings of gender in the U.S. "obesity epidemic" (*Fat-talk Nation*), clinical medicine (*Under the Medical Gaze*), and China's one-child policy (*Governing China's Population*, *Just One Child*).

MATTHEW C. GUTMANN is Professor of Anthropology at Brown University. He works on gender, politics, and health in Mexico and China.

CASEY HIGH is a social anthropologist who works with Waorani communities in Amazonian Ecuador. His recent book is entitled *Victims and Warriors: Violence, History and Memory in Amazonia* (U Illinois Press)

DOROTHY L. HODGSON is Professor of Anthropology at Rutgers University. She is a historical anthropologist who works on the cultural politics of gender, ethnicity, and social change in Tanzania.

JENNIFER JOHNSON-HANKS is Associate Professor of Demography and Sociology at the University of California, Berkeley. She is author of *Uncertain Honor: Modern Motherhood in an African Crisis*.

CINDI KATZ teaches at The Graduate Center of the City University of New York. Her research addresses social reproduction, global economic restructuring and everyday life, and the politics of knowledge.

DON KULICK is Professor of Anthropology in the Department of Comparative Human Development, University of Chicago. His most recent book is *Loneliness and its Opposite* (with Jens Rydström, 2015).

CARRIE M. LANE is an anthropologist and Associate Professor of American Studies at CSU Fullerton. She is the author of *A Company of One* and is currently researching the professional organizing industry.

THAÏS MACHADO-BORGES is Associate Professor in Social Anthropology and researcher at the Institute of Latin American Studies, Stockholm University, Sweden.

SABA MAHMOOD is Professor of Anthropology at the University of California, Berkeley. She is the author of *Politics of Piety* and *The Minority Condition*, and co-author of *Is Critique Secular?*

CHARLENE E. MAKLEY is Professor of Anthropology at Reed College in Portland, Oregon. Makley has conducted ethnographic research since 1992 in Tibetan regions of China.

CHANDRA TALPADE MOHANTY is Distinguished Professor of Women's and Gender Studies and Dean's Professor of the Humanities at Syracuse University.

RICHARD MORA is an Associate Professor of Sociology at Occidental College. He serves on the Editorial Board of *Gender & Society*.

MARY H. MORAN is Professor of Anthropology and Africana and Latin American Studies at Colgate University. She has conducted research in and about Liberia since 1982.

AIHWA ONG is Professor of Anthropology at the University of California, Berkeley. Her research has focused on modernity, transnationalism, citizenship, global cities, and migration in Southeast Asia, China, and the United States.

SHERRY B. ORTNER is Distinguished Professor of Anthropology at UCLA. Her most recent book is *Not Hollywood: Independent Film at the Twilight of the American Dream*.

CHERYL R. RODRIGUEZ is a feminist anthropologist and Chair of the Department of Africana Studies at the University of South Florida.

SUSAN CAROL ROGERS is Associate Professor of Anthropology at New York University. Her ongoing ethnographic research in rural France has covered a range of topics including family life and economic change, rural tourism, and urban imaginaries.

ALISON ROOKE is a Senior Lecturer in the Sociology Department at Goldsmiths and Director of the Centre for Urban and Community Research.

SHARON R. ROSEMAN is Professor in the Department of Anthropology at Memorial University of Newfoundland and a specialist on gender, class, and labor in Galicia.

LOUISA SCHEIN teaches Anthropology and Women's/Gender Studies at Rutgers. She authored *Minority Rules:*

The Miao and the Feminine in China's Cultural Politics (Duke 2000).

NANCY SCHEPER-HUGHES is Chancellor's Professor and Chair of Medical Anthropology at the University of California, Berkeley. She is the author of *Death Without Weeping: the Violence of Everyday Life in Brazil* and co-editor of *Violence on the Urban Margins*.

RICHARD A. SCHROEDER is Professor and Chair of Geography at Rutgers University. He is the author of *Shady Practices: Agroforesty and Gender Politics in The Gambia* and *Africa After Apartheid: South Africa, Race and Nation in Tanzania*.

LYNN STEPHEN is a cultural anthropologist whose interdisciplinary research illuminates challenges facing Mesoamerican indigenous peoples, particularly in relation to gender, race, migration, violence, and low-intensity war, and their responses to these challenges.

KIMBERLY THEIDON is a medical anthropologist who focuses on Latin America. She is the Henry J. Leir Chair in International Humanitarian Studies at the Fletcher School, Tufts University.

KATH WESTON is a Professor of Anthropology at the University of Virginia. Her latest book is *Animate Planet: Making Visceral Sense of Living in a High-Tech Ecologically Damaged World* (Duke UP).

KRISTA VAN VLEET conducts research in Bolivia and Peru on gender and kinship, affect and narrative, violence, and religion. She is Associate Professor of Anthropology at Bowdoin College.

PATRICIA ZAVELLA is an anthropologist and Professor in the Latin American and Latino Studies Department at the University of California, Santa Cruz.

Additional Resources for Teaching and Learning

I. RECOMMENDED FILMS TO ACCOMPANY TOPICS AND READINGS

2: Power, Agency, and Structure

Voices Unveiled: Turkish Women Who Dared (2010, 69 mins)

I Am a Girl (2013, 88 mins)

Made in India: A Film About Surrogacy (2010, 97 mins)

3: Gender, Sex, and Sexuality

Orchids: My Intersex Adventure (2010, 60 mins)

Intersexion (2011, 44 mins)

You Don't Know Dick (1997, 58 mins)

4: Complicating Gender

Maid in America (2005, 57 mins)

Black Women On: The Light, Dark Thang (1999, 52 mins)

Between Light and Shadow: Maya Women in Transition (1997, 27 mins)

Living on the Fault Line, Where Race and Family Meet (2007, 56 mins)

5: Politics of Representation

I Am a Man: Black Masculinity in America (1998, 60 mins)

Miss Representation (2011, 90 mins)

6: Growing Up Gendered

Straightlaced: How Gender's Got us All Tied Up (2009, 68 mins)

Playing House (2004, 75 mins)

7: Language and Performance

Gender & Communication: Male-Female Differences in Language and Non-Verbal Behavior (2001, 42 mins)

8: Bodies/Embodiment

Killing Us Softly 4: Advertising's Image of Women (2010, 45 mins)

Red Moon: Menstruation, Culture & the Politics of Gender (2009, 53 mins)

Body Image: The Quest for Perfection (2000, 30 mins)

9: Mediated Lives

Searching 4 Sandeep (2007, 55 mins)

Writing Desire (2000, 23 mins)

10: Gender at Home

Dadi's Family (1988, 58 mins)

Chronicles of a Savanna Marriage (1998, 56 mins)

11: Gender at Work

Poto Mitan: Haitian Women, Pillars of the Global Economy (2009, 50 mins)
Dish: Women, Waitressing and the Art of Service (2010, 58 mins)
Transnational Tradeswomen (2006, 63 mins)

12: Gendered States

Through Chinese Women's Eyes (1997, 52 mins)
The World Before Her (2012, 90 mins)

13: Global Connections of Life, Love, and Labor

Tokyo Girls (2000, 58 mins)
Indian Cabaret (1985, 60 mins)
Girl Model (2011, 76 mins)

14: Structures of Violence

War Takes (2002, 78 mins)
To See If I'm Smiling (2007, 59 mins)
Invisible War (2012, 93 mins)

15: Politics of Human Rights and Humanitarian Interventions

Aidependence (2014, 90 mins)
Saving Face (2011, 52 mins)
Pray the Devil Back to Hell (2008, 72 mins)

II. SOURCES FOR CLASSROOM FILMS AND VIDEOS

Women Make Movies: http://www.wmm.com
Alexander Street Press (includes streaming video): http://www.academicvideostore.com
Media Education Foundation: http://mediaed.org
Documentary Educational Resources: http://der.org

Berkeley Media LLC: http://berkeleymedia.com
California Newsreel: http://newsreel.org
PBS POV "Documentaries with a Point of View": http://www.pbs.org/pov/

III. FILM REVIEWS

Films for the Feminist Classroom (critical reviews of relevant films): http://ffc.twu.edu

ARD—the Anthropology Review Database: http://wings.buffalo.edu/ARD/